THE USES
OF PSYCHIATRY
IN THE LAW

THE USES
OF PSYCHIATRY
IN THE LAW

A Clinical View of Forensic Psychiatry

WALTER BROMBERG

Q QUORUM BOOKS
WESTPORT, CONNECTICUT • LONDON, ENGLAND

Library of Congress Cataloging in Publication Data

Bromberg, Walter, 1900-
   The uses of psychiatry in the law.

   Bibliography: p.
   Includes index.
   1. Forensic psychiatry. 2. Insanity—Jurisprudence.
3. Forensic psychiatry—United States. I. Title.
K487.P75B76   614'.19   78-22724
ISBN 0-89930-000-6

Library of Congress Catalog Card Number: 78-22724
ISBN: 0-89930-000-6

First published in 1979

Quorum Books, a division of
Greenwood Press, Inc.
51 Riverside Avenue, Westport, Connecticut 06880

Printed in the United States of America

10 9 8 7 6 5 4 3 2 1

Contents

Illustrations

Preface

This work attempts to join the two disciplines, law and psychiatry, in their common interest of human engineering. In essence, both are concerned with modifying human misbehavior. In criminal law, and some aspect of civil law, the legal system serves justice by the correction of wrongs; psychiatry, psychology, and psychotherapy attempt through various methods to better human misbehavior. The purpose of this book is to identify areas where psychiatry and psychology are useful in the modern legal process. It gives equal weight to the contributions of both disciplines, with full awareness that the law is the ultimate arbiter in the task of tranquilizing social frictions caused by misbehavior and mental vagaries. It is hoped that students and practitioners of the legal process in relation to mental problems, and students and practitioners of mental illness in relation to the law, will benefit from this study of dual intervention in the lives of those whom society singles out for correction and/or restoration to their place in the community.

The technique employed is to explore the limitations of psychiatric thinking and to assess its advantages and liabilities in areas of the law where such concepts have relevance. Case reports to illustrate legal decisions and practices have been culled predominantly from my work on the East and West coast. It is hoped that the case reports will bind psychiatric evaluations to the requirements of the law, sometimes successfully, sometimes the reverse. In all interpretations of case law and of psychologic knowledge, I take full responsibility.

This project arose from a series of lectures I gave to law students of the McGeorge School of Law, University of the Pacific, on psychiatry and the law. In amplifying the material, the main areas wherein psychiatric help is sought and given in the law are covered. The details of legal technicalities and psychiatric niceties are necessarily minimized. The emphasis is on the mainstream of forensic psychiatry encountered in the clinic, office, hospital, penal institutions, attorneys' offices, and courtroom. The work is intended to be a clinical approach to forensic psychiatry; as such, it is comprehensive but not exhaustive.

My acknowledgments cover the many attorneys for whom I have evaluated clients, the judges before whom I have appeared, and teachers and associates with whom I have worked for over half a century. From discussions, teachings, and rulings from the bench, I have clarified my thinking about psychiatric implications in the law. The influence of all has been profound. Some of my mentors and associates have passed on; some are engaged elsewhere. Not only fellow workers, but also patients, prisoners, plaintiffs, and defendants, have helped balance evaluations and shed new light on old problems. Although they are too numerous to mention individually, my gratitude is extended to all.

While the gathering of cases for this work started at Bellevue Psychiatric Hospital in New York City, the Court of General Sessions, New York County (now the Criminal Courts), and the Forensic Psychiatry service of Kings County Hospital, Brooklyn, New York, it continued in California and other western areas. The collation of the material was done at the McGeorge School of Law, University of the Pacific, Sacramento, California. To Dean Gordon D. Schaber who encouraged the effort and provided student grants for legal assistance and to Professor Stuart A. Brody with whom the work was discussed in its early stages, I give my thanks. Librarian Alice Murray and her assistant Dennis Stone as well as the research librarians were most helpful with legal references; Joyce (Rivers) Mansfield, J.D., Henry V. (Hank) Griffin, J.D., and Cecil Bishop, LLb., were tireless in their assistance with the tedious task of searching out legal decisions. I owe a debt of gratitude to Jan (Pryor) Root, administrative assistant to the Center for Legal Advocacy (more widely known as the "Courtroom of the Future" at the McGeorge School of Law), whose typing and retyping of the manuscript was a model of dedication. To all who tangentially or directly assisted in this undertaking, I tender my appreciation and thanks.

Walter Bromberg, M. D.

THE USES
OF PSYCHIATRY
IN THE LAW

1

Introduction

This work explores those areas in the law in which psychiatry is involved. It provides only the essential legal decisions and commentaries wherein psychiatry, psychology, and neurology play a role in the investigation, settlement, or court trial of contested issues.

Hence, the purpose of this work is to record the present-day involvement of neuropsychiatry in all applicable branches of legal practice. Its philosophic basis is the common aim of attempting to manage human misbehavior. Both law and psychiatry, in spite of their differences in conceptualization, procedures, and techniques, seek to codify, understand, and correct human misbehavior through punishment, rehabilitation, and psychotherapy, respectively. Viewed broadly, the law codifies misbehavior in terms of degrees of crime, while psychiatry codifies maladaption in terms of diagnoses. The law aims to assess responsibility for misbehavior, i.e., crime, through the concept of intent, specific or general; psychiatry aims to assess the genesis of criminal action via study of the criminal's mental conflicts and personality trends. The law's goal is to modify behavior through punishment, rehabilitation, or requiring restoration of loss, as in tort cases; psychiatry's goal is to modify misbehavior through medical therapy or psychotherapy. The justification for law is the attainment of justice in our socioeconomic milieu; the justification for psychiatry is balancing the individual's bio-psycho-social system. The law began in the ideal of justice; psychiatry grew out of the need to help distraught humans. Laws evolved from the social conscience; psychiatry evolved from magic and mysticism, to which were added philosophic idealism, medicine, neurology, clinical psychiatry, and psychology. Both disciplines represent attempts at a kind of social engineering.

Both law and psychiatry advanced through intricate living experiments in directing human behavior, through trial and error, or, more accurately, trial and success. Both have traditions and precedents. It was inevitable that they would meet on the battleground of the evaluation of wrong-doing in daily life. Just as the law has advanced into areas of social living—civil rights, workmen's compensation, social welfare, public education, and family law, to name a few, so has psychiatry emerged from its preoccupation with the insane and neurotic patient. Psychiatry and psychotherapy have broadened from a medical specialty to a point at which they spill over into community health areas, involving companion arts and sciences such as psychological counseling, crisis intervention, and education of the handicapped.

In exploring those areas in which psychiatry and law meet, the fact cannot be avoided that opposition to the spread of the mental sciences in the legal processes has become vigorous in recent years. The objection of many jurists and legal scholars to the increased participation of psychiatrists in court trials is well known (see Chapter 2), but opposition to the proliferation of psychiatric activity in the law has also developed from the ranks of sociologists, civil rights workers, and psychiatrists. Prominent among the psychiatrist group is Karl Menninger who thinks the psychiatrist does not belong in a court of law and Thomas Szasz.[1] Szasz inveighs against their use in these words: ". . . coercion and deceit are rampant in the legal and social uses of psychiatry—beginning with the pseudomedical definitions of mental illness, and ending with the tyrannical abuses of psychiatric power in cases of political and other offenses." Dr. Szasz' campaign to disenfranchise the entire profession has received support from some segments of the public interested in preserving civil rights. The director of the National Institute of Mental Health, Dr. Bertram Brown, concerned over reduction in funds for mental research, commented in an article: "Claims have been made by psychiatrists that 'psychiatry is dead' and that 'mental illness is a myth' and many lay people have attacked the entire field as devoted to brainwashing and mind control rather than healing."[2] Researchers of more moderate stripe[3] agree that psychiatric diagnoses are relatively unreliable. Others point to the "little value" of such diagnoses in legal proceedings because the "judgment of psychiatrists is no more reliable than those of the general public."[4]

In discussing the intrusion of new views into the law, an English legalist (1974) remarks, in a restrained mood, that the criminal law, "an essentially fluctuating thing . . . interpreted in accordance with the spirit of the age . . . must carefully tread a path between undue flexibility and resistance to new theories from outside the law."[5]

While the controversy continues, the psychologic disciplines have been, and continue to be, used in the legal process. We will now turn our attention to this development.

The Early Uses of "Psychology"

It is difficult to pinpoint the time when physicians were called in to pronounce an accused insane within the meaning of the definitions then recorded. In the early days of the ecclesiastical courts, during the Middle Ages in England, the pronouncement of idiocy or insanity was the function of the presiding bishops. As secular courts took over these functions, judgment as to what constituted madness and idiocy became the function of the court and lay witnesses. Sir Matthew Hale agreed with the general principle that an insane man was not a competent witness "[I]f prevented from recalling the matter on which he is to testify from understanding the questions put to him."[6] In the same connection, a child was said to "want discretion" up to the age of fourteen, although Sir William Holdsworth, the British legal historian, points out that Lord Hale found some children at the age of seven years to be good witnesses in sexual cases "if they were bright enough." The actual definition of insanity from a judicial viewpoint arose from canon law, as indicated in the first available test, enunciated by Bracton, archdeacon of Barnstable (1265): "An insane person is one who does not know what he is doing, is lacking in mind and reason and is not far removed from the brutes."[7] Lord Twiss, who edited and translated Bracton's codification of Anglo-Saxon law, notes that Bracton as ecclesiastical judge tried to explain to his "savage countrymen [the] benefits to be derived from an equitable system of law . . . drawn from the rich fountain of Roman jurisprudence."

In any event, the test laid down by Sir Matthew Hale in 1671 for legal insanity, using the then current term *melancholia*, stated: "Such a person is laboring under melancholy distempers hath yet ordinarily as great understanding as ordinarily a child of fourteen years hath, is such a person as may be guilty of treason or felony." The level of "understanding" placed at fourteen years had been further defined by Fitzherbert in 1535: "An idiot is such a person who cannot account or number 20 pence, nor tell who was his father or mother, nor how old he is."[8]

The records do not make clear whether medical men were asked to make these decisions, but a shift in accent as to the elements of insanity can be observed in the Arnold case[9] tried in 1724 in London. Arnold, allegedly a "madman," shot and wounded Lord Onslow.

Twenty-two witnesses testified that Arnold "talked to himself . . . broke out in passions of cursing or foolish laughter . . . talked to inhuman creatures . . . said Lord Onslow was in his belly and was the occasion of his trouble . . . [and] was a known lunatic." The only witness who appeared to have been an expert was a Mr. Allen, a commissioner of the peace, who examined Arnold in the House of Correction and testified that "he seems as sensible as myself or any person in this court." After a full discussion of Arnold's "lucid intervals," Judge Tracy presented the jury with a test in his charge:

. . . not every kind of frantic humour . . . points him out to be a madman as is exempted from punishment: it must be a man totally deprived of his understanding and memory and doth not know what he is doing, no more than an infant, than a brute, or a wild beast.

By the end of the eighteenth century, physicians were beginning to be recognized as having a special knowledge of madness. In England in 1788, the Drs. Willis, John and Francis, attended King George III for his "phrenzy fever" on the occasion of one of his depressive attacks.[10] During later manic attacks, Drs. Baker and Heberden were consulted as the British public became aware of the king's "slight derangement." On this side of the Atlantic, Benjamin Rush, a student of Dr. William Cullen of Edinburgh University, wrote his textbook of psychiatry,[11] while Philippe Pinel in France, through his widely read and translated treatise, established psychiatry as a branch of medicine.[12] Still, psychiatrists were only infrequently called into court to decide the question of madness among criminals.

The confusion, even embarrassment, of judging irresponsibility for crime because of insanity is illustrated by a trial in New York (1823) in which Eliza Tripler was accused of stealing five silver spoons from the home of her employer, Mr. Stonehalf. The defense was that Eliza had fallen on her head causing "strange conduct." The judge commenting that "[n]o question can ever come before a court and jury so embarrassing to consider . . . as cases of real or alleged insanity," settled the problem by remarking: "Insanity is calamity enough without inflicting the pain of a conviction."[13]

In English courts, too, judges struggled with a definition of insanity which would satisfy the requirements of law. Sir James Stephen in his *History of the Criminal Law in England* (1883)[14] is authority for the statement: "From the time of Lord Hale to our own no legal writer of authority has discussed this matter on its merits . . . the principles of

law by which the relation of insanity to crime may be determined."
The cases were determined by a "direction to the jury by a single
judge." For example, in 1812 a change in emphasis from "deprivation
of understanding" to "distinguishing good from evil" crystallized in
the *Bellingham* case (1812).[15] The accused had killed the chancellor of
the Exchequer; his plea of not guilty was based on statements of those
who knew him—friends, relatives, and neighbors—that he was of "infirm mind and very much deranged," although one witness stated that
"no one medical gentleman practised in disorders of the brain had
ever been called to his assistance." After sifting the testimony of lay
witnesses, Lord Chief Justice Mansfield addressed the jury, saying:
"The single question was whether, when he committed the offense,
he had sufficient understanding to distinguish good from evil, right
from wrong and that murder was a crime not only against the laws of
God [but] against the laws of his Country."

In other cases such as *Hadfield*, which influenced the so-called
M'Naghten rule promulgated in 1843, the skill of the attorneys in
urging delusion as a test for irresponsibility for murder virtually became medico-legal doctrine. Sir Stephen pointed out that Erskine in
Hadfield's case was "greatly admired" as an orator and that his
"speeches, though poor reading" were those of an "admirable advocate" and "verdict-getter" sufficient to cause the judge, Lord Kenyon,
to stop the prosecution with a directed verdict of acquittal. Erskine's
statement of delusion as the test of legal insanity (1800) was influen-
tial: "[B]y insanity, I mean, that state when the mind is under the
influence of delusions, where the reasoning proceeds upon something
which has no truth . . . but vainly built upon some morbid image
formed in a distempered imagination."[16]

In the early part of the nineteenth century, a body of writings had
grown concerning the medico-legal status of mental disease in England, France, and Germany, but it remained for Dr. Isaac Ray in the
United States to forge the field of forensic psychiatry practically
singlehanded. His *Treatise on Medical Jurisprudence of Insanity*
(1838) stated in its preface: "The English language does not furnish
a single work in which the various forms and degrees of mental derangement are treated in reference to their effect on the rights and
duties of man."[17]

Ray bridged a gap between "madness" and "insanity," noting that
popular notions derived from "wretched inmates of madhouses, whom
chains and stripes, cold and filth" had reduced to "the stupidity of an
idiot . . . the fury of a demon" left no room for a real analysis of mental

disease. Perhaps there was a "great prevalence of insanity" at the time Ray worked, or a clearer recognition of it sufficient for Ray to write, in criticism of Lord Hale's "child of fourteen" test:

In the time of this eminent jurist [Hale], insanity was a much less frequent disease than it is now. . . . Those nice shades of the disease in which the mind, without being wholly driven from its propriety, pertinaciously clings to some absurd delusion, were either regarded as something very different from madness, or . . . too far removed from the common gaze.[18]

Lunatic asylums during the eighteenth century were indeed "Bedlams," places of horror for patients and spectators alike. However, during the last quarter of the century and gathering strength in the first quarter of the nineteenth century, physicians were altering the foul-smelling "Lunatick" houses to medically supervised asylums and retreats. Doctors, having to do more for their patients than bleed, purge, chain, and fetter them, were gradually forced to study their charges and to classify and analyze the mental diseases presenting themselves, to the point where a clinical science of psychiatry evolved.[19] It was from this vantage point that physicians like Isaac Ray and Benjamin Rush introduced psychiatric thinking to the courtroom in criminal trials.

In the civil law, commissions *de Idiota Inquirendo* and commissions *de Lunatico Inquirendo* and Against *Persons non Compotes mentis*[20] existed for many years under common law. Until the early 1800s, insanity was a cause for voiding a marriage, a will, or a contract if agreed to in a Court of Chancery or by an established commission *Lunatico Inquirendo*. Still the major channel for the entry of psychiatry into the law was in criminal trials.

To trace the evolution of the mental experts' participation in court deliberations through the nineteenth and twentieth centuries would entail a lengthy and fascinating piece of history beyond our present purpose. As Zilboorg remarked, "What we call today 'the legal aspects of psychiatry' is a recent development."[21] And a distinguished jurist, Edward DeGrazia, wrote:

. . . there was a vastly greater difference between the intelligence of the court and the jury than there is now, and the tendency was for the learned and great judges to bestow their learning very liberally upon the ignorant and degraded jury by way of instructions. . . . the use of experts as witnesses to give opinions on scientific subjects was comparatively unknown.[22]

Suffice it to say that this evolution has widened to include consideration of all aspects of the mental and physical life impinging on criminal behavior. The new slant encompasses more than mental disease:

The psychiatrist perceived his discipline's entrance into criminology as subserving the ultimate effect of humanizing the criminal law and possibly humanizing the criminal himself. He asks, "Is it too much to expect that the illumination which psychology can provide into the unconscious influences on criminal behavior may make the criminal law responsive to the needs of society and the offender?"[23]

The significance of the clinical approach to forensic psychiatry is the ascendance of a dynamic, behavioral view of human beings in conflict with society and the law. Similarly, in the civil area, the legal significance of mental illness, personality distortions, neurotic tendencies, intrafamilial tensions, and stress reactions are weighed with regard to domestic and marital conflicts, custody problems, and personal injury litigation.

Notes

1. Thomas Szasz, *Law, Liberty and Psychiatry:* 240, Macmillan Co., New York (3d printing, 1968).

2. Bertram S. Brown, *The Crisis in Mental Health Research*, 134, no. 2, Am. J. of Psych. 118 (Feb. 1977).

3. J. E. Helzer, Lee Robins, et al., *Reliability of Psychiatric Diagnosis*, 34 Arch. of Gen. Psych. 132 (Feb. 1977).

4. B. J. Ennis and T. R. Litwack, *Psychiatry and the Presumption of Expertise*, 62 Calif. L. Rev. 693 (1974).

5. George W. Keeton, *English Law:* 331, David and Charles Ltd., Newton Abbott Devon (1974).

6. Sir William Holdsworth, *A History of English Law* 9: 186, Methuen and Co. Ltd., and Sweet and Maxwell, London (reprinted 1966).

7. Henrici de Bracton, *Angliae Legibus et Consuetudinibus* 2, ed. by Sir T. Twiss, Longman and Co., London (1879).

8. Fitzherbert, quoted in J. Michael and H. Wechsler, *Criminal Law and Its Administration:* 807, Foundation Press, Brooklyn, N.Y. (1941).

9. T. B. Howell, *A Complete Collection of State Trials and Proceedings of High Treason and Other Crimes* 16:695, T. C. Hansard, London (1812).

10. Manfred Guttmacher, *America's Last King. An Interpretation of the Madness of George III:* 284 et seq., Chas. Scribner's Sons, New York (1941).

11. Benjamin Rush, *Medical Inquiries and Observations Upon Disease of the Mind,* Kimber and Richardson, Philadelphia (1812).

12. Philippe Pinel, *A Treatise on Insanity in Which Are Contained the Principles of a New anl Practical Nosology of Maniacal Disorders,* translated from the French, Sheffield, England (1806).

13. *People v. Tripler,* in J. D. Wheeler, *Criminal Cases:* 48, Banks and Gould, New York (1854).

14. Sir James Fitzjames Stephen, *A History of the Criminal Law of England* 2: 151, Macmillan Co., London (1883).

15. George D. Collinson, *A Treatise on the Law Concerning Idiots, Lunatics and Other Persons Non Compotes Mentis:* 666 et seq., W. Reed, London (1812).

16. 27 St. Tr. 1281 (1800). Quoted in Stephen, *History of Criminal Law:* 159.

17. Issac Ray, *A Treatise on the Medical Jurisprudence of Insanity:* 48, Charles Little and James Brown, Boston (1838).

18. Ibid.: 13 (5th ed., 1871).

19. Walter Bromberg, *From Shaman to Psychotherapist, A History of Mental Healing*, Henry Regnery Co., Chicago (1975).

20. Collinson, op. cit.: 5, 554, 603.

21. Gregory Zilboorg, *Legal Aspects of Psychiatry in One Hundred Years of American Psychiatry:* 507 et seq., Columbia U. Press, New York (1944).

22. Edward DeGrazia, *The Distinction of Being Mad*, 22 U. of Chi. L. Rev. 339 (1954-1955).

23. Seymour L. Halleck and Walter Bromberg, *Psychiatric Aspects of Criminology:* 3, Charles C Thomas Publ., Springfield, Ill. (1968).

2

The Psychiatrist Before
the Law

The intrusion of legal rules into a neuropsychiatric examination occurs only when such examination, written or oral, is brought before a judge and jury. Otherwise, the report of an examination, evaluation, or summary of treatment follows the usual medical form. An attorney requesting an evaluation of a client may suggest consideration of certain points of concern to him in dealing with the courts, third parties, workmen's compensation bodies, or other attorneys; he or she may need certain questions answered or certain areas explored. While the physician may feel the questions are unanswerable, unscientific, or of no medical consequence, he is obligated to consider and attempt to answer them. For instance, in matters of criminal responsibility involving questions of knowledge of "right" and "wrong," the psychiatrist may, as Guttmacher noted some years ago,[1] have no means of estimating "the degree of 'ethics' in a person," or he may be unwilling in a civil case to assign a "cause" for the patient's complaints. But once medical, psychiatric, or psychological material is given in a report or as testimony before a court or administrative hearing, it is thrown into the crucible of the adversary proceeding. It is here that the medico-legal conflict is engendered. It arises in the course of expert testimony, but its seeds live in the past—in the law's rationale of dispensing justice and medicine's rationale of dispensing solace. In exploring how psychiatry is used in the legal process, it would be well to meet this sometime impasse head on.

The Medico-Legal Conflict

The law complains that the psychiatrist deals with disturbances of feelings and emotion common to all persons and on which anyone may express an opinion. Hence, he invades the area of "common sense" with his presumably exact information and formulated opinions. Lawyers complain that the expert uses unnecessarily complex language and concepts (frequently termed "medical gobbledygook"); that he talks down to the judge and jury; and that he accepts an assignment (except where the court orders the examination) from the side which pays him best—that he "hires himself to give his special knowledge for value received."

Psychiatrists, on the other hand, are uneasy in contributing their knowledge and experience under the restrictions of legal procedure. This uneasiness may vary from mild dislike to embarrassment, anxiety, even panic, or simply dissatisfaction and anger. The obvious cause is the contentious atmosphere of the courtroom. On the face of it, these reactions may seem surprising because the psychiatrist usually works in situations of conflict, since mental illness, including neurosis and personality disturbances, is born of conflict and thrives thereon.

Consciously or otherwise, the psychiatrist takes his stance as a lineal descendant of the priest, shaman, and medicine man in intuitively assuming the position of authority in medical matters. Indeed, the tradition and training of psychiatrists tend to develop this posture of authority. Thus, when cross-examiners do not accept this authority without question, anxiety or even outright anger may arise. Some have advised psychiatrists to give a wide berth to being subjected to cross-examination. This posture has resulted in an open division within the profession.

A few years ago, one of America's leading medico-legal experts advised his colleagues to avoid the forum:

It is most pertinent to differentiate between the doctor of medicine who is engaged in the business of detection of crime or who otherwise serves the ends of penal justice, and the psychiatrist who is called upon to examine and testify as to the mental condition of a given defendant. . . . such a doctor is merely a specialist who hires himself to give his special knowledge . . . for value received; he is not a physician, not a healer, not a servant in the ministry of medical mercy.[2]

Although it is natural for a physician to dislike the maneuvers of a trial, the nature of judicial truth depends on the criss-cross reduction of claims and assertions, memories, screen-memories or half-memories, through cross-examination, despite the purist view espoused by Zilboorg and others. Cross-examination may not winnow out every grain of truth, but it helps to level out unavoidable differences reported by two observers of the same phenomenon. Moreover, cross-examination involves the credibility of witnesses, expert and otherwise, extending to their interpretation of facts, their prejudices, unconscious biases, clarity of thought, and validity of logic.

The lawyer is entitled, even taught, to attack credibility directly or through stratagems and tricks in the cross-examination procedure. To the medical man these tricks smack of indecency; to the lawyer they constitute the essence of his skill. The doctor regards these stratagems at best as a game and at worst as a shabby and sadistic attitude on the part of the lawyers, calculated to denigrate psychiatric opinion and knowledge. Herein arise the witness's tension and anxiety with its defensive anger or embarrassment.

The expert psychiatric witness sees an entirely different picture spread before him in the courtroom than is perceived by the attorneys and judge. The cross-examining lawyer is intent on building up his own or destroying the opponent's case; he has no personal animus against the witness, although an aggressive spirit against an expert witness is far from unknown.

More than one lawyer has expressed his experiences with an adverse witness in saying "I tore him to ribbons," thus indicating his pleasure at reducing presumed truth to falsity. On a more urbane level, a competent lawyer once remarked to an equally competent medical witness after two days of parry, defense, and counterattack in court, "Doctor, it's all a matter of semantics, isn't it?" Whereupon, the doctor said drily, "It is."

From the psychiatrist's position, as captive in the witness stand, he is vulnerable to attack with little chance for personal defense. To the beleaguered witness, attorneys in court may be classified in several functional groups—a classification[3] made without malice and with the highest regard for attorneys on the firing line.

1. The "country lawyer" type, who claims to know nothing. He stumbles over technical words and wants to oversimplify human actions and thus take the meat out of the psychiatrist's explanations, rendering them as meaningless gobbledygook for the jury. He insists on the plainest of words in the testimony, thus trying to obscure nuances of feelings and reactions in the defendant that represent the heart of mental dynamics.

2. The "plodding" type, who hovers over each symptom and sign in turn and who delights in pinioning the expert on obscure findings. He discusses the Romberg test and the reflexes, inquires into the blood pressure, and may even dip into such esoteric areas as a cephalin flocculation test, glucose tolerance test, or details of neuroanatomy in order to test the extent of the expert's knowledge. He has usually checked the answer the night before in a standard textbook.

This type is enamored of negative findings because then he can proceed from a deductive point of view to show that if a certain disease has a standard clinical picture, then each symptom should be presented in a given case so diagnosed. Thus, if schizophrenia involves "flattened emotion," and this has not been detailed by the expert witness as a finding, it implies a lack of carefulness or personal veracity on the part of the examiner.

3. The "unctuous" type, who is excessively polite. He apologizes for taking up the doctor's valuable time and refers to him as a "man of science," setting him up for a devastating blow through some bit of evidence that he conceals to the last moment. Here the psychiatrist-witness feels like a butterfly on a pin. The lawyer often presents the damaging bit of information obliquely, at the end of an innocuous interchange, by prefacing it with a disarming "by the way" comment.

4. The "blustery" type, who wades into the witness eager for a one-round knockout, i.e., for immediate destruction of credibility. This bullying approach may spread to include personal references to the witness, his fee, his loyalty to the defense or the prosecution, and his social relationships with attorneys. This type sometimes imitates a tremor or a muscle tic, saying with unconvincing naiveté, "If I had this, would you say I'm neurotic?"

5. The ostensibly "know-nothing" type, who wants each psychiatric (or ordinarily descriptive) word defined in detail. Such a cross-examiner will inquire into such general constructs as "nervousness," "clinical," and "mental." He will belabor the absence of "objective" signs in neurosis and then ask if it isn't true that the word "psychosis" is a fancy way of saying "kookie." He may plaintively complain that there are too many schools of psychiatry and that no layman could possibly understand all "those big words," or he may bring up the name of "Frood" (Freud) in apparent perplexity. The latent purpose here is to emphasize the confusion, obscurantism, and mysticism of psychiatrists.

There are other roots for the discomfort of honest, competent psychiatrists in court. One is their inability to explain views of the psychological life that may appear peculiar to laymen who are not accustomed to thinking in terms of conscious and unconscious mentation. Another reason is the basic difference in the logic employed by each discipline. In the legal setting it is mainly deductive, while in the medical setting it is mainly inductive. One resulting difficulty is that legal thinking tends to be atomistic, while medical thinking points toward a holistic view of man. Each discipline has not only an intellectual but also an emotional loyalty to its own logical preconceptions.

In spite of these understandable difficulties, the expert witness must observe certain rules imposed by the court and the system of jurisprudence.

RULES AFFECTING EXPERT WITNESSES

As in the case of other expert witnesses, the psychiatrist or neurologist is expected to have special knowledge, skill, training, and experience in order to testify as to matters at issue in a trial. To qualify as an expert, a medical man must present evidence of having "knowledge, skill, experience, training and education" in his given field in consonance with standards of other specialists working in the same area.[4] Once qualified, the expert is expected to conform to certain basic principles and postulates of court practice. These will be set down in an informal manner, but are grounded on case law and accepted legal rulings.

(1) Attendance in response to a subpoena is compulsory under pain of a contempt of court citation. A doctor so summoned must testify as to what he knows concerning the patient he has examined and treated, although he need not qualify as an expert. The expert usually contracts with the attorney for his appearance in court, although the court does not always support this stance.

(2) On a subpoena *duces tecum*, the witness must bring whatever documents, records, or notes he possesses which are relevant to the case in court. A *duces tecum* subpoena merely guarantees the presence in court of pertinent records. Their admissibility in evidence is subject to the decision of the presiding judge.

(3) A medical expert must be qualified by the attorney who calls him, by reciting his professional education and training as well as his practical experience in the field relevant to the issue before the court. Thus, not only his academic degrees, but also the extent of his experiences in cases similar to the one at trial, need to be brought out.

(4) The psychiatric expert is expected to answer the questions put to him in his most direct manner without embellishment or resort to technical language. Although many questions are posed requesting a "yes" or "no" answer, this is not always possible. In such a case, the witness is permitted to explain to the court why he cannot supply a "yes" or "no" answer, or he can request permission to qualify his answer.

The expert witness is expected to testify from his personal observation and examination of the accused or the plaintiff, and from medical records unless disqualified by hearsay rules. He may also rely on observation in the courtroom. The opinion finally delivered should be based on the facts ascertained, the steps in reasoning employed, and the conclusion at which he arrived. An opinion is given within "medical probability," not "possibility." A "guess," "impression," "speculation," or "belief" is to be distinguished from an opinion. An opinion is a final judgment made after consideration of available facts; as such, it approximates truth. In ordinary language, the term *opinion* carries the value of a "belief," defined in Webster's Dictionary as "acceptance of something as true whether based on reasoning, prejudice or the authority of the source." A legal opinion is less a belief than a reasoned conclusion. Richardson discusses these distinctions as they apply to witnesses:

An opinion in a legal sense is something more than mere speculation or conjecture. It is usually conceived as a belief which is stronger than a bare impression. . . . For instance, a physician may have an opinion based on reasonable medical certainty; on the other hand, a layman may know that at a certain time the wind was blowing very strongly and have no real knowledge regarding its speed as measured in miles per hour. It is easy to see which would be the more valid opinion.[5]

Present-day dynamic psychiatrists attempt to present more than an opinion as they recount their reasoning leading to the conclusion. In an old California case (1911), in ruling on an action for divorce on the ground of insanity, the court said:

Expert witnesses may give their opinions concerning the mental condition of a person. They are not restricted to the mere declaration of an opinion that the person is or is not of sound mind, but may state the nature and extent of the deficiencies, if any, which they believe to exist.[6]

Hearsay, especially where historical facts in a given case are provided by a relative, is not admissible for consideration by a medical expert. Therefore, where possible, the history should be taken from the patient directly. On the other hand, use of a medical textbook to impeach a witness on cross-examination is generally accepted as an exception to the hearsay rule.

Richardson has summarized this situation:

As independent evidence to prove the truth of the facts, asserted medical treatises usually are not admitted. . . . The limitations of the majority rule have been severely criticized as permitting, under the guise of cross-examination, the admission of statements of learned treatises not to impeach the expert's knowledge but for the real purpose of getting such statements into the record.

The American Law Institute, Model Code of Evidence, Rule 529 favors frank admission of this testimony as substantive evidence. It provides: "A published treatise, periodical or pamphlet on a subject of history, science or art is admissible as tending to prove the truth of a matter stated therein if the judge takes judicial notice, or a witness, expert in the subject, testifies that the writer of the statement in the treatise, periodical or pamphlet is recognized in his profession or calling as an expert in the subject."[7]

Hospital records and charts are admissible in evidence since these records are analogous to those kept by other business organizations. The general rule of evidence permits entries made in the regular course of duty or business to be admitted in evidence where the declarant is unavailable. Some courts consider the person making the entry to be "unavailable" where it is certain that if called to testify, such a person would have no present recollection of the facts and could only testify from the facts as recorded. Routine entries in the chart made by nurses and attendants are thus admitted as part of the witness's testimony.

On the Witness Stand

The behavior of the expert witness on the stand is prescribed as much by tradition as by the rules of evidence. He is expected to speak in understandable, nontechnical English; to refrain from lecturing the jury or presenting a dissertation on the subject under discussion; to avoid witticisms or sallies against the cross-examiner; or to offer help in forming questions. It is self-evident that the expert is not to be an advocate for either side, nor is he permitted to indulge in a battle of wits with the cross-examiner (a temptation difficult to withstand on some occasions). The witness's duty is restricted to presenting his finding and opinion together with the reasons therefor. In offering an opinion and the reasons for it, he is prohibited from using hearsay material, except that in developing the case history—the so-called longitudinal view of a patient's difficulty—information given by relatives is often permitted by the judge. In the instance of a hypothetical question propounded to the witness, which is supposed to include all evidence adduced, the expert is not allowed to alter the presumptions should he feel the picture presented is one-sided.

Cross-examination of a witness is the "heart of the case" and the occasion for most psychiatric discomfort. The main purpose of this part of the trial is to destroy or injure the witness's credibility. For the purpose of impeachment, the opposing party has the right to elicit contradic-

tory evidence or opinion, if possible, and to develop the witness's reputation (bad preferably) for truth, honesty, and integrity. The cross-
examiner has the right to question the type of practice, the fees charged,
the education and experience, and even the state of health and age of
the expert. Any writings by the witness may be examined, and statements relevant to and contradictory of the testimony given may be
explored. From this position, the cross-examiner often tries to impugn
bias in the witness by trying to establish that the expert is "plaintiff or
defendant" oriented. For men experienced in the medico-legal field,
the imputation often is made that they are "professional witnesses."
Although this may have been the case in the past, present-day professional standards for specialists make it unlikely. The implied accusation made by cross-examiners attempting to reduce a witness's credibility: "Isn't it a fact that you are a professional witness?" can be
answered: "Yes, I am a professional and I am a witness."

With regard to the question of the impartiality of a psychiatric witness, it has been suggested that the "battle of experts" can be scaled
down by having court-appointed impartial examiners. Professor Goldstein of Yale University discusses the disadvantages of this proposal.[8]
He points out that while such a system sounds plausible on the surface,
it would diminish the cross-examination by giving "special weight of
probity to testimony of one witness." He argues that impartial experts would "deny the full range of relevant testimony" to the jury
and that "we must beware lest a single-minded search for 'the truth'
obscure the fundamental insight of the adversary system." From a different angle, Dr. Bernard Diamond makes the incisive comment that
"objectivity is a myth"[9] and that the best intentioned psychiatric
expert is unwittingly a "potent advocate" in that a dynamically oriented psychiatrist may be introducing elements which lead to "reforms
of the law."[10] (See discussion of the Gorshen and Wells cases, p. 73).
Certainly in testifying at trials for defendants accused of murder, the
position of the psychiatrist as citizen might lead to an identification
"with the defendant or with society, usually the latter." The use of a
neutral expert in court trials has been under intensive discussion, particularly during the 1960s. A symposium in the *Temple Law Quarterly*,
1961, covered the subject in detail; it indicated that such eminent
legalists as Professor Wigmore, Judge Learned Hand, and others had
recommended this move decades before. Earlier (1956), an American
Bar Association committee made the same recommendation indicating
that it would "relieve court congestion . . . improve the process of
finding medical facts . . . have a prophylactic effect on presentation
of medical testimony in court."[11] However, a thorough analysis of the

use of impartial experts by Elwood Levy of the Philadelphia bar (1961)[12] summarized the experiences of judges in federal and state courts along the Atlantic seaboard: "Neither a prophylaxis for medical testimony nor supposed diminution of trial time is the coin with which to purchase shrunken constitutional guarantees . . . impartial proposals such as the impartial medical plan have no place within the framework of trial by jury."

From the psychiatrist's standpoint, the expectation that an expert would be "free from fees" if court-appointed and "able to testify as a scientist" is valid theoretically but leaves no room for the delicate nuances entering into a subjective judgment. On balance, it would seem that the adversary system with opportunities for cross-examination and rebuttal of witnesses provides the best basis for operation of what Goldstein calls the "pragmatic genius of the Anglo-American system."

Qualifying the Expert

The direct examination develops the psychiatric aspects of the case for the accused or the plaintiff. In using experts, the attorney may forestall troublesome questions by qualifying his expert with care. This qualification will establish his knowledge of the field, aid in credibility-anticipation, and possibly remove some of the sting of cross-examination. An example of a thorough qualification of a neuro-logic-psychiatric expert, Dr. Martin Towler, by Melvin Belli in the Jack Ruby trial[13] follow:

(After identifying the doctor)

Q. And what is your speciality in the medical profession, doctor?
A. I specialize in neurology and psychiatry.
Q. Are you on the staff of any hospital in Texas?
A. I am on the staff of the University of Texas Medical Branch Hospital, in Galveston.
Q. Do you do any teaching?
A. I am a professor of the Department of Neurology and Psychiatry, in the Medical Branch in Galveston.
Q. Let me go back, Doctor, and ask you about your qualifications so that we will know who you are. You were graduated first from what school of learning, before you took your medical work?
A. I took my pre-medical training at the University of Texas in Austin. Then I graduated from the University of Texas Medical Branch in Galveston.
Q. After your graduation there, did you specialize?
A. I took the required additional six years of training and qualifications for the Board in Psychiatry and Neurology.
Q. You are a diplomate, are you not, in your specialty?

A. I am a diplomate of the Board of Neurology, American Board of Neurology and Psychiatry.
Q. In Neurology and Psychiatry. Is there likewise a Board to which those proficient in their arts, are certified in electroencephalography?
A. There is an American Board of Electroencephalography. I have been certified to that Board.
Q. How long have you been certified in electroencephalography?
A. Since about 1948 or '9, I am not sure about that year.
Q. Do you read your own electroencephalograms?
A. Yes, sir, I do.
Q. Have you done any writing in your particular field?
A. I have written articles on neurology, psychiatry and electroencephalography.
Q. Have you seen many or any epileptic cases in your career?
A. I have seen a great many.
Q. Could you tell us roughly, how many electroencephalograms, in your career, you have read? Would that run into thousands or what?
A. I read approximately four thousand a year, and I have over quite a few years.

The Direct Examination

The purpose of the direct examination of an expert is to bring the findings and conclusion of the examiner before the jury. The attorney, after he has established the expert's background, training, and experience, brings out the salient findings and establishes as much of the material as would present a clear picture to the jury of the mental state of his client. All aspects of the case at issue, civil or criminal, are laid out in sequential order to support the final opinion of the witness. The witness, of course, follows the attorney's progression, but may, in a situation where a dynamic interpretation may be in order, attempt to introduce psychologic detail subject to objections by opposing counsel. At times, counsel for the defendant in a criminal case may present the whole picture through a hypothetical question addressed to the expert witness. This was the situation in a murder case where the accused was convicted on three counts of first degree murder and five counts of kidnapping; the murders were of a doctor, his daughter, and his wife, in that order. The first two homicides were not defended; the third became the main subject of this part of the testimony (see Chapter 6). The expert had been qualified: [14]

Q. Now have you had occasion to examine the defendant in this case, John C.?
A. I have.
Q. And for what period of time, total, did you examine him and work with him?
A. I saw him February 22nd at the County Jail for a period of more than four hours, and I saw him again last night at the County Jail for about a little more than an hour.

Q. During that time, did you conduct certain tests, medical, psychiatric or both with respect to Mr. C.?

A. I gave him a brief neurological examination. I couldn't do it completely, and then most of the time I spent in an interview and observations and getting details on his background, mental condition, and so on.

Q. In addition, did you have an opportunity to acquaint yourself with the facts of this case as alleged by the People?

A. Yes, I read the records extensively.

Q. Now let's assume, Doctor, that Mr. C. has testified in this case that he was involved with a group originating in the bay area who—to whom only one individual was known to him by the name of Rod, that as a result of his involvement he went to the ranch of a Clayton B. G., a veterinarian in the Willows area, and that he further testified under oath that he assisted in taking, against their will, apparently, Doctor G., who is a veterinarian in his 50's, his 13 year-old daughter who he gave into the charge of a person he alleges to be his confederate, Rod, and that he thereafter personally took, again, presumably, against their will, the 22 year-old son of Doctor G. and Nancy G., the wife, a lady in her 50's, now if you know the record and the pleadings with respect to this matter and you've indicated that you've read them, Mr. C. is being accused of personally being responsible for the deaths of the 13 year-old girl, Lisa G., of the veterinarian, Clayton B. G., as well as —these deaths were alleged to have occurred by garrotting with bailing wire. The death of Nancy G. is alleged to have occurred as a result of a single gunshot wound from a large caliber high velocity gun.

Now Mr. C. denies having any personal involvement with the deaths of the girl, the 13 year-old girl, and father. On the other hand—and he further denies there was any prior plan to kill the 13 year-old girl or her father or for that matter the 22 year-old son or his mother. However, in this the defendant has admitted on the stand under direct examination and further under cross-examination that he was present when Mrs. G. was shot in a field to which he transported her, that the gun had been fired and that he was aware shortly thereafter that she was either dead or she had been shot. Now assuming those facts, Doctor, and assuming what your examinations have disclosed with respect to Mr. C., what would be your opinion as to his medical psychiatric frame of mind throughout this area starting with the beginning of the hypothetical?

District
Attorney: Your Honor, may I interpose an objection at this time? May we approach the Bench?
(Bench conference.)

The Court: Let the record show that the objection to the last question is sustained. Will you please reword your question, Mr. S.?

Mr. S: All right, your Honor, bearing in mind the hypothetical we were discussing.

Q. My question to you is as a result of your background, your studies, your interviews with the defendant, your knowledge of the facts of this case. Have you formed any opinion with respect to the defendant's probable state of mind at the time of the occurrences that are alleged here?

A. I have.

District
Attorney: I'm going to object, your Honor, as vague and ambiguous . . .

The Court: Objection is over-ruled.

Mr. S: You may answer, Doctor. Go ahead.

A. It's my opinion that he was in a dissociative state . . . sometimes known as a fugue state, F-U-G-U-E state. When a person acts without full conscious knowledge of what he's doing.

And to explain that, we have to go back to the background and get the whole picture of the personality.
The main features are that the—

District
Attorney: I'm going to object, your Honor. It's non-responsive.

The Court: Sustained.

Mr. S: What part of it, your Honor?

Court: After he said, defines it, then he's not responsive. When he starts to lecture on what he did.

District
Attorney: Move to strike the balance.

Court: It will be stricken . . .

Mr. S: Now Doctor, you've stated an opinion, and I would ask you at this time to state, what did you use to form the basis of your opinion?

A. Well, the first element was the history of C.'s personal development. And the first element that I considered was the fact that early in life, between the ages of nine and twelve, he's described as a wild individual. They'd been to a psychiatrist following some school disruption. And some years later, in his adolescence, he was taken to a psychiatrist after some legal episode.

That the history states that he had a very stormy marital situation which culminated in a finding of his wife being unfaithful, and this gave him a tremendous emotional reaction which lasted for weeks and months.

And that the present situation which you're asking me about occurred in an area where he had taken his wife, lovers' lane, at one time, and later for reconciliation.

And that the emotional reactions about the infidelity and his wife's leaving him were strong elements that synthesized in him, made him blow up . . .

I further consider the fact that sometime in September, which was shortly after his wife finally left . . . he engaged in behavior which I would describe as psychotic, that is, mentally ill. That he was disconnected in speech. That he hallucinated; that is, he talked to people who weren't there. He thought he saw people in an orchard that were not in fact there. That he was wild and fighting, out of control, and out of contact with reality. That this subsided after a while when he left the area.

That later on, when involved in this ride with two people, he was under the instructions of a certain alleged person. And that this involved doing something which he had never done before, namely: Shoot someone. That the emotional impact so overthrew his control, his conscious control . . . that during the time of the shooting of Mrs. G. he did not have a full sense of consideration and deliberation.

And this I call a disassociative reaction or a fugue state . . . I've seen a few cases of this type, where there's a big conflict . . . which floods up and overthrows conscious control for the moment.

I also considered the fact that he described what we call a Deja vu, D-e-j-a v-u, which means a feeling of having already done this before. . . . It occurs to many people, particularly people who are depressed, sensitive people. That what they've done . . . they've done before in some peculiar sense of remote behavior. And this represents to us the presence of a serious emotional conflict . . . with a change in consciousness, not the clarity that one has in ordinary situations.

And all things I think lead to this state which I think impaired the capacity to think, to meditate, to form a judgment.

Q. You say to think and form a judgment. Would you say that the conditions that you feel as a result of your knowledge and study and exposure to Mr. C. would reflect on his ability to maturely and meaningfully premeditate and deliberate upon a crime such as a homicide?

A. Yes, I think it influences whatever deliberation means, which means to make a judgment, to think of consequences. And at that point he didn't have that capacity by virtue of this emotional exposure.

District
Attorney: Your Honor, if I may, I hate to interrupt the Doctor. I believe it's non-responsive to the question, if I understand the response.

From the position of the expert witness who wishes to detail all he has uncovered about the case at issue, objections by the opposing counsel may be disturbing. These objections can be legally realistic or general demurrers that an explanation given by the witness is "vague" or ambiguous. Thus, an analysis of the defendant's background and emotional reactions is often blocked. However, when such material forms the grounds for the expert's opinion, it may be admissible. The witness then can elaborate on the history and the total situation as permitted by the judge. In general, the extent of information to be testified to has been discussed with counsel before the court hearing so it will coincide with the defendant's counsel's strategy. Sometimes the hypothetical question outlines the underlying psychiatric problem in the defendant, often it does not. In cases of not guilty by reason of insanity (not the situation in the case of John C.), a dynamic interpretation is of less moment than a descriptive diagnosis of the defendant.

The Cross-Examination

The purpose of the cross-examination is, as noted, to expose the witness's credibility, to contradict the evidence adduced, to minimize its significance, and to point up the expert's bias in his testimony. The rules of evidence allow the cross-examiner to point up hearsay and to impeach the witness; an unwritten law permits the cross-examiner to try to nettle the expert and so to introduce confusion or at least contradiction in his testimony. From the standpoint of the witness, these techniques, though valid, can be countered by honest, careful answers to the questions proposed, by restricting the testimony to what is known, and by resisting any tendency to argue with the cross-examiner. Testifying in court for the psychiatrist or psychologist is unquestionably a trying experience. On leaving the stand, he can feel that his "truth" has been distorted or macerated and that he has been pilloried in "having to fend off serious attacks upon his dignity, his honesty and his intelligence," as Seymour Halleck puts it.[15]

A transcript of the cross-examination of the author's testimony in the trial of Jack Ruby[16] illustrates some of the principles outlined above.

The direct examination by Mr. Belli summed up the conclusion reached; that Jack Ruby was an unstable personality verging on psychopathic personality, that he suffered several depressions and at least one head injury, and that he was an aggressive, impulsive individual whose personality could be described as "epileptoid" and whose fugue state (at the time of the murder) lay within the limits of psychomotor epilepsy. The last question of the direct examination was:

Q. All right, now, did you find any manic depressive traits within this brittle personality, and your epileptoid personality—pathology?
A. Yes. You see the total picture—I called it complicated earlier, it's complicated in this sense. There is a basic emotional instability which leads into depressions. And there has been a history of several in this case. There is also the organic background which merges with the instability; the background being that of the epileptoid personality or the epilepsy equivalent. So the two elements come in here, as I study this case, both organic and psychological.

The cross-examination by Mr. Wade, district attorney of Dallas County, considerably abridged, follows:

Q. Doctor, you mentioned that you had been on the staff out at Mendocino State Hospital in California from August 1950 to April, 1951, I believe—September 21st, 1951?
A. About fourteen months, yes.

Q. I believe there was some difficulty there with the rest of the staff, between you and them, isn't that right?

A. No...

Q. On how to handle sex offenders?

A. Difficulty between me and the Director of the Department of Mental Hygiene.

Q. You thought that sex criminals that you had—they were all sex criminals, weren't they, of some sort?

A. Yes, the group I had.

Q. I believe that it was your recommendation that they be released in the community and run around loose, isn't that right?

A. No—no. I was called to conduct this research project, and I did. And part of my research was to treat them, and part of the treatment resulted in some benefit. And then arose the difficulty in my idea and the Director of Mental Hygiene's ideas, and that was the thing. It was the conflict of ideas.

Q. Isn't it a fact that your idea was that in rehabilitating them, they should have furloughs out among the citizens there?

A. That was the interpretation put upon it by the Department of Mental Hygiene. It was different from mine. I said that they shouldn't be locked up behind stone walls, if they were better; and that the process of treatment involved some freedom on the grounds. And that's the exact situation. And the Department had other ideas...

Q. I know you became Clinical Director but on September 21st or thereabouts, "He was given notice that he was rejected as a permanent employee in this clinical job for the reasons given below."

A. After fourteen months activity the conflict between myself and the Director was such that I had to stop work. I was not rejected. I had the job, but there was a conflict, so I ceased working there...

Q. Well, did they turn you down or didn't they?

A. Well, I lost the hearing, if that's what you mean. The conflict there was with the Department, and I was an individual.

Q. Now Doctor, on another subject, you have testified, of course, a number of times for Mr. Belli and his firm, is that right?

A. Not a number of times. One or two cases from his office, yes.

Q. Tell the Jury how many, exactly, you have now, Doctor, one, two, three, four or five? You know how many you have testified in for him or his firm previous to this.

A. Yes. To my recollection, two, that I remember now.

Q. Are you telling the Jury positively that two are all you have testified in?

A. That's my best recollection now, yes.

Q. That is for him or any member of his firm?

A. Yes.

Q. And in this case, since you have worked on it, I believe they pay you $350.00 a day, is that right?

A. That would be usual, yes.

Q. Now, as a matter of fact, Doctor, you don't even agree with the Texas law on this right and wrong test on insanity, do you, in your book?

A. Yes.

Q. You know what the McNaughton [sic] rule is, don't you?

A. Yes.

Q. As a matter of fact, in a lot of these books, you disregard—you disagreed with that rule, isn't that right?

A. I recognize the rule. I have ideas about it, yes.

Q. I mean you don't even agree that should be the test in a case of this kind?
Mr. Belli: I think there is a lot of people that don't agree with. . . .
Mr. Alexander: Now, your Honor, he doesn't need any coaching from Mr. Belli.

Q. (By Mr. Wade): Now, Dr. Bromberg, tell the Jury specifically what you are diagnosing this trouble as.

A. I am diagnosing him as a epileptoid personality, with epileptic equivalent, and an extremely unstable makeup, which dips into depressive episodes at certain times in his life.

Q. Well, are you saying he is a psychomotor epileptic? You can answer the question whether you think he is or isn't.

A. Yes. He has that condition. He suffers from that condition. . . .

Q. Well, now, let's go next, would you say he is a manic-depressive?

A. I say he has depressions—had depressions.

Q. I believe you testified on the other hearing though, that you diagnosed it as manic depressive?

A. Yes. Those depressions which he had come under the heading of manic depressive psychosis. . . .

Q. As a matter of fact, Ruby doesn't even fit the description you have given in your book for manic depressive, does he?

. . .

A. Well, the textbook is only a wordy description of many kinds of people. That's just a symbol of the condition. And no textbook fits any case specifically, exactly.

Q. Well, I want to know just what was going on, epilepsy or manic depressive, or something else? . . .

A. This man is a basic psychotic personality, meaning emotional instability, throughout his life. He has an epileptoid personality, with occasional psychomotor seizures. He has depressions, which trigger off these epileptic equivalents. That's the total diagnosis in a nutshell.

Q. As a matter of fact, in your book you wrote, you found that epileptic criminals—is a minor factor in major crime and had practically no percentagewise, that it was minor, isn't that right?

A. Well, that refers to all major crimes, the total picture of major crime.

. . .

Q. And I believe you wrote another book, "Crime in the Mind," didn't you?

A. Yes sir.

Q. Page 71 . . . "The implication that hidden epilepsy manifested in a fugue state or post epileptic automatic furor, is the cause of otherwise inexplicable violence, carries less validity at the present time."
Does that sound like you?

A. That was written in 1948, yes.

Q. 1948. Have you changed your mind on that since?

A. No. I believe what I said. And there are cases that do have validity.

Q. As a matter of fact, when you and Dr. Guttmacher were talking to Ruby, he was asked by Dr. Guttmacher, "Why didn't you shoot the second time?" And he told you all, "The police grabbed my hand."

A. I don't recall that . . .

Q. Your diagnosis is depending on what he told you, is that right about it? Does that enter into your diagnosis?

A. Part of it, yes. It has to do with it, yes.

. . .

Q. Doctor, would it change your thinking about him any—assume he did remember all this and didn't tell you about it.

A. Well, if he remembered it and didn't tell me, I wouldn't know that he remembered it. I can only tell what he remembered, from what he told me. . . .

. . .

Q. Suppose when, after arrested, after talking immediately with Dr. Holbrook, or the next day, and not telling him any of the things that he told you about all this episodic behavior; and then his lawyers announced that he was temporarily insane on the day of the killing, and immediately after Mr. Belli got in the case, publicly, talking to him at various times.

And then when he gets to you—when certain other psychiatrists got to see him, he refused to talk to them, representing us, our psychologists, on advice of lawyers. And then—

Mr. Tonahill: That's prejudicial. The law doesn't refuse him the right to talk to them, Your Honor.

We ask for a mistrial.

Court: Overrule your objection.

. . .

Q. And suppose that when he gets to you he can't remember anything about it. I know you are good at reading people's minds, but when he sits down, he doesn't remember anything other than saying, "I am Jack Ruby."

If all those facts were so, would it alter your opinion in any way?

Mr. Tonahill: Now, Your Honor, the trouble with that question, particularly the last part of it, is that all those facts aren't so. Some of them are absolute misrepresentations.

Q. Just assume they are, Doctor. . . .

A. If he didn't say the things he said to me, that he did say, and his behavior was not what he said, that it was, the situation being entirely different, it is conceivable that a different conclusion would come from that material.

Mr. Wade: I believe that's all.

Re-Direct Examination by Mr. Belli:

Q. Doctor, is there anything I could have said to him as a lawyer, or a doctor, a psychiatrist, a priest or a holy man, or a legal man, that could have changed his electroencephalogram?

A. No, definitely no.

Q. Is there anything I could have said to him, in the same category, one or all of them, that could have changed his Rorschach examination?

A. No, nothing you could say could have changed that.

Q. Is there anything that I could have said to him, or could have done to him, or for him or that anyone else could have said to him or have done for him, or administered to him—

A. Nothing.

Q. —that would change the MMPI test, the Bellevue Wechsler test, memory recall test, or any of the other nine basic psychological tests?

A. Nothing.

Q. A man with an unstable personality, and a man with psychomotor epilepsy pathology, if he were living in a city like Dallas, and the events that happened here, would that agitate anybody with that type of personality?

A. I feel it would.

Q. And what is it that triggers these men off, with this unstable personality and psychomotor epilepsy equivalent. Is it auditory or olfactory, visual or psychic stimuli?

A. Well, there's two groups of stimuli; One is physical, that is fatigue, sometimes alcoholism, or any physical illness; second, his great emotional shock or great emotional agitation will trigger off these seizures.

Q. How long do you think he has had these conditions that you have observed in him?

A. I think that he has suffered from epileptoid personality most of his life. I think he has been a sick man, sometimes the sickness hasn't risen to the level we call an illness; sometimes it has. I think that's the basic personality that he has had all of his life. . . .

. . .

Re-Cross-Examination by Mr. Wade.

Q. Doctor, was Dr. Shafer's psychological report instrumental in your findings, help you in your findings?

A. It confirmed my clinical diagnosis, yes. It confirmed it.

Q. It confirmed it. Was that confirming, the part where he ruled out manic depressive in his report, where he said there couldn't be any manic depressive here? You read that, didn't you?

A. I have his report, yes.

Q. You read where he ruled out schizophrenia and manic depressive?

A. I don't recall that particular part, but I can find it.

Q. Page 4, you can look at it, about four lines—just read the first four lines.

A. Yes, I see it.

Q. What does it say?

A. A number of other diagnostic possibilities have been considered and ruled out . . . borderline schizophrenia, manic depressive, psychosis, paranoid state and severe recent brain damage or deterioration. . . .

Q. Is that report—you say that confirmed your report, you say it is manic depression, didn't you here?

A. Well, I make the diagnosis. This is a laboratory test.
Dr. Schafer assays diagnostic possibilities. That's his discussion, but I say that the tests corroborate my clinical diagnosis.

Q. Well, he says that the test does not indicate manic depressive, doesn't he? Well you didn't agree with him on that.

A. No, he is a psychologist and I am a psychiatrist. I am a physician, and we make diagnoses. A psychologist makes reports of tests. It's a different situation there.

Q. And there wasn't any indication up here at the City Hall that he was trying to kill himself, when he killed Oswald, was there?

A. I didn't hear there was, no.

Q. He didn't tell you there was, did he?

A. No.

Q. How far did he tell you he was away from Oswald?

A. Well, as he came down the ramp, he first encountered Oswald within ten or twelve feet from where he stood. That's a clear perception on his part, as I remember.

And the next clear perception, he knew, that he was on the concrete floor of the ramp.

Apparently he advanced in those few steps in an automatic way until he was closer.

. . .

Q. He didn't remember being two feet away from Oswald?

A. That was my discussion of it. That was not a clear memory.

Q. Look on Page 12 of your report, "That it flashed through his mind as he saw Oswald, that Oswald was a smirking Commie—a Commie Rat, and he took another stride, his hand in his pocket. By this time he was within two feet of Oswald." That's in your own report!

A. These are my notes in the report. I believe that this phrase, "Smirking, a Commie Rat," is a retrospective confabulation. I don't think he was clear enough at that time to formulate those concepts.

Q. You don't even believe that was so, when he told you.

A. I said his words, but I think they were what we call retrospective falsification, they were fitted in.

Q. He had a tendency—grandiose tendency, I believe is what you testified before?

A. Yes.

Q. Is that right?

A. Yes, that's correct.

Q. He had a feeling—you get the impression he liked to be in the limelight or in the center of things, didn't you?

A. That is correct.

Q. And he had a feeling of wanting to be a hero, is that right?

A. A martyr, rather. He had a definite Messianic trend, his motto being to rescue the Jewish people from the charge that they haven't got guts, to put it in his words.

Q. He also told you that he wanted to prove that Jews did have guts, didn't he?

A. Yes, he said that many times.

Q. He said that many times. As a matter of fact, he was upset over that Bernard Weissman ad. He discussed the Bernard Weissman ad that was in the paper.

A. Yes.

Q. He had the feeling that someone had put that name "Weissman" in there to somewhat adversely affect the Jewish people, isn't that right?

A. Yes, he did think that.

Q. Don't you think, Doctor, that shooting a man on television, before quite a
   number of people, would have the effect of a person having grandiose tendencies, would have the effect, he thought, of making him a hero?
A. I feel at that time he had no such thought because his consciousness was suspended; he was in turmoil and agitation.

Re-Direct Examination by Mr. Belli:
Q. Doctor, you know that Mr. Belli hadn't even seen this man until two weeks
   after the jail—I mean Dr. Holbrook had examined him and found him to have
   an unstable—u-n-s-t-a-b-l-e personality? You know that from history, don't
   you?
A. Yes...
Q. You used the word "Messianic" trend. What was that expression or what is
   that word?
A. Well, that refers to the idea that a person thinks he is the savior of the race,
   so to speak, the Messiah, one of the Messiahs, you know; and people who
   think that they are the Messiah for any group of people have a delusion that
   they are going to save the race for the salvation of man, and so on. And he
   had that idea for years. It popped up all through his history.

. . .

The Deposition

A deposition of a psychiatric expert is, as with all other witnesses,
part of discovery procedures. The attorney opposing the one for whom
the expert will testify conducts the examination. A court reporter is
present, the witness is sworn, and objections are recorded, but no rulings are made on the testimony. The purpose of the deposition is to explore the opinions of the witness and the material on which he or she
based his or her opinions. The material may be used for possible impeachment at the subsequent trial and to preserve evidence "for use at
the trial if the deponent becomes unavailable" and for possible cross-
examination.

There are other legal uses of the deposition but for the psychiatric
expert it functions chiefly as a final statement of his findings and conclusions of the case in hand. Since the deposition is taken as a sworn
statement, it befits the expert witness to regard it as equivalent to testimony in court, even though the atmosphere during a deposition (taken
in an office) is less contentious than a court appearance.

For this reason, the witness should not be misled in regarding the
deposition as less exacting than a court appearance. Since the procedure
of direct and cross-examination have been outlined above, nothing is
gained by reprinting a deposition here.

The re-direct, re-cross, rebuttal, and re-rebuttal and *voir dire* are
legal procedures utilized by attorneys and imply no special psychiatric
activity.

The Neuropsychiatric Written Report

The vastly more frequent use of neuropsychiatric expertise is not on the witness stand, but in written reports to judges, attorneys, administrative referees, and probation and parole officers. The format of such reports, usually in the medical tradition, covers the history, abstracts of documents from other physicians and hospitals, findings on examination, analysis of the current problem, and conclusions. If specific legal questions are asked, the answer is given following the medical conclusions, as in the case of workmen's compensation cases (where degrees of disability are requested), or in questions of proximate cause in personal injuries or criminal responsibility in response to legal tests. The desiderata of clarity, objectivity, and completeness are as essential in written reports as they are on the witness stand. A recent symposium on the written psychiatric report (arranged by the American Academy of Psychiatry and the Law, 1977, with psychiatric and judicial authorities) touched on some do's and don'ts of pragmatic value and will be outlined here.

Judge David O. Boehm of the New York Supreme Court recommended to the psychiatrists that the report start with the conclusion, and then present its justification through enumeration of the findings and reasons therefor. Dr. Seymour Pollack of the Institute of Psychiatry and the Law, University of Southern California, warned the psychiatrist not to "play lawyer" by reciting case law or to turn his report into a "legal brief." Attorney Michael Perlin, director of the New Jersey Division of Mental Health Advocacy, indicated the need for "simple English" and suggested that books on literary style were "better preparation" for the psychiatric report than any "law book or medical text."

Dr. Jacques Quen of the Psychiatric Department, Cornell University School of Medicine, urged that the psychiatrist be "authoritative but non-authoritarian." Dr. Robert Newman, director of the Department of Psychiatry, Louisiana State University, School of Medicine, advised that "the report should not be cluttered up with references to the medical literature."

An attorney recommended that the patient's informed consent should be obtained if "court action is anticipated."

The comments of these experts, in addition to the features in medical reports written by every physician, cover the situation adequately. The complexity of the case under review and the medico-legal implications obviously direct the length of the written report. Two case reports are presented below, each with a special problem requiring analysis: one criminal, one civil.

Case Number 1: Criminal

Dear [Attorney-at-Law]:

The patient was seen in this office on August 6, 19-. At that time, a full report from the Sheriff's Office, the Indictment, interviews with the various witnesses and the details of the armed robbery and kidnapping were at hand and studied carefully. The patient and his wife were interviewed, together and separately.

PAST HISTORY:

The patient is a man of thirty-two who was born in Idaho, but has been living in Northern California most of his life. After high school he enlisted in the United States Navy, where he spent four-and-a-half years. He received an Honorable Discharge and the only difficulty he had was as Captain's Mast for alcoholism and apparently some altercation with an officer. Following that, he worked in construction and lumber; and for five-and-a-half years as an iron worker. For the last few years, he has been developing his own auto repair business. He was married for eight years, has one child; the difficulties in his life revolve around a marital problem and his financial difficulties.

The marital situation will be discussed first:

The wife, aged thirty-two also described the marriage as full of tension and bickering from the very start. She relates that the two important sources of irritation were: First: the mother-in-law, whom she describes as an overbearing woman who was closely tied to the son (the husband), and was vitally interested in his welfare to the point that she entered into the business. She had free access to the office, as did the wife. Apparently, some years ago, the mother-in-law beat up the wife, and more recently when they were both in the office, an altercation developed and the mother-in-law struck and bit the wife. The patient was working on a car at the time and he came over and found them both on the floor with the mother-in-law over the wife. This tension persisted and it seems that the patient was unable to settle the problem on either side.

However, prior to that, there had been a long series of disagreements between the patient and his wife, mostly as the result of what the wife calls an attitude of arrogance and domination. The patient, on the other hand, claims that the wife was overanxious to know what he was thinking and there was a total breakdown in their communication. This situation culminated in his leaving to see his father in Idaho or to go to see an old girlfriend and thus try to settle the marital disharmony.

The second element in his frustration and emotional agitation was the fact that he was already behind some $2,500.00 in expenses in his business and unpaid taxes.

PERSONAL HISTORY:

The patient, as noted, is thirty-two. He has never had any major physical or mental disturbances. He did have one arrest for drunk driving for which he paid a fine. He drank occasionally, but never to excess except for that one episode and has not used drugs. He describes himself as a hard-working man, content with very little, and both the patient and his wife agree that he worked as long as twelve or fourteen hours a day in order to liquidate his debts and get on a good footing in his business. He feels that he is a man of "basic instincts" by which he means he likes a home, a steady job, he loves to work and is very efficient at it and he is intent on making his own way in the world. His sexual activity was rather routine prior to his marriage and he claims since that time that he has had no extra-marital relationships. Of his family, he has four siblings who are apparently well-adjusted; a father who is a machinist and working in Idaho and who is divorced from the mother; a mother, who is said to be an alcoholic, although otherwise, apparently an on-going personality.

PSYCHIATRIC EXAMINATION:

The patient is a man of high average intelligence. His answers are responsive and he is able to explain his actions fairly well. He makes the point that when he left home on May 5th he had it in his mind to develop a permanent solution to his marital disharmony. Despite the patient's claim that he is a hard and steady worker, there is a marked degree of emotional instability and impulsiveness in this man. Undoubtedly, he was under pressure from his mother and from his wife which may have interfered with his judgment.

THE OFFENSE:

The patient's account of the offense indicates that he left his home and had gone to another town to seek out a girlfriend he knew once. When he found that she was not available, he turned and was returning home, having not quite decided whether or not to do so. Then suddenly he realized he had very little money. He saw a bar and the idea suddenly came to him to attempt a robbery. As soon as he entered the bar, the thought struck him that what he was doing was "stupid" and he then made preparations to leave. His discharging the six bullets from his revolver, he states, was only a defensive maneuver, after he had been shot at by the bartender. His escape, or attempted escape from the police, in which he was driving at a high speed, was in response to a panic reaction. As he drove along at high speed, he was aware that he had done something contrary to his nature and something very fool-hardy in retrospect, and this increased his panic. It is noteworthy that the patient says he had only several beers in the early part of that day, May 5th, and that he submitted himself to an examination by the police and that he did have 0.1% alcohol in his blood test according to official reports.

DISCUSSION:

The picture here is not entirely clear except that the patient was under great stress, both from the marital point of view and from his attempt to recoup his losses and pay his debts. He was also involved in an intramural tension between his mother and his wife that seemed to brook no solution. He was completely discouraged by his wife's lack of softness and insistence on probing into his feelings and felt that he had come to the end of his rope.

CONCLUSION:

From a technical point of view, this patient is not insane and is able to stand trial, to understand the nature of the defense and assist in his defense. There is, however, the circumstance that he was emotionally disturbed and that he was in a panic, was undecided as to how to conduct his life and how to solve the dilemmas in which he found himself. As a consequence, his act in the bar was impulsive in that the actual entering of the bar to acquire money was on the spur of the moment and not done with deliberation.

It is the professional opinion of this examiner that he did not have a specific intent to commit assault upon the man who was shot and that he had no specific intent to kidnap a woman who was in the bar. However, from the analysis of his mental state, this examiner cannot state that he was in such a mental condition as not to form the intent to commit a robbery.

Sincerely yours,

Case Number 2: Civil

In the following personal injury case, the problem revolved around the patient's refusal to submit to a laminectomy. The attorney's questions, that is, whether her denial of surgery was psychologically motivated, are answered at the conclusion of the report.

Dear Attorney at Law:

The patient was seen on February 8, 1977. At that time complete reports were available from examinations by Drs. A, B, C, D, and Dr. F, a chiropractor. In addition, there were reports of the myelogram. These conditions, particularly those of Dr. C, cover the period from November 6, 1975, to January 24, 1977. Without going into detail on the various examiners and their findings, it is granted that she had an injury to her back on November 6, 1975, by lifting a six-gallon carton of milk. She also had a positive myelogram in January of 1976, locating a disc protrusion and probable herniation at the L-5 and L-4 level, and a questionable defect at L-5, S-1.

HISTORY:

The history indicates that the patient was born in Oklahoma, but came to California at the age of six. She had two years of high school and then started to work. She was married at eighteen, and has had three marriages. The first one lasted two years; and the second one lasted about ten years, ended in divorce, but she had two children from that marriage, now grown. Her third marriage has lasted fourteen years and is quite satisfactory; her husband is forty-four and the patient is fifty-five. He is a truck driver and they have a small piece of land with some cattle and the usual husbandry. They have been active on this ranchette, and both the patient and her husband have worked steadily to keep the ranchette going. In her own family her mother is still living and in her 80's. Her father died about the age of seventy, and the siblings are in good condition. No nervous or mental disease in the family. The patient's medical history indicates that she had a hysterectomy some time ago, and had a fracture of the foot some years ago, but otherwise she has been well and active. She did all the chores on the ranchette and was active all day prior to November 6, 1975. It is noteworthy that between the second and third marriage she was single for about four years and maintained and brought up her sons at that time without any help.

On November 6, 1975, the patient was lifting a carton of milk, and had a severe pain in her back. It was located across the sacroiliac area with the pain extending down the left leg. From that time on, in spite of treatment by a chiropractor for a month and a half and medications, she had persistent pain. The pains are described as stretching across the lower back extending into the left leg, which then becomes numb. She also feels weakness in the calf muscles and the thigh muscles on the left side, and has cramps in the muscles of the foot, the calf, and the thigh, particularly the posterior aspect. She is unable to sit, to climb, to bend, to get in and out of a tub, and has difficulty in sleeping because of the pain. To use her words she is "never comfortable." The numbness which started in the left leg occasionally goes to the right, and with this there are headaches and difficulty in walking.

NEUROLOGICAL EXAMINATION:

The patient is a woman of average height and good development.

Gait: She walks extremely slow, favoring her left leg, and with some difficulty in extending the leg forward to a sufficient degree to take a full step. She is unable to stand on the left leg without aid, and can stand on her right leg with difficulty.

Reflexes: The reflexes in the upper extremities are normally present. In the lower extremities there is definite absence of reflexes at this time, even with the Jendrassik's maneuver on the left side. The right reflex appears more strongly with the reinforcement maneuver. There is no Babinski, but there is difficulty in extending the left big toe, as well as slow movements of the toes on request, resembling a foot drop.

Coordination: Essentially negative.

Sensation: The patient has a general hypesthesia and hypalgesia over the whole left lower extremity, and at times, in the chest and in the upper part of the arms. This extends to temperature, but not to vibration, and to pin-point and touch. In fact, she has difficulty in discriminating between pin-point and touch in the entire left extremity going beyond the knee.

Cranial Nerves: Essentially negative.

Physical Examination: The patient showed marked tenderness on pressure of all the muscles of the paravertebral groups on both sides starting with the trapezius and going down to the paraspinal muscles inserted in the ilium. There is also considerable tenderness in the sacroiliac area at the T-12 and L-5. There were no specific spasms encountered, although the muscles in the lumbar region are somewhat tense.

PSYCHIATRIC EXAMINATION:

The patient is intelligent, makes responsive answers, and is oriented and clear. She describes her symptoms precisely, and during the examination she has to stand up even though she is in a hardbacked chair, because of the ache across her back. All of her movements are slow, particularly sitting and standing. She says she is unable to lie on the floor because she has difficulty in getting up. As far as her housework is concerned, she is unable to bend, and therefore, cannot vacuum or do any work except perhaps standing up when doing the dishes. All of her activities are slowed up, and her social life is diminished.

PERSONALITY ANALYSIS:

The patient describes her reluctance to have a laminectomy as urged by some physicians because she was "scared of surgery." She makes it clear that when she says she was "terrified" of surgery, she meant that it is her experience that many people who have had laminectomies or disc difficulties have not been helped, in fact have been worse after the operation. Add to this, the fact that she had two experiences in her family in which her mother-in-law was treated surgically for a minor procedure and died on the operating table, and a father-in-law who also had an inoperable cancer of the liver who died three days post-surgery. However, she does not place these in any more than normal perspective, but accents the fact that people do not do well after surgery in her lay experience, but adds that if it be true that the disc would deteriorate in time and she was paralyzed or disabled more than now, she would submit to surgery.

DISCUSSION:

The picture must be approached first as that of an individual with a definite LUMBROSACRAL SPRAIN about a year and a quarter ago, with a LEFT SCIATIC SYNDROME. This is demonstrated by the pain, difficulty in loco-motion, the absent AJ, and the sensory signs. The second point is the sensory signs which are a little excessive, but do not correspond to the glove and stocking type characteristic of hysteria. There is rather a generalized sensitivity which sometimes occurs in back injuries which spreads cephalad up to the shoulder and neck region and distally to the buttocks and the calf muscles. This can be re-garded as an overflow sensory reaction to an original left sciatic nerve pressure which must be combined with the fact that this woman is sensitive to pain. Another point is the fact that she seems to have difficulty in moving her toes and particularly the extensor hallucis on the left side in the manner of a myotonia. There is a slowness in voluntarily moving these muscles, and this examiner can-not place this entirely to her wish—in fact, she tries hard to move her toes and only slowly is able to overcome the apparent hypertonicity of these muscles, i.e. the peroneal muscles in the left foot.

From the standpoint of her personality one must conclude that she is the average American woman, of average or even better intelligence, who has ad-justed to her life pattern well and rationally, who shows no signs of definite neurosis, nor of hysteria, nor malingery. What we are faced with here is a lady who is sensitive to the dyskinesias caused by the injury, and probably has a LOW PAIN THRESHOLD.

CONCLUSION:

The spread of sensory changes throughout the entire left side, the sensitivity to palpation of the back muscles can be labeled a FUNCTIONAL OVERLAY.

In this examiner's opinion the patient is disabled from her work at the present time.

It is strongly recommended, however, that she has physical therapy consisting of massage, active and passive movement, ultrasonic stimulation, and steam packs, as well as considerable encouragement and sympathetic, though vigorous, handling.

In answer to your specific questions:

(1) The patient does not suffer from a severe psychological disability which precludes her for surgery. She has an attitude toward surgery derived from her common everyday experience, and a degree of low tolerance to pain.
(2) This psychological disability is not total, but her physical disability is total.
(3) The psychological disability has been stimulated or provoked by the industrial accident.
(4) My prognosis, as noted above, is fairly good, providing she has the treatment as outlined.
(5) My comment would be that her attitude toward surgery is self-protective, but not such as would not yield to real necessity for surgery or to a reasonable explanation by a prospective surgeon.

Thank you for referring this case to me.

Sincerely yours,

Notes

1. Manfred Guttmacher, *Principal Difficulties with the Present Criteria of Responsibility and Possible Alternatives:* 171, Am. Law Inst. Model Penal Code No. 4, Philadelphia (1955).

2. Gregory Zilboorg, *The Reciprocal Responsibility of Law and Psychiatry,* The Shingle 83 (Apr. 1949).

3. Walter Bromberg, *Psychiatrists in Court: The Pyschiatrist's View,* 125 Am. J. Psych. 296 (April 1969).

4. *Admissibility of Expert Testimony. Weinstein's Evidence* 3: Sec. 702(02), Matthew Bender Co. (1977).

5. James R. Richardson, *Doctors, Lawyers and the Courts:* 282, W. H. Anderson Co., Cincinnati (1965).

6. *Dunphy v. Dunphy* 161 Calif. 380 (1911).

7. Richardson, *Doctors, Lawyers, and the Courts.*

8. Abraham S. Goldstein, *The Psychiatrist and the Legal Process: The Proposal for an Impartial Expert and for Preventive Detention,* 23 J. Orthopsych. 123 (1963).

9. Bernard L. Diamond, *The Fallacy of the Impartial Expert*, 3 Arch. of Crim. Psychodynamics 221 (Spring 1959).

10. Bernard Diamond, *The Psychiatric Advocate*, 1 J. Psych. & L. 5 (Spring 1973).

11. S. Polsky et al., *Symposium on Expert Testimony*, 34 Temple L. Q. 357 (1961).

12. Elwood Levy, *Impartial Medical Testimony*, 34 Temple L. Q. 416 (1961).

13. *State v. Jack Ruby*, in *Trial* 6: 59, Matthew Bender Co. (Dec. 1964).

14. *People v. Card*, Merced Super. Ct., Calif. no. 8077 (1975).

15. Seymour Halleck, *A Critique of Current Psychiatric Roles in Legal Process*, Wisc. L. Rev. 379, 395 (1966).

16. *The Trial of Jack Ruby*, 6, no . 4, Trauma 215 (1964).

3

By Reason of Insanity

The main difficulty in applying psychiatric knowledge to cases alleging insanity before the court is the translation of "psychosis," a psychiatric concept, to "insanity," a legal one. The obviously psychotic person who perpetrates a crime presents no medical problems for the expert and few legal problems for the court and defense or prosecuting attorneys. More puzzling are the cases where it is difficult to draw the fine line dividing those who have a psychosis not amounting to legal insanity from those who are technically insane. The question then becomes one of how the psychiatric decision is made in conformity with legal rules established by statute and case law decisions. Although the law on criminal responsibility for capital crimes has been settled, the theoretical and practical problems raised by *close* cases have been debated for the past century or more, and are still being debated. This chapter describes the complex skein of legal logic and psychiatric thinking that has surrounded the subject.

The issue of responsibility for major crime rests on the accepted dictum that each accused person is presumed to be sane unless proved otherwise. Conviction or acquittal on a murder charge involves a determination of the capacity or incapacity to form an intent to murder. The basic doctrine of *mens rea* states that a person of unsound mind, or one of defective intelligence, is incapable of forming an intent to kill. This principle has been fundamental in jurisprudence for at least a millennium in all cultures. According to anthropologist E. Adamson Hoebel of the University of Minnesota, the same idea is embedded in the laws and political structure of primitive tribes. Among the Ashanti, a tribe on the Gold Coast of West Africa whom Hoebel studied,[1] careful attention was given to the question of intent in Ashanti murder trials. He writes: "A mens rea had definitely to be established. Otherwise a plea of accidental homicide would hold and the slaying would be accepted as the action of an evil spirit misdirecting the activity of the killer." One can almost sense the term *evil spirits* being substituted for insanity!

The Problem of Insanity in Homicide

In our sophisticated society, the degree of mental illness that directs the killer becomes the test of responsibility for the crime. A case of homicide is presented here in order to introduce the modern tests for avoiding responsibility due to insanity. Although the homicide was apparently a volitional act and no insanity plea was made, the case still raises the issue of mental abnormality. A young man in his late twenties whom we shall call Henry was accused of stabbing a man in the back thirteen times and leaving him dead.[2]

Henry, who made his living through petty theft and burglary, obtained a job as short order cook. On the evening of the crime, he wrapped his boning knives in an apron, left his job and was picked up by a man dressed in silk pajamas. They drove to the country where a homosexual act was committed with the agreement of Henry.

Henry's account of the crime pointed towards a dream-like state which, combined with impulsive knifing, suggested an automatic act, neither premeditated nor deliberated. He said: "He was leaning over from the driver's seat, well, going down on me. Something went on in me, kind of revolted . . . I reached over for my cook's tools. I grabbed the knife . . . I plunged it into his back. I don't remember the rest." When he reached town, he saw blood on his hands. "I came to . . . It was kind of like being drunk."

He left the victim, fled the area in the car, and was apprehended in another state. There was no resistance; in fact, Henry told the police: "I did it, I don't know why." His airy speech was unlike what the police expected from a seasoned miscreant.

Thorough examination, both psychiatric and psychologic, resulted in a finding of a psychopathic personality, "with primitiveness of thinking, an emotional blandness, inability to empathize and egocentricity." Henry's legal defender was piqued by his ready confession, airy manner, and interest in poetry. Further study revealed a homosexual tendency and an unusual fascination with Oscar Wilde's writings, especially his fairy tale, *The Happy Prince*. [The tale is of a bejeweled statue of a prince in a medieval town, who asked that his sapphire eyes, gold leaf, precious jewels in his sword be given to the poor of the town, leaving only base metal which was melted by the townspeople. But the heart of lead would not melt.] Henry wanted to be the Prince, a "Christ-like figure who gives his all. . . ." He recognized his masochistic identification with Wilde's Prince.

Throughout the examination, Henry displayed a blandness and aloofness surprising to his legal defender and psychiatrists. "I am destined for the gas chamber," he said, "I have an inclination for that."

There was no claim of insanity but the question arose whether a person in an emotional dreamland, a schizoid reverie, could deliberate and premeditate. The defense psychiatrist described the murder as occurring in a homosexual panic:

Q. Now, Doctor, do you attach any true significance to the fact that this particular event happened during the commission of a homosexual act?

A. Yes, I do. I think that the impact of a homosexual act somehow started the train of reactions which resulted in this impulsive killing. Some sort of a sudden realization occurred, a revulsion, that set off in its train this impulsive act and that interfered with whatever deliberation might have been possible. That is why I say his capacity to deliberate was impaired.

In the cross-examination as to the deliberation issue, the District Attorney focused on the grasping of the knife through which the slaying occurred:

Q. It would likewise then be possible that in reaching for the knife he could be reaching for something he would recognize as a potentially lethal weapon?

A. You are asking about knowing [his knowledge]?

Q. Yes, sir.

A. With respect to knowing, I think he knew what a knife was when he saw a knife; he possibly knew what a knife was when he felt that knife.

Q. Could you give us your opinion as to the point after the incident, or during the incident, when the defendant did regain his full capacity, when his capacity was no longer impaired?

A. We are speaking about capacity to premeditate and deliberate?

Q. Yes.

A. Which is different than knowing?

Q. Yes.

A. The point at which he regained his capacity to deliberate, I think, was when he came to in the drive-in (after the murder).

Other experts, however, did not agree that the defendant's emotional explosiveness impaired his capacity to premeditate. One expert witness pointed to behavior after the crime that disclosed an apparent rationality and with it a capacity to premeditate. The cross-examination of this witness by the defense follows:

Q. Now, the fact that he is leaving the scene—you said he did all these things, went to the car, drove away—the fact that he scattered the belongings from the wallet throughout the area and the fact that he dropped some of his own objects that would identify him, you say that tells you that he had the capacity to premeditate?

A. That is one of the points, yes.

Q. And that indicates to you, Doctor, that he had the capacity to premeditate and deliberate. Is that right?

A. Yes, he was wanting to get rid of the objects.

Q. . . . does it appear strange to you that a person who had this tremendous capacity wouldn't go back and remove these instruments and hide them?

A. Yes, I think here we have to realize that a psychopath, a character neurosis, is a very egocentric person and they feel that many times they would not be apprehended, whereas somebody else would. This is a part of their psychopathy.

Q. And did you take that into consideration in formulating your opinion in this matter?

A. I did.

Q. Will you tell us, Doctor, what indicates to you that the defendant did have the capacity to deliberate and premeditate?

A. Well, I found no evidence of any mental illness; he didn't feel there were any outside influences that had any bearing on him. . . . In fact, he is the least unstable person that has taken the witness stand in this trial . . . he has restraint and calm and speaks to the point.

Another expert witness agreed on the serious personality distortion present, stating that Henry "did have the ability to premeditate and deliberate the killing." He could not say, however, that the prisoner "actually had so deliberated or premediated."

After prolonged argument and summation by counsel for both sides, instruction by the judge, and consideration by the jury, a verdict of second-degree murder was brought in, indicating agreement that the accused could not be guilty of first-degree murder in view of impaired capacity to premeditate his crime.

A severely schizoid or psychopathic individual is, of course, not insane. The point at which a person who is admittedly of abnormal mental makeup can be designated irresponsible for crime depends on legal criteria. As indicated in the opening chapter, the search for a workable formula occupied centuries of English jurisprudence, culminating in the M'Naghten opinion in 1943.

The M'Naghten Opinion

Daniel M'Naghten (this version of his name has been chosen since it is so rendered in Clark and Finnelly) was a Scotsman with a long history of persecutory delusions. At his arraignment after arrest for shooting Mr. Drummond, secretary to Sir Robert Peel, supposing Drummond to be Peel, M'Naghten said:

The Tories in my native city have compelled me to do this. They follow and persecute me wherever I go, and have entirely destroyed my peace of mind. . . . I believe they have driven me into consumption. . . . They have accused me of crimes of which I am not guilty; they do everything . . . to harass and persecute me; in fact, they wish to murder me. . . .[3]

The trial before Chief Justice Tindal and Justices Williams and Coleridge and a jury in Old Bailey enlisted many lay, and several medical, witnesses. The opening speeches of the solicitor general for the queen and Lord Cockburn for the defense recited the law on irresponsibility for murder up to that time in great detail. Medical witnesses, particularly Dr. E. T. Monro, with "thirty years of experience in insanity," unanimously concluded that M'Naghten was insane at the time of the shooting. Justice Tindal then stated to the jury: "I have undoubtedly been struck . . . by the evidence we have heard . . . from medical persons who have examined as to the state of mind of the unhappy prisoner . . . the whole of medical evidence is on one side. . . ."

He then asked the jury members if they wished to find M'Naghten "not guilty on the grounds of insanity." They assented. On the court's order, the prisoner was remanded to Bethlehem Hospital, and later he was transferred to Broadmoor Asylum as a "criminal lunatic" where he died twenty-two years later.

Many protested the defendant's acquittal. Queen Victoria wrote to Lord Peel:[4]

We have seen the trials of Oxford and M'Naghten conducted by the ablest lawyers . . . and they *allow* and *advise* the Jury to pronounce the verdict of *Not Guilty* on account of *Insanity* when everybody is morally convinced that both malefactors were perfectly conscious and aware of what they did. . . .

The English public was equally angered at this decision. The House of Lords, after debate, suggested that the justices be questioned "as to the law of England on this topic." Five specific questions were put to the judges:

I.

What is the law respecting alleged crimes committed by persons afflicted with insane delusions, in respect of one or more particular subjects or persons: as, for instance, where at the time of the commission of the alleged crime, the accused knew he was acting contrary to law, but did the act complained of with a view, under the influence of insane delusion, of redressing or revenging some supposed grievance or injury, or of producing some supposed public benefit?

II.

What are the proper questions to be submitted to the jury, when a person alleged to be afflicted with insane delusion respecting one or more particular subjects or persons, is charged with the commission of crime (murder for example) and insanity is set up as a defense?

III.

In what terms ought the question to be left to the jury, as to the prisoner's state of mind at the time when the act was committed?

IV.

If a person under an insane delusion as to existing facts, commits an offense in consequence thereof, is he thereby excused?

V.

Can a medical man conversant with the disease of insanity who never saw the prisoner previously to the trial, but who was present during the whole trial and the examination of all the witnesses, be asked his opinion as to the state of the prisoner's mind at the time of the commission of the alleged crime, or his opinion whether the prisoner was conscious at the time of doing the act, that he was acting contrary to the law, or whether he was labouring under any and what delusion at the time?[5]

Chief Justice Tindal, speaking for fourteen of the fifteen judges, started his answers by noting:

The Medical Evidence was: that persons of otherwise sound mind, might be affected by morbid delusions: that the prisoner was in that condition: that a person so labouring under a morbid delusion might have a moral perception of the right and wrong but that . . . it was a delusion which carried him away beyond the power of his control . . . that he was not capable of exercising any control over acts which had connection with his delusion. . . .

Some witnesses who gave evidence, had examined the prisoner, others formed their opinion on hearing evidence given by other witnesses.

The answers are epitomized by the universally known rule:

that to establish a defense on the ground of insanity, it must be clearly proved that at the time of the committing of the act, the party accused was labouring under such defect of reason, from disease of the mind, as not to know the nature and quality of the act he was doing, or if he did know it, that he did not know he was doing what was wrong.

The answer to question IV is not particularly pertinent today (partial delusion). The answer to question V regarding the hypothetical question stated in part: "But where the facts are admitted or not disputed, and the question becomes substantially one of science only, it may be convenient to allow the question to be put in that general form. . . ."

The "right and wrong test," as it came to be dubbed, was imported from England and embodied in the statutes of many states of the Union from 1850 onwards. Soon after its promulgation, however, attacks centering on its emphasis on cognition mounted in intensity. Almost immediately, Isaac Ray[6] in America criticized the M'Naghten test: "Without mentioning all the objections to which this test of responsibility is liable, it is enough to say that it furnishes no protection to that large class of the insane who entertain no specific delusion, but act from momentary irresistible impulses, or diseased moral perceptions." By the fifth edition of his treatise (1871), Ray lashed out at the unitary and misguided attitude of English judges toward the insane criminal: "Such a remarkable doctrine [the M'Naghten rule] as this can have sprung from only the most deplorable ignorance of the mental operations of the insane." Ray's objection rested chiefly on the exclusion of the "irresistible impulse" theory from M'Naghten. Ray posed the question, as it arose in many cases of homicide where particularly heinous crimes occurred: if intellectual impairment (as in delusional insanities) renders the individual not responsible for criminal acts, why should not volitional impairment relieve him of responsibility? If the will of the accused was under the domination of uncontrollable impulses and emotions, why was not "volitional" mental disease an adequate defense?

Early Criticism of M'Naghten

Much of the pressure that psychiatrists have exerted against the right and wrong test arose in connection with the conflict over "moral insanity" and the "irresistible impulse" theory. Dr. Isaac Ray, then America's outstanding forensic psychiatrist, linked moral insanity and irresistible impulse as evidence of a wider spectrum in mental illness than had been accepted up to that time. Dr. Ray's fight for recognition of "moral insanity" as a type of insanity was accepted by most mental specialists in this country, including the founders of the American Psychiatric Association. The *American Journal of Insanity* of the period was full of discussions spurred on by Dr. Ray. Chief Justice Shaw of Massachusetts was even influenced to charge the jury in a murder case (1844)[7] that "the irresistible and uncontrollable impulse" exempted the defendant from criminal responsibility.

Reaction to the M'Naghten rule in American courts and among American psychiatrists was strongly negative. An editorial in the *Journal of Insanity* (1847) inveighed against the rule in these biting words: "It is singular indeed for judges in these States to instruct juries, not in the words of our own statutes, but according to what they suppose the law to be in England."[8] Sir James Stephen in analyzing the M'Naghten opinions[9] (1883) made the much-quoted comment: "every judgment delivered since the year 1843 has been founded upon an authority . . . in many ways doubtful." He objected to the generalized nature of the answers given by the justices since "they were mere answers to questions which the judges were probably under no obligation to answer and which the House of Lords had probably no right to require an answer. . . ."

Sir James understood keenly that the measure of responsibility for crime was not cognition, i.e., knowledge of right and wrong, but

a delusion . . . never or hardly ever stands alone but is in all cases the result of disease of the brain which interferes . . . with every function of the brain, which falsifies all the emotions, alters in an unaccountable way the natural weight of motives of conduct, weakens the will and sometimes . . . so enfeebles every part of the mind. . . .

The authority of Lord Stephen, added to the insistent voice of Isaac Ray, did not completely convince the judiciary that the M'Naghten test was what Stephen called an "antiquarian curiosity." Indeed, early in the controversy (1845) the lord justice in a Scottish case of murder told the jury: "they were not to consider insanity according to the definitions of medical men—especially such fantastic and shadowy definitions as are to be found in Ray, whose work was quoted by the counsel. . . ."[10]

In 1869, Judge Doe of New Hampshire in a masterful opinion rejected the M'Naghten rule as being legally unsound: "if the expert testifies that . . . his [the accused's] disease has overcome, or suspended or temporarily or permanently obliterated his capacity of choosing between a known right and a known wrong . . . [it] is a matter of fact for the jury (i.e. not a matter of law)."[11] In joining the psychiatric critics of M'Naghten, Judge Doe sided against reactionary attitudes towards psychiatrists in England as represented by the lord chancellor's statement in the House of Lords (March 1862): "The introduction of medical opinions and medical theories into this subject has proceeded upon the vicious principle of considering insanity as a disease."[12]

Nevertheless, judges were faced with practical problems to be solved. In an oft-quoted Mississippi case (1879) involving a woman's plea of "impulsive insanity" (claimed to have been produced by menstrual difficulties), the court considered the question of "moral, emotional or impulsive insanity" in relation to responsibility for homicide. The accused, "in the dead of night, while her husband lay sleeping on a common bed, split open his head with a hatchet, without provocation or motive . . ." Justice Chalmers, in reviewing the case stated (in part):

The law is not a medical nor a metaphysical science. Its search is after those practical rules which may be administered without inhumanity, for the security of civil society. . . . And therefore, it inquires, not into the peculiar constitution of the mind of the accused, or what weakness, or even disorder, he was afflicted with, but solely whether he was capable of having, and did have, a criminal intent.[13]

A western court (Utah), on the other hand, adopted a less disunited view of the personality. It ruled that an individual who knows right from wrong, but whose mind is so deranged or disordered by mental disease that "it fails to function and cannot direct or control the acts of the person so afflicted, is and should be recognized as being legally insane." The opinion continues: "Volitional ability to choose the right and avoid the wrong is a fundamental in the required guilty intent of one accused of crime as in the intellectual power to discern right from wrong and understand the nature and quality of his act."[14]

By 1939, the legal standard remained undimmed. The California courts repeated their dedication to the "all or none" character of criminal irresponsibility: "Insanity is either a complete defense or none at all. There is no degree of insanity which may be established to affect the degree of the crime."[15]

Until the American Law Institute worked on its Model Penal Code and the M'Naghten rule was liberalized in the *Wolff* case in California (1964, see below), a "narrow literal reading" of the test remained the law in all states except New Hampshire.

Still, medical experts and some attorneys objected. Their reasons can be summarized as follows: (1) the questions and answers were intended to cover only cases of delusional psychosis; (2) the answers were premised upon psychopathological notions out-of-line with current psychiatric concepts; (3) issues of "right" and "wrong" belong to ethics, not to psychiatry; (4) the older "faculty" psychology wherein cognition was a separate faculty from emotion has been discredited in view of the modern holistic or integrated view of man's mental structure; (5) psychiatry used different criteria than did the law in gauging mental illness; thus Dr. Zilboorg's plaint (1939):

When they all individually and jointly [judges, lawyers and jury] ask me whether the defendant is in my opinion insane, I must candidly state, if I am to remain true to my professional knowledge and faithful to my oath, first, that I do not understand the question, and second, that since I do not understand . . . I do not know whether the defendant is insane or not.[16]

Some years before (1915), Judge Nott had answered this complaint:

The law has laid down what may be termed a working rule . . . and, while medical men may criticize that rule . . . yet when you see . . . its extreme simplicity, the ease with which it can be applied . . . I am not aware of any better working rule that these medical men or anyone else has ever put forward.[17]

The Continuing Controversy

The difficulties psychiatrists were experiencing in translating misbehavior (i.e., crime) from dynamic into legal terms stemmed from the broader view of the human personality contributed by psychoanalysis. Freudian insights, which were enlivening clinical psychiatry during the third and fourth decades of this century, were being applied to criminal actions. Freud's intuitive flash that guilt preceded rather than followed crime led to other discoveries of the influence of the unconscious on deviant, as well as everyday, behavior:

Paradoxical as it may sound, I must maintain that the sense of guilt was present prior to the transgression, that it did not arise from this, but contrariwise—the transgression from a sense of guilt. These persons we might justifiably describe as criminals from a sense of guilt.[18]

Much research with criminals, both juvenile and adult (Healy, Alexander, Karpman, Lindner, Foxe, Diamond, and Bromberg), using the psychoanalytic format, produced a dynamic criminologic psychiatry that sought to understand crime as the result of unconscious *and* conscious pressures. This new orientation brought psychiatrists face to face with two difficult problems—the influence of emotion and cognition (knowledge) and the free-will determinism dilemma. Both areas bore a direct relation to the practical job of testifying in court on issues of responsibility for criminal acts. The question, diagrammatically stated, was: Is a criminal guided by intellect alone, by knowing right from wrong? The answer to the cognition problem (i.e., whether "knowing" can stand alone without considering the emotions) was voiced by Franz Alexander, a leader in psychoanalysis, and by Hugo Staub, his German co-worker, a lawyer and psychoanalyst: "Psychoanalysis considers the human psychic apparatus as a system which is fully, and without a single gap, determined by psychological and biological causative factors."[19]

The issue of free will versus determinism remains an unsolved philosophic puzzle, each concept having its adherents. Many feel that the problem bears no relation to the insanity issue. According to Fingarette: "[T]he law is founded on the necessity to distinguish between the actions of a man . . . done freely or done under compulsion. The assumption that such distinctions presuppose some metaphysic doctrine involving free will is common in legal circles but it is a false assumption."[20] This legal scholar insists that insanity is not a technical notion but rather a "layman's term referring to grave personal defects in ways intelligible to the ordinary man." The test, Fingarette concludes, "lies in the notion of rationality . . . [of] mental capacity . . . relevant to the crime."[21] Professor Jerome Hall, on the other hand, understood the human admixture of cognition and emotion behind criminal action. In upholding the validity of the M'Naghten rule, he wrote:

Moral judgment (knowledge of right and wrong) is not reified as an outside, icy spectator of a moving self. On the contrary, the corollary is that value-judgments are permeated with the color and warmth of emotion—as is evidenced by the usual attitudes of approval that coalesce with right decisions. Indeed all action, especially that relevant to the penal law, involves a unified operation of the personality. . . . The McNaghten rule provide an analytical device for dissecting this action.[22]

The Dynamic Psychiatric View

The effect of this controversy on the legal definition of insanity was practically nil until the determinism theory, i.e., that a person's acts are determined by unconscious drives as well as conscious motivations, began to be asserted in criminal trials. By the late 1940s, psychoanalytic concepts had colored psychiatric practice to the point where antisocial behavior was regarded as occasioned by unconscious determinants, just as neurotic symptoms had been found to be based on the conflict between unconscious impulses and an unyielding superego. In the courtroom, psychiatric experts testified about the dynamics of the individual case in explaining their opinions (see the Diamond and Gorshen case, Chapter 4), while seasoned psychiatric criminologists (Wertham)[23] expounded the psychologic meaning of insanity in cases of violent crime. In fact, some members of the legal profession were visibly concerned lest the logic of the M'Naghten rule be undermined. A committee of the American Bar Association "viewed with alarm . . . the spread of psychoanalytic doctrines which tended towards determinism."[24]

The Group for the Advancement of Psychiatry attempted to reconcile the legal principles of insanity with the assessment of "ego impairment" as propounded by dynamic psychiatry. Their statement (1954) put the total situation clearly:

Ego impairment would appear to be a direct measure of responsibility. Ego impairment implies lessened control in maintaining behavioral norms of social interaction. In law, such would be the basis of exculpation. On this level of abstraction the lawyer and psychiatrist can agree. The psychiatrist can determine that ego impairment exists and the lawyer can transpose the fact into his terms of intent and responsibility.[25]

Still, opportunities to demonstrate the use of dynamic psychiatry in court were not too numerous. The following case presents some of the difficulties in translating a dynamic view of an accused's state of mind into the legal rules concerning irresponsibility for crime.

The accused, a former policeman, a known alcoholic, shot and killed his divorced wife before a witness, a taxi driver who had delivered the wife in front of her home. The accused, waiting for her in the attempt to effect a reconciliation, wanted to talk to her in private but the victim refused.

She asked the taxi driver to wait until she locked the house so she could return to town. The accused then shot her three times and as she fell in full view of the driver, he said: "Roll her over and see if she is dead." He then walked to a bar, after throwing his gun over a hedge en route, and was having a few drinks when apprehended by the police.

At the trial, the taxi driver testified that the accused appeared to be neither "drunk nor crazy . . . but deliberate and cold" at the time of the shooting. As the case unfolded upon examination, what appeared to be "deliberateness" in his actions seemed more likely to be an aspect of an alcoholic delirium. Examination in the county jail made within twenty-four hours of the crime demonstrated confusion and vivid hallucinations which lasted seven days. On questioning, the accused said:

The last thing I remember I was at a bar drinking whiskey . . . and then sitting in a bar with detectives around questioning me . . . suddenly all the faces materialized . . . the next thing I knew I was in the Chief's office and then I was on top of a cliff. Then I was on top of the hotel and they were doing the same thing. They were cutting babies up. They had no clothes on. I recognized some of the babies. They were my sister's. My boy was one thrown over the cliff. Everybody I knew was thrown over the cliff. Yesterday, I could see my sister's babies when I looked at the wall. There were cages moving up and down.

A fellow prisoner who observed the accused from the moment of his jailing reported:

He looked everybody over in a wild sort of way. He yelled, "I know too much, they are going to get me." He snatched things out of the air. He got a razor, turned his face to the corner and was going to cut his throat. I twisted his arm down and pulled the blade out. After the first night, I saw him urinate in a cup, drink it and toss the urine over his head like a shower.

Because the material in the delirium was so expressive of an obvious psychosexual problem, the accused was studied in the jail and, for several months, after conviction on death row in the Nevada State Prison. In this classic case of alcoholic delirium tremens, the psychologic defenses of dismemberment and castration fear were plainly visible.[26] For example, the accused said openly:

I was on the top of a cliff, a high cliff. They had wheel-barrows to cut babies up in. Heads, legs, and everything. Somebody took my sister's children and killed them. They tied them up with wire and burned up their feet. I could see children jumping up and down screaming. They would put different pieces of different bodies in wheel-barrows and dump them off the cliff. My brother got word of this and got some Rangers with blue or green coats and they were going to kill the people on top of the hotel. At the hotel there was a big Texan with a big knife. They were cutting men's penises off and shoving them in their mouths. They cut the testicles off too and put a piece of plaster over it.

As the delirium faded and his confusion decreased, the accused was able to relate snatches of the hallucinations he had experienced:

While I was seeing babies cut up and so forth, I also saw a man put in a coffin and put in the cement. Some of the men they cut, they, I mean by the gang that was doing all this—made them stand over a bucket and bleed in it before putting tape on them.

The theme of fear of passivity, of loss of maleness and being transformed into a woman ("bleed into a bucket"), clearly showed the dynamics behind the murder. Even more significant were his associations as to what the taxi driver witness testified he had heard: "Roll her over and see if she is dead." The accused had no memory of this remark; in fact, he had an amnesia for the shooting. The remark was interpreted as a condensation of two ideas—aggressive impulses towards women and a defense against his unconscious fear of being a woman. In the delirium, the remark meant: "Roll her over and see if she is a woman" (i.e., "Am I a woman?"). The cold tone ascribed to the accused by the taxi driver at the time could be recognized as an isolation of affect, that is, a separation of emotion from the underlying idea. In such situations, the ego cannot stand so revolting an idea and hence shuts off the emotion that ordinarily would accompany the horrifying idea of being turned into a woman.

Although this technical interpretation was not voiced by the present author in the witness box, the fact was testified to that the homicide occurred while the accused was in an incipient alcoholic psychosis. The history of the accused was reviewed: he was a heavy user of alcohol since his eighteenth year; he was a tense, hyperactive, impulsive youth, characteristics which "set him apart" from his companions; a physician had warned him that he was "losing his mind" from "alcoholic poisoning of the brain" within a year before the crime; three months before the shooting he lived in a befuddled, dull state; and eight days before the murder he was apprehended by a sister with a gun aimed at his temple, intent on suicide. Overall, there was good clinical reason to believe the accused had been in a fugue state for several days before the homicide and that chronic alcoholism had impaired his capacity to know right from wrong.

The jury did not accept this testimony supporting the plea of not guilty by reason of insanity. They brought in a verdict of guilty of first degree murder, and the judge assessed the punishment as execution in the gas chamber. An appeal was taken[27] to the Supreme Court of Nevada on the theory that "a review of the record will show that he has proven, by a preponderance of the evidence, that he [the accused] was insane when the shots were fired." The court, pointing to the insufficiency of the evidence presented by the expert, said:

The jury by its verdict found the defendant sane at the time of the homicide. Dr. Bromberg, a witness for the defense, after testifying on direct examination as to the accused's mental condition, was asked on cross-examination, "Doctor, in your diagnosis of this fugue, did you know that the defendant, after shooting his wife, had disposed of the gun and after being arrested showed the officers where it was?" Objection was made on the ground that the question was unfair. . . . We do not agree with this contention. The witness was in no way misled by the question. . . . As no error appears in the record, the judgment and order denying a new trial was affirmed. . . .

Since a jury's decision is guided predominantly by the testimony heard, tempered by the judge's instructions, the expert's opinion need bear no greater weight than that of a lay witness. The differing effect on a jury of lay and expert witnesses was similarly at issue in a Florida case, *Hixon v. State of Florida* (1964),[28] in which a man shot his ex-wife on a chance meeting in the street. The accused, a patient in an Ohio state hospital for several years, had escaped, seeking his wife in Florida. At the trial, the lay witnesses, two deputy sheriffs, a reporter, and an attorney who observed Hixon to be "intelligent and mentally normal" soon after the crime testified in that vein. Four psychiatrists, upon examination, unanimously agreed that the defendant had been and was schizophrenic at the time of the shooting and hence irresponsible by virtue of not knowing right from wrong. The jury, however, convicted Hixon of first degree murder. He was hospitalized as criminally insane. Four years later, upon release from the hospital, Hixon appealed to the Florida Court of Appeals on the ground that he had been insane at the time of the crime. The Appeals Court reversed the conviction, saying:

The exclusive rule in Florida is M'Naghten. . . . [if] accused was insane of "continuing nature" prior to the commission of the act . . . [he is] presumed to continue up to the time of commission of the act.

Lay witness testimony is meager evidentiary matter against the total evidence that defendant was insane at the time of killing his former wife.

Where expert testimony was accepted on its face value, the question of irresponsibility was referred back to the M'Naghten rule.

Broadened Applications of M'Naghten

The phrase "continued insanity" connotes legal recognition of the chronicity of mental diseases such as schizophrenia. In one sense, it harks back to the nineteenth-century concept of insanity as a unitary condition.[29] In another sense, the concept relates to the total involvement of the personality with the disease. Legal scholars appreciate this broadened view of mental disease. In this connection, Weihofen suggests: "If the word 'know' were given this broader interpretation, so as to require knowledge 'fused with affect' and assimilated by the whole personality—much of the criticism of the knowledge test would be met."[30] This wider view of mental disease in relation to irresponsibility for crime was utilized by Justice Schauer of the Supreme Court of California in the *Wolff* case (1964).[31] He reduced a conviction of murder in the first degree to second degree by offering a more liberal interpretation of knowledge of right and wrong. In support of his ruling, he commented: "knowledge should have an affective meaning."

The case concerned a fifteen-year-old boy who struck his mother with an axe handle on the head, rained blows on her, and, when she attempted to run away, choked her to death. Examinations by psychiatrists demonstrated impulsive behavior, bizarre ideas, sexual confusion, and other evidences of markedly impaired judgment. For example, the defendant told the doctors he "needed to get his mother out of the way" as he planned to entrap seven girls in his home for sexual purposes. At the trial, police officers testified that on surrendering himself after the crime, he had been "calm and coherent" and knew what he was doing at the time of the crime. For example, his answer to an officer's question: "You know the wrongfulness of killing your mother?" was, "I did. I was thinking of it. I was aware of it."

In his appeal decision, Justice Schauer agreed that "[t]his admission, coupled with the defendant's uncontradicted course of conduct . . . constitutes substantial evidence from which the jury could find the defendant legally sane at the time of the matricide." But he also accepted evidence from expert witnesses that Wolff suffered from schizophrenia and as such was not a fully normal or mature, mentally well person. "The extent of his understanding, reflection upon it and its consequences, appears to have been materially . . . vague and detached." Rejecting the defendant's claim of legal insanity because he had been diagnosed as schizophrenic, the court continued: "[t]o accept the defendant's thesis would be tantamount to creating by judicial fiat a new defense plea of 'not guilty by reason of schizophrenia.' To do so . . . would be bad law and apparently still worse medicine." Nevertheless, the justice's acknowledgment of the defendant's emotional "detachment," in spite of his "knowledge of the right," led to establishing a wider parameter in applying the M'Naghten rule. In other words, knowledge of right and wrong has to be joined with appropriate emotion to satisfy responsibility for crime.

A further attempt to broaden psychiatric testimony in its application to the legal test of insanity was embodied in the *Durham* decision.[32] As Alexander Brooks commented in 1974: "Born in 1954, it enjoyed a turbulent existence . . . [It] produced a wealth of insanity defense jurisprudence unrivalled elsewhere."[33]

The rule enunciated by Circuit Judge Bazelon in the *Durham* case departed from the M'Naghten opinion; it stated: "An accused is not criminally responsible if his unlawful act was the product of mental disease or mental defect." This rule (which became known as the "product test") was welcomed by expert witnesses in that all relevant evidence as to the mental condition could be presented to the jury. Many legalists, however, found it lacking in guidelines and impermissibly broad. Other defects were pointed out: "[Durham] does not face the question of how extensively capacity must be impaired to call for holding the defendant irresponsible."[34] Similarly, Dr. Roche wrote: "From the side of psychiatry, there is a general expression of relief from the onus of M'Naghten, but a lingering uneasiness both for the definition of 'disease' and 'defect,' and an uncertainty that troubles the psychiatrists in determining the casual nexus between disease and an unlawful act."[35]

Some years after its promulgation, the *Durham* decision was discarded. Judge Barnes in *Sauer* (1957) had realized that

The release of psychiatrists from the "strait jacket" of M'Naghten rules can hardly be regarded as a panacea for the problems of communication from medical expert to layman. This communication is a semantic problem that faces judges and attorneys daily. It is difficult to solve, but the solution may better lie, not in the layman accommodating the specialist, but rather in the adjustment by the specialist of his technical vocabulary to the language of the layman.[36]

In *U.S. v. Brawner* (1972), [37] the court stated:

We have decided to adopt the ALI rule as the doctrine excluding responsibility for mental disease or defect. A principal reason for our decision to depart from the Durham rule is the undesirable characteristic . . . of undue dominance by the experts giving testimony . . . the "product" concept did not signify a reasonably identifiable common ground . . . shared by non-legal experts, and the laymen serving on the jury. . . .

Shortly before criticism of *Durham* became general, the American Law Institute (ALI) had grappled with the possibility of establishing a test that covered areas of total personality impairment in criminal insanity pleadings.

The American Law Institute Test

In the tentative draft of 1958,[38] of which Professor Herbert Wechsler was the recorder, the formulation for an improved test for criminal responsibility stated: "A person is not responsible for criminal conduct if at the time of such conduct as a result of mental disease or mental defect, he lacks substantial capacity either to appreciate the criminality of his conduct or to conform his conduct to the requirements of law." A final draft of the Model Penal Code (1962) substituted the word "wrongfulness" for "criminality," so that the final version read: "A person is not responsible for criminal conduct if at the time of such conduct as a result of mental disease or defect he lacks substantial capacity either to appreciate the wrongfulness of his conduct or to conform his conduct to the requirements of law." The essential improvement over M'Naghten was use of the word "appreciate" rather than "know" to include the full meaning of cognition with its emotional component. Circuit Court Judge Kaufman (Second Circuit, 1966) in *U.S. v. Freeman*[39] agreed that the American Law Institute test "provided the jury with a workable standard . . . [allowing] the most modern psychiatric insights" to be received in testimony. The judge recognized that this test for irresponsibility "makes no pretension at being the ultimate in faultless definition"; still, he felt it was an "infinite improvement over the M'Naghten rules."

The consensus of opinion was that this broadened test was preferable to M'Naghten and its enactment into statutes in New York, Kentucky, Illinois, Massachusetts, Maryland, Vermont, Missouri. Several federal circuit districts followed. The California Supreme Court in 1978 also upheld the ALI test.[40] As Judge Kaufman had anticipated, criticism of the ALI test was forthcoming: Dr. Manfred Guttmacher, in lengthy correspondence with Professor Wechsler during the drafting period, arrived at the conclusion that it would be wise to "do away entirely with a definition of insanity and have psychiatric opinion used only in determining fitness to stand trial and assisting in disposition after trial."[41]

Others in the early phases of the discussion pointed to M'Naghten's validity in considering the importance of rationality in human affairs and in the judgment of criminal responsibility. "Does the defendant have the competence to understand ordinary everyday . . . actions and the ordinary consequences of these actions?" Professor Jerome Hall asked with regard to the relation of a common-sense view of responsibility to the legal test:

These are the simple formulations of the M'Naghten rule. . . . The problem of criminal responsibility makes sense only if human responsibility makes sense.

Thus our problem is an aspect of the central question in any human being's life, his stand vis-a-vis the world, especially whether moral obligation, freedom and responsibility have meaning for him.[42]

The complexity of the subject made it difficult to balance psychiatric thinking about mental disease with legal criteria. Professor Goldstein of Yale University summed up the impasse:

The new rules which appeared on the scene in the 1950's represented a flight from law. They swung from the extreme of abandoning the effort to frame a legal standard, giving the matter entirely to the jury, to the opposite extreme of trying to give the matter almost entirely to the psychiatrists. The first never won favor; the second has seen the medical-seeming standard shaped by an adversary system into something as much legal as medical. In reaction against both extremes, the American Law Institute resumed the effort to frame a standard which joins medical science and social purpose. Its proposal solves most of the problems generally associated with the older rules while at the same time representing the same line of historical development.[43]

While the American Law Institute test improved the opportunity to present psychiatric testimony reflecting the nuances of emotional reactions of persons accused of crime, it excluded "abnormalities manifested only by repeated criminal or otherwise anti-social conduct." But cases arose where crime was the outcome of transient emotional explosiveness or a warped sense of reality of the sociopath, indistinguishable from the so-called continuous insanity. This difficult clinical distinction is presented in detail in Chapter 5. For the present, its relation to legal tests for insanity is outlined in the *Currens* case, as enunciated by Chief Judge Biggs of the Third Circuit Court of Appeals.[44]

The Currens Modification

At the age of twenty-two, Currens purchased a car under false pretenses, then drove it to a distant state where he abandoned it. The defendant was arrested, and tried and convicted in the U.S. District Court for Western Pennsylvania for violating the Dyer Act (1958). He appealed on the grounds that the court had charged the jury using the M'Naghten rule, whereas psychiatrists had found him hysterical and emotionally unstable "to the degree affecting his judgment." Opinions varied as to his capacity to confer with counsel, but prolonged examinations at the Lewisburg Federal Penitentiary and the Federal Medical Center in Missouri resulted in labeling Currens as displaying "explosive and irrational conduct, hypochodriacal tendencies and apparently valid amnesia" for his theft. A battery of psychological tests, including the Rorschach ink-blot test, pointed to a "disturbed and possible disintegrating personality" whose reality contact was "seriously weakened." The defendant's record, including eight arrests prior to the Dyer Act arrest for forgery, impersonating an officer, and other offenses, was studied during hospital observation under varied conditions. All examiners agreed with the final evaluation of sociopathy with the development under stress of schizophrenic signs of undifferentiated type. Currens advanced the not guilty by reason of insanity plea when the appeal was heard in 1961.

The particular feature of the *Currens* decision rested on Judge Biggs' analysis of the psychopathic concept in relation to the accepted medico-legal maxim that "the psychopathic personality is not insane." After a thorough study of the psychiatric literature on the subject, he concluded that this notion could not be maintained in the face of clinical evidence. In his decision he wrote that he could not hold with the common finding that sociopathy is "insufficient to put sanity in issue." Rather, he felt that "all pertinent symptoms of the accused should be put before the court and jury . . . the totality of symptoms . . . to arrive at criminal responsibility." Essentially, he wished to avoid the cognitive aspect of the test for insanity by substituting "the substantial capacity to conform his conduct to the requirements of the law" in place of the phrase "substantial capacity to appreciate the criminality of his conduct," as stated in the American Law Institute Model Code test. Although the judge found the ALI test more applicable to the defendant at bar than M'Naghten or Durham (the latter had been urged by Currens' attorney), he wished to modify the phrase "appreciation" for criminality as indicating "knowledge" in favor of "conforming . . . to the law."

The charge which Judge Biggs found acceptable to a jury stated:

If you the jury believe beyond a reasonable doubt that the defendant, Currens, was not suffering from a disease of the mind at the time he committed the criminal act charged, you may find him guilty. If you believe that he was suffering from a disease of the mind, but believe beyond a reasonable doubt that at the time he committed the criminal conduct with which he is charged he possessed substantial capacity to conform his conduct to the requirements of the law he is alleged to have violated you may find him guilty.

Unless you believe beyond a reasonable doubt that Currens was not suffering from a disease of the mind or that despite that disease he possessed substantial capacity to conform his conduct to the requirements of the law . . . you must find him not guilty by reason of insanity.

Thus, your task would not be completed upon finding, if you did find, that the accused suffered from disease of the mind. He would still be responsible for his unlawful act if you found beyond a reasonable doubt that at the time he committed that act, the disease had not so weakened his capacity to conform his conduct to the requirements of the law which he is alleged to have violated. . . .

Judge Hastie, who dissented in part, pointed out that Judge Biggs' charge to the jury sounded like the "irresistible impulse" test. Nevertheless, he agreed with the *Currens* test as propounded.

In spite of attempts to make insanity tests more palatable to psychiatrists testifying in court by means of the American Law Institute Model Code insanity test, many remained convinced of the adequacy of M'Naghten. Law Professor Livermore and psychology Professor Meehl wrote a paper in the *Minnesota Law Review* with the self-revealing title of "The Virtues of M'Naghten" which analyzed the psychological implication of the test.[45] They suggested that if the three factors "tokening" rational thinking are considered—motivational factors, emotional disruptive factors, and reasoning defects—an estimate can be made of whether an accused can or cannot "reasonably be expected to comply with the law." These indices, they assert, can be developed from M'Naghten and can point directly to responsibility or irresponsibility for criminal acts.

In the same direction, Justice Gunn of the Minnesota Supreme Court ruled in a murder case, *State v. Rawland* (1972),[46] that "competent evidence relating to cognition, volition, and capacity to control behavior" could be offered in testimony where M'Naghten was the controlling statute. The case concerned Rawland, a teacher in his thirties who was convicted of second degree murder, as sane, following the stabbing of his father to death. His claim that he suffered from "defect of reason" at the time of the stabbing was denied by the trial judge, even though four psychiatrists, including one who treated him for an extended period before the crime, diagnosed him as a longstanding schizophrenic. Since the defendant was ruled not to have suffered from defect of reason, he appealed on the grounds that the Minnesota statute embodying the M'Naghten test was unconstitutional. The presiding Supreme Court judge, in a lengthy and well-reasoned decision, ruled that Rawland did indeed suffer from "defect of reason" and that "evidence . . . should be received freely . . . [of] the entire man and his mind as a whole," a statement by U.S. Supreme Court Justice Blackmun which Justice Gunn quoted with approval. The Minnesota statute was declared "not unconstitutional" but the defendant was ruled not guilty by reason of insanity.

It is a commentary on society's fascination with insanity and murder that the lay press at times becomes embroiled in the adequacy of tests for insanity and hence criminal irresponsibility. In a recent issue of the *Saturday Review*, a professor of educational philosophy wrote of the American Law Institute's "substantial capacity test" that it was a "merger of the M'Naghten and Durham rules . . . [which] served little purpose except to compound the difficulties of both standards."[47] Yet, in spite of caviling within and without the law, interference with responsibility for crimes because of mental aberrations of any kind requires psychiatric evaluation to aid the court in unraveling such kaleidoscopic kinds of human behavior. A case of murder in the first degree, *State v. Kessler* (1967),[48] acquitted by reason of insanity, illustrates the function of the American Law Institute's "substantial capacity" test in New York State:

The accused, a medical student of very superior intelligence, with a background in an elite preparatory school and a leading Eastern University, was suspended from his medical class in his 2nd year, because of disruptions in his classes and harassment of his professors with repetitious questions and comments, related to his intense interest in drug experimentation. He had previously made a brilliant record in his studies but began to plan what he called a "research to outdo Freud." "I wanted to make a name for myself . . . to do something outstanding. . . . I took drugs to know how it feels to be schizophrenic."

A few weeks before the homicide, the subject was admitted to Bellevue Hospital in a toxic, confused state. Released after five days, he continued to experiment with hallucinogenic drugs. Two days prior to the homicide, he consumed several LSD cubes, sodium amytal capsules, a quantity of gin and ethyl alcohol. On the morning of the crime, he telephoned his mother-in-law in the presence of his wife. (Both women had complained of his uncontrolled experiments.) Four hours later, his mother-in-law was found in a pool of blood in her kitchen; the coroner found 102 stab wounds in her body. The accused's jacket button and a bloody towel were found in the apartment. The perpetrator was readily apprehended.

The accused was admitted to the Prison Ward of the Kings County Hospital within a few hours of his arrest. He was agitated, talked under pressure but able to respond; he claimed complete amnesia for the crime.

"I don't remember a thing. I was trying to be schizophrenic. I took LSD and three quarts of alcohol in two days. The alcohol was cut half and half with water. I remember seeing a white figure on a blue background. It was a brilliant blue. I saw things turned from blood to wax. I don't remember anything since yesterday at 1:30. They say I killed." (cries)

"Every time I took LSD I took notes. . . . Once I started to write a paper, 'Does the fetus masturbate?' I saw myself dead on the living room floor and shrink smaller and smaller. . . . I am absolutely convinced 100% . . . that schizophrenia is not a psychogenic illness."

As he improved, his discussions took on a scholarly, although still dysjunctive air; he spoke learnedly about his theory of schizophrenia involving the chemistry of serotonin and how LSD could be isolated in the brain by electron-microscopy. He said:

"Since I started taking LSD I began having personality changes. The first time I took it I was extremely nervous and had paranoid ideas in that I thought that people were watching me."

Q. Did you always have the idea of doing something scientific and outstanding?

A. Yes. . . . The last three years I had the desire to do something outstanding in the field of science and make a name for myself. I don't think that is being sick.

Q. What do you think was the psychic transformation that went on with you?

A. After I started taking LSD I found I would be depressed and tense. I developed a terrific amount of anxiety and depression which lasted about a week and petered off for a while. The last time the anxiety lasted about a month.

An initial psychometric test made soon after admission to the hospital resulted in an I.Q. of 135 verbal and 90 performance. Two weeks later, the test was repeated with a verbal score of 142 and a performance score of 128. It was assumed that his toxic state had reduced his visuomotor and verbal facility; the psychologist classified him as of Very Superior Intelligence. The projective tests, Rorschach, Bender and Goodenough-Machover Figure Drawing, however, demonstrated vast "inferiority feelings with paranoid elements." The prisoner's free floating responses were characterized with raw sexual fantasies: in one instance he voiced a memory of himself as a little boy sitting in the bathroom "slipping down the seat." The terror of "slipping," the psychologist pointed out, apparently "led to a frantic search for achievement and success at any price." It also appeared from the tests that "while the subject came close to the borderline of schizophrenic thinking he still possessed enough critical judgment to recover from losing himself in irrational bizarre fantasies."

A study of his life activities was undertaken. In his adolescence, the prisoner had been known as a harum-scarum youth, given to pranks during his college days, albeit an excellent student. At one point he was asked to leave college in the 3rd year; at another, he was sent to a psychiatrist. In medical school, his behavior led to being referred to a professor of psychiatry for an opinion. Some of the instructors considered him actively psychotic; others regarded the prisoner as eccentric and narcissistic. Others pointed to a paranoid trend.

A month's study of the accused resulted in a final diagnosis of Personality Disorder, Paranoid type and Drug Intoxication at the time of the crime. He was reported to be able to confer with counsel in his defense and competent to stand trial. This psychiatric evaluation was transmitted to the district attorney.

At the trial, one year later, the defendant's condition at the time of the crime in the light of "substantial capacity test" was subjected to the American Law Institute test, the law in New York. The defense psychiatrists testified that defendant was suffering from schizophrenia and was temporarily insane at the time of the murder: the prosecution experts testified that he had substantial capacity to understand and appreciate the consequences of his act.

The defense attorney contended that the hallucinatory drugs consumed played a direct role in the homicide and that the defendant "suffered total amnesia," a condition during which he did not know or appreciate the consequences of his act. The district attorney restated the testimony that the accused was basically an eccentric, narcissistic, psychopathic personality who used drugs as a shield. The defense attorney characterized his client as a man "verging on genius who lapsed into psychotic episodes." The district attorney told the jury that if he were acquitted, he would have "created a perfect crime."

The jury of 11 men and one woman reported themselves deadlocked. On three occasions, they asked for a repetition of the psychiatric testimony. Finally the jury returned a verdict of not guilty by reason of insanity.

The acquitted man was ordered to a mental hospital by the judge. After three months, he was released as no longer mentally ill. He was returned to a civilian mental hospital on two other occasions by the judge, but released after a short period each time.

The interpretation of that accused's behavior at the time of the crime, vital in answering the question of capacity to appreciate the wrongfulness of his act, raises complex problems. One of the puzzling features of the case was the 102 stab wounds delivered to the body of the victim. At the trial, the defense assumed it to be direct evidence of insanity. But the absence of apparent motive stood in strange contrast to the manner of the assault. There had been no strong antagonism by the accused towards his mother-in-law, no prior indications of physical or social aggression, aside from his flamboyant and egotistical style. In the search for an explanation of the stabbing, a probable motive advanced at the trial by the prosecution psychiatrist was that suicidal impulses were turned to homicide under the clouding influence of drugs ingested during two days before the crime. This dynamic viewpoint indicated that deep dissatisfaction with an unattainable ambition, under the defensive shield of the drug intoxication, erupted in the compulsive form of the assault—the multiple stabbings. Suicide-turned-homicide is a well-recognized mechanism.[49] Whether this compulsive, unconscious behavior constitutes "lack of substantial capacity" became the jury's task to decide. In any event, this case brought up the question of motive in homicide, either expressed or covert, and its place in psychiatric analysis of irresponsibility for crime.

Motivation and Irresponsibility

Although motivation is an important concern for psychiatrists in studying murderous behavior, it is not of paramount importance to the law. "Intent" is, of course, vital in adjudicating guilt. Intent is distinguished from motive in that intent represents the wish to affect a certain result, i.e., assault or murder, while motive is understood to mean that which incites or causes a person to act. The law does not inquire into motivation for murder but focuses on intent. In an Idaho case (*State v. Stevens*, 1969),[50] appealed to the Idaho Supreme Court on error of the trial court which "refused to prove motive" in a larceny case, the court ruled as follows: "Motive generally is defined as that which leads or tempts the mind to indulge in a particular act . . . [it] differs from intent [in that its] purpose is to use a particular means to effect a certain result. Motive . . . is not considered an essential element of any crime unless made so by statute." The irrelevance of motive in the question of guilt or innocence is settled law since the requisite intent and act in a murder case can lead to a guilty verdict if no motive is ever established.[51] Still, this dictum has given way to a broader view in California jury instructions, which permit consideration of

motive or lack of motive as a circumstance in the case. Presence of motive tends to establish guilt. Absence of motive may tend to establish innocence. You will therefore give its presence or absence, as the case may be, the weight to which you find it to be entitled.[52]

In a complex case,[53] a man was accused of giving his lifelong friend vitamin capsules which contained cyanide. (Considerable confusion existed as to whether the accused had knowingly placed cyanide in the vitamin capsule.) An appeal on a conviction of murder in the first degree by the Supreme Court of California resulted in a remand for a new trial because no motive or intent had been shown. The prevailing opinion, concurred in by four justices (while three dissented), stated: "The absence of motive . . . furnished one element for consideration by the jury. . . . The general rule is absence of motive tends to support the presumption of innocence."

The more customary disclaimer that motive is not an essential element of crime does not remove motive from its place of interest among those concerned with homicide. Traditionally, motivations for murders are placed in two broad classes: (1) *rational*, for profit, status, or political reasons; and (2) *emotional*, for reasons of jealousy, resentment, revenge, or defending one's honor. The latter motivations are usually bracketed as "crimes of passion" which are regarded as requiring less premeditation and deliberateness than are specific intent crimes. What is lacking is an analysis of the psychologic background of "crimes of passion." Psychiatrists have been concerned that motivation for violent crime has received little attention. Guttmacher and Weihofen in their *Psychiatry and the Law*[54] ask for a reexamination "of the criminal law dogma that motive is irrelevant."

The present author has studied conscious and unconscious motivation in three hundred murder cases.[55] Obviously, the several examiners of a murder or other type of crime might have developed varying hypotheses concerning motivation in a given offender. Rather than be an impediment to justice, this diversity might make legal tests of insanity more humanistic; it would flesh out the bare bones of responsibility required in the legal tests of insanity. Although the study was not statistical, the motivation fell into the following broad groupings in order of frequency:

Redress of wrong: Humiliation on a conscious level as revenge, and reaction to inferiority feelings on an unconscious level.

Hostility released by alcoholism with possible unconscious latent homosexual elements.

Sexual inadequacy: By both sexes as in triangle murders where both heterosexual and homosexual jealousies motivate the crime.

Hyperkinesis in youth: Where destruction is the outcome of extension of motoric tendencies. These include the so-called thrill homicides of older persons.

Extension of the pubertal destructive urges in adult (sociopathic) offenders; the "sadistic" killer.

Despoiler reactions: Destruction of attractive young females based on an unconscious intolerance of young males to female beauty. Includes hatred of the procreative function of females.

Maternal destroyer: Infanticide by women. The crime of Medea wherein those who create may destroy. Often in depressed, mentally ill offenders.

Suicide turned into homicide.

Panic reactions: As in robberies where guilt develops a panic or fear of self-injury as the motive.

Wanton reactions: Among psychotic (paranoid or organically ill offenders).

For profit or status: Among professional gangsters or political assassins.

The study was initiated to present murder from the witness stand as a multidetermined event and possibly to develop a basis for a future preventive program. In the former situation, it was envisioned that interpretations of motivation would enrich, rather than confuse, a jury's perception of the individual whose criminal responsibility it was called upon to decide. This view, however, has been countered by the recent movement in several quarters to abolish the insanity defense and the psychiatrists' participation therein (Guttmacher, Menninger, and others). Professor Allen's statement, "The dichotomy between the 'Mad' and the 'Bad' is a patent absurdity,"[56] summarizes the view that the psychiatrist's contribution is best made after the question of guilt or innocence in a murder case is resolved.

Notes

1. E. Adamson Hoebel, *The Law of Primitive Man:* 235, Harv. U. Press, Cambridge, Mass. (1964).

2. *People v. Henry* (sic) (County of Sacramento, Calif., 1958).

3. *Daniel McNaughton, His Trial and the Aftermath*, ed. by Donald J. West and Alexander Walk, Gaskell Books, Headley Bros., Ashford, Kent (1977).

4. Ibid.: 9.

5. 8 Eng. Rep. 718 (1843) House of Lords; Clark and Finnelly 200. Quoted in William Lawrence Clark and W. L. Marshall, *A Treatise on the Law of Crimes:* 342, 6th ed. rev. by M. F. Wingersky, Callaghan & Co., Chicago (1958).

6. Isaac Ray, op. cit.: 48.

7. Gregory Zilboorg, *Legal Aspects of Psychiatry:* 519.

8. Ibid.: 565.

9. Sir James F. Stephen, op. cit.: 151 et seq.

10. Quoted in Ray, op. cit.: 63 n. (5th ed.).

11. *State v. Pike*, 49 N.H. (1 Shirley) 399 (1870).

12. Quoted in Ray, op. cit.

13. *Cunningham v. State*, Sup. Ct., Miss., 56 Miss. 269 (1870).

14. *State v. Green*, 78 Utah 580, 6 Pac. 2d 177 (1931).

15. *People v. Cordova*, 14 Calif. 2d 308, 94 Pac. 2d 40 (1939).

16. Gregory Zilboorg, *Misconceptions of Legal Insanity*, 9 Am. J. Orthopsych. 540 (1939).

17. *People v. Purcell*, Ct. Gen. Sess. (N.Y., 1915).

18. Sigmund Freud, *Criminality from a Sense of Guilt* 4, Collected Papers trans. by Joan Riviere, Hogarth Press, London (1950).

19. Franz Alexander and Hugo Staub, *The Criminal, the Judge and the Public*: 70, Macmillan Co., New York (1931).

20. Herbert Fingarette, *The Meaning of Criminal Insanity*: 81, U. of Calif. Press, Berkeley (1972).

21. Ibid.: 249.

22. Jerome Hall, *General Principles of Criminal Law:* 499, Bobbs-Merrill Co., Indianapolis (1947).

23. Frederic Wertham, *The Show of Violence*, Doubleday Co., New York (1949).

24. Wilbur G. Katz, *Law, Psychiatry and Free Will*, 20 U. of Chi. L. Rev. 397 (1954-1955).

25. Group for the Advancement of Psychiatry, Report No. 26, Criminal Responsibility and Psychiatric Expert Testimony (1954).

26. *State v. Butner*, 66 Pac. 127 (Nev., 1949).

27. Walter Bromberg, *A Psychological Study of Murder*, 32 Int'l. J. of Psychoanalysis Part II (1951).

28. *Hixon v. State of Florida*, 165 So. Rept. 2d 436 (1964).

29. *One Hundred Years of American Psychiatry:* 205 et seq., Columbia U. Press (1944).

30. Henry Weihofen, *Insanity as a Defense in Criminal Law*, Chap. 7, Commonwealth Fund, New York (1933).

31. *People v. Wolff*, 394 Pac. 2d 959, 61 Calif. 2d 795, 40 Calif. Rptr. 271 (1964).

32. *Durham v. U.S.*, 214 Fed. 2d 862 (D.C. Ct. App., 1954).

33. Alexander Brooks, *Law and the Mental Health System:* 176, Little, Brown & Co., Boston (1974).

34. Herbert Wechsler, *Criteria of Criminal Responsibility*, 22 U. of Chi. L. Rev. 367-86 (1955).

35. Phillipe Roche, *The Criminal Mind:* 252 Farrar, Straus & Cudahy, New York (1958).

36. *Sauer v. U.S.*, Cir., 9th Dist. (1957).

37. *U.S. v. Brawner*, 471 F. 2d 969 (D.C. Ct. App., 1972).

38. American Law Institute, Model Penal Code, Tentative Draft no. 4, Philadelphia (Apr. 1955).

39. *U.S. v. Freeman*, 357 Fed. 2d 606 (1966).

40. *People v. Ronald Drew*, 22 Calif. 3d, 333 (1978).

41. Manfred Guttmacher, American Law Institute, App. B: 170.

42. Jerome Hall, *Mental Disease and Criminal Responsibility—M'Naghten Versus Durham and the American Law Institute Tentative Draft*, 33 Ind. L. J. 212 (1958).

43. Abraham S. Goldstein, *The Insanity Defense:* 84, New Haven and London, Yale U. Press (1967).

44. *U.S. v. Currens*, 290 Fed. 2d 751 (1961).

45. Joseph M. Livermore and Paul E. Meehl, *The Virtues of M'Naghten*, 51 Minn. L. Rev. 789 (1967).

46. *State v. Rawland*, 199 N.W. 2d 774 (1974).

47. Richard Gambino, *The Murderous Mind: Insanity v. The Law*, Saturday Review 10 (Mar. 18, 1978).

48. Stephen Kessler, Indictment no. 1431/1966, County of Kings, N.Y.

49. Karl M. Menninger, *Some Sidelights on the Psychology of Murder*, 81 J. Nerv. & Ment. Dis. 442 (1935). G. Zilboorg, *Psychoanalytic Aspects of Suicide*, 14 Int'l. J. of Psychoanalysis 387 (1933).

50. *State v. Stevens*, 454 Pac. 2d 945 (1969).

51. *State v. Guilfoyle*, 145 A. 751.

52. California Jury Instructions, Crim. 2.51 (Evidence and Guides).

53. *People v. Albertson*, 145 Pac. 2d 7, 23 Calif. 2d 55 (1944).

54. Manfred Guttmacher and Henry Weihofen, *Psychiatry and the Law:* 402, W. W. Norton, New York (1952).

55. Walter Bromberg, *Motivation in Murder*, Unpublished study (1977).

56. Richard Allen, *The Insanity Defense; an Uncertain Future*, 58, no. 4 M. H. 4 (1974).

4

Partial or Diminished Responsibility

As the material in this chapter shows, it can be stated as a general proposition that dynamic psychiatry has exerted an influence on legal decisions which permits a lesser degree of mental illness than insanity to reduce the degree of a crime. Partial responsibility does not acquit the accused, but it often reduces the level of a crime charged, as from first to second degree murder. In one of the early cases, *U.S. v. Fisher* (1945),[1] where this principle was urged, the accused was said to have exhibited a grade of mental illness; "though not so pronounced as to come within the tests of criminal insanity, [it] may nevertheless negate the particular intent requisite to the crime charged."[2] Thus, some types of mental illness may preclude deliberation in the crime of homicide but not demonstrate sufficient "defect of reason" to obscure knowledge or appreciation of right from wrong.

The doctrine of diminished responsibility has a history reaching back to the sixteenth century. For example, Dr. Ray[3] quotes Lord Hale as being uneasy in differentiating total from partial insanity:

It is difficult to define the invisible line that divides perfect and partial insanity; but it must rest upon circumstances duly to be weighed and considered . . . lest on the one side there may be a kind of inhumanity towards defects of human nature; or, on the other side, too great indulgence given to great crimes.

Mental disorder which mitigates punishment for major crime, though it does not excuse it, has been recognized in many European countries[4] and increasingly so in this country. Professor Weihofen in discussing *Fisher* pointed out that "borderline or partially" insane persons should merit less punishment than sane criminals because they are less capable of understanding the wrongfulness of their act. Aside from this humanistic attitude mitigating punishment, the effect of borderline mental conditions on the specific intent crimes is an important facet of the diminished capacity plea.

Changing Attitudes: Moral Versus Legal Wrong

Before detailing the cases which tend to establish the diminished responsibility doctrine, it might be helpful to note some of the forces that have pointed to this direction. One of these factors is the reduced moral impact of punishment on offenders, especially the young. This trend is the result of major attitude changes, spurred by the civil rights push of the past two decades, that "crime is less an evil and more an experience, less an injury than an assertion of rights."[5] Aggression has been discovered to be a "human right" in the lexicon of the revolting young, and therefore punishment for wrong-doing is regarded less as moral reprobation than as a legal stricture. In a way, this change in social value given crime and punishment has been mirrored in the shift from "moral" wrong to "legal" wrong in jury charges.

From early days in the common law, the criminal actor's choice of "right" and "wrong" and knowledge of these choices rested on the "law of God and nature," often quoted as the "law of God and man." Justification for punishment was predicated on knowledge of this principle. Kant (1785) expressed the moral basis of the criminal law: "The Penal Law is a Categorical Imperative: and woe to him who creeps through the serpent-windings of Utilitarianism to discover some advantage that may discharge him from the Justice of Punishment, or even from the due measure of it."[6]

Many judges have since expressed the same sentiments in legalistic terms. Judge Cardozo, in a New York's *Schmidt* case (1915), reiterated this axiom: "Knowledge that an act is forbidden by law will permit the inference that . . . it is also condemned as an offense against good morals . . . [it is] impossible to say . . . there is any decisive adjudication which limits the word 'wrong' to legal as opposed to moral wrong."[7]

Professor Weihofen, however, has shown that social attitudes toward punishment for crimes have softened over the decades, and with it a subtle shift from "morally wrong" to "legally wrong" has appeared in court decisions.[8] The phrase "legal wrong" carries less of the condemnatory force inherent in Kant's Categorical Imperative than is reflected in "moral" wrong. The first is against the law of the land, the second against an immutable eternal principle. A hint of this change in emphasis can be seen in a South Carolina case (1957). On an appeal from conviction where the accused had claimed insanity at the time of the crime of murder, the Supreme Court of South Carolina said: "The test is the capacity or want of it sufficient to distinguish moral or legal right from moral or legal wrong and to recognize the particular act charged as morally or legally wrong . . . is to be determined by the jury."[9] Whether the doctrine of partial responsibility owes its development to softened social attitudes towards punishment reflected in the law is a matter of conjecture.

The Fisher case, referred to above, raised the issue of partial responsibility to a valid legal doctrine. Although Justice Reed for the U.S. Supreme Court decided against the appeal from a death sentence, the case brought to the fore the whole issue of mental illness, not amounting to insanity, when offered in mitigation of punishment. Briefly, the facts were as follows. Fisher, a Negro working as a janitor in the Library of Congress, had learned that a female librarian considered his work slack. Justice Frankfurter, in a dissenting opinion, reviewed the essential facts:

On the fatal morning, Miss Reardon, the victim, told Fisher that he was not doing the work for which he was being paid, and in the course of her scolding called him a "black nigger." This made him angry—no white person, he claimed, had ever called him that—and he struck her. She ran screaming towards a window. Fisher ran out of the room and up the stairs. Her screaming continued. At the top of the stairs he saw a pile of wood lying by the fireplace. He seized a piece of wood, ran down the stairs and struck her on the head. The stick broke and he seized her by the throat. She continued to scream until she went limp. He then dragged her to the lavatory and left her there while he went back to clean up the spots of blood. She recovered sufficiently to scream again, and he returned to the lavatory and cut her slightly with a knife he carried in his pocket. The importance of the screaming is a key to the tragedy. It is difficult to disbelieve Fisher's account that he never wanted to kill Miss Reardon but only wanted to stop her screaming, which unnerved him.

Justice Frankfurter concluded: "The evidence in its entirety hardly provides a basis for finding of premeditation."

At the original trial, psychiatrists for the defense testified that Fisher was "below average with minor stigmata of mental subnormalcy." One expert testified that he was a psychopathic personality of a predominantly aggressive type. Others stated that Fisher, by reason of a deranged mental condition, was unable to resist the impulse to kill. The prosecution countered with competent evidence that the petitioner was capable of understanding the nature and quality of his acts. In the face of these differing opinions, the jury concluded that the accused was criminally responsible. The defendant appealed on the grounds that the trial court refused to instruct the jurors that, in determining whether he was guilty of murder in the first or in the second degree, they should consider the evidence of the accused's psychopathic aggressive tendencies, low emotional response, and borderline mental deficiency. It was conceded that the aggregate of these factors was not enough to support a finding of not guilty by reason of insanity.

Even though the Supreme Court upheld the jury's verdict, Justice Reed stated:

It may be that psychiatry has now reached a position of certainty in its diagnosis and prognosis which will induce Congress to enact the rule of responsibility for crime for which petitioner contends. For this Court to force the District of Columbia to adopt such a requirement for criminal trials would involve a fundamental change in the common law theory of responsibility.

In another dissent, Justice Murphy analyzed the new doctrine evoked by Fisher's attorneys in remarking:

The existence of general mental impairment, or partial insanity, is a scientifically established fact. There is no absolute or clear-cut dichotomous division of the inhabitants of this world into the sane and the insane. Between the two extremes of "sanity" and "insanity" lies every shade of disordered or deficient mental condition, grading imperceptibly one into another.

More precisely, there are persons who, while not totally insane, possess such low mental powers as to be incapable of the deliberation and premeditation requisite to statutory first degree murder.

Building on Justice Murphy's admission that psychiatric knowledge, though limited in scope, could help juries in the "baffling psychological factors of deliberation and premeditation," Weihofen and Overholser asked "why defense counsel have not urged the proposition more often."[10] They added a prophetic note:

On careful analysis the Fisher decision appears to be more a victory than a defeat for the proposition that partial insanity may reduce the degree of a crime. It is true that the majority of the Court found no error in the trial judge's failure to give an instruction based on this theory. But the Court did not deny its soundness.

The new prominence given by the Fisher case to the theory that mental disorder may affect the degree of a crime will almost certainly result in its being urged more often and more articulately than it has been hitherto.

Weihofen's and Overholser's prediction has been borne out since the Fisher case, in diminished responsibility pleadings. Of necessity the irresistible impulse theory was involved as was the psychopathic personality problem. The latter is discussed in Chapter 7; the irresistible impulse theory, which remained operative as an acceptable defense in seventeen states until 1952, requires mention here.

Irresistible Impulse Theory as Partial Responsibility

The control of one's actions through the will has been a basic tenet in man's thinking since the time of Aristotle. Interference with the will by mental disease has been recognized as indicating irresponsibility where the will was overthrown by "uncontrollable impulses." This doctrine, expressed in various forms, was accepted by some judges during the nineteenth century, under the influence of the then prevalent psychiatric opinion that homicidal mania and moral insanity were valid clinical entities. In a nineteenth-century Massachusetts case,[11] Judge Gibson confirmed the irresistible impulse as a valid defense: "There is a moral or homicidal insanity consisting of an irresistible inclination to kill or commit some particular offense. There may be an unseen ligament pressing on the mind, drawing it to consequences which it sees but cannot avoid . . . a coercion . . . incapable of resistance." Dr. Ray espoused this doctrine with great vigor, as judged by his writings in his *Medical Jurisprudence*:

[W]e have an immense mass of cases related by men of unquestionable competence and veracity, where people are *irresistibly* impelled to the commission of criminal acts while fully conscious of their nature and consequences . . . they are not fictions invented by medical men . . . but plain unvarnished facts as they occurred in nature. . . .

Others were not so convinced, however. Ray quotes an English judge (1848) on "uncontrollable impulse": "[This] opinion should be scanned by juries with very great jealousy and suspicion because it might [be] a perfect justification for every crime committed." It should be remembered that homicidal mania in which the uncontrollable impulse is manifest without other psychiatric signs was a respectable diagnosis to explain otherwise inexplicable homicides until the late nineteenth century. Indeed, most of the cases where irresistible impulse was used as a defense were united with this diagnosis. That an element of propaganda existed in the efforts of Ray and his contemporaries to push the irresistible impulse defense can be seen in the comments of a medico-legal historian that forensic psychiatrists in the nineteenth century "saw in the doctrine of irresistible impulse the most powerful wedge which could be driven [into] . . . the petrified log of traditional criminal law."[12]

Where used currently, the general rule is:

Irresistible impulse as recognized by the courts is an impulse induced by, and growing out of, some mental disease affecting the volitive, as distinguished from the perceptive powers, so that the person afflicted, while able to understand the nature and consequences of the act charged against him and able to perceive that it is wrong, is unable, because of such mental disease, to resist the impulse to do it. It is to be distinguished from mere passion or overwhelming emotion not growing out of, and not connected with a disease of the mind.[13]

After years of discussion in psychiatric and legal areas, the use of irresistible impulse in defense has fallen into disuse, except as allowed in a few states and the District of Columbia. Zilboorg's requiem written in the 1940s sums up the situation regarding this defense: "as to the irresistible impulse, it crept in, so to speak, here and there, but it never gained the popularity it deserved. . . . Moral insanity lingered on for another twenty years, then imperceptibly died out."[14]

In spite of this dirge, impulsive conditions do occur and are observed clinically. Whether such compulsions are irresistible or simply not resisted is of less moment to psychiatrists than to judges and juries who have the duty of assigning guilt or innocence to an act attributed to impulsive or compulsive behavior. Weihofen sets forth the reasons why the courts of most states have rejected the irresistible impulse defense: "(a) The belief that no such disorder is in fact possible, (b) if it does exist, it is too difficult to prove to be allowed as a defense, (c) it is a dangerous defense to society, (d) statutes setting forth the right and wrong test as the only criterion of responsibility prevent courts from adopting any other tests."[15]

A Michigan case, *U.S. v. Pollard* (1959),[16] illustrates the persistence of the irresistible impulse test in a slightly different form. Pollard was a Detroit police officer regarded as a "well adjusted, highly intelligent officer [with] a pleasing personality and happy disposition." Two years after a traumatic event in his life—his wife and infant child had been brutally beaten and killed by a drunken neighbor—he became involved in a series of bank robberies. During this period of mourning, Pollard had been observed to be silent and morose while on duty, chronically depressed, sobbing and crying, threatening suicide. He made a plea of insanity at the time he committed the robberies. His psychiatrist reported that at the time of the attempt "he was suffering from a diseased mind which produced an irresistible impulse to commit the criminal acts." Two other psychiatrists agreed that Pollard suffered from a "traumatic neurosis" or "dissociative reaction," although he knew the acts were wrong. A thorough study of the accused at the Medical Center in Springfield, Missouri reported that

a dissociative state may have existed and his actions may not have been con-sciously motivated. . . . It is our opinion that during the period in question, Pollard, while intellectually capable of knowing right from wrong, may have been governed by unconscious drives which made it impossible for him to adhere to the right.

Lay witnesses testified that he was despondent, agitated (at times "beating the wheel of his car"), abstracted, and depressed. Another witness, a police lieutenant, contradicted these statements: he testified that "his efficiency record rating was more effective than his service [had been] prior to his wife's death."

In his analysis of the case, Judge Levin recognized the unanimity of the psychiatrists' opinion but wrote: "there are compelling reasons for not blindly following the opinions of experts on controlling issues of fact." He also cited the federal courts' approval of a test of insanity that included the irresistible impulse test in this form (*Davis v. U.S.*, 1897):

[I]nsanity . . . means such a perverted and deranged condition of the mental and moral faculties as to render a person incapable of distinguishing between right and wrong . . . yet by his will, by which I mean the governing power of his mind . . . has been otherwise than voluntarily so completely destroyed that his actions are beyond his control.[17]

The judge agreed that the "profession of psychiatry . . . [made] vast areas of information available through its efforts" and noted that the experts indicated the accused's "unconscious desire to be apprehended and punished" (because of deep guilt). Nevertheless, the judge decided that "the defendant's entire pattern of conduct . . . militated against" the experts' opinion. In sum, the District Court exercised its independent judgment "by weighing the case in its entirety, as opposed to being bound by what might be considered uncontradicted expert opinion . . . and that the defendant committed the acts for which he is charged and that when he committed them he was legally sane."

The case was appealed to the U.S. District Court, which reversed the judgment.[18] The court argued that "in the opinion of psychiatric and medical experts, a dissociative reaction resulted in Pollard's commission of the acts." They gave credence to the irresistible impulse theory: "When there has been created by the evidence, a reasonable doubt as to whether the accused person acted under an irresistible impulse, the burden is upon the prosecution to establish beyond a reasonable doubt that he did not act under an irresistible impulse." Whether this test in the jurisdictions of most states would pass muster is questionable in spite of clinical findings that dissociative reactions (also known as conversion hysteria) do occur. Although such mental states do not qualify as insanity in a legal sense, they are linked to mental states that form the basis for pleas of diminished capacity.

A Definitive Case of Diminished Capacity

Mental conditions that "negate the intent requisite to a crime charged" vary in degree, from subnormal intelligence to "states of nervous tension," or any illness that interferes with premeditation or deliberation. In fact, according to Witkin, the defense of diminished capacity has, in recent decades, become "firmly established in California law"[19] and elsewhere. The case of *People v. Wells* is a California landmark case[20] involving the issue of whether a "state of nervous tension . . . actuated by fear" could vitiate malice aforethought in a charge of assault. The defendant, a life-prisoner named Wells, had struck a guard in the state's prison, a crime which is covered under Section 4500 of the California Penal Code: "Every person undergoing a life sentence in a State prison of this State, who, with malice aforethought, commits an assault upon the person of another . . . by any means of force likely to produce great bodily injury, is punishable with death."

The circumstances in *Wells* were that the defendant had been taken to the warden's office on a charge of misconduct. He became noisy, angry, and insolent, and the warden asked him to leave. Outside the office, the defendant sat on the floor, refusing to return to his cell. A prison guard, a man named Brown, entered the hall, and the defendant seized a heavy crockery cuspidor, threw it at Brown, injuring him severely. Wells testified he had no intent to strike Brown but picked up the cuspidor to defend himself from another guard, one Robinson. The state's testimony was that Wells had "malice for all officers" and threw the cuspidor with "malice aforethought." The trial judge disallowed evidence from the prison doctors and a psychiatric consultant who testified that the defendant was suffering from an abnormal mental condition at the time he injured Brown, namely, a state of tension induced by fear. The expert defined the state of tension as "a condition in which the whole body and mind are in a state of high sensitivity to external stimuli." Counsel for the defendant, therefore, asserted that Wells did not act with malice aforethought.

Wells brought the case to the Supreme Court of California on appeal, citing, among other assertions, that evidence of a mental state negating malice aforethought had been disallowed by the trial court. In analyzing this contention, the court agreed that evidence that the defendant "suffered from an abnormal mental state (not insanity), i.e., fear of personal safety," should properly be received. Further, it stated that "if a qualified expert [said] he acted from genuine fear rather than revenge," the testimony should have been received. Commenting that Wells had "conducted himself according to his own standard of conduct" rather than the institution rules, the court affirmed the denial of

a new trial but ruled that the medical and psychiatric evidence should
have been admitted "but the error was not prejudicial." The Supreme
Court's reasoning about malice aforethought, a primary factor in specific intent crimes, bears restating:

Since the crime defined in the section quoted above "necessarily involves proof
of a mental state (specific intent or motive amounting to malice aforethought)
... the prosecution ... was allowed to introduce evidence from which it could
be inferred that he bore such "malice aforethought" toward prison guards as a
class and toward Brown in particular. Here, the offer was to show not insanity,
but a lack of mental capacity to have malice aforethought, but, rather, the fact
of nervous tension and that the particular tension was directly relevant to the
issue of "purpose, motive, or intent," i.e., to the critical question as to whether
defendant's overt act was done with "malice aforethought" or was actuated by
fear, genuine although unfounded in ultimate truth. This evidence was admissible
... refusal to admit such evidence allows one to be convicted ... without proof
of the requisite mental intent specified by the statute ... constitutes a denial of
due process of law.

The Wells decision did not directly involve diminished capacity to
have malice aforethought but was "directly relevant to the issue of
purpose, motive or intent." Some ten years later in *People v. Gorshen*
(California, 1959),[21] the central issue was that the defendant "did not
have a mental state which is required for malice aforethought or premeditation . . . by virtue of an underlying schizophrenic condition,
from which the accused suffered." Gorshen, a longshoreman, shot and
killed his foreman in the presence of police, for which he was found
guilty of second degree murder in a trial without a jury. The defendant appealed that psychiatric testimony established that he did not
act with malice aforethought and "did not intend to take human life
. . . . therefore should be acquitted." The case as detailed in the Supreme Court's ruling is of acute psychiatric interest.

The record discloses the following events leading up to the homicide: At 5 p.m.,
on March 8, Defendant reported to the dispatching hall. Between 6 and 7 o'clock
he and a fellow worker ate and consumed a fifth of a gallon of sloe gin. Defendant worked until 11 p.m. Between 11 and 12 o'clock defendant and fellow
worker ate and consumed a pint of sloe gin. Shortly after 12 midnight O'Leary,
the foreman told defendant to go to work. Defendant threw the glass to the
deck, exchanged a "few words" with O'Leary, and went to work. Thereafter
O'Leary told defendant that he was drunk and was not doing his work properly
and directed defendant to go home. They argued, defendant spat in O'Leary's
face, and O'Leary knocked defendant down and kicked him. At the request of
other workers O'Leary walked away from defendant. Defendant threw a piece
of dunnage and brandished a carton at O'Leary.
Paul Baker, a "walking boss" took defendant to a hospital. Defendant was

bleeding and bruised; his left eye was swollen shut and a deep cut under it required 5 to 6 stitches. Defendant drove to his home, got a .22 caliber automatic pistol which contained 2 bullets, fired one shot in his living room, put the gun in his apron, and drove back to the pier. He arrived there about 30 minutes after he had been sent home and went into the ship looking for O'Leary.

O'Leary warned the police, who searched Gorshen on the pier, finding no gun. One of the officers described defendant as "angry," "almost tearsome," "emotional," but not incoherent or boisterous.

O'Leary and Nelson then appeared. Defendant shot. The single bullet entered O'Leary's abdomen, killing him. The officers subdued defendant after a brief struggle.

Defendant had a very good reputation for peace and quiet and did not usually drink to excess. During the 15 years he had known O'Leary prior to the night of the homicide they had been friends and had had no trouble. Defendant's recollection of the events of that night was "kind of hazy." He considered it unfair of O'Leary to order him to go home but to retain the fellow worker with whom defendant had been drinking.

"The argument starts about he wants me to go home and I . . . tell him that I intend to wait until business agent comes in, so apparently he, he hit me and knocked me off, off the floor and when I jump up, he got on and hit me again, and that's—then I tried to defend myself. I, I didn't hit him . . .; he was apparently too fast for me or stronger, bigger." Defendant did not recall throwing a piece of dunnage or brandishing a carton or threatening to go home and get a gun. When he discharged the gun in his home, "I didn't know it was on the safety or not, I was shaky. I didn't know what I was doing."

Dr. Bernard L. Diamond, who examined the defendant, testified as follows:

That defendant suffers from chronic paranoiac schizophrenia, a disintegration of mind and personality. For 20 years defendant had trances during which he hears voices and experiences visions, particularly of devils in disguise committing abnormal sexual acts, sometimes upon defendant. Defendant recognizes that these experiences are "not real" but believes that they are "forced upon him by the devil."[22]

Apparently, the defendant, prior to his examination by Dr. Diamond, had not disclosed to anyone these experiences, nor those that follow. A year before the shooting the defendant (who was fifty-six years old at the time of trial) became concerned about his loss of sexual power. With this concern, his sexual hallucinations increased in frequency, and his ability to work became increasingly important to him as a proof of his manhood. Dr. Diamond's analysis continued: "On the night of the shooting, O'Leary's statement that defendant was drunk and should leave his work was to defendant the psychological equivalent of the statement that 'You're not a man, you're impotent, . . . you're a sexual pervert.' " Then, according to the defendant's statements to Dr. Diamond, O'Leary applied to the defendant an epithet which indicated sexual perversion. At this point, according to Dr. Diamond's opinion, the defendant was confronted with

the imminent possibility of complete loss of his sanity. . . . [A]s an alternative to total disintegration . . . , it's possible for . . . an individual of this kind, to develop an obsessive murderous rage, and unappeasable anger. . . . The strength of this obsession is proportioned not to the reality danger but to the danger of the insanity. . . . [F]or this man to go insane, means to be permanently in the world of these visions and under the influence of the devil. . . .

The defendant told Dr. Diamond that from the time he was taken to the emergency hospital until the time of the shooting:

That is all I was thinking about all of this time is to shoot O'Leary. I forgot about my family, I forgot about God's laws and human's laws and everything else. The only thing was to get that guy, get that guy, get that guy, like a hammer in the head.

In the opinion of the doctor, the defendant acted almost as an automaton:

[E]ven the fact that policemen were right at his elbow and there was no possibility of getting away with this, still it couldn't stop the train of obsessive thoughts which resulted in the killing. . . . [H]e did not have the mental state which is required for malice aforethought or premeditation or anything which implies intention, deliberation or premeditation.

The trial court stated at some length the matters which it considered in reaching its decision. It said,

Up till the time that Dr. Diamond testified in this case, there was no explanation of why this crime was committed. [The doctor is] the first person that has any reasonable explanation. Whether it's correct or not, I don't know. . . . [I]f I would follow Diamond's testimony in toto, I should acquit this man. I'm willing to go on record, that in all probability his theories are correct . . . that he had no particular intent to commit this crime.

The court accepted the doctrine laid down in *People v. Wells*, namely, that on the trial of issues raised by a plea of not guilty to a crime which requires proof of a specific mental state, competent evidence was admissible that mental abnormality not amounting to legal insanity could negate malice aforethought. The judge agreed with Dr. Diamond's explanation, giving his opinion of the "medical essence" of "malice aforethought," to wit, "whether an individual performs an act as a result of his own free will or intentionality, or . . . whether the action is directly attributable to some abnormal compulsion or force, or symptom or disease process from within the individual." The trial court's judgment of second degree murder was upheld by the Supreme Court of California whose summary gave validity to the diminished capacity plea in this instance. It stated: "In other words, within the area of culpability for the crime charged, the testimony of the expert apparently created a reasonable doubt that the homicide was murder of the first degree but not that it was murder."

The important principle of diminished capacity in murder cases where the defendant did not have the specific mental state essential to entertain malice aforethought was reestablished in *People v. Conley*, a California case (1966),[23] which involved a first degree murder conviction. The defendant claimed amnesia for the shooting of his victims, resulting from alcoholic intoxication. A physician testified that his blood showed 0.21 percent alcohol, sufficient to "impair his judgment"; a psychologist testified that Conley was in a "dissociative state [with] personality fragmentation." The Supreme Court reversed the conviction stating: "although expert testimony is necessary for diminished capacity based on mental disease or defect . . . [it is] not essential to prove diminished capacity because of intoxication." The court added that "nonexpert" observation and testimony was sufficient in the latter situation.

The effect of *Conley*, characterized as a "special adaptation of the Wells-Gorshen rule . . . where there is evidence of diminished capacity to deliberate, premeditate, harbor malice aforethought or to form an intent to kill," was to formulate jury instructions in California law,[24] consonant with the decision. The instructions in cases of murder and voluntary manslaughter read:

If you find from the evidence that at the time the alleged crime was committed, the defendant had substantially reduced mental capacity, whether caused by mental illness, mental defect, intoxication, or any other cause, you must consider what effect, if any, this diminished capacity had on the defendant's ability to form any of the specific mental states whether he was able to form the mental states constituting either express or implied malice aforethought, you cannot find him guilty of murder of either the first or second degree.

Furthermore, if you find that as a result of mental illness, mental defect, or intoxication, his mental capacity was diminished to the extent that he neither harbored malice aforethought nor had an intent to kill at the time the alleged crime was committed, you cannot find him guilty of either murder or voluntary manslaughter.

Diminished Capacity and Alcoholism

A mental condition for which a defense of diminished capacity has been frequently urged arises in alcoholic offenders. Here, periods of confusion, amnesia for the crime, uncontrollable craving for continued drinking (dipsomania), "blackouts," fugue states, and impulsive, often wanton, aggression point to the possibility of the diminished capacity defense. Clinically, these conditions fall under several recognizable heads: acute and chronic alcoholic intoxication, delirium tremens, alcoholic deterioration (alcoholic dementia), alcoholic paranoia, pathological intoxication, and two conditions rarely involved in criminal acts— Korsakow's syndrome and acute hallucinosis. The law, however, does not differentiate these diagnoses, asking only if a mental disease (resulting from alcoholism) rendered the accused incapable of entertaining specific criminal intent or unable to know right from wrong or unable to conform his conduct to the requirements of law. If the answer is in the negative, alcoholism in any form constitutes no defense against a criminal charge since drinking is a voluntary act.

This settled rule has an ancient lineage. In the seventeenth century, Sir Matthew Hale enunciated the principle of alcoholism and crime with a clarity that underlies today's rulings. He wrote of "dementia affectata, namely drunkenness":

This vice doth deprive men of the use of reason, and puts many men into a perfect phrenzy; and therefore . . . such a person committing homicide . . . shall suffer for his drunkenness answerable to the nature of the crime occasioned thereby . . . by the laws of England such a person shall have no privilege by this voluntary contracted madness, but shall have the same judgment as if he were in his right senses.

To this flat statement, Lord Hale added the exception:

That although the simplex phrenzy occasioned immediately by drunkenness excuses not the criminal, yet . . . if . . . an habitual or fixed phrenzy be caused . . . [this] puts the man into the same condition in relation to crimes, as if the same were contracted involuntarily at first.[25]

This seventeenth-century summation of the law on alcoholism and crime is, in the words of a Maryland justice (1968), "substantially that followed by the courts in the United States."[26] Justice Orth of the Court of Special Appeals went on to diagram the situation, admittedly "an oversimplification":

[T]he majority [of courts] distinguished between (1) the mental effect of voluntary intoxication which is the immediate result of a particular alcoholic bout; and (2) an alcoholic psychosis resulting from long continued habits of excessive drinking. The first does not excuse responsibility for a criminal act; the second may. . . . The cases usually refer to the first category as a "temporary" insanity and the second category as a "permanent," "fixed," or "settled" insanity.

An early American case (*State v. Haab*, Louisiana, 1901)[27] re-affirmed the established rule. The prisoner, convicted of first degree murder, appealed on the grounds that a medical expert had testified that the accused suffered from delirium tremens before the crime. The trial judge had expressed himself as "denying" the testimony of Dr. Maylie since Haab's alcoholism only

temporarily destroyed his mental soundness. . . . It makes no difference [whether] you designate the temporary effects of his excesses as "ordinary drunk," "drunk to stupefaction," "delirium tremens," "drunk to frenzy, insanity, etc." . . . This was not delirium tremens but merely affliction with that nervousness [that] always accompanies immoderate indulgence in alcohol.

The Supreme Court of Louisiana confirmed the conviction, noting that the trial judge made one remark "that might well have been omitted"—that in denying Dr. Maylie's testimony the court may have communicated its negative "impressions or opinions" to the jury.

The various clinical complications and mental states caused by alcoholism present considerable difficulties in actual forensic practice. For example, a common defense for criminal behavior cited by offenders is the so-called blackout, a lay term signifying a syncopal attack which may be brief or prolonged and accompanied by amnesia. As is well known, at some time in his drinking career the alcoholic finds that he cannot account for a number of hours during a drinking spree. During that time he talks, acts, and moves in his accustomed way without any consciousness of what he has done or memory thereof. He may also have committed violent acts or have behaved contrary to his accustomed manner during this period, with an amnesia for these occurrences the next day. Motor behavior carried out in the absence of consciousness is called a flight or fugue. It is allied to the automatism discussed in Chapter 6.

The validity of a fugue state with subsequent amnesia in a criminal case is always subject to disbelief. The alcoholic offender with a history of blackouts can reasonably maintain a claim of amnesia for a crime. However, if one reviews his behavior in detail with him, one can obtain flashes of memory, so-called islands of memory, that rise disconnectedly in a fog of forgetfulness. Witnesses who observe the criminal to be clear in speech and purposeful in action can only testify

to an apparent presence of mind since the fugue state as well as amnesia is an entirely subjective phenomenon.

The degree of intoxication sufficient to bring out an "absence" similar to petit mal epilepsy is unknown. It is a fair assumption that an
intimate relationship exists between the repressed urges in the individual and his intoxication, but the presumption of unconsciousness
in such cases raises legal problems relating to the ultimate question of
criminal responsibility. That cases where "blackouts" are claimed are
rarely clearcut is illustrated in the following:

Abel C., a man in his late 40's, wearing dark glasses, his hand in his pocket
simulating a gun, approached a teller in a bank. He demanded "all the money
. . . I can shoot or bomb . . . stay alive . . . no alarms or noise. . . ." Abel was
soon captured and $1100 recovered. His insistence on complete amnesia for
the event led to a question of competency to stand trial as well as sanity at the
time of the crime.

Study of his life pattern pointed towards alcoholism, with a history of several arrests for bad checks, four state hospital admissions and a term at a rehabilitation center.

Of the robbery charge, the prisoner knew almost nothing. He claimed he
was on the job working for an auto parts firm; that he was seized with a compulsive feeling of some kind, became confused, started drinking, and found
himself in another city. He didn't remember being in a bank, had only the
vaguest memory of being questioned. The prisoner said, "I can't believe I would
do a thing like that." The entire episode he described was "like a kaleidoscope,
a rush of things, nothing sequential."

The accused related that after pressures from the job began to build up; he
got "uptight" and "the wheels go round"; he became depressed and developed
an irresistible craving for alcohol and he "flipped out." A middle-aged man,
Abel's manner was apologetic; he talked in a halting way, especially when trying
to reconstruct the events of the robbery. He maintained that the episode was
shrouded in confusion and amnesia. As the interview proceeded, he showed an
obviously superior intelligence. His memory for impersonal events was excellent, his vocabulary more than adequate.

Reexamination 8 months later revealed continued amnesia for the offense.
The accused seemed genuinely concerned with "the pressure they put on me"
preceding the robbery because the firm he worked for used "hot cars . . . I
fronted for them." He insisted the F.B.I. "called me all the time . . . watching
me because I was an ex-con . . . it made the wheels spin in my head."

In spite of an element of exaggeration in his denial of awareness of his
acts, it was concluded the amnesia was partly hysterical and partly
secondary to alcohol. The defendant was convicted but was placed
on probation.

Not uncommonly, an unclear case may be dealt with legally in less
clinical fashion. In a New Jersey case (1962)[28] where the accused was

convicted of murdering his wife, the accused contended that heavy drinking preceded the crime. The trial judge excluded the defense since alcoholism had not altered premeditation. On appeal, the Supreme Court of New Jersey ruled that "a trial judge may exclude evidence when probative value is meager."

The chronic alcoholic involved in crime presents puzzling problems to the courts. In discussing decisions covering alcohol and crime, the American Law Reports annotations maintain:

The problem is permeated with all the difficulties implicit in . . . the concept of criminal intent, with its nebulous distinctions between malice, general criminal intent, and specific intent. There seems to be no doubt that the moral disapprobation of the courts . . . for drunkenness, had a distinct effect upon the development of the law.[29]

Alcoholic Mental Diseases and Irresponsibility

The point at which chronic alcoholism progresses to mental illness, as delirium tremens, alcoholic paranoia, or deterioration, is difficult to determine; the effect on judgment, reality testing, and appropriateness of behavior can develop insidiously. Such a situation was seen in the case of Smith, a forty-two-year-old man, evaluated prior to being charged with willfully threatening the president of the United States. His criminal record indicated wife beating, assault with intent to commit murder, auto theft, aggravated assault, and narcotics charges. The defendant readily admitted to twenty arrests for intoxication, as well as an undesirable discharge from the army and a period in a mental hospital in Georgia. His consumption of wine and beer was practically continuous for the preceding five years. In statements to the Secret Service, the accused stated:

"I do not like the Vietnam War started by President Nixon. I would harm the president if I could, any way I could. I have a grudge against Mr. Nixon because of a lot of friends of mine were killed on account of him. I swear by God, I would kill him if I had the chance. . . ."

At the time of the examination the accused denied any thought about killing President Nixon, saying he was out of his head during this time. He recalls seeing terrifying objects: snails, animals, rabbits, etc. All he remembered was that the President's welfare check was about to be tricked out of him and that he was still hearing peculiar voices. He smelled peculiar odors, he heard people as if on "concrete" and heard birds whistling. Sometimes he heard a murmuring and a man calling his name. . . . They told him that he was "the worst thing God created . . . the lowest thing in the world." Sometimes he felt as if piano wire were out over his face; as if it were cutting into his cheek "but when I looked, I found my face was normal."

Smith was obviously in an acute alcoholic delirium with visual and auditory hallucinations and probably somatic delusions as well.

In the condition called alcoholic deterioration or chronic brain syndrome due to alcoholism, hospitalization for a prolonged period often affects the outcome of the legal situation:

A man, aged 69, was charged with attempted murder. He had been drinking in a bar with his sister-in-law where he met a stranger, inviting him to the former's home for continued drinking. After a night of wassail, the woman staggered into the street, bleeding from a knife wound in the back. The accused stated that he remembered nothing from mid-night until he found himself on the street in the morning. He admitted seeing blood on his sister-in-law's dress sometime during the night. The young stranger was absolved.

The accused's history indicated life-long alcoholism with a record of 27 arrests and incarceration for drunk and disorderly conduct, vagrancy, public intoxication, check forgery, etc. He related "black outs," dizziness and numerous intestinal complaints. Examination demonstrated arteriosclerosis with hypertension and, from a mental point of view, confabulations, lack of goal idea, confusion, perceptual difficulties. Psychological tests showed confusion on the Bender test, and on the Rorschach test, "paucity of responses, spacial confusion, delayed responses" and other organic indicators. The Goodenough-Machover Draw-a-person test showed weakness of his mental organization, sexual conflict (impotence), and an uncertain sense of body integrity.

A diagnosis of chronic brain syndrome, alcoholic deterioration and cerebral arteriosclerosis was made. The accused was transferred to a state hospital for six months on a stipulation of incompetency to stand trial. Because of the probability that he did not know the nature and quality of his act at the time of the offense, and because the inflicted wound turned out to be superficial, the prosecution agreed to drop the charges, and the accused remained in the state hospital.

Alcoholic paranoia, a chronic though rare type of mental disease, less often encountered in criminal cases, is to be distinguished from episodes of jealousy and accusations of infidelity during an alcoholic spree or period of heavy drinking. The presence of paranoid ideation during the sober period differentiates this mental disease from the frequent paranoid-like accusations of infidelity among intoxicated persons. This is not uncommon in intrafamily arguments. A murder case wherein a man killed his wife, believing her to be unfaithful when he was intoxicated (*People v. Juarez*, California, 1968),[30] presents this problem. *Juarez* urged a diminished capacity defense, claiming the trial court on conviction committed error in failing "to take into consideration all the evidence bearing on the issue." One psychiatrist testified that the accused suspected his mate, the victim, to be involved with another man, thus diagnosing him as an alcoholic paranoid. Another equally competent psychiatrist received a history that the defendant,

Juarez, knew his "paramour had been faithful" while he was sober. The second expert gave the opinion that the defendant was not psychotic at the time of his criminal act and that the murder was the act of an "unstable, immature man under the influence of alcohol." On an appeal to the conviction, based on the second doctor's testimony, and on corroboration by lay witnesses, the appeal court affirmed the original judgment.

The condition known as pathological (alcoholic) intoxication presents baffling elements in the determination of responsibility for violent crime. In this type of case, a special sensitivity to alcohol is assumed existing often in combination with an inherently unstable personality. The distinguishing characteristic of pathological intoxication is the onset of wild aggressiveness after a few drinks, sometimes as few as one or two. Kolb, in his standard textbook,[31] describes the condition as

much more striking in the severity of symptoms than ordinary drunkenness. . . . The onset is dramatically sudden. Consciousness is impaired . . . activity is exaggerated, impulsive and aggressive, even to the point of destructiveness . . . the disorder lasts from a few minutes to a day or more and is usually followed . . . [by] amnesia for the episode.

To this clinical description, Dr. Kolb adds: "There is an increasing tendency to consider that such episodes with . . . crimes of violence are really instances of psychomotor epilepsy released by alcohol in persons predisposed to such seizures."

In the current diagnostic manual of the American Psychiatric Association (1968), pathological intoxication is considered a species of psychosis, an organic brain syndrome.[32] It is renamed idiosyncratic intoxication in the draft of the *Diagnostic Statistical Manual* III (1978).[33] In these cases, the electroencephalographic readings are not usually pathological; therefore, the assumption that they are allied to the epilepsies is still open to question. However, it is probable that the syncopal attacks bear some relation to vascular sensitivity in the cerebral circulation. In any event, the behavioral picture is specific in that violent aggression, often of a wanton, purposeless character, follows the imbibing of a few drinks, followed by amnesia after the attack. Before a typical case is related, it should be noted that the courts do not always accept pathological intoxication as rendering valid a plea of diminished capacity. In a Colorado case,[34] a defendant's argument that he suffered from "an acute mental disturbance . . . manifesting excitement, or confusion, and hallucinosis followed by amnesia and diagnosed as pathological intoxication," was denied by the court. The following case can be correctly regarded as one of pathological intoxication.

The accused, a powerfully muscled young man of nineteen, known as Bill, was involved in three assaults on girls after drinking bouts, the last leading to a charge of murder. The pattern of his behavior was sufficiently stylized to warrant detailed description.

Bill's early history disclosed rheumatic heart disease with headache during adolescence which preceded the criminal assaults. As an adolescent, he came home mildly intoxicated, became disruptive, slamming dishes in the kitchen, at which his father loudly scolded him. Unexpectedly, he lashed out at his father; many blows were exchanged but his father prevailed. Bill went into the house, fell on the couch and "blacked out." Upon awakening, he had no recollection of the episode.

The accused's boyhood and adolescence before he joined the army showed no abnormalities. He traveled in a typical circle of high school athletes who followed the procedure of having sexual relations with "factory girls." It is noteworthy in view of the following history that he said he never talked about intimate sexual activities with his friends. Sexual activity was treated on a puberty level, usually after drinking, with girls jointly used by other boys.

The first aggressive episode followed a drinking party with friends on a furlough. The youths picked up a girl known to be promiscuous. The two companions had intercourse with her, followed by Bill. Sitting in a car, he started caressing her when suddenly he struck her several sharp blows to her face, seized her by the neck, ripping off her clothing with his free hand. After intercourse, he returned her home and was surprised to find his hands bloody.

Two months later at another party, while on leave from the Army, he drank with a girl. They necked and went outside with obvious sexual intent. Suddenly, he punched her two or three blows in the face. He remembers this episode, because he was then attacked by eight of her friends, who proceeded to beat him up. He returned to camp and remarked to his mother that he had better see a psychiatrist, in view of the two blackouts he had experienced.

Several months later, he attended an American Legion Party, invited by his parents. He drank a little, then met a girl whom he invited outside. In his car they embraced, then suddenly he delivered two sharp blows to her face. Outside the car, he pushed her behind a billboard where she fell. He choked her, hit her again four or five times, ripped off her dress and started to palpate her vulva. The girl went limp. No sexual intercourse was attempted. Leaving her behind the billboard, Bill returned home, again covered with blood, and passed out on the couch. The charge was murder and rape.

A careful study was done with negative neurological findings. Psychological testing showed some immaturity and lack of emotional control (Rorschach test). The Machover Draw-a-Person test, scored by Dr. Karen Machover, showed impoverished self-esteem, resentment toward females with unconscious fear of female genitalia, in short, a "global character disorder with acute disturbance in the sexual area."

A final report advised the court that Bill demonstrated diminished capacity to premeditate at the time of the homicide by virtue of pathological intoxication. The wanton, aggressive behavior in a situation which would be expected to yield gratification, the amnesia following the attacks, the initial stimulation by a few drinks, the lack of awareness of his behavior, all confirmed the diagnosis. The accused plead to second degree murder and second degree assault, thus the death penalty for murder in the first degree was reduced to a prison sentence.

Unconsciousness and Diminished Capacity

The hypothesis of a criminal act occurring during a state of suspended consciousness, followed by amnesia, presupposes a degree of unconsciousness at the time of the crime. Such lack of awareness is usually imputed either to intoxication or to organic brain disease, including epilepsy or head trauma. This complex neuropsychiatric area is discussed in a later chapter. For the present, the relation between diminished capacity and unconsciousness from any cause is pursued.

Unconsciousness per se during a violent act has been upheld as conferring irresponsibility. The California Penal Code recognizes this situation. Judicial instructions as to alleged unconsciousness during a crime state:

Where a person commits an act without being conscious thereof, such act is not criminal even though if committed by a person who was conscious, it would be a crime.

This rule of law applies only to cases of the unconsciousness of persons of sound mind, such as somnambulists or persons suffering from the delirium of fever, epilepsy, a blow on the head or the involuntary taking of drugs or intoxicating liquor, and other cases where there is no functioning of the conscious mind.[35]

Proof of such a state depends on objective signs beyond the offender's statements. For example, a man in a barroom fight was struck on the right side of the face, fracturing the cheekbone and the bones of the orbit as he fell against a metal edge of the bar. He immediately got up, drove home, secured a gun, returned, and shot his assailant. He claimed no awareness from the moment he was struck until he was brought to a hospital. Clinical examination confirmed the fractures and consequent brain concussion. Spinal fluid examination disclosed evidence of hemorrhage within the meninges. The accused stated:

We were playing pool . . . Guy called me a f———p———. Blows were passed. The next thing I remember, I am on the floor, with pain in the right side of my face and a feeling as if a blood vessel inside my head burst. . . . My next memory is that I am standing looking at Gene who is behind the bar and I am saying, "Call the police quick."

The plea of murder in the second degree was accepted by the court on the basis of neuropsychiatric testimony of unconsciousness due to brain concussion.[36]

In *People v. Huey Newton*, this defense of unconsciousness from a gunwound in the abdomen, preceded by a blow to the face, was advanced in an appeal from a conviction of voluntary manslaughter of a police officer.[37] The accused testified that he was struck in the face by a police officer who was investigating a homicide. Dazed, the accused remembered nothing until he arrived at a hospital; he had no knowledge of how he came there. Apparently, the police officer shot the defendant as the latter shot the former. At the moment of being struck, Newton was aware only that he "heard an explosion . . . and a sensation of hot soup in the stomach." He then lapsed into unconsciousness. The Appellate Court reviewing the trial proceedings noted that Dr. Bernard Diamond had testified that one who had been shot "in the abdominal cavity [could have] a profound reflex shock reaction with loss of unconsciousness for a short period of time up to ½ hour." On the presumption that Newton fired a gun "while and not before, he was in a state of unconsciousness," the court ruled that unconsciousness "was a complete defense . . . negating the capacity to commit any crime at all."

However, in another California case,[38] wherein two defendants pleaded diminished capacity from unconsciousness due to intoxication by alcohol and drugs (LSD) to murder and robbery charges, the court stated:

Unconsciousness is ordinarily a complete defense to a charge of criminal homicide. (Pen. Code. Sec. 26, Subd. 5) If the state of unconsciousness results from intoxication voluntarily induced, however, it is not a complete defense. (Pen. Code. Sec. 22) Thus, the requisite element of criminal negligence is deemed to exist irrespective of unconsciousness, and a defendant stands guilty of involuntary manslaughter if he voluntarily procured his own intoxication.

Unconsciousness secondary to narcotic or tranquilizing drugs presents a relatively new problem in homicide cases. In a 1961 Minnesota case,[39] the accused claimed he was *involuntarily* intoxicated by a drug prescribed by his physician. The accused was convicted of hit and run and assault. He appealed on the grounds that the trial court erred in refusing to instruct the jury on the defense of temporary insanity due to involuntary intoxication. Three days before the incident, the accused had been given Fluphenazine (Valium) by his doctor for backache. This medication had a "strange" effect on him, so that he remembered nothing of the accident or the assault on the policeman that followed. In reversing the conviction and ordering a new trial, the appeal court commented: "Four different kinds of involuntary intoxication have been recognized: Coerced intoxication, pathological intoxication, intoxication by innocent mistake, and unexpected intoxication resulting from the ingestion of a medically prescribed drug." The Veterans Administration doctor who treated the accused testified that "drowsiness, fatigue, ataxia and confusion [were] the normal side effect of Valium . . . with hyperexcitability, although more rare, was a possible side effect." In agreeing with the appellant that the prescribed drug Valium rendered him "unexpectedly intoxicated to the point of unconsciousness, incapable of controlling his actions and thus not criminally responsible," the Appeals justice laid down the requirements that:

> the defendant must not know . . . that the prescribed drug is likely to have an intoxicating effect . . . that the prescribed drug . . . is in fact the cause of the defendant's intoxication at the time of his alleged criminal conduct . . . that the defendant, due to involuntary intoxication, is temporarily insane . . .

In a dissenting opinion, Justice Rogosheke declared:

> In my view, Section 611.026 has no application to the defense asserted because involuntary intoxication due to the ingestion of a medically prescribed drug is simply not a form of mental "illness" or "deficiency" as those terms are commonly used. To describe the asserted mental state of defendant in this case as one of insanity stretches that word far beyond its ordinary meaning and gives Section 611.026 a construction it is doubtful was ever contemplated by the legislature.
>
> In my opinion, the defense of involuntary intoxication does not rest upon so tenuous a statutory basis.

The increased use of addictive and hallucinogenic drugs in violent crime may increase the incidence of diminished capacity pleas. Lysergic acid, phenylcyclidine, mescaline, and other drugs that disturb perception, induce confusion, and possibly stimulate brain areas serving motor actions resulting in homicide may occasion medical states that could impair deliberation and premeditation. As with the problem of alcoholic intoxication, this is a difficult area in which to evaluate a mental state at the time of a criminal act within the limits of legal criteria.

Notes

1. *U.S. v. Fisher*, 328 U.S. 463 (1945).
2. Henry Weihofen and Winifred Overholser, *Mental Disorder Affecting the Degree of a Crime*, 56 Yale L. J. 959 (1947).

3. I. Ray, *Medical Jurisprudence*: 11.

4. Henry Weihofen, *Mental Disorder as a Criminal Defense*: 175, Dennis and Co., Buffalo, N.Y. (1954).

5. Walter Bromberg, *Is Punishment Dead?* 127 Am. J. Psych. 163 (Aug. 1970).

6. Immanuel Kant, quoted in *The Science of Right*, Encyclopedia Brit. 11: 489, Chicago (1952).

7. *People v. Schmidt*, 216 N.Y. 324, 110, N.E. 945.

8. Henry Weihofen, *Insanity as a Defense in Criminal Law*: 40, Oxford U. Press, London (1933).

9. *State v. Allen*, 98 S.E. 2d 826.

10. Weihofen and Overholser, op. cit.

11. *Commonwealth v. Mosler*, 4 Penn. St. 264.

12. Gregory Zilboorg, *One Hundred Years of American Psychiatry*: 502, Columbia U. Press, N.Y. (1944).

13. 14 Am. Juris. 753.

14. G. Zilboorg, *One Hundred Years of American Psychiatry*: 514.

15. H. Weihofen, *Mental Disorder as Defense*: 95.

16. *U.S. v. Pollard*, 171 F. Sup. 474 (Mich., 1959).

17. *Davis v. U.S.* 163 U.S. 373 (1897), 17 S.C. 360.

18. *U.S. v. Pollard*, 282 F. 2d. 450 (6th Cir., 1960).

19. B. E. Witkin, *California Crimes*: 140, 1975 Supp., Bancroft-Whitney Co., San Francisco (1975).

20. *People v. Wells*, 33 Calif. 2d, 330 (1949).

21. *People v. Gorshen*, 51 Calif. 2d 716, 336 P. 2d (1959).

22. Bernard Diamond, *With Malice Aforethought*. 2 Arch. Crim. Psychodynamics 1 (1957).

23. *People v. Conley*, 64 Calif. 2d 310 (1966).

24. California Jury Instructions, Part 8, Sec. 8.77 (1976 rev.).

25. Lord Hale, *Please of the Crown* 1: Chap. IV, 29 (1949 ed.)

26. *Parker v. State*, 254 A. 2d, 391 (1969).

27. *State v. Haab*, 29 So. Rept. 725 (1901).

28. *State v. Hudson*, 38 N.J. 364, 185 A. 2d 1 (1961).

29. Am. L. Rep. 3d, 8: 1236 (1966).

30. *People v. Juarez*. 258 Calif. A. 2d, 349, Calif. Rept. 630 (1968).

31. Lawrence C. Kolb, *Modern Clinical Psychiatry*: 209, W. B. Saunders Co., Philadelphia (8th ed., 1973).

32. *Diagnostic Statistical Manual*: 6, Am. Psych. An., Washington, D.C. (2d ed., 1968).

33. *Diagnostic and Statistical Manuals*, DM III: Am. Psych. An., Washington, D.C. (Draft, 1978).

34. *Martinez v. People*, 124 Colo. 170, 235 P. 2d 810 (1951).

35. California Jury Instructions, 3d rev. ed., Sec. 4.30, West Publ. Co., 1970.

36. *People v. Colton (sic)* Super. Ct., Calif., no. 22126 (1959).

37. *People v. Newton*, 87 Calif. Rept. 394 (1970).

38. *People v. Graham*, 78 Calif. Rept. 217, 71 C. 2d 303.

39. *City of Minneapolis v. Altimus*, 238 N.W. 2d (1961).

5

Competency to Stand Trial

The common law has long held that "an accused could not be required to plead to an indictment or be tried for a crime when he was so mentally disordered that he could not meet the common law test of competency."[1] Indeed, our system of justice is based on the capacity of one charged with a crime to prepare a defense within the meaning of due process. Mental competency to stand trial was not unknown to the older psychiatrists, as observed by Dr. Ray in his celebrated *Medical Jurisprudence*:[2] "In those cases where there are some but not perfectly satisfactory evidences of insanity, the trial or sentence should be postponed, in order that opportunity may be afforded to those who are properly qualified for observing the state of the prisoner's mind." In his day, insanity may have been loosely related to competency to stand trial, for he astutely observed that in "many cases, where the issue of insanity was doubtful at trial . . . [it could be] . . . veiled from observation, as never to be suspected even by the most intimate associates of the patient." In any event, competency to stand trial is now a settled requirement in American courts, and it is to this situation that psychiatrists are most often asked to contribute their expertise. Compared to psychiatric referrals for the insanity defense, "thousands are committed each year for . . . pretrial competency examinations," according to the National Institute for Mental Health research report (1972).[3]

The question of competency to stand trial has grown out of the common law. The three-pronged test encompasses the accused's capacity (1) to understand the nature and purpose of the proceedings against him, (2) to comprehend his condition in reference to such proceedings, and (3) to assist counsel in preparing his defense.[4] This determination involves many more psychiatric combinations and permutations than appear to confront the examiner in estimating the

89

presence of insanity and the capacity to appreciate the criminality of the accused's conduct. In the competency determinations, for example, a gradation of emotional reactions occurs, ranging from a minor depression to catatonic regression. In insanity examinations, one may find a continued mental illness, paranoid schizophrenia, a paranoid state, organic brain syndrome, or mental deficiency. On the other hand, the conditions that bring about incompetency to stand trial usually are briefer episodes, thus illustrating the ego stresses attending the prospect of imminent conviction and eventual punishment. Since such ego pressures are often related to guilt feelings of which the accused is not aware, these emotional states may cover the whole scale of human reactions.

It may be helpful to regard the varied mental states met with in determinations of competency to stand trial as a paradigm of levels of defense to any threatening situation. In social life, for example, denial of a reality situation may start with a slight bending of the truth in the interest of lending gaiety to conversation. Playful exaggeration leads to the white lie, then to prevarication that glosses over an unpleasant truth, and finally to an alleged or true forgetting of the situation, virtually an amnesia. Such maneuvers, allowable in social life, become a psychic necessity for the prisoner facing trial. Thus, in the offender facing an indictment can be seen denial of the act itself, then lying with a shift of the burden to another, a rationalization, and finally an alleged or real amnesia for the act itself. Thus, the sequence that is experienced is conscious suppression, merging into repression (on unconscious basis) and amnesia. This can be called the *dynamics* of the situation. When the unconscious irritant, the guilty feeling beneath, becomes too painful, the behavior spreads to a mental state, the so-called prison psychosis.[5]

Pseudo-Imbecility or the Buffoonery Syndrome

The prison psychosis often starts with a buffoonery syndrome. The development is easily discernible. The prisoner, on sensing his dangerous situation, assumes a vacant, preoccupied expression, becomes bewildered and depressed, sometimes mute. As the stresses of a trial and imprisonment become formidable prospects, he may move to an agitated depression or break into episodes of wild, destructive behavior in a setting of confusion; or the stunned ego may take another route toward denial by development of a buffoonery syndrome or the condition called pseudo-imbecility. A variant of the latter reaction is the Ganser syndrome, originally considered a specific mental illness of hysterical type.[6] The syndrome to which Ganser drew attention (he called it a "hysterical twilight state") is characterized by approximate answers to the point of absurdity (hence *vorbei reden*—to speak close to). Thus, a patient will say "2 and 2 make 3," or "New York City is in New Jersey," or "Chicago is in Indiana," thus betraying specific knowledge that is distorted within approximate limits. This kind of pointed stupidity is seen during incarceration, in jail preliminary to trial, but rarely at the time of apprehension. Ganser's syndrome, in both pure and impure forms, may include obvious foolish behavior of infantile character that suggests conscious malingery.

The two cases reported here reflect a pseudo-imbecility syndrome not yet fixed into the Ganser form.

A. and M., both in their early 30's were arrested after a bank robbery during which they stole $42,000. According to the Federal Attorney, their modus operandi consisted in assuming disguises, approaching the tellers of the bank with drawn pistols, removing money from the cash drawers, then driving off in a waiting car. They were soon apprehended.

A's history indicated a background of aggressive crime. At the age of 17 he received a two-year sentence for theft in Louisiana. A year after completion of a prison term, he was convicted of armed robbery for which he served five years at San Quentin and two and a half at Folsom Prison in California. Upon his release he developed a heroin habit. Within six months he was charged with possession of a dangerous weapon, a charge that was reduced to a misdemeanor with subsequent release from custody.

On examination, A's manner was of a dissembling childishness. When called into the interview room, he approached it with a bewildered expression, staring at the examiner but obeying the simple request to sit at the table. He seemed confused by initial amenities and refused to answer specific questions. His expression later became surly with a show of aggression.

The answers given, when insisted on, were out of context: often A. would repeat the question turning it back to the examiner in a surly manner. A part of the interview follows:

Q. What is the charge against you?
A. Don't cost me nothing.
Q. Were you arrested?
A. You're crazy; didn't arrest me. Why were *you* arrested?
Q. Do you use drugs?
A. Don't you? You will.
Q. Were you born in 1941?
A. That's a Goddam lie. Born in '50.
Q. Ever work?
A. Don't remember.
Q. Where are you now?
A. In the Goddam room with you.

At the end of the interview, A. stood up abruptly, shaking the examiner's hand. The defendant appeared to be playing a part, to appear brutish, stupid, remote.

Physically he bore a close resemblance to Bill Sykes as portrayed in the British version of Oliver Twist, in expression, manner and features almost as if he consciously mimicked Dicken's boorish character.

M. gave his history in a rambling manner: he apparently spent two years in an institution for the criminally insane and for several months in a psychiatric hospital.

Similarly, M. came into the examining room in an obviously bewildered state. He made a move to leave as soon as he entered and seemed confused at being asked to sit down. His movements were restless; he looked away from the examiner and demanded to know who he was. On being given an explanation, he quieted down but still looked dully around the room.

The defendant's answers give a picture of the attitude and mental status of the defendant:

Q. What is the date?
A. No.
Q. Your age?
A. Don't know.
Q. Why are you here?
A. It's another bag; I see through it. Do what you want. I know the C.I.A.
Q. Did you do a robbery?
A. Shit on that. Get the fucking game going. You can charge me with rape, or anything.
Q. Do you have an attorney?
A. A policeman.
Q. Why are you here?
A. I took money from the fucking F.B.I. Played with his dogs. Don't know the whole trip. You can't fight city hall.

After a while, defendant M. became more cooperative and resigned to his position; his answers were more in line with the intent of the questions. It became obvious that he was impatient for the whole process to be over and that he accepted his position as defendant for the charged crime.

Both offenders were adjudged competent to stand trial.

The Ganser Syndrome

It is generally agreed that reactions of this type are especially likely to arise from a basic instability such as is predictable in psychopathic personalities. Often, however, the reaction may start as a conscious effort to prolong the legal proceedings, a kind of legal strategy among prison-wise individuals. Prisoners who have had contact with psychiatrists or psychologists are able to simulate mental illness to a realistic degree; such success may elevate a prisoner's narcissism to the degree of providing a "secondary gain" by virtue of outwitting his medical examiners. In some cases, simulation invades the ego to the extent of developing regression into psychosis. In the case to be presented, however, the simulated incompetency lasted for a relatively short time. The case concerns a well-known criminal, Kayo Konigsberg, indicted for extortion and felonious assault.[7] The background of this defendant provides a rationale for the mental state he presented on examination for competency to stand trial.

The defendant, aged 40, had a record of impulsiveness, aggression and incorrigibility in his early years.

From the age of 17 to 21 he had been arrested on 22 occasions for disorderly conduct, traffic violations (6), battery and assault (5), fugitive from justice (6), robbery, criminally receiving (5). A conviction of robbery resulted in a sentence of 14 years. While awaiting transfer to the New Jersey prison, the prisoner was examined by a psychiatrist with a finding of "Mental Deficiency with Schizophrenic tendencies."

The defendant was admitted to the New Jersey State Hospital because of sullen, belligerent behavior and apparent delusions that the police wanted to kill him. A three month period of observation resulted in a diagnosis of "No Psychosis, Psychopathic Personality." A psychologic test indicated "High Average Intelligence (with an I.Q. of 110) in a negativistic personality."

In the prison he was re-examined because of extreme belligerence towards the guards, assaultiveness and claims of harrassment by officials. A diagnosis of "No Psychosis, Psychopathic Personality" was again entered. Two years later, another examination was undertaken because of uncooperative, argumentative behavior and a hunger strike. This examination resulted in a diagnosis of "Sociopathic Personality Disturbance: Anti-social Reaction."

Further study at two year intervals altered the diagnosis to "Unstable Psychopath . . . Paranoid Personality" with a comment by the examiner . . ."The prisoner has Paranoid attitudes characterized by general suspiciousness . . . at bottom a fear of being annihilated, compensated for by outward display of strength and preoccupation with principles of right and wrong." The prisoner was paroled after serving 7 years.

On release he became involved in hijacking and loan sharking for which activities charges of criminally possessing stolen property and extortion and assault followed. After indictment the defendant was transferred to the Federal Medical Facility for study, then retransferred for the trial in New York County. At the Federal Institution he was alleged to have "suffered a stroke with brain damage." Attorneys for the defendant claimed ". . . he was insane from 1950 up to 1966 (time of examination)." Some of the staff diagnosed the prisoner as a Ganser Syndrome but the Chief Psychiatrist had certified him as insane.

The current charge related to Konigsberg stripping the victim to the waist, beating him with a rubber hose and threatening to throw him out of the window. The extortion involved return of $100,000, which had been improperly sequestered by stockbrokers, themselves barred from Wall Street for illegal practices.

Prior to the examination, material was made available indicating that while in Federal custody he had filed suits against the Attorney General of the United States, a federal judge, the doctor in charge of the Federal Medical Facility, and the Director of the Bureau of Prisoners for "cruel and inhuman punishment." Prison officials generally agreed that the defendant was a "terrifying human being" but well versed in the criminal law. Although never charged with murder, it was rumored that the defendant had throttled, shot and beaten people in his position in the underworld.

At the examination, Konigsberg entered the room, his left hand in a paralytic position, his face flattened on the left side, staring at the examiner with unblinking eyes. He appeared to have pulled up the right side of his mouth to effect a paralytic look. The right leg was circumducted when walking. Other neurological signs were negative. Responses were brief, often absent. His manner was surly but one detected a faint air of mockery and a kind of quiet pleasure in his inappropriate answers.

Q. How do you feel?
A. No answer.
Q. It is said that you had a head injury 2 years ago?
A. I don't care about that . . . they are plotting . . .
Q. Who is?
A. Don't worry about that. You are trying to fool me.
Q. How much is 3 and 6?
A. I told you there is nothing wrong with me.
Q. Do you understand me?
A. They are plotting against me.

Continued observation led to a final opinion that the prisoner was a simulator, able to understand the charges against him and of assisting in his defense. The diagnosis of "Sociopathic Personality with a suggestion of Ganser-like Syndrome" was entered. The defendant was returned for trial.

At the trial, which extended over many weeks, the defendant appeared pointedly disheveled, wearing a "mismatched jacket and pants and a King of Clubs beard" according to a reporter, sitting impassively and disinterestedly. Suddenly he shouted to the bailiff: "I'm going to sit where I want or I'll bang this chair over your head."

This presaged the defendant's entry into the case as his own lawyer. The next day he arrived in court cleanshaven, wearing, in the words of a New York Times reporter, "a dark, two-button suit with double-vested jacket, a neat white shirt, and a dark tie." Konigsberg discharged his lawyer, whom he now called a "spy," he announced: "Harold Konigsberg will be represented by himself and Judge Roy Bean. Because he don't write too good, he needs the presence of his wife at the counsel table.". . . Then he added, "When I kill a person, they can't find any bodies."

With this new alignment, the trial became a travesty.

"Your Honor," said Kayo, "You are dishonest, unAmerican, a liar, a sneak, and a conniver . . ."

As the trial wound on, Konigsberg insulted the judge daily, alternately offering him orange juice from his counsel table, shouting, mimicking and deriding the Court, District Attorney and witnesses.

"Your Honor," Konigsberg said, leaning over the counsel table threateningly, "my wife and I have seen you wink at the D.A. on three occasions. Once you conspired with my attorney, Miss Kahn, a spy. I move for a mistrial on the grounds you are in cahoots with the D.A." Then suddenly and confidentially, "Do you want some orange juice? It's healing."

Cross-examining the witnesses who testified against him, he insisted that they were criminals, that it was all one big plot.

"I'll teach you Judge. The jury's tired of your nonsense. You run some court of justice." He conferred with his wife, who served as his clerk and assistant, then turned towards the judge, who had advised him to cut his cross-examination short. "Talk up, Judge. I don't want to be a lip reader. Don't tell me when I'm through with a witness. I'll tell you."

After weeks of extended cross-examination of the witnesses, the defendant addressed the court: "You've heard of the Gettysburg address? Well, that's nothing compared to my summation."

At the conclusion of the trial, Konigsberg's conviction for extortion brought a sentence of forty-four years in a New York State prison. This type of bizarre, zany defense is, of course, highly unusual. But as an indication of specific antisocial aggression of the true sociopath, whether hidden in mockery of legal principles or expressed in regressive syndromes, Konigsberg's subsequent behavior is worth noting. On return to the federal facility to finish his original sentence, the prisoner continued his legal harassment of the officials. The following year, he brought a writ of habeas corpus accusing the psychiatrist in charge, Dr. Ciccone, of cruel and unusual punishment and denial of constitutional rights, and the facility staff of "harassing, degrading and confusing me." Some of his complaints bordered on petulance and zaniness; yet, they were so arranged as to mimic the law's respect for human rights. In his brief he complained that:

"the respondent has been kept from a full-handled toothbrush, clean sheets and blankets, art supplies, diary . . . pen, pencils, paper, carbon paper, legal materials. . . . The food placed on the floor in front of the isolation cell (it remained there for 10 to 12 minutes) had dust stirred into it from officer's shoes, it was available to cockroaches . . . in fact one cockroach was seen on the food . . . lack of religious services on Friday nights . . . being transported from Missouri to New York (for the extortion trial) incognito without informing his attorney or wife as evidence of denial of constitutional rights . . ."

A federal judge ruled on the prisoner's brief that there was no evidence either of violation of constitutional rights or of cruel and unusual punishment, except that there was "some merit to a few charges," such as the charges of Konigsberg's inability to have a rabbi in attendance for religious services. He ordered such services be made available. He also noted that the respondent was a "man of unusual and complex personality . . . [who takes] great pride in physical prowess."

This case proved to be a caricature of insanity under conscious control of the prisoner—a rare occurrence. More frequently, but still uncommon, is the regression to a catatonic state by prisoners in peril of execution after conviction. The stimulus of the original buffoonery syndrome advancing to a psychosis became evident in the case of the two Esposito brothers facing first degree murder convictions (1942).[8] The press dubbed them the "Mad Dog Killers."

The two brothers, heavily armed, ran amuck in a crowded section of New York City after a robbery with resultant killing of two citizens including a policeman and wounding of several others.

At their arraignment on first-degree murder charges, the brothers began to act peculiarly, showing increasing dullness and confusion. Where they had been noted by many to be alert, street-wise gangsters before the murder and during the street battle, they became dull, stupid and unresponsive. At the hospital the younger, Louie, aged 29, said, in response to the examiner's questions, "I don't feel so good; come around another time." When asked what his occupation was, he responded, "Make dolls." When questioned as to how he made them, he said, "Cut them out of anything" (pointing to bed linen). When asked for his father's name, his answer was "Which father?" In response to a question as to why he did not answer questions, he wrote as follows: "Don't talk in the enemy camp." When asked his name, he wrote, "Sir John Garibaldi." He seized a piece of paper on which he had been writing, tore it into bits, pushed it into his mouth, made chewing movements and then spit out the paper. Asked what he had been eating, he wrote, "chicken."

The behavior of Harry, his 35 year old brother, pursued a similar course under custody. During the first month after the offense, he showed signs of mental confusion. In response to an examiner's questions, he disclaimed any knowledge of past events and began to act in a manner which was considered obvious malingery by the examining physician. For instance, he would take a hard-boiled egg which he had for breakfast, place it on the floor and, on his hands and knees, push it around with his nose. On another occasion, while taking a showerbath, he put the soap in his mouth.

Because of the presence of a strong element of malingery, a commission appointed to decide on their sanity considered the reactive psychosis to be comparatively superficial. The brothers were declared legally sane and able to stand trial.

During the trial of the brothers, 3 months after the offense, their behavior became progressively worse. Louie assumed a fixed posture; his head was bent, his expression was at times reflective, then depressed, apathetic and bewildered. Harry's behavior was characterized by gargoyle-like grimacing, by periods of tremendous preoccupation with pieces of paper in his hands, by restless movements and episodes of excitement. There were periods of weeping and childish tantrums when he struck his head against the table. At one point the accused smeared feces on their clothes to the consternation of the Judge and jury. Their behavior persisted throughout the presentation of evidence, the testimony of expert psychiatrists, deliberations of the jury and their verdict, and the pronouncement of death sentence by the presiding judge.

En route to prison a sudden flurry of fighting, shouting and wild resistance occurred, but in prison they returned to a torpid, mute state, refused to eat or to wear clothes, tore up the bedding and had to be kept in isolation. They remained mute, bewildered, completely regressed, diagnosed as Catatonic Schizophrenics by the prison psychiatrist.[9] The death sentence was carried out 8 months after incarceration on the assumption that they were legally sane.

The Dynamics of Prison Psychoses

From a dynamic point of view, these reactive psychoses represent introjected rage. The anger ordinarily pointed at society and agents of law enforcement now becomes insupportable anguish: the aggressive criminal cannot tolerate his fury at being caught. The feelings can be so strong that they overwhelm the ego, appearing as a severe depression or a regression to mutism or destructive behavior. It is not without reason that this type of mental condition rendering an accused incompetent to stand trial is seen among aggressive criminals, notably murderers and armed robbers and in felony murders. It is as if the enormity of their daring automatically stimulated a guilt reaction in spite of their surface callousness about human destruction.

This type of prison psychosis, usually transitory, I have called "protest psychosis."[10] It was seen in pure culture among black prisoners in the New York area, stimulated by the civil rights struggle in the United States during the 1960s. The symptomatology for which the term protest psychosis was suggested was influenced by more than personal pressures within the offender. It drew force from social needs (the civil rights movement), was dipped into religious doctrine (Black Muslim group), was guided in content by African subculture ideologies, and was colored by denial of Caucasian legal and social values and hostility thereto.

The inmates of the jail, King's County, Brooklyn, N.Y., to be described here were referred by attorneys, judges, and prison doctors because of sudden destructive behavior in the courtroom during trial or pleading, thus necessitating evaluation for competency to stand trial. The prisoners were diagnosed as schizophrenic psychoses or schizoaffective conditions when admitted to the prison ward, King's County Hospital, whereas they actually expressed hostility to a threatening and hated situation. Investigations by a psychologist, Dr. Franck Simon, a native of Haiti who was aware of the content of African ideology, and by myself proved that the reactions, bizarre though they were, rested on a denial of white language and cosmology. The seriocomic expression of the prisoners' protest, evident in their mental content—delusions, illusions, disorientation, paranoid coloring, and grandiosity—functioned as a denial of Caucasian values in Western civilization.

A negro of 22 was indicted for murder, with a previous record of three assaults but no mental illness. The patient was referred from the House of Detention because of bizarre behavior.

On admission he said: "I growl sometimes." (what makes you growl) "All lions growl." (are you a lion) "Yes, can't you tell." (He says he growls and does it on request and then says apologetically) "I don't growl so good. I was an angel." (How did you get there) "The people took me away, way up above the clouds. You see the building that God lives in. He is in a big room. You have to get permission to see it. God was way down the aisle. He asked what He could do for me and I said I had a problem. I make $30,000.00 a day and I spend it all." (Where are you now) "This is a wide open country. You can see so far. You can see trees and grass and people walking. It is not the United States. It could be Africa. The place is called Opeenoba."

"I have a lot of names." (tell me a few) "Leo, Clefus, Edward. A lot of them that I use; George, Clarence."

On the ward the patient asked for medicine for his fangs. He asked for raw fish and raw meat. Often he stood next to the television box "absorbing electrical energy" which will result in total darkness in about three weeks. When pressed for explanations, he became angry: "I am not supposed to be answering you at all... I have my orders.... I have been advanced."

As the regression continued, the delusional material took on a more familiar aspect: he talked about absorbing energy from other people and that a total blackout would occur in three weeks. The prisoner stood motionless for hours at a time, saying when "enough energy is absorbed I will go into space"; people are "putting white powder in my food."

The patient was committed to a State Hospital, remaining there for eleven months, and discharged as recovered, able to stand trial.

A second prisoner charged with robbery, was referred to the hospital because of mutism, destructive behavior (burning blankets in his cell, and self-inflicted wounds on his head). On admission prior to trial, he was agitated, confused, talking incessantly and required restraint. His expression was empty. When pressed for an explanation he said: "My original language was stolen from me by the slave master and in English I cannot say the word." He referred to his Islamic "language" as his "original language." He stated that this original language has come back to him "slowly."

(what was your original language) Arabic. (can you use it now) I can speak it. (just say a few words) To say hello, I would say jambool. (how did the original language get stolen by slave masters) They cut our tongues out—tied us up. (how long ago) 400 years ago. (what about the last 200 years) Over in the South picking cotton.

The prisoner improved rapidly. The later interview indicated his rationality: (you pray in what language) Native tongue—Arabic to some extent. (you were born in Washington, D.C., how do you know the language) Met people, Afganistan, etc. (what do you think will be the result of race fighting) I don't know. Blacks going to take over the country. President told James Brown thanks for helping out your country. (what do you think will be the windup of all this) Don't know. (what do you think the best windup) Peace. (you have dreams) No and I don't take medication. (anything else you want to tell me) My name is Pooki Ali—righteous name.

The psychiatric conditions encountered in judging competency to stand trial vary greatly. Moreover, the unexpected turns in the accused's reactions tax diagnostic efforts. For example, transitory states of intoxication from alcohol or drugs, episodes of organic confusion, and emotional outbursts affecting mental clarity often clear up quickly.

Emotional reactions such as depressions sometimes persist or even merge into chronic psychoses. Furthermore, chronic psychoses which are in remission may exacerbate under the stress of confinement and the imminent trial. On the other hand, persons with a history of chronic illness, e.g., schizophrenia, who appear to be stabilized may maintain their apparent composure at the time of examination for competency to stand trial. Hence, the presence of a longstanding mental illness may influence the examining psychiatrist to find incompetency where there is none within the legal definition of competency. Again, the problem of utilizing the accepted legal definition of a "settled" or "continued insanity" will produce difficulties in matching it to psychiatric concepts of "remission." The case of W. H., aged thirty-nine, indicted for bank robbery, is a case in point of "settled" insanity:

The prisoner, arrested for bank robbery, was remanded to the Federal Medical Facility for observation by the court. He remained there for five months and on his return changed his plea to "not guilty by reason of temporary insanity."

The history indicated that the prisoner was committed to a State Hospital in California at the age of thirteen, then over a period of twenty-one years had been a patient at seven state hospitals in California, Wyoming, Colorado, Oregon, with re-admissions two and three times at several hospitals. There were also arrests for burglary and robbery of a bank, the occasion for some of the hospital admissions. One diagnosis was recorded as "Permanent (continued) Schizophrenia."

On examination, the prisoner showed disorganization in thinking and a paranoid attitude towards physicians, court officials and attorneys with whom he had contact. He insisted that the offense of bank robbery was due to a "toxic condition" due to sensitivity to the drug Prolixin and "semi-starvation" from two months residence with the Salvation Army before the crime. Nevertheless it was concluded that the prisoner was competent to stand trial.

Three months later the prisoner was re-examined. His activity in the jail was destructive, his behavior psychotic. At the State Prison, where he was sent for safe-keeping, the prisoner demonstrated an advance in his mental illness. The chief psychiatrist at the prison indicated that his behavior for about a month had been disorganized, aggressive and destructive. He had flooded his cell, threw water at the attendants, blocked the door and keyholes to prevent his enemies from "killing me." On one occasion he burned up his mattress; on another he destroyed the toilet bowl. Again, he sharpened a coil from his mattress and further braided his sheets into strips with obvious suicidal intent. He had thrown feces at attendants, made claims that a man was coming through the toilet bowl to kill him, etc.

At the time of the current contact, the defendant refused to answer any questions. He was agitated and aggressive in expression and demeanor towards the examiner. For a few minutes he threatened to put on a "blow up" if questioned. His behavior, for example, stuffing the door with paper wads to prevent people from coming into his cell was dictated by paranoid ideation.

At other times the defendant expressed himself normally to other inmates

and sometimes to the attendants. Some of his behavior was obviously childish;
e.g., he was concerned lest an inmate might gain entrance to his cell through
the common waste pipe connecting the two toilets in his and the adjoining cell.
At other times he would discuss medication with the physician in a normal and
knowledgeable way.

It was agreed that the prisoner was involved in a Prison Psychosis with a
schizophrenic background. One reported opinion stated that his psychotic behavior rendered him incompetent to stand trial. Another found him competent.

The prisoner was tried, convicted, and sentenced to the federal penitentiary. He served five years, was released to a halfway house, violated parole on two occasions, and returned to the penitentiary where
the psychiatric staff again found him mentally ill. Seven years after
the original sentence, the inmate was found to be "suited only to shel-
tered environment" when discharge was contemplated. In a word, his
history clearly indicated a chronic "settled" insanity which permanently impaired his capacity to ever make an independent adjustment.

Indices of Incompetency

The shifting character of the accused's mental states while incarcerated awaiting trial, as well as the emotional outbursts that sometimes occur in the courtroom during indictment or trial, complicates
the determination of competency. Dr. Robey, who has discussed the
problem in some detail,[11] points to the need to evaluate the prisoner's
susceptibility to decompensation under stress of the trial. This pressure might result, and has resulted, in violent behavior, depression,
suicide, and other signs of regression. Robey's checklist for psychiatrists who are called on to estimate incompetency conveniently sur-
veys all the possibilities involved in such determinations.

1. Comprehension of court proceedings (including cognition, orientation, ap-
   perception and judgment)
   Surroundings
   Procedures
   Charges (including the nature of the charges and complexity of the case)
   Verdicts
   Penalties
   Legal Rights
2. Ability to advise counsel
   Facts
   Plea
   Legal strategy
   Maintaining relationship with lawyers
   Maintaining consistency of defense
   Waiving rights

Interpreting witnesses' testimony
Testifying if necessary
3. Susceptibility to decompensation while awaiting or standing trial
Violence
Acute psychosis
Suicidal depression
Regressive withdrawal
Organic deterioration

Robey's checklist, which had a wide circulation among attorneys and court officials, suggested to McGarry and associates at the Harvard Laboratory of Community Psychiatry that there is "an appetite for greater clarity and comprehensiveness in competency determinations." To supply this need, a multidisciplinary team of lawyers, psychiatrists, and psychologists, under the leadership of Dr. Louis McGarry, developed "clinical criteria for competency to stand trial." They rated the accused on a five-point scale: [12]

1= total lack of capacity—a mute or incoherent person or a severe retardate.
2= severe impaired function.
3= moderately impaired function.
4= mildly impaired function—little question of adequacy.
5= no impairment.

The categories tested follow in abbreviated form:

1. Appraisal of available legal defenses: accused's awareness of possible defenses.
2. Unmanageable behavior: appropriateness of accused's verbal and motor behavior, i.e., possibility of disruption in court.
3. Quality of relating to attorney: ability to trust and communicate with attorney.
4. Planning of legal strategy: appreciation of lesser plea bargaining.
5. Appraisal of role of (a) defense counsel (b) prosecuting attorney (c) judge (d) jury (e) defendant (f) witnesses.
6. Understanding of court procedures: events of trial and their import.
7. Appreciation of charge: concrete understanding of the charge.
8. Appreciation of range and nature of possible penalties.
9. Appraisal of likely outcome: realistic assessment of outcome.
10. Capacity to disclose to attorney available pertinent facts surrounding the offense: a consistent, rational, relevant account of the motivational and external facts.
11. Capacity to realistically challenge prosecution witnesses: recognition of distortion in prosecution testimony.
12. Capacity to testify relevantly: ability to testify with coherence, relevance and independent judgment.
13. Self-defeating v. self-serving motivation (legal sense): capacity to protect himself through legal safeguards.

The detailed outline proposed by McGarry and his associates seems at first blush to resemble overkill, a too-minute analysis of the accused's ability to confer with counsel and understand the charge against him. The bald fact, however, is that many unexpected situations arise out of incompetency claims, not to mention the strategic value to the defense of having an accused remain in a hospital, if found incompetent, until witnesses have disappeared and public furor has quieted in a case of public concern. There are intricate questions to be solved: amnesia during an offense and at the time of trial; the effectiveness of drugs to keep a prisoner in remission from a mental illness sufficient to stand trial; the problem of mentally deficient persons who will never "recover" their rational understanding of court proceedings. These are matters for both judicial and medical determination.

Yet, criticism has been levied against psychiatrists entering into the determination of competency. Slovenko, for example, asks why psychiatrists are needed in a "purely operational procedure [asking] whether the person understands the charges and can assist counsel."[13] He explicates his stand as follows:

The point is that fitness to stand trial can be measured by an ordinary view. Psychiatric examination does not further the inquiry. For the literal application of the test, the judge can by himself make as valid a decision as anyone on the basis of a few ordinary and simple questions put to the defendant.

This type of criticism must be weighed against the basic fact that each accused has a constitutional right to due process, and one who is not competent to stand trial cannot avail himself of that right. In *Pate v. Robinson* 1966,[14] the U.S. Supreme Court ruled that the prosecution of a defendant who was legally incompetent at the time of trial "violates due process" even though he is alleged to have waived a hearing on his competency to stand trial.

The accepted test for competency follows that enunciated in *Dusky v. U.S.* (1960).[15] It is relied on to cover any mental abnormality that may be urged by the court or attorneys which interferes with competency to stand trial. "The test must be whether he has sufficient present ability to consult with his lawyer with a reasonable degree of rational understanding—and whether he has a rational as well as factual understanding of the proceedings against him." Still problems arise: a markedly subnormal defendant would be unable to satisfy *Dusky* since he is by definition of "defective" intelligence. Further, in the case of an amnesiac, "factual understanding" of the charge against the defendant would be hampered by lack of memory, and hence he would be unable to assist counsel.

Amnesia in Competency Hearings

Amnesia itself is a puzzling phenomenon. From a clinical and legal point of view, the causation of the amnesia, whether organic, emotional (hysterical), or malingered, is pertinent to the determination of competency. The duration of amnesia is likewise significant: that caused by organic deficits (brain injury, and so forth) is apt to be permanent, whereas the hysterical type is apt to be temporary. The general rule is recorded in the *American Law Review*:

[T]he general rule that amnesia, in and of itself, is no defense to a criminal charge unless it is also shown that the accused, at the time of the act, did not know the nature of the act and that it was wrong. The fact that the accused is subsequently unable to remember the crime is, in itself, no proof of his mental condition when the crime was performed.[16]

An Arizona case, *State v. McClendon* (1968),[17] treated the amnesia problem extensively. McClendon shot his ex-wife in the head, then inflicted a head wound on himself; he claimed amnesia for the event. He was convicted of murder. On appeal, the Supreme Court of the state reversed the conviction, stating:

The trial court abused its discretion in denying the defendant's motion to postpone trial and commit the defendant to an institution when it appeared that defendant was suffering from an amnesic condition of undetermined duration. We held that it would be a reproach of justice . . . if a man, while suffering with amnesia of an uncertain type and extent, was compelled to go to trial when the possibility existed that a further examination would reveal his condition to be temporary and susceptible to treatment.

In the trial court, several examining psychiatrists testified that the defendant's amnesia, apparently fixed, related specifically to the crime act. The court conceded that "precedent of this area is meager and questionable," but in consideration of all the testimony, the court found McClendon sane, rational, and competent in all respects

except that he is suffering from amnesia, which prevents him from recalling the facts and circumstances immediately surrounding the alleged crime. This amnesia would appear from the testimony of the experts to be relatively permanent in nature, at least it is apparent that a reasonable amount of treatment will not effectuate a recovery of the defendant's memory.

The court finds that the defendant understands the nature of the charges pending against him and is able to assist counsel with the exception of being able to relate to his counsel the facts and circumstances surrounding the alleged crime.

The legal significance of a prolonged or irreversible amnesia is that it leaves open the possibility that the defendant's knowledge at the time of the crime may be affected, thus rendering him unable to confer with counsel. In a case where a defendant suffered a serious head injury with obvious brain damage, *U.S. v. Wilson*,[18] it was adjudged that "extrinsic information" was available to the defendant to allow him to overcome his lack of knowledge of the crime. In *Wilson*, the accused committed several crimes (robberies and car thefts), suffering a severe head injury during a chase by police. His amnesia was global for the crimes: memory was absent for several hours before the crimes (retrograde amnesia) and for three weeks thereafter (anterograde amnesia). After prolonged observation and study at the Washington (D.C.) Hospital Center, he was returned to court as mentally well "other than amnesia." Although Wilson sustained a left-sided partial paralysis and brain damage, the reporting physicians stated the accused had a "rational and realistic understanding of the nature of the charges against him, based on information given him since his injury . . . the amnesia is permanent, and . . . does interfere with the patient's ability to assist counsel in his defense." The examiners added that the prisoner "could synthesize an accurate historical picture of what certainly must have happened."

The issue before the District Court in the District of Columbia was "whether standing alone his absence of present independent recollection of events of the afternoon . . . renders him unable to properly assist in his defense." Balancing all factors, including "the public's interest in bringing the morally responsible to bar and the right of an accused to a fair trial, the court concluded that Wilson was not incompetent to stand trial, since "information necessary to the construction of a defense" was available to both prosecutor and defense counsel. In Judge McGuire's specific wording:

[T]he rule to be applied in this case is whether insufficient information concerning the events at the time of the commission of the crime and evidence relating thereto is available to the defense so that it can be said that the presence of such an amnesia as we have here precipitates a situation in which defendant's memory is indeed a faculty crucial to the construction and presentation of his defense. Accordingly, since there has been no showing of the unavailability from sources extrinsic to the defendant of substantially the same information that his present independent recollection could provide if functioning, defendant's motion to be adjudged incompetent to stand trial is denied.

This ingenious legal solution of the incapacity of the defendant "to disclose to the attorney available pertinent facts surrounding the offense" (McGarry, point 10, above) does not completely remove the psychological significance of amnesia in court trials. It is obvious that the claim of amnesia is impossible to deny or corroborate since it is essentially a subjective experience. There is a patent selectivity in hysterical amnesia for criminal acts where chiefly those details surrounding the offender's crime are forgotten while other facets of his life are remembered—name, work record, marriage, children, and so forth. In the organic amnesia, following head trauma, arteriosclerosis, senility, or the like, neither the crime detail nor other aspects of the offender's life can be recalled. This difference between two types of amnesia is sometimes suggestive of malingery, especially the fact that personal identification is often forgotten. Paul Schilder[19] has studied the meaning of amnesia in relation to the total personality and makes the point that amnesia represents a "turning away from experience" in general terms. In the specific situation of the person who appears in a distant locality without any memory of his identity (hysterical amnesia), the so-called victim of amnesia is impelled to "run away from the place where he lives."[20] This basic pattern of avoidance, which Schilder felt was deep in everyone's personality, makes it difficult to be certain that the criminal who alleges amnesia, except in organic brain cases, has "suffered" from amnesia.

Varieties of Amnesia

The courts have agreed that for practical purposes, amnesias can be placed in two categories: *temporary*, i.e., treatable by psychologic means, and *permanent*, i.e., resistant to treatment methods. The methods of uncovering an amnesia are threefold: (1) a meticulous search for memories through a "fine-tooth comb" interrogation of each moment of the crime period, (2) hypnosis with a similar interrogation aimed at reliving the situation, and (3) a sodium amytal interview utilizing the same procedure as above. These techniques rarely result in recovery of full memory; often one gets fragments of recall or dreams that reenact vivid features of the event. Out of these fragments, over a period of time, memories of the whole episode may return. Organic cases may also recall islands of memory, patches of fleeting incidents, alternating with the so-called lacunae of memory, but the total picture cannot be reconstructed by the patient/defendant. The more serious the organic injury—brain laceration, contusion, or hemorrhage—the more likely it is that the amnesia is permanent. A recital by observers of the incident (as a criminal act or accident) often aids the dissolution of an amnesia. In the following example of temporary amnesia, a robber, under hypnosis, fell asleep and dreamed of a robbery. He reported the dream on awakening. Discussion of the dream and a few reported facts restored his memory of the crime.

An enlisted man in the U.S. Navy, aged 27 had stolen a service revolver from his superior officer the day before the offense with the intention of committing suicide. He had been under considerable emotional stress for some time. The prisoner had gone to see his wife, to whom he had been married more than six months. The marriage had never been consummated and during the period of marriage the situation had been unsatisfactory for both individuals. About midnight, on leaving her, he was tense and even dazed; his marital and life situation appeared to present no prospect of solution. He went down to the river to contemplate shooting himself, but returned and held up a motor car with two occupants, taking their valuables and forcing them to drive with him downtown. Finally one occupant shouted within hearing of a policeman and the prisoner fled.

On his arrest, he had no memory of the robbery and abduction.

Memory itself is an unsolved neurophysiological problem. In the words of Suarez and Pittluck,[21] "a wholly adequate definition of memory has bedevilled psychologists for generations." These authors restate the processes of memory: (1) registration of an impression, (2) retention of the impression, and (3) recall or retrieval of the idea, now a memory. Other authors, Koson and Robey,[22] formulate the process slightly differently: (1) formation of the memory trace, and (2) recall of the memory. They point out that alcohol, drugs, or a psychosis impair memory formation, whereas brain damage impairs recall. From a medico-legal point of view, the important aspect of these distinctions is that injury to the recall process is more apt to be permanent, whereas impairment of the formation process may be reversible. Such diagrammatic propositions are not always easy to substantiate in practice. Perhaps the better part of wisdom is to echo the statement of Suarez and Pittluck, namely, "the complexity of the process called amnesia . . . supports the notion of an elaborate admixture of organic and psychogenic factors."

The law regards the defense of amnesia in criminal matters with less question than do mental experts. A case in point is *Thomas v. State* (Tennessee, 1957)[23] wherein a man charged with grand larceny of a car, reckless driving, and leaving the scene of an accident claimed lack of criminal intent because of amnesia before and during the crime. The defendant appealed the conviction to the Supreme Court of Tennessee, relying on testimony in the trial court that he was "severely intoxicated" at the time of the offense. The higher court affirmed the conviction, ruling that amnesia was no defense and that

failure to remember later, when accused what happened during the crime is in itself no proof of the mental condition when the crime was performed. . . . Since there is no evidence as to the effect of amnesia upon the defendant's mind, the defense is not available any more than that of drunkenness.

The use of the sodium amytal interview in uncovering an amnesia may be determinative and effective, or it may not. In the case to be presented of a woman accused of mortally shooting her husband after a day of drinking, the amnesia for the mortal shot was fixed.

The accused, a woman of 44, fired two shots from a revolver at her husband after a drinking episode, the first passing between his legs to the floor, the second striking him in the heart. The victim died of the second bullet. The accused had no memory of the shootings.

Her life revolved around her family and husband, the latter a chronic alcoholic. The history indicated hours spent in bars, threats against the accused, promises to do better. The day before the offense, both the victim and accused continued drinking, resulting in a hangover on both their parts. The next day, the pair spent the day in a bar with friends. The accused recalled all of the events during the day of the crime except the actual squeezing of the trigger. No signs of mental illness appeared.

A "fine-tooth comb" inquiry of the pertinent events was undertaken.

The day of the crime was spent drinking in a bar with a friend, Gary. This consumed the early morning and the whole afternoon until about 5:00 o'clock. The patient remembers about that time her husband, who was drunk, pulled out a knife and placed it in a position as if to cut her. She called out, "Don't cut me," and some other drinkers in the bar knocked the knife out of the husband's hand. Following this, an altercation with some young man took place and the patient drove her husband home, after 7:00 p.m.

At that point the victim slapped and kicked her and then said, "I'll show you," and went for the gun in a nightstand near their bed.

The patient reached for the gun herself knowing the danger and got it before he did. She held it in her hand and phoned for the friend, Gary, to come over since her husband was "on the rampage." While she held the gun in her right hand, pointed toward her husband, he took the phone from her and continued to talk to Gary inviting him to the house and joking in the usual manner. As he was holding the phone in his right hand he took a swipe at her with the left in the direction of the gun. (Gary recalled hearing a shot fired and recalled her husband say over the phone, "She shot between my feet.") The husband hung up the telephone instrument and walked toward the kitchen saying, "Let's not fight, let's get some coffee." The accused held the gun as he made his way toward the kitchen door. At that point he said, with astonishment, "You shot me right through the heart" and died. She saw blood on his shirt front as he fell. She placed the gun in the kitchen and then thought immediately of how to get help.

The patient had no memory at all of the second shot. She did recall having placed the gun on safety as she left the bedroom, went to the kitchen, at the door of which her husband lay on the floor.

A sodium amytal interview was conducted at a hospital in order to see if the amnesia was fixed in her mind. The patient was given 7½ grains of sodium amytal intramuscularly because her veins collapsed; she was put into a semi-hypnotic trance. The questions were the same as given in the interview.

Q. Did he knock you down and kick you?
A. Yes. He said, "I'll show you" and started for the bedroom.
Q. What then?

A. I got up and went to the bedroom, too. . . . I guess we both got to the bedroom door at the same time and he went around the bed and I went across
the bed. . . . It [the gun] was in the nightstand. I had the gun in my hand
. . . I told him to get back in the other room. . . . I don't recall yelling . . .
I might have. . . . I told him to sit down "You're not going to beat me anymore." I told him I was going to call his friend. (She dialed with her left
hand, and asked Gary to come over, holding the gun with her right hand.)
Q. What did he do?
A. He said, "Well, I wish you wouldn't call him." On the phone, I asked Gary
and his wife to come over. Then my husband wanted to talk to Gary. I
handed him the phone. . . . He reached for the phone, I was upset and
crying, I was hurt. . . . I had to get the gun before he did. . . . I thought I'd
be killed. . . . He was laughing [husband]. He said I shot between his feet
to Gary on the phone. He was laughing to Gary. "They might come over."
Then he said, "Let's quit the fighting and I'll get some coffee."
Q. What were you thinking then?
A. I would give the gun to Gary and I wouldn't be afraid of him anymore. I
hoped someone would come over so he would behave. He was grabbing for
the gun while he was on the phone. He leaned over and swung at me. I
just told him he wasn't going to beat me.
Q. Do you remember pulling the trigger for the first shot?
A. No. I put the gun on safety and the next thing he stands there and says "you
shot me" . . . "No, I didn't dear." He pulled his shirt and said, "Yes, you
did, right in the heart." I just wanted to sober him up. He started to walk
into the kitchen and got to the kitchen door and fell.

Under the amytal, the accused was unable to recall the act of pulling
the trigger for either shot, although she was aware that she put on the
safety catch as a routine, automatic act. The district attorney accepted
the amnesia as valid: the accused was acquitted in a preliminary hearing since the prosecutor would be unable to present the grand jury
with evidences of specific intent on the part of the accused.

It is not surprising that defenses based on amnesia present unusual
pleas. Recall, as a function of memory, is a private experience for
everyone including criminal defendants, since recall of memories is
under the influence, in part at least, of emotional states, i.e., whether
the memory is acceptable to the individual's ego. This truism has been
recognized by many judges faced with amnesia cases in criminal situations. For example, in *Parson v. Anderson* (Delaware, 1972),[24] a convicted murderer claimed amnesia for the crime some seven years after
conviction and imprisonment. Parson, the prisoner sentenced to be
hanged, served a writ of habeas corpus on Warden Anderson, claiming
that his amnesia for the offense entitled him to a retrial. Several mental
experts had examined the defendant, all agreeing that the amnesia "was
partial, genuine" but that he was "not psychotic at the time of the
examination." It should be noted that Parson was convicted for the

murder of a fifteen-year-old babysitter whom he had attempted to rape. The original jury found him guilty without a recommendation for mercy. A rehearing was held eight years later by the U.S. Court of Appeals, Third District, which concluded that a current assessment of the prisoner's mental state at the original trial was "impossible." Further retesting under hypnosis and sodium amytal corroborated the amnesia. The examiners concluded: "[His] amnesia was probably genuine and would persist as long as it remained in Parson's self interest not to retrieve the lost facts from his subconscious."

The Court of Appeals denied request for a new trial on the basis of alleged incompetency eight years before. They noted:

Observation of Parson during the trial left "no doubt as to his ability to fully understand and to assist counsel in all phases of the case except, of course, the happening of the crime itself." The defendant took extensive notes and following the trial made a comprehensive, intelligent and clear four or five minute statement to the court why he thought the trial had not been a fair one. He praised defense counsel's work during this statement.

The defendant presented a second writ to the Court of Appeals[25] to reconsider the issue of whether amnesia at the time of the original trial would provide a defense for not pleading insanity. The court responded in ruling against the writ:

the evidence was of physical nature . . . [samples of Parson's blood, fingernail scrapings and pubic hair] . . . the amnesia did not meaningfully affect the availability of this type of defense. . . .
Because the defense's trial strategy deliberately omitted a defense based on insanity, Parson cannot now be heard to contend that the defense was unavailable to him because of his amnesia. Therefore, we hold that, in the context of this case, the fact that the defendant suffered amnesia as to the commission of the crime, does not, in and of itself, render the defendant incompetent to stand trial.

The Legal View of Incompetence

There are many legal situations in which competence is called into questions. As reviewed in a 1961 article in the *Yale Law Journal*,[26] these comprise: (1) at the preliminary hearing, (2) before a grand jury, (3) at arraignment, (4) before or during trial, (5) on appeal, and (6) prior to execution. In addition, motions can be made for competency examinations of defendants (7) for discovery or suppression of evidence, (8) as assistance to the accused's lawyer, (9) for a sanity commission appointment, (10) for a stay of proceedings, (11) for a new trial where new evidence appears concerning the cure of a mentally ill accused, (12) for a writ of error corum nobis, and (13) a writ of habeas corpus.

One of the minor problems of incompetency relates to individuals who appear to have regained their competency while under treatment in a hospital, only to fall back into incompetence when treatment is abandoned. The question then becomes whether improvement under drug or other therapy satisfies the legal criteria of ability to understand the proceedings against them and assist counsel in their defense. This situation was met and answered in *State v. Rand* (Ohio, 1969).[27] Staff psychiatrists of the Lima State Hospital, Ohio, where the defendant had been remanded, testified after a period of treatment (through tranquilizing drugs) that "Rand was a very good patient, cooperative, a very good worker when on medication. Without medication he breaks down." In deciding whether the defendant had removed his incompetency through medical treatment, the court questioned the attending psychiatrist:

Q. . . . with drugs, in your opinion, would Mr. Rand be able to counsel . . . with his attorneys in his own defense?
A. Yes.

Accordingly, the court held that the defendant was competent to stand trial, under "properly administered tranquillizing drugs that permit him to counsel with his lawyers."

While the psychiatrist's task is clearly to estimate the capacity or incapacity of the defendant to understand the proceedings against him, the legal standard has been criticized as "imprecisely formulated." David Bacon,[28] writing in the *Southern California Law Review*, has suggested that the competency tests should be based on "the chance of the accused prevailing at trial"; the current tests, Bacon feels, are "overbroad." The logic behind his notion is best expressed in his own words:

The test should evaluate the effect of an aberration in perception, memory, and coherence and the accused's chance of prevailing at trial. Every accused who suffers a diagnosable mental disorder possesses two defenses. First, there is the defense that the accused can tender if the court permits him to stand trial. The second is the defense he could present but for the psychiatric disorder. To each defense a chance of prevailing at trial can be assigned. If for both defenses the chances are equal, the aberration does not infringe the state interest in the accuracy of adjudication; the accused should be permitted to stand trial.

In effect, this test would inquire into whatever prejudice an accused's mental condition would exert on his chance for prevailing at trial;

the diagnosis, psychopathology or dynamics of the psychosis, emotional state, amnesia, or other mental disability are of only contributory importance. In addition, Bacon suggests a special pretrial conference between the prosecutor, defense lawyer, and psychiatrist/psychologist to ascertain whether the clinical findings would enhance or decrease the accused's success at trial.

The subject of competency tests was reviewed in extenso by Judge Tomson of New York in *People v. Valentino* (1974).[29] In this case, three psychiatrists agreed that the accused "suffered from mental disease" and hence was incompetent to stand trial. Judge Tomson took the occasion to analyze the extent of the psychiatric-legal problem of competency, commenting that the legal test requires less of a defendant: "The true test is the ability to fullfill his role at trial." The judge's statement put the indices of competency squarely in legal perspective.

In determining competency there has been a tendency to assign the defendant a key role at trial and to demand of him at times what may be a too high level of performance....

What witnesses to call, whether and how to cross-examine . . . which motions to make is the province of the lawyer upon consultation with his client. Although the judge agrees "psychiatric testimony" is essential to any intelligent evaluation of the defendant's capacity to stand trial . . . the psychiatrist's expertise is medical, not legal, despite the invention of "forensic psychiatry."

Following the recommendations of the Special Committee on the Study of Commitment Procedures and the Law . . . relating to incompetents . . . of the New York City Bar (1968), Judge Tomson suggested the following criteria for competency:

(1) Is the defendant oriented as to time and place?
The defendant must have a minimal contact with reality. This encompasses the basic human functions that are automatic to all but the seriously mentally ill. An accused must appreciate his presence in relation to time, place and things.
(2) Can the defendant perceive, recall and relate?
These abilities should be familiar as three of the four necessary qualifications of witnesses. Recollection is used not as pertaining to the events underlying the charge, . . . but in the more basic sense of ability to recall sensory perceptions from one moment to the next.
(3) Does the defendant have at least a rudimentary understanding of the process of trial and the roles of the judge, jury, prosecutor and defense attorney?
(4) Can the defendant, if he wishes, establish a working relationship with his attorney? (If the accused is so delusional or paranoid that he will not trust his counsel or tell him the true facts, then he would be incompetent.)
(5) Does the defendant possess sufficient intelligence and judgement to listen to the advice of counsel and, based on that advice, appreciate (without necessarily choosing to adopt it) that one course of conduct may be more beneficial to him than another?

(6) Is the defendant's mental state sufficiently stable to enable him to withstand the stresses of the trial without suffering a serious, prolonged or permanent breakdown?

The guidelines laid down by the judiciary are not far distant from those worked out by psychiatrists (Robey, Koson, and McGarry). The psychiatrist addresses himself to the task of interpreting the defendant's mental life in the context of legal tests concerning the trial, the defense, and the attorney's role. His tools are the defendant's history, verbal productions, reactions to questions, estimated mental capacity, and mental function. These data are viewed in relation to the integrity of the ego at the time as it is influenced by the presence of mental disease or defect. This amounts to an estimation of the defendant's ego strength in the face of the imminent trial. Just how to measure "ego strength" is itself a problem since the concept of "ego" is amorphous yet realistic. Ego strength is built up of childhood experiences, resistance to life traumas, developmental (physical) background, social experiences, and the like. Estimation of ego strength, although admittedly an unmeasurable quantity, depends on the psychiatric examiner's knowledge, intuition, perception, and experience.

Notes

1. J. H. Hess, H. B. Pearshall, D. A. Slichter, and H. E. Thomas, *Criminal Law—Insane Persons—Competency to Stand Trial*, 59, no. 7 Mich. L. Rev. 1078 (1961).

2. Ray, op. cit.

3. Monograph: *Competency to Stand Trial and Mental Illness*, Crime & Delinquency Issues, Nat'l. Inst. Ment. Health, Final Report, No. 7ROI 18112-01, Rockville, Md. (1972).

4. Hess, Pearshall, et al., op. cit.: 1078, 1080.

5. Walter Bromberg, *The Liar in Delinquency and Crime. The Nervous Child*: no. 4, 351 (1972).

6. Sigbert Ganser, *Ueber Einen Eigenartigen Hysterischen Dammerzustand*, 30 Arch. f. Psych. 633 (1898).

7. *People v. Konigsberg*, Indict. no. 4725-63 (New York County, 1966).

8. *People v. Esposito*, 39 N.E. 2d 925, N.Y. Ct. App. (1952).

9. Ralph Banay, psychiatrist, Sing Sing Prison, New York, Personal Communication (1940).

10. Walter Bromberg and Franck Simon, *The Protest Psychosis, A Special Type of Reactive Psychosis*, 19 Arch. of Gen. Psych. 155 (Aug. 1968).

11. Amos Robey, *Criteria for Competency to Stand Trial. A Checklist for Psychiatrists*, 122, no. 6 Am. J. Psych. (Dec. 1965).

12. L. McGarry et al., *Handbook, Competency to Stand Trial and Mental Illness*: *Assessment Instrument*, 99-116 Nat'l. Inst. Ment. Health, Washington, D.C. (1973).

13. Ralph Slovenko, *Psychiatry and the Law*: 93, Little, Brown & Co., Boston (1973).

14. *Pate v. Robinson*, 383 U.S. 375 (1966).

15. *Dusky v. U.S.*, 362 U.S. 402 (1960).

16. ALR Digest, 46 ALR 3d 551.

17. *State v. McClendon*, 103 Ariz. 105, 437 P. 2d 421 (1968).

18. *U.S. v. Wilson*, 263 F. Supp. 528 (1966).

19. Paul Schilder, *Mind: Perception and Thought in Their Constructive Aspects*: 384, Columbia U. Press, New York (1942).

20. Milton Abeles, and Paul Schilder, *Psychogenic Loss of Personal Identity*, 34 Arch. Neur. & Psych. 587 (1935).

21. John M. Suarez and Tyler A. Pittluck, *Global Amnesia: Organic and Functional Considerations*, 3 Am. Acad. Psych. & L. Bull. 17 (1976).

22. Dennis Koson and Amos Robey, *Amnesia and Competency to Stand Trial*, 120 Am. J. Psych. 588 (May 1973).

23. *Thomas v. State*, 301 S.W. 2d 358; 261, 201 Tenn. 645 (1957).

24. *U.S. ex rel. Parson v. Anderson*, 354 F. Supp. 1060 (1972).

25. *U.S. ex rel. Parson v. Anderson*, 481 F. 2d 94 (1973).

26. *Amnesia: A Case Study in the Limits of Particular Justice*, 71 Yale L. J. 109, 122 (1961).

27. *State v. Rand*, 247 N.E. 2d 342 (Ohio, 1969).

28. David L. Bacon, *Incompetency to Stand Trial: Commitment to an Inclusive Test*, 42 So. Calif. L. Rev. 444 (1969).

29. *People v. Valentino*, 356 N.Y.S. 2d 962 (1974).

6

Convulsive States and Violent Crime

Since Hippocrates in 400 B.C. named it the sacred disease because of its presumed supernatural origin, epilepsy or "fits" have intrigued medical men and laymen alike. The diverse and spectacular manifestations of this disease, in a person apparently healthy between seizures, readily suggested an extrahuman causation. The aura with its strange sensory experiences—a rush of heat in the chest, a foul smell, a buzzing sound, deja vu phenomenon, the flailing of the limbs, tonic and clonic movements and post-seizure confusion, the odd momentary blankness of petit mal—all contributed to the notion that some "taint" was at work in epilepsy.

Epilepsy and "Homicidal Mania"

The kinship between explosive behavior, assaultive actions in emotionally unstable persons, and epilepsy was persuasive among older authorities. Thus Esquirol,[1] the pupil of Pinel in nineteenth-century France, and Isaac Ray in this country stoutly maintained that homicidal mania existed among epileptics. Esquirol further identified "masked epilepsy" in his widely read treatise (1838) as automatic behavior supplanting the convulsion. Gowers, the eminent English neurologist, recognized "automatic actions" as a clinical entity (1885),[2] but he did not elaborate on its criminal consequences. His description of automatic actions avoided the question of whether they were "true epileptic events," i.e., psychomotor seizures or merely post-ictal actions, but he commented that he could not "discard the older view" that automatic actions were true epileptic seizures. Gowers was concerned with the medico-legal problems involved: "These automatic actions are . . . of practical importance on account of their medico-legal aspect since they sometimes have the aspect of voluntary actions.

It is, indeed, often not easy to convince observers that these actions are not deliberately volitional and intentional. . . ."

The literature prior to the use of the electroencephalogram (about the 1940s) continued to unite "acts of violence [and] automatisms instinctively motivated."[3] Jelliffe, one of the earliest to bring psychological concepts into relation with organic conditions of the nervous system, reasoned that post-ictal unconsciousness allowed emergence of primitive, "instinctive" impulses, a kind of infantile reaction to utter helplessness. Jelliffe and Pierce Clark,[4] in trying to understand the epileptic furor, "a veritable wild man . . . [who] is liable to kill anyone who approaches," sought an explanation in emotional instability exploding during unconscious periods after the seizures. This corner of psychoanalytic-physiologic theory, although relatively neglected since the electroencephalogram has come into use, may still explain certain unclear assaults in emotionally unstable persons. It may, at least, shed light on the so-called epileptic rage taken to indicate proneness to violent crime.

Before this relation of emotional outbursts and violence is outlined, however, it should be noted that today's neurologists disclaim any relation between epilepsy in any form and homicide. In 1975, James Lewis, an American neurologist, wrote in the *Journal of the American Medical Association*[5] that the alleged cause of post-ictal violence among temporal lobe epileptic patients was "clinical lore." In fact, he called the epileptic "rage" reaction a "myth" since his experience indicated that "unmotivated assault" has not been found among brain disease sufferers and that the "episodic dyscontrol," a phrase coined by Karl Menninger to cover abrupt violence in unstable individuals, could be due to a "sick brain or sick society." Moreover, from a medico-legal viewpoint, Lewis characterized the defense of Jack Ruby as suffering from psychomotor epilepsy as "too improbable to have been fiction."

The fact remains, however, that explosive rage is a common human experience whether expressed verbally or physically. It is also a fact that nature provides us with a clear analogue of human explosiveness in earthquakes, volcanos, tornados, and avalanches. These experiences during the past 10,000 years have so impressed the human psyche as to be represented in the legends, myths, and religions of all cultures. It is fair to say that the paradigm of man's violence to man is the convulsion in nature. The Bible reflects a cataclysmic event in the "loud voice" that precedes the rebirth of the true believer. Some Christian sects assert the "loud cry" will herald the end of the world. One sect speaks of an "avalanche of natural disasters" announcing the end of human life; vast troubles like floods, fire, thunder, and destruction are freely predicted as prophetic cosmic occurrences. In a word, the *anlage* of the killer's explosive impulse lies in a deep reservoir of feelings in all humans, the Jungian collective unconscious. It is psychologically reasonable to say that this dread of explosive happenings, with its cosmic connotations, is projected to the epileptic and is even dimly accepted by the latter in his unconscious, as Jelliffe suggested years ago. In any event, this psychological background of human violence should be recognized when appeals for diminished responsibility are offered the court and jury in cases of wanton homicidal aggression.

Absences, Fugues, and Violent Crime

The relation between "absences," "fugues," or post-convulsive aggression has been accepted more readily by neuropsychiatrists and courts in Europe than in the United States. For example, a Polish investigator (1963) analyzed a series of 250 cases of epileptics concerned with crime and concluded that "epilepsy, compared with other diseases, is not so haphazardly connected with delinquent behavior as was previously thought."[6] An Australian psychiatrist reported a recent case (1963) of psychomotor epilepsy with positive electroencephalographic findings in a man whose previous character made his criminal act "quite unlikely."[7] Similarly, two Italian researchers found a correlation between antisocial behavior patterns and the localization of epileptogenic foci. In the words of these authors, "The epileptic personality represents a mental condition which decreases the subject's will power at the moment of the crime."[8]

In Scottish and English law, automatism as a defense has achieved a respectable status. English authorities have urged relief of criminal responsibility for those suffering from automatic behavior.[9] However, in an Irish case, the plea that psychomotor epilepsy was validly a "defect of reason from disease of the mind," hence sufficient to excuse one Bratty for strangulating his victim during a "blackout," was rejected.[10] The trial judge refused to instruct the jury that automatic behavior during a blackout was sufficient to acquit unless an insanity defense was urged. On appeal to the House of Lords, Viscount Kilmuir, as judge, stated: "Conduct of defendant might be compatible with psychomotor epilepsy . . . (as disease of the mind affecting the reason.) But it must be presented as something other than defect of reason from disease of the mind. . . ."

Other English and French authorities have been chary of attributing aggressive behavior to the psychomotor seizure itself. Gastaut and Broughton "attribute the motor activity of the psychomotor seizure to the confusion itself."[11] They further analyze the activity as a function of (1) the degree of confusion, (2) the "inner" drives of the patient, (3) environmental possibility for self-expression, and (4) deep-rooted infantile or symbolic behavior, the last-named being "often antisocial."

In the United States, the opinions of neurologists specializing in epileptic phenomena can be summed up in Dreifuss' statement: "Automatisms are not usually associated with violent behavior."[12] Dr. Feldman (1977) followed up 137 epileptic patients for fourteen years and found only 6 who showed "remarkable behavior disturbance," including violent behavior. This investigator also denies the concept of "epileptoid personality" (see the discussion of Ruby's personality below), recognized as one which is overreligious, rigid, egocentric, and self-righteous. He suggests that this type of behavior is attributable to the "threat of recurrence of a seizure" which would render a person "suspicious, anxious, shy, irritable, even paranoid." A study of 150 patients with psychomotor epilepsy, analyzed by Radin (1973),[13] found that "psychomotor seizures as a general rule are not associated with aggressive or destructive behavior . . . [although] it is conceivable that the patient if restrained during confusional states, might react in a defensive manner that could be interpreted as goal-directed assault." It can be concluded that the clinician who treats epileptics is in general agreement that psychomotor epilepsy (the preferred term is now *complex partial seizures*) is not associated with violent acts or crime.

In criminal cases, the defense of a "fugue state" occurring as part of the psychomotor pattern has been raised on the basis of diminished responsibility, especially when the convulsive seizure has involved alcoholism or drugs. An illustrative case is that of *People v. Baker* (California, 1954)[14] wherein a forty-four-year-old man with a history of mental dullness (IQ of 70) and verified epilepsy since the age of fifteen, was accused of killing his wife by two blows to the head. There were no witnesses. Prior to the crime, the defendant had been committed to a state hospital on three occasions, had been treated by a physician with dilantin and phenobarbital for years, and had been observed to be in a "clouded" state on many occasions. One physician who had treated the patient for several years noted him to show "glossy" speech, incoherence, and a "drowsy and dazed" state on examination soon after the crime. The official diagnosis at the hospitals to which he had been admitted in the past was epilepsy with clouded state, convulsive seizures and psychosis. In addition, the defendant was observed to have had several convulsive seizures and periods of unconsciousness in a local hospital. Lay witnesses agreed that during periods when the defendant was free "from the effects of his disease . . . [he] had a friendly, sunny, harmless disposition . . . [and] that the Baker family life was harmonious during these intervals. . . ."

The three court-appointed psychiatrists who examined the patient-defendant reported Baker was insane at the time of the crime. One psychiatrist "intimated" that the prisoner was malingering or that he had taken an overdose of anti-epileptic medication; opposing this testimony was that of twenty physicians who had examined and diagnosed the defendant. In accordance with the majority opinion of the examining psychiatrists, the defendant was committed as insane to a state hospital from whence he was returned for trial in two years as sane. The trial court found him guilty of murder in the first degree; he was sentenced to death (1953). On automatic appeal, the defendant contended that the trial judge's instructions to the jury were "prejudicial, unclear and ambiguous," based on the fact that "proof of a permanent insanity prior to the commission of the crime raised a presumption that such insanity continued to exist until the time of the offense." On review by the Supreme Court of California, the justices conceded the case "to be a very close one on the question of guilt, sanity, and premeditation [but] the errors [by the trial court] substantially and prejudicially affected the rights of the defendant." The errors referred to were contained in the trial court's charge to the jury that "permanent insanity . . . raised the presumption that such insanity continued to exist . . . at the time of the crime." The defendant's claim of "ambiguity and prejudicial [jury] charge" was upheld by the Supreme Court on the basis that the trial judge had made two statements in direct contradition: "conclusive presumptions are not rebuttable" and "*any* such presumption . . . may be overcome by contrary evidence" in the same charge. The justices reversed the conviction and ordered a new trial, stating:

Although moronity and the mental condition caused by epileptic seizures, unless they amount to unconsciousness, are not included with the exempting provisions of Section 26 of the Penal Code, nevertheless these conditions may indicate some lack of a "healthy and robust mind" and do have bearing on the question of the capacity to premeditate and deliberate.

Types of Epilepsy and Criminal Responsibility

The imputation that violent behavior is attributable to epilepsy in any form is fraught with difficulty. Emotional explosiveness and violent acts may be found in other mental conditions—severe alcoholic and drug intoxications, unstable psychopathic personalities, impulse disorders (Frosch and Wortis),[15] hyperkinesis, even the psychotic character.[16] This no-man's land where emotional instability and organic brain conditions meet presents complex problems for all concerned. Although the electroencephalograph aids in differentiating some of the conditions listed above, the medico-legal situation is often far from clear. A Kentucky case, *Cooley v. Commonwealth* (1970),[17] illustrates one aspect of this complexity.

The defendant, Cooley, stabbed his brother to death while in an altercation about a car; both had been drinking. A passerby attempted to intercede, taking a knife away from the defendant after the stabbing and knocking Cooley to the ground, whereupon, in the words of a witness, Cooley "commenced to twitch and jerk spasmodically and otherwise manifest symptoms of an epileptic seizure." The history stated that the defendant had been epileptic for eight years prior to the crime. He also claimed amnesia for the stabbing and for all subsequent events. The defense was fashioned around a probable psychomotor seizure occurring during the impulsive murder. The gist of the medical defense can be learned from the report of the psychiatric testimony, namely:

[T]he appellant was suffering from psychomotor epilepsy which is not a form of insanity in that it is not psychological but is a manifestation of a mental defect or disease. He further testified that victims of psychomotor epilepsy are susceptible to grand mal seizures and that one of the stages of psychomotor epilepsy is a state of automatism during which the subject of the attack is not aware of his actions and of which he later has no memory. This state of automatism may last for a matter of seconds to a matter of days depending upon the situation in each particular attack.

The trial court convicted the defendant of voluntary manslaughter. The case was appealed to the Court of Appeals of Kentucky. The grounds of unconsciousness during an automatic act as part of an epileptic convulsion was reviewed by the higher court. They affirmed the conviction, deciding that "a defense of epilepsy did not go to the question of [having] sufficient reason to know what he was doing. . . . No specific instruction on epilepsy was required as long as a general instruction on insanity was given."

On the other hand, a showing of psychomotor epilepsy combined with alcoholic intoxication in a California case[18] resulted in a reversal of a conviction of second degree murder by the Court of Appeals. Dr. George M. Thompson had diagnosed the defendant as having psychomotor epilepsy "precipitated by alcohol . . . [in that] . . . a person who is abnormally susceptible to small amounts of alcohol may have a psychomotor seizure and attack . . . often carries out abnormal behavior frequently assaultive in nature." Dr. Thompson had performed an electroencephalographic test, and then an "alcohol activated" one using two ounces of alcohol which produced "spikes" on the tracing. Another neurologist, Dr. Guy Hunt, diagnosed the defendant as exhibiting a "chronic adult maladjustment syndrome with paranoid trends." Both experts accepted the claim of amnesia for the stabbing and bludgeoning of the victim and agreed that "because of his impairment, . . . brain damage . . . defendant would not be able to deliberate and weigh the consequences of his acts." Justice Garbert ruled that "in this case there was sufficient evidence present on the issue of diminished capacity to require the instruction be given on the court's own motion."

Without witnessing a seizure shortly before or at the time of a crime, the existence of epilepsy or post-convulsive furor or psychomotor seizure depends chiefly on the subject's history and an electroencephalographic tracing of wave-and-spike type. In criminal cases, the diagnosis is ordinarily made in retrospect by the expert witness, by the history, and by tracing the subsequent amnesia which does not constitute a defense of irresponsibility for crime unless a loss of consciousness has occurred. This situation developed in *People v. Williams* (California, 1971)[19] wherein the defendant walked into an eye clinic where "he had never been a patient" and shot an optician point-blank "with whom he had no connection." In a bifurcated trial, the jury returned a verdict of guilty of first degree murder and sane at the time of the crime. The defendant appealed to a higher court, on grounds of unconsciousness at the time of the crime and total diminished capacity to form the intent to murder. After reviewing the psychiatric evidence, which consisted of careful examinations by three psychiatrists and a positive brainwave tracing for psychomotor epilepsy, the Court of Appeals reversed the judgment. The reviewing court pointed out that it was error to charge the jury that the "defendant was conscious by reason of his mutually conceded conscious-like act," contrary to the expert's testimony that in psychomotor epilepsy "he who appears conscious is actually not conscious."

More striking, however, is the witnessing by a jury of an actual seizure during a trial. While it is not conclusive proof that an epileptic attack occurred during a murder, it at least constitutes undeniable proof of epilepsy.

During Mardi Gras week in New Orleans, a millionaire visitor had been found in a hotel room garotted, his skull crushed by a blunt object. The accused, known as a roustabout and sometime homosexual prostitute, was indicted, tried and convicted of 1st degree murder with a death sentence. The apprehension of the accused followed an unusual circumstance. He had gone to a Veterans Hospital because of an attempted suicide and while there complained to the staff that he had a dream, after seeing the victim's picture on a television newscast, that he had murdered someone. He had no waking memory of such an occurrence.

After three years imprisonment on death row, the Supreme Court[20] of Louisiana reversed the conviction on grounds of prejudicial error by the District Attorney, who implied from the manner in which the defendant viewed certain photographs of the scene of the crime "that he was familiar with the actual scene." Since the defendant did not take the stand, the Justice ruled the "implication . . . infringed defendant's constitutional privilege against circumstantially forced self-incrimination." A new trial was ordered.

On the second trial, Prof. Hubert W. Smith, Professor of Legal Medicine at Tulane University and M. Zelden, a New Orleans attorney, developed a history of the defendant indicating unpredictable, explosive behavior from childhood, numerous arrests for thefts, burglaries, antisocial acts in the U.S. Army and several mental hospital admissions. On two occasions he had been diagnosed as "Acute Schizophrenic Reaction," later changed to "Psychopathic Personality"; in the Army he had been shot in the head while escaping custody. Throughout his life, he had "spells" characterized by pallor, sweating, wild outbursts of violence followed by amnesia. Five weeks before the crime, the defendant had been in a State Hospital in Kansas for three and a half months with a diagnosis of "blackout spells with amnesia, alcoholism, homosexuality, psychotic tendencies, explosive hostility and emotional outbursts."

After elopement from the hospital, the defendant spent some time in New Orleans where, according to the police he had been picked up on a routine arrest for investigation; a police official noted an "obvious mental" condition. This observation was made three days before the murder; moreover, during the following two days, records of the Charité Hospital revealed two emergency room admissions—one for "fits" occurring on the streets and a second for "maniacal behavior" in the Police Station.

When this author entered the case, review of the history pointed toward a long history of automatisms and post-ictal behavior: in one episode, the defendant had thrown a fellow serviceman off a train, in another, he had successfully fought off 4 policemen, in a third, he had assaulted his wife, then fled his home in Kentucky, lived in another state for three months with no memory of his flight. All these "spells" were preceded by a headache and accompanied by amnesia. It was this history that stimulated the search for the pre-homicide history of "fits" in the local hospital. Even more strange was the suicide attempt which resulted in a Veterans Hospital admission with its subsequent *deja vu* phenomenon in a dream.

During the examination, an "absence" was observed: the defendant suddenly became pale, his neck and facial muscles tensed, speech stopped and he was abstracted for about 60 seconds.

Subsequently under hypnosis, some details of the crime were uncovered. These were testified to at the retrial: namely, that he had met the "old gentleman" on the street, that the victim offered him a meal, inviting him to his hotel room, that the victim (known as a notorious homosexual) had propositioned the defendant (also known as a sometime male homosexual). However, revulsion seized the defendant when the victim, stroking his thigh asked to be urinated upon. "It was different," testified the defendant, "It was something awful. I picked up my clothes, wanted to leave in disgust. . . . That's when he said something about that 'bitch,' my wife, and I hit him. That's all I remember though I tried for three years to recall the rest."

Although no electro-encephalographic tracing could be secured, a diagnosis of Epileptic Equivalent in a Psychopathic Personality was advanced by the defense attorneys, the basis for a not guilty by reason of insanity plea.

The State's experts agreed to the psychopathy and paranoia, emphasizing the homosexual panic but insisting that the epileptic equivalent was "feigned" as was the amnesia and clouded state during the assault on the victim. Defense testimony emphasized that the murder occurred during an "absence" and that the defendant was not malingering and, in fact, had a life-long history of "equivalent" seizures.

Testimony was presented in detail by both sides.

At the end of a long day of cross-examination, on redirect the defense lawyers put the hypothetical question "whether with a reasonable degree of medical certainty, the defendant, at the time of the attack on the victim, was sane or insane." On my answering that he was insane, "A most remarkable thing happened, involving one of the most dramatic moments in the history of criminal trials," to quote an eye witness, a reporter for the New Orleans Times Picayune.[21]

"The accused, Hoover, who had been sitting placidly at the counsel table, leaped to his feet, screaming, I'm not insane, I'm not insane. Two large bailiffs, one seated on each side of Hoover, sought to hold him, but he raised his arms with an enormous show of power, lifting the two heavy officers of the law like corks, and tossing them aside. He stood for a moment, then turned, punching wildly at his attorney and attendants who moved to overpower him. After a brief, wild struggle, he fell to the floor, his pupils fixed, his eyelids twitching spasmodically, his muscles rigid, his pulse slow, his breathing labored. Within a few seconds his composure was regained. A scene of bedlam reigned in the courtroom. Spectators dashed out as though they feared for their lives."

The turbulence described by the journalist was not exaggerated. When quiet was restored, testimony continued. The jury returned with a verdict of technical guilt with recommendation of mercy, thus avoiding the sentence of death.

Pros and Cons Re the Psychomotor Defense

With the increasing recognition of automatism and psychomotor seizures as clinical entities, and its presentation as a legal defense, there has developed a corresponding interest in the relation of epilepsy to crime. This renewed interest was stimulated by the defense of Jack Ruby of not guilty by reason of insanity, based on psychomotor epilepsy as advanced by Attorneys Belli and Tonahill (1964). The clinical picture of psychomotor epilepsy featured by mumbling, champing movements of the jaw, purposeless fidgeting by buttoning and unbuttoning a garment, smacking of the lips, restlessness, irritability, and "even pugnacity when restrained"[22] had been accepted by neurologists. Parenthetically, the present author witnessed such a "blind roving" in a young male patient during a petit mal type of seizure: the patient was a proven epileptic. While trying to restrain the patient from colliding with a bookshelf in his "absent" state, he automatically and forcibly pushed me away. It was the possibility of such behavior occurring during an assaultive crime that attracted medico-legal attention. The concordance of aggressive behavior in an emotionally unstable individual with a background of psychopathic traits and explosive physical violence and a type of psychomotor variant electroencephalographic tracing formed the basis for the defense hypothesis of Belli and Tonahill in the Ruby case.

Specifically, a December 1963 article by Frederick Gibbs, one of America's foremost encephalographers, and his associates reported that a psychomotor variant type of seizure discharge occurred in 0.05 percent of 50,000 electroencephalographic readings, consisting of "notched waves of five to six cycles per second . . . associated with fourteen to and six positive spiking."[23] Gibbs noted that the psychomotor variant in his cases was "not associated with clinical manifestations," i.e., actual behavioral disturbances.

These findings were similar to those reported by Dr. Martin Towler in his electroencephalographic examination of Jack Ruby. This approach was roundly criticized in many quarters. In 1963, Marshall Houts, editor of *Trauma*, an authoritative digest for attorneys, wrote of the trial transcript: "It is this maudlin script, all 663 pages of its medical psychological and psychiatric testimony, that screams out of the real lesson of Jack Ruby, the clarion message that *psychiatric testimony should never be permitted in the courtroom*. . . . There is no logical or practical place for them."[24]

Psychiatrists were also disturbed by the plea of psychomotor "fugue" state, though less shrilly than Houts. In a letter to the *Journal of the American Psychiatric Association* (June 1974), Dr. Nathan Rickles deplored the conflicting testimony in the Ruby trial: "Once again futility, controversy and confusion were displayed. . . . Six experts testified and, like adversaries lined up on opposing sides of a giant tug-of-war, gave conflicting reports."[25]

The National Epilepsy League was concerned over the implication that epilepsy was related to violent crime. The Board of Directors of the league issued a fact sheet to "correct mis-statements about epilepsy" and to counter the implied relationship between homicide and epilepsy.

Clinical investigators reported their experiences which negated the joining of aggression and epilepsy. After treating 15,000 epileptic patients "on every social level" over the years, Dr. Samuel Livingston reported that "crimes committed by these patients was no greater than . . . that in a similar number of non-epileptic persons."[26] Livingston's statement appeared as an editorial in the *Journal of the American Medical Association* (1964) to combat "the completely presumptive classification of epilepsy with murder throughout the Jack Ruby trial." In 1976, Sigal stated that "Aggressive and libidinous . . . aspects of psychomotor seizures . . . [are] founded in science fiction rather than scientific research."[27] Not only the area of psychomotor seizures, but also that of the "epileptoid personality," was studied, a description given less credence in recent years than a century ago. However, one study by Harvard investigators Bear and Fedio[28] found that the personality characteristics of "obsessiveness, circumstantiality, religious interest, anger, emotionality and aggression" were present in patients with temporal lobe epilepsy (psychomotor), but not in a control group of neurological patients without seizures. In general, up to the time of this writing, the majority of opinion of neurologists and specialists in seizure disorders is that there is no correlation between aggressive or violent acts and any type of epileptic phenomenon.

The Jack Ruby Case

Because of the conflicting medico-legal feelings surrounding the unique murder of Lee Harvey Oswald, assassin of President John F. Kennedy, by Jack Ruby, the case is presented here in all of its medico-legal behavioral intricacies.

For the sake of an accurate record, it should be noted that attorneys Belli and Tonahill were concerned lest their client's emotional instability may have hidden a deeper mental condition. In consultation with Professor Hubert Winston Smith of the Law-Science Academy at the University of Texas, Austin, they regarded the Ruby case as ideal for "bringing dynamic psychiatry into the evaluation of criminal behavior."[29]

The facts surrounding the murder of Oswald are as follows:

A little after 11:00 A.M., on November 25, 1963, Jack Rubenstein, AKA Jack Ruby, a fifty-two-year-old, Dallas night club owner, entered the Western Union Office on Main Street, Dallas, a little more than one-hundred yards from City Hall which housed the Police Station. "When I was finished sending the money [to an employee] curiosity got the best of me." A crowd had gathered opposite the building. A police car was poised at the head of the ramp leading to the jail exit, the driver talking to a police officer directing traffic from the building. At that moment, Ruby walked down the ramp, apparently unseen by the officers, melting into the crowd of reporters at the open door to the jail. ". . . so I walked down . . . nobody around me . . . I thought I might get a scoop for my friends at the radio station." Suddenly, he saw Oswald, manacled to two detectives, at the jail exit. "He had a very smirky, cunning, vicious look like an animal." Ruby was aware of a flash of revulsion. Hugh Aynesworth, a reporter among the newsmen, saw Ruby push forward at the instant, holding his gun within inches of Oswald's abdomen.

Ike Pappas, a newsman for a New York radio station, whose microphone had been thrust up to Oswald's face a second or two before the fatal shot recorded this tape:

There's the prisoner.
Do you have anything to say in Defense? (Sound of a shot)
There's a shot.
Oswald has been shot—Oswald has been shot!
A shot rang out—mass confusion here. (Noise—brief silence)
There's mass confusion here—rolling—fighting.
As he was being led out—
He is being led back—
Looks like he was thrown to the ground.
The police have the entire area blocked off.
"Everybody stay back; everybody stay back" is the yell.
(Parts are indistinguishable to Court Reporter)
(Brief Silence)
To get in the last question—to ask him whether he had anything to say in his defense and a split second later the shot rang out.
Toward the left. When Oswald came out he had the same look on his face that he always does or has—and it sounded like a loud fire-cracker rang out, he grabbed his side and said "Ow," and fell back to the ground.
(Parts of playback indistinguishable to Court Reporter)
Dark hat—stocky—put the gun right in his belly—
One of the wildest scenes I have ever seen.
Let me see if I can reconstruct it. Lee Harvey Oswald was coming out in the garage, in the police headquarters at Dallas, he was being removed by Captain Fritz. They were going to take him—to the county jail.
I said "Do you have anything to say in your defense?"
Immediately after that the shot rang out. The man rushed up and jammed the gun right into Oswald's stomach and fired one shot. Oswald was carried back in the hallway. One man wearing a black hat rushed up and jammed the gun in his belly, fired once.
Oswald doubled up and said, "Oh," fell on his knees.
There was a tremendous struggle.
He appears dead.

Ruby's statement of the incident was that he walked down the un-guarded ramp, and the next thing he knew he was on the concrete floor with two men struggling for his gun. He recalled crying out with astonishment, "You don't have to beat my brains out. I'm Jack Ruby. I'm not somebody who is a screwball." The tape did not pick up any remarks by Ruby. When his gun was wrested from him, detectives immediately took him upstairs to the jail. Detectives Harrison, Clardy, and Sergeant Dean questioned Ruby who was alleged to have said, some ten minutes after he was removed from the scene to the jail above, "I hope I killed the son-of-a-bitch. . . . I intended to get three shots off . . . I did it to show the world Jews have guts. . . . I did it so Jackie Kennedy would not have to come to Dallas for trial." The accused was indicted and charged with first degree murder.

An initial psychiatric examination was performed by Dr. John Holbrook, a Dallas psychiatrist, on November 25, 1963, the day after the crime. He found the accused "knew the nature and consequences of his acts at the time."

A neurological examination was ordered by Judge Joe Brown at the defense lawyers' request and with the prosecution's agreement. It was performed by Dr. Martin Towler of Galveston and was supervised by Dr. Robert Stubblefield, chairman of the Department of Psychiatry, Southwest Medical School, and Dr. John Holbrook of Dallas. The thorough examination at Parkland Hospital conducted on January 28-29, 1964, produced no positive results except the electroencephalographic records, which were interpreted by Dr. Towler to show abnormalities in the shape of "waves and spikes . . . [indicating] . . . a seizure disorder . . . in the category of a psychomotor variant." Dr. Towler, himself an experienced electroencephalographer, recognized the condition as identical with that described by Dr. Frederic Gibbs of Chicago, in a December 1963 issue of *Neurology*. The records which Dr. Towler sent to Dr. Gibbs resulted in his confirmation: "Seizure discharges, of the psychomotor variant type," he wrote, " . . . appears independently in the left and right and mid-temple areas and spreads diffusely. . . ."

The examination of the accused by Dr. Manfred Guttmacher, chief psychiatrist of the Baltimore Supreme Bench, and by myself was conducted on December 21 and 22, 1963, in the Dallas County Jail.

Physically, Ruby was of medium height and well muscled, with no signs of physical disease. His speech, delivered with machine-gun like rapidity, suggested a slight lisp, but the words were well articulated, accompanied occasionally by faintly feminine gestures. The interviews actually became monologues, often circumstantial, interrupted only by our answering a few of Ruby's questions. His expansiveness alternated with periods of depression, punctuated by tearfulness.

His notions about diet, his business problems, his inner feelings of racial sensitivity, and his reactions towards President Kennedy and "the family" and towards Dallas poured out in a flood of disconnected phrases, malapropisms, and Damon Runyonesque expressions.

The medical history was significant: two head injuries, one by the butt of a gun which he shrugged off, and a second ten years later caused him to be hospitalized in Chicago with a diagnosis of brain concussion. The loss of the terminal joint of the fore-finger of his left hand, bitten during a brawl, and four gonorrheal infections and occasional attacks of bronchitis, treated successfully, were accepted as inevitable with his way of life.

Interest was drawn especially to the history of emotional depressions Ruby suffered: the first after the murder of Leon Cooke, a friend and idol, which lasted for months. No medical aid was sought at the time. A second depression of more serious nature, occurred in 1952 following a failure of his Silver Spur Club. Overcome by depression and severe apathy, Ruby holed up in a hotel room for 2 months in Chicago, seeking no medical help. For five months this despondency persisted, gradually lifting spontaneously. A third episode on the President's death.

Aside from these depressions, there was ample evidence of a severely unstable personality in spite of his self-evaluation. "I've got a tremendous amount of conceit. I am a gregarious guy. I can't stand having anybody put me down." That he was sensitive, impetuous, demanding nurturance in the form of praise and affection to support his low self-esteem with physical aggressiveness, was obvious to every one who knew him. "I am a very vain person. When I put the C.D.R. in my coffee and made my hair deteriorate, I stopped it."

His health attitudes attracted our attention. Among other medications, Ruby had taken Preludin, a reducing drug, explaining that "it makes you a positive thinker, you don't have any inferiority, your reflexes are great . . ." Drugs attracted him as supplements to exercise and a selected diet: "They keep you from laying down and wanting to take a nap. It takes out your procrastination." Combining C.D.R.—a type of food supplement, with alcohol, "makes me nasty and very argumentative." During his machine-gun recital of health-giving substances, Ruby took a small picture of President Kennedy with a black border and Catholic prayers on the reverse side, out of his pocket, looking at it fondly, tears welling up in his eyes. Then, abruptly, "I am one of the most colorful persons you ever met, and I went with the most gorgeous girls in town. . . ."

The full flavor of the accused's mental state can best be presented by a paraphrased account of the story Ruby spewed out during the examinations.

On the morning of Friday, November 22, 1963, Ruby arrived in the cafeteria of the Dallas News about 11:00 a.m. for the ritual placing of the week-end advertisement for his Carousel Club. He liked to write his own copy, aiming to outwit his competitors: "I like a lot of class. . . . I know the semantics of words." According to Hugh Aynesworth, a seasoned staff writer for the *Dallas News*, later the *Dallas Times-Herald*, who knew Ruby well, the balding entrepreneur was at home with newsmen. He ate a "late breakfast," chatted leisurely with a couple of men for about an hour, then asked for John Newnam, advertising manager for the News. Retiring to the advertising department at about 12:10 p.m. to compose his material, Ruby talked to a few men in the office: Said one, "he rambled on and on in his usual grandiose, expansive, grating manner."

At about 12:35 p.m., Ruby became aware of a sudden hush in the ordinarily bustling office. He looked up from his work. Typewriters had stopped clacking; there was a tense, shocked stillness. "What's the matter?" he asked. "What's happened"?

Somebody told him, "The President has been shot." Advertising copy in hand, he gasped, feeling as if he had been physically struck. He stood; he sat; he felt sick. Within minutes the announcement came of the President's death.

The news of Kennedy's death stunned Ruby. He felt gaspy, a tightness gripped his chest; he could think of only one thing, to call his sister, Eva. Ruby reached for a phone saying to John Newnam near him, "The town is so blemished it will be dormant." The call connected, Ruby tried to answer Eva's babbling voice. "He was precious," sobbed Eva. His throat tightening, he said partly into the phone, partly to his neighbor, "I'll have to leave town. I feel like a nothing person. . . . I don't want to live anymore . . . Dallas is ruined." Turning to the phone he cried to Eva, "I'll have to close the club [Carousel Club]. I'm afraid I'll crack up."

The next day and a half were spent in mourning interspersed by frantic hyperactivity and breastbeating. Reacting to Eva's anguish, interrupted by bursts of anger at the GO HOME YANKEE billboard signs he had seen, he said to anyone who would listen:

Why did they do it, why did they do it. . . . such a beautiful man . . . that poor woman . . . poor John-John and Caroline—without a father.

In Dallas, I am a foreigner. I feel I represent my people inwardly. I am known as a tough Jew—a live one. Jews are blamed for so many things.

I was carried away in mourning, more than when my father died or if my brother had been killed.

Such a beautiful man and wonderful family. . . . I was dried out from crying.

Studies of the defendant's background pointed to significant factors in his personality development: a chaotic early life in a disorganized family, interrupted schooling, and an introduction into street life as a huckster in adolescence. Ruby's father, a soldier in the Russian Army during the Russo-Japanese War, carried the Cossack spirit to America. The boy's father called Jack "Little Cossack." "He was extemporaneous, I was the same way . . . he was very belligerent, we were always ashamed. I am the same way. I blurt out, that's why I don't have ulcers," Ruby explained.

By early manhood, Ruby was assured the reputation of a quixotic character on Maxwell Street. With duty in the U.S. Army in World War II over, he fell into a life of hucksterism, of petty, then larger, businesses, night club ownership, and round-the-townmanship. Minor offenses brought him into contact with the petty underworld. His life was a saga of turbulence, opportunism, and *Chutzpah*. *Chutzpah*, a Jewish word covering a combination of effrontery, gall, and energetic interest, was Ruby's hallmark. At once feisty, sudden to anger, yet kind to those in trouble, Ruby was propelled by a hidden spring of concern for justice. Stories of Ruby's "craziness" were legion. Hugh Aynesworth, the reporter who followed Ruby's career in Dallas over the years, witnessed a scene in which Ruby threw an unruly customer in one of his clubs bodily through the door. Aynesworth also saw him slash a man across the chest with a bottle for some trivial indiscretion. Ruby was known to have hauled men across the bar for obscene remarks and to have assaulted a customer in his Vegas Club.

Many described Ruby as a "bully . . . arrogant, a mean little man." Others found him kind to those in trouble, a lover of dogs and cats whom he called "my children" (he kept ten dogs and six cats), a man of sudden, unexpected generosities. Dallasites were ambivalent: "[H]e looked like a tough, stand-up comic," wrote Ken Biggle of the *Dallas News;* "a very emotional man," said the girls in the club; "a character in a business of characters," opined another writer; "A great patriot," said George Senator, his roommate; "not that patriotic," reported exotic dancer Julie Taylor.

Dr. Guttmacher and I perceived a psychotic tone to Ruby's productions, a basic looseness of reality appreciation, an intellectual disorder not readily visible on the surface, obscured by malapropisms but recognizable as disorganized thinking. These findings, his depressive affect and emotional instability and his defensiveness against self-deprecatory feelings by overmasculinized behavior, pointed to the probability that Ruby had lived a subclinical psychosis most of his life.

Psychological examinations by Dr. Roy Schafer of Yale University provided corroboration of the clinical evaluation. Using the Adult Intelligence Scale; projective tests such as the Rorschach, Draw-a-Person (Goodenough-Machover), Thematic Apperception, Word Association and Sentence Completion tests; and the Bender Gestalt and other tests for visuo-motor function, Dr. Schafer reported confusion, disorientation, loosely organized thought, and distorted perceptions sufficient to suggest "some form of physical impairment of brain function." The inappropriate speech, fragmented word usage, disjointed syntax, poorly integrated body image, and feelings of self-denigration and worthlessness, occurring in a setting of emotional instability and depression, paralleled our psychiatric observations. It appeared to Dr. Schafer that Ruby's responses were "very similar" to those obtained from patients with psychomotor seizures. Moreover, the psychologist commented that Ruby's "religious preoccupation and pietistic expressions" suggested a personality makeup seen in persons with convulsive disorders, i.e., the so-called epileptoid personality.

The intensive psychiatric-social-cultural study of the defendant, supported by the psychologist's investigation, resulted in a recommendation that the defendant was psychotic. This was based on Ruby's looseness in reality appreciation; an intellectual disorder not readily visible on the surface since it was obscured by malapropisms; and disorganized thinking in the presence of marked depressive affect and emotional instability—all of which suggested a current psychotic state superimposed on a lifelong subclinical psychotic personality. In addition, he displayed a tendency toward paranoid coloring. The whole could have fitted a functional or organic psychosis. From a medicolegal point of view, it was suggested that the murder occurred in an unstable, explosive, inferiority-driven man, whose depression over the death of President Kennedy was intensified by an unconscious identification with the president, heightened by racial and religious sensitivity. The crime was the result of an automatic act beyond the defendant's control.

Attorney Belli requested a bail hearing in order to present enough evidence of mental illness in his client to guarantee a complete psychological and neurological examination outside the jail environment. The hearing on January 20 and 21, 1964, allowed a thorough review from the witness stand of Dr. Schafer's and my own findings and opinions as outlined above. Judge Brown agreed to a full battery of neurological tests under the supervision of Dr. Robert Stubblefield, after the medical testimony was heard. The bail request was withdrawn.

A few weeks later, the defense made a motion for change of venue from Dallas for reasons of prejudice. Belli and his associates had gathered considerable evidence concerning the attitude of some sections of the Dallas public for months prior to President Kennedy's tragic entrance into the area. The local feelings which Belli attempted to use in his plea for a change of venue are summarized by the following newspaper advertisement:

"WELCOME MR. KENNEDY

   TO DALLAS...

A city so disgraced by a recent liberal smear that its citizens have just elected two more Conservative Americans to public office.

WHY is Latin America turning either anti-American or Communist, or both, despite increased U.S. Foreign Aid, State Department policy, or your own Ivy-Tower pronouncements?

WHY has Gus Hall, head of the U.S. Communist Party praised almost every one of your policies and announced that the party will endorse and support your re-election in 1964?

WHY have you scrapped the Monroe Doctrine in favor of the "Spirit of Moscow?"

The advertisement bordered in black, ended:

MR. KENNEDY, as citizens of these United States of America, we DEMAND answers to these (12) questions, and we want them NOW.

THE AMERICAN FACT-FINDING COMMITTEE

BERNARD WEISSMAN
Chairman

P.O. Box 1792—Dallas, Texas

(Political advertisement paid for by Bernard Weissman)

Although the thrust of this diatribe was against communism, the undertones of religious bigotry were unmistakable. The use of a presumably Semitic name, Bernard Weissman, in the advertisement in the *Dallas News*, inflamed Jack Ruby. A more moderate impression was given by Dr. Frederick Carney, professor of Christian Ethics at the Perkins School of Theology. In his testimony at the change of venue trial, Carney agreed that there was "considerable intolerance . . . in the tortured city" before November 22, 1963.

Those who knew the temper of Texas recognized the atmosphere of hate. "GO HOME YANKEE" signs appeared on Dallas streets. Chief of Police Jesse Curry of Dallas was aware of the virulence of right extremists: "They threaten to upset the stability of the whole city," he wrote in retrospect: "Dallas in the fall of 1963 was a city of mixed emotions." While he was arranging security measures for the president's visit to Dallas on November 22, Chief Curry counted thirteen extremist groups under surveillance. These included the Indignant White Citizens Council, the General A. Walker's Group, and the Texas White Citizens Council. They planned to picket the presidential party; handbills had been distributed along the motorcade route among the gathered crowds. One pictured Kennedy both in profile and full face.

WANTED FOR TREASON

THIS MAN is wanted for treasonous activities against the United States:

The Trial

Judge Brown denied the motion for a change of venue. A plea of not guilty by reason of insanity was entered, and the trial began in Dallas in early March 1964. The psychiatric testimony began on March 9, 1964. On direct examination Dr. Roy Schafer testified in depth concerning the various psychological tests he had performed; his testimony led to the conclusion that Ruby "did have organic brain damage, and that the most likely specific nature of it was 'psychomotor epilepsy.'" District Attorney Henry Wade indicated that, as a psychologist, Schafer had no medical opinion as to whether Ruby knew "right from wrong" at the time of the crime. Dr. Martin Towler, the next witness, a neurologist and electroencephalographer, stated that Ruby's brainwave tracings showed "paroxysmal discharges to five to six per second slow wave activity . . . appearing spontaneously in both temporal areas." On cross-examination by the district attorney,[30] Towler included a "fugue" state as part of the clinical picture:

Q. Now, you are familiar with—we had some testimony about a fugue state here. Do you know something about that Doctor? Now, is it your opinion . . . that he suffered from psychomotor epilepsy?
A. Yes. I thought of him as having a type of seizure disorder that we refer to as psychomotor variant. . . . A fugue state can be part of a psychomotor variant. It need not be.
Q. As a matter fact, they wouldn't perform any purposeful behavior while in a fugue state, would they?
A. They could perform what seemed to be purposeful behavior.

Dr. Guttmacher's testimony centered on his opinion that the accused was not "capable of distinguishing right from wrong and realizing the nature and consequences of his act at the time of the alleged homicide." The testimony ranged widely over areas of heredity (Ruby's mother's mental illness), of a weakness of ego structure that allowed hostile impulses to erupt, of unconscious psychosexual conflicts, epileptoid personality and depression, emotional instability, and paranoid tendencies. Summarizing his testimony on direct examination, Dr. Guttmacher stated:

Q. Will you give your full, detailed opinion with reference to his condition?
A. Well, I concluded that we are dealing with a person with a damaged brain, who's been subject to pathological—that is, abnormal mood states . . . who has persistently demonstrated a very poor control of aggression by episodic and explosive outbursts . . . and in all probability precipitating the episode of automatic behavior completely beyond his control.

The issue of psychomotor epilepsy and the probability of Ruby having committed the homicide during an epileptic seizure of some type was minimized during the witnesses' testimony, although the notion of "ego rupture" under extreme stress was clearly stated. Under cross-examination of Dr. Guttmacher by the prosecutor:

Q. Leaving out psychomotor epilepsy or—what did you call it? Acute dissociation or rupture of the ego?
A. Yes, episodic dyscontrol, yes.
Q. Is that what is known as a functional mental psychosis?
A. It would be functional, not organic. But people who have organic brain disease are more prone to develop such a condition, but it is not in itself an organic condition.

I was the last defense witness, and my testimony can be summarized as follows: (See transcript of cross-examination in Chapter 2.)

The murder was committed under the surge of conscious hate and the unconscious conflicts. Described as a man of quick movements, quick reflexes, a man geared to action, the shooting was automatic and instinctive. This condition is well known among individuals of the epileptic constitution or the aggressive psychopathic type. It amounts to a Fugue state wherein physical acts are consummated automatically, without conscious thought, within the patient's usual pattern of behavior.

The prosecution's experts were uniform in denying the specificity of the electroencephalographic tracings. Dr. Sheff Olinger, a neurologist in Dallas, testified that the changes in Ruby's tracing were "nonspecific" and that Dr. Gibbs' "psychomotor variant" was different from psychomotor epilepsy. In sum, Dr. Olinger's testimony matched that of Dr. Stubblefield, Dr. Holbrook, Dr. Peter Kelloway, director of the Laboratory of Clinical Encephalography, Dr. Earl Walker, neurosurgeon of Johns Hopkins University, Dr. Robert Schwab of Harvard University Medical School, and Dr. Francis Forrester of the University of Wisconsin Medical School. All of these experts agreed that the encephalographic findings in Ruby's case were not significant, that psychomotor epilepsy during the shooting by Ruby was implausible, that organic brain damage was an unsupportable diagnosis in the case at hand, that the psychological tests were inconclusive of paranoia, and that there was no real evidence of a post-ictal state or a fugue state. The answer of Dr. Ronald McKay, past president of the American Neurological Association, on direct examination, characterizes the prosecutor's experts' testimony:

Q. Let me ask you, Doctor, would a person in an ictal or psychomotor seizure
   state, pick out a moving target from a crowd, move in on it and shoot that
   target from close range and then have recall of it?
A. No sir.

The appearance of Dr. Fred Gibbs of Chicago as a defense witness was
anticlimactic. After considerable discussion of the psychomotor variant
tracing diagnosed by Dr. Gibbs, the issue of Ruby's insanity at the time
of the shooting was broached to the witness. His answer to a previous
question was, "I said the electroencephalograph could not say anything
about psychosis." Then:

Q. Doctor. . . . Do you have an opinion from your electroencephalogram as to
   whether Jack Ruby knew the difference between right and wrong and
   understood the nature and consequences of his acts on November 24th?
A. I have no opinion.

After the attorney's summation and the judge's charge, the jury
found Ruby guilty of murder in the first degree, the penalty—death.

Epilogue in re Ruby

Following the verdict, while attorneys were preparing an appeal before the Texas Court of Criminal Appeals, reports filtered out of the
county jail that Ruby was mentally disturbed. During the night of
April 25, 1964, Ruby had dashed his head against the cell wall. Dr.
Louis West of the University of Oklahoma Medical School was called
in to examine the prisoner. He found Ruby to be in need of immediate
hospitalization: "his reasoning was impaired, his delusions of his family
tortured by 'medieval methods,' unshakeable."[31] Two other psychiatrists, Dr. Stubblefield and Dr. W. R. Beavers, appointed by the court
in April 1964, found Ruby "acutely mentally ill . . . [with] depressive
and paranoiac trends"; they agreed that suicide was a danger and psychiatric treatment imperative.

In June 1964, Dr. Emmanuel Tanay, a forensic psychiatrist from
Detroit, made a study of the mountain of notes Ruby had written in
his cell during the jury verdict, in addition to a thorough analysis of
the subject's background. He indicated that Ruby suffered from a
chronic schizophrenic psychosis of paranoid type, lasting "at least"
since February 1963, and further, that at the time of Oswald's assassination, Ruby was "incapable of exercising conscious control over his
actions" by virtue of a dissociative reaction. Dr. Tanay filed his lengthy
report to Attorney Clayton Fowler on June 17, 1964.

Dr. Tanay's opinion seconded that of Dr. West in January 1965 and, later, that of Dr. Werner Tuteur, a psychiatrist brought in by Elmer Gertz, a Chicago attorney who headed the team of lawyers hired by Ruby's family to prepare an appeal (July 1965).[32] Dr. Tuteur found Ruby's delusional system to be well organized by July 1965. The accused had told the psychiatrist that the "strip teaser made me go to the Western Union to wire her money . . . [it was] timed just right to shoot Oswald." The psychiatrist felt the paranoid psychosis had existed for "four to five years."[33] It was clear that Ruby's mental illness had deepened. During 1965 and 1966, notes and letters smuggled out of Ruby's cell referred to his "plan" to circumvent the massive destruction of Jews which Ruby was convinced was imminent. "Someone must get to England, France and Israel and tell the right people what has happened to the Jews so they can prepare. . . . If they would kill a man like Jonas Salk . . . then it must be true."

On June 13, 1966, a sanity hearing was held in which Ruby's lawyers did not participate for technical legal reasons. Testimony from officers in the jail was heard, of which these statements were samples: "Jack is a pretty good gin rummy player. . . . he loved to read, having a very fine mind." The jail physician reported that the prisoner worked crossword puzzles well, and a deputy sheriff testified that "he never noticed any delusions" in his charge's actions. The jury trial found him sane.

Meanwhile, an appeal to the Texas Court of Criminal Appeals[34] was heard, and a reversal of the original verdict of guilty was ordered on October 5, 1966. The justices ordered a new trial and change of venue. "Jack Ruby was forced to trial under the most adverse, unusual and extraordinary circumstances. . . . the established legal principles of law in this state and nation cried out for a change of venue . . . which would guarantee Ruby the fair and unprejudiced trial which he failed to receive."

As plans for a new trial were in preparation, the prisoner developed symptoms of invasive cancer throughout the body — lungs, lymph nodes, liver, and brain. He died on January 4, 1967, still not legally convicted of a murder witnessed by at least 10 million viewers.

In retrospect it is evident that the neuropsychiatric complexities running through Ruby's attorneys' presentation (electroencephalographic tracings, personality analysis, psychometric test results, emotional instability, psychomotor epilepsy) taxed the jury of laymen in a state where M'Naghten was the legal test for insanity. Texas law then required that the defense bore "the burden of proving insanity by a preponderance of evidence." Since 1964, Texas law has modified the insanity test in response to the "trend away from M'Naghten" in favor of the Model Penal Code test. The test was adopted in 1974 and states:

It is an affirmative defense to prosecution that, at the time of the conduct charged, the actor, as a result of mental disease or defect, either did not know that his conduct was wrong or was incapable of conforming his conduct to the requirements of the law . . . characterizing insanity as an affirmative defense preserves the burden of proof that previously existed on the issue.[35]

The evidence was insufficient to convince the jury either that Ruby suffered from psychomotor epilepsy, episodic dyscontrol, or fugue states, or that he was insane at the time of crime. Tom Howard, Ruby's first attorney until he was displaced by Belli, intended to have his client plead to murder without malice on the premise that Ruby "acted under rage sufficient to make a person of 'ordinary temper' kill . . . although Ruby's was by no means an ordinary temper."[36] A writer for the *Saturday Evening Post*, whose story about the trial prompted a defamation of character suit by Attorney Belli,[37] offered this advice: "The real tragedy, as far as the defense was concerned, is that if Gibbs had been willing to testify from the beginning, Belli would have discovered the mistake and, presumably, abandoned the EEG machine . . . and gone on to build a solid psychiatric case. . . ."

Perhaps this comment from a layman is not without value in its understanding of jury psychology. In retrospect, the hypothesis of "episodic dyscontrol," clinically accurate though it was, strained the perception of laymen. On the other hand, a study of 130 patients with a history of violent attacks, i.e., episodic dyscontrol, against "people, walls, furniture, self" by Dr. Bachy-Rita and associates[38] at the Harvard Medical School and the U.S. Naval Hospital, Philadelphia, gave significant results. These investigators found electroencephalographic abnormalities among 79, or 29 percent of the patients. They concluded that the relation of "episodic dyscontrol to minimal brain was suggestive" since a number of their cases presented a history of head injuries, birth injuries, and febrile conditions in childhood.

The possibilities of a psychosis, suggested by indications of a paranoid attitude and disorganized thinking observed in Ruby in the early examinations, conceivably might have appeared more plausible to a jury. The agitated depression following Kennedy's assassination in an unstable man might have masked early signs of a mental condition which flowered during the two and a half years Ruby remained in jail awaiting a retrial.

In my own considered opinion, Ruby lived a subclinical psychosis most of his life. As further corroboration of the diagnoses of paranoid psychosis established by Drs. West, Tanay, Stubblefield, Tuteur, and others, a study of the accused's doodles and letters produced signs of serious personality conflicts such as might precede psychotic decom-

Design drawing by Jack Ruby. Drawn while in jail.

pensation, i.e., a mental breakdown. These precisely drawn designs, numbering about two hundred, constituted one of Ruby's main activities in jail. Some of this material, given to me by Dr. John Lattimer of Columbia University, was studied by Dr. Donald Uhlin and his staff in the Art Department at California State University, Sacramento (Plate I). Dr. Uhlin,[39] an expert in the psychopathology of art productions by mental and neurotic patients, a field stemming from the Draw-A-Person (Goodenough-Machover projective test), found indications of

strong efforts to structure and maintain the ego. The symmetry of these drawings indicates paradoxical feelings associated with sexual ambiguity.

The forms utilized reflect this dichotomy in that the rectangle is generally considered masculine while the diamond shape is strongly feminine.

Further, they indicate a concrete, rigid personality exercising over-control; everything must be in its place, nothing can be disorderly.

The textured drawings with their shaded areas and linear reinforcement, (much redrawing), reveal a high level of anxiety as well as indications of a paranoid or pre-paranoid personality.

With the exception of the Draw-A-Person test drawings (Plates II and III), the doodlings and letter-writings[40] were made entirely spontaneously without any knowledge that the material would become subject to psychological study. The stylized drawing of a woman's face (Plate II) was given a "blind-analysis." The indications were

a degree of self-identification and perhaps egocentricity. The emphasis upon the hair suggests virility striving (in contrast to) feminine identification in the heavy emphasis on eyes, eyelashes and the full feminine mouth. The "crisp" line quality suggests some degree of impulsivity. The total impression is that of a subject strongly identified with the figure as a self-image.

Blind analysis of Plate III by Professor Tarmo Pasto,[41] indicating a "valid projection of self," revealed

a highly impulsive, insecure individual with ill-concealed homosexual problems. Over all, the inner-openness (no cuff lines, poor articulation of limbs, no definite closures separating body, limbs and head relationships) indicates a person who acts before he thinks . . . spear-like arms and fingers [indicate] violence . . . lack of hair indicates doubts as to virility . . . the homosexual component expressed in . . . open crotch area, avoidance of a seam in sexual area . . . phallic tie. . . .

A further blind analysis by Dr. Karen Machover[42] stressed "a danger of aggression in the speared fingers . . . effeminate hip formation (bolero

Draw-A-Person test drawing of woman's face with portion of letter written by Jack Ruby.

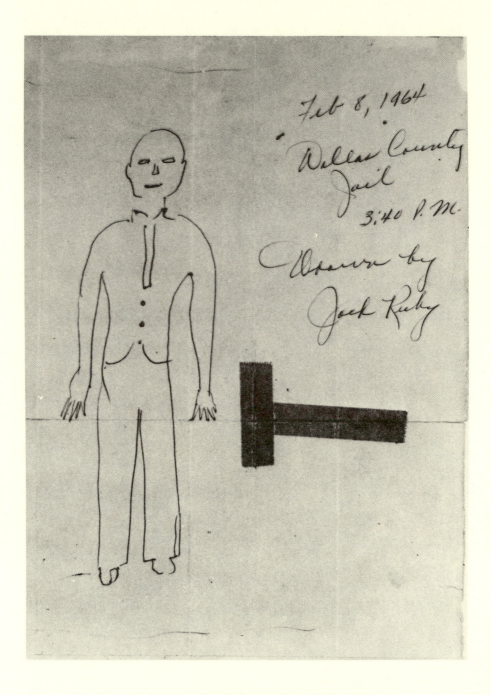

Draw-A-Person test drawing of male figure done by Jack Ruby.

effect) . . . gaps in drawing of feet indicating loss of consciousness . . . vestigial ears showing paranoid tendency . . . .

Analysis of drawings is but one aspect of the projective test battery, but it is a sensitive indicator of the subject's inner perception of self. As such, it aids the analysis of the total personality configuration of the subject under study. The handwriting displays a meticulous, compulsive style, done with precision that seems to betray a strong effort to control paranoid ideation.

Although this type of intensive psychological study of an accused does not answer any legal test, it might provide evidence of psychological conflicts that would corroborate a clinical diagnosis.

Notes

1. J. R. Esquirol, *A Treatise on Insanity:* 845, trans. by E. K. Hunt, Lea and Blanchard, Philadelphia (1838).

2. W. R. Gowers, *Epilepsy and Other Convulsive Diseases: Their Causes, Symptoms & Treatment*, Wm. Wood Co. (1885), reprint by Dover Publ., New York (1964).

3. Smith E. Jelliffe and William A. White, *Diseases of the Nervous System: A Textbook of Neurology and Psychiatry:* 961, Lea and Febiger, Philadelphia (4th ed., 1923).

4. L. P. Clark, *Nature and Pathogenesis of Epilepsy*, N.Y. Med. J. (Dec. 1915).

5. James A. Lewis, *Violence and Epilepsy*, 232 J.A.M.A. 1165 (June 1975).

6. L. Uszkiewiczowa, *Criminality of Epileptics and Some Questions of Giving Opinions in Cases of Epilepsy*, 15 Archiwum Medycyny, Psychiatrii Sadowej 1 (1963).

7. H. G. Stevenson, *Psychomotor Epilepsy Associated with Criminal Behavior*, 50 Med. J. of Australia (Melbourne) 784 (1963).

8. G. Amati and D. Ragozino, *The Epileptic Personality and Its Criminologic and Forensic-Psychiatric Aspects* 3 Folia Psychiatria 269 (1964).

9. L. M. Leigh, *Automation & Insanity*, 5 Crim. L. Q. (Dept. of Justice, Ottawa) 160 (1962).

10. *Bratty v. Attorney General for Northern Ireland*, 3 weekly, J.R. 965 (1961).

11. Henri Gastaut and R. Broughton, *Epileptic Seizures:* 126, Charles C Thomas, Springfield, Ill. (1972).

12. F. E. Dreifuss, *Differential Diagnosis of Partial Seizures with Complex Symptomatology* 11:193 in *Advances in Neur.*, Raven Press, New York (1975).

13. Ernst A. Radin, *Psychomotor Epilepsy and Aggressive Behavior*, 28 Arch. of Gen. Psych. 210 (Feb. 1973).

14. *People v. Baker*, 42 C. 2d, 550, 268 P. 2d 705 (1954).

15. John Frosch and Bernard Wortis, *A Contribution to the Nosology of Impulse Disorders*, 111 Am. J. Psych. 1 (Aug. 1954).

16. John Frosch, *Psychoanalytic Considerations of the Psychotic Character*, 18 J. of Am. Psychoanalysis A. 24 (Jan. 1970).

17. *Cooley v. Commonwealth of Kentucky*, 459 S.W. 2d, 89 (1970).

18. *People v. Austin*, 270 C.A. 2d, 845, 99 Calif. Rptr. 1541.

19. *People v. Williams*, 32 C.A. 3d; 99 Calif. Rptr. 103 (1971).

20. *State v. Hoover*, 54 So. 2d, 130 (1951).

21. *New Orleans Times Picayune:* 1 (Oct. 26, 1952).

22. Roscoe L. Barrow and Howard Fabing, *Epilepsy and the Law*, 14, Hoeber, New York (2d ed., 1966).

23. F. H. Gibbs, C. L. Rich, and E. L. Gibbs, *Psychomotor Variant Type of Seizure Discharge*, 13, no. 12 Neurology 991 (Dec. 1963).

24. *State v. Jack Ruby*, 6, no. 4 Trauma 4.1 (Dec. 1964), ed. by M. Houts, Matthew Bender & Co., San Francisco (1964).

25. Nathan K. Rickles, *The Ruby Trial*, 188, no. 10 J.A.M.A. 939 (June 1974).

26. Samuel Livingston, *Murder and Epilepsy*, 188 J.A.M.A. 172 (Apr. 1964).

27. M. Sigal, *Psychiatric Aspects of Temporal Lobe Epilepsy*, 163, no. 5 J. of Nerv. and Ment. Dis. 348 (Nov. 1976).

28. David Bear and Paul Fedio, *Quantitative Analysis of Interictal Behavior in Temporal Lobe Epilepsy*, 34 Arch. of Neur. 455 (Aug. 1977).

29. Hubert Winston Smith, Personal Communication (1963).

30. 4 Trauma, op. cit.: 24.

31. Louis J. West, Personal Communication (1965).

32. Elmer Gertz, *Moment of Madness. The People v. Jack Ruby*, Follet Publ. Co., Chicago (1968).

33. Criminal Code, Vernon's Texas Penal Code, Chap. 8, Sec. 8.01; Crim. Proc. Chap.

34. *Ruby v. State*, 407 S.W. 2d 793 (Tex., 1966).

35. Criminal Code, Vernon's Texas Penal Code, Chap. 8, Sec. 8.01; Crim. Proc. Chap. 46, Art. 46.01 (1977).

36. Joyn Kaplan and Jon R. Waltz, *The Trial of Jack Ruby:* 22, Macmillan Co., New York (1964).

37. *Belli v. Curtis Publ. Co.*, 24 C.A. 384; 102 Calif. Rptr. 122.

38. George Bachy-Rita, John Lion, Carlos Clement, and Frank Ervin, *Episodic Dyscontrol: A Study of 130 Violent Patients*, 127 Am. J. Psych. 1473 (May 1971).

39. Donald Uhlin, *Assessment of Violence Prone Personality Through Art*. Symposium, World Congress of Psychiatry, Honolulu, Hawaii (Aug. 1977).

40. Sherwood Morrill, former chief document examiner, California State Bureau of Criminal Identification.

41. Tarmo Pasto, director, Ars Gratia Hominis Project, California State University, Sacramento, Calif. (1965).

42. Karen Machover, consulting psychologist, Kings County Hospital, Downstate Medical Center, Brooklyn, N.Y. (1965).

7

Psychopathic (Sociopathic) Personality and the Law

The psychopathic (sociopathic) personality presents more of a psychiatric and criminologic problem than a legal one. In court trials, psychiatric evaluations of sociopaths are sought chiefly when transitory mental states or emotional outbursts suggest a possible lack of awareness at the time of criminal offense. In sentencing procedures, such offenders who contribute largely to recidivism, and in parole board hearings, the troublesome question of prediction of further aggression often arises. In penal institutions, the psychopath can become a disciplinary problem, thus negating rehabilitative measures. In mental clinics and hospitals, the psychopath is a constant block towards treatment efforts. This elusive constellation of mental characteristics weaves in and out of the criminal and to a lesser extent, the civil law, like a Fata Morgana, an evil daemon. What is the significance of this diagnosis in medicine and in the law?

Evaluation of the Psychopathic Concept

The terms *psychopathy* and *sociopathy* are usually referred to as a diagnostic wastebasket and are a source of confusion, even consternation, to both the legal and psychiatric professions. Descriptive terms for this troublesome behavior pattern have been legion, shifting with the ebb and flow of psychiatric theory. Cason, writing in 1943,[1] found no less than 202 technical terms and phrases in the literature denoting the psychopathic personality. They ranged from "abnormal character" to "constitutional psychopathic inadequate," the terms designed to unite "pathology" with the "psyche." To appreciate the confusion, one must dip briefly into psychiatric history.

The initial step in the evolution of the psychopathic concept came in 1806 with the publication of Phillippe Pinel's treatise.[2] The famed liberator of the insane in revolutionary France brought diagnostic order to the virgin field of psychiatry by separating out the group of patients who presented emotional troubles without perceptible impairment of reasoning power. He considered this new class of mental disease to be the result of a perversion of "affections and moral" feelings: a *manie sans delire*, i.e., insanity without delusions. Alienists of the time recognized that many persons who were not laboring under insane delusions, but were nevertheless quite "mad," fell into this class.

Contemporaneous with Pinel, a London specialist, J. H. Cox,[3] described "among varieties of maniacs met within medical practice" a full panorama of idiosyncratic personalities who might be regarded today as eccentrics, neurotics or psychopathic persons.

who...take violent antipathies, harbor unjust suspicions, indulge strong propensities, affect singularities in dress, gait and phraseology; are proud and conceited; easily excited and with difficulty appeased; dead to sensibility, delicacy and refinement . . . prone to controversy . . . always the hero of their own tale, using hyperbolic, high-language to express the most simple ideas. . . .

Persons of this description to the casual observer might appear activated by a bad heart, but the experienced physician knows it is the head which is defective.

This portrait of a "variety of maniacs" seems to have been neglected until 1835 when Pritchard[4] introduced the term *moral insanity* to include those whose "passions acted involuntarily . . . without any disease of the understanding . . . [with] morbid perversion of affections, inclinations, temper, habits, moral disposition and natural impulses." Pritchard's concept was welcomed and quickly adopted on both sides of the Atlantic. Among others, Isaac Ray readily accepted the diagnosis because the inclusion of moral insanity within medical respectability allowed alienists to testify in court with assurance. The concept was reckoned a defect in the basic physical-psychological makeup of a person, a true pathology of the psyche—*psycho-pathic*.

The concept of inherent defect (Lombroso called it an "atavism") remained in the literature and in the minds of psychiatrists. In 1891, Koch introduced the term *psychopathic inferior*,[5] and Adolph Meyer modified it to *constitutional psychopathic inferior* (1905).[6] As will be shown presently, this accent on inferiority, presumably on a genetic basis (some authors added the notion of "degeneracy" or "depravity"), had a decided influence on the prevailing view of the psychopath. Meanwhile, many tried to define this group more accurately. During the first quarter of the twentieth century, the German school of psychiatry emphasized the psychic structure of the psychopath, i.e., the temperament;[7] British workers stressed distortions in the moral sense, i.e., defect in the inhibitory faculty;[8] American investigators pointed to difficulties in social adjustment, i.e., excessive demands from the environment.[9] This view of the inelasticity of the psychopath's ego, his inability to adjust to society, led Partridge, in 1928, to suggest the now commonly accepted term *sociopathic*. Further refinement of the concept led in two directions: the structural, i.e., organic and the dynamic. The organic was exemplified by Cleckley's description of the psychopath as suffering from a "semantic dementia," that is, a disease characterized by the use of words without appreciation of their meaning.[10] The second, dynamic orientation, particularly espoused by Franz Alexander,[11] considered the psychopath as a character neurosis whose antisocial behavior and callousness functioned as a hard carapace, a cover for neurotic conflicts: the tough exterior hid the soft underbelly of dependence on a rejecting society. Whatever theoretical concept is held, there is general agreement that the sociopath is a calloused, egocentric individual with little anxiety or guilt, unable to form permanent emotional relationships or to profit from punishment and impatient to postpone gratification in favor of immediate impulsive satisfaction of his needs and desires.[12] But like all characterizations of "types" of individuals, the criteria of lack of anxiety and inability of profit from punishment have been eroded (see the case of John Card, below). Out of these wide differences of opinion, the diagnosis of psychopathic (sociopathic) personality is usually attached to the antisocial type. This suffices for legal purposes; undeniably, the psychopath is a "troublemaker" acting contrary to mores, customs, and laws.

A deeper analysis demonstrates a different picture. In a word, the sociopath acts out those antisocial elements (conscious and unconscious) which are hidden, controlled, or suppressed among the law-abiding population.[13] He is the scapegoat of our own controlled antisociality. In supplying this means of expiation for society, he perceives society's unconscious hostility towards him, reacting by withdrawing into an antisocial community (the gang) and the underworld. One can say, *Society loves its crimes but hates its criminals*. The sociopath is dimly (or acutely) aware of this paradox. He intuitively perceives his "pariah" position in society, reacting thereto with hostility and crime. Like a psychologic boomerang, society's revulsion is returned manyfold. The recidivist, the professional criminal, the gangster may be intuitively aware of this peculiar bond between the wrongdoer and the conformer. Those who study or attempt to treat sociopaths should also be aware of this intricate subterranean relationship.

Nevertheless, the courts are obliged to pass judgment on the mental state of these individuals. The transitory mental upsets and the effect on criminal responsibility are major problems confronting the legal process. To aid the courts, psychiatrists must be able to distinguish between insane, neurotic, and sociopathic criminals. The insane offender has already been dealt with; a few words on the neurotic criminal are now in order.

The individual with a neurotic problem is rarely, except in sentencing, the subject of inquiry for legal purposes. In sentencing, the judge is faced with the alternatives of incarceration or probation with a recommendation for psychotherapy. The issue is never that of criminal irresponsibility or diminished capacity. The neurotic who acts out his or her conflicts in misbehavior is mentally clear and often intelligent, but is unable, without help, to control his impulses. Such cases call for extended psychotherapy; the sentencing judge, recognizing the neurotic element running through the crimes (often a compulsive shoplifter or compulsive forger), orders psychotherapy as part of the probation program. This was the situation with Mrs. O., a fifty-three year-old woman afflicted with a severe mysophobia (fear of germs and dirt) but otherwise mentally clear.

The offender, arrested for the third time over 12 years for shoplifting, usually of small inexpensive items, had suffered from fear of death and funerals from an early age. When a playmate passed away, her family had insisted the child be buried in a white, angelic costume: this impressed Mrs. O., to the degree that she suffered a revulsion to death, later transformed to an obsessive fear of dirt.

In later life Mrs. O.'s phobia extended to money, to touching persons or things. Her behavior was controlled by fears of contamination to a severe degree. For example, at a market, she would not allow the checker to touch either the money she offered or the objects purchased. Both would be left on the stand. Her restrictions became so severe that she could not enter a restaurant, was forced to wash and re-wash her money—both coins and paper money—slept in a car because she could not abide anyone touching her bed clothes and had to throw away bits of soap used in washing her clothes, as each bit became contaminated.

Her shoplifting consisted in two plums and a TV guide which she placed in her bag to avoid their being "dirtied" by other hands.

The district attorney dropped the charges of petit larceny on the assurance that psychotherapy would be sought.

It has been said that the neurotic suffers within himself because of his conflicts, whereas the sociopath causes society to suffer through his misbehavior. This distinction is generally valid, but it should be remembered that the varied group of psychopaths includes, besides criminal offenders, visionaries, eccentrics, revolutionaries, and even geniuses.

The Legal Position

As far as legal process is concerned, the dynamics of sociopathy is of merely academic interest, although it may be significant in penal institutions where rehabilitation is attempted. In relation to culpability for crime, the criminal process excludes psychopathic or defective delinquent behavior as a basis for an insanity defense. The New York Penal Code[14] states boldly: "A morbid propensity to commit prohibited acts, existing in the mind of a person who is not shown to have been incapable of knowing the wrongfulness of such acts, forms no defense to a prosecution thereof."

In a slightly different form, the American Law Institute Model Code adds to its proposal for a modern insanity test: "As used in this Article, the terms 'Mental disease or defect' do not include an abnormality manifested only by repeated criminal or otherwise antisocial acts."[15] The courts have been firm in excluding sociopathy from the rubric of mental disease or defect, as witness a U.S. Circuit Court ruling in *McDonald v. U.S.* (1962)[16] wherein the judge commented on the plea of a mentally subnormal appellant whose IQ of 68 (moron level) was held to confer irresponsibility for crime. The judge said:

[N]either the court or jury is bound by *ad hoc* definitions or conclusions as to what experts state is a disease or defect. What psychiatrists may consider a "mental disease or defect" for clinical purposes, where their concern is treatment, may or may not be the same as mental disease or defect for the jury's purpose in determining criminal responsibility. Consequently, for that purpose the jury should be told that a mental disease or defect includes any abnormal condition of the mind which substantially affects mental or emotional processes and substantially impairs behavior controls. . . . Since the question . . . is ultimately for the triers of fact, obviously the resolution cannot be controlled by expert opinion.
. . . What we have said however, should in no way be construed to limit the latitude of expert testimony.

A dissenting judge in *McDonald v. U.S.* [17] even more firmly expressed the court's dissatisfaction with the varying views of "psychopathic" persons by experts. Psychiatry's attempt to present an "entering wedge" to legal logic in pointing to the basic abnormality of the sociopathic personality was dealt with in these terms:

The rulings (above) . . . have been especially necessary because of the frequent alternation and expansion of the definition of "mental disease" by those experts who appear most frequently as witnesses in this jurisdiction. They suddenly reclassified psychopathic (sociopathic) personality as a mental disease in re Rosenfield, 157 F. Supp. 18 (D.C. 1957); they reclassified emotionally unstable personality as a mental disease in Campbell v. U.S. supra; they reclassified narcotic addiction as a mental disease in U.S. v. Carroll, Crim. No. 383-62 (D.C. June 28, 1962). . . . I think it is obvious that the new classifications were made by the doctors for clinical purposes only, for demonstration is not needed to make it plain that these conditions newly called "mental diseases" are not such in the legal sense. Until now, this court has allowed the shifting winds of expert nomenclature to control its decisions.

Nevertheless, psychiatrists, notably Bernard Diamond,[18] objected to the restriction of the term *sociopathy* to "abnormality manifested only by repeated or otherwise antisocial acts." A thorough discussion of the M'Naghten, Durham, and American Law Institute tests for irresponsibility in *Wade v. U.S.* (1970)[19] brought to the fore the issue which Dr. Diamond was championing. Quoting the expert's objection that the American Law Institute's "purported definition of psychopathic personalities . . . discriminates against economically poor defendants who are less likely to produce expert testimony disclosing mental illness beyond criminal or otherwise antisocial conduct," Judge Ely said:

Even more important than the need to preserve the insanity defense . . . is society's need to be protected from potential recidivists. Persons who may be labeled by experts as "psychopathic" include those who are seriously ill and who are incapable of persistent, ordered living of any kind.

An extended discussion of the psychopath problem is found in *Campbell v. U.S.* (1962)[20] wherein a defendant convicted of robbery appealed on the grounds that he was suffering from an "emotionally unstable personality," and hence his crime was the "product of a mental disease or defect" as embodied in the Durham decision when in use in the District of Columbia Circuit Court. Psychiatrists of the St. Elizabeth's Hospital staff who, in 1957, had administratively recorded sociopathic personality as a mental disease, testified in Campbell's case that he "reacted with excitability and ineffectiveness . . . showed poor judgment and had difficulty relating to people around him." The U.S. Court of Appeals, District of Columbia, reversed his conviction on technical grounds. Significantly, Judge Warren Burger, then of the Court of Appeals, dissented. Focusing on the reversal of Campbell's conviction, Judge Burger inveighed against the "administrative" device of changing the classification of "various abnormal mental conditions" as was done in *Wade*. His dissent in *Campbell* stated:

The majority is again giving judicial approval the extraordinary process by which a small segment of the medical profession alters the scope of the law of criminal responsibility by the simple device of "administratively" expanding the

definition of mental disease. . . . This was done once before by changing the
definition of mental disease to include psychopathic or sociopathic personality
which like "emotionally unstable personality" was not classified as a mental
disease when we adopted the "disease-product" test (i.e., the Durham rule).

Judge Burger went on to say:

There was no *medical* significance or consequence to this "administrative"
change. But there was an enormous *legal* consequence . . . for now the showing
of one of these newly classified "diseases" places on the government the burden
of proving beyond a reasonable doubt that the act charged was not a product
of this new "disease."

The essential factor in this discussion of psychopathic personality as a
condition making for irresponsibility is that, in the court's words, "a
jury ought to be told plainly that they *alone* are to determine whether
in fact a 'mental disease' exists because that is an issue of fact . . . ."

The Classification Dilemma

Justice Burger's vigorous criticism of the shifting diagnostic postures
of psychiatrists toward "abnormal mental conditions" reflects the
changing attitude of psychiatry towards antisocial behavior. Psychiatry is responsive to changes in social mores and values. It is also responsive to "advances" in medicine, especially in the area of mental and
emotional problems as they move from an accent on psychologic causes
to organic-biochemical explanations. One may view the changing concept of the psychopath at worst as caprice (as does Justice Burger)
and at best, as the result of the slow, heavy "advance" of the mental
sciences. As the historical sketch in the early part of this chapter suggests, the attempt to encapsulate a type of character in a single word,
i.e., a diagnosis, is difficult. The official *Diagnostic Manual of the
American Psychiatric Association* (1968 edition) placed the sociopath
in the category of personality disorders in order to differentiate this
class from psychotic individuals. The projected revision of the *Diagnostic and Statistical Manual* (draft of 1978), not yet adopted, retains
the sociopath as a personality disorder, while it removes cases of drug
dependence—opium, heroin, marijuana, hashish, and the like—to a class
known as substance use disorders. Adult antisocial behavior, as well
as adolescent antisocial behavior, is placed in a class designated as conditions not attributable to mental disorder.

The shades and nuances of individual behavioral aberrations are not
easily classified. For one thing, our society's changing values, varying

from permissiveness to authoritarian suppression, imprint themselves on the individual. For another, typology is an unsatisfactory way of dealing with individuals. The diagnostic categories overlap in a given individual. For example, an antisocial person may at the same time display sexual deviation, and an emotionally impulsive offender may also display paranoid tendencies. Furthermore, maladjusted behavior changes with reactions to life pressures and to advancing age. Thus, emotional immaturity in a young sociopath gives way to a mature attitude as life experiences modify his attitude toward society. Several decades ago, the Gluecks[21] demonstrated this evolution in their followup study of five hundred juvenile delinquents. They found, as have many others, that "with the passing of years . . . [there was] . . . a steady diminution of youths who continued to be offenders; by the time delinquents reached the age of twenty-nine, 40% ceased to be criminals. . . . the natural process of maturation offers the chief explanation of this improvement."

But the process of maturation—the acceptance of adult community values and decrease of maliciousness in pubertal boys, and an appreciation of the need for social controls—does not occur in all youthful offenders. When social and emotional immaturity persists to adulthood, it becomes sociopathy. Expected and allowable rebelliousness among youths becomes a fixed pattern of antisociality in adult life; the natural hypermotility (overactivity) of adolescence becomes impulsivity and wanton aggression; and avoidance of tender feelings towards sexual objects remains as sadism among adult sociopaths.[22] Mental dullness short of deficiency is one factor that seems to fixate the psychopathic pattern; another factor is identification with a subculture of egocentric aggression; a third is the emotionally inflexible, basically poorly integrated person whose uneven development can be observed early in life. This represents the classic *psychopath* whose emotional emptiness makes crimes like homicide a meaningless event in their lives. Fred, incarcerated for robbery, was such an individual.

Fred's peculiarities started with sex play with ponies. At the age of 12 he wondered "how it would be like to be with a horse." He tried it alone, then regularly. "I would sneak out of the house and do it to a pony." It was because "I never learned to masturbate." Just before his 17th year, he dropped out of school, lived in an apartment with a friend and started drinking.

His first arrest was for burglary at age 16, for which he received one year's probation. He was warned for numerous curfew violations. The subject spent 40 days in the county jail for possession of a needle (drugs). He was arrested for passing a bad check, received 21 days and was required to make restitution ($75.00). At age 20 he was involved in a robbery of a bar and was sent to the

California Youth Authority for a diagnostic workup. Following that the subject was sent to the county jail to serve a one year sentence.

At the county jail, he and a companion managed to escape. In the process of escape, a homicide occurred, and Fred was charged with murder in the first degree. His abbreviated description of the crime follows:

A door was open and Mike and I slipped out, got under the fence, not detected by guards. Ran over open fields in direction of a college. We were cold and wet. Got to a house, broke in through a broken window and inspected house.

Found money, dry clothes, a .22 rifle, and a .22 pistol. Took both and dressed in clothes. On way out, met the owner, returned in car with wife and children. I said, "We want your car." The man advanced on Mike, who shot him in the trunk (points to left side). I shot him in the leg. The wife drove away. I felt panicky; the man asked for a tourniquet and Mike tied his leg, then he got killed. We ran.

The psychiatric examination was made during Fred's incarceration in jail while on the first degree murder charge.

He related experimenting with marijuana, then "speed" which had been injected in his vein prior to the robbery. He tried LSD; had two bad trips, and also tried heroin occasionally. On drugs he would feel "pulled into himself." He thought about seeing a psychiatrist in a clinic, but did not pursue it.

The next year he met a woman, age 31, with whom he became friendly, then intimate after several months. The latter was frigid; she could not achieve orgasm unless she masturbated. He states that he related his sexual relations with horses to her; it excited her. They lived together for ten months, then he married her.

By that time, the affair was becoming unsatisfactory; at times his wife would ask him to spank her. Now he says, "I should have beaten her; that would cure her frigidity." They lived together for a while. Finally, he began to spend more time away from his wife. The defendant had several homosexual experiences, both active and passive. There was no money passed during the homosexual encounters. He was picked up on several occasions by motorists when "we did everything."

The defendant complained that he was aware something was wrong with him from early life. For one thing, he had no control over his pony-compulsion. For another, he could not talk to people, especially girls and women. "I have a short speech," meaning he has few words to say with women. The defendant complained he had few friends; he couldn't get in with the "drug culture" because those people were "mellow."

He had several "slumps" wherein he became paranoid; people talked about him. At the time of the robbery he was in such a slump. "I had to do something to pull me out." At that time he was on "speed." He felt people were "down on me." At night he would feel he was losing his mind. . . . "I fell into a world of my own."

The defendant explained that when he gets in a "slump," tension builds up and he must break out. These episodes were present when a child. "The feeling builds up and it becomes a cumulative bad feeling" which must be worked out. He feels his mother, or women could help him.

The subject described his mental state as being "on the edge of a whirlpool." He became withdrawn at times and felt his "mind was caving in." When on "speed," he felt "paranoid," would stay in his room but tried to act normal to throw his parents off the track. At times he "doubted myself"; this awareness of something wrong had been with him for several years.

During the examinations the patient was cooperative; he became slightly tense when reciting sexual exploits, but told them freely. At times he suddenly blocked, looking off in the distance. His language was generally good, even sophisticated at times, indicating high average intelligence. Psychological tests, including the Rorschach and Draw-a-Person tests corroborated the clinical findings of emotional flatness, inner tension, paranoid attitudes, sexual conflicts, confusion and a "shrunken ego."

The examinations resulted in a diagnosis of a severe psychopathic personality with schizoid traits and psychosexual conflicts. A longitudinal scrutiny of Fred's life demonstrated a succession of chaotic acts assuming the function of overcoming inner tensions. His "acting out" represented inability of ego control of inner excitement, with occasional dips into a transitory psychosis.

Fred's attorney pled him guilty; he received a life sentence. During his incarceration in prison, he became involved in an assault with a knife on a fellow inmate and in the subsequent fight lost an eye. Under pressure of conflicting loyalties to ethnic prison groups, the prisoner, who was Caucasian, developed a paranoid psychosis. Transferred to a hospital for the criminally insane, the subject regressed to the level of a chronic hostile paranoid state, unamenable to treatment nine years after the original crime.

Personality Types, Other Than Antisociality

Personality disorders, other than the antisocial type, include paranoid, litigious, emotionally explosive, hysterical, sexual, and drug dependent groups. Personality groupings vary—sometimes the inadequate and schizoid types are included. As noted above, the phrases "personality disorder" and "sociopathic personalities" are often interchanged, depending on the time period and attitude of various examiners. A few groups that become involved in the law will be discussed here.

The *paranoid* personality has not attained the level of a paranoid psychosis: his ideation is short of a delusional system. These individuals are hypersensitive in their contacts, sensing humiliation where none is intended. Their attitudes, best described as an extension of the super-sensitive person with paranoid coloring or tendency, is manifested in the litigious personality. This type of individual elevates his or her suspiciousness to the level of a public charge against a person or institution, thus forcing litigation in matters better solved in a public rather than a personal way. Such individuals may present charges to the district attorney in the interest of a "cause" aimed at alleviating a social problem. The delusions, such as they are, constantly shift with little of the attendant grimness of the true paranoiac's persecutory trends. Herbert S., a man of twenty-five years, came to attention on his arrest for possessing and selling marijuana to a minor.[23] He pleaded guilty, then reversed his plea. The judge sentenced him to five months in the county jail suspended, with three years probation, pending psychiatric examination.

The probationer's behavior was rather odd. Once he fractured his femur while attempting to steal a "flag from a flagpole" for unknown reasons. While recuperating in a convalescent home, he became incensed over what he considered "deficiencies" in management. He arranged a transfer of a patient with the help of a nurse with whom he later lived in a common-law relationship. Herbert began a campaign to bring these irregularities to the court's attention, without success. The campaign to bring the convalescent home-owner to book fizzled out.

At another time he wished to leave the state temporarily but refused to sign a waiver of extradition because a "multi-millionaire" might have a warrant for his arrest—grounds unknown. Contact with the probation officer was accompanied by statements that "someone was following" him, or that he "feared for his life." As a cook in a restaurant, he left after a short time because he was aware "something illegal was going on," notably that the police who frequented the eating house were charged half-price for their food.

In a lengthy letter to the court he stated:

"I sincerely hope that upon investigation . . . a smoother workable relationship between myself and the Department of Probation will be established. . . . I formally request that I be reassigned a Deputy Probation Officer of less irrationality and who possesses a greater respect for the principles of law and government and our Nation, State and Country."

Herbert's past history featured several arrests for armed robbery, sale of drugs to minors, disorderly conduct, and a suicidal attempt. There was also an admission to a state hospital, from which he was discharged in a brief time with a diagnosis of antisocial personality.

The current psychiatric examination uncovered a man who talked with considerable vigor, utilizing legalistic terms and an officious manner. He stressed his capacity to do private legal research. His strong social conscience led to uncorrected public disgraces about which he badgered the American Civil Liberties Union. Utilizing mispronounced and inappropriate legal phrases, he insisted that the legally constituted authorities were unable to carry out their

functions. Behind the over-dramatization and grandiosity lay undeveloped paranoid trends not sufficiently entrenched to invade his ego.

A final diagnosis was rendered the court that Herbert was not psychotic, but rather was a paranoid personality with a litigious bent and
a hypomanic behavior pattern.

Allied to the litigious personality is the political extremist whose
paranoid tendencies fit well into subversive organizations. Whereas the
litigious individual seeks to bring his complaints and investigations to
court in quasilegal form, the agitator uses illegal means through a na-
tionalistic or political group. The agitator's paranoia is mixed with
revolutionary fervor, an identification with political power, and a tendency towards illegal aggression. Thus, Tony G. was charged and
convicted by a federal jury for unlawful possession firearms, interstate
transportation of ammunition, and obliteration of serial numbers on a
machine gun.

Tony was raised in a middle-class environment. He presented no problems as
a child until the 14th year when he was discovered to be afflicted with muscular
dystrophy. Shortly after this traumatic experience, he left school and began to
associate with delinquent boys.

As he grew older, Tony built up a distorted and systematized concept that
there was an impending revolution against our Government to be perpetuated
by left-wing militants. At the same time he saw himself as the object of hostility
from those militant groups. He believed that the agents from the Alcohol, To-
bacco and Firearms Division of the U.S. Government had him under constant
surveillance.

Married and working as a mechanic and later an armorer (apparently for
extremist groups), Tony and his wife became involved in arming political
sympathizers against the revolution. An investigator for the United States Attorney, accompanied by an informant, met Tony and his wife to engage in a
discussion which included such topics as the right of citizens to bear firearms
against the militant left-wing liberal groups operating in the United States at
the time (1970). Tony's eagerness to quash the revolution led him to sell a
Sten submachine gun, a Schmeisser submachine gun, an M-3 and an Ingram submachine gun to the Federal agent. Further investigation revealed a workshop
for machining weapons, ammunition, numerous weapon parts, a flare gun,
shells, etc. Found also were 5,000 amphetamine pills.

Contrary to the usual paranoid psychotic, Tony spoke freely about
his political ideas, asserting his constitutional right to bear, sell, trade,
and transport arms. His position was firmly stated:

The reason for my involvement, in the situation which I am faced with, is the
love of my country and to defend it at all costs against the growing threat of

the communist revolutionaries and radicals which are tearing our nation apart through strife and terrorism.

Since the court had asked for an analysis of the offender's personality in relation to the possibility of probation, the final report advised the court that the defendant "could be a danger to society if permitted to continue his interest in guns from a social rather than individual point of view. His identifications are with power, governmental power, and he should be strictly enjoined from his previous associates. His love of intrigue is strong. . . ."

The litigious person is benefited neither by imprisonment nor by psychotherapy. Examination develops nothing of a psychiatric nature which could be used in defense.

The chronic swindler, often called a hysterical-swindler, has gained that characterization because his misrepresentations (impersonating an officer, practicing medicine without a license, posing as an entrepreneur) gratify grandiose fantasies and feelings of omnipotence. Although larceny by trick, conspiracy to defraud, embezzlement, or obtaining money under false pretenses are penal code terms for swindling in the various jurisdictions, the crime descriptions do not always match the techniques used. Thus, New York Penal Law[24] places larceny by trick, embezzlement, obtaining money under false pretenses, and stock frauds under larceny (Section 155.05). Illinois includes impersonating an officer, confidence games, intent to defraud, and forgery under deception (Article 17).[25] California statutes list fraudulent representation or pretense, forgery of credit cards, and obtaining telephone or telegraph services by fraud under larceny (Theft, Title 31, Section 484).[26] The recent tendency is to consolidate offenses like false pretenses, swindling, embezzlement, and even extortion under theft (Texas, Section 31.02).[27] In general, theft constitutes a single offense superseding the separate crimes noted. As Professor Inbau and associates comment in their *Criminal Law and Its Administration*: "There is little justification for the distinction between larceny by deception and larceny and embezzlement."[28]

The psychologic profile of the swindler is close to that of the conversion hysteric. Hiding behind the unctuous manner, hypnotic fluency of speech, and dramatic aura can be seen the basis for this pretentiousness in an emotionally starved childhood. This was the finding of Karl Abraham,[29] one of the pioneer psychoanalysts in Germany who studied the impostor, pathological liar, and swindler. The impostor, utilizing gaudy uniforms and high-sounding titles, is less common in this country than in Europe, but the confidence man is still a form-idable criminologic problem.[30] In illustration of this type of personality disorder, the cases of two "noblemen" of Russian birth charged and convicted of larceny by trick (New York), are outlined below:

Count D. and Professor S. were indicted for larceny by trick. Count D., un-usually amiable and persuasive, described himself as belonging to the ousted Russian aristrocracy, claiming to be a graduate of the University of St. Peters-burg. He gave evidence of having wide knowledge and good comprehension. He related that he had come to this country to arrange colonization in Nicaragua for expatriated Russian nobility, a plan which was to net him $50,000 a year. He lived in fashionable hotels and spent his time among people of wealth. He had been arrested and discharged for uttering a worthless check in Berlin some years before.

The co-defendant, "Professor" S., spoke English haltingly, claimed to have studied at the University of St. Petersburg. He assumed a ponderous, confused air, giving the impression that he was absorbed in scientific problems.

The victim, a successful business man, was introduced to the Count and the Professor, and given a preliminary showing of their counterfeiting process in action. The Professor bathed a one dollar bill in acid until the original was bleached white and the numbers erased. In the presence of the victim, the bleached bill and one of a larger denomination were wrapped around a pencil. With utmost carefulness and gravity, the Professor rolled the pencil, around which were the tighly wrapped bills, across the floor, again and again. The victim watched the procedure narrowly. The process was interrupted by a solemn, critical examination of the pencil following each rolling. After about six hours of this activity, when the victim was on the point of fatigue, the Pro-fessor opened the package disclosing the newly-formed ten dollar bill.

The victim, impressed by the meticulous care and scientific precision of the experiment, was convinced. At the next meeting he brought $25,000 in bills in a package, which were to be changed to bills of higher denomination. At this session, the Professor, in mixing the two chemicals, made an error and nausea-ting fumes arose which overcame the victim. The Count and the Professor, profusely apologetic, rushed out to bring restoratives for the victim, who found when he came to, that his package of $25,000 had been replaced by one con-taining worthless paper.

The psychology of forgery differs from that of swindling only in that the trickery employed is less devious. In that respect, forgery and, to a degree, embezzlement lie closer to extortion. In extortion, authority and its implied force convince the victim to part with money, while in forgery, the authority of a written instrument accomplishes the same objective. In both crimes, the offenders exercise a basic need to expand their egos, to command a granting of their wishes by the flourish of a signature or threat of force. In extortion, the motive is obvious; in forgery, it is covert. Experienced law enforcement agents recognize the forger as an addictive personality; he rarely changes his behavior, even after punishment by imprisonment. Similarly, the extortionist whose disregard of society's approved business methods is part of his antisocial bent is developed from the ranks of the openly aggressive. For this reason, both groups can be classed as sociopaths. Although commonly not considered suitable for a defense of not guilty by reason of insanity or even diminished capacity, the psychological underpinnings of the forger and the extortionist cause them to border on, or fall into the realm of, psychopathology. The offender whose misappropriation of funds is cited below illustrates similar psychologic mechanisms to those found in forgers and embezzlers.

M. M., an attorney, after six years of successful practice found himself harrassed by creditors following a period of over-extended life style. He had speculated in a land venture and building program, which after two years caused him to borrow a substantial amount of money. In trying to make up his losses, he appropriated large amounts from his clients' recoveries, applying them to his large indebtedness. The result was a charge of grand larceny and a subsequent charge by the Bar Association for unethical conduct.

During this anxiety-provoking period, M. M. was tense, worried and confused to the point of being unable to carry on his practice.

The essential points of his history are that he graduated from a fully accredited law school, passed the bar examination, and soon developed a blooming practice. He was known as a colorful personality who relied on his flamboyance to impress his clients. It was generally agreed that he was an engaging personality from his early days, who loved ostentation and exaggeration in his life style.

The patient talked rapidly and well and had a charming manner about him. There was a certain flair which one sees in hysterical-swindler types. Underneath his free-flowing manner, however, there was a marked degree of immaturity. There was a certain self-excusing tendency in this man, a certain glibness and looseness in his thinking. He answered questions, and elaborated his answers somewhat, but once he got rolling it was almost impossible to stop him, even though his conversation was cogent.

The psychological tests brought out three points: a degree of depression, interference with his thinking process because of nervous tension and inner conflict.

At times his answers were well integrated, well organized and convincing. At other times, the response to the Rorschach cards showed a poverty of response. Sometimes he verbalized and mixed his perceptual process with his thinking pattern; for example, he kept saying "I notice," "I'm not sure," "it appears," "my first impression," "for some reason," as if he were unable to really set down what he saw or what he thought. In addition, the inter-weaving of verbalization was done with a great amount of charm and humor, as if he were observing himself and trying to cover up some deeper difficulty in perception with his thought processes.

He did recognize he had a compulsion to be always known as a successful man, and was aware that he exaggerated and prevaricated to the end that he would be regarded as a successful attorney.

Review of the psychological tests showed that the defendant displayed slight thinking difficulty in the sense that he waved aside obvious rational conclusions, substituting grandiose ideas. Further signs of a psychopathic personality of the hysterical swindler type appeared, but this examiner was unable to say that he was mentally ill at the time of his defalcation. He did know right from wrong, even though he had a compulsion to avoid the right.

Extortion, Kidnapping and the Psychopath

The crime of extortion and/or kidnapping, committed by mentally clear offenders with a specific momentary purpose in mind, rarely calls for psychiatric evaluation. This generalization, however, must be tempered by consideration of those kidnappers whose crime is an act of revenge (as in a custody fight) or the result of depression such as among women who abduct babies to supply the emotional needs of an impoverished ego. More commonly, kidnapping for ransom is carried out by sociopathic persons, often with a prison record for robbery or extortion. Psychologically, kidnapping is akin to extortion, with its identification with power and authority, the use of crude force, and the intent of financial gain. The case detailed below adds one element, probably more universal among such criminals than is realized, namely, a perception of what is best described as the heroic mold. This term was coined to characterize the exaltation, the feeling of infallibility, and the excitement of adventure observed in psychopaths who embark on daring crimes. The thrill distorts their judgment and the feeling of control obscures their humanity, as among kidnappers. In one psychologic sense, the kidnapper resembles the compulsive gambler who sets himself against implacable fate. He hopes to overcome Lady Luck with the power of magic; the law of averages "must" sometime operate in his favor.[31] When the gambler's winnings or losses mount to dizzying sums, he loses his grip on the value of the money for which he strives. The excitement of gaming transforms money into valueless pieces of embossed metal or printed paper. So too with the psychopathic kidnapper whose plans are smudged by the excitement of the deed and the anticipated chase.

The offender at hand[32] embodied the essence of immaturity. Youthful braggadocio combined with a calculated plan which dissolved to panicky indecision when the reality of his crime finally assailed him. The result was a third unplanned killing and a second kidnapping.

John's sociopathic profile had been evident for some time. Arrested for juvenile offenses, he became involved in stealing hay from the fields, a profitable type of theft. Arrested five times, John received probation and later, a brief stay in the county jail. In spite of this, John continued to steal hay, drive to the city and sell it for increasing amounts of money.

These night thefts crowded out his usual occupation of cord-wood dealer. Returning from the city with large amounts of cash caused a crisis at home. His wife threatened to leave him, which she did with another man taking the children with her. This event pushed John into a brief psychotic episode from which he recovered. Bitterness over her infidelity burned deeply into him. He turned to the "gang" in the city with whom he claimed he became persuader, body-guard for the "boss" and driver of the getaway car. As a muscular 6 foot 2 inch, in his 27th year, John acted as a chauffeur for the gang, John learned how to shoot "if a gun is stuck under your chin." He learned how to "rip a man's chest open with your fingers and pull his heart out." He also learned how to impersonate an officer, how to use a zap for unruly customers, and how to carry a pair of hand-cuffs and a .45 pistol in his belt. "I got a security officer's uniform. Say you want to do a burglary, you walk into a house, saying you wanted to check security. You ask questions—when you leave the house—you learn the place."

To the examiner, he confided: "Sure, I can get you anything you want. Identification permits, phoney licenses, gun permits . . . you gotta know the right people."

"I was in a $250,000 shake down once," he confided. "You don't ask questions because they can get to your children. You never ask for money; you wait and somehow it comes through."

His coolness under pressure and his alleged disregard for human life were invaluable assets to his new employers. "The way I figured it, I wouldn't live old."

A few days later, after conviction for triple murders and kidnapping, John remarked while sitting on Death Row in a prison: "I'm the smartest in the family. Life and money have no value to me. I just wanted to do something big and different. . . . I rebelled. I wanted big money. It was an ego trip."

The details of John's involvement in the crime for which he was sentenced to the gas chamber, differed completely from those advanced by the sheriff. Scrupulous investigations conducted by detectives indicated that the persons to whom John allegedly sold his stolen hay were in fact legitimate business men, dealers in fire-wood and feed; none had any connection with the underworld characters. Whether he participated in an extortion gang or played out a fantasy remains undetermined.

According to the prisoner's version, the gang sent one Rod to ask if he wanted to make some quick money. Already in debt for $4,000 (how he managed this debt in view of successful larcenies was never explained), John readily assented. "There was no fee in it, just what the boss said. I was to do a job. Then the boss would help me some time." The simple plan called for John's demanding $15,000 from a local veterinary, reputed to have welched on a drug transaction with the gang. The plan outlined by Rod seemed simple enough. The two were to await the doctor's return from his animal hospital one evening, then request the money using any convenient method—gun or knife or other—to persuade the victim to part with the money.

The next day under an alias and alone he sought to buy a car at the victim's home. Refused, he returned the following day with the same request. His unnecessary persistence struck the young son as odd, but he passed it off as a clumsy intrusion.

On a summer evening, John and Rod appeared before the home in time to intercept the doctor and his 14 year old daughter. Key in hand, Lisa was opening the door when she was ordered to turn around. "I had the 30.06 rifle and Rod had a 38 revolver; he covered the Doc and I covered Lisa. We didn't plan to hurt anybody. I made a motion for the girl to say nothing. Then Rod told me to get the wire out of my truck and break it into pieces. He was my boss, so I did what he told me."

About 7 p.m. on this hot valley evening, Rod proceeded to wire the doctor and his daughter, their wrists behind their backs. They marched the be-wired pair into the grove, some 150 yards from the house. Turning from the pair, still wired at the wrists, the prisoner insisted that was the last he saw of father and daughter.

The next day, a neighbor noted a foul odor issuing from the grove. The sheriff, notified, found two putrifying bodies a few yards apart at the foot of two trees. The autopsy report stated: "The male body had been strangled by wire between the thyroid cartilega and hyoid bone, with three stab wounds in the chest. The girl's death was from strangulation by wire."

Meanwhile John had stopped the son and wired his hands behind his back, explaining that his errand was to obtain the $15,000, that his father owed the gang for a "dope deal." Casually entering the home with the youth, John explained in more detail to the doctor's wife, his request for money.

Unaware of the fate of her garotted husband and daughter, the doctor's wife assented to the plan to get the money from the bank the next day. After requesting the son to sweep away tire tracks from the driveway, John drove the pair to a neighboring town where he placed them in a motel under his guard.

The kidnapping was anything but threatening. The prisoner slept outside the room he provided for his captives, treated them well at breakfast the next morning, and tested the doctor's wife's trustworthiness by ordering her to cash a $200 check in the local market.

At 10:30 that morning the group casually approached the bank. The doctor's wife's alternatives were clear: "Get as much money as you can. Don't tell the police. If you do, you'll never see your husband or daughter again." The victim, her leg in a cast from a healing fracture, hobbled into the bank. She sought the bank manager and a hurried conference followed. Stunned, he ordered a teller to note as many numbers on the bills as possible, then deliver $5,000 to his client. The transaction was carried out swiftly, without disturbing the measured pace of the bank. When the doctor's wife emerged from the bank, she passed the money to her captor. They drove off. John said gruffly: "Did you talk . . . if you did, your people will be dead."

The day was consumed in aimless driving along country roads. Several times John stopped to telephone Rod, presumably for instructions. He bought food, distributing it amiably to his captives. The sporadic travel continued until they came to a grain field.

Gun in hand, the kidnapper ordered the pair to sit on the grass in a clearing. He sat opposite, telling them that Rod had ordered him to scare or kill them. Doggedly, the prisoner explained he worked for the "gang": "If you don't do what they say, they'll kill me or I might die in a gun battle."

The discussion was dispassionate and deliberate. The conversation drawled on for more than an hour. They talked of life and death. Suddenly the prisoner's philosophic attitude evaporated. "I was getting up the nerve to shoot them," he confided later.

He twirled his gun ostentatiously around his forefinger. The finality of death settled on the trio. The doctor's son leaned over to kiss his mother good-bye. John turned away, getting a shot off into the trees. As he followed the shot contemplatively, the son stood up, streaking towards a tall stand of tulle shoots bordering the open fields. John started to pursue the youth but soon turned back. Standing about 8 feet away from the doctor's wife, who sat on the grass, her encased leg comfortably stretched before, he pumped a shot into her body. Instinctively, he jumped into his car and tore out of the clearing into the road. The investigators later found blue paint scrapings on the fence post, the carefully closed gate strewn across the road.

Later, in custody, the prisoner explained his feelings during that moment: "I got scared when the boy ran. Rod told me to kill them but the boy disappeared in a gully behind the tulles. I felt funny, like in a dream, like something I had done before. That place was a lover's lane. I took Sue [his wife] there once. I didn't feel the gun go off. When I looked down on the lady and saw her dead, it was like something I had been through before. I couldn't breathe. It was like I saw Sue lying there and that guy with the beard. . . . Right then my idea was to get out of the country quick. Someplace where they don't like cops or Americans. Maybe Russia. I felt funny in the head, so I jumped in my car, jammed out of the field and drove fast down the road, must have been going 100 miles an hour. Then I seen a house and pulled into the driveway."

The cottage proved to house a widow with three children. Pushing open the door, bent over as if in pain, John mumbled something about a car accident down the road and "was her husband home," so he could get some help. When the woman answered "No," he strode into the room, his gun pointed at her, saying "Don't run, I've already killed three people. I need your car. There won't be no trouble. Get in with your kids. I'll take care of your kids," he reassured the mother, "We're going for a little ride."

The little ride lasted 7 days, carrying them through Nevada's brown deserts, Utah's mountains, and back to California. The captives, adjusting to this burly, good-hearted man, accepted the food and lodging he provided them without question. The leisurely, gypsy holiday approached the idyllic.

"I was so happy," John later reminisced in prison. During the trial, Mrs. C. as State's witness recounted their meanderings through the countryside: "It was like a family outing," she said.

On the third day, he pulled up to a used-car lot, bought a Chevrolet for cash, leaving Mrs. C.'s car by the roadside. A few days later he dropped the Chevy, buying a Buick. Every morning at about 10 a.m. he made phone calls, presumably to his boss for instructions. The calls were to Mae, his girl friend. The police meanwhile had tapped Mae's phone. They heard snatches of conversation—"I'm in Washington. Got to meet you. I'll tell you where to meet me. My kids are in danger. I love you. Ah-huh. What'll I do? Wait, I'll call tomorrow."

Another day: "Mae, I lost my children for good. Have the cops been there?" "No," she lied, "it's OK." "Yeah, I'll call again." More calls, more snatches of conversation: "Mae, I'm in California. Meet me in Truckee. I got to save my kids from the gang."

On the seventh day, John drove his captives to a California valley. Selecting a grove of trees along the road, he tied the kidnapped family to trees, leaving them food and clothes. The next morning, on the streets of Truckee, he was approached by three men who surrounded him with quiet deliberateness. " 'I'll bet these are F.B.I.,' I said to myself and sure enough one stepped up to me, showing his I.D. card, saying, 'F.B.I.' It was just like in the movies."

The arrest was made without difficulty. In answer to the agents' questions, the prisoner gave the stock answers about Rod, his bosses, and the gang's threatened reprisals against his children. He was returned to the county jail, and an indictment was brought before the grand jury of three counts of first degree murder and five counts of kidnapping. The trial, held in a distant town on a change of venue order, was lengthy, and the prosecution's case detailed. John's defense lawyer labored to present a picture of diminished responsibility sufficient to reduce the charge from first to second degree murder. (See Chapter 2 for direct examination.) John's confused, vacillating state during the first kidnapping and homicide of the doctor's wife, and his reversion to a kindly parental role during the second, argued for lack of premeditation for the crimes. The carefully drawn psychological picture of an unstable sociopathic personality, shot through with streaks of immature dependence, was discounted by the jury. They found the accused guilty on all counts. The judge sentenced him to death under the "special circumstances" provision of California law.

On Death Row, the prisoner began to insist he had not killed the doctor's wife. Each rethinking of the crimes solidified the mirror image of the truth. Imagination fixed the fantasy of Rod, the accomplice, into a tenuous web of near reality. The story of Rod and the gang grew to a certainty on Death Row. Rehearsing the crime over and over, embellishing his involvement with the gangsters, lent a reality to his story. He began to fear that the "boss" could send his henchmen to "get" him in prison. There was no expression of regret for the killings; his worry was that entrance into the "big time" had been foreclosed for him. He wavered between the fading fantasy of heroic heights and the actuality of his earlier premonition—"I won't live old."

The case and the followup present nothing of legal significance beyond the plea for diminished responsibility which was discarded by the jury. However, study of this sociopath permitted a view of the dynamics of his character structure, namely, the alternating presence of dependent passivity and aggression, held in check with difficulty by an unstable ego. His behavior during the kidnapping demonstrated his conflict; John's indecisive rides through the countryside with both sets of captives betrayed the tenuousness of his heroic stance. Strong dependency feelings towards women and children arose to struggle with his fantasy of gangland associations. Unacquainted with psychological concepts, John only was aware of a curious deja vu experience at the moment he shot the doctor's wife. The grove, where the shooting occurred, a lover's lane for local youths, had served him as a rendezvous some years earlier with Sue, then his wife-to-be. The fusion of images involving the two women that arose in his mind represented a compromise between dependent cravings and violent impulses. The prisoner's softness towards his second group of captives, almost a paternalism, was in marked contrast to his ruthless disposal of the three victims. During the kidnapping of Mrs. C. and her children, one can interpret his frequent calls to Mae as denoting infantile yearnings for approval and nurturance. "Mae, do you love me? Are they after me?." Translated into psychologic terms, his pleas meant "Does anybody want me? Does anybody love me?" In this emotional state, the FBI agents were both captors and rescuers.

The Puzzle of Psychopathy

The psychological analysis of a murderer advanced above is of less concern to the legal process than to penologists and criminologists with whom sociopaths make contact some time in their careers. The many attempts to understand the genesis of this condition, chiefly with an eye to treatment or prevention, have included consideration of grinding poverty, insanity, psychopathic inferiority, hostility towards parents, compulsive neurosis, climatic influences, psychedelic "freak-outs," XYY chromosomes, endocrine glands, unresolved Oedipus complexes, primitive personalities, alcoholism and drug usage, alcoholic forebears, beetling brows, and bumps on the skull. Each of these factors has been dissected, scrutinized, accepted, and relied on, but finally discarded.

Recently, an organic etiology has been sought. The electro-encephalograph in the 1940s-1950s showed specific brainwave changes in many psychopaths, but more recent work (1969)[33] demonstrates no specific electrical activity in the sociopath's brain. The presence of chromosome differences found in some murderers (the XYY syndrome occurring in tall, muscular men with a history of violence) did not hold up in studies involving large groups of aggressive men. Nielsen's study in Europe[34] found that 10 men out of 232 examined in an institution for criminal psychopaths demonstrated "major chromosomal abnormalities."

In this country, over one hundred XYY karyotypes have been detected in criminals,[35] but researchers have concluded that "the available evidence" has been "too equivocal" to establish a structural, organic background for murderous and antisocial tendencies. On the other hand, many investigators agree that sociopaths develop "from inborn or early acquired cerebral dysfunction and disturbed parent-child relationships," as Maughs[36] suggested.

With no agreement as to the causes of the condition, empirical methods of treatment have been extended on many fronts. These include individual psychotherapy, group and milieu therapy, and behavior modification in penal institutions. These attempts to treat sociopaths are outlined in Chapter 8 where the use of voluntary and legally enforced therapy is discussed. The most noteworthy of such attempts was at the Patuxent Institution in Maryland, established by legislative act in 1951. Its purpose was to "protect society from the segment of the criminal population who probably will again commit crimes . . . if released on the expiration of a fixed sentence." The population committed to Patuxent by the court, if determined to be "defective delinquent," was sentenced to a "fully indeterminate sentence from one minute to life."[37] The therapy consisted of group and milieu therapy, educational and vocational training, and a "form of behavior modification." After considerable experience, the Maryland legislature repealed the indeterminate sentence necessary for prolonged treatment of the sociopath or "defective delinquent" housed at Patuxent. In 1977, the involuntary commitment of recidivists was rescinded except for certain three- and four-time offenders; incarcerated prisoners were permitted admission if they wished "treatment."[38]

In effect, indeterminate sentences with the attendant treatment program for sociopaths (defective delinquents) were abandoned because they provided only limited benefit to society. Among "hard core offenders, the re-arrest rate was reduced to the level of other offender groups."[39] Considering its only moderate benefits, the procedure was too costly. Another factor in terminating the Patuxent experiment was society's "disenchantment with the correctional model or medical model for handling the crime problem . . . specifically psychiatric treatment . . . and the emphasis on constitutional rights of the individual."[40]

The puzzle remains, and so does the reality that the sociopath taxes the resources of the laws, the courts, penal institutions, and psychiatrists.

Notes

1. H. Cason, *The Psychopath and the Psychopathic*, 4 J. Crim. Psychopathology 522 (1943).

2. P. Pinel, *A Treatise in insanity in which are contained the principles of a new and more practical nosology of maniacal disorders than has yet been offered the public, exemplified by numerous and accurate historical relation of cases from the authors of public and private practice, with plates illustrative of craneology of maniacs and idiots*, trans. from the French, Sheffield, England (1806).

3. J. H. Cox, *Practical Observations on Insanity*, Murray, C. and R. Baldwin, London (2d ed., 1806).

4. J. C. Pritchard, *A Treatise on Insanity and Other Disorders Affecting the Mind*, Sherwood, Gilbert and Piper, London (1835).

5. J. Koch, *Die Psychopathischen Minderwertigkeiten*, Maier, Ravensberg (1891).

6. A. Meyer, *Reports of the N.Y. State Pathological Institute*, Utica, N.Y. (1904-1905).

7. Eugen Kahn, *Psychopathic Personalities*, Yale U. Press, New Haven, (1931).

8. W. Lewis, *A Text-book of Mental Diseases*, Chas. Griffen and Co., London (2d ed., 1899).

9. G. E. Partridge, *A Study of 50 Cases of Psychopathic Personality*, 7 Am. J. Psych. 953 (1928).

10. Hervey Cleckley, *The Mask of Sanity*, C. V. Mosby Co., St. Louis, (2d ed., 1950).

11. Franz Alexander, *The Neurotic Character*, 11 Int'l. J. Psychoanalysis 523 (1930).

12. L. C. Kolb, *Modern Clinical Psychiatry*: 496.

13. Walter Bromberg, *The Treatability of the Psychopath*, 110 Am. J. Psych. 604 (Feb. 1954). Walter Bromberg, *Dynamic Aspects of the Psychopathic Personality*, 17 Psychoanal. Qt. 58 (1948).

14. Penal Code, Sec. 34. McKinley's Consolidated Laws of New York, West Publ. Co., St. Paul, Minn. (1975).

15. American Law Institute, Model Penal Code (Final Draft) (1962).

16. *McDonald v. U.S.*, 312 F. 2d 847, 851, D.C. Cir. Ct. (1962).

17. Ibid.: 861.

18. Bernard Diamond, *From M'Naghten to Currens and Beyond*, 50 Calif. L. Rev. 189, 193 (1962).

19. *Wade v. U.S.*, 426 F. 2d 64, 72 (1970).

20. *Campbell v. U.S.*, 307 F. 2d, 597 (1962).

21. Sheldon Glueck, and Eleanor Glueck, *500 Criminal Careers*, Alfred A. Knopf, New York (1930).

22. Walter Bromberg, *Emotional Immaturity and Antisocial Behavior*, J. Clin. Psychopath. 423 (Jan. 1947).

23. *People v. Herbert S.*, Sacramento County, no. 43919, Filed Jan. 1, 1974, Viol. Health & Safety Code, Calif. Sec. 11360 & 11361.

24. McKinley's Consolidated Laws of New York, Annotated Book 39, Penal Law, Sec. 155.05: 110-12, West Publ. Co., St. Paul, Minn. (1975).

25. Illinois, Annotated Stat., Smith-Hurd, Chap. 38, Art. 17, West Publ. Co., St. Paul, Minn. (1977).

26. West Publ. Co., Annotated California Codes, Vol. 49, Penal Code Title 13, Chap. 5, Sec. 484, West Publ. Co., St. Paul, Minn. (1970).

27. Vernon's Texas Codes Annotated, Penal Code Section 31.02, Penal 3, p. 266, West Publ. Co., St. Paul, Minn. (1974).

28. F. E. Inbau, J. R. Thompason, and J. B. Zagel, *Criminal Law and Its Administration*: 305, Foundation Press, New York (1974).

29. Karl Abraham, *The History of an Imposter in the Light of Psychoanalytic Knowledge*, trans. by A. Strachey, 4 Psychoan. Qt. (1936).

30. Walter Bromberg and S. Keiser, *A Psychological Study of the Swindler*, 94 Am. J. Psych. 1441 (1938).

31. Walter Bromberg, *Crime and the Mind. A Psychiatric Analysis of Crime and Punishment*: 262, Macmillan Co., New York (1965).

32. *People v. John Card*, Case no. 8077 (County of Merced, Calif., 1975).

33. A. A. Sayed, S. A. Lewis, and R. P. Brittain, *An Electroencephalographic and and Psychiatric Study of 32 Insane Murderers*, 115 Brit. J. Psych. 1115 (1969).

34. J. Nielsen and T. Tsuboi, *Correlation Between Stature, Character Disorder and Criminality*, 116 Brit. J. Psych. 145 (1970).

35. S. Kessler and R. H. Moos, *The XYY Karyotype and Criminality*, 7 J. Psych. Res. 153 (1970).

36. Sidney Maughs, *Psychopathic Personality*, 10 J. of Crim. Psychopath. 249 (July 1949).

37. Jonas R. Rappeport, *Enforced Treatment—Is It Treatment?*, 2, no. 3 Bull. Am. Acad. of Psych. and the L. 148 (Sept. 1974).

38. Art. 27, Para. 643 B, Mandatory Sentences for Crimes of Violence. Art. 31 B (rev. 1977).

39. Henry J. Steadman, *A New Look at Recidivism Among Patuxent Inmates*, 5, no. 2 Bull. Am. Acad. of Psych. and the L. 200 (1977).

40. Peter P. Legins, *The Patuxent Experiment*, 5, no. 2 Bull. Am. Acad. of Psych. and L. 116 (1977). The entire Vol. 5 issue of the Bulletin is devoted to the Patuxent Institution.

8

Sexual Crimes and
Sexual Psychopathy

Murky as the sociopathic problem is in relation to criminal law, that of sexual deviation is even more opaque. Because laws regarding sexual offenses carry the heritage of biblical proscriptions and age-old taboos, they maintain some of the aura of sinfulness. Still, attitudes toward sexual crimes have varied with the changing mores of historical periods. The biblical admonition "There shall be no whores of the daughters of Israel, nor a sodomite of the sons of Israel" (Deut. 23:18) was not necessarily followed in all cultures and epochs. Judge Morris Ploscowe, in tracing the evolution of the law of sexual crimes,[1] notes that the common law in England took a "comparatively liberal attitude" toward sex expression during the post-Renaissance period. "Fornication was no crime. . . . Adultery was not a punishable offense [but] the sanctions of the common law were involved when sex activity created public scandal . . . [or] out-raged decency." Earlier, Ploscowe adds, "incest, fellatio, cunnilingus, adultery, fornication, and mutual masturbation could be brought before the Ecclesiastical Court and the Church of England." Although Lord Stephen in his *History of English Law*[2] comments, "Nearly every secular law enacted by early English kings was coupled with an ecclesiastical code . . . ecclesiastical courts extended jurisdiction to "incest, bigamy, acting as a procuress, abortion, overlying children, assault with intent to ravish."

Sexual Crime, Society, and the Law

Secular courts gained control over sexual crime during the seventeenth century in England, but religious influence remained strong among legal authorities. In his *Commentaries*, in the section "Crimes Against Nature," Blackstone wrote: "I will not act so disagreeably a part to my readers as well as myself . . . to dwell any longer on a subject the very nature of which is a disgrace to human nature, a crime not fit to be named."[3]

In the United States, particularly in the states formed from the thirteen Original Colonies, the statutes concerning sexual crimes which derived from the common law retained a connotation of abhorrence. For example, under Massachusetts law[4] "Unnatural and Lascivious" acts against a child under sixteen years of age (pedophilia) and "Lascivious Cohabitation" (common law relationship) were bracketed under crimes against chastity. The statutes of Rhode Island[5] defined sexual crime in terms reminiscent of older attitudes: "Every person who shall be convicted of the abominable and detestable crime against nature, either with mankind or beast . . ." The New York Penal Law has been modified since the early nineteenth century (1816) when a New York judge in a case involving a school master charged with "gross indecency toward certain young females"[6] refused to "stain the purity of the page" with an exact description of the accused's acts. Evidence at the trial was forthcoming that the teacher had his charges recite standing beside his desk in such a way that he could palpate their buttocks and genitals without being observed by the other students. At trial, the judge stopped a recital of the details because "sufficient evidence had been proved . . . and the court would not hear details so disgusting."

The twentieth century brought a different attitude towards sex crimes among the judiciary. Wingersky, editor of Clark and Marshall's *The Law of Crimes* (1958), quotes a federal judge (1951): "Planted by superstition and watered by ignorance, taproots of our criminal law concerning sex offenders and offenses lie deeply embedded in a compost of religious notions of sin and legal ideas of crime."[7] Many enlightened jurists have called for an objective view of sexual crime, as reflected in recent legislative enactments. The current Penal Code of New York (1972)[8] lists sexual crime in four major categories: (1) sexual misconduct, (2) consensual sodomy, (3) rape, and (4) sexual abuse. Sex-related offenses are listed in other sections describing deviate sexual behavior such as public lewdness, bigamy, adultery, incest, and endangering the welfare of a child. Wisconsin has avoided the phrase "crime against nature";[9] its statute against sexual perversion states: "[It is] a crime to commit abnormal acts of sexual gratification involving the sex organs of a person in the mouth or anus of another. . . ." California law, on the other hand, includes under crimes against the person and against public decency and good morals, rape, abduction, carnal abuse of children, and seduction; bigamy, incest, and the crimes against nature are listed in a separate chapter of the Penal Code.[10] Among other jurisdictions, Texas has adopted the phrases "deviate sexual intercourse" (fellatio or pederasty), "sexual contact" (touching the genitals or anus or breast of a female ten years or older), and "sexual intercourse" (rape or aggravated rape).[11] The phrase "lascivious intent" is not used in the definition of other sexual crimes such as public lewdness, indecent exposure, sexual abuse of a child, and homosexuality. In the legislative attempt to clarify and simplify the law on sexual crimes, Texas has supplanted the phrase "carnal knowledge," with its implication of "fleshiness and sensuality" (Oxford English Dictionary), with the simple phrase "sexual intercourse."

In many states, the recent tendency has been to reduce the use of emotionally laden pejorative terms like "degenerate" and "perverse" to "deviancy," or in the case of homosexuality, to a "different sexual orientation." The main thrust of sexual crime laws is the maintenance of public and private decency and the reduction of emotional and physical hurt to the victim, as well providing possible treatment for the offender. Emphasis is on matching the danger to public health and safety with the severity of the crime; the "psychopathy" of the offender with the likelihood of persistence in sexual misconduct. For example, California statutes direct that an act of oral copulation with a person under fourteen years (or more than ten years younger than the perpetrator, or compelled by violence or threat of harm) is a felony for which punishment of two to four years in state prison is mandated. "One who exposes his person, or private parts thereof, in any public place" is guilty of a misdemeanor. Under Texas law, aggravated sexual abuse of a child involving serious bodily injury, kidnapping, and the like is a first degree felony, while adult homosexual deviate conduct "with another individual of the same sex" is a Class C misdemeanor. Examples such as these can be cited in forty-eight other states of the Union. The point is that the etiology and psychopathology of the deviation and motivation of the particular crime are of secondary importance far behind the primary aims of public safety and decency.

In assessing public offensiveness among specific sexual offenders, complications arise: the several crimes are not specific unto the perpetrator. For instance, a homosexual may engage a youthful partner at one time and thus be liable for a felony charge, or he may choose an adult partner at another, holding himself open for a misdemeanor. If he is discreet and the act is carried out in private, no legal penalty is incurred. A fetishist may restrict himself to collecting boots or youths for their sexual stimulation, or he may engage in homosexual relations with minors when the occasion arises.[12] Soliciting for male prostitution on the part of a youth merits a charge of "disorderly conduct" in California and elsewhere,[13] or it may be elevated to a felony if robbery or assault occurs. Finally, the range of deviation that is reported to authorities must be viewed in terms of the tremendous social changes that have affected sexual mores and morals since early in the century. Particularly is this operative in sexual psychopathy laws which developed just prior to this social reevaluation. Before the hazy and complex area of legislation on sexual psychopathy is discussed, psychiatry's contribution to legal sanctions against sexual criminals will be surveyed.

Psychiatric Contributions to Deviate Sexuality

The modern attitude of objectivity towards sex in general and sexual deviations in particular is considered to have been ushered in by Krafft-Ebing, Havelock Ellis, and Sigmund Freud, each from a slightly different viewpoint. Victor Robinson, the medical historian, in an introduction to Krafft-Ebing's groundbreaking work *Psychopathia Sexualis* (1882),[14] regarded "the foremost figures in the Sexual Science of the Twentieth Century" to be Iwan Bloch, Magnus Hirschfield, Havelock Ellis, Sigmund Freud, with Krafft-Ebing as "the true founder of sexual pathology." The medical profession, except for a small band of alienists dealing with criminals, did not immediately accept this new work, whereas Havelock Ellis's books and, surreptitiously, Krafft-Ebing's volume made an abiding impression on the literate public. In his introduction to the English edition of *Psychopathia Sexualis*, Robinson commented on this public fascination with sexual deviation: "Psychopathia Sexualis became the Adolescent's handbook, but countless elders also tasted the forbidden apple in secret. . . ." In a sense, the productions of these and other leaders became the pornography of their times.

This new interest was not reflected in laws or legal practice until well into the twentieth century. Krafft-Ebing complained that "law and jurisprudence have thus far given but little attention to the facts of psycho-pathology," while he perceived that "in no domain of criminal law is cooperation of judge and medical experts so much to be desired." Obviously, sexually deviated activity was not unknown in Europe, but according to Fielding Garrison in his standard *History of Medicine* (third edition, 1921),[15] it had not become a social or legal problem in this country:

[T]he question of sexual perversion and the crimes resulting from it, for which in young, healthy frontier communities like the United States no special provisions had been necessary in criminal procedures until the crowded condition in modern cities brought the unsavory subject to the surface. . . .

Public interest in sexual "degeneracy" remained sub rosa, while the law remained starkly punitive. The attitudes toward sexual psychopathology are suggested by Oscar Wilde's imprisonment in England for homosexual intimacy with Lord Douglas (1895), the charge of obscenity against Havelock Ellis, Freud's ostracism from society and psychiatric respectability ("It was considered bad taste to bring up Freud's name in the presence of ladies"[16]), and "The Whole Book (Psychopathology of Everyday Life) reminds one much of the thinking of primitive minds, of persons with unscientific, uncritical . . . ideas."[17] Even Bernard Glueck, a pioneer in psychiatric criminology, spoke of sexual perverts (psychopathic) in his epochal report from New York's Sing Sing Prison (1918),[18] and Arthur Foxe, working in Dannemora State Prison, New York, classified homosexuals as "Perverted Characters" in the 1930s.[19]

The Background of Sexual Psychopathy Laws

The enormous mushrooming of psychoanalytic interest and study during the third and fourth decades of this century brought an acute interest in psychosexuality to the mental sciences. What were considered perversions now proved to be part-instincts of human development. As Fenichel phrased it: "Freud discovered infantile sexuality and disclosed that the sexual aims of the pervert are identical with those of children . . . ."[20] The concept that perversions represented an arrested development in the maturation of the sexual impulse placed them in the "psychopathic" column in most psychiatric texts. The sexual deviate, being neither psychotic nor mentally deficient, lay somewhere between neurosis and personality disorder, close to the sociopathic character diagnosis. Thus, Paul Friedman, writing in the *American Handbook of Psychiatry* in the 1950s,[21] set down the "major sex perversions" as overt homosexuality, pedophilia (child molesters), fetishism, transvestism (clothing of opposite sex), exhibitionism, voyeurism (peeping), sadomasochism, zoophilia (bestiality), necrophilia (love of the dead), masturbation (questionably), and group perversions (orgies). He added obscenity and pornography as being "closely related to exhibitionism and scoptophilia."

For several decades, however, it was agreed that sexual deviates

belonged under the heading of personality disorder,[22] while the sociopathic personality category referred to antisocial persons (see Chapter
7). Modern students of homosexuality, such as Irving Bieber and associates,[23] place the condition close to the neurosis: "In our view, every
homosexual is in reality a 'latent' heterosexual" (1962). Bak and
Stewart refine a few deviate types in dynamic terms:

[T]he fetichist, exhibitionist and transvestite all deal with castration anxiety
engendered by the lack of resolution of their bi-sexuality. . . .
    [They] search for the phallic female . . . the fetichist invents one, the ex-
hibitionist hopes to see one, the transvestite is one. . . .[24]

Studies by psychoanalysts did not go beyond homosexuality among
males and females under office treatment; they rarely included deviates, such as pedophiles, who made up the bulk of sexual criminals. The
type of offenders the courts had to deal with included aggressive, even
murderous, criminals, and the designation of personality disorder with
an analysis of underlying neurotic elements held no significance for
the courts, or for the public for that matter. Many psychiatrists persisted in utilizing the "sexual psychopath" description. Morgan and
Lovell expressed it as follows: "The psychopath becomes a sexual
psychopath when he commits a sex crime or it is considered he has had
propensities in that direction."[25] The essential point was the "propensities to commit sex crimes, interpreted as "utter lack of power to
control sexual impulses."[26] The first sexual psychopathy law appearing in Illinois (1938) stated:

Any person suffering from a mental disorder who is not insane, nor feeble-
minded, whose mental disorder has existed for more than a year, and whose
mental disorder is coupled with propensities to the commission of sex offenses,
is hereby declared to be a criminal sexual psychopath.

Other states which adopted sexual psychopathy laws were Michigan
(1939), California (1939), Minnesota (1945), and Massachusetts
(1947). The laws were directed toward persons with "criminal propensities" (Michigan), with "irresponsibility for sex conduct and
dangerous to others" (Minnesota), with "habitual course of misconduct in sexual matters, who lack power to control sexual impulses"
(Massachusetts). The California Code defines a sexual psychopath as
one "who is affected in a form predisposing to the commission of
sexual offenses and in a degree constituting him a menace to the health
or safety of others."[27] Further characteristics set forth in this legal
definition are that he has involved "a child under the age of fourteen

in a sexual act . . . or has had a previous sexual offense . . . or (as listed) in codes of other states, as Wisconsin, Illinois, etc.) has uncontrollable impulses towards abnormal sexual acts."

Since psychiatrists were called upon to consult with the courts regarding the "psychopathy" of indicted or convicted offenders, they were asked to fit their knowledge of sexual deviancy into the legal scaffolding. The crux of the matter centered on whether the deviation was *fixed* in the offender's personality, that is whether a compulsive, and hence uncontrollable, quality accompanied his sexual impulse.

The numerous writings and discussions on the subject can be summarized by a report which the Group for the Advancement of Psychiatry (GAP) rendered in 1949[28] for the guidance of courts and legislatures. The GAP committee, whose membership included Philip Roche, Manfred Guttmacher, Hervey Cleckley, and myself, made a thorough analysis of the problem and offered this definition. A sexual psychopath . . . is guilty of repetitive, compulsive acts . . . carried out to the point of community intolerance . . . manifesting a heedless disregard of consequences . . . seeking to attain ultimate expression even if momentary obstacles are encountered.

The initiation of sexual psychopathy laws followed public reaction to a series of horrifying, often mutilating sex crimes throughout the country, well publicized in the press. An outraged public clamored for the segregation of "sex fiends" from society. Agitation for restrictive laws was aided by such authorities as J. Edgar Hoover, director of the FBI, whose article *How Safe Is Your Daughter?* appeared in the *American Magazine* in July 1947. The protection of society was the first request made of the various legislatures, and rehabilitation, if possible, a second. It was understood that sexual psychopaths were neither insane, mentally defective, nor normal and that the statutes represented a "new approach to an age-old" problem.[29]

The intent of the legislation is to treat the sexual psychopath by confinement in a mental health facility until he is "cured" or improved sufficiently to take his place in society. The statutes, therefore, are not criminal statutes.[30] One accused of sexual offenses can be given a separate hearing before trial on the issue of sexual psychopathy as a civil matter before the criminal aspect is dealt with. The New Hampshire courts in *In re Moulton* (1950)[31] expressed the principles underlying the sexual psychopathy acts that hold for all states enacting such laws, when they held that "the statutes provide for care, treatment, segregation and rehabilitation of sexual psychopaths . . . the objectives are remedial, therapeutic and preventive and seek to protect society . . . within the framework of a special statutory method which is civil rather than criminal . . . ." The place of confinement of one adjudged to be a sexual psychopath is necessarily a hospital, not a prison or jail. The superintendent of such an institution has the duty of reporting to the judge whether rehabilitation is possible and completed. If not, the patient is returned to court for further criminal action.

Legal objections to the sexual psychopathy laws on behalf of the person so designated have been numerous: e.g., denial of due process; question of constitutionality; validity of the state's police powers; the fact that "one member of a medical staff" can release a patient or block it; discriminatory because it "carves a class out of a class"; double jeopardy; conflict with the provision against self-incrimination. Some of the objections are frivolous, and some valid. An example of the frivolous is an Illinois case[32] in which a man indicted for taking indecent liberties with a female child appealed on the grounds that two psychiatrists who diagnosed him a sexual psychopath had given their signed reports to the jury. The Appellate Court ruled that "although it was not proper procedure," a reversal "with such report not being taken by the jury" would have produced no difference in the verdict. One valid objection to the statutes often noted is that time spent in a hospital until the individual is either cured or no longer a menace can be much longer than a determinate sentence for the alleged crime in a prison. Appeals courts have answered these objectives in the negative, based mainly on the need to maintain public safety through segregation of dangerous sex offenders.

The legal status of the indeterminate sentence for sexual psychopaths was tested in *Specht v. Patterson* (1966), a Colorado case in which the accused was sentenced for "one day to life." Both the District Court and the Supreme Court of Colorado approved the legislative act mandating an indeterminate sentence for one who "threaten[ed] bodily harm or [was] a habitual offender." The defendant petitioned the U.S. Supreme Court[33] because there had been no hearing on the fact of sexual psychopathy beyond a psychiatric report. Justice Douglas ruled that the defendant was not afforded the "safety of due process" at trial since the defendant was deprived of the "right to be heard, to confront witnesses, the right of cross examination and to offer evidence on his own . . . ." Quoting a Pennsylvania statute, Justice Douglas said: "due process cannot be satisfied by partial or niggardly procedural protection."

Based on *Specht*, the New York Court of Appeals remitted for resentencing a man whose psychiatric report "merely states that the defendant has a sociopathic personality without a favorable prognosis . . . [or] any discussion of the defendant's sexual problems . . . ." In

People v. Bailey (1968),[34] the defendant had been given an indeterminate "one-day-to-life" sentence for various sex offenses under New York Penal Law 2189a. In remanding for resentencing, the Court of Appeals remarked that

the most basic concepts of justice and fairness require that the defendant be given an opportunity to participate in a fact-finding process which could result in his imprisonment for life. . . .

The psychiatric report is inadequate if it does not state the risk to society involved in the defendant's immediate release with or without treatment and defendant's potential for responding to treatment.

Treatment of the Sexual Psychopath

The indeterminate sentence principle is aimed at facilitating treatment and rehabilitation. The New York, like the Colorado, statute and the statutes of other states emphasized the treatability of the sexual psychopath. Segregation of the sexual psychopath from society, the first aim of the statute, was easily accomplished; treatment and rehabilitation were more difficult. Early attempts utilizing psychoanalytically oriented therapy to realize these desiderata were sporadic. Foxe reported treatment of a sodomist in a New York penitentiary in the 1930s.[35] Robert Lindner, in his widely read book *Rebel Without A Cause*,[36] described hypoanalysis of a psychopath in a federal penitentiary. Dr. Ben Karpman, who spent a lifetime at St. Elizabeth's Hospital, Washington, D.C., studying sociopaths and sexual deviates, described the results of his work in a volume which provided little therapeutic information but much description of sexual deviancy. The present author initiated intensive psychotherapy on a few probationers, including pedophiles, at the Court of General Sessions in New York during the late 1930s, an outpatient activity continued during the 1940s by Dr. Ralph Banay and Dr. Melitta Schmiedenberg in Kings and New York counties. These scattered reports of treated cases indicated only meager success. The type of sexual offender available for outpatient treatment was chiefly minor offenders—exhibitionists, homosexuals, and some pedophiles—since dangerous sexual psychopaths were usually incarcerated.

A direct therapeutic attack on sexual psychopaths was initiated by the California Department of Mental Health in 1950 at Mendocino State Hospital, a designated institution for offenders committed under California's statute. Since individual psychotherapy was impractical, group therapy was undertaken on seventy-five certified sexual psychopaths[37] whose offenses varied from incest to lewd and lascivious conduct from various jurisdictions in the state. The main emphasis was on psychodrama and milieu therapy with tacit understanding that society and the community, as well as the therapists involved, were aware of the existence of conscious and unconscious bias against sexual deviation. The atmosphere was as free as possible within confines of the institution; authoritarianism was played down. Acting-out was encouraged in an atmosphere of socially acceptable play (during psychodrama), demonstrating other-than-conscious motives without the use of complex interpretations, in "a way no patient could avoid." Freeing the patient from the tremendous sense of guilt under which all sex offenders of normal intelligence labor was a recognized prerequisite for any intensive therapy.

As a consequence of this new approach, increasing socialization of patients with reduction of guilt feelings occurred, and a strong reaction against any treatment for sexual psychopaths simultaneously developed within and outside the hospital. Public feelings exerted pressure through administrative channels to discontinue the program. The point of very briefly outlining this attempt to treat the sexual psychopath by other than punitive methods by the present author and associates is to show the importance that social feelings play in the total universe of sexual deviation.

Group therapy as a method of thawing out the psychopath to prepare him for insight development and to acquaint him with emotional factors in the background of his deviation was continued, after several years, in the Atascadero State Hospital, California, then designated as a hospital for the criminally insane. Dr. Karl Bowman reported (1956) 7.4 percent recidivism from this institution after one year of "treatment."[38] Survey from a similar program in a Colorado institution gave the same recidivism result; namely, 7 percent of discharge patient-deviates were returned. The generally encouraging results, or at least the less fearful attitudes of the public towards deviates, helped the California legislature to soften the term *sexual psychopath* to "mentally disordered sex offender" in the Code.[39] This change in accent from relative indifference to hopelessness to a cautious optimism in the treatment of homosexuals and other deviates was reflected in a comment (1963) by the then director of the California State Department of Mental Hygiene: "[Since] 1939, when the original sex psychopath law was enacted . . . we have gained considerable experience which indicates that certain individuals are helped by hospital treatment and others are not."[40]

Other methods of therapy were employed besides traditional psychotherapies;[41] behavior modification, organic (castration and endocrine) methods, aversion treatment, and neurosurgery, including lobotomy and freezing or injection of the hypothalamus and amygdala, were all attempted. The results were indifferent, although changes in homosexual orientation have been reported through behavior modification and avoidance therapy.[42] Considerable interest during the 1970s was elicited in this area, but the difficulties—lack of criminal validity of sexual psychopathy statutes, ambivalence of the public regarding sexual deviance, prediction problems among sexual criminals, inadequate followup, and factors of informed consent to treatment— were formidable. Many have urged that sexual psychopathy laws be repealed. Among others, Thomas Szasz claims the designation of sexual psychopath as "medically sick" is a political, not medical, one,[43] and Slovenko has dubbed the program at the Atascadero State Hospital (California), which admits indicted sexual psychopaths from the courts, a "fraud and a hoax."[44] Criticism, both legal and psychiatric, has been widespread. In a recent white paper by the Group for Advancement of Psychiatry (April 1977), the conclusion reached by the Committee on Law and Psychiatry, after a detailed study of the situation, called for repeal of sexual psychopathy statutes as a "beginning step toward justice . . . [and that] . . . the term 'sex psychopath,' which is devoid of psychiatric meaning, should cease being used."

In spite of considerable disenchantment with sexual psychopathy laws and the possibilities of successful treatment, the need for their consideration remains undiminished. Many cases are counseled in outpatient clinics and therapists' offices if on probation and are treated in group therapy sessions in institutions. In the main, the results in terms of insight and a reintegration of psychosexuality within the patient's ego are only modestly successful. Still, the statutes remain in the codes of many states, and psychiatrists are called to determine the presence or absence of sexual psychopathy as defined.

Legal Criteria

The statutory requirement for a finding of sexual psychopathy in many states closely matches that of California.

Section 5500: Mentally disordered sex offender means any person who by reason of mental defect, disease, or disorder, is predisposed to the commission of sexual offenses to such a degree that he is dangerous to the health and safety of others. Whenever the term "sexual psychopath" is used in any code, such term shall be construed to render to and mean a "mentally disordered sex offender."[45]

The final draft of the American Law Institute Model Penal Code covering sexual offenses[46] has simplified definitions of sexual crime. The proposed code classifies the crimes as:

Section 213.1 *Rape*, intercourse by a male with a female "not his wife": (use of force, threat or kidnapping, use of drugs or intoxicants to prevent resistance; female under 10 years; unconsciousness of victim; includes sexual intercourse per os or per anum).

  Gross Sexual Imposition: (threat to prevent resistance "by a woman of ordinary resolution"; mental disease or defect in the victim; false supposition that offender is her husband).

Section 213.2 *Deviate Sexual Intercourse*, refers to a person engaging in such acts with another: (use of force, threat or kidnapping; use of drugs or intoxicants; person less than 10 years old; victim is unconscious; includes intercourse per os or anum; includes intercourse with an animal).

  By Other Imposition: (engages or forces another to engage in intercourse if threat used; mental disease or defect in victim; if victim unaware of sexual act being committed).

Section 213.3 *Corruption of Minors and Seduction*, (refers to both persons as in 213.1 and 213.2; victim is less than 16 years of age or actor 4 years older than victim; actor is guardian or responsible for welfare; if victim is in custody of the law or in a hospital; promise of marriage not meant to be fulfilled).

Section 213.4 *Sexual Assault*, (refers to a person who subjects another, not his spouse to such acts; sexual contact is any touching of sexual or intimate parts of the person . . . [to] arouse or gratify sexual desire of either party . . . [or] sexual contact offensive to the other person).

Section 213.5 *Indecent Exposure*, (refers to a person other than spouse; for purposes of arousing or gratifying sexual desire in himself or others, exposure of the genitals "under circumstances . . . conduct is unlikely to cause affront or alarm").

There have been other attempts to redefine two vital aspects of sex crime legislation, namely, dangerousness and the right to privacy, especially consensual acts among homosexuals. The issue of whether an adjudged sexual psychopath is a danger to the health and safety of others is crucial to his admission to a hospital and to his release. Robert Sadoff, writing from Pennsylvania, suggests viewing such individuals as belonging to two classes: (1) aggressive sexual deviates—rape, lust murder, sadomasochism, necrophilia, sodomy, pedophilia, and (2) anonymous deviates—exhibitionism and voyeurism, frottage, obscene calls, and letters and fetishism.[47] Such a classification would accentuate the primary legal problem, namely, dangerousness.

The prediction of dangerousness among all criminals, particularly sexual offenders, is admittedly difficult, if not impossible. The Group for Advancement of Psychiatry, Committee on Psychiatry and the Law, after reviewing the evidence of the sexual psychopath's future behavior, made the flat statement: "Predictions about sexual danger-ousness are unreliable." Another psychiatric commentator, Dr. Daniel Jacobs, points to the nub of the problem in saying: "(The) absence of any clear written criteria for psychiatric evaluation . . . leaves the examining physician with only the broadest concept of what is expected of him."[48] Dr. Jacobs made the further valid comment that few examiners are free from a subtle bias against deviation and that bias inevitably enters into their final evaluation.

Formal proceedings in sexual psychopathy statutes in the several jurisdictions follow certain fixed principles, although details may vary in the different states.[49] The basic principles—protection of society by segregation of the sexual psychopath; treatment of and rehabilitation of the subject; civil nature of the proceedings; a sexual offense charge, without any criminal charge or display of sexual deviation; a jury trial or hearing before a judge; examination and certification by two or three psychiatrists or physicians; right of appeal and review; discharge from confinement when "no longer a menace" or recovered; return to court for sentence—hold for most states. The California statute[50] reflects the major steps in certification of the sexual psychopath. The procedures in the Welfare and Institutions Code of that state illustrate the application of such laws. Under the old law, now superseded but only moderately changed, a person can be examined for sexual psychopathy, i.e., mentally disordered sex offender,

When a person is convicted of a sex offense involving a child under 14 years of age and it is a misdemeanor, and the person has been previously convicted of a sex offense in this or any other state,
or,
When a person is convicted of a sex offense involving a child under 14 years of age and it is a felony,
or,
When a person is convicted of any sex offense, the trial judge on his own motion, or on the motion of the prosecuting attorney, or on application by affidavit by or on behalf of the defendant, if it appears to the satisfaction of the court that there is probable cause for believing such a person is a mentally disordered sex offender within the meaning of this chapter may adjourn the proceedings or suspend the sentence, as the case may be, and shall certify the person for hearing and examination by the superior court of the county to determine whether the person is a mentally disordered sex offender within the meaning of this article.

The procedure for such determination as amended by Section 6307 (1976) is as follows:

The judge shall appoint not less than two nor more than three psychiatrists or certified clinical psychologists, each of whom shall be a holder of a valid and unrevoked physician's and surgeon's certificate, each of whom has directed his professional practice primarily to the diagnosis and treatment of mental and nervous disorders for a period of not less than five years, to make a personal examination of the alleged mentally disordered sex offender, directed toward ascertaining whether the person is a mentally disordered sex offender.

(6308, 1976) Each psychiatrist or psychologist so appointed shall file with the court a separate written report of the result of his examination, together with his conclusions and recommendations and his opinion as to whether or not the person would benefit by care and treatment in a hospital. At the hearing each psychiatrist or psychologist shall hear the testimony of all witnesses, and shall testify as to the result of his examination, and to any other pertinent facts within his knowledge, unless the person upon advice of counsel waives the presence of the psychiatrist or psychologist and it is stipulated that their respective reports be received in evidence.

One new step in the amended (1976) section states: "If the proposed commitment is contested by either the defendant or the People, one of the psychiatrists or psychologists so appointed may be designated by the defendant and one by the People."

The procedure for commitment for an indeterminate period has been superseded by Section 6316. It states that if the mentally disordered sex offender can benefit by treatment, he may be ordered to a state hospital, county mental health facility, or private mental health facility, or the court has the discretion of returning the subject to court for "suitable disposition" of the crime. Should the report state that the subject "will not benefit by care or treatment in a state hospital or other facility," he may be returned to court for further action. A significant change in the matter of disposition or commitment to a state hospital was the removal of authority to commit an offender for "an indeterminate period." For those mentally disordered sex offenders who commit a felony after July 1, 1977, the term of commitment means the "longest term of imprisonment which could have been imposed including the upper term of the base offense. . . ."

Conflicts in Managing the Sexual Offender

The finding of a mentally disordered sex offender as a civil action presents certain practical legal difficulties. For example, in a Florida case, *Huckaby v. State* (1977),[51] a defendant was convicted of forceful rape on his eleven-year-old daughter with a sentence of execution. Huckaby had continued sexual relations with three daughters for a period of fourteen years until it came to light during a divorce proceeding. Testimony during the trial established that he exposed his family to a "nightmarish life of brutality, fear and sexual assaults . . . for twenty years." The defendant appealed from the trial court conviction on grounds that he had not been given a hearing under the Mentally Disordered Sex Offender Act (Chapter 917, Florida Code) and that "kinship in criminal incest . . . bars criminal prosceution under rape." Psychiatric testimony indicated that he was a "schizoid personality" and that he had been diagnosed previously as schizophrenic or possible organic brain syndrome in a state hospital. On appeal, the Supreme Court of Florida, considering the mental aspect of the case as mitigating circumstances ("The heinous and atrocious manner in which this crime was perpetrated . . . was the direct consequences of his mental illness"), vacated the sentence of death but affirmed life imprisonment. The court held that the trial judge "abused his discretion in refusing to schedule a hearing under Florida Code," i.e., the Mentally Disordered Sex Offender Act which provided that treatment be given the offender so designated.

Agreement of psychiatric findings in a given subject with the requirements of the mentally disordered sex offender law is often incomplete. When psychiatric unanimity is lacking, the final decision falls back on legal criteria. *People v. Burnick* (California, 1975)[52] provided an instance of such a disagreement. In this case of child molesting, the testimony of three psychiatrists before a trial court differed: Dr. Davis testified to the defendant's dangerousness to the health and safety of minors as a pedophile; Dr. Coburn diagnosed the defendant as neither a pedophile nor a homosexual, but rather an immature and depressed individual, not dangerous to others; and Dr. Tweed testified that the offender was not a pedophile, of immature personality makeup, and not dangerous. Since the standard of proof had been "a preponderance of evidence"[53] and the psychiatrists were two to one against designating the defendant as a mentally disordered sex offender, the state appealed the case to the California Supreme Court. Justice Mosk, delivering a majority opinion, decided that the "accused" must have the full panoply of protection of due process (Fourteenth Amendment) which requires "proof beyond a reasonable doubt." This change to "beyond a reasonable doubt" would in the future alter the weight given psychiatric testimony. Thus, Justice Burke in his dissenting opinion in *Burnick* commented: "It is no longer hearsay to question the reliability of psychiatric predictions."

Psychological analysis of a defendant does not easily mesh with legal standards, even in the hands of honest, competent psychiatrists. The problem is bringing psychological observations into line with legal requirements of "dangerousness to others" and of "potential benefit from treatment." As Judge Ploscowe, writing in 1960, pointed out: "Few branches of the law have shown such a wide divergence between actual human behavior and stated legal norms. Sexuality simply cannot be realistically confined within present legal bounds."[54] The variety of human sexual responses, the ebb and flow of social morality, and changes in accepted values necessarily alter psychiatric opinion. The psychiatric goal of understanding the place of the sexual impulse in the ego configuration of the defendant must find an accommodation to social norms and legal rules; sexual misbehavior and psychopathology must be fused in the psychiatrist's thinking. He or she must be able to sift through the denials and conflicting stories of complainant and defendant, to differentiate between aggressive or purely sexual impulses, and to unravel the ego-value to the offender of each. It would be helpful then to review the psychopathology of sexual deviance as the psychiatrist sees it.

Clinical Profiles of the Deviate: Statutory Rape

Unlawful sexual intercourse with a female under the age of eighteen years (California)[55] or seventeen years (New York),[56] who is not the wife of the perpetrator, is called statutory rape. Since the sexual impulse is heterosexual, no issue of deviancy arises, and the main problems relate to the age of consent of the "victim" and the possibility of mental defect vitiating her capacity to give consent. The precise definition of mental defect is not set down in the statutes: in the New York Code, it is defined as "mentally defective or mentally incapacitated or physically helpless";[57] in the California Code, it is defined as "incapable of giving legal consent through lunacy or other unsoundness of mind."[58] Statutory rape often occurs as a partially compliant act on the part of the complainant.

D.T., a 29 year old coach and teacher in a high school was accused by two of his students, aged 14, of furnishing them marijuana and having sexual intercourse with one of them on several occasions at his apartment. There was no accusation of force used except the implication on the part of the complainant that the defendant's seduction was the compelling factor.

Study of the defendant showed him to have been a successful coach, known as a "mod" or "in" person, "swinger" with a weird sense of humor according to his contemporaries but a good teacher. He had been admonished by the administrator for being "too free with girls in his class" but had no previous charges. His history was given freely, his answers responsive to sexual questions, his sexual life being heterosexual, with several engagements and affairs but no marriages. As a well-developed, athletic person he gave the impression of libertinism without any deviate indications.

The complaining witness and her girl friends were studied through their mutual correspondence and a full report of the police interrogation. The quotes and actions, on the part of the complaining witness, indicated that this girl had good sexual knowledge, based on some actual experience, that her statements about the defendant developed out of a wish to have relations and also humiliate him. Her statements demonstrated an adolescent, immature air about them. Undoubtedly D.T. and the complaining witness talked about sexual matters rather freely as he did with others.

The correspondence between the two girls (examination of the victim was not permitted) showed their sexual sophistication, their rivalry as to sexual attractiveness, represented a mixture of experience, wishes and fantasies of a sexual nature.

It was reported to the defense attorney that the sexual intercourse between the defendant and victim may have been aided by the defendant's general jocosity and euphoria and the complainant's submission to the seduction.

An examination at the penal institution confirmed the primary opinion that he was not a sexual psychopath. The defendant was placed on probation by the judge.

Forceful Rape

Unlawful sexual intercourse accompanied by threats or actual infliction of bodily injury or any form of forcible compulsion constitutes forceful rape. It is acknowledged by many that the sadistic, destructive impulse overwhelms the sexual stimulus in forceful rape. The aggression can occur before or after the rape; use of a knife or a gun, actual beating, or painful manipulation of the victim's genitalia is not uncommon. Dr. John Macdonald, who devoted a whole volume to the subject of rape (1971),[59] reminds his readers of the viciousness of some gang rapes by adolescent groups. He comments on the "overt disdain for girls, combined with homosexual overtones: among adolescent group rapists," a finding I myself also encountered and named the despoiler syndrome.[60] It rests upon an unconscious envy of the female, expressed by an urge to destroy or despoil feminine beauty and refinement. Intolerance of feminine aesthetic appeal receives reinforced vigor from sadistic feelings joining the uprush of sexual excitement. The *despoiler reaction* or *overt disdain*, as Macdonald identifies it, is especially evident in rape murders and lust murders. As an exercise in domination, it is present in all forceful rapists who betray their defensive need to belittle the sexual object. What appears to be an insatiable sexual appetite (satyriasis) proves to be a cover for unperceived hostile impulses. The sexual behavior of young Horner, charged with forcible rape and assault with intent to murder, illustrates these points.

After a boyhood punctuated by juvenile offenses of various types, Horner, when he was sixteen, married a girl of fourteen. From this time on, his life was oriented around sexual relations—with his wife, girl friends, prostitutes, and pickups. There was no doubt that the loose organization of his family—his father and brother had both been involved in cases of incest—formed a background wherein sexual license had attained a fixed social value; he could not be content with fewer sexual contacts than several a day. Often he would meet women in bars who were willing to have sexual relations with him, but what he yearned for was an aggressive mastery of the women. When Horner determined to have intercourse he carried a knife with which to threaten his sexual partner, sometimes assaulting her by punching her with his fists. Once sexually stimulated, he could not rest until satisfaction was obtained through injury to his victim.

In the case for which he was examined,[61] Horner had picked up a partner in a barroom. They arranged a tryst. While preparing for intercourse, the accused's excitement increased; the young woman became frightened and resisted. Horner produced a knife and proceeded with the sexual act. As resistance increased on the woman's part, he slashed her throat with the knife.

A conviction of felonious assault and attempt to commit murder was upheld.

The Homosexual Offender

The life pattern of practicing homosexuals does not generally lead to criminal offenses. The professed "gay" person lives in an esoteric environment of his own making, with a partner and friends of his own choice, without coming into conflict with the law. Should he leave his group and associate with youths for sexual purposes, he may then be arrested and charged if the sexual objects are under the age of consent. There is a complicating factor to be considered in charges made by a youth against an adult homosexual, namely, that the easy compliance of a well-developed boy of fourteen to sixteen to the requests of the gay person may foreshadow a latent homosexuality which frightens the youth to the point of complaining to authorities. An adult homosexual may then be indicted after an association that gave every appearance of being a consensual homosexual affair.

Guy D., a tall, well-developed boy of 16 accused his uncle who shared a room with him in a family of eight children, a disabled father and a vigorous mother intent on developing her career in social work. The sexual acts between the uncle, a man in his 40's, and the complainant covered a period of nine months.

The sexual acts started with mutual masturbation, progressed then to anal intercourse, and oral copulation. Guy professes no experience with masturbation prior to this and did not know of sodomy. He states he objected to the latter practice but submitted because of the money involved and the general feeling that they were "friends." The defendant apparently expressed his love for the complainant and the complainant felt a lesser degree of this feeling. "Love notes" were exchanged; their association included going out until early morning hours, driving around and indulging in sexual play. The relation was explained to him "like marriage" and Guy accepted this explanation with moderate remonstrances, and a continuing supply of money.

The notes indicated sexual interest on both sides: "Wake me up or I will cut your nuts out and make you eat them, Guy." "I don't like to see you sick . . . but that way I can tell you how much I love you because I love you so much it is pitafal [sic] . . . I love you the same you Love me But I Don't show it like you and I dont want a girl or someone younger I just want you and only you and I will try anay [sic] way to keep you. Do you want to [picture of penis with pubic hair] [picture of penis with a drop-crude drawing], Guy D."

Investigation of the complainant's activities revealed definite autoerotic tendencies compatible with homosexual tendencies. For example, the subject stated he placed marbles in his rectum on several occasions just to see "how it would feel." He also placed marbles in his mouth and on one occasion swallowed a penny purposely to "see if I could do it." He used other objects in both rectum and mouth, i.e., a toothbrush, his fingers, and an enema with peroxide to "open me up." He claimed these activities were his own idea.

On re-examination with the new information, Guy's attitude changed from that of a professedly naive boy to one of sophistication. The notes exchanged between the defendant and Guy, written with spelling and syntax of a child, did not represent his true mental potential. On psychological tests, particularly the Rorschach test, he demonstrated significant homosexual interests. The material indicated regression to pre-genital stimulation (anal penetration and urethral introduction of foreign objects) with full awareness of homosexual acts.

The report to the defense attorney pointed to definite deviate tendencies on the part of the complainant, with evidences of a passive approach to men, under which hid strong aggressive features. His manipulations made seduction by an older man plausible and ordinary male friendships could be interpreted as homosexual advances.

In this connection, examination of the alleged victim may, as in the case described, shed light on the sexual relationship reported. Bender and Blau, in an early study of female and male child victims of homosexual and heterosexual "attacks,"[62] remark that "these children undoubtedly do not deserve the cloak of innocence with which they have been endowed by moralists, social reformers and legislators." In recent years, psychiatric and psychologic examination of a child victim has been requested as the right of the accused to discovery.[63] While generally this "right of a defendant to pretrial inspection of the prosecutor's evidence . . . rests with the trial court's discretion," some courts have rejected this "inherent power." They agree that such power is to be exercised only "in the absence of substantial corroborative evidence of the crime." In view of present-day permissiveness of sexual relations, experienced psychiatrists have often requested an opportunity to examine the victim of both rape and homosexual crimes, while the courts have as often refused on several bases, one being that the "credibility of witnesses and the weight of their testimony are questions for the jury."[64]

The bisexual who may have given up life as a gay under pressure from society or his spouse occasionally reverts to a "fling" with any available male under alcoholic influence or in a period of stress or anxiety. Karpman found that the rationalization offered for these falls from grace was that they provided the act greater potency and stronger gratification.[65] Another rationalization is the bisexuals' complaint of their spouses' lack of passion, but Karpman more correctly states the case in his aphorism: "every bi-sexual carries in his psyche a pervasive inner need for homosexual indulgence." Similarly, unmarried men, or those without heterosexual experience until their middle years, find reasons in a busy life for lack of sexual expression. Sometimes a revered social role such as that of a clergyman or dedicated teacher may serve to cover repressed homosexual leanings. These individuals may find their interest in helping people or in engaging in altruistic enterprises suddenly shattered by newly discovered homosexual yearnings. Such persons do not recognize themselves as latent homosexuals, shunning both male and female close associations to vent their deviate impulses among children. They thus become one type of pedophile, a group that occupies a large segment of criminal sexuality.

The Pedophile and His Crimes

The term *pedophile* is more precisely a psychiatric descriptive designation than a legal one. Pedophiles brought before the court may have indulged in homosexual acts with boys, attempted intercourse with female children, exposed their genitals to children, or fondled, palpated, or performed masturbatory acts or any form of erotic activity with a child. The legal offenses covering pedophilic behavior are designated "sodomy," "carnally abusing a minor," "impairing the morals of a minor," "lewd and lascivious conduct," and so on, depending on the statutes of a particular jurisdiction.

The large number of pedophiles who pass through the courts may be separated into broad groups in relation to the underlying pathology of the offender, as offenders motivated by (1) pansexual drives, i.e., excessive sexual impulses gratified by any sex object, (2) sexual neurosis and psychopathy, or (3) organic brain disease (senile psychosis, cerebral arteriosclerosis, mental deficiency) or functional mental illness (e.g., schizophrenia).

The usual profile of the pedophile is of a social failure, a lonely middle-aged man afflicted with anxiety concerning his sexual potency.

A large number give histories of impotence or partial impotence. It is evident that the pedophile's inferiority feelings lead him to search for younger and less formidable love objects, whose ignorance would prevent his deficiencies from becoming obvious. The child sexual object, replacing the unattainable adult female, saves the offender's ego from psychic traumata that might prove destructive to his mental equilibrium.

The mainspring of this sex drive proves on analysis to be the wish to be a child again, a regression to an earlier period when the sexual instinct was expressed in partial impulses of playing, seeing, smelling, touching, and so on. Disappointment with the spouse for one reason or another stimulates infantile yearnings. What appeared to be satisfactory in the tedium of marriage now appears in its true light. The yearning for ineffable satisfaction passes beyond the wife to the loving, permissive mother of old who, in retrospect, seemed to have allowed the boy-child full play for his sexual fantasies. Thus, when the spouse passes her sexual prime or loses interest in her husband, his infantile needs reassert themselves. This regression to an infantile psychosexual position occurs silently; the pedophile knows only that he has become aware that gratification of the wished-for kind is possible only with the child love-object. To the older pedophile, the switch in sexual object seems natural and unremarkable.

Hence, the older pedophile openly describes the stimulation offered by children as the cause of his offensive behavior; he often justifies his acts as a privilege that age confers.

The claim made by older pedophiles that the children they offend against are, under cover of innocence, unduly enticing has been the subject of studies in recent years. The analysis of the criminal-victim relation, first intensively studied by Von Hentig,[66] postulated that the potential victim often attracts his or her attacker out of a "mutuality" existing between them. On one hand, this mutuality can be recognized as an unconscious seduction on the part of the victim, and on the other, as a reading of this trend that coincides with the pedophile's desires. The psychologic situation between offender and victim in incest cases has a similar background.

In recent years, the accepted description of the pedophile as a middle-aged, inferior-feeling social isolate has altered in favor of younger, vigorous, but neurotic younger men. The following case is an example of the pedophile with a latent homosexual trend, eventuating in child molesting:

Father K., an Episcopal priest of 43, was arrested for molesting several minors in and around his swimming pool at his home. A graduate of a representative university, an officer in the U.S. Air Force with a good record, graduate of a seminary, K. was an attractive, vivid and open personality, well liked by his parishioners and effective in his ministry. He claimed his sexual life was nil, being absorbed in his work; although his church sanctioned marriage, he never married, had two "broken" engagements and no real friendships with women.

The charges, substantiated by neighbors and the child victims aged eight through eleven, relate to his freedom in swimming nude with the children in his pool, kissing and mutually masturbating the boys and palpating them with evident sexual excitement. Charges of oral copulation at first denied were later tacitly admitted. Police investigators found pornographic literature in his study, particularly a privately printed collection of nude figures of boys.

K's reaction to the charges led to a depression, accentuated by an ecclesiastical court hearing by his superiors and a recommendation that he resign from the church. Under psychotherapy the accused regained some of his ebullience, uncovering a narcissistic, moderately exhibitionistic personality; one who made a deliberate effort to "look good." Projective testing by a psychologist confirmed these findings; the tests showed sexual identity conflicts, strong achievement strivings without capacity for sustained effort.

Contact with the accused made clear the neurotic drives behind his vocation as a minister. Not diagnosed as a Sex Psychopath (Mentally Disordered Sex Offender), it was recommended to the court that the accused quit the ministry and find his own level in commerce. He was placed on probation.[67]

Sexual Neurosis Versus Sexual Psychopathy

The younger group of men charged with molesting minors presents the picture of sexually competent persons, often embroiled in custody fights tinctured by strongly aggressive feelings against the ex-wife. Their sexual preferences are not necessarily homosexual but are plainly in response to the struggle for power (and custody of children) between the accused and the mother of the children. It is a common finding that the wife or ex-wife has been apprised of the subject's deviate activity for some time before a charge is brought. This delay in bringing up a charge can be dictated by an unconscious desire to placate the accused because of some vaguely perceived disinterest in women, or by a strategy to let the man flounder in his deviancy, to his eventual discomfort and her enjoyment at his discomfort. The law rarely looks beyond the acts of the defendant into the neurotic tangle of the adult couple in such cases; the chief concern of the courts is the presence or absence of sexual psychopathy. The case presented here illustrates a neurotic pedophilia.

S.S., a tall, vigorous, successful business man of 36 was charged with Violation of Penal Code Section 288, described as oral copulation and an "infamous crime against nature" on his daughter and son, ages 16 and 14 respectively. His denial of the offenses was covered by a recital of a stormy marriage to the mother of the children, followed by divorce. The accused described the woman as a "hateful bitch," vindictive, sexually cold. On re-marriage, he characterized his present wife as an ideal partner and woman, his marriage as "excellent." The charges arose from contact with the children during visits afforded by the divorce agreement.

The background of S.S. indicated several areas of stress. His father was described as an extremely aggressive man, born in Russia with no insight or sympathy for his son. The defendant left home at an early age and made his way, including service in the Air Force, from the age of 14. His attitude towards his father, whom he plans never to see again, was brusque, obscene and bitter. Clearly of high average or superior intelligence, the defendant claimed his entire life had been given a "sour taste" because of early experiences at home; a " vicious father" and "mousy" mother.

During the interviews, his language was brusque, he had nothing but a most aggressive and disdainful attitude toward his first wife. He had not been close to his children either. He imputed all his trouble to his first wife, saying that she went beyond that of acts of an outraged wife, namely burning his Internal Revenue Service records, and then turning him into the Internal Revenue.

From the standpoint of his sexual life, he claims that he never was particularly strong sexually, although he had affairs starting at the age of 15, with a girl, then intermittent contacts with girls during his first marriage, at which time he felt definitely rejected sexually by his wife. Since he has been re-married he has no complaints whatsoever and never had any interest in other women. He denied any interest in perversions except those variations now credited with normal intercourse.

The examinations of S.S. concluded with a diagnosis of sexual neurosis based on a simultaneous identification with his father and a repudiation thereof and of all male figures. Not enough evidence of persistent deviate behavior or imminent threat to others was present to classify the defendant as a mentally disordered sex offender.

Examinations by two other psychiatrists resulted in a different diagnosis from that offered above. Both felt the accused was a mentally disordered sex offender within the meaning of the law, although one of the examiners commented that the sexual activities "have only involved his children." This examiner also advised against sending the defendant to a state hospital, suggesting counseling on an outpatient basis. He further suggested that the mother of the children be investigated because "One is concerned that she allowed herself to use what had happened more in vindictiveness than for the childrens' benefit."

Some students of the subject feel that sexual crimes cannot always be neatly classified as homosexuality, exhibitionism, voyeurism, pedophilia, and so on. Offenders often cross lines. Slovenko, in an article entitled "Everything You Wanted to Have in Sex Laws,[68] asks: "There are many laws on sex. . . . To what extent are these laws necessary?"

Why, he asks, cannot "non-sex laws" covering aggression be used for forcible rape, sexual psychopathy, or indecent behavior towards minors? Slovenko makes the valid point that many crimes denoted sexual are in truth assaults or nuisance behavior (i.e., voyeurism). Whatever the dynamics in a rapist or pedophile may prove to be, the law has the duty of protecting the public from danger or indecency. The psychiatrist with a dedication to clinical discipline may discern neurotic regressions in sex offenders (pregenital impulses that demand gratification) that do not have a fixed "propensity" towards sexual deviation. This difference in psychiatric attitudes toward sexual offenses is presented in the following murder case which, though not strictly applicable to sex crimes, does shed light on a real medico-legal dilemma. The dilemma is the conflict between dynamic interpretation of human behavior and the law's insistence on free will in criminal acts (see judges' opinions below).

The defense attorney in a New Jersey murder case employed a psychoanalytically trained psychiatrist, Dr. Willard Gaylin, to testify on the dynamics of the defendant.[69] His testimony in essence was that the defendant "was a passive-dependent type with aggressive features ... [who] ... under stress ... in a life situation where he was unable to cope ... had distorted his personality mechanism to the point ... that he acted in a semi-automatic way" at the time of the crime. The trial court admitted the testimony only for the purpose of fixing the punishment, adding: "the evidence [by the psychiatrist] ... was unreliable or too speculative or incompetent when tested by concepts in the law...." On appeal before the New Jersey Supreme Court, Justice Francis recalled Dr. Gaylin to court. Dr. Gaylin repeated his testimony and in a lucid exposition was permitted to conclude that "[this] man is a helpless victim of his genes, life environment ... that unconscious forces dictate his behavior." The court answered the appeal by stating: "if the law were to accept such a medical doctrine ... the legal doctrine of *mens rea* would all but disappear from the law." More central to the issue under discussion was Justice Weintraub's remarks in his concurring opinion, namely: "Dr. Gaylin's view seems quite scientific. It rests upon an elementary concept of cause and effect ... a dead-end approach to the mystery of our being. ... Dr. Gaylin wisely leaves that subject to the philosopher...."

Applying this view to the sexual offender problem bypasses dynamic concepts, the whole concept of polymorphous perverse instincts, evident in the variegated expression of the human sexual impulse. This is not to say that the courts are blind to the presence of sexual deviation;

indeed, the sexual psychopathy laws represent an infelicitous attempt to separate out that compulsive sexual behavior which constitutes a danger to society from those behaviors that constitute a nuisance at best and an aesthetic affront at worst. The crux of this dilemma is seen in the certification of an offender as a sexual psychopath where the offender's behavior was clearly of neurotic nature. The case was that of a nineteen-year-old, charged with prowling, peeping, illegal entry of a house, and rape.[70]

There had been several complaints of a prowler who peeped into windows of a given neighborhood over a period of six months. He had been observed leaving the back door of a home by two passerbys and was readily apprehended.

The offender readily related that he had an "uncontrollable urge" to prowl at night. He agreed with the complainants that he had climbed into a room of one home to obtain a better view; that he entered another home through a bedroom window; and that he had been observed standing on a box under a window in yet another home. On one occasion, he seized a woman who had walked out of her house to a washhouse a few feet away, placing his hand over her mouth, told her not to scream and keeping her face turned away from him at all times.

According to the police report, the victim, a Mrs. D., stated that the subject talked to her for approximately thirty minutes and during this time he related that he had known her before. She asked him what brought all of this on and he related, "Oh, a smile or two." Shortly thereafter the subject told her to get down on the grass on her hands and knees, next to the washhouse, under the light. The subject got down behind her and performed an act of sexual intercourse with her. During the act, the subject asked her if it pleased her or if she was enjoying it, to which she replied that it, "Is not very good, is it?" The accused was apparently disappointed at this. They both then stood up and the subject continued to keep her facing away from him, apologizing for what had happened. She told the subject that he ought to get a girl to go with him and he would not have to do something of this nature and he stated that he "Liked older women like her." Mrs. D. related that the subject did not harm her and had been very gentle. She had thought it was much better to submit to the subject rather than have him hurt her or her children.

Prior to examinations of the accused by the present author, two psychiatrists had certified the accused as a mentally disordered sex offender and had recommended hospitalization for observation and treatment. One examiner commented on his "impulsiveness and immaturity," and the other, on his "inadequate personality and underlying mental disturbances of a serious nature." A third psychiatrist, called at the insistence of the defense attorney who did not agree with the sexual psychopath classification, felt the certification in accordance with the code was "moot." This examiner considered the stresses assailing the defendant—a brother killed in Vietnam and his wife on the verge of bearing his first child—to cause a regression into "infantile voyeuristic behavior." The judge ordered the defendant committed to the Atascadero State Hospital for the ninety-day observation period prescribed by the current statute.[71] There a final adjudication of mentally disordered sex offender was made, with the recommendation that he be returned to court as "unable to utilize treatment and still a danger to society."

Examination by the present author revealed a somewhat different picture and interpretation.

His first arrest at the age of 14 was for drinking. This was repeated during the next two years about five times. On the last occasion he was made a ward of the court and placed on probation. Following that, there were several (3-4) traffic violations including driving without a license for which he was fined. His actual sex life started at 12 years as an experiment but that relations with high school girls started about the age of 16. He had a steady girl in school, and later went with a girl about seven months when he was 18 years old. It was shortly after this that he met his wife; he claims to have been faithful to his wife. There is little indication in the marriage that he had perverse sexual impulses.

The defendant appeared to be of high average intelligence. Thorough ventilation of his sexual feelings brought out definite evidences of neurotic origin. This is illustrated by his closeness to his peers in their common activity and his daring in prohibited things such as drinking, stealing, etc. He needed the support of other males to neutralize his own (unconscious) fears of not being masculine enough. The use of drugs resulted from a wish not to appear timid or cowardly.

A careful psychological test was administered. On the Rorschach Test, the defendant showed sexual shock reactions. Thus, he responded to the Sex Shock Cards with a long reaction time—51 seconds. (Card VI). Since Card VI elicits associations of the male sex organ far more frequently than associations of the female genitals, Card VI Shock is commonly interpreted as ambivalence and conflict pertaining to the male's sexual activity. On the Machover, Draw-A-Person Test, the subject omitted the nose on both figures. The nose is considered to be a sexual symbol, the penis.

The picture that emerged was that of a youth interested in gaining acceptance by his peers by being a "swinger," afraid of nothing and willing to take a "dare." Earlier in high school he was interested in athletics but in common with many well-developed high school youths, considered the ordinary outlets for physical energy too "establishment" for his tastes. There were indications that he was thoughtless, hyperactive, and juvenile in his attitude toward the law and authority.

The subject's behavior was juvenile, opportunistic and reckless. In the same sense, his sexual activities were spurred on by anxiety to establish his manhood.

On these bases, a diagnosis of Sexual Neurosis was made. It was recommended to the court that Gary was a good prospect for psychotherapy, particularly since he had been brought up abruptly to face society's rules and sanctions against breaking those rules.

Offenses Against Public Decency

Of the sexual acts prohibited by law, some are admittedly "normal" and some deviated. The deviated include fetishism, necrophilia, bestiality, sadomasochism, obscene telephone calls and writings, homosexuality, and transvestism. Others are "normal" in essence—exhibitionism, voyeurism, prostitution, procuring, bigamy, adultery, and fornication. Mental scientists are greatly interested in the former, but law enforcement agencies have no special interest in either group beyond their capacity to offend public decency and hence cause mental distress.[72] Some of these offenses are victimless, some contrary to human dignity. With the changes in social values given sexual experience in this era, the degree of disapprobation embodied in the law seems unrealistic. Our society has become scoptophilic (i.e., takes pleasure in looking), to witness motion pictures, magazines, advertisements, and novels extolling sexuality. Nevertheless, the law makes a distinction between purposeful voyeurism of humans and that involved in printed material; between actual exhibitionism and that conveyed in artistic productions.

Voyeurism and Exhibitionism

It is a psychiatric truism that exhibitionism and voyeurism are two sides of the same coin. The peeping tendency among neurotics, or scoptophilia as it is technically termed, has been analyzed minutely. Most analysts find scoptophilia to be a defense against castration anxiety. As Fenichel puts it, "Voyeurs are fixated on experiences that arouse castration anxiety, either the primal scene or the sight of adult genitals."[73] For reasons that dip into society's attitude toward viewing the male genitals, exhibitionism has aroused public disgust and anger. The technique of indecent exposure has been modified somewhat by the automobile; the motorcar symbolizes the fleeting character of the exposure that the exhibitionist wishes to enact. A common type of exhibitionism is that of a young man in a motorcar who drives alongside girls and women, presents his penis to them in a moment of their unawareness, and drives off, masturbating either at that time or later.

The psychologic meaning of exhibitionism has been debated. Rickles, for example, imputes early psychologic traumata due to a dominating mother as the effective factor in a high proportion of exhibitionists.[74] Others consider the act a wish to arouse the female sexually; more sophisticated investigators feel it is performed to reassure the exhibitionist of his own masculinity. From the considerable number of cases studied by this author, a somewhat different view has been developed.

The exhibitionist presents an attitude that demonstrates aggression, rather than seduction, toward women. One must recognize, of course, a degree of sexual excitement in the offender, but the exhibitionist asserts his male prowess only to deny the female and to express his contempt for her. He symbolically shakes his penis at women as he might shake his fist. The reaction of the woman is as important to the exhibitor as are his own sexual feelings: women must be shocked or dismayed, or there is no pleasure in the act. That shock or dismay is a sign of their perception of his contempt or resentment. When an occasional woman victim smiles indulgently or with amusement, the exhibitor usually runs off in confusion and embarrassment. Flight from the scene is a better indication of his libidinous interest in women than is the exhibition itself. Exhibitionism is seduction without a female, an invitation to pleasure that is immediately denied.

The offense of obscene telephone calls fulfills the peeping tendency in an indirect way. Anonymous calls to a home, inquiring preferably of the woman answering whether intercourse is being, or has been, performed, vicariously gratifies the caller's voyeuristic tendencies. This form of sexual stimulation, occurring predominantly among adolescents, is invested with an infantile aura, reminding one of Fenichel's interpretation of castration anxiety arising from witnessing the primal scene. Anonymous callers are rarely apprehended, and the opportunity of examining such an adult offender is uncommon. One such case was as follows:

Jack, aged 40, a telephone repairman, had made unsolicited calls to women subscribers. The conversations, jocular at first, became salacious, and finally lewd. Since the caller spoke in a voice of simulated tenderness and playfulness, and was a member of the telephone company's staff, the women were loath to complain. Whereas the initial calls were only mildly indecent—"I'll make the (telephone) bell soft and sexy for you, baby"—then gradually developed an air of lewdness—"My wife has a bad back, honey; I'd like to get into your pants . . ." Finally, one subscriber heard remarks of obvious indecency: "You're good enough to eat, honey—to eat pussy, I mean . . ." The repairman was tracked down and an arrest made, but no charge was brought. The telephone company discharged the worker, with a strong recommendation that he undergo psychiatric treatment.

The patient had been considered a competent, trustworthy worker with an exemplary home life. Nothing in his marriage or sexual life pointed toward deviation. A handsome man, trimly and powerfully built, his wife spoke of him as restrained and tender in sexual feelings; his friends knew him as suave, personable, and witty. During the early interviews, the patient was evaluated as an Urmensch ("primitive man"), a designation applied by Freud to men endowed with an animalistic, primitive sexual organization.

Psychological projective tests (the Rorschach), however, developed indications of repressed aggressive attitudes toward women, poor emotional controls, and a confusion of male and female identification; this, in contradistinction to his apparently strong drive toward women. Because of his flair for adornment with striking clothes and his unctuous talkativeness, the suspicion of a latent homosexual component arose as the interviews progressed. This could not be substantiated until suddenly, some three months after treatment had begun, his wife reported coming upon her husband in an act of oral copulation with an adolescent relative in their home. The substitution of oral aggression toward women, via the phone calls, by homosexual acts shed new light on the patient's obscene calls. They could now be seen as representing a furtive means of expressing, through his pseudo-heterosexuality, an unconscious projection beyond the woman on the phone to the invisible man of the home. The jocularity for which the patient was noted among his fellow workers and his seductive, playful manner with women proved to be unconscious defenses against latent homosexual impulses.

The situation outlined above was repeated in a female obscene caller —itself a rarity—charged with disturbing the peace.

The offender, Joyce, a slim, wiry woman of forty-two, had been known in her neighborhood as unpleasant and verbose. In recognition of her masculine manner, she had been nicknamed "Tommy." The neighbors, independently of each other, considered her a "trouble maker"; she accused women of "tapping her wire," intercepting her phone calls, implicating her with the sheriff, and so on. The criminal situation came to light when Joyce poured out her venom over the telephone. What started as seductive conversation (Joyce disguised her voice to appear to be an intoxicated man) became bitter invective. She accused her women friends of sexual perversions of an oral type (cunnilingus) and insisted in telling them smutty stories over the phone, particularly ones featuring this perversion. Finally, she was brought to court. The resulting psychiatric examination revealed a primitive, aggressive person, whose instability, perseveration, paranoid attitudes, and restricted mental content suggested an organic brain condition.

The obscenity which Joyce repeatedly expressed in her telephone calls confirmed the theory that for her the telephone exerted a magical influence over a distance. The anonymity of the caller is common, increasing their fantasied domination of the captive audience.

Flights of deviate sexual fantasy are not limited to the spoken word. Salacious letterwriting comes into the legal arena when it is sent to an unwilling recipient who reports it to the postal authorities subject to U.S. Code, Title 18, "Mailing of Obscene Material."[75] The opportunity to examine an obscene letterwriter presented itself in a man of forty referred for determination of the degree of sexual psychopathy and/or psychosis by the court.

The defendant, an ordained minister of a Protestant denomination, now engaged in selling an "achievement program" for business executives, had been divorced some three years before his present second marriage. The first marriage had produced 5 children and was regarded as successful until the separation. The second marriage, he claimed, was also successful sexually and socially. He himself was a vigorous, well spoken, outgoing individual. From his high school days, he had been imbued with an evangelistic interest in the Christian life, had developed a system of "positive self-affirmation" through religious means which he was now marketing. A female high school teacher who had organized a Christian fellowship in his school is credited for putting him on the path of evangelism.

While living with his second wife, the defendant wrote a series of letters to this high school teacher (whom he had not seen for years) relating his sexual excitement and vivid fantasies of their projected intimacies. The letters were received through the mail several times a week over a 3 month period; in addition, the defendant enrolled his fantasied enamorata in sex clubs who deluged her with pornographic material.

The letters started: ". . . I'm so excited thinking about you . . . 24 hours a day . . . I love you . . . I want to make love to you sexually . . . I can teach you things about erotica that will turn you on to *Life* . . . Deep down you have wanted to experience sexual liberation . . ."

The missives were in the form of a dream in which he and his phantom enamorata indulged in sexual practices and conversation with abandon.

I had stopped by your house to tell my identity . . . You were ready . . . within minutes you had a big Orgasm. "Give me all your love juice, Lover, every drop." The following morning . . . my cock stuck up your pussy from the rear. "You sang a little tune—'fuck me in the morning, fuck me in the evening, be my love'n Baby and fuck me all the time.' Then you got on your knees, stuck your big, fat ass in the air and said "Oh Lover, lick my ass-hole honey and suck my clitoris . . ."

This transport of orgiastic excitement appeared to be similar to the coprolallia of the regressed schizophrenic. But his ego integration, his apparent success in promotion campaigns with business executives, and his clarity in discussing impersonal topics placed his productions in a different light. The defendant's written splurge of genital fantasy did not "constitute a menace to the health and safety" of others but was contrary to the postal code. Psychologically, the written productions were reminiscent of a masturbatory experience. A smirking tone ran through his one-way correspondence addressed to a lady who had inspired an evangelical fervor in him as a schoolboy. It was as though in one outpouring, he neutralized the *leit-motif* of his adult life, his religious dedication.

Transvestism and Transsexualism

Dressing like and becoming the opposite sex are necessarily matters of sexual deviancy, but they can be viewed as matters of sexual preference. The male transvestite wishes to produce the illusion of being female by clothing, manner, and gait and speech usually in the privacy of his home. The female transvestite aspires to the illusion of masculinity through vesture, movements, and the like. The transsexualist, on the other hand, if a male, desires to be emasculated, to have a vagina formed surgically, and to receive hormones that might result in female breast formation. The female transsexualist wishes to reduce breast tissue, promote hairy growth through hormones, to deepen the voice, if possible to obtain a penis, and to adopt the attitudes and habits of a man.

In both cases, an emotional identification with the opposite sex is the basic reason for desire to change. Such persons suffer intensely from inner conflict and social obloquy as they struggle in a world of clearly defined sexual identities. From a medico-legal point of view, this condition is of little consequence except for the legal problem of obtaining judicial permission to change names. Both the transvestite and transsexualist come to psychiatric attention because of depression and acute feelings of rejection. Since the 1950s when the following case was studied, there has been a relaxation in social attitudes towards this condition.

Tommy, when first seen appeared to be a muscular person, hair clipped and combed in mannish fashion, dressed in slacks, jacket and a man's shirt, talking crisply but with evident agitation. Life had become intolerable for her: dressed as a man, walking down the street with swinging stride, passersby and children at play gazed at her curiously, or a child might stop her, asking in innocent arrogance, "What are you?" Only at home was she comfortable, able to lounge about, smoke her pipe, work at the carpentry she loved. Her menage included a "wife," a homosexual partner who maintained her feminine role. The immediate cause for consultation was the imminent withdrawal of the "wife," who had decided to marry, giving up this pleasant, but abnormal life. Tommy had been dedicated to her transvestite life for as long as she could remember, the "wife" lost interest in this deviated situation. Tommy's depression was real and acute—a major problem in her life.

Counsellors of many types had advised Tommy to give up her dream of becoming a man. Already jilted in two "love affairs" with women, Tommy was despondent. She had determined to seek medical help for the longed-for final transformation: surgical amputation of her breasts, hormonal treatment to reduce her rounded abdomen, increase the body-hair growth, deepened voice, and reduce or halt menstruation. As a basically well-developed female of normal contour, the wisest counsel seemed to be to persuade Tommy to resume the life that her genes had decreed for her. Her determination to have her sex changed could not be shaken—the usual satisfactions of femininity left her cold.

The immediate problem was treatment for the depression and a legal change of name and sexual habitus if this could be secured. An endocrinologist had already treated her over several years with glandular preparations, which had accomplished some of the aims desired in voice, structure, hairiness, menses. If she dressed as a man and used her natural speaking voice she was looked at in disbelief. Once a policeman stopped her while driving, asking for her license, and could scarcely be convinced that she owned the car registered in a female name.

Consultation with legal authorities as to statutory provisions for changing her "official sex" resulted in the finding that nothing in the law permitted a judge to grant her this transformation. Although the right of a woman to wear men's clothes and to "register" as a man (or the reverse) was given legal sanction in Germany before World War I, and in Denmark later[76] when voluntary castration was approved if the patient's sexuality made "him prone to commit crimes, thereby making him a danger to society or when it involves mental disturbance, to a considerable degree, or social deterioration," no such law was found in any jurisdiction in the United States.

Tommy insisted on visiting Denmark to see what aid could be obtained there. The Danish Ministry of Justice (1955) had meanwhile become chary of legally handling cases from other lands, in view of the publicity given cases like Christine Jorgensen. They regretfully refused to invite the patient to Denmark. She remained in a state of dissatisfaction, rendered acute from time to time by her insistence on dressing as a man.

It must be borne in mind that there has been a tremendous change in public acceptance of transsexualism and other sexual deviations during the past two decades. This change in values is reflected in the law. For example, the California Penal Code (Section 318.6) prohibits "any live acts, demonstrations or exhibitions which occur in public places . . . involv[ing] the exposure of private parts or buttocks . . . or the breast of a female participant . . ." but adds: "The provisions of this section shall not apply to a theatre, concert hall . . . primarily devoted to theatrical performances."

The New York Code is even more specific in defining prohibited material under Section 235.20 (disseminating indecent material to minors). Nudity is defined as

the showing of the human male or female genitals, pubic area or buttocks with less than a full opaque covering, or the showing of the female breast with less than a fully opaque covering of any portion thereof below the top of the nipple, or the depiction of covered male genitals in a discernible turgid state.

Pornography and Indecency

Since decency is the controlling criterion in laws against pornography selling, standards for limitations of sexual impulses and desires becomes the problem. How to measure the influence of "hard-core" pornography or how to set standards of obscenity is a cultural-moral question with which the law has struggled for a long time. The basic principle was laid down in an English case, *Queen v. Hicklin* (1868).[77] Hicklin had published and sold 203,000 copies of a book titled *Confession Unmasked: shewing the depravity of the Romish priesthood . . . questions put to females in confession*. He claimed the book "related to impure and filthy acts, words, and ideas." Hicklin's counsel urged that the book was intended to "expose the immorality of the confessional" and that it was a "controversial book." Chief Justice Cockburn, after agreeing that "the mere use of obscene words . . . does not make the work obscene," laid down the following test:

I think the test of obscenity is this, whether the tendency of the matter charged as obscenity is to deprave and corrupt those whose minds are open to such immoral influences, and into whose hands a publication of this sort may fall . . . suggest to the minds of the young of either sex or even to persons of more advanced years, thoughts, of a most impure and libidinous character.

The significant American case heard, *U.S. v. Roth*,[78] by a New York court, then the U.S. Circuit Court of Appeals (1957), stated that Section 1141 of the New York Penal Law "should only apply to what may properly be termed, 'hard core' pornography," which "lacks serious literary, artistic, political or scientific value." The *Roth* court furnished this crucial test: "Obscene material is material which deals with sex in a manner appealing to prurient interest . . . [by] the average person, applying contemporary community standards . . ." On appeal to the U.S. Circuit Court (Second Circuit), an explanatory note was added, namely: "The correct test is the effect on the sexual thoughts and desires, not of the 'young' or 'immature' but of average, normal adult persons."

The pruriency test, as it came to be known, was added to by the patent offensiveness test occasioned by a U.S. Supreme Court appeal in *Manuel Enterprises v. Day* regarding a magazine for homosexuals.[79] Here the test was "whether the material is so offensive on its face as to affront current community standards of decency."

The landmark case which partly confirmed *Roth* and laid down the current criteria is *Miller v. California*,[80] decided in the U.S. Supreme

Court (1973). This case, relating to mailing unsolicited sexually explicit material, had been found contrary to California's Penal Code, Section 311.2, resulting in a conviction in the trial court, affirmed by the Appellate Court in California. The appeal to the highest court was answered by Chief Justice Burger with dissents by Justices Douglas, Brennan, Stewart, and Marshall. In essence, the ruling decision found that "obscene material was not protected by the First Amendment"; that a state law that regulates obscenity should use these guidelines:

whether "the average person applying community standards" would find that the work, taken as a whole, appeals to prurient interest, whether the work depicts or describes, in a patently offensive way, sexual conduct . . . whether the work, taken as a whole, lacks serious literary, artistic, political or scientific value.

Justice Burger, conceding that the "sexual revolution" of recent years may have had "useful byproducts in striking layers of prudery from a subject long irrationally kept from needed ventilation," said that those selling hard core material were liable to legal sanctions. In a similar case, *Paris Adult Theatre v. Slaton* (1973),[81] the Supreme Court found that the state of Georgia could establish its own standards within the parameters of *Roth* but that "correlation between obscene material and crime was arguable . . . [even though] there are not scientific data which conclusively demonstrates . . . connection between antisocial behavior and obscene material."

The specific point to which the last case addressed itself, the influence of pornography on potential sex offenders, may be one upon which psychiatrists or psychologists (more recently sociologists and educators) may be called to testify. The question in that situation becomes "when sexual thoughts and desires stimulated by prurient material are translated into criminal action." One can rephrase the question by asking when and whether pornographic material invades the private thoughts and images of persons exposed to it to effect a reaction. There is, of course, no ready answer to these questions. What is being dealt with here is breaking the seal of psychologic privacy through communication of sexual ideas. Obscenity is not an absolute; its ultimate influence depends on the use it is put to in the individual. What is being legislated in the various statutes is the invasion of sexual privacy. This complex situation was the issue of an allegedly lewd motion picture in which a movie critic and the present author were asked to testify regarding its literary and artistic value in spite of its portrayal of sexual deviancy.[82]

The film portrayed a brothel in a Latin American country with activities of the prostitutes but without actual sexual performances. A revolutionary group invaded the brothel, presumably to interrupt the proceedings. Their chief then engaged in sadistic acts with the women, whipping them until blood appeared, tieing them to a steel bar over their heads and visiting other sexual indignities on the women.

Although the prostitutes assumed alluring postures and moved in suggestive manner, no males were depicted in the film. The total message was to show the cleansing effect of a possible revolution on bourgeois activities.

The defense of "redeeming literary and political" value was disallowed by the lower court and retrial was denied. The theatre owners were fined in the basis of infraction of a local ordinance.

Crimes of Normal Sexuality

Crimes expressing normal sexual impulses, such as statutory rape, incest, fornication, adultery, bigamy, and prostitution, rarely require psychiatric testimony. Of this group, incest perpetrators are occasionally examined because of their surface resemblance to pedophiles. However, the psychological atmosphere surrounding incest differs from that of pedophilia: the victim may be a submissive accomplice or may accept paternal lovemaking as a pubertal daughter's advantage in her unconscious adversary position vis-à-vis the mother. On the perpetrator's side, although guilt is evident, examination reveals a self-excusing attitude, less evasion, and a greater reliance on a wife's neglect and unattractiveness or alcoholism as rationalizations for this practice. Among incest offenders there is a tacit acceptance of a patriarchal privilege foreshadowed in the Bible that belongs to the head of the tribe. Psychiatrically, one finds chiefly a grudging acknowledgment that what was done was wrong in the eyes of the law but little of defense mechanisms, neurotic conflicts, or impulsiveness.

Prostitution and prostitutes were formerly the subject of psychiatric study, particularly in the attempt to find psychopathy or mental dullness among its practitioners. The older literature regarded these women as mentally retarded, neurotically frigid, schizoid or antisocial psychopaths. This simplistic classification does not hold in modern times, although neurotic strains may be buried in the personality of many prostitutes, as well as drug addiction and egosyntonic relationships with antisocial persons. In male prostitution, a relatively new and increasing field of antisociality, the lure of money far outweighs an inner homosexual inclination, although homosexuality may occasionally prove to be the case.

The expert's function in examining the sexual offender is not limited to the determination of psychopathy. The goal of the psychiatrist or psychologist may be to aid the court or attorneys in evaluating clues for an unapprehended offender, in attempting to answer questions of motivation in a suspect, in estimating the possibilities for treatment, or in estimating the degree of "prurient sexual interest" in a motion picture or book. The defense attorney may require assistance in interpreting the sexual behavior of a complaint or the credibility of denial in an accused. Sometimes a reconstruction of the alleged offense based on a psychiatric analysis of both parties may be helpful to both prosecutor and defender.

Notes

1. Morris Ploscowe, *Sex and the Law*: 138, Prentice-Hall Co., Englewood Cliffs, N.J. (1951).

2. Sir James Stephen, *History of Criminal Law*: 397.

3. Sir William Blackstone, *The Commentaries on the Laws of England*, 4:218 (4th ed.), Adapted to the Present by Robert M. Kerr, J. Murray, London (1876).

4. Massachusetts General Laws, Chap. 272, Sec. 16, West Publ. Co., St. Paul, Minn. (1970).

5. General Laws of Rhode Island, 3:38, reenacted 1969, Chap. 10, Sec. 11, Bobbs-Merrill Co., Indianapolis (1969).

6. *People v. Jenner*, City Hall Recorder, 1816, N.Y. Ct. Gen. Sess. of the Peace, New York.

7. Clark and Marshall: 669, rev. by Melvin F. Wingersky, Callaghan & Co., Chicago (6th ed., 1958).

8. New York Penal Code, Sec. 130, McKinley Annotated Laws (1972).

9. Wisconsin Statutes, 41, Annotated Pocket Part, West Publ. Co., St. Paul, Minn. (1976-1977), Sec. 944.17.

10. California Penal Code, Title 9, Sec. 261 and 281, West Publ. Co., St. Paul, Minn. (1970).

11. Texas Penal Code, Sec. 21.01, Title 5, Chap. 21, Sexual Offenses (1975).

12. *Thermond v. Superior Court*, Solano County, Calif., 49 Calif. 2d 17, 314 Pac. 2d 6 (1959).

15. Fielding Garrison, *History of Medicine*: 739, W. B. Saunders Co., Philadelphia

14. Richard Von Krafft-Ebing, *Psychopathia Sexualis, a Medico-Forensic Study*, Eng. adaptation. Pioneer Publ., Inc., New York (12th ed. rev., 1947).

15. Fielding Garrison, *History of Medicine*: 739, W. B. Saunders Co., Philadelphia (3d ed., 1921).

16. Walter Bromberg, *From Shaman to Psychotherapist*: 202, H. Regnery Co., Chicago (1975).

17. Meyer Solomon, *Psychopathology of Everyday Life. A Critical Review*, J. Abnormal Psych. 23 (Apr. 1916).

18. Bernard Glueck, *A Study of 608 Admissions to Sing Sing Prison*, 2 Ment. Hygiene (Jan. 1918).

19. Arthur Foxe, *Classification of the Criminotic Individual*, in *Handbook of Correctional Psychology*, E. M. Linder and R. V. Selinger, eds., Philosophic Lib., New York (1947).

20. Otto Fenichel, *The Psychoanalytic Theory of Neurosis*: Chap. 16, 342, W. W. Norton, New York (1945).

21. Paul Friedman, *American Handbook of Psychiatry*, 1:593, Basic Books, Inc., New York (1959).

22. American Psychiatric Association, *DSM* 2 (1968).

23. Irving Bieber, et al., *Homosexuality, a Psychoanalytic Study of Male Homosexuals*: 220, Basic Books, Inc., New York (1962).

24. Robert C. Bak and Walter Stewart, in *American Handbook of Psychiatry* 3:297 (2d ed., 1974).

25. Quoted in R. F. Schlesinger and E. F. Scanlon, *Sex Offenses and the Law*, 11 U. Pittsburgh L. Rev. 636 (1949-1950).

26. American Law Reports, Statutes Relating to Sexual Psychopaths, 24 ALR 2d (1952).

27. Welfare and Institutions Code, State of California, State Printing Office, Sacramento, Calif. (1955), Chap. 4, Sec. 550.

28. Group for the Advancement of Psychiatry, Psychiatrically Deviate Sex Offenders, Report no. 9, Topeka, Kans. (1949).

29. 24 ALR 2d: 351.

30. Ibid.: 352.

31. *In re Moulton*, 96 N.H. 370, 77 A 2d (1950).

32. *People v. Clymer*, 326 Ill. App. 468, 62 NE 2d m 129 (1945).

33. *Specht v. Patterson, Warden*, 386 U.S. Reports, 605 (1966).

34. *People v. Bailey*, 21 N.Y. 2d 588 (1968).

35. Arthur Foxe, *Classification of the Criminotic Individual*, in *Handbook of Correctional Psychology*: 24.

36. Robert Lindner, *Rebel Without a Cause*, Grune & Stratton, New York (1944).

37. Study by Mendocino State Hospital of seventy-five certified sexual psychopaths.

38. Karl M. Bowman and Bernice Engle, *Certain Aspects of Sex Psychopath Laws*, 114 Am. J. of Psych. 583 (Feb. 1958).

39. State of California, Senate Bill 1040, Chap. 4, Welfare and Institutions Code (approved July 1963).

40. State of California, Department of Mental Hygiene, Letter No. 2329, Dr. D. Lieberman, director (September 1963).

41. Group for Advancement of Psychiatry, *Psychiatry and Sex Psychopath Legislation: The 30's to the 80's* 9, no. 98 (Apr. 1977).

42. D. H. Barlow, *Increasing Heterosexual Responsiveness in the Treatment of Sexual Deviation*, 4 Behavior Therapy 655 (1973).

43. Thomas Szasz, *The Right to Health*, 57 Geo. L. J. 734 (1969).

44. Ralph Slovenko, *Psychiatry and the Law*: Chap. 12.

45. Welfare and Institutions Code, State of California, 1967, Art. 5, Sec. 5500, amended by stat. 1968.

46. American Law Institute, Model Penal Code, 1968, Art. 213, Sec. 213 et seq.

47. Robert L. Sadoff, in *Comprehensive Textbook of Psychiatry* 2, ed. Williams & Wilkins Co., Baltimore (1975).

48. Daniel Jacobs, *Psychiatric Examination in the Determination of Sexual Dangerousness in Massachusetts*, 10 New England L. Rev. 85 (1974-1975).

49. Incompetent Persons, 41 Am. Juris. 2d, Sec. 49 et seq.

50. Welfare and Institutions Code, State of California, Sec. 5500 et seq., amended 1976, Sec. 6302 et seq.

51. *Huckaby v. State of Florida*, 343 So. 2d 29 (1977).

52. *People v. Burnick*, 14 Calif. 3d 306 (1975).

53. California Welfare and Institutions Code, Sec. 6300.

54. Morris Ploscowe, *Sex Offenses: The American Context in Law and Contemporary Problems*: 217, Duke U. Press, Durham, N.C. (1960).

55. California Penal Code, Title 9, Sec. 261, 6.

56. New York Penal Code, Sec. 130.25.

57. New York Penal Code, Sec. 130.05.

58. California Penal Code, Sec. 261.

59. John M. Macdonald, *Rape, Offenders and Their Victims*, Charles C Thomas Springfield, Ill. (1971).

60. Walter Bromberg, *The Murder and the Murderer: The Destroyer and Creator*, 2 Arch. of Crim. Psycho-dynamics 523 (1957).

61. *People v. Horner (sic)* Super. Ct., Stanislaus County, Calif. (1962).

62. Lauretta Bender and Abram Blau, *The Reaction of Children to Sexual Relations with Adults*, 7 Am. J. Orthopsych. 500 (1937).

63. 18 ALR 3d, 1433.

64. *Wedmore v. State*, 237 Ind. 212, 143 NE 2d, 649.

65. Ben Karpman, *The Sexual Offender and His Offenses*, Julian Press, New York (1954).

66. Hans Van Hentig, *The Criminal and His Victim*, Yale U. Press, New Haven, Conn. (1948).

67. *People v. Cate*, no. 41518, County of Sacramento, Calif. (1972).

68. Ralph Slovenko, *Everything You Wanted to Have in Sex Laws*, J. of For. Sci. 118 (Oct. 1972).

69. *State v. Sikora*, 219 A. 2d 193 (1965), 44 N.J. 453.

70. *People v. Gary (sic)*, County of Yuba, Calif., no. 15 A 15826 (1971).

71. California Welfare and Institutions Code, Sec. 6316.

72. California Penal Code, Title 9, Sec. 261 through 318.6.

73. Fenichel, op. cit.: 347.

74. Nathan Rickles, *Exhibitionism*, J. B. Lippincott Co., Philadelphia (1950).

75. U.S. Code, Title 18, Sec. 1461.

76. Danish Sterilization & Castration Act, no. 176 (1955), no. 130 (1929).

77. *Queen v. Hicklin*, L. R. Vol. 3 Q.B. 360; Clowes & Sin, London (1868).

78. *U.S. v. Roth*, 237 F 2d, 796 (2d Cir., 1956); 354 U.S. 476, 1 L. Ed., 1498 (1957).

79. *Manual Enterprises v. Day*, App. D.C., 1962, 82 Sup. Ct. 1432, 370 U.S. 478, 8 L. Ed. 2d, 639.

80. *Miller v. Calif.*, 98 Sup. Ct. 2607 (1973).

81. *Paris Adult Theatre v. Slaton*, 98 Sup. Ct. 2628 (1973).

82. *People v. Blumenfield*, Sacramento County, Calif. Mun. Ct. (1969).

9

Drug Addiction
and Crime

Like sexual psychopathy, the subject of drug addiction inhabits the borderland of two disciplines, law and psychiatry. Again like sexual gratification and sexual deviation, drug use and drug abuse are motivated by psychological and physiological needs and cravings. For centuries, no criminal sanctions existed against the use of opiates. Ancient Greek physicians knew of the effects of opium and prescribed it freely; in the fifteenth century, Paracelsus, the medical iconoclast, introduced laudanum to his Materia Medica. Recognition in the Western world of drug addiction as a "vice" and/or a medical condition is less than two hundred years old. John Lettsom, a prominent London physician, wrote the first paper on the subject in 1789.[1] The derivation of morphine from opium in 1806 and the further derivation of heroin from morphine in 1898 made drug addiction a familiar aspect of medical practice. Dr. Alexander Wood's invention of the hypodermic needle (1855) popularized the use of morphine for painful conditions. During the Civil War, the injection of morphine to deaden the agony of gunshot wounds was so general among Union troops that addiction to morphine became known as the "Army Disease."[2]

During the nineteenth century, narcotic drugs attracted the attention of the literati and demi-monde in Europe and this country. At the turn of the twentieth century, its use had spread to the point where it began to be a public health issue for which legal sanctions seemed indicated. Medically induced drug addiction in cases of incurable cancer were treated without hindrance by physicians, but the growing number of dillettante addicts was decried by law enforcement officials.

Alienists classified these users as emotionally disturbed. "The victim of drug habits," wrote Dr. Charles L. Dana, an eminent New York neurologist,[3] in 1905, "belong as a rule to the more degenerate types of phrenasthenias (neurotics)." Transition from a private vice to a law enforcement problem followed the organization of the International Commission on Opium in Shanghai in 1909. The governments of European nations and the United States, alarmed by the insidious increase in opium use consequent upon its exportation from China, organized the commission which, by 1912 at the Hague Opium Convention, agreed to restrict the use of the drug to medical practice.

With the passage of the Harrison Narcotic Act (1914) ("passed partly to carry out a treaty obligation" according to Rufus King),[4] what was a medical curiosity and an intriguing psychologic condition at best, and a difficult-to-treat-illness at worst, became a serious public health hazard. This evolution invaded psychiatric, sociologic, law enforcement, and legal areas.

The Evolution of Drug Addiction Problems

The Harrison Narcotic Act of 1914[5] merely made it unlawful to "dispense, produce, import, manufacture, compound, sell, distribute, deal in or give away" any narcotic drug without registering with and purchasing a special tax stamp for $1.00 from the collector of Internal Revenue. Physicians prescribing morphine, heroin, or cocaine were excluded from the criminal sanction. With slight modifications, the Uniform Drug Law has become the law in forty-six states, Puerto Rico, and the District of Columbia; the remaining four states have enacted their own narcotic laws. A later interpretation of the act, encompassed in Treasury Department regulations, seemed to change the purport of the Harrison Act. It stated that "any use of narcotics for the purpose of satisfying the demands of the addiction itself is illegal."[6] The term *addict* was not in common use until the Bureau of Narcotics of the Treasury Department triggered national anxiety by referring, with the aid of the press, to the growing "dope menace." The advent of worldwide drug usage followed World War II. In 1948, the World Health Organization developed and maintained an entire section devoted to the international problem of drug addiction.

The dangers of the "dope menace" became entwined with increasing lawlessness in the 1920s when cocaine was indicted as the cause of violent crime in the South among blacks,[7] and heroin as an instigator of robbery and homicide in large metropolitan centers. The sinister connotation of illegal drugs was further intensified by the rise of marijuana use, first in the South, then in larger northern cities. For some reason, the spread of marijuana (weed, grass, pot) gave rise to a greater degree of panic than the insidious increase in heroin usage. Fanned by the Federal Bureau of Narcotics' admonition during the 1930s against marijuana as the royal road to violent crime and addiction, the press picked up the alarm. *The New York Mirror* (1933), among others, published a feature article titled "Loco Weed, Breeder of Madness and Crime." The zeal of the Federal Bureau of Narcotics in furthering legislation among the states branding marijuana as a stimulus to crime culminated in the Federal Marijuana Tax Act of 1937. Although, like the Harrison Act, it was only a registration and tax procedure, the intent was to discourage the use of marijuana by fines and prison sentences, chiefly because it was believed to be an inciter of aggressive, violent behavior. Much legislation in the several states was directed against the drug traffic and gang activities in the black market, but the inclusion of marijuana with narcotic drugs, New York (1944)[8] (since amended), bespoke the anxiety engendered by illegal drugs just prior to the end of World War II.

Paradoxically, as penalties against drug addiction became more severe, the "drug culture" expanded. Up to the 1970s, punishment for sale and use of narcotic drugs, often including marijuana, called for a life sentence in New York; five years in California; and life imprisonment in Louisiana, Arizona, Missouri, Montana, Texas, and Ohio.[9] In practice, however, sentences were often lighter, depending on the number of convictions and other factors, such as appeals on the basis of "cruel and unusual punishment." Nevertheless, one effect of severe punishment for selling or using illegal drugs seemed to have a reverse effect—an ever-widening nonconformity with respect to drugs. It also led to movements for decriminalization of marijuana. This rebellious attitude was enhanced by the Mind Expansion cult during the 1950s and 1960s. Led by Tim O'Leary's sloganeering "turn on, drop out" movement, many youths responded by resorting to marijuana, LSD, amphetamine, psylocybin, mescaline, heroin, and, later, cocaine, partly in willful nonconformity to statutes against drug usage in the various states.

The ebb and flow of statutory sanctions against narcotic drugs bears a direct relation to public attitudes. As the antiestablishment spirit of the young in the 1960s lost some of its vigor, public distrust of marijuana (but not of heroin) also faded. The pervasive use of "pot" on many levels of society, with no corresponding increase in violent crime due to marijuana, tended to support demands for decriminalization of the drug. Much psychiatric study of the behavioral effects of drugs—

though still controversial—reduced the fear of marijuana addiction, specifically of mental dullness or other permanent toxic effects, its aphrodisiac effect, and its predisposition to homicide or assault. As a consequence, many states have cut their penalties drastically. For example, Oregon (1973) made possession of one ounce of marijuana a civil violation punishable by a fine of $100.[10]

The new approach in Oregon, the first state to decriminalize the drug, has been branded a success. Contrary to expectations, there was no "dramatic increase" in marijuana use. After 1973, other states reduced the status of marijuana use, possession, or sale of small amounts to misdemeanors (from felonies) or removed the act from the crime category. Some states legislated marijuana charges as civil offenses meriting fines, embarked on treatment programs, and permitted expunging records of the charge. The turnabout concerning marijuana's "vicious" influence has been thoroughly reviewed in a publication of the New York University School of Law titled *Recent Trends in State Drug Legislation*.[11] For our present purpose, the California and New York drug law modifications, which represent different approaches to the growing problem, are described in detail below.

The New York law, passed in 1973, included marijuana, hallucinogenic drugs, methadone, and narcotics as "dangerous drugs,"[12] possession or sale of which constituted a felony. Thus, possession or sale of a controlled drug such as heroin of ½ ounce or more, ½ ounce of marijuana, or twenty-five or more marijuana cigarettes constituted a Class D felony.[13] In a 1975 revision, methadone was excluded, but ⅛ ounce of narcotic drug (such as heroin or cocaine), ½ ounce of amphetamines, and 1 mgm. of LSD were placed in the Class C felony group. Marijuana was excluded, but "concentrated cannabis" was added by the 1977 amendment. Actually, the 1977 amendment (Article 221) brought marijuana into the misdemeanor class when possessed "up to two ounces." The general attitude was expressed by the New York legislature in saying about the "recreational use of marijuana" that "arrests, criminal prosecution and criminal penalties are inappropriate for people who possess small quantities of marijuana for personal use." Still, mandatory terms were specified for various felony classes. Treatment was emphasized but proved ineffective. The harshness of New York drug laws was aimed at the "twin problems of addiction and crime."[14]

The California law, enacted in 1975, sought to reduce penalties for marijuana while stiffening penalties against heroin.[15] For possession of less than 1 ounce of marijuana, the penalty is a fine of $100, with provision for "diversion", i.e., an "education and treatment program" for repeat offenders. Further, those arrested for possession, "giving away," or transporting less than 1 ounce of marijuana cannot be booked by the arresting officer. Thus the offense is removed from the criminal category and is in fact called an "infraction." In contrast to this decriminalization of moderate use of marijuana is the intensification of penalties of heroin possession. Use for sale of more than ½ ounce of heroin was increased to a mandatory sentence of five years to life. The law also penalizes use or sale of amphetamines, concentrated cannabis, barbiturates, peyote, and cocaine, with an escalator clause for second or third offenses.[16] Regarding hard drugs such as heroin, the new Code makes sentences "mandatory" and prohibits probation or suspension of execution of the sentence.[17] The thrust of the new laws was to eliminate sellers, pushers, and providers through long imprisonment, not unlike the intent of the New York law.

In spite of the stricter narcotic laws in many states and greater leniency governing marijuana, the flow of illegal drugs continues unabated and has even increased. The editor of *Contemporary Drug Problems* (1975) has summarized the situation: "The drug crisis of the 1960's was not resolved in the 1970's: all that happened was that a few prominent politicians proclaimed what most people wanted to hear . . . the 'war' is being won." Perhaps because of its relation to hashish through the active cannabis principle (cannabinol), its lurid history, and its presumed connection with crime, marijuana has attracted much attention from law enforcement agencies and psychiatrists. Beginning in the 1930s, its social effect on the American scene has been tremendous. The flavor of some early reactions can be gauged by a comment of a right-wing group, the American Coalition, which testified in the 1930s before a congressional committee: "Marijuana perhaps now the most insidious of our narcotics, is a direct by-product of unrestrained Mexican immigration. . . ."[18]

Psychiatric View of Addiction

The literature on marijuana far outdistances that on heroin, cocaine, or opium during the last three decades. Marijuana was originally considered a cause of insanity in India and Africa. Clinical investigation of cannabis effects started in Germany and France in the early 1930s in relation to mescaline whose hallucinogenic properties had been known for years. Aside from papers of criminologic interest (e.g., Dr. Fossier's article in the *New Orleans Medical Journal*, the "Marihuana Menace," in 1931)[19] the earliest clinical study of cannabis intoxication in this country issued from the Bellevue Psychiatric Hospital,

New York. The present author's study (1934)[20] of eleven cases of
mental reactions resulting from marijuana usage showed transitory and
moderately prolonged reactions with anxiety, euphoria, depression,
body-image distortion, and panic reactions. Some of the cases developed schizophrenic-like psychoses engrafted on the acute intoxication.
Five years later, twenty more cases were reported,[21] sufficient to
classify the reactions into (1) acute intoxications and (2) toxic psychoses "often superimposed on a basic functional mental disturbance."
As the use of this drug spread, much research developed, notably a
study ordered by Mayor La Guardia through the New York Academy
of Medicine (1937). A select committee analyzed every aspect of drug
usage using psychological, sociologic, and psychiatric experts. Key
findings were the lack of "mental or moral deterioration" among prolonged users and the absence of any relation between criminal action
and marijuana smokers. This report by Allentuck and Bowman (1942)[22]
received wide publicity and considerable criticism since public attention had been riveted on the crime-inducing quality of marijuana and
the "stepping stone hypothesis"[23] that marijuana inevitably led to
heroin or cocaine. Essentially, the question under debate was the addictive aspect of marijuana. In the early paper by the present author,[24] it
was concluded that habituation was not a chemical-psychological one,
but rather a "sensual addiction in the service of the hedonistic elements
of the personality." Users on many levels of society were unanimous in
pointing to the pleasant lethargy and relaxation induced by the drug.
Marijuana users tended to congregate within their own groups, leading
law enforcement officials to lump them with psychopathic, i.e., criminal
persons. With the acquisition of more experience, a controversy developed between sociologists and mental health experts who foresaw
moral deterioration in marijuana "addicts" and those who regarded it
as relatively harmless. The latter lumped "emotional dependence" with
"drug habitation," to the end that they saw psychopathy in all illegal
drug users. Sociologist A. R. Lindesmith, working with drug culture
groups, denied the "psychopathy" of the addict, explaining:

[Those who] studied addicts only after addiction . . . do not tell us how those
traits which were the result of addiction were separated from those that were
the causes of addiction. . . . The unspoken assumption is that any trait which
distinguishes addicts from non-addicts is ipso facto a criterion of abnormality. . . .[25]

Further apologists of the "drug way of life" insisted on the normality
of mind expansion and the drugs which attained this desired state. Thus,

a novelist wrote: "With the help of heroin, one is no longer grotesquely involved in becoming, one simply is."[26] But those who tried to therapeutize the user held different views. Dr. Robert Felix refined the psychopathic concept to encompass the special state of the addict.[27] He employed the term *psychopathic diathesis or predisposition* to describe persons not falling into the usual category of psychopath, yet showing "borderline maladjustment." The U.S. Public Health Service summed up the majority view (1963): "It takes three things to make an addict—a psychologically maladjusted individual, an available drug and a mechanism for bringing them together."[28]

On the issue of criminality and drugs, wide differences of opinion existed. Everyone agreed that heroin or cocaine addicts were major factors in burglary, robbery, and larceny because of their constant need of money for drugs, but few were of the same opinion regarding marijuana. During the early years (1930s), the Bureau of Narcotics insisted that homicides and assaultive crime were stimulated by marijuana, while psychiatric investigators (Bromberg, Allentuck, and Bowman) denied this relationship. Of 16,854 drug offenders in the Court of General Sessions, New York County, which processed felonies, during the period of 1932-1937,[29] only 135 were charged with marijuana possession and use. The conclusion of Allentuck and Bowman some seven years later, when marijuana use had spread in New York City, was in a similar vein: "Marijuana is not a determining factor in the commission of major crime."[30]

The Vietnam War brought a tremendous escalation of narcotic usage of heroin or heroin combined with hashish to these shores, in addition to the already extended use of marijuana in the young civilian population. This put a different light on the question of marijuana addiction. Although heroin and cocaine claimed a growing number of adherents, scientific and public interest still converged on marijuana. During the 1970s, an enormous literature grew up around scientific and clinical use of the drug. The indices of addiction—increased tolerance, symptoms of withdrawal, and increased dependency—were recognized. Hardin and Helen Jones (1977), summarizing the pharmacological and clinical work done on marijuana users, insisted that neurological, medical, and psychiatric sequellae follow prolonged use: "The list of altered functions . . . is long: changes in personality, memory, facial expression, thought formation, mood, motivation, skin color and motor coordination. . . ."[31]

While this scientific evidence was accumulating, reduced criminal sanctions against marijuana were being enacted into law. The sharp division between "hard" drugs and marijuana was being eroded from the standpoint of the experimenters[32] and clinicians. Most psychiatric observers held to the view that hard drug addicts and some marijuana users, especially among the young, could correctly be called abnormal personalities, if not psychopaths. The Council on Mental Health of the American Medical Association had already expressed this view (1963): "There is a general agreement among all students of addiction that addicts have personality aberrations and that these psychiatric conditions preceded and played an important role in the genesis of addiction...."[33]

Meanwhile, methadone was introduced by Dole and Nyswander in New York City[34] as a means of blocking the physical effects of heroin. On extended trial, however, it was to be itself an addictive drug. Under medical control, methadone allowed heroin addicts to pursue their social and industrial life but at the cost of another addiction. It appeared then that an addictive personality, or an abnormal personality akin to psychopathy, which lacked the capacity to give up immediate gratification for a larger ideal—social conformity—was a major factor in the whole problem of addiction. This designation is of more than academic importance because it underlies the larger question of how the state can enlist its police powers to regulate the use of habit-forming drugs in the interest of public health.[35] In other words, if addiction is a "disease," or even a facet of a personality disorder, does the state have the right to regard it as an offense?

Legal Reflections on Addiction

The fine line between drug addiction, a disease, and the criminal use of a prohibited substance was redrawn in the landmark decision of *Robinson v. California* (1962).[36] Robinson was convicted by a jury in the Municipal Court of Los Angeles of having used narcotics, as evidenced by needle marks in the antecubital space of his elbow. The California Code (1962) stated in Section 11721: "No person shall use, or be under the influence of, or be addicted to the use of narcotics" except if administered by a physician. The crime was a misdemeanor for which a term of not less than ninety days nor more than a year was prescribed. An appeal to the Appellate Division of the Los Angeles Superior Court upheld Robinson's conviction but left some doubt as to the constitutionality of "being a drug addict." The case reached the U.S. Supreme Court where Justice Stewart delivered the opinion on the issue whether "the status of narcotic addiction" is a criminal offense per se. Regarding the California law, Justice Stewart decided:

We hold that a state law which imprisons a person thus afflicted as a criminal, even though . . . he has never been guilty of any irregular behavior there, inflicts a cruel and unusual punishment in violation of the Fourteenth Amendment. . . . Even one day in prison would be a cruel and unusual punishment for the "crime" of having a common cold.

In the course of his opinion, Justice Stewart agreed that the power of the state to regulate the "vicious evils" of the narcotic drug traffic was valid and that it could take several forms—"criminal sanction, program of compulsory treatment . . . requiring involuntary confinement, public education," but that "narcotic addiction is an illness." In this opinion, he was vigorously seconded by Justice Douglas: "If addicts can be punished for their addiction, then the insane can also be punished for their insanity." Justice Douglas quoted a lurid (and medically unfounded) description of addiction from the *New York Law Journal* (1960):

To be a confirmed drug addict is to be one of the walking dead. . . . The teeth have rotted out . . . the gall bladder becomes inflamed . . . membranes of the nose turn a flaming red . . . veins collapse and livid purple scars remain. Good traits of character disappear and bad ones emerge, imaginary and fantastic fears blight the mind and sometimes complete insanity results. . . .

Justice Douglas then concluded:

In Section 5350 of the Welfare and Institutions Code, California has expressly provided for civil proceedings for commitment of habitual addicts. Section 11721, is in reality, a direct attempt to punish those the state cannot commit civilly. . . . We would forget the teachings of the Eighth Amendment if we allowed sickness to be made a crime and permitted sick people to be punished for being sick. This age of enlightenment cannot tolerate such barbarous action.

In his dissent to *Robinson*, Justice Clark made a distinction between the addict who is so voluntarily and one who has lost his self-control over the habit. He pointed out that the California statute imposes a county jail term for "volitional addicts" (Section 11721) in the hope that incarceration will stir them to rehabilitation, whereas one who has "lost the power of self-control" in relation to drug usage, i.e., is ill, is provided for by Section 5355 of the California Code as a civilly committed hospital patient. Justice White, who also dissented to *Robinson*, called the volitional user a "redeemable" addict and properly subject to criminal sanction. In other words, Justice White concluded, it is not "cruel and unusual punishment" to convict someone for an addiction which is voluntary since such a person is not, by statutory definition, an ill person.

The effect of *Robinson* was extended to alcoholic cases where the condition of chronic alcoholism, a disease, was considered a "status" and hence not subject to punishment as a crime. In *Driver v. Hinnant* (1966),[37] a man convicted of intoxication on a public highway or a public place as a misdemeanant appealed his conviction. The U.S. Fourth Circuit Court of Appeals ruled that the North Carolina statute invoked in *Driver* was unconstitutional under the Eighth Amendment (cruel and unusual punishment) because a chronic alcoholic is "powerless to stop drinking" and lacks evil intent and consciousness of wrongdoing. However, in 1968, *Powell v. Texas*,[38] an alcoholic charged with being drunk in a public place sought appeal under the Eighth and Fourteenth Amendments, pleading that he was afflicted with the disease of chronic alcoholism. The case went to the U.S. Supreme Court, where on a five to four decision the conviction was not found to be cruel and unusual punishment. The majority of the Court felt that the states could not be compelled to excuse behavior based on an "alcoholic compulsion" as maintained by the appellant. Five years later, in *United States v. Moore*,[39] the issue of whether a "non-trafficking addict" could be convicted arose. Moore claimed he was driven by an "overwhelming compulsion" to use illicit drugs. On a five to four decision, the Court of Appeals (Washington, D.C.) affirmed the conviction, in part on the argument that, though a "craving" for drugs cannot be punished, the "acts which give in to that craving" are punishable, i.e., criminal. A commentator[40] suggests that the basic question of criminal responsibility is involved in the drug addict who has lost "specific intent" because of loss of control due to drug addiction.

Sociology of Drug Addiction

Drug addiction as a "disease" has enormous sociological as well as psychological implications. Its contagiousness flows from the subculture of users that seduces, then cajoles, and finally threatens the new user to join the "establishment." The user of illicit drugs joins a specious fellowship, united by a specific language and attitude that inevitably become antisocial. The use of drugs does not start as an illegal activity, but it leads to burglary, theft, robbery, and possibly murder as the need for continued supply manifests itself. Sometimes the induction into addiction has no relation to the subculture of the streets, as with patients with incurable disease or with doctors and nurses who are in contact with legal medications. Sometimes use of illegal drugs starts as a social grace; it can be combined with a testing-of-the-limits in defiance of society's disapproval, as in the young. The potential addict joins a community of persons who feel they have the power to "kick it" when they wish, whose narcissism becomes fused with the general air of rebelliousness of the group. With full intellectual knowledge of the effect of drugs on the body, they indulge in a kind of social masochism, an unconscious need to suffer before they gain sufficient self-esteem to take their place in the world. In this psychological sense, the type of drugs consumed makes little difference as long as they induce body-image changes, mood elevation, or "mind expansion"; they may be morphine, heroin, cocaine, barbiturates, marijuana, hashish, amphetamine, codeine, demoral, dilaudid, quaalude, or any one of a dozen of tranquilizers, soporifics, or narcotics. The more exotic the name of the drug—Angel Dust, Purple Dot, Acapulco Gold, or Orange Sunshine (LSD)—the more exciting the experience. From prolonged use, a chemical and psychological dependence develops and simultaneously the need for contact with the drug subculture. Thus, social and individual factors entwine in those who become immersed in the drug life-pattern. Whether this pattern leads directly to criminal action depends on economics as well as sociopathic tendencies since undoubtedly many addicts have enough funds to avoid criminal actions. The wealthy, adjusted addict is excepted in this discussion.

The case of a twenty-three-year-old male, whose story could be multiplied in every jurisdiction in this country, serves as a paradigm of one type of criminal eventuality.

Martin T., aged 23 was arrested for driving while intoxicated and felonious assault on a police officer. His history started when he dropped out of high school in the second year when he entered the "drug scene." From that time Martin worked sporadically, married at an early age followed by an annulment within a few weeks. He was on "speed" (amphetamines) for about three years, then "reds" (barbiturates), LSD and other drugs. On two occasions he had "bad trips" after using LSD: he became confused, thought the leaves on trees were talking to him, that his mind was "a piece of cake." During the last "trip" he became involved with the traffic incident.

There had been several admissions to hospitals, a sentence to the Youth Authority and arrests for possession of drugs. Care by a psychiatrist in the intervals between hospitalization, availed little. Martin became involved with the Hell's Angels, sold drugs as a "candy man" in the Haight-Asbury drug culture in San Francisco.

The offense for which Martin was arrested followed a psychotic episode which started with his taking about a pint of vodka and some hasheesh, following injection of LSD. This LSD was given him by a friend and was called "Orange Sunshine," being apparently mixed with some other drug. A short time after he took it, he had a terrific panic, fear of dying, thought that his lung

wound of an earlier stabbing was causing a further collapse: he started screaming for help and was brought to the hospital. In a complete panic, didn't know
where he was, felt that he was about to die, and made plans how he would be
buried. The patient then felt that he was in a coffin, which is how he interpreted the gurney stretcher; he remembers being in a car, but he called it a
sailboat, remembers his violence there when he tried to smash his hands through
a glass window and finally put his head through the window; and he felt that
the fluid they were giving him was embalming fluid.

From a study of his pre-arrest personality, it was evident that Martin was an
immature, suggestible young man, not particularly resourceful but possessed
of good basic intelligence. (His father was a respected minister.) A deep-seated
negativistic attitude towards authority was evident in the Rorschach and Draw-
A-Person tests.

The felonious assault charge upon the officer was dropped and the psychiatric
report recommended probation with strict supervision and intensive psychotherapy.

A second and more serious case socially was that of Frank D., thirty
years old, convicted of first degree murder. A plea of diminished
capacity based on the toxic psychosis due to drug intoxication at the
time of the crime was disallowed by the trial court.

Frank D., represented the classic course of a social psychopath, dedicated to an
antisocial life. His juvenile record started at 14 years, succeeded by three years
in a Federal Penitentiary for a drug smuggling operation, and two years more
in State's Prison for drug selling. Avowedly, he allied himself with the drug
world, calling himself an "outlaw" with pride, identifying himself with "my
people."

The instant offense occurred while he, Bud and Bud's wife were in a motel
room in order to settle the triangle induced by Bud's absence from his wife's
side during a prison sentence. The three consumed amphetamine, "reds" and
possibly other drugs during the prolonged discussion. Bud then laid down to
rest, and after further discussion, Frank stabbed and cut Bud's throat under the
pretext that the latter was one who had killed a "brother," meaning a close
associate in the gang. Both the woman and the offender were confused and
excited by an evening of drug ingestion. The wife asked Frank, "Is he dead
yet," thinking in her confusion that it was indeed the man who killed Frank's
"brother." To answer this, Frank slashed the deceased's throat decisively, a second time.

On gaining awareness in jail, Frank recognized his illusion, insisting that he
would never have killed a man "over a woman." His discussion of his life-style,
the difference between himself and associates of the "straight world" contained
a little more than immature grandiosity. An underlying paranoid strain and a
degree of judgment impairment was evident in his thinking. However, it was
apparent that the homicide was committed under the influence of a toxic state.
The wanton nature of the crime fell into the same pattern as a murder done by
Frank's "brothers" when, some months before, they had disposed of a rival by
decapitating him, cutting off one hand and dumping him in the river.

Governmental Control of Illegal Drugs

The ceaseless struggle of the U.S. Bureau of Narcotics against narcotic drugs smuggled in from foreign countries was buttressed in 1968 by the formation of the Drug Enforcement Administration.[41] This agency added to its narcotic drug efforts control over "abuse or trafficking in central nervous system depressants, stimulants, and hallucinogenic substances by the Controlled Substances Act of 1970."[42] Under the president's reorganization plan, the new bureau was charged with responsibilities for developing overall federal drug law enforcement startegy programs, planning, and evaluation; full investigation and preparation for prosecution of suspected violators under all federal drug trafficking laws; and full investigation and preparation for prosecution of illicit drug suspects involving contraband seized at U.S. ports of entry and international borders. Also included in responsibilities were supervision of all relations with drug law enforcement officials and the regulation of the legal manufacture of drugs and other controlled substances under federal regulations.

Among the functions of the Drug Enforcement Administration was the authority to provide "grants to States . . . and to public or non-profit agencies . . . to collect, disseminate educational materials"; to encourage research and extend treatment; to control legal and illegal drug distribution; and to register "every person who manufactures or distributes" such drugs. Definitions, penalties, and legal procedures for those who violate provisions of this act are included. For physicians, a significant part of this detailed act is the "Controlled Substances" portion which establishes five schedules, as abstracted:

Schedule I: Drugs with a high potential for abuse with no currently acceptable medical use. Examples of Schedule I: Heroin, morphine, marijuana, L.S.D. . . .

Schedule II: Drugs with high potential for abuse but with currently accepted medical use. Examples of Schedule II: Opium derivatives, methadone, cocaine, amphetamines, methaqualone. . . .

Schedule III: Drugs with potential for abuse "less than drugs in Schedule I and II: may lead to moderate or low physical dependency or high psychological dependence." Examples of Schedule III: barbiturates, amphetamine, and limited concentrations of codeine. . . .

Schedule IV: Drugs with low potential for abuse, accepted medical treatment use, may lead to limited physical or psychological dependence. Examples of Schedule IV: phenobarbital, meprobamate, paraldehyde, chloral hydrate. . . .

Schedule V: Drugs with low potential for abuse, accepted medical treatment and limited dependence "relative to drugs in Schedule IV." Examples of Schedule V: medications with "non-narcotic drugs mixed with limited quantities of narcotic drugs" for antitussive and antidiarrheal purposes. . . .

In case of improper prescription of drugs in Schedules I and II, the sentence is imprisonment for not more than fifteen years, a fine of $25,000, or both; for Schedule II, imprisonment for five years and a fine of not more than $15,000, and so on.

The government's intent through the Federal Food, Drug and Cosmetic Act is to restrict unauthorized transactions in drugs under the controlled substance schedule. Records for Schedules I and II must be kept separate from drugs in other schedules. Each "legitimate handler of controlled drugs"—importer, manufacturer, pharmacy, hospital physician, or researcher—must register with the Drug Enforcement Administration and obtain a specific registration number. In addition, doctors are limited to prescription *only* after an examination of the patient during a bona-fide patient-physician relationship where the examination leads to a prescription that would be beneficial to the patient. In a 1959 Georgia case, *DeFreese v. U.S.*,[43] a physician sold as many as 20,000 "bennies" (benzadrine tablets), 20,000 amphetamine tablets, and 1,000 phenobarbital tablets to a narcotic agent posing as a truck driver for cash. After conviction in the District Court, the doctor appealed to the U.S. Court of Appeals, Fifth Circuit, on the grounds that the law was not applicable to wholesale sales. The Appeals Court confirmed the conviction since no medical examination had been made before the sale. The doctor appealed a second time, claiming the drugs had not been shipped interstate, but this contention was easily disproven since they were manufactured in New Jersey. In general, the courts have ruled that prescribing controlled drugs must be in the "course of professional practice."[44]

In a Washington, D.C., case (1974), *U.S. v. Moore*,[45] a physician had registered under the controlled drug act for using methadone to treat addicts. Dr. Moore sold methadone in large quantities without medical examinations to addicts in an office at the entrance of which stood two armed guards. At his trial before the District Court, the doctor admitted that his practice was "irregular," but he insisted his sales to addicts were in good faith on the theory that large amounts of methadone would saturate the heroin addicts and induce a "strong psychological desire" to remain off the drugs. The prosecution insisted that his treatment schedule had "no medical purpose" and that he was in fact a "pusher." Conviction was on the basis that Dr. Moore had no authorization to so dispense methadone without examinations.

Appeal to the U.S. District Court of Appeals (Washington, D.C.) resulted in a reversal by Chief Judge Bazelon on the grounds that the appellant was exempt from prosecution on a specific section (841) of the District of Columbia statute. The federal prosecutor then appealed the case to the U.S. Supreme Court (*U.S. v. Moore*, 1975)[46] where Justice Powell read the majority opinion. It stated that a "registered physician can be prosecuted under Section 841 when his activities fall outside of the usual course of professional practice." The District Court of Appeals' verdict was reversed, the original conviction affirmed, and the general principle laid down that the appellant's activity "exceeded the bounds of professional practice."

In sum, the Controlled Substances Act and drug legislation of the several states cover every contingency of drug abuse, while providing for extensive programs for education and prevention. This latter aim reaches far beyond forensic psychiatry into a social area of vast dimensions. The medical and pharmacologic literature on drug addiction is large, but it contains relatively few forensic implications. The individual addict presents problems in therapy to internists and psychiatrists willing to treat such cases, whereas drug traffic is a low enforcement problem with sociological, even international and political implications.

Notes

1. Fielding H. Garrison, *History of Medicine*: 372, W. B. Saunders Co., Philadelphia (3d ed., (1921).

2. Narcotic Drug Addiction, Mental Health Monograph 2: 1, U.S. Department of Health, Education, & Welfare, Bethesda, Md. (1963).

3. Charles L. Dana, *Textbook of Nervous Diseases*: 962, Wm. Wood, New York (7th ed., 1908).

4. Rufus G. King, *The Narcotic Bureau and the Narcotics Act: Jailing the Healers and the Sick*, 62 Yale L. J. 736 (1952).

5. Harrison Narcotic Law, c. 1.38 Stat. 785.

6. U.S. Treasury Department Regulation No. 5, Art. 167 (1957).

7. Dennis Helms, Thomas Lescault, and Alfred Smith, in *Contemporary Drug Problems* 4: 195 (1975).

8. New York Penal Code, Book 39, Part 2, Sec. 11751 (1944).

9. Annual Survey of American Law: 343, Oceana Publ. Inc., Dobbs Ferry, N.Y. (1977).

10. Oregon Rev. Stat., Sec. 167.207 (1) (1974).

11. See note 9, ibid.

12. New York Penal Code, Sec. 220.00.

13. New York Penal Code, Art. 220.00.

14. *Recent Trends in Drug Legislation*: 353.

15. Gerald F. Uelman, *California's New Marihuana Law*, 5 Calif. State Bar J. 27 (1976).

16. California Penal Code, Sec. 11350 et seq.

17. California Penal Code, Sec. 1203.07.

18. David F. Musto, *The American Dream*: 220, Yale U. Press, New Haven, Conn. (1973).

19. E. A. Fossier, *The Marihuana Menace*, 84 New Orleans Med. & Surg. J. 247 (1931).

20. Walter Bromberg, *Marihuana Intoxication. A Clinical Study of Cannabis Sativa Intoxication*, 91, no. 2 Am. J. Psych. 303 (Sept. 1934).

21. Walter Bromberg, *Marihuana, A Psychiatric Study*, 113 J.A.M.A. 4 (July 1939).

22. S. Allentuck and Karl Bowman, *The Psychiatric Aspects of Marijuana Intoxication*, 99 Am. J. Psych. 248 (1942).

23. Lester Grinspoon, *Marihuana Reconsidered*, Harv. U. Press (1971).

24. Bromberg, *Marihuana, A Psychiatric Study*: 26.

25. A. R. Lindesmith, *Dope Fiend Mythology*, 31 J. of Crim. L. and Crim. 199 (July 1940).

26. Alexander, Trocchi, *Cain's Book*: 98, Grove Press, N.Y. (1960).

27. Robert H. Felix, *An Appraisal of the Personality of the Types of the Addicts*, 100 Am. J. Psych. 462 (1944).

28. Narcotic Drug Addiction, Monograph 2: 5, U.S. Dept. H.E.W.

29. Bromberg, *Marihuana, A Psychiatric Study*: 20.

30. Allentuck and Bowman, Mayor's Committee on Marihuana, Book 3 (1944).

31. Hardin Jones and Helen Jones, *Sensual Drugs: Deprivation and Rehabilitation of the Mind*, Cambridge U. Press, Cambridge (1977).

32. Ibid.: 251.

33. Council on Mental Health Report, 139 J.A.M.A. 962 (Sept. 1963).

34. V. P. Dole, and M. Nyswander, *A Medical Treatment for Diacetylmorphine (heroin): A Clinical Trial with Methadone Hydrochloride*, 193 J.A.M.A. 646 (1964).

35. *Whipple v. Martinson*, 256 U.S. 41 (1921).

36. *Robinson v. California*, 370 U.S. 660 (1962).

37. *Driver v. Hinnant*, 356 F. 2d 761 (4th Cir., 1966).

38. *Powell v. Texas*, 392 U.S. 514 (1968).

39. *U.S. v. Moore*, 468 F. 2d 1139, Dist. Ct. App., D.C. (1973); *U.S. v. Moore*, 94 Sup. Ct. 298 9 (1973).

40. I. Sullivan, *Criminal Responsibility and the Drug Dependence Defense—A Need for Judicial Clarification*, 42 Fordham L. Rev. 361 (1973).

41. E. Lewis and W. M. Leuck, *Medical Practice Under the Law. Drug Enforcement* 4, no. 3:18 U.S. Dept. Justice, Washington, D.C. (1977).

42. Public Law 91-513, Oct. 27, 1970, U.S. Statute at Large 84: 1236, U.S. Government Printing Office, Washington, D.C. (1971).

43. *DeFreese v. U.S.*, 270 F. 2d 730 (1959) in *DeFreese v. U.S.*, 270 F. 2d 737.

44. *White v. U.S.*, 299 F. 2d 813 (1968).

45. *U.S. v. Moore*, 506 F. 2d 426: Cir. (D.C. Cir.), 1974.

46. *U.S. v. Moore*, 96 Sup. Ct. 335 (1975).

10

Family Law and Psychiatry

Divorce and, to a lesser extent, annulment form a screen upon which emotional pressures in marriage are writ large. Marriage calls for a full armamentarium of adaptive powers in each partner. When adaptation to new stresses fail, be they financial, sexual, emotional, parental, or social, basic inadequacies in either party rise up as neurotic signposts. Most often, the tensions evoked do not qualify for a specific diagnosis. It is recognized that marriage can be a breeding ground for dissension. As Floyd Dell, the novelist, put it some time ago: "Marriage is an iniquitous institution arranged by the Devil himself." The emotional difficulties that surface appear as depressions, hysterical episodes, emotional explosions, assaults, claims of insanity in the other spouse, and personality clashes.

The legal procedures invoked to grant a divorce rest upon the same emotional conflicts that ordinarily are overcome, neutralized, compensated for, or obscured in a successful marriage. Hostility is overcome by compliance, temperamental differences are neutralized by mutual interests, psychosexual preferences are modified by love, opposing life-styles are covered by generosity of spirit, and avarice is obscured by false liberality. These human reaction formations dissolve on the occasion of divorce. The law accommodates these nuances of feelings in its statutes and judicial rulings, but when clashing claims resist adjudication, psychiatric assistance may be needed to evaluate the depth and reversibility of conflicting personalities. This is especially true in custody problems attendant upon divorce, as well as in annulment.

Mental Illness and Matrimonial Problems

The presence of mental illness can prohibit a marriage legally, or it can be the basis for annulment and for divorce. This bald statement has many ramifications. Indeed, Judge Ploscowe and his associates in their treatise *Family Law* observed: "insanity as a concept has occasioned a crazy quilt pattern in family law."[1] In the common law, a feebleminded or insane person could not contract a legal marriage because such a one was "unable to understand in a reasonable manner the nature and consequences of the transaction, i.e., consent to marriage." This notion has been embodied in the statutes of most states. The principle involved is that of voidable and void marriage. In the voidable, the validity of the marriage can be attacked; in the void, it has no legal force from the beginning. The significance of a void versus a voidable marriage arises in relation to legitimatization of any children of the marriage and to property rights. These problems come up primarily in annulment proceedings. A marriage based on circumstances which make it voidable (or capable of being annulled) is in existence until it is declared void by a court and is only void from the time it is so declared. A "marriage" based on circumstances which make it "void" never existed *ab initio;* it still requires a declaration of nullity by a court before it can be said not to have existed,[2] but it is then void from the beginning. An infinite variety of situations arises in litigation relating to mental illness and marriages. In California, if one party is of "unsound mind unless after coming to reason, the parties freely cohabit," the marriage is voidable.[3] In New York, the marriage of a "lunatic" can be voided at any time during the continuancy of the lunacy or after the lunatic's death by a relative "who has an interest to void the marriage."[4]

Psychiatrists are not often involved in marriages prohibited because of mental illness, but they may be called to testify as to the lack of capacity to "reasonably understand" the nature and consequences of the marriage transaction.[5] Such cases usually come to attention through the objections of relatives whose pride, progeny, or property are involved. In the following case, the parents of a mentally ill young woman sought psychiatric and legal advice to prevent her marriage to a young man who himself had recovered from a schizophrenic episode.

Roger, the only son of an educated couple became confused during his first year in college. He was depressed, and felt hopeless and inadequate with suicidal thoughts. A complete estrangement followed between himself and his parents who sought to impress him with Christian Science doctrine. He refused treatment and left home.

Moving to Washington, D.C., Roger enrolled in a university but continued depressed. In a trance-like state, he attempted a hold-up but was shot in the thigh by a policeman. Hospitalized at St. Elizabeth's Hospital, he was diagnosed as paranoid schizophrenia. The charge was dropped and the patient was released after two years of treatment at the age of 22 to be followed by a private psychiatrist. He improved slowly over five years when he met the girl, Iris, with whom he became infatuated. Her parents sent her to Europe with a brother to escape Roger's attentions. On her return she became acutely, then chronically insane and was declared to be incurable by competent psychiatrists in a leading sanatorium in the east.

Meanwhile, Roger had improved under psychotherapy to the point of obtaining a responsible job with a large organization. He insisted on visiting the girl in the hospital but was prevented through an injunction secured by the parents on advice of psychiatrists that it would worsen the patient. Roger prevailed and the pair were married secretly while the patient was on leave. Subsequently the girl improved sufficiently to leave the hospital. The husband, aware of possible annulment proceedings on the part of his wife's parents, requested an examination, which was done with the following report.

The patient complained only of spotty memory defects. She had been treated with electro-shock therapy and with Insulin therapy at the hospitals in which she was domiciled. In spite of this, she was able to do work requiring close attention and had a comprehending mind. During her period out of hospitals, it should be noted that she took courses at a community college, achieving a degree of A.A.

Her physical health was good; she had interest in sports and social events, was alert and displayed no emotional blocks or other residuals of mental illness. She had considerable insight into her mental breakdown, being aware of the place of stresses in her life and their potential to cause trouble. She had calculated all these risks and had balanced them against her normal wishes and aspirations as a woman in our culture. It was noteworthy also that the hallucinations and delusions from which she suffered at the time of her hospitalization had been erased from her mind through the shock therapy.

In the opinion of the examiner, the patient Iris had suffered from schizophrenia, paranoid type. However, at the examination no evidence of this condition was present. She appreciated the forbearance and steadfastness of her husband, understanding his personality and the history of a breakdown in his case, and was able to balance all these factors as would any mature person.

The patient was able to contract a marriage, conduct business and manage her own affairs; she was mentally competent from a psychiatric and legal point of view.

The marriage continued uncontested by the parents of the bride.

Annulment, Divorce, and Insanity

The grounds for divorce or annulment of a marriage are numerous and closely similar in the fifty states. Grounds for divorce include adultery, incurable insanity, mental cruelty, alcoholism, conviction of a felony, drug addiction, desertion, impotence, refusal to bear a child, excessive sexual demands (nymphomania and satyriasis), incompatibility, failure to provide for a spouse, bigamy, "intoxication and loose habits." The categories in which psychiatric attention is sought are mainly mental illness, sexual problems, mental cruelty, and alcohol and drug addiction. There are many other grounds—incest, physical cruelty, separation, stubborn silence, unchastity, contracting a venereal disease, and connivance—all of which have little or no relation to psychiatric evaluation.

The fact of "incurability" of mental illness is dictated primarily by psychiatrists. For example, in New York annulment can be granted to the spouse of an incurable mental patient after the latter has been insane for five years or more.[6] The procedure for establishing incurability[7] specifies that "three physicians, recognized authorities on mental disease, appointed by the court, all agree on incurable insanity . . . [but] the judge is not bound by this opinion." In California, the decision as to incurability also rests with psychiatrists as in *Wirz v. Wirz* (1950)[8] wherein denial by the trial court of the husband's suit for divorce was appealed. At the initial trial, Dr. Walter Rapaport, superintendent of Agnews State Hospital, testified that the wife was a chronic manic depressive psychotic, but the trial judge disregarded this opinion. On appeal, the appellate justice reversed the denial, referring to "medical expert opinion evidence":

The Question is the quantum of proof . . . [necessary] . . . to establish "incurable insanity" . . . absolute certainty is not required . . . [only] moral certainty or proof which produces conviction in the unprejudiced mind.
    The trier of the fact is not entitled to . . . disregard uncontradicted, entirely probable testimony of unimpeached witnesses.[9]

The general rule is that, in addition to the testimony of the treating psychiatrists, the mentally ill spouse must be incurably insane or confined to a state hospital or other institution for a period of three to five years immediately preceding filing of the action. The time varies in the several states: the Alaska Code prescribes eighteen months; Nevada, two years; and Washington, "at least two years . . . due to chronic mania or dementia."[10] Maryland adds "that such insanity is permanently incurable with no hope of recovery" to the requirements that the patient "is confined to an insane asylum, or hospital . . . for not less than three years" and is certified by "two or more physicians competent in psychiatry."[11] Delaware law states that a "mentally retarded, epileptic or chronic and recurrent mentally ill person . . . [who] has been under the supervision or care of an institution for mental disease during a period of five years" is subject to divorce by a spouse. Delaware further requires a report from a five-member commission consisting of

the State psychiatrist, . . . a licensed physician . . . an attorney . . . two laymen of good character. . . . If the report of this commission shall be that the person is mentally retarded, epileptic, or a chronic or recurrent mentally ill person, and has been . . . in an institution for five years . . . the Superior Court may grant a divorce . . .[12]

The Delaware commission's judgment was questioned by one appellant,[13] after the trial judge denied the petition of the husband because the commission had adjudged the wife mentally ill rather than adjudicated her *de lunatico inquirendo* as prescribed by statute. On appeal to the Supreme Court of Delaware, Chief Justice Wolcott, although recognizing that adjudication was a judgment "by exercise of judicial power," decided that the commission's adjudgment satisfied the laws. He therefore remanded the case to enter a divorce decree.

In all jurisdictions, the basic test is whether the insane party is capable of understanding the obligations assumed in the marriage. This rule, present in the common law, has been invoked in the enormous variety of divorce pleadings that face the judiciary. For example, one question arose as to the parameters of insanity. An early California case (1911), *Dunphy v. Dunphy*,[14] concerned an annulment from a marriage contracted during an alcoholic spree by an only son of wealthy parents; the son was conceded to be a wastrel and chronic alcoholic. The court acceded to the claim that the husband was "too intoxicated at the time of marriage [with] no comprehension of the nature and effect of the marriage ceremony." The young man's guardian added that his ward was of "unsound mind." The annulment was granted. The wife of four days appealed, indicating that Dunphy had cohabited with her with a conscious wish to marry. On appeal before the Supreme Court of California, several physicians testified that excessive and prolonged drinking of alcohol brought about "an organic change in the brain." The chief justice remarked that up to that time (1911), "This court has never had occasion to define the degree of unsoundness of mind which will authorize a judgment annulling a marriage."

The justice considered the assertion that Dunphy was of "unsound mind" in these terms: "[T]he question of what is an unsound mind must, in cases of this character, be determined by the same tests which are applied in any case where it is sought to set aside the contract or other act of a person alleged to be insane. . . ." Based on the testimony of the physicians, the annulment was sustained.

The capacity to appreciate the obligations of marriage brings up other considerations. In one New Jersey case, a wife obtained a divorce from a husband who had been confined in a mental hospital for the requisite period (twenty-four months) as a paranoid schizophrenic. The husband appealed on the grounds that he had been given a number of leaves from the hospital during the two years; thus, he claimed "non-continuous hospitalization."[15] The Superior Court affirmed the "divorce from bed and board," ruling that

the non-institutionalized spouse, he or she, needs and is entitled to a partner in the household, and a surrogate parent for the children, if any. . . .
. . . A patient who is confined to a mental hospital and who will not be discharged unless approval is given by the medical staff is not the spouse of a viable marriage.

Earlier, a similar result was reached by a New York court in *Weiss v. Weiss* (1961).[16] In this suit for annulment the wife-defendant contended that remissions in her illness which permitted her release from the hospital for periods of time during her marriage were proof that her illness was not "incurable." This constituted her defense to the annulment. The court responded:

The fact that an illness has responded to treatment does not necessarily establish that it is not incurable. . . . [The law] is not intended to grant the right of divorce (or annulment) only from those persons who are so violently insane that they have to be incarcerated at all times. The test is not the manifestation of the mental disease. It is permanence and incurability.

Some states refuse to provide insanity as grounds for divorce or annulment, especially when the insanity of a party occurred after a valid marriage had begun. This was the case in Iowa (*Punelli v. Punelli*, 1967[17]) wherein a husband obtained a divorce on the grounds that his wife, a mentally ill person, demonstrated "cruel and inhuman behavior," including physical violence. The wife appealed to the Supreme Court of Iowa on several grounds, among them that there had been insufficient evidence of her mental incapacity. In this regard, Justice Mason commented: "Our problem is not with sufficiency of evidence . . . but with responsibility for the [cruel and inhuman] acts." He ruled that a divorce cannot be granted "if the acts complained of were the result of mental illness . . . for which the guilty party is not responsible." The Supreme Court reversed the lower court's decree of divorce and remanded the case for a hearing as to the wife's responsibility. In this situation, the lack of ability to comprehend the "inhuman" acts because of mental illness became a defense to divorce. Even in those states where insanity is not a ground for annulment or divorce, the actions of the "insane" party will provide grounds for a divorce based on the general concept of "breakdown of the marriage relationship," a "no-fault" concept which is rapidly becoming generally accepted. This concept is set out in the Iowa Code which prescribes as grounds for divorce: "Breakdown of the marriage relationship to the extent that the legitimate objects of matrimony have been destroyed and there remains no reasonable likelihood that marriage can be preserved."[18]

Indeed, the very complexity of divorce and annulment grounds resulted in the formulation of the Uniform Marriage and Divorce Act, adopted by the American Bar Association in 1974.[19] The act provides for "irretrievable breakdown of the marriage" as the sole ground for dissolution of marriage. Nine states had accepted this simplification by 1974. Even so, there are many situations that call for psychiatric opinion and testimony. One of these of particular interest to the medical expert is that of sexual disability as grounds for divorce and annulment.

Sexual Disabilities in Divorce and Annulment Proceedings

Impotence on the part of a husband is frequently a legal ground for divorce or annulment. The California Code states that a marriage is voidable, such that an annulment may be granted if "either party was, at the time of marriage, physically incapable of entering into the married state and such incapacity continues and appears to be incurable."[20]

The legal test is whether the man can maintain an erection sufficient to penetrate; inability to impregnate, i.e., sterility, is not a bar to the marriage. Furthermore, as set forth in one California case (*Stepanek v. Stepanek*, 1961),[21] the impotence has to be incurable, and the plaintiff must show "clear proof of the permanent and incurable physical incapacity" to establish this fact.

In this case, a woman of thirty-eight, claimed that her husband, a man of sixty-six, was impotent because of high blood pressure and excessive drinking. The husband denied the claim, although he admitted he had married "partly for companionship because at his age a person would have to." After receiving a deed to real estate, the wife petitioned for annulment. The petition was denied on the grounds of "absence of evidence that the condition appears to be incurable."

Impotence sufficient for a legal attack on a marriage may be psychological or physical, and if it is known to the husband before the marriage, it may authorize granting of an annulment and may even constitute fraud. In recent years, the term *physical causes* have included psychological impotence, and judges have recognized that sexual debility is treatable.

The basic premise that impotence when "incurable" "violates the very law of nature" is a carryover from ecclesiastical law of centuries ago, but it is still adequate grounds for divorce in twenty-six states and for annulment in eighteen states.[22] The occurrence of impotence early in marriage, when medical advice is sought, is usually dealt with by referral to a urologist to ascertain the possible presence of a physical defect of the genital organs. Rarely is a physical cause found since most cases of impotence are of a psychological nature. However, as the two cases to be quoted demonstrate, men without sexual experience before marriage can suffer from inability to carry out normal intercourse with a spouse for unperceived organic reasons.

A woman of 24 married a man of 26 with a congenital defect of the penis (hypospadias) for which he had had partial surgical repair as a child. Penetration was impossible however, and the wife suggested consultation with a urologic surgeon. On completing the repair of the hypospadias so that the urethra terminated at the distal end of the penis, intercourse became possible. No legal action was taken and the couple adopted a child to their mutual satisfaction.

The second case involved a neurologic disorder—multiple sclerosis of moderate to severe degree—which made intercourse increasingly ineffective.

A couple met in college, both aged about 24 years, and finding themselves congenial, decided on marriage. Neither had sexual experience before marriage. First attempts at sexual intercourse were mildly successful but as the marriage progressed, the husband became more and more impotent. The wife developed a depression and a state of nervous tension. Both were seen and it was soon evident that the husband had a nervous system affliction.

Neurological examination demonstrated incoordination, muscle weakness in the lower extremities, urinary difficulty, ataxia and reflex changes. A diagnosis of multiple sclerosis was made. Divorce was sought and obtained without contest. The wife re-married, had three children in a successful marriage.

Psychogenic impotence rests upon various neurotic factors. Latent homosexuality, unconscious hostility towards females, and neurotic inhibitions of various types, including cultural and familial pressures, have been encountered in cases sent for treatment. This very common difficulty comes before a legal tribunal chiefly under the insistence of the wife or relatives. As is well known, the fact of the marriage tie can occasion impotence where potency was normal outside of marriage or with other partners. Occasional religious differences between the pair, with strong reactions to cultural identifications on either side, can contribute or precipitate the impotence. Two cases reveal the operation of these factors.

A young rabbinical student married to a Jewess became so deeply immersed in his philosophical studies that he spent little time with his wife. Upon her request for sexual activity on the honeymoon and thereafter, the husband stated he preferred to regard her in a spiritual way. He considered marital sex to be an intrusion on the spiritual relationship, in spite of counsel by his teachers to the contrary. The wife sought a religious divorce (the "get" based on the Talmudic teaching—"If a man vows he will not have intercourse with his wife . . . he is compelled to divorce her").[23] She also sought a legal annulment, which was granted.

* * *

Owen D., a scientist with a doctorate from a leading eastern university, met and courted a young woman with comparable education. The girl was Catholic and the man Protestant. During the courtship, the wife-to-be noted a lack of ardor although Owen was acceptable socially. Both the mother of the affianced and the girl herself considered Owen as "emotionally frozen." He gave every appearance of enjoying their active social life but never mentioned anything of his intimate thoughts, desires or wishes, accepting the plans presented by the girl without comment. At one point he said, "Sex is for after one marries." He was observed to be fastidious and "over organized." There had been no sexual life on his part prior to the marriage, at the age of 31.

No intercourse was attempted on the honeymoon. For a month they lived a celibate life when the wife left in anger at the non-consummation of the marriage. After an annulment was granted, the husband entered psychotherapy, with achievement of potency. He met a Catholic girl with whom he had an affair until marriage was proposed and rejected by the girl on religious grounds. Two years later, the relationship continued but doubts began to arise regarding his sexual competence. The problems reached a solution when, a year later, Owen met and married a Protestant girl with whom he had a gratifying life in every respect.

The psychological factors which impede successful penetration are manifold. Anxiety, or performance anxiety as it is now called,[24] is a frequent cause which may progress to a phobic reaction against any physical contact with the partner on a neurotic basis or simply as "embarrassment or maidenly reluctance" to engage in sexual relations. The latter cause obtained in a Georgia case (1941),[25] wherein the wife petitioned for divorce, while the husband requested annulment on the grounds that the marriage was never consummated because of alleged impotence. The wife, however, testified that she suffered embarrassment at his weakness but complied sexually. The presiding judge held for the wife since she claimed impotence was not shown to have been "incurable" and hence was not a valid claim on the husband's part.

A woman's inability to perform intercourse is usually the result of psychological factors causing involuntary spasm of the vagina, a condition known as vaginismus, analogous to impotence in men. Sometimes it does not reach the point of inability to allow penetration, but it causes pain on intercourse, known as dyspareunia. If vaginismus makes penetration impossible, it becomes the basis for annulment, since the legal test, as indicated in the New York case just quoted, is the "physical capacity" to consummate marriage. Similarly, the California law states that "the ability or inability for copulation, not fruitfulness," is the legal test for annulment.[26]

In a case treated by this author, a mature man, married to a compatible wife, planned to have a family but found intercourse impossible because of the wife's vaginismus. Before an annulment was initiated, the pair sought psychiatric help. A course of hypnotherapy, concentrating on the wife's fear of penetration based on a lifelong inferiority neurosis, brought symptomatic relief. Her unconscious fear of adopting the role of wife and mother was dealt with by using posthypnotic suggestion. After three months of normal sexual life, the patient reported that she was pregnant.

Indignities—Grounds for Divorce

The number of sexual difficulties that intrude on a marriage, exclusive of impotence in a husband and inabilty to conceive in a wife, are usually placed under the rubric of indignities. In an earlier edition of his *Divorce and Annulment* (1895), Nelson cites "peccadilloes; annoying habits; disagreeableness," even "moral and religious differences," as not necessarily grounds for divorce.[27] More recently, the term *indignities* covers a wide range of offensive behavior which may or may not dip into objectionable sexual activity. Much of this behavior is lumped under the term *sexual mismating*[28] and includes dissatisfactions of both parties, infidelities, excessive sexual demands, complaints such as "made to feel like a prostitute," "boasting of affairs," and other such complaints as are familiar to confidants of the parties. Indeed, claimed indignities can be very diverse. In *Robinson v. Robinson* (1957),[29] wherein the wife threw a dinner plate at the husband, struck him with a broom, bit him, yelling "Murder, Murder," removed a strong box containing $30,000 belonging to him, spit at him, and the like, a Pennsylvania court declared:

An indignity to the person is an affront to the personality of another, a lack of reverence for the personality of one's spouse. It consists of various acts, so varied, in their nature that the courts have not undertaken to define the offense in more than general terms. But the offense is complete when a continued and persistent course of conduct demonstrates that the love and affection upon which the matrimonial status rests has been permanently replaced by hatred and estrangement.

A more modern statement with due regard to psychological factors and a less stereotyped "ideal" marriage pattern is that enunciated in a Florida case, *Firestone v. Firestone* (1972).[30] In this case, both individuals had wealth and social station: "Extreme cruelty as ground for divorce is relative . . . determined by the degree of one's culture, his emotions, nervous reaction or moral sense. . . . The rapid change in social conventions may generate conditions that bring on extreme cruelty." The legal test for indignities that support a divorce decree remain "that [which] causes mental torture, undermines the health or tends to dethrone the reason of the other."

From a psychiatric point of view, such indignities described from the statutes as "mental cruelty" sufficient for a divorce can rest on disabling neurosis, incipient psychoses, personality peculiarities, plain pique, or sadistic attitudes. Such categories as verbal abuse, stubborn silence, nagging, humiliation in public, and obscene language, which tend to "induce mental or physical hurt on the object of misconduct," have been grounds for divorce.[31] Obviously, each such charge must be evaluated on the basis of an analysis of each party's personality, cultural background, and mental health. In states where "no fault" divorce laws are in effect, as in California, judges may request opinions, when custody problems arise, from marriage counselors in the family court departments or from psychiatrists or psychiatric social workers in private practice. Consultants of this sort are commonly requested by attorneys prior to filing a divorce petition to rule out actual mental illness or serious neurotic problems better solved by psychotherapy than by divorce. Such a situation is outlined in this case:

A couple in their middle 40's, married for 22 years developed sufficient intra-familial tension to contemplate legal separation. The husband and wife ran an active business which suffered from a burglary accompanied by a beating of the wife by the assailant. The tension existing prior to this incident now became "unbearable." Recriminations from the woman toward the man took the form of complaints of "being tied down," violent outbursts, both physical and verbal. The husband's complaints were of tremendous hostility of the wife towards him and of the threat to break up a meaningful relationship of 22 years and to destroy an active and successful business.

The husband had been an outstanding executive in government service before opening the business; the wife had been an entertainer in early life and presented the picture of an attractive, well-groomed, intelligent woman. During the interviews, bitter attacks by the wife on the husband were counter-balanced by a thrust of blame by the husband due to her "inferiority neurosis." Psychotherapy at intervals over a period of two years availed nothing.

The wife was hospitalized after an episode in which she threatened to shoot the husband and exhibited a flurry of paranoid accusations and extreme hysterical over-reactions. Physical examination including an electroencephalogram (based on the suspicion of an "epileptoid personality") was negative. However, the stream of invective, the aggressive attitude and the hysterical frenzy during the brief psychotic episode seemed to support a diagnosis of hysterical psychosis. Her brittle attitude at times had a schizoid flavor which alternated with depression and guilt over her aggressive attitude towards the husband. He showed marked dependence on his wife, mixed with distress over his rejection.

Eventually, a separation was effected and finally a divorce. The wife sought other male relationships and attempted to develop her own career. Although both parties were able to perceive the psychologic problem between them, no effective change could be accomplishd. The divorce was granted on the basis of "irreconcilable differences."

Custody and Parental Mental Problems

The basic issue in decreeing custody of children after a divorce revolves around the established principle, as stated by Nelson,[32] and agreed to by all courts:

The court must be guided in determining the custody of minor children [in that] the best interests and welfare of the children is the paramount consideration; the dominant thought is that children are not chattels to be disposed of according to the wishes of the parents or anyone else. . . .

The usual procedure has been to place children in the custody of the mother, especially when they are of "tender age." This so-called tender age doctrine has recently come under attack as prejudicial to fathers. According to a Kansas decision (1975), it is only one "important factor to be considered in determining how a child's interest and welfare are best served,"[33] and in California (1972), it was deleted from the statute.[34] Generally, however, few awards of custody of small children to the mother are challenged except where the "best interest of the child" principle appears to be violated. The recent trend in custody law is toward treating parents equally, with more custody awards being granted to fathers and occasionally with both parents retaining joint custody or with sole custody regularly alternating between them.

Although the "best interest of the child" principle is universally accepted, some experts insist that the phrase is "amorphous," requiring, beyond a judicial decision, an analysis of the personalities of the contesting parties in custody proceedings and their probable effect on the child.

Professor Henry Foster of New York University feels that "the assistance of social scientists and experts is essential if the decision is in fact to be in accord with the 'best interest of the child'."[35] Anna Freud and co-workers, in *Beyond the Best Interests of the Child* (1973), plead for a translation of "what we know from psychoanalysis about growth and development" of the child to "procedural and substantive guidelines . . . [of] actual judicial decisions."[36]

In accordance with this view, psychiatrists and psychologists have been increasingly involved in custody conflicts, especially when the demand is made that a child be removed from custody based on the custodial parent's mental health, life-pattern, and sexual or other "intemperate behavior." The Code in California, for example, lists seven reasons for removal of a child from custody of a parent, two of which are of concern here:

(a) When the parent suffers a disability because of the habitual use of alcohol or (nonmedical) controlled substances, or is morally depraved,
(b) or the parent is declared mentally deficient or mentally ill by a competent court and the State Director of Mental Hygiene or the superintendent of a State Hospital where the parent is hospitalized certifies as to mental deficiency or mental illness such that the parent will not be capable of supporting or controlling the child in a proper manner.[37]

Beyond the judicial granting of custody at the time of a divorce decree, the issue of changing custody arises some time later. Removal of a child from custody of a mentally ill parent presents little difficulty when psychiatric examination certifies that the parent is incurably ill.

More weighty problems develop when a noncustodial parent or relative alleges that the custodial parent is morally depraved, has intemperate habits, or is otherwise unfit for custody. The exact legal meaning of "moral depravity" is not defined in the law, but the phrase usually denotes immoral sexual behavior, alcoholism, or drug abuse. It is often cited by grandparents or interested relatives, including the noncustodial parent, when a liaison is uncovered existing between the custodial parent and another man or woman. The implication is that contact by the child or children with the enamorata will result in emotional harm to the minors. Among actual cases, the range of conduct claimed by the term *depravity* can range from claims of "numerous heterosexual and homosexual affairs" to sexually molesting a minor (daughter or son), a criminal record, use of obscene language before a child, and drug abuse. The court is concerned essentially with the effects of "moral turpitude" on the minors.

In practice, claims of deleterious influence on a child are made by the ex-spouse or in-laws, after a visit to the noncustodial parent. Such claims are often made when the noncustodial parent is found to be living with a new partner or is remarried, as in the following example.

Dolores, aged 31, divorced her husband after a year of marriage. The husband, a stable man with close relationship to his parents, insisted that the couple live next door to his parents. His superficial reason was that the grandparents could be of aid to them. Dolores found the marriage intolerable: the husband was "tied to his parents." Before the divorce, a child was born who became the grandparents' pride. The divorce followed one year of marriage. One of the complaints of the grandparents revolved around Dolores' friendship with the family doctor who understood her virtual exclusion by the grandparents from the family circle. The divorce court awarded custody to the mother, with visitation rights to the husband who always took the three-year-old boy to his parents' home. As time wore on the child, on his return to his mother after weekend visits, showed hysterical tantrums, loss of appetite, marked insecurity and "nervousness" for several days after the paternal visit. Accusations on either side increased: the grandparents and husband claimed that Dolores' friendship with the doctor was the cause of the boy's nervous symptoms

Under the whiplash of the grandparents, the husband petitioned the court to remove his son from the custody of the mother on grounds that she was "unfit," citing the close friendship with the doctor. The judge requested psychiatric study of all parties followed by a report.

Examination of the boy revealed a tense, wary lad just over three years, obviously bright and just as obviously attached to his mother. Interviews with the grandparents, ex-husband, Dolores and her doctor friend made it clear that the outspoken antagonism of the husband's family was the stimulus for the child's emotional turmoil.

The report of the court recommended changing the visitation rights to avoid bringing the child into contact with the grandparents. The court confirmed the earlier custodian rights of Dolores and agreed with the visitation rearrangement.

In some situations, grandparents (or other close relatives) have requested that the relation of parent and child be "severed" because of mental illness or "depraved" conduct on the part of the parent. In a California case, *Zimmerman v. Zimmerman* (1962),[38] the grandparents of a child petitioned the court to "free her from the custody and control of her parent," in this case the mother. Two years before, the child, Rene, had been declared a ward of the Juvenile Court at the age of seven; her father had died when she was two. The mother's home was found to be unfit for Rene; the mother had entertained men "at all hours," drinking, and sexual activities "were carried on . . . many of them in the presence of the child." It was further alleged that the mother "habitually used vulgar and profane language . . . in the child's presence." After the allegations were found to be true, the child was made a ward of the court until the age of eighteen years. The mother assented to the charges but made an effort during the next two years to rehabilitate herself after a period in a state hospital. In spite of this effort, the grandparents petitioned for "termination of all parental control [and] severance of the relationship between child and parent" on the grounds that the mother was depraved at the time of the hearing. This petition was denied by the court and the denial was upheld by the Appellate Court. The child remained with the grandparents, but the request for the vital "termination of the parental relationship," virtually a disowning of the child, was rejected.

In this case, sexual irregularities on the part of the mother were acknowledged. Generally, sexual deviation practiced on the children by an ex-husband becomes the reason for requesting change of visitation rights. Whether the charges are true or, as is often the case, exaggerated, or even trumped up by the mother or grandparents, such a complaint reflects the animosity that existed between the parents prior to the divorce. Long-held adult hatreds expressed as conscious or unconscious sexual jealousies between the parties become enlarged as they are projected on the screen of custody and visitation rights. The children involved become the pawns of this continued struggle. The recriminations that flow back and forth between the parents generally rest on deep feelings of rejection in the ex-wife and unrealized dependence feelings in the ex-husband. The courts consider this psychological interplay to be of primary interest only when overt acts react on the best interests of the child. Clinical experience has shown that sexual acts performed on children by an ex-husband are not the consequence of a mentally disordered sex offender, but rather the result of frustration in a man humiliated by wifely rejection and belittlement. The following complex case illustrates the interplay of these psychological forces.

Wes Rutter was born out of wedlock but adopted in infancy to the Rutters. His childhood, school days and graduation from a junior college followed a normal pattern. He married at 19 to a wife who brought one child to the marriage which Wes adopted. A second child was born to the couple. Soon the union turned sour, featured by bickering and accusations of coolness by Wes towards his wife, Emily. During these years, Wes turned to his stepdaughter for comfort. On the suggestion of his wife, according to Wes, that the child learn the facts of life, she encouraged him and the girl to bathe together. This led to intimacies between the 7 year old girl and Wes in which palpation, intercourse per femora and oral play became a frequent occurrence.

The marriage meanwhile deteriorated: Emily refused Wes' sexual advances and she herself sought a lover. With this and two years of sexual misconduct with the child, Emily suddenly announced she "hated . . . his guts" and filed for divorce. A short time after this was finalized, Wes met a young woman with whom he was entirely compatible and whom he planned to marry. Because Wes had been convicted of molesting a minor and placed on probation on promise of seeking treatment, visitation rights had been denied him.

Thorough study produced no evidence in his past life of sexual deviation tendencies. Following prolonged psychotherapy and completion of his probation, he petitioned the court to create visitation rights for his two children.

On a hearing before the judge, further treatment was arranged as a condition of visitation rights. It was reported to the court that, after three years of therapeutic contact, including group therapy, "the petitioner's sexual misconduct was not based on sexual psychopathy but was the result of frustration and emotional dissatisfaction with his first wife. . . ." It was further recommended that visitation rights be permitted at his home in the presence of his present wife, a woman of stability with insight into the complex emotional problems in which the petitioner had been involved.

The court ruled favorably on this recommendation, and granted the visitation rights previously denied.

The writings and case decisions on custody problems are extensive. The *Painter v. Bannister case* (1966)[39] received wide publicity. It involved the efforts of a father to regain custody of his little boy after he voluntarily placed the child with grandparents for what the father thought was a temporary period. In this case, there was no question of "moral depravity" of the father, or even of "fitness." The case revolved around the issue of "the best interest of the child" based upon a psychologist's evaluation of the varying life-styles of the contesting parties. The case is reported in full in Brooks' *Law, Psychiatry and the Mental Health System*[40] with notes and commentary. Here is only the merest outline of the case:

Mark Painter, aged 7 years, was living with his maternal grandparents in Iowa when his father, now remarried after the child's mother died three years before the current action, sought to regain custody. The appeal court was asked to decide between the rightful parent, the father, Mr. Painter, and the grandparents, the Bannisters. The latter lived in a conservative Iowan community, whose citizens were church-goers, interested in college education for their children and generally stable, conventional, middle-class people. The father, Painter, was a free-lance writer and photographer, living a "Bohemian life" in Northern California, "a romantic and dreamer" according to an Iowan psychiatrist. He was an agnostic "or atheist" with leanings toward Zen Buddhism. The Bannisters were 60; Painter was in his mid-20's. The father had already established himself, but planned to move and live in an artist colony near San Francisco.

Dr. Glen Hawks, a child psychologist of Iowa State University, had made a thorough study of Mark, his grandparents and their community. He testified that if the boy were to go to his father "the chances of his going wrong" were very high. Dr. Hawks found Mark to have a superior I.Q.; he felt Mr. Bannister had become Mark's "father figure" and that the "biological father" was less important to a boy's development than the person with whom he developed an identification; that the boy's anxiety and uncertainty would be better handled with his grandparents. Dr. Hawks testified at length concerning the stable relationship the Bannisters had developed with Mark and the difficulties to be anticipated in relating to his father.

The Iowa Supreme Court ruled that the boy should be left with the Bannisters despite the trial court's award of custody to the father, and the trial court record indicated they felt the Iowa psychologist's testimony was prejudiced and exaggerated. Justice Stuart of the Iowa Supreme Court stated, "We place a great deal of reliance on the testimony (as shown in the written record) of the child psychologist" and conclude that since the primary consideration was the best interest of the child and the return of custody to the father was likely to have a seriously disturbing effect on the child's development, this fact must prevail."

The Painter case may be used as a legal precedent for future judicial decisions in custody cases. It is an example of not only legal but also psychological, sociocultural, and familial patterns considered and balanced in an effort to determine how these factors may affect the child. At the beginning of his decision, Justice Stuart stated, "Legal training and experience are of little practical help in solving the complex problems of human relations." Child analysts who have studied all stages of child development stress the importance of genuine affection, stimulation, and unbroken continuity in a young child's contact with adults, beyond the need for a father-figure for the boy and mother-figure for the girl.[41] Anna Freud and co-workers emphasize the totality of influences on a child. Although Justice Stuart acknowledged that life with Mark's father would provide intellectual stimulation and a wider horizon for the boy's growth, he proclaimed that stability of the home was more important for a proper development of a child.

Nationwide, however, others arrived at different opinions in the Painter case. Law journal articles critical of the decision appeared.[42] A book written by Mr. Painter about his losing battle for his son[43] aroused widespread sympathy and indignation. Specifically in reaction to the case, the California legislature revised the civil code,[44] setting up a priority list within which the "best interest" doctrine must be considered. This list gives first priority for custody to the parents. It is clear that, besides prognosis, the psychiatrist in custody cases must maintain an objective attitude (as was not the case with Dr. Hawks in testifying for the Bannisters) in projecting the effect of parents and social pressures and opportunities on a child's development.

Psychiatric testimony or reports regarding the mental health of those seeking custody has been challenged on the grounds of privileged communication between psychiatrists or psychologists and the patient. This issue arose in *Atwood v. Atwood* (Kentucky, 1976)[45] where a mother of three appealed a prior award of custody to the father. The award had been based on a charge that she was "mentally ill," having been seen by two psychiatrists on at least eight occasions. The expert's depositions had been considered in the initial court's award of custody to the father. The mother appealed the doctor's opinions to the Supreme Court of Kentucky, which upheld the award and ruled that the psychiatrist privilege in civil cases held except where

[t]he mental condition is introduced . . . and the judge finds it more important to the interests of justice that the communication be disclosed than that the relationship between patient and psychiatrist be protected. . . . The custody statutes (KRS 421. 215 (3) (c)) . . . place the mental conditions of all family members squarely in issue.

Adoption and Mental Problems

The principle of "best interest of the child" holds in adoption proceedings as well as in custody cases.

Because of the renewed interest in adoption and custody proceedings in states where the "no fault" divorce has been enacted, it is noteworthy that Michigan[46] defined the "best interest of the Child" standard in their Child Custody Act of 1970. The factors to be considered by the court include: the love, affection, and other emotional ties existing between the parties and the child; the capacity . . . of the parties to give the child love, affection, and guidance . . . educating and raising the child in its religion and creed if any; the capacity of the parties to provide the child with food, clothing, medical care, or other remedial care . . . ; the permanence, as a family unit, of the proposed custodial (or adoptive) home; the moral fitness of the parties. In addition, in custody problems, the act added: the length of time the child has lived in a stable, satisfactory environment . . . ; the home, school, and community record of the child; the reasonable preference of the child, if . . . the child be of sufficient age to express preference; the mental and physical health of the competing parties.

In the California Civil Code,[47] after the procedure for initiating adoption proceedings is started, and a report and recommendation from the Department of Health is received by the judge (Section 227), "The court must examine all persons appearing before it pursuant to this section, each separately, and if satisfied that the interest of the child will be promoted by the adoption . . . may make and enter a decree of adoption."

There are two reasons for rejecting adoptive parents: unsuitability of the home and unsuitability of the petitioners. In the second case, the social worker makes a negative recommendation when the adoptive parents demonstrate physical disability, mental illness, or moral unsuitability. The indices of unsuitability in the home lie beyond psychiatric purview. With regard to personality deviations, mental illness, moral turpitude, or any disturbing behavior, these can be cited by the psychiatric social worker, which may or may not be corroborated by medical consultants.

The importance of estimating prognosis in a prospective adoptive parent alleged to be mentally unfit, particularly with an infant child, is seen in *Geller v. Los Angeles County Department of Adoptions* (1968).[48] Here, an infant in the care of adoptive parents was removed from their home and committed to the County Department of Adoptions because the "petitioners are not suitable for this minor child." At the initial trial a Dr. Walters who examined Mrs. Geller found that she was "apprehensive and guarded" about her previous depressions, that her condition was a recurrent one, and that there was a strong probability that she would need "psychiatric care in the future." The petitioners appealed, including in their grounds the claim that the trial judge was "irrevocably biased against all prospective adoptive parents who had had psychiatric treatment in the past."

The psychiatric question at issue revolved around Dr. Walter's report which diagnosed Mrs. Geller as having a "long standing passive-aggressive character disorder . . . which will undoubtedly develop into psychiatric symptoms in the future." The consultant also stated that Mr. Geller had "substantial feelings of inferiority." On the other hand, a Dr. Conrad, who had treated the patient for two years for depression, asserted that "to conclude that someone with an inferiority complex makes a poor parent was 'far fetched . . . [since] depressive reactions are as common as tonsillitis'." The Court of Appeals ruled that psychiatric conflict in evidence "must be resolved by the trial court" and affirmed the earlier decision.

Psychiatric problems other than depression have been invoked to counter adoption and custody awards, notably homosexuality. As social attitudes towards homosexuality become more permissive in some segments of the country, the courts are now finding this issue arising openly in custody cases. In a 1967 California case,[49] a mother, admitting that she was a homosexual "engaging in sexual acts with other females," was denied custody of her daughter by the trial court. She appealed, and the Appellate Court ruled that the trial court "failed in its duty to consider all the evidence . . . as to how the welfare of the child best be served," in holding that the mother was unfit "on the

basis that she was a homosexual as a *matter of law*." The Appellate
Court also stated that the trial court had discretion beyond ruling the
mother was unfit "as a matter of law." More particularly, in a more
recent California case (1975),[50] the mother, a homosexual living with
another woman, intended to "bring up her daughter in that environment." When custody was refused her and an appeal was taken, the
Appellate Court ruled: "In exercising a choice between homosexual
and heterosexual households for purposes of child custody a trial court
could conclude that permanent residence in a homosexual household
would be detrimental to the children and contrary to their best interests." The role of the psychiatrist or psychologist in evaluating the
influence of either parent in adoption and custody situations would
be to evaluate the influence of homosexual attitudes and conduct upon
the child in the future.

Clearly, objectivity is an important element in such emotion-laden
situations, and one must be aware of the influence of "counter-
transference" in the examiner. Beyond these considerations, there are
guidelines for planning a child's future as developed by experts in child
psychiatry. Dr. Herbert Modlin of the Menninger Foundation, summarizing extensive experience with neglected orphanage children over
two decades, divided the developmental levels as follows:

The FIRST two years of a child's life, the *pre-verbal* period require "good
mothering" with all the emotional nurturance and "atmosphere of affection and
solitude" it implies,
    The SECOND phase (three to six years) needs both male and female figures
(not necessarily biological parents) to develop "sexual identity, love, dependence
and self-concept,"
    The THIRD phase (six to twelve years) a period of defining and consoli-
dating basic personality traits and learning stress-handling techniques, requires
a "home atmosphere . . . [with] predictable, trustworthy people with whom the
child can interact meaningfully,"
    The FOURTH phase of normal adolescence, a "transition stage period of
severe upheaval and change" needs parents with a pliable personality in addition
to "external parental controls, as church, school, social controls."[51]

These stages of development must, of course, be viewed in relation to
the adoptive or custodial parents' capacity for emotional security, their
social and cultural level, the educational possibilities of the child, and
the innate intelligence and physical condition of the child. The following case involved some of these considerations:

A young couple, aged 23 and 27 respectively sought to adopt a child. The social
worker denied the petition because she found the wife to be emotionally unstable, e.g., crying without adequate cause.

The petitioner was seen by a psychiatrist: her complaint was that she was depressed because "she had been prevented from adopting a child." Fertility tests on the husband showed 50% motility in his sperm count. The wife had been one of eight children, she had one year of college training, was bright, talked rapidly and complained that she was over-sensitive and cried easily.

She was found not to be depressed but emotionally unstable to a degree. Her judgment was good, she carried her responsibilities well but showed diffuse anxiety and over-reactions to minor stresses in her life.

A final diagnosis of no psychosis but a personality make-up of a "quick re-actor" type, just short of emotional instability was made. She was regarded as basically a good candidate for adoption. The patient was much relieved with this opinion, freely expressed, losing much of her anxiety, of what she considered some type of biological inferiority.

The adoptive parents may occasionally find the child to be physi-cally or mentally afflicted and may then wish to rescind the adoption. In such cases, there is a provision in the California Code for a petition to set aside the adoption.

If any child heretofore or hereafter adopted . . . shows evidence of being feeble-minded, epileptic or insane as a result of a condition prior to the adoption and of which the adopting parents had no knowledge . . . a petition setting forth such facts may be filed and if such facts are proved to the satisfaction of the judge the adoption may be set aside.[52]

This uncommon situation occurred in the following instance:

The adoptive parents of a child, received when he was about one year old, began to notice that the child developed a gait disturbance as he began to walk. It was in the nature of the so-called "scissors gait" characteristic of cerebral palsy. Soon the child showed slowness in talking, inability to play with other children and generally mental dullness. The child was brought to an orthopedic surgeon at the age of three years who diagnosed a "tendency toward spasticity in the lower extremities." The child was seen by a neuropsychiatrist who felt there was an indication of cerebral palsy with a possibility of mental retardation. The adoption was set aside.

Sterilization

Laws permitting sterilization of mental defectives stemmed from the eugenic movement of the late nineteenth century which hoped to control the rising tide of crime by reducing the progeny of the feeble-minded. It was regarded as constitutionally permissible to prevent the procreation of "moral degenerates" by sterilization. In *Buck v. Bell*, a Virginia case (1927),[53] sterilization applied to inmates of mental in-stitutions was reviewed by the U.S. Supreme Court. Justice Holmes placed the imprimatur of the Court on this practice in saying: "It is better for all the world, if instead of waiting to execute degenerate offspring for crime, or to let them starve for their imbecility, society can prevent those kind who are manifestly unfit from continuing their kind."

For some years, the law in several states upheld the validity of involuntary sterilization of institutional and prison inmates afflicted with "hereditary forms" of insanity or imbecility, as in Oklahoma's Habitual Criminal Act (1935).[54] By 1917, the laws of sixteen states permitted involuntary sterilization of persons certified by heads of institutions as feebleminded, epileptic, moral degenerate, or sexually perverted, including "habitual criminals." The number had risen to thirty-two states by 1942 but fell when these statutes were declared to be unconstitutional in 1942 in *Skinner v. Oklahoma*[55] because the "habitual criminal" need not have committed acts involving moral degeneration. Meanwhile, scientific support for sterilization of persons who were supposedly genetically "unfit" faded until it was recognized that there was no justification for sterilizing sexual or any other offenders.[56]

Still, sterilization through vasectomy and fallopian tube ligation, to reduce the probability of mentally defective progeny, was permitted in California and twenty other states as recently as 1968.[57] The California Welfare and Institutions Code, Section 7254, permits eugenic sterilization to

Any person lawfully committed to any state hospital . . . who is afflicted with . . .
a) Mental disease which may have been inherited and is likely to be transmitted to descendants.
b) Mental retardation in any of its various grades.
c) Marked departures from normal mentality.
The Superintendent of the state hospital . . . shall certify such opinion to the Director of Mental Health and shall . . . give written notice of such certification to the patient, known parents, spouse, adult children or guardian . . . with provisions for hearing by the Director of Mental Health in case of objection. . . .

Involuntary sterilization has been subject to legal attack on many grounds, particularly its constitutionality, its abuse of police power of the state, the question of cruel and unusual punishment, arbitrary classification of inmates of institutions, and so on. Judicial answers to these legal attacks have varied. As the *American Law Review* put it, "they do not establish a trend but rather a pattern of alternating periods of approval and disapproval of the statutes in question."[58] For example, an Alabama statute which permitted the assistant and superintendent of the Partlow School for mental defectives to "prescribe for treatment of inmates . . . [if] they deem it advisable . . . [are] authorized and empowered to sterilize any inmate,"[59] was ruled unconstitutional by three judges called to settle the issue of constitutionality in 1973. Regarding the statute involved (Title 45, Section 243, Alabama Code), they stated: "The sterilization *vel non* [or not] of mentally retarded inmates cannot be left to the unfettered discretion of any two officials or individuals."

Since sterilizations were proceeding "in certain instances" in spite of the declaration of unconstitutionality, Chief Judge Johnson of the U.S. District Court covering Alabama in 1974 set out certain standards in order to provide a "full panoply of constitutional protection" for the inmates subject to involuntary sterilization.[60] In addition to legal safeguards, this protection consisted of a Review Committee which was required to approve the decision to sterilize prior to surgery. The commission, in addition to physicians, attorneys, women, and "minority group members," was to include a resident (inmate) of the Partlow State School. Judge Johnson added that all information should be available to the director and that the "inmate understands the nature and consequences of sterilization . . . and has formed, without coercion, a genuine desire to be sterilized. . . ."

A recent case (1976) in North Carolina[61] faced the question of constitutionality differently. The subject was a minor with an IQ of 40, hence a "proper subject for sterilization . . . [who] . . . unless sterilized would procreate a child or children who would have serious physical, mental or nervous disease or deficiencies."

The director of social services for the county requested an order to comply with the law, but the minor's attorney petitioned that the request be quashed. The Superior Court judge agreed, finding the law to be unconstitutional. The state authorities then asked for a review of the case, and Judge Moore of the Supreme Court of North Carolina ruled, after consideration of all factors, that the law was *not* unconstitutional. He added that medical "evidence must be clear, strong and convincing before an order [for sterilization] may be entered."

The Delinquent Child

Children come under legal surveillance and mental observation and evaluation for two general reasons: as behavior problems and as delinquents. Neglected or abandoned children also come under Juvenile Court jurisdiction. Child psychiatrists and psychologists have dealt in depth with this extensive field. The present relatively brief discussion focuses on a few salient medico-legal involvements of children in trouble with the law.

Children subject to Juvenile Court supervision include a large group, ranging from "immoral or indecent conduct, growing up in idleness

and crime, incorrigibility, habitual truancy, begging, violation of any
ordinance (curfew) or law (burglary, murder, rape, sexual offenses,
selling narcotics, etc.).''[62] It has been traditional to treat juveniles differently from adults coming before the courts. The basic philosophy
of the juvenile process is to remove children from the punitive atmosphere of the criminal courts and to handle them through informal
private hearings without juries and with the paramount goal of nurturance and rehabilitation, not punishment. The thrust of juvenile
proceedings was expressed by Miriam Van Waters in the 1920s: "The
Juvenile Court is conceived in the spirit of a clinic.''[63] This principle,
forged in the heyday of the child guidance movement, promised to
concentrate on rehabilitation and treatment through psychiatric techniques. However, because juvenile delinquents in time became involved
in more serious offenses than truancy or waywardness, the legal defenses and right to due process to which an adult criminal is entitled
were urged as the right of juveniles also. As a result, several crucial
decisions were handed down which dramatically changed the criminal
juvenile's position before the law. Without abstracting the immense
amount of litigation resulting in bringing the Juvenile Court closer to
adult courts, the significant steps will be outlined.

In 1966, the U.S. Supreme Court in *Kent v. U.S.* held that bringing
a sixteen-year-old boy before an adult court was in accordance with
juvenile law in the District of Columbia. This law allowed the judge
to remand a juvenile to the U.S. District Court (D.C.) by "waiving
jurisdiction after a full investigation" by the judge. Since the charges
against the boy were serious—housebreaking, robbery, and forcible
rape—the two psychiatrists and a psychologist expressed the opinion
that Kent showed "severe psychopathology," a plea of not guilty by
reason of insanity was entered and the offender was committed to St.
Elizabeth's Hospital. An appeal was taken, heard by the U.S. Supreme
Court on the issue of a waiver of a juvenile to an adult court.[64] Justice
Fortas, delivering the majority opinion, ruled that a juvenile offender
was entitled to the "basic requirements of due process and fairness."
In that opinion it was pointed out: "In practically all jurisdictions,
there are rights granted to adults which are withheld from juveniles."

The next year (1967), the decision in *Kent* was clarified and expanded in *In re Gault* (an Arizona case)[65] by according juveniles the
right to counsel and to cross-examination of witnesses, the right against
self-incrimination, and the right of confrontation. Indeed, according
to Justice Black's concurring opinion, "I think the Constitution requires that he (infant or adult) . . . be tried in accordance with the
guarantees of all the provisions of the Bill of Rights made applicable

to the States by the Fourteenth Amendment." Then in 1970, in *In re Winship*,[66] the further "constitutional safeguard of proof beyond a reasonable doubt" and "trial by jury" were added to the rights accorded in *Gault*. *Winship* was a New York case involving a twelve-year-old boy charged with theft under the New York juvenile law in which "the standard of proof is less rigorous than in criminal cases." Here Justice Brennan answered the question, "whether proof beyond a reasonable doubt is among the 'essentials of due process and fair treatment'" in the positive. Finally, in 1971, the issue of a jury trial for juvenile offenders was discussed in *McKiever v. Pennsylvania*[67] in which a sixteen-year-old boy was charged with robbery, larceny, and receiving stolen goods. Justice Blackmun of the U.S. Supreme Court gave the majority opinion that jury trial for juveniles should be abolished. The dissent of Justice Douglas, however, continued the movement to render juvenile offenders triable under the jury system for serious crime. He stated: [T]he juvenile court initially was created as a social experiment, it has not ceased to be part of the judicial system. . . .

These safeguards for juveniles have been criticized by, among others, Justine Polier,[68] a New York family court judge. She writes: "It has become increasingly clear that neither a factory model of efficiency in social agencies nor due process in the courts is adequate to meet the social problems that confront them." Professor Jerome Miller,[69] in discussing the future of juvenile law, comments: "Even if the Juvenile Court system had been totally effective in its substitution of treatment or rehabilitation for punishment, with a 'clinical' rather than punitive approach, the constitutional basis for such an approach would still be an open question."

In the main, these legal safeguards have not disturbed the basic philosophy of the juvenile court process. The total proceedings are alien in principle to the criminal process. The differences can be readily seen in the following: A juvenile is not "arrested," but he or she is "taken into custody" without a warrant; a petition is prepared by an intake officer rather than an indictment or information being prepared by the district attorney; the minor is held in detention, not "incarcerated" in the county jail, the court acting as *locus parentis*; there is no provision for bail for the juvenile. The probation officer can dismiss the matter at intake and no acquittal of the charge is necessary; a hearing is held on the petition and there is no trial; the records of a juvenile hearing are confidential, whereas the proceedings of a court are in the public domain. A duly appointed referee or judge may hold the hearing for a juvenile; a judge officiates in a criminal arraignment or trial. A psychological or psychiatric examination may be ordered by a judge, referee, or probation officer if sufficient signs of mental disorder appear in the child; only a judge may order a psychiatric examination in a court of record. The services of "such psychiatrists, psychologists or other clinical experts as may be required to assist in determining the appropriate treatment of the minor" are provided in the juvenile code; county funds pay for psychiatric examinations ordered by the county courts.[70]

Clinical Material

The psychological and psychiatric literature on the effects of neglect and maternal deprivation on behavior problems in children is vast. Autism, mental retardation, adolescent rebelliousness, neurosis of childhood, hyperkinesis, identity crisis, immaturity, reaction to cultural restrictions, pubertal fantasy, and inferiority feelings compensated by aggression have been abundantly explored. Similarly, the emotional and cultural factors in child criminal offenders have been plumbed. In juvenile court situations, a psychological and psychiatric report to a judge helps determine probation or rehabilitation in a training school, but has less specific meaning than in an adult court with adult offenders, except where *Kent*, *Gault*, and *Winship* decisions function. Most, if not at all, states make statutory provisions for mental examinations of juveniles, as in Florida where after adjudication by a judge examination preliminary to treatment may be ordered.[71]

The protean manifestations of juvenile psychopathology demonstrate how closely delinquent acts mirror those of adult offenders in today's world. The wide gap that was presumed to exist between the mental structure and function of children's psyches and those of adults has narrowed to the point where motivations for delinquency and criminal acts are practically indistinguishable. Three cases of juveniles will be cited, culled from many of like nature, to illustrate sexual aggression in a seventeen-year-old youth, social aggression in a fourteen-year-old girl, and wanton assault in a twelve-year-old boy.

One afternoon, a housewife was backing her car out of her driveway when she became aware of a youth's face at the car window. Suddenly pulling the door open, the seventeen-year-old boy, brandishing a knife, ordered her to drive them to a "lonely spot." The housewife induced him to allow her to re-enter her home. There the youth insisted that "she draw the drapes and disrobe" explaining that he had never seen a "naked lady" before. The victim refused, whereupon he placed a knife at the throat of her three-year-old child, repeating his demand.

With desperate courage, the mother responded with a well-placed blow to her tormentor's head, after which he left the house quietly.

The history of his delinquencies, waywardness, incorrigibility, armed robbery and kidnapping, had a most ominous ring.

Three years before the current offense Larry had ordered a girl of eight, at knife-point, to disrobe and dance for him in an abandoned building. He tried to set fire to the child's hair, then forced her and her five-year-old brother to accompany him to a restroom adjoining a motel, where he attempted intercourse with the child unsuccessfully.

Although an early psychological test indicated an IQ of 98 on the Binet-Simon test, Larry was unable to write, print his name, spell or read. It was found that Larry had not the slightest notion of the phonetic value of letters.

Larry was recognized as an "anxiety-ridden" boy with emotional thinness and a quixotic manner. He revealed a curious mixture of infantility and adult behavioral patterns. His sexual exploits, on the surface quite daring and sadistic, of which he was admittedly ashamed, were fraught with the quality of a sexual fantasy. Although this split in feeling and behavior suggested schizophrenia, there was little else to support this disgnosis in this desperate, "impulse-ridden" boy.

Several of the examiners were impressed with this bizarre behavior and schizophrenic attitudes. Two years earlier, other examiners found motor incoordination so extreme as to suggest organic brain disease.

The treatment recommended for Larry included a return to a Youth Authority institution for prolonged retraining, since he was ill-equipped to return to the social world. For a year and a half, he was given academic training in remedial mathematics and remedial English, as well as industrial training in garment making. As time progressed, Larry's senseless aggression seemed to decrease; his emotional relationship with his parents improved and his daydreams of bizarre sexual conquests faded to a sexual curiosity normal for a boy of his age, and were replaced by a more natural attitude, attended by normal emotions.

By the time Larry attained his nineteenth birthday he showed a semblance of stability, although to some observers he appeared emotionally retarded. Organic brain defect was no longer suspected. Without the tools of social relatedness (the ability to read and write), Larry had frozen to a quixotic, schizoid level, from which he gradually emerged.

Larry's female counterpart showed her aggression and rebelliousness through her sexual attractiveness. Rather than travel Larry's torturous neurotic route toward realization of fantasied sexual potential, Darlene plunged into her chosen misbehavior with relish:

In her fourteenth year, Darlene had changed from a docile child to a sexually promiscuous incorrigible girl. Her misconduct came before the juvenile court when she was discovered to have charged a nineteen-year-old youth with "molesting her," when in fact, she had been promiscuous with him and several boys in the neighborhood for months.

Two days after she was cited as a juvenile delinquent by officers in a juvenile division, a policeman, catching up with an erratically driven car, was surprised to find an intoxicated fourteen-year-old girl at the wheel. Investigation of Darlene's behavior led to recommitment to the juvenile court on a charge of "being in danger of leading a lewd life."

Darlene, blasé, her expression immobile, described her sexual freedom with several boys in her group. She told how she masturbated two boys in the presence of three other juveniles; how she led a gang of openly promiscuous girls into petty larcenies. Her gang—"My own personal gang"—made capital of their new-found freedom; they were obscene and completely undisciplined, truant from school, rarely at home at night. Their routine of escapades included stealing liquor, getting "dead drunk," and having intercourse with any boy who presented himself. In Darlene's case, contact with a psychiatrist initiated by an anxious mother, had produced little help. The doctor suggested an early marriage, a solution that the mother considered impractical.

Social investigation proved Darlene's accusation that her mother was aggressive and unloving and her father a "namby-pamby," to be generally untrue. She spoke disparagingly of her mother, calling her an "old grapefruit." With fine sarcasm, she expressed the opinion that her mother was a "phony" because she wore "falsies," and spent much time and energy "prettying" herself. The mother, tense, anxious, smartly dressed in comparison with the studied sloppiness of Darlene, entertained no perception of the basic struggle between her daughter and herself on the ground of sexual attractiveness.

It was apparent from the examinations that Darlene possessed an adequate intelligence, characterized by one examiner as "very astute." Although she impressed some as "emotionally flat," her inner aggression was obvious. On the surface she appeared self-assured, but underneath there was a marked sensitivity and a marked aggression, particularly toward parent-figures. She regarded her sexual exploits in a naturalistic way; she felt there was nothing particularly antisocial about them, because of the changing attitudes in girls throughout the nation.

Because Darlene's conduct was regarded as a precursor to psychopathy, the juvenile judge committed her to a correctional institution for girls.

The recent increase of aggressive crime among juveniles—homicide, mayhem, assault, armed robbery, and forceful rape—has stimulated state legislatures to enact laws such as is included in the California Code.[72] In Section 707 of the Welfare and Institutions Code, a juvenile can be found unfit for treatment as a juvenile and be remanded to an adult court when he or she has (1) a degree of criminal sophistication, (2) is not rehabilitatable, (3) has a poor previous record, (4) has previously failed at rehabilitative efforts, and (5) is alleged to have committed a grave offense. Tom, aged twelve, represents such a situation:

Quietly watching television with his mother one evening, Tom suddenly, in his mother's words, "began to look strange. . . ." She noticed that his eyes bulged and that he was foaming at the mouth. Without a word he pulled a knife from his pocket and plunged it into his mother's chest. The knife-blade was deflected by a rib so that only a laceration of the chest wall occurred. The offense was doubly unexpected because there had been no previous delinquencies on Tom's part, no intra-family tension, nothing but the history of a quiet, withdrawn, self-absorbed boy of fifteen.

A thorough social history provided little information beyond his parents' lack of perception of his indwelling character. The direct interview with the delinquent provided a history: Tom claimed that he had "blacked out" at the time of the offense. He recalled nothing in the television presentation that had excited him—it was a musical comedy of the ordinary type—but in speaking of it he began to elucidate (with no insight into its significance) his daydreams and fantasies. They dealt with exaggerated accounts of body injury, of how to fight, and so on. This fifteen-year-old boy prattled on in a childish manner, making such statements as "If I fought with a fellow I would break his arm off and hit him over the head with it." When questioned further he said he would break the arm off at the shoulder to get a longer piece to use; this fantasy gave him a "good feeling." This material was given in a flat, matter-of-fact tone, in marked contradiction to what he actually did as a fighter. Tom admitted that when he actually was brought face to face with an opponent he would "grab him, not punch him, and rough him up," in obvious ignorance of the art of self-defense. The disparity between what he imagined he could do and his actual behavior with his peers was extraordinary. Tom had no perception of the reality meaning of the aggressive, sadistic fantasies he tossed off so glibly.

It was difficult to assess the so-called seizures that Tom's mother described. There had been no history or findings of epilepsy. The knife used by Tom, a filed-down Japanese sword that Tom claimed he used as an all-purpose knife, was described with boyish enthusiasm. But other indications of neurotic sadism appeared unexpectedly. Tom talked spontaneously about his fantasies when at his mother's request he washed her back when she bathed. He recognized that a few years earlier he had been aroused sexually by this practice, but now, he said, "it doesn't bother me any more." It is interesting that his mother, who was so alarmed and perplexed at the attack, said she treated sex rather casually in the home and "hid nothing" from her son.

The father, a career man in the Navy, away from home more than half of each year, was described as a heavily tattooed man of massive proportions. The mother herself was described by one observer as "a diminutive woman of nondescript features." It was evident that the mother had no notion of the florid sexual fantasies that filled Tom's mind. On the surface he appeared to be emotionally flat, almost barren; beneath the surface one could sense the seething emotion and sexual aggression. His ready talk about breaking arms off, a feat that he pictured with childish ease, undoubtedly was related to unconscious castration fantasies—a displacement from below upward. In this sense, the "blackout" can be regarded as due to a hysterical repression of sexual ideas that simultaneously warded off overwhelming sadistic fantasies threatening to flood his ego.

In making evaluations of the young offender leading to testimony in court concerning irresponsibility for crime or diminished capacity, the special nature of juvenile aggression must be considered. The fact that juvenile aggression has spread over a wider variety of crimes than a generation or two ago is often interpreted as "psychopathic behavior" falling close to, if not within, the rubric of mental disease. In assessing the psychopathology of juvenile and adolescent delinquents, social factors arising from youth subcultures must be carefully calibrated. It is a matter of daily experience that the pubertal and adolescent universe is committed to behavior and attitudes opposed to those of the adult world. The ever-changing social patterns of the young are evident in speech, dress, recreation, sexual practices, and alcohol and drug usage. Rather than constituting "psychopathic" traits, these practices should be considered maneuvers to test the reality of power fantasies that lie behind the "machismo" of tough delinquents. In this context, delinquency and serious crime become adventures in testing the limits of the adult world's permissivity. Juvenile delinquency among males is a way-station from fantasy to the actuality of envied masculine adult power.

Of these dynamics, the juvenile is unaware; he is too involved in his inner emotional turmoil, too ready to accept the moral support and strength he receives from his "club" or "gang," too willing to defy the law in concert with his fellows. In this situation, crime is not "crime" but an expression of group power, a phenomenon that Fritz Redl, the child psychiatrist, called "group intoxication." For the lone juvenile offender, the cause of his or her deeds must be found in the inner recesses of his mind and his or her place in society.

Whether present-day juvenile aggression is a byproduct of a permissive society, the result of decay of the traditional family group, the product of free expression in the media, or simply an explication of individual freedom for which everyone in the Western world strives is beyond precise explanation. In any case, the present misbehavior of children in our culture raises new problems of a legal, psychological and social nature.

Notes

1. Morris Ploscowe, Henry F. Foster, and Doris J. Freed, *Family Law*: 255, Little, Brown & Co., Boston (2 ed., 1972).

2. *In re Gregorson's Estate*, 116 P. 60, 160 C. 21 (1911).

3. California Civil Code, Sec. 4424 (c).

4. Laws of New York, Domestic Relations Law, Sec. 140 (c).

5. Ploscowe, et al., op. cit.: Chap. 2 and 3.

6. Domestic Relations Law, Sec. 140(f), New York.

7. Domestic Relations Law, Sec. 141 (3), New York.

8. *Wirz v. Wirz*, 96 Calif. App. 2d 171; 214 P. 2d 839 (1950).

9. *Mantoya v. Bratlie*, 33 Calif. 2d 120; 199 P. 2d. 677.

10. Ploscowe, et al., op. cit.: 466.

11. Maryland General Laws, Art. 16, Sec. 26.

12. Delaware Code, Title 13, Domestic Relations, Sec. 1522 (10).

13. *Glisson v. Glisson*, 237 A. 2d 393 (Del., 1967).

14. *Dunphy v. Dunphy*, 161 Calif. 380; 119 F. 612 (1911).

15. *E. Plaintiff v. F. Defandant*, 118 N.J. Super. Ct. 491 (1972).

16. *Weiss v. Weiss*, 31 Misc, 2d 221, N.Y.S. 2d 296 (1961).

17. *Punelli v. Punelli*, 149 N.W. 2d 784 (1967).

18. Iowa Code.

19. Uniform Marriage and Divorce Act, Desk Guide, Family Law Reporters, Bureau of National Affairs (1974).

20. California Civil Code, Sec. 4425 (f).

21. *Stan Stepanek v. Stepanek*, 193 Calif. App. 2d 760: Calif. Rptr. 793 (1961).

22. Ploscowe, et al., op. cit.: 231

23. Rev. Dr. A. Cohen, *Everyman's Talmud*: 169, E. P. Dutton Co., New York (1949).

24. Helen S. Kaplan, *The New Sex Therapy*, Brunner-Mazel, New York (1974).

25. *Long v. Long*, 13 S.E. 2d, 349 (1941).

26. California Civil Code, Sec. 4425, note 22.

27. William T. Nelson, *Nelson on Divorce and Annulment* 1: Sec. 3.06 Callaghan, Chicago (2 ed., 1945).

28. *Bobst v. Bobst*, 347 Penn. 411; 54 A. 2d 898 (1947).

29. *Robinson v. Robinson*, 183 Penn. Super. Ct. 574; 133 A. 2d 259 (1957).

30. *Firestone v. Firestone*, Fla. 263 So. 2d 223 (1972).

31. Ploscowe, et al., op. cit.: Chap. 3.

32. *Nelson on Divorce* 2: 212.

33. *Hardenburger v. Hardenburger*, Kans. 532 P. 2d 1106 (1975).

34. California Civil Code, Sec. 4600.

35. Henry Foster, *Family Law*, 36 N.Y.U. L. Rev. 629 (1961).

36. Jos. Goldstein, Anna Freud, and Albert Solnit, *Beyond the Best Interests of the Child*, Free Press (Macmillan), New York (1973).

37. California Civil Code, Sec. 232 (3, 4, 5).

38. *In re Rene Zimmerman, A Minor: Zimmerman v. Zimmerman*, 206 C.A. 2d, 835; 24 Calif. Rptr. 329 (1962).

39. *Painter v. Bannister*, 258 Iowa 1390; 140 N.W. 2d 152 (1966).

40. Alex Brooks, *Law, Psychiatry and the Mental Health System*, Little, Brown & Co., Boston (1973).

41. Goldstein, Freud, and Solnit, op. cit.

42. Leonard V. Kaplan, *An Academic Lawyer Plays Arm-Chair Analyst*, 46 Neb. L. Rev. 759 (1976).

43. Hal Painter, *Mark, I Love You*, Simon & Schuster, New York (1968).

44. California Civil Code, Sec. 4600.

45. *Atwood v. Atwood*, 550 S.W. 2d 465 (Ky., 1976).

46. Michigan Compiled Laws, Child Custody Act: 91, Annot. 722.2 (1970).

47. California Civil Code, Sec. 226, 226.6, 227.

48. *Adoption of Baby Schroetter, A Minor, Geller v. Los Angeles Co. Dept. of Adoptions*, 261 C.A. 2d 365; 67 Calif. Rptr. 819 (1968).

49. *Nadler v. Superior Court*, 266 C.A. 2d 523; 63 Calif. Rptr. 352 (1967).

50. *Chaffin v. Frye*, 45 C.A. 3d 39; 119 Calif. Rptr. 22 (1975).

51. Herbert Modlin, American Bar Association Proceedings, 1963, Discussion on Family Law.

52. California Civil Code, Sec. 227b.

53. *Buck v. Bell*, 274 U.S. 200 (1927).

54. Habitual (Criminal) Sterilization Act, Okla. Title 57, Sec. 171 (1935).

55. *Skinner v. Oklahoma*, 62 Sup. Ct. 1110; 316 U.S. 535 (1942).

56. Ben Karpman, *The Sexual Offender and His Offenses*: 564, Julian Press, New York (1954).

57. Sterilization of Criminals, etc., 53 ALR 3d, 960.

58. 53 ALR 3d, 965, op. cit.

59. *Wyatt v. Alderholt*, U.S. Dist. Ct. Ala., N.D. 368, Fed. Supp. 1382 (1973).

60. 368 Fed. Supp. 1383 (1974).

61. *In re Sterilization of Joseph Lee Moore*, 221 S.E. 2d 307 (1976).

62. Sol Rubin, *The Law of Juvenile Justice*: 9, Oceana Publ. Co., Dobbs Ferry, N.Y. (1976).

63. Monrad G. Paulsen and Chas. H. Whitebread, *Juvenile Law and Procedure*: 2, Nat'l. Council of Court Judges, Reno, Nev. (1974).

64. *Kent v. U.S.*, 383 U.S. 541, 86 Sup. Ct. 1045 (1966).

65. *In re Gault*, 387 U.S. 1, Sup. Ct. 1428 (1967).

66. *In re Winship*, 397 U.S. 358, 90 Sup. Ct. 1068 (1970).

67. *McKiever v. Pennsylvania*, 403 U.S. 528, 91 Sup. Ct. 1976 (1971).

68. Justine W. Polier, *The Juvenile Court*, Family L. Q. Arno Press, New York (1974).

69. Jerome G. Miller, *The Juvenile Court*: 229, Family L. Q. Arno Press, New York (1974).

70. California Welfare and Institutions Code, Sec. 827; Sec. 741 (1976).

71. Florida Statutes, West Publ. Co., Annot. Title 5, Chap. 39, Sec. 39.08.

72. California Welfare and Institutions Code, Sec. 707 (1976).

11

Mental Competency

The use of psychiatric experts in will contests, to prove or disprove testamentary capacity in deceased persons, was not always warmly welcomed by the courts. No more weight is given a psychiatric opinion of the mental state of the maker of a will than that of a relative or layman who was acquainted with the deceased. Dr. Isaac Ray, champion of forensic psychiatry during the last century, insisted on the "honorable place of" psychiatric testimony in will cases.[1] Apparently, he experienced some opposition to such use because he wrote of an "Angell Will" case in 1863.

In the litigation of a will, a wide range of inquiry is opened, a larger variety of relations is exposed, than is permitted or required in that of a crime or a contract. The investigation may extend over a life-time and be pushed into the inner recesses of the inner life . . . to show the full significance of . . . a trait . . . [and] the operations of the mind, sound as well as unsound . . . to reconcile seeming discrepancies of testimony. . . .

Despite Ray's plea for psychiatric participation in will cases, opposition persists. Professor Green wrote in 1944, "Courts have occasionally stigmatized expert psychiatric testimony as the weakest and most unsatisfactory kind of evidence or as valueless."[2] Psychiatrists have also complained that psychiatric expertness in will matters abases the profession. Zilboorg, in writing the history of one hundred years of American forensic psychiatry[3] in 1944, commented:

The psychiatrist who undertakes to form an opinion in [will] cases . . . appears in court not as a physician . . . but as a citizen who possesses certain special knowledge which the law does not possess but . . . which the law is willing to buy and use. [He] . . . is at best a skilled worker making an honest living and at worst, the willing servant of the law . . . dealing with property rights.

In more accusatory terms, Dr. Thomas Szasz claimed in the 1960s that psychiatrists "exercise social control" by their appearance and testimony in court, tantamount to "a threat to a free society, because it is based on mysticism and deceit, not rational thought and honesty."[4]

Undoubtedly, a cloud of suspicion hangs over the use of psychiatric testimony in will cases, in large part because the contestants (and presumably the experts) have an undiluted interest in the money involved. Whether experts should be subject to guilt by association is a matter of individual judgment, but testamentary capacity does involve mental disorders of varying degrees and is clearly an appropriate area for psychiatric inquiry and opinion.

Legal Criteria

The basic principles in will-making is that the testator must have a "sound mind, or sound mind or memory, or sound and disposing mind and memory."[5] A "sound mind" is equated with a "sane mind," although this supposition has been debated by legal scholars. In this connection, the authors of the respected text *Page on Wills* note: "Language of this sort lays down no precise standard. . . ."[6] In fact, they state:

Testamentary capacity does not require a normal mind, nor is it necessary that the testator should be free from prejudice or able to reason logically . . . [he may] be below the generally accepted standard of morality . . . be obscene and indecent . . . be insane in the medical sense . . . or [have] an impaired and defective memory . . . [and still] have sufficient mental capacity to make a will.

The accepted legal standard in all states is that the testator must know (1) the extent and nature of his estate, (2) the nature of the testamentary act, and (3) the identity of his beneficiaries and their relationship to him or her. In general terms,

The law has taken the position that so long as a person is able to understand and bear in mind, in a general way, the nature, worth and extent of his property; and his relations to persons around him, including the names and identity of the persons who are to be the objects of his bounty; and the nature and effect of the act of will making; he should be accorded testamentary freedom notwithstanding his mind might be diseased, feeble, or deranged so far as other affairs and matters of life are concerned.

These standards bring up numerous legal problems, but present interest dictates that only those abnormal mental states will be discussed that might void a probated will.

The major conditions that could invalidate a will are mental deficiency; delusions, the product of insanity; and senile dementia or other organic brain disease, although the fact of senility in itself is not sufficient to deprive a testator of power to make a will. The insane delusion "must be one which is not based on evidence" in distinction to a "mistake which is susceptible of correction." The use of alcohol (habitual intoxication) or drugs does not invalidate a will if at the time of making it the testator "had the requisite understanding." Moreover, any debilitating disease, extreme weakness, paralysis, or epilepsy does not prevent a testator from making a valid will, nor does eccentricity, religious fanaticism, contact with departed souls, extreme vindictiveness, or other emotional condition function to prevent will-making.[7]

In re Murray's Estate (Oregon, 1944)[8] illustrates a legal analysis of the "unsound mind" concept.

Mrs. Murray, aged 74, made a will in January 1940, and died in November of that year.

Her will directed the executor to reduce the estate, both real and personal, to cash and then dispose of it by three bequsts, as follows:

"A one-third part thereof to First Hebrew Christian Synagogue, 2209 Michigan Avenue, Los Angeles, California.

"A one-third part thereof to Portland Hebrew Mission, 2406 Southwest First Avenue, Portland, Oregon.

"A one-third part thereof to Four Square Gospel Church, 1403 Seventh Street, Oregon City, Oregon."

The trial court voided the will on grounds that Mrs. M. was of unsound mind at the time of making the will. An appeal was entered based on the fact that even though the testatrix had become a religious fanatic after death of her husband the year before, she was sane. The secretary who typed her will testified that Mrs. M. was "sane, never another thought." The executor of the estate, Hankins, testified concerning the First Hebrew Christian Synagogue: "They are a religious, a very fanatical religious group, but that doesn't mean they are crazy."

Eight witnesses, long-time friends and neighbors of the testatrix testified as to Mrs. M.'s erratic behavior, her hallucinations and confused speech. One testified: "The way she acted I thought she was off balance. If I would get up and act that way in church you would say I was ready for the insane asylum." Another witness recounted that he found Mrs. M. "Sometimes quite loud, and she couldn't sit down nowheres, it seemed when I have seen her, . . . her lips were moving like as though she was listening to herself. She would sit in a steady stupor, like, and her lips would be moving, and sometimes she would make motions like she was just in earnest. . . ."

Dr. A. H. Huycke, a qualified physician, testified to extended experience in the examination of many persons concerning sanity, and in answer to a hypothetical question, gave an opinion that the assumed facts could denote insanity but did not necessarily do so. The assumed facts did, however, denote senility, senile decay, and he added: ". . . in that case, a person senile to that extent probably wouldn't in my opinion, be very clear on her ideas of business."

The Supreme Court of Oregon, after reviewing the record, ruled that the "proponents failed to sustain the burden of proof upon the issue of testamentary capacity. Her peculiar religious beliefs . . . dominated and controlled her mind . . . touching on the subject matter of the will," hence destroying her testamentary capacity. The lower court, which had voided the will, was upheld by the supreme court of the state.

Medical Criteria

Of all the physical and mental disabilities which can affect the capacity to make a will, senility and its associated mental states are most frequent. The peculiarities of the aged, their memory lapses, emotional changes, and shifts in interest may often appear to amount to mental disease. However, a fine line between testamentary incapacity and eccentricity must be drawn in each case. At the present time, the whole class of senile conditions is lumped together in the American Psychiatric Association Nomenclature (1968 edition) as "Organic Brain Syndrome associated with Senile Brain Disease."

The 1978 draft of the *Diagnostic Manual* of the American Psychiatric Association lists senile states under the heading *Dementias* arising in the senium and presenium (*Progressive Idiopathic Dementia*, senile onset) and (*Progressive Idiopathic Dementia*, presenile onset). The third heading, *Multi-Infarct Dementia*, presumably covers cerebral arteriosclerosis or other organic brain diseases. For present purposes and for better understanding of the intricacies of the senile states, three distinct entities can be distinguished: presenility and senility, senile psychosis, and cerebral arteriosclerosis. With a compilation derived from many authorities, the present author differentiates the three conditions as follows:[9]

Presenility and Senility: This condition shades from "advancing age" to normal "old age." Mental changes as listed below fall into the group of Senility *without* psychosis.

The specific mental signs of senility vary in constancy and intensity. In general, if the symptoms are exaggerated they shade into the second category, namely Senile Psychosis.

The signs of presenility or senility are:

1. Furtive development.
2. Anxiety, depression, and melancholia.
3. Beginning memory defects.
4. Reduction in interest in ordinary attractions of life.
5. Beginning restlessness or confusion, especially at night, with or without delirium of transitory type.
6. Inability to assimilate new ideas of others.
7. Egocentricity.
8. Labile or unstable feelings.
9. Suggestibility in the presence of stubbornness.
10. Poor impressibility (inability to learn new things).
11. Beginning ethical or moral obtuseness.
12. Possible temporary sexual excitement.
13. Gaps in memory with confabulations inserted.
14. Living more and more in early life (memories).
15. Critical ability decreased.
16. Frequent irrational financial transactions or gifts.
17. Perception and attention decrease.
18. Disturbed orientation—mistakes day for night and vice versa.

The signs of senile dementia or senile psychosis are:

1. Reaction to trivia with excessive emotion.
2. Emotional lability.
3. Tendency towards empty chatter or monosyllabic speech.
4. Possible delusions of grandeur.
5. Possible delusions of poverty and/or sin or of being persecuted and robbed.
6. Hypochondriacal tendencies become marked.
7. Hallucinations as part of a delirium merging into dreamlike states.
8. Well-developed delirium which is occupational in nature. (At this point the condition is called presbyophrenia):
   Constant activity, and fussing about things misplaced, confusion of time, confusion of speech; i.e., half words, part words, and repeated words (echolalia).
9. Untidiness about person, severe tremor interferes with handwriting.
10. Physical disorders—appetite decreased—poor coordination—weakness and clumsiness, also loss of sphincter control.

Cerebral Arteriosclerosis may occur earlier in life: Mental symptoms are the results of disturbances of blood supply in various parts of the nervous system. The symptoms are apt to be less insidious and more demonstrable on examination:

1. The organic signs and symptoms are: headache, tinnitus, dizziness, paralysis, aphasia, visual disturbances, hearing diminution, high blood pressure, heart irregularities, etc.
2. The mental or psychic symptoms are:
   a. Emotional instability with explosive outbursts.
   b. Memory disturbances especially for recent events.
   c. Impaired orientation.
   d. Not too marked changes in fundamental personality.
   e. Depression with ideas of suicide.
   f. Anxiety related to their physical handicap.
   g. Paranoid states often involving relatives or those close to the patient.
   h. Aphasia and mental confusion.

Competency and Wills

Evaluation of a testator's capacity to make a will after his or her demise requires a different approach than obtains in other medico-legal situations. Habits, behavior in different situations, attitudes, customary speech, and even anecdotes are gathered from relatives, neighbors, nurses or attendants, and friends. The home is inspected, if possible, and the arrangements and conditions noted; letters, diaries, books, and food supplies are scrutinized in the attempt to reconstruct the decedent's personality. Whether a clinical diagnosis can be developed out of these observations is less important than establishing abnormalities of memory, intellectual function, and mental clarity before and during the signing of the will in question. The following case illustrates this kind of reconstruction.

H.S. a bachelor, died on March 1, 1966, at the age of 82 years. Since the death of his sister in 1961, with whom he had lived in a large apartment in New York City, the deceased remained in the same home.

His Will, executed on December 20, 1961, a few months after his sister's death, left $3,000 to a cemetery, with detailed instructions about the care of his father's plot; $3,000 to his sister, who died; $3,000 to his nephew; $2,000 to his nephew's wife; and $1,000 to each of the nephew's two children. The residuary estate, amounting to about $1,000,000 was left to religious institutions, each gift to be memorialized by a bronze plate in honor of his two unmarried sisters.

The Will was admitted to probate but his nephew, H.S.'s only living relative, contested the Will. The nephew, a stock broker, was frequently called by the decedent for advice about investment but he never put orders through the nephew's firm. The latter and his wife visited H.S. frequently offering to clean his apartment, which he refused.

His contacts were almost nil; he talked to his lawyer occasionally, but no other person after Lillian's death was invited to the home or called by the decedent, except his nephew.

The superintendent of the building who knew him for 4 years said that H.S. usually didn't know what he was doing, that he had a very hot temper, that "you had to be careful what you said to him, and that he would launch into a terrific scolding on the slightest occasion." He made no friends in the building.

He never spoke of any occurences later than 1920. The photographs on his wall were of old associates, especially military, and notes in his diary concerned older associations, sometimes as far back as 1908, with very little of current interest. In the years prior to 1961 he had a keen interest in politics. After that he was restricted in his ideas and interest and showed some evidence of confabulation. He showed mental dullness and a non-reactivity; for example, the telephone would ring for minutes at a time and he wouldn't answer the phone. When he did, there were long pauses in his speech. He didn't seem to comprehend what was said to him when his nephew called.

When H.S.'s sister died in August of 1961, he showed a depression that lasted for years until his death in 1966. On the telephone and in ordinary conversation he would weep spontaneously when even casual impersonal material was brought up, particularly immediately after her death. When invited out to dinner or for a ride he would say "I won't go without her . . . it wouldn't be the same." When the telephone caller would simply inquire as to how he was, he would say "I am broken up" and would cry spontaneously; his attachment to his sister was extreme. It showed a marked emotional dependence which is characteristic of a man whose ego is no longer independent and self-sufficient.

After her death, he lived on the barest essentials, crackers and milk. His appearance changed markedly. Whereas he previously had been a careful, even dapper dresser, he now was untidy, wore his clothes until they were threadbare, had no interest in keeping himself up. The decedent never made dinner for himself nor did he ever go out for dinner, even at weekly intervals, whereas he would be enthusiastic about the dinners his sister had prepared. He showed an inability to assimilate new ideas of others. He was quite unstable. He would go into a rage over minor matters whereas before his emotions were adequate to the occasion. His landlord said he would often be irascible about minor details to the point of absurdity. He became monsyllabic. His answers would be "yes" or "no." His callers "could not get anything out of him."

He had always been friendly to his nephew's children and wife, evincing a normal interest in them, as would any grand-uncle. After his sister's death he paid little attention to them.

A visit to H.S.'s apartment which the present superintendent said were typical of the last four years, showed extreme dirt and disorder. Three-year-old newspapers were crumpled on the floor under the chair facing the television set. Empty tins and boxes were scattered around the kitchen and other rooms. Boxes of graham crackers, which were his chief food, were on the dining room table along with empty cardboard boxes. The bathroom basins were discolored. The furniture was old. He slept in an old-fashioned, brass bed. His sister's room was left just as it had been at the time of her death.

H.S. kept detailed records of his investments, and prepared his own income tax returns. His check stubs were carefully filled out. He apparently knew his assets, but his way of living casts doubt on whether he understood what money meant.

His checkbooks showed only small gifts to charities, the largest being an annual contribution of $25.00 to the Y.M.C.A., except for a $1,000.00 gift to the Building Fund of Kismet Temple.

The total picture emerging was that of a man whose character had gradually and irreversibly changed; his shrinking interest in the world about him precluded acceptance of the amenities of life. His depression was chronic. The diagnosis was (1) Chronic Brain Syndrome, associated with Senility. (2) Chronic Depression.

H.S.'s mental condition at the time of his making a will in December, 1961, indicated that the decedent was unable to appreciate the "natural objects of his bounty," by virtue of oncoming senility and a chronic depression. The will was successfully overturned.

H.S.'s mental condition at the time of his making a will in December 1961, indicates that the decedent was unable to appreciate the "natural objects of his bounty" by virtue of oncoming senility and a chronic depression.

A common claim of survivors in the instance of an inequitable will, is that of delusions entertained by the testator at the time of will-making. These can be delusions of infidelity on the part of a wife, of grandiosity with overestimation of the deceased's estate, or impoverishment with a corresponding minimization of his or her estate. Delusions can appear which may be a reflection of a transitory emotional state, a mistake, or a fixed delusion regarding a beneficiary. The law makes a clear distinction between a "mistake" in judgment or a "belief based on false or insufficient evidence" and an insane delusion. For example, the delusion that a reputed son of a testator was not in fact his son because of infidelity on the part of his wife must rest on a fixed, false belief "incapable of being removed by reason" to be considered a delusion. The oft-quoted *In re Coffin case* (New Jersey, 1968)[10] demonstrates these distinctions:

Edward W. Coffin, Sr., the testator, a wealthy man, left a will which did not acknowledge his son, an only child. The son, Edward W. Coffin, Jr., contested the will, claiming that his father had not been competent at the time he made the will (August 1962), in that at the time his father had had an insane delusion that Coffin, Jr., was not in fact his natural son.

Edward Warren Coffin, Jr., was conceived and born as the result of a casual and brief affair between Coffin, Sr., and Edna Sullivan in February 1924. Later, Miss Sullivan told Coffin she was pregnant. Coffin, who believed that Miss Sullivan was promiscuous, refused to believe that her pregnancy was the result of his sexual relations with her. Finally, Coffin agreed to marry Miss Sullivan in order to legitimate the child, on condition that they obtain a divorce shortly thereafter. They were married in April 1924, and, after a weekend "honeymoon," never again lived together as husband and wife.

Coffin, Jr., was born in November 1924. Coffin, Sr., never recognized the boy as his son. He obtained a divorce in February 1926. Except for a few brief encounters shortly afterward, Coffin and his former wife never saw each other again. Nor did he see his son until 1965.

Forty-one years later, in October 1965, father and son met for the first time. Coffin, Sr., was happy and acknowledged Coffin, Jr., as his son, apparently because he saw a close facial resemblance.

Coffin, Sr., had made a will in August 1962, leaving 50 percent of his estate to the First Church of Christ Scientist in Boston and 50 percent to a friend, Mrs. Newitt. On December 21, 1965, Coffin asked his attorney to change his will to include his son and his grandchildren but Coffin never saw the draft because he died the very next day, thus leaving the August 1962 will as his final testament. Coffin, Jr., contested the probate of the 1962 will. The question in the case was whether Coffin was competent when he made that will.

Dr. Henry Davidson, an eminent psychiatrist and author of Forensic Psychiatry (2d ed. 1965), was called to testify on behalf of the son. Prior to giving his testimony, Dr. Davidson was presented with all the facts of the case. He also read a number of letters written by Coffin in 1924. Dr. Davidson's opinion was based heavily on the 1924 letters written by Coffin, Sr. Thus, his opinion as to Coffin's mental condition in 1962 was based largely on evidence of behavior in 1924.

The lengthy testimony given by Dr. Davidson developed from his diagnosis of a paranoid condition with delusions of grandeur and of infidelity concerning his wife and the birth of their child.

Q. Specifically, sir, what if anything in these writings heretofore examined reveals any personality trait of the writer?

A. All right. Now, you understand, of course, that nobody makes a diagnosis based on an isolated phrase. I mean that the picture of the personality reflected in the whole run of the writings is necessary.

These writings reflect a strongly paranoid person. One of the characteristics of a paranoid person is the feeling of persecution. Now, in the letter addressed to Mr. Brown, he speaks of, "That they made slanderous charges against me." In another letter which was addressed, "My dear Tom:" he says, "People are constantly belittling my knowledge and ability."

Secondly, there are a group of references in this letter to ideas of grandeur. In the letter he wrote to Mother Audrey in the convent. "I suppose," he said "I am skilled in the laws relating to this better than any lawyer," and in a letter that he wrote to "My dear Tom," he said "I have trouble convincing my brother-in-law that I know some law. It is hard to convince him that I know what I am talking about."

There is an air of self-righteous resentment in these letters. For example, the letter to Mr. Brown, where he speaks of an effort to extort money, the letter in which he speaks of people making criminally slanderous charges, and that is his term, a letter to his wife in which he said you tried trickery— "the lawyer tried trickery with the idea to get future business for himself."

He wrote a letter to Mr. Brown, the same Mr. Brown, in which he says, "Does your work with personnel cover blackmail for your concubines?"

To his own lawyer, Mr. Hawkin, he wrote, "You did your best to duck, to crawl out and evade my request."

In another letter to Mr. Hawkin he said, "This shows more clearly than words the treacherous nature of your legal work."

Another characteristic of paranoid people is the feeling that others spread lies about them. He refers to criminally slanderous charges. He characterizes the type of slander and he says that, "You and Miss Van Winkle . . ." whoever she is—"are contemptible liars." In another letter he said, "You brand yourself as false." He identifies someone as a blackmailing shyster, Stohlman.

Now, a characteristic of paranoid thinking is that the delusional system does not change to grow or except after a very strong—well, sometimes a person gets older and it merges with senility. It merges with senile delusions too.

Cross-examination:

Q. Now, Doctor, would you say this definition of an insane delusion was correct: The mind's spontaneous conception and acceptance of that as a fact which has no real existence except in its imagination and in its persistent adherence to it against all evidence?

A. It is only partly correct. It goes back to the question you asked me in the first place. If a person believes that he is more intelligent than he really is or a woman believes that she is more beautiful than she really is, it is hard to say whether it is a delusion or a mistaken idea.

I think you would have to get into the definition of a delusion the possibility of a distortion of a fact which would also be a delusion, not the mere invention of a fact from the mind.

Q. Would you say that a person was suffering from an insane delusion if he had heard some report on the outside and that he misinterpreted it in his mind and had acted on the basis of that interpretation?

A. It would depend on his interpretation of this . . .

Q. Doctor, suppose this man had received from a source on which he relied information to the effect that his wife before they were married had gone out with a man who had the reputation of being a fast man. And that he was married and that she had gone out with another man who had the reputation of being an unsavory character and was known to be going around with young girls and suppose the wife said to this source of information that she knew them both well and that she went out with them frequently and that they were quite as fast as they were reputed to be and suppose the wife said to this source that she had had relations with the person who was now her husband, that he had used contraceptives on all occasions but one and then said: "You bet any other man I went out with took pains to protect me." She then stammered and said: "I mean if I had ever gone out with any other man that way he would have protected me."

Suppose the person who was the source of this information then had asked the wife if she did not realize what would happen if she went to the apartment of the person who later became her husband and suppose she said: "Of course, you poor fish, that's what I went for."

Now, would you say that would cause any doubt as to the chastity of his wife in her premarital relations and doubt as to the legitimacy of the son that she bore seven months after the marriage?

A. If that is all there was to it and there were no other evidence of emotional or mental illness in the man, I would say you cannot infer mental illness from that.

The appellate division of the New Jersey court heard the appeal from a judgment of the county court denying probate to the decedent's will, dated August 25, 1962. The ground was that, at the time the will was executed, the decedent lacked testamentary capacity because he was suffering from the insane delusion that the caveator was not his son. Judge Sullivan wrote the opinion for the court in which it reversed the trial court and directed that the will be admitted to probate. The opinion states:

> The burden of establishing lack of testamentary capacity is on the one who contests the will being offered for probate. This burden must be sustained by clear and convincing evidence. . . . Furthermore, it is incumbent upon the caveator to establish lack of capacity at the time the will was executed. . . . Indeed, he must show that the disputed will was the product of the decedent's insanity.
>
> An insane delusion which robs an individual of testamentary capacity is a false belief based upon incidents "existing only in the diseased imagination of the deluded party." Rather, an insane delusion is a false and fixed belief not founded on reason and incapable of being removed by reason.
>
> We have carefully reviewed the record and find that the totality of the proofs does not establish that at the time the will was executed decedent was suffering from an insane delusion which robbed him of testamentary capacity. Decedent's belief over the years that caveator was not his son was based on some evidence. Decedent had information given him by his wife, as to her relations with other men, which led him to believe that he was not the father of her child. . . . He might have been mistaken in his belief that did not make it an insane delusion. Moreover, the record demonstrates that decedent did not persist in his belief after he met caveator and apparently saw a strong physical resemblance. In short, neither the elements, nor the indicia, of an insane delusion were made to appear.
>
> The judgment denying probate is reversed and the matter remanded with direction to admit decedent's will to probate.

Another common claim is that drugs are administered to induce a testator to change his will, a charge rendered into legal language as "undue influence." A contest on the ground of "undue influence" is usually based on the suggestibility of elderly or senile individuals, or of seriously ill or dying persons, on the theory that failing memory and confusion intensified by drugs tend to increase suggestibility. This situation obtained in a California case where a successful physician changed his will while in the hospital some six days before he died of an invasive cancer.[11] Dr. F. entered a hospital on February 1, 1959, executed the contested will on March 31, 1959, and died on April 5 of that year. In the new will, he changed the provision of a prior will, dated February 12, 1959, which provided the sum of $100,000 to his sons on a life insurance policy, in favor of his longtime office nurse whom he planned to marry, naming her residuary legatee. The trial court and jury found for the contestants (ex-wife and sons) on the grounds that the testator lacked testamentary capacity and that "undue influence" had been exercised by the office nurse.

An appeal was heard by the Supreme Court of California. Justice Tobriner examined the medical testimony of one physician that the sedative Butisol which the patient received, "clouded his thinking and made him groggy: it tended to decrease his ability to think clearly." Another physician testified that the deceased showed "certain personality quirks" during his hospital stay. The justice balanced this testimony against that of witnesses to the signing of the second will that "he was of sound and disposing mind," and he concluded that there was no basis for denying probate of the will. Justice Tobriner's analysis stated:

Both witnesses to the will expressed the opinion that Dr. F. was of sound and disposing mind at the time he signed it. One witness testified that the doctor sat on the edge of his bed and joked about the "grand opening" the next day, referring to an exploratory operation. This case turns solely upon the issue of whether substantial evidence supports the findings of the jury that the involved will is invalid because the testator lacked testamentary capacity to execute it and because one M.T. exerted undue influence upon him. We have concluded that, without doubt, the record does not sustain a finding of lack of testamentary capacity.

Turning to the second basic issue of the case, the finding of the jury that M.T. unduly influenced the testator in the making of his will, we note at the outset that the right to testamentary disposition of one's property is a fundamental one which reaches back to the early common law; "the right to dispose of one's property by will is most solemnly assured by law, and . . . does not depend upon its judicious use." (*In re McDevitt's Estate* [1892] 95 Cal. 17, 35, 30, P 101, 106.) M.T. had the opportunity and motivation to influence the doctor but it is insufficient to [indicate] undue influence. . . . [It was not] the pressure which overpowered the mind and bore down on the volition of the testator at the very time the will was made.

Mental Competency and Contracts

The phrase "contractual capacity" covers that portion of the law of contracts which demands that the parties have the mental capacity to enter into an agreement. The usual test is: Did the party *understand* the nature and effect of the transaction in dispute? "A person entirely without understanding has no power to make a contract of any kind."[12] Mental illness or mental retardation alone will not be sufficient to render a person incompetent to contract. Since understanding a particular transaction is of the essence, a mentally ill person may be incompetent for one purpose—for example, purchasing property in a complicated financing transaction—although competent for another contract, as purchasing a pair of shoes.

Professor Green has summarized the legal viewpoint:

Courts have devised certain standards for determining whether or not mental disease . . . is sufficient to destroy capacity to enter into a binding agreement or to make a valid will. . . . Standards vary . . . one common element [is that] the mental disorder, in order to destroy capacity, must impair the capacity of the individual to understand the transaction in question.[13]

Psychiatric thinking in relation to psychosis, senility, or mental deficiency must be narrowed down to the "understanding test" where testimony is given relating to a contract dispute. For example, a delusion of grandeur, in a manic psychotic believing himself to have been chosen by God as a latter-day Noah to purchase a yacht, would void an agreement to purchase a boat. However, hypomanic patients may have cognitive understanding of a transaction but may be unable to control their overactive behavior. The following New York case illustrates the use of psychiatric testimony in a case of manic depressive psychosis decided by Judge Meyer.

The evidence demonstrates that from April until July, 1961, plaintiff was in the depressed phase of a manic-depressive psychosis and that from August until the end of October he was in a manic stage. Previously frugal and cautious, he became more expansive beginning in August, began to drive at high speeds, to take his wife out to dinner, to be sexually more active and to discuss his prowess with others. In a short period of time, he purchased three expensive cars for himself, his son and his daughter, began to discuss converting his Long Beach bathhouse and garage into a 12-story co-operative and put up a sign to that effect, and to discuss the purchase of land in Brentwood for the erection of houses. In September, against the advice of his lawyer, he contracted for land at White Lake in the Catskills costing $11,500 and gave a $500 deposit on acreage, the price of which was $41,000 and talked about erecting a 400-room hotel with marina and golf course on the land.

On September 16, 1961, he discussed with Mr. Kass, defendant's president, the purchase of the property involved in this litigation. It was agreed the parties would meet for contract that afternoon.

. . . On the following Monday morning, plaintiff transferred funds from his Long Beach bank account to cover the check. Between September 23 when the contract was signed and October 8 when plaintiff was sent to a mental institution he continued to show signs of mental disturbance.

On September 25 plaintiff saw Dr. Levine as a result of plaintiff's complaint that his wife needed help, that she was stopping him from doing what he wanted to. He was seen again on September 26 and 28, October 2 and October 8, and hospitalized on October 8 after he had purchased a hunting gun. Dr. Levine, Dr. Sutton, who appeared for defendant, and the hospital all agree in a diagnosis of manic-depressive psychosis. Dr. Sutton's opinion, based on the hospital record and testimony of plaintiff's wife and Dr. Levine, was that plaintiff was subject to mood swings, but that there was no abnormality in his thinking, that his judgment on September 23 was intact.

The contract of a mental incompetent is voidable at the election of the incompetent (Blinn v. Schwartz, 177 N.Y. 252) and if the other party can be restored to status quo rescission will be decreed upon a showing of incompetence without more.

In the instant case the contract concerns vacant land and is executory and though plaintiff caused some digging to be done on the premises, the proof shows that the land has been levelled again. Clearly, the status quo can be restored and plaintiff is, therefore, entitled to rescission if the condition described meets the legal test of incompetence.

Whether under the latter test a manic will be held incompetent to enter into a particular contract will depend upon an evaluation of (1) testimony of the claimed incompetent, (2) testimony of psychiatrists, and (3) the behavior of the claimed incompetent as detailed in the testimony of others.

In the instant case, plaintiff did not testify at the trial but his examination before trial was read into the record. It shows that he understood the transaction in which he was engaged, but throws no light on his motivation. But the rapidity with which plaintiff moved to obtain an architect and plans, hire laborers, began digging on the property, and his journey to Albany to obtain building approval, all prior to title closing are abnormal acts. Viewing those acts in the context of his actions, the court is convinced that the contract in question was entered into under the compulsion of plaintiff's psychosis. That conclusion is contrary to the opinion expressed by Dr. Sutton, but the court concludes that Doctors Levine and Krinsky as treating physicians had the better basis for the opinions they expressed. In any event their opinions are but confirmatory of the conclusion reached by the court on the basis of the evidence above detailed.

Accordingly, defendant's motions at the end of plaintiff's case and of the whole case, on which decision was reversed, are now denied, and judgment will be entered declaring the contract rescinded and dismissing the counterclaim.[14]

Incompetency Proceedings re: Property

Legal hearings concerning incompetency to manage one's affairs cover many life situations beyond that of will-making. They may be represented in allegations by relatives or close friends that a person is unable to manage his or her property because of extravagance, poor judgment, or mental confusion. The older law, borrowed from England, branded such a person *non compos mentis* if his incompetency was proven; thus the contract or agreement he or she made was rendered void. The general rule now is that a person who does not understand the nature of the transaction in which he or she is involved and its effect on his property is "incompetent" to make a contract or a will. This "understanding" test does not depend on mental or physical infirmity, or even senile dementia or other psychosis.

Indeed, in the case of elderly persons, the ruling in a Michigan case[15] holds generally:

Weakness of mind or forgetfulness are not sufficient to invalidate a will if it appears that the testatrix (or testator's) mind was capable of attention and an exertion when aroused and was not imposed upon. The weak have the same right as the prudent and strong minded to dispose of their property.

A similar case illustrating the same principle was that of *Cundick v. Broadbent* (Wyoming, 1967)[16] wherein the older rule: "if his mind was merely confused or weak so that he knew what he was doing yet incapable of fully understanding the terms and effect of his agreement, he could indeed contract, but such contract would be voidable at his option" was replaced by a newer view: "in recent times courts have tended away from the concept of absolutely void contracts toward the notion that even though a contract can be said to be void for lack of capacity to make it, it is nevertheless ratifiable at the instance of the incompetent party," as stated by the U.S. District Court of Appeals.

The facts in the case were that Cundick sold his land, livestock, and equipment with the consent and approval of Mrs. Cundick. There was no claim of mental incompetency at the time the agreement was signed. A month later, Mrs. Cundick elected to nullify the contract on the basis of Mr. Cundick's mental incompetency, and hence that the agreement was *void ab initio*. At the trial, all the physicians who examined the appellant three years before and one year after signing the contract agreed that Cundick was mentally incompetent to enter into a contract. The family physician diagnosed the condition as "depressive psychosis." Two neurosurgeons examining the subject at the time of request for rescission of the contract established a diagnosis of "presenile or premature arteriosclerosis . . . and atrophy of the frontal lobes." They agreed, as did a psychologist, that Cundick was a "confused and befuddled man with very poor judgment." On the other hand, there was lay testimony that he showed "nothing unusual" during and before the transaction. On appeal, the U.S. District Court, after examining the medical testimony at the initial hearing which was in conflict with the laymen's testimony, ruled that "expert evidence does not foreclose lay testimony concerning the same matter which is within the knowledge and comprehension of the lay witness. A lay witness may tell all he knows about a matter in issue even though it may tend to impugn the conclusions of the expert."

The final decision of the U.S. District Court ran against the appellant, the wife. The presiding justice stated that Cundick's acts during the transaction

> were the acts, conduct and behavior of a person competent to manage his affairs. . . . As applied to the critical issue of incompetency . . . when the medical testimony . . . is considered in the context of all that was said and done, it does not carry the heavy burden of proving that Cundick was incompetent.

However, a dissenting opinion by one of the circuit judges gave greater weight to the opinion of the medical experts, which was "positive, convincing and undisputed." He pointed out that during the period of the negotiations, "every pertinent act by Cundick was performed under the guiding hand of . . . his wife, his lawyer or some other person." It was further noted that the value of the property was much in excess of what the defendant paid for it. The judge's dissent was based on the "weak understanding" of Cundick:

> Even though a mental condition may not amount to legal insanity, it may be sufficient to result in an inequity between the parties properly to be considered . . . in determining whether a transaction vitiated by fraud, either actual or constructive. . . . It is inconceivable to me that any mentally competent person . . . would dispose of his interests at a price equal to less than one-half of the actual value. I would reverse . . . in favor of the appellant.

As is clear from the decisions, the ruling criterion is whether a person can manage his affairs "unassisted." This issue arose in an Oklahoma case heard by the Supreme Court of the state.[17] Armstrong, the appellant, who had been judicially declared incompetent, sold 160 acres before he was adjudged to be incompetent. His mother, who owned the property jointly, desired to set aside the conveyance and was advised by an attorney to have Armstrong declared incompetent and to appoint a guardian preliminarily. This was done. The guardian, one Martin, then contracted with the lawyer who successfully recorded the moneys for the sale, which sale was confirmed by the court.

When Armstrong was restored to competency, he challenged the fees paid the guardian for the sale of the property. Armstrong contended that the petition for the incompetency proceedings did not allege him to be "insane or mentally incompetent to manage his property," but only that he was an "incompetent person." In reviewing this contention, the Supreme Court of Oklahoma laid down the following rule:

> The phrases, "incompetent," "mentally incompetent" and "incapable," as used in Section 851 and 852, 58 O.S. 1941, mean any person who, though not insane,

is, by reason of old age, disease, weakness of mind, or from any other cause, unable unassisted to properly manage or take care of his property, and by reason thereof would be likely to be deceived or imposed upon by artful and designing persons.

The issue of competency often arises with regard to elderly persons whom the court wishes to protect from those "who would take unfair advantage" of the infirm individual. Fraud and undue influence are frequently claimed in conjunction with a transaction with an elderly, senile, or otherwise incapacitated person. Thus, in *Garland v. Allison*, a North Carolina case,[18] an eighty-six-year old man executed a deed for ten acres of land at a time his heirs claimed he was "physically infirm and mentally incompetent." They also claimed that no money was paid for the property and that receipts presented in court were "forgeries." The heirs also alleged that the purchaser had been given "notice of the incapacity" of the subject. The defendants denied these allegations, insisting that the subject was competent at the time of the sale and that $1,500 had been paid him as "fair value" for the land. A jury found for the heirs. On review, the Supreme Court of North Carolina ruled that "there was ample and persuasive evidence of the mental incompetency of the grantor . . . and that he [the grantee] had notice of the incapacity and when there is notice of incapacity fraud is presumed."

From the cases cited, it is evident that a medical diagnosis encompassing mental symptoms such as confusion, transitory disorientation, illusions, abstract thinking difficulty, and impaired judgment, adding up to a chronic brain syndrome, has only relative validity in court contests. The Supreme Court of Wyoming, deciding an involved insurance case,[19] made the comment regarding a doctor's testimony: "A condition which may be described by a physician as senile dementia may not be insanity in a legal sense." It is likewise clear that descriptions of behavior, samples of conversation, observed reactions, and attitudes towards and knowledge of the transaction in question are more valued in court than a mere diagnostic label. Furthermore, an opinion expressed by a physician that an incompetent person is now "free of symptoms of his illness and able to handle his own affairs and manage his money" is inadequate in a legal setting. A New York judge, in hearing a petition to discharge a veteran as competent to manage his property,[20] commented of a physician's statement: "I examined the petitioner. . . . I found him to be free of symptoms of his illness and able to handle his own affairs. . . . I am of the opinion that he should be considered competent.

The general conclusory statement of a physician that he had examined petitioner and found him free from the symptoms of his illness . . . is insufficient. There is nothing to indicate that the physician—upon whose statement all the dependents lean—specializes in the treatment and care of persons with mental illnesses, and he does not state the facts upon which his expressed opinion is founded.

Other Areas Involving Competency

Beyond instances of contracts and wills, there are several areas where mental competence may be at issue: competence to commit a tort, to manage one's own affairs, to testify as a witness, and to hold a job,[21] some of which are discussed here. In all these situations, the basic principles of "capacity to manage his or her property and affairs" holds, and psychiatric testimony is used to help decide this issue. Since there has been, and will continue to be, a bulge in the proportion of the elderly in the country's population, disturbances in memory and dullness of mental acuity or shrewdness in business matters must be differentiated from such senility as will impair management of one's affairs. For example, in a North Dakota case[22] a woman sold property held in joint tenancy by her deceased husband and herself to their son far below its actual value. A psychiatrist testified after examination that Mrs. F. had an IQ of 67 as a result of "advancing age," although previously "her judgment in practical matters was average." The Supreme Court of the state reversed the earlier incompetency finding since the woman "understood the meaning of joint tenancy" and had carried out her husband's wishes to help their sons start their farming careers.

The question of the competency of elderly persons who are not senile or psychotic, but not in possession of their full functions, resolves itself into an estimation of practical management of ordinary life problems. Dr. Leifer of Syracuse University expressed this difficult-to-decide situation: "The problem of determining the kind of performance which represents good or poor management is . . . easy at the extremes: in the middle ground no amount of scientific evidence will be helpful . . . [the] kinds of performance [considered] as good or poor management [is] a matter of personal taste."[23]

As a practical matter, statutes in several states, among them California, Arkansas, North Carolina, and Pennsylvania, provide for guardianship in cases of "senility," "extreme old age," "mental informities of old age," and the like.[24]

Competency to Hold a Job

Competency to maintain a job has developed into an issue with the growth of governmental bureaus as well as large corporations whose complex departmentalization sometimes invites personality clashes. Such situations arise when a worker or supervisor develops a paranoid attitude or displays emotional instability which impairs the smooth operation of an office or personnel relations. Personality disorders or frank psychoses may stimulate discord among the personnel, or ethnic conflicts may touch off deep-lying prejudices that eventuate in emotional outbursts. Most large corporations employ psychologists or psychiatrists to screen out disaffected employees or those in upper echelons who show mental disturbances. In state or government service, there are internal appeal mechanisms to test incompetency in particular jobs. However, these cases may require final adjudication in a court where "mental disability" sufficient to discharge a worker may be contested. In these situations, a psychiatric analysis is often requested to establish the extent of the mental disability, if any, and whether it is sufficient to destroy tenure or other agreed-on rights. The following case pinpoints the implied psychological areas:

Grace T., a 33 year old teacher with more than seven years experience was accused of "acts of unprofessionalism and aggravation of members of the teaching staff" as well as physical violence to students in the 5th grade. This and other complaints led her principal to recommend suspension to the Supervisors of the school district on the grounds of reasonable cause to believe Grace T. is suffering from a mental illness of such a degree as to render her incompetent to perform her duties according to Section 13411 of the Education Code.

A panel of three psychiatrists was appointed to examine the teacher under the section "Suspension of permanent employee due to mental disability." Their examination concluded with the finding: ". . . the most appropriate diagnosis in this case is . . . *Schizophrenic reaction, Paranoid* type . . . incompetent to perform her duties. . . ."

Grace T.'s attorney objected to the suspension, citing the lack of "procedural due process . . . confrontation and cross-examination of witnesses . . . the rights of discovery of documentary evidence . . . and the right to be represented by a psychiatrist or physician of her own choice."

Because the current author had examined the teacher some six years before in another contest, he was asked to re-examine her. The resulting picture reported to the attorney was *Cyclothymic Personality Disorder* with *Hypomanic* episodes and *Sociopathic Personality* features.

The first examination presented a clear picture of a hypomanic individual. An abstract of the first contact is illuminating:

"She comes in on time, dressed neatly, her hair long and fixed in a fairly attractive manner. She immediately shakes hands with the examiner and sits down and starts to talk. At first her talk is quite confusing because it is given rapidly, sometimes wittily, and jumps around from subject to subject. It was impossible to make a consecutive record of her conversation, but the following would be a good sample: She said, "I studied at the University of Nevada. I was in the psychology class. It was all by accident. I walked in, being a biology major, and they were talking about rattlesnakes fighting each other and I became 'hooked' on it and stayed and changed my major to psychology. There are 'crazy' students in psychology. I fracture the language. I'm also a part time tax consultant. My specialty was jazz dancing. I was a radio announcer in Reno. I am an under-active thyroid on the reverse type. My kids call me a 'perambulating garbage can.' I do social work as a 'for kicks.' I have a crazy personality which is 'inane'—that's a family joke. . . ."

The patient's statements were delivered with machine-gun rapidity. As the interview progressed, her dramatic manner and flirtatious smile became more controlled. Later examinations demonstrated less flighty speech and an attempt to explain some of the changes, detailed below.

She does admit that she gets angry from time to time and as she puts it, "if you cut in front of me with a car, the air would be blue with swearing," and then she goes on to say that she learned how to swear from the school children where she learned the various dialects from black children from Louisiana or Texas or in the Eastern Southern states.

In discussing her alleged striking of the children she said she took karate and then offered to remark that she is half black and half Comanche.

The background for the teacher's examinations was complex. It started with manifold complaints against Grace T. within and outside the classroom. The complaints started with observations of her fellow teachers that she "rambled," showed lack of judgment and tact in handling children and their parents, allowed a "breakdown in control of her classes" and was "agitated" by "events in her personal and professional life." She is said to have made derogatory statements about her colleagues, of having struck students on the hand with a ruler, of pulling a student's ears, of hitting them when they struck her, of embroiling her class in constant turmoil. A sample of her reported behavior as offered the examining psychiatrists and the Supervisors of the School Board provides the flavor of Grace's comportment:

"Ms. T. became involved in an altercation with Student 'F' in her classroom. The class was dismissed by Ms. T. for recess. Student 'F' remained. Ms. T. hit student 'F' with a pointer. Student 'F' took the pointer from Ms. T. and broke it. Ms. T. then procured a ruler. The ruler dropped on Student 'F's' nose and it began to drip blood. Then Ms. T. hit Student 'F' in the nose, and the blood flowed freely from his nose. Thereafter, Ms. T. was discovered in the classroom attempting to stop Student 'F's' nose from bleeding. Approximately 3/4's or more of a cup of blood had been lost by Student 'F.' Ms. T. accused Student 'F' of slapping her and knocking her glasses onto the floor."

Her personal history was exotic and dramatic. Married on two occasions, the first husband died in an auto accident with their two children. The second marriage ended in divorce because, she stated, "He worked for the Mafia." There were several suicide attempts, a claim that she had been pregnant five times, and a period of questionable sexual activity. Nevertheless, Grace was of superior intelligence, and had graduated from a university, obtained a teaching credential, qualifying in a special educational field.

Although the subject was diagnosable as psychotic at various times, an analysis of her personality could be summed up as a *Cyclothymic Personality* with *Hypomanic* episodes, and *Sociopathic Personality*.

On the basis of her incompetency, the school district placed Grace on "Mandatory sick leave" of two years following the report of three designated psychiatrists. The subject then, through her attorney, filed an action in the Superior Court. Prior to trial of that action, wherein the panel of psychiatrists testified as to the mental illness (Schizophrenia, Paranoid type), the current author was deposed. The sections of the deposition pertaining to the diagnosis and its bearing on "incompetency to perform her duties" follow.

Q. What is a cyclothymic personality?
A. A person who is subject to alternating elation, depressive feelings and behavior.
Q. As a—
A. People who have mood swings is one way of expressing it.
Q. Are people with cyclothymic personalities considered to be mentally ill?
A. It is under the categorization of a personality disorder, which is a mental illness. It is really a personality deviation, but it is placed under the mental illness diagnostic system of the American Psychiatric Association.
Q. What is the difference between a cyclothymic personality and a manic-depressive psychosis?
A. One aspect of a psychosis is a divorcement from reality, and the other is a series of mood swings, either elation or depression, not yet reaching the level of a psychosis, an illness. Perhaps it would be best to say a personality disorder is a borderline state.
Q. I'm sorry. What do you mean by borderline?
A. Borderline between normality and psychosis.
Q. Does the condition of a cyclothymic personality ever develop into manic-depressive psychosis?
A. It may.
Q. You used the term "hypomanic" and the term "hypomanic state" in your report. Can you tell me what those are?
A. Hypomanic means less than maniacal, but it is a matter of degree.
Q. What types of symptoms characterize a manic state?
A. Extreme activity, disconnection of speech, pressure of speech, grandiosity, circumstantiality, and mostly pressure of activity.
Q. Flight of ideas?
A. Flight of ideas.
Q. What is a flight of ideas?
A. Just what it says. The ideas do not follow in a sequential order. They jump around.
Q. Flit from one topic to another?
A. Right.
Q. So when you use the word "hypomanic" then, if I could try to put it in layman's terms, you are referring to a type of manic state, but one of lesser degree or lesser quantity, if you will, than the state normally called manic?
A. That's correct.
Q. Doctor, when examining a person, who we will say for the moment, hypothetically, does have a manic-depressive psychosis but is in a state of remission—

Q. Can the diagnosis be one of a cyclothymic personality?
A. It can if the life history matches the cyclothymic pattern.
Q. Have you recently read this report, Doctor, from the Medical Center concerning her treatment there between November 2, 1975, and November 6, 1975?
A. I have read it.
Q. In the first paragraph of—I'm sorry—second, under designation history, you find the words that the symptoms resulting in her treatment there during the period November 2 through 6, 1975, were increased motor activity, rapid speech, insomnia, extreme combative, and threatening behavior. Are those types of symptoms consistent with your diagnosis?
A. Yes.
Q. Are they consistent with the diagnosis of schizophrenic reaction paranoid type?
A. Not in my opinion.
Q. Why not?
A. Because the essence of schizophrenia is an emotional flatness, aloofness. And this is a picture of an over-active, aggressive person, in line with my second diagnosis of sociopathic personality.
Q. What type of—could you please tell me what a psychopathic personality is?
A. Yes. It is a personality type which tends toward antisocial, destructive, aggressive behavior, and is built in the bone, so to speak, or starts at an early age, six or seven or eight, and is a pattern of behavior.
Q. Would you characterize it as an illness?
A. That is a moot question. I think it belongs in the category of mental deviation, but when this psychopathic personality goes into episodes, those are acute illnesses, may last an hour or two or a day or two days. At that time you could say she was psychotic. When she attains the ordinary level, it is a question of whether you want to call it a psychiatric category or not.
Q. Were you able to reach any opinion as to whether she was competent to perform a teaching assignment?
A. It would depend upon the kind of students she had and the type of environment she was in. My reading of this woman is that she is a highly individualistic, independent person, and perhaps in a special school where the environment is conducive and doesn't rub against her sensitivity, she might have been a very excellent teacher.

At the trial before a judge without a jury, the court confirmed that the plaintiff "suffered from a mental illness of such a degree to render her incompetent to perform her duties at the time of the original charges." However, the subject had meanwhile improved under Lithium medication. She filed an appeal to the District Appellate Court which denied the suspension but recommended settlement of back pay. Her emotional instability decreased rapidly. The subject obtained a position other than teaching with a state department, maintained good control over her behavior, and was well adjusted two years after her appeal.

Competency to Testify as a Witness

The competency of witnesses to testify has relevance to credibility, particularly in criminal cases where the outcome of a given trial may well hang upon their testimony. This is a principle long embedded in the law, the precise point being whether the witnesses' ability to tell the truth is impaired by mental defect or disease, childhood, senility, or other condition. The modern criteria of competency to be a witness do not vary greatly from those enunciated by Lord Hale in the sixteenth century, as quoted by Lord Holdsworth: insanity was an "absolute bar [from] recollecting the matter on which he is to testify, from understanding the questions put, from giving rational answers."[25] Children under fourteen years were also disqualified since they "wanted discretion."

In modern times, competency to testify as a witness is generally presumed, but the witnesses may be disqualified if insanity, mental defectiveness or moral depravity, infancy (under the age of fourteen years), or intoxication are "made to appear."[26] Instances in which the expert is asked for an opinion as to incompetency are relatively infrequent since the judge has the opportunity to disqualify a witness (1) by observing him during trial or on the stand, (2) by observing him during *voir dire*, (3) by testimony of other witnesses, and (4) during direct or cross-examination. The fact of an earlier period of insanity or mental hospital residence is in itself not disqualifying since the effect of derangement must relate to the "subject of the testimony." The essential points as laid down by Wigmore, to be established by the judge with or without the aid of psychiatry, are the "capacity of observation, the capacity of recollection, and [the] capacity of communication."

Witnesses have been excused from testifying by a judge, but the use of psychiatric opinion as to incompetency to testify seems to have been stimulated by the landmark case of *U.S. v. Hiss* in 1950.[27] Alger Hiss, a State Department "career man," had been indicted by a federal grand jury as a communist and a member of subversive organizations chiefly on the basis of accusations by Whitaker Chambers, a writer and journalist, that Hiss "turned over documents of the State Department" to foreign governments. Dr. Carl Binger, a psychiatrist and psychoanalyst, had never examined Chambers. Nevertheless, he testified that Chambers was a "psychopath, unreliable as a witness, a pathological liar," and, as Dr. Meyer Zeligs' later analysis indicated, "paranoid and grandiose."[28] Dr. Binger's opinion, as an expert, was based primarily on Chambers' writings. His testimony detailed such bits of behavior as "repetitive lying, stealing, withholding the truth, bizarre and unusual acts, panhandling, play-acting and assuming false names, instability of attachment, pathological accusations."

The expert's lack of legal sophistication and medico-legal experience made him a ready victim to Prosecutor Thomas Murphy's vigorous cross-examination which virtually destroyed Dr. Binger's diagnosis. "Most psychiatrists," wrote Weihofen and Guttmacher,[29] "agree that the Binger testimony was unfortunate." Nevertheless, the court allowed the expert's testimony:

> The outcome of this trial is dependent to a great extent upon the testimony of one man, Whitaker Chambers. . . . The existence of insanity or mental derangement is admissible for the purpose of discrediting a witness. Evidence of insanity is not merely for the judge on the preliminary question of competency, but goes to the jury to affect credibility.

The Hiss case aroused interest in medico-legal circles because, as David Saxe maintains, "The Hiss case has had a salutary effect in generating interest in psychiatry testimony as a vehicle for more effective and legitimate impeachment procedures."[30] On the other hand, Alexander and Szasz, in consonance with their general disparagement of psychiatry in the courts, state in relation to incompetency testimony in the case of contracts:

> We favor doing away with the legal recognition of mental incompetency as a ground of avoiding contracts. . . . we believe that this policy is most consistent with traditional moral aims of the Anglo-Saxon law . . . namely, the expansion of the scope of individual self-determination and protection of personal dignity. . . . [We] rank . . . these values . . . higher than security or mental health. . . .[31]

The matter of credibility of witnesses received a test in a California case where a charge of involuntary manslaughter was brought against a psychiatric technician in the Modesto State Hospital (*People v. McCaughan*, 1957).[32] The technician was required to spoonfeed a seventy-one year-old patient. The patient subsequently died, allegedly from the use of "improper force," according to witnesses who were all mental patients on the ward. The technician was convicted, and on appeal, the case went to the Supreme Court of California. The justices affirmed the conviction, but in relation to the testimony of the mental patients, they suggested exercise of

> great caution in qualifying as competent a witness who has a history of insane delusions relating to the very subject of inquiry in a case in which the question

is not whether or not an act was done but rather, the manner in which it was done . . . [and whether] . . . testimony as to details may mean the difference between conviction and acquittal.

In general, the courts support the "rights to contest the issue of competency." In *State v. Butler* (New Jersey, 1958),[33] the state Supreme Court upheld this right in a case of murder to which one Coleman was the only witness. The defendant Butler requested a mental examination of Coleman after the state had conducted such an examination, which apparently reported the witness as competent. The trial court denied the defendant's motion on the grounds that "competency [was] for determination by the court alone" since it was an *ex parte* question. On appeal, the New Jersey Supreme Court ruled that

"[the] ex parte decision at the trial . . . deprived the defendant of substantial rights to contest the issue of competency and to supply the jury with pertinent evidence on the important problem of credibility." The defendant had received and introduced into evidence a report from a Maryland State Mental Hospital that Coleman had been diagnosed a few years before the crime under consideration as a "chronic brain syndrome, associated with convulsive disorder with behavior reaction, with moderately defective intelligence but not psychotic."

In lesser grades of mental abnormality in a witness, competency as in a "true psychopath" depends on the same tests as for a mentally ill person. Thus, in an Illinois case, *People v. Nash* (1966),[34] the trial court denied a petition for psychiatric examination of a witness who had been described as a psychopathic personality in a prison report some ten years earlier. The state Supreme Court upheld the lower court's denial: "A psychopath has the capacity to observe, recollect and communicate and is therefore a competent witness. . . . The question is whether it is permissible to show that he is a psychopath in order to impeach his credibility." The reviewing tribunal went on to remove the imputations possible in a psychopathic diagnosis by adding:

[It is] permissible to show that a witness . . . has a bad reputation for truth and veracity. . . . it would seem unnecessary to raise the issue of whether a witness is a psychopath, from which a jury could infer that he possesses the characteristics of untruthfulness, when direct evidence of a witness's reputation for truthfulness is admissible.

Following is a case in which a psychiatric diagnosis invalidated the competency of a witness.

A 21 year old black youth, indicted with four co-defendants in the murder of a policeman, turned state's evidence before the Grand Jury. His charges were dropped and the defendant's attorney requested a psychiatric examination because of a history of head injury, alcohol and drug intoxication with hallucinations which made his competency to be a witness suspect. The witness had stated that he was "pretty sure" one of his co-defendants had shot the police officer while the latter was driving in a squad car. The presiding judge ordered the examination but the youth objected and a thorough history of his medical records and observation in court served as material for the psychiatric report. The issue presented by the attorney was the competency of the subject to recall and recollect and communicate the material which he was to testify.

The subject had a long history of mental troubles. At the age of 14 he suffered an accident, accompanied by unconsciousness, followed by dizziness, numbness of the extremities due to apparent brain concussion. At the age of 17 he started using drugs at which time he suffered a compound fracture of the skull, by a hammer blow at the hands of an unknown assailant. The skull was depressed, the brain lacerated with hemorrhage in the brain substance. Subsequent to the injury the patient was aphasic. An electroencephalogram was reported positive. Six months later cranioplasty was performed with insertion of an acrylic plate.

During the next two years the patient was treated for alcoholic intoxication, drug intoxication with hallucinatory episodes. The patient had used "speed," barbiturates, lysergic acid, glue sniffing in varying amounts sufficiently to keep him confused, insomniac and hallucinating much of the time, including the period in which he had allegedly heard a co-defendant plan the crime of murder. At one time he saw "blood on the street . . . elephant brains" reporting dreams of catastrophic nature. His speech difficulties persisted.

At the trial the significant testimony indicated that the subject suffered from "impaired judgment and lack of control over his impulses and emotions" subsequent to his brain damage, combined with "excessive and persistent drug intoxication," the latter within a short period before the trial at which he was to testify. The subject was ruled incompetent to testify.

Other areas requiring competency in a legal action include competency to be a juror, competency to be executed, and competency to give "informed consent." These situations involve psychiatry to a minimal degree. Competency to give consent for psychosurgery has also become a problem during the recent controversy regarding selective lobotomy for violent behavior. (The lead case in this area, *Kaimowitz*, is discussed in Chapter 16.)

In general, the rule in the case of competency to be a juror is whether the subject is of "normal mind at the time of trial."[35] The issue of a juror's competence is occasionally raised by a defendant who has been convicted of a crime. The law in general is that jurors may be excused for mental illness or other mental or moral disability. For example, the West Virginia law excludes "idiots, lunatics, paupers, habitual drunkards or those convicted of infamous crimes" for jury duty.[36] In a 1973 case, *State of West Virginia v. Johnson*,[37] a defendant convicted of using a controlled substance (lysergic acid) appealed conviction from a circuit court on the grounds that a juror had been mentally ill. The state Supreme Court ruled against him, supporting the trial court and stating that "mere eccentricity or radical belief does not disqualify a juror" as long as a juror is "free from legal exception." An older Texas case, *Ex Parte Lovelady*,[38] heard before the Court of Criminal Appeals in 1948, brought the issue of a juror's former state hospital commitment to the fore. The defendant had been convicted by a jury of murder in the first degree for which the penalty was death. He appealed on several grounds, one of which was that the foreman of the convicting jury should have been disqualified because of insanity in the past. The foreman had been a resident of a state hospital for eight years a few years prior to his jury service but had regained his sanity at the time he was appointed to jury duty. Two physicians who had known him testified that he was sane and "not impaired enough" to be disqualified. A psychiatrist who did not examine the juryman testified as an expert that the juryman had "permanent and fixed insanity" on the basis of an original diagnosis of luetic (syphilitic) brain disease. Lay witnesses who were acquainted with the foreman for years testified that he ran his business well, showing no signs of mental trouble. The court overruled the psychiatrist's opinion on the basis that although the law (Civil Code, Texas, Article 616) disqualified a juror as insane, his ability to "transact his own business with intelligence" was sufficient evidence to qualify him.

The unique situation of competency to be executed has been tested in *Solesbee v. Balkcom* (1950),[39] heard in the U.S. Supreme Court. A condemned convict in Georgia became insane after sentence of death had been pronounced. Three psychiatrists examined the subject, finding him sane. The defendant appealed through a writ of habeas corpus on the grounds that execution of an insane person violated the Fourteenth Amendment. The Supreme Court, reviewing the issue of constitutionality of the Georgia law, concluded with Justice Black writing the opinion: "The power to reprieve has sprung from the same source [as] the power to pardon," namely, the governor of the state, aided by doctors "specially trained in appraising the elusive and often deceptive symptoms of insanity." Justice Frankfurter wrote a dissenting opinion, asking in effect, "May a State, without offending Due Process put an insane man to death?" The justice answered: "Not to kill such an insane man 'has its roots in our English common law heritage,' no less deep than not to convict him without a hearing."

Notes

1. Gregory Zilboorg, *Legal Aspects of Psychiatry*: 525.
2. Milton D. Green, *Proof of Mental Incompetency and the Unexpressed Major Premise*, 53 Yale L. J. 271, 284, 285 (1944).
3. Zilboorg, op. cit.: 512.

4. Thomas Szasz, *Law, Liberty and Psychiatry*.

5. William H. Page, *The Law of Wills* 1:593, rev. by W. Bowe and D. Parker, W. H. Anderson Co., Cincinnati (1960).

6. Ibid.: 598.

7. Ibid.: 636 et seq.

8. *In re Murray's Estate: Hankins v. Mabee*, 144 P. 2d 1016 (Oreg., 1944).

9. Collated from a large number of references in the medical literature.

10. *In re Estate of Coffin*, 103 N.J. Super. Ct. 1, 246 A. 2d 489 (App. Div., 1968).

11. *In re Estate of Fritschi*, 384 P. 2d 656 (Calif., 1963).

12. California Civil Code, Sec. 38.

13. Green, op. cit.: 273-74.

14. *Faber v. Sweet Style Manufacturing Corporation*, 242 N.Y. Sup. 2d 763 (1963).

15. *In re Getchell's Estate*, Mich. Sup. Ct., 295 N.W. 360 (1940).

16. *Cundick v. Broadbent*, 383 F. 2d 157 Cir., 10th Cir. (Wyo., 1967).

17. *Armstrong v. Martin*, 223, P. 2d 1072 (Okla., 1950).

18. *Garland v. Allison et al.*, 19 S.E. 2d 245 (1942).

19. *Kaleb et al. v. Modern Woodman of America*, 64 P. 2d 605 (1937) (51 Wyo., 116).

20. Application of George Abrams, an Incompetent Person, 119 N.Y.S. 2d 894 (1960).

21. Alex Brooks, op. cit.: 1000 et seq.

22. *In re Guardianship of Eleanor Frank*, 137 N.W. 2d 218 (N. Dak., 1965).

23. Ronald Leifer, *The Competence of Psychiatrists to Assist in the Determination of Incompetency: A Skeptical Inquiry into the Courtroom Functions of Psychiatrists*, 14 Syracuse L. Rev. 564, 567 (1963).

24. George Alexander et al., *Surrogate Management of the Property of the Aged*, 21 Syracuse L. Rev. 87 (1969).

25. Sir W. Holdsworth, *A History of English Law* 9:186, Methuen & Co., London (3d ed.).

26. John M. Wigmore, *A Treatise on Evidence* 2: Book 1, Title II, Sec. 492 et seq., Little, Brown & Co., Boston (3d ed., 1940).

27. *U.S. v. Hiss*, 88 F. Supp. 559 (Cir., 1950).

28. Meyer Zeligs, *Friendship and Fratricide, An Analysis of Whitaker Chambers and Alger Hiss*, Viking Press, New York (1967).

29. M. Guttmacher and Henry Weihofen, *Psychiatry and the Law*: 364.

30. David Saxe, *Psychiatry, Psychoanalysis and the Credibility of Witnesses*, 45 Notre Dame Lawyer 238 (1970).

31. George S. Alexander and Thomas Szasz, *From Contract to Status via Psychiatry*, 13 Santa Clara Lawyer, 537 (1973).

32. *People v. McCaughan*, 317 P. 2d, 974 (Calif., 1957).

33. *State of New Jersey v. Butler*, 143 A. 2d 530 (1958).

34. *People v. Nash*, 222 N.E. 2d 473 (Ill., 1966).

35. Corpus Juris, Secundum, Juries, Sec. 208.

36. West Virginia Code, Chap. 53, Art. 1, Sec. 2.

37. *State of West Virginia v. Johnson*, 201 S.E. 2d (1973).

38. *Ex Parte Lovelady*, 207 S.W. 2d 396 (Tex., 1948).

39. *Solesbee v. Balkcom*, 339 U.S. 9 (1950).

12

Commitment Problems
and Practice

To Protect the Public

The evolution of psychiatry during its two hundred year history has been intimately bound with the problems of involuntary commitment of the insane. Before psychiatry became a medico-social enterprise, "madmen" and those who showed "losse of right witte, feebleness of brayne, phrensie"[1] were lumped together with criminals, prostitutes, beggars, and vagrants in Bedlam and similar institutions in Europe. From the eighteenth century when Lunatick Asylums, Mad Houses, and Retreats grew in number, in accordance with the new humane trend towards the insane, admissions to these institutions were made at the request of "a poor officer or a relative."[2] Soon reputable doctors objected to the "advertisements of lunatic establishments" under the superintendence of their respective authors,[3] to no avail. Beginning in the 1830s, however, psychiatrists led by Isaac Ray began to denounce "despotic superintendents" who controlled the lives of the inmates and to question the "propriety of confinement" without medical or psychiatric examination. Indeed, it was not generally recognized that insanity was a "disease" rather than an "awful visitation from Heaven that no human agency can reverse."[4] It required several generations of psychiatrists to convince the American public that insanity was treatable.

At its annual meetings from 1844 to 1875, the Association of Medical Superintendents of American Institutions for the Insane voted a series of resolutions, a veritable Magna Carta for the insane. It opened with the resolutions:

1. Insanity is a disease—to which everyone is liable,
2. Properly and promptly treated, it is about as curable as most other serious diseases,
3. In a great majority of cases, it is better and more successfully treated in well-organized institutions than at home. . . .[5]

In addition to these efforts of psychiatrists, a swell of resentment by the public against the "railroading" of patients into asylums led to legal regulation of commitments. The case of Mrs. Packard who was committed to the Illinois State Hospital on the petition of her husband alone, in the 1860s, led to the formation of the Association for the Protection of the Insane. The organization's active campaign culminated in a bill presented to the New York State Legislature in 1882. The bill which passed the Assembly but failed in the Senate provided:

That no person be admitted to the asylum as insane except by court order after a "trial" of the "accused" . . . and a verdict of insanity by a jury of twelve men; that such trial shall be conducted in all respects as a trial for felony with the right to call witnesses, challenge jurors. . . .[6]

The reform movement was opposed by doctors, among others. An editorial in the *Philadelphia Medical Times* (July 1882) sheds light on the mocking tone of those who decried the association's efforts:

We were not surprised at the "proceedings of the National Association for the Protection of the Insane." . . . Reporters disguised, forcing their way into insane hospitals in order to make a sensation and earn their penny a line, lawyers over-brimming in court with philanthropic eloquence . . . learned judges on their benches . . . doctors eager for notoriety and fees, have made such a din that a quiet voice asking for protection for the sane is not to be heard. . . .

The usual practice until the twentieth century, when state hospitals came under the supervision of the State Departments of Mental Hygiene, was commitment through a writ of *de lunatico inquirendo* certified by the court. By the 1920s, most states had developed Departments of Mental Hygiene with rules for certification by examinations by two physicians following a petition of relatives or officers of the peace, and final commitment by a judge of a court of record. In some states, the examining physician could be a doctor who had practiced a specified number of years. In more recent times, the physician was required to be a psychiatrist qualified by the state. The term *examiner in lunacy* was replaced by the term *qualified psychiatrist* (New York State, circa 1930); the word "insane" was gradually supplanted by the phrase "mentally ill." The right of writ of habeas corpus was retained with consideration for a jury trial, if requested, before a judge of a court of record. Since the question of "dangerousness to self or others" was (and still is) vital in dealing with mentally ill persons, many statutes provided for detention of the insane in jails pending transfer to state hospitals. As late as 1933, fourteen states still detained such persons in legal custody, pending a trial on the "charge of insanity."

Under the stimulus of various movements for social reform during the first decade of this century, the National Committee for Mental Hygiene (organized in 1909 under the whiplash of Clifford Beer's book *A Mind That Found Itself*),[7] started a national campaign to better the lives of the insane. The campaign involved exposing brutality and abuses in the state hospitals, providing legal protection for hospital inmates, and raising the "standard of care for those in danger of developing mental disorder or actually insane." Dr. Thomas Salmon, the first medical director of the committee, started his work in 1912. He investigated a Southern State County Poor Farm and "found a 'yard man,' formerly a trolley car conductor taking care of the insane . . . three or four remained in cages all day, on stone floors instead of on green grass. . . ."[8]

In more sophisticated areas, the domiciles of mental patients were less primitive. When the present author started his career at Manhattan State Hospital on Ward's Island, New York, in 1928, dungeons, then unused, where maniacal patients had been placed for safety, occupied the basements of massive buildings housing hundreds of patients. A brief description of a hospital of an admittedly higher grade than greeted Doctor Salmon, and of a decade later, will illustrate the problems that faced the early mental hygienists.[9]

The main structures of Manhattan State Hospital, fronting on East River, were replicas of those designed by Kirkbride in the 1850s. Spacious high-ceilinged halls surrounded by wards and single rooms, a sitting room lined with wooden chairs, and a nurses' station and office near the entrance constituted the approved plan. The buildings that housed the "back wards," including the Inebriate Asylum built in 1854, appeared more antiquated as one moved away from the Administration Building. Here patients of all varieties — cases of dementia praecox, melancholias, manics — whiled away their years. The more disturbed were ordered to sit in straightback chairs, while the more compliant pushed a heavy wooden block across the hall for the obvious purpose of polishing an overpolished floor. There was no communication between patients and little with the nursing staff; some argued with imaginary foes outside the windows; some sat in Rodinesque immobility; some giggled foolishly. During the nonwork hours, the halls looked like an old Hogarth print. Occasionally, a crackling laugh issued from an upstairs window, or a grunt from a restrained manic broke the empty hum.

In the morning, long lines of ragtag patients filed from the halls under attendant-guards, en route to menial jobs in the laundry or on the grounds. The men dressed in ill-fitting drab clothes, a cloth cap set at an idiotic angle, and talked and gesticulated to themselves. The women patients, in clumsy shoes and dun-colored dresses, giggled or mumbled to the morning air. Occasionally, one would depart from the file to emphasize a point to an imaginary persecutor or to lunge at a vexing enemy. The scene was dreary, hopeless, eternal.

The Insanity Law under which the Manhattan State Hospital functioned, passed in 1896 (Chapter 545, Section 60), prescribed that the state was "entrusted with the duty to protect the community as well as the alleged insane from his deranged acts." With the exception of the malaria treatment for general paralysis, therapy beyond cathartics, sedatives, and tonics was rarely discussed. Until the mid-1920s, the lack of trained psychiatrists made treatment "inapplicable."[10] Custody was the main consideration. Involuntary commitments to state hospitals followed certification procedures signed by a judge of a court of record. As Dr. Henry Davidson remarked, ". . . the court's approval of the psychiatrist's recommendation . . . [was] only a *pro forma* endorsement of the medical decision."[11] By the 1930s and 1940s, the tone of mental hospitals had changed markedly. Admissions on a voluntary basis were encouraged, and a dynamic view of mental disease was gradually introduced. Other factors were the modernization of treatment through insulin and electroconvulsive therapy, the use of psychotropic drugs, a softening of the milieu in the hospital, and the use of ancillary workers in occupational, group, and recreational therapies. By the 1960s, a storm of protest against arbitrary commitments by psychiatrists eventuated in demands for more legal protection of involuntary patients. This thrust brought many changes in commitment procedures, in part through a sustained attack on the traditional province of the psychiatrist in legal areas. The result has been a veritable medico-legal revolution.

The Revolution in Involuntary Commitment

The opening salvo in the revolution can be said to have been initiated by Dr. Thomas Szasz' rejection of mental illness as a *myth*.[12] In numerous publications since 1960, Szasz and his followers have insisted that mental illness is simply "a problem in living" and that psychiatrists are superfluous, if not dangerous, in their social control of persons through autocratic psychiatric diagnoses and commitments. Within a decade, this view made a deep impression on socially minded psychiatrists and psychologists, and extended an indirect influence on the judiciary and legislatures. More careful attention was paid to safeguarding the rights of incarcerated patients and criminals. At about the same time, another influence, even more powerful and pervasive, especially among minorities, made itself felt in the demand for increased educational and socioeconomic rights. This movement derived its strength from the civil rights agitation of the 1960s. The consequence for forensic psychiatry, where it took the form of the Szaszian implosion, was a reduced reliance on psychiatric judgments. For the law, the consequence was a series of judicial rulings and legislative acts that implemented civil rights for patients. These two forces interdigitated to evolve into current medico-legal procedures.

An early study by Stanton and Schwartz (1954),[13] that preceded the revolution, scrutinized the effect of traditional psychiatric policy and practice in state hospitals. Sponsored by the National Institute for Mental Health, these authors uncovered a basis for questioning whether the whole gamut of "treatment" in the mental hospital was dedicated to the needs of patients or was really aimed to supply the needs of doctors and administrators. They asked whether the total hospital "milieu" was indeed directed toward the betterment of the inmates. It was a serious charge, and the impact of this study was evidenced in a decade when the mammoth move to bring patients back to their communities instead of institutionalization in isolated areas was set in motion.

The movement to abolish mental hospitals in favor of community resources received added impetus from a widely read book by Erving Goffman (1961), *Asylums*.[14] Studying the sociology of mental institutions, Goffman described the process of transforming patients into "institutional units" rather than free individuals. According to Goffman, the patients in submitting to a process that "strips away their identity" lost their individuality and spirit under the rationalization of "treatment." Recently (1977), several psychiatrists have reexamined Goffman's views, concluding that hospitalization in a state hospital may be the "choice for some patients."[15] In any event, once the community mental health program came into general use, the state hospital population dropped spectacularly. Illinois housed 49,000 patients in state institutions in 1959, but only 13,000 in 1977; the New York State Hospital census dropped from 85,000 in 1964 to 26,700 in 1977; California witnessed a shrinkage of state hospital patients from 36,000 in 1967 to 16,000 in 1977.[16]

Community mental health programs became a reality with the passage of the Community Mental Health Centers Act by Congress in 1963.[17] State hospital systems phased out in the larger states as the machinery was devised to shift acute and chronic patients to community clinics, outpatient departments, halfway houses, and acute psychiatric services in general hospitals. The move was of "such magnitude that . . . it was described as mental health's third revolution" (1967)[18] in the words of two investigators at the Laboratory of Community Psychiatry, Harvard Medical School. Other commentators assigned the "geometric growth" of community mental health activities to the "increase in the number of mental health personnel and the participation of local, state and federal governments in financing these methods. . . ."[19] In general, the movement focused the attention of legal scholars on cognate problems like freedom for chronic patients in hospitals, dangerousness of nonhospitalized persons, and the efficacy of treatment given in the traditional hospital manner. Legislative action encouraged development of planned community mental health facilities, many times without adequate personnel or financing, as in California with the passing of a Community Mental Health Services Act in 1970.[20] Its preamble typifies the legislative intent: "[T]he legislative intent [is] to end inappropriate, indefinite, and involuntary commitment of mental disordered persons and persons impaired by chronic alcoholism, and to eliminate legal disabilities. . . ."

Attacks on treatment espoused by psychiatrists, its inadequacies and cruelties, continued among Szaszian followers, then by sociologists and lawyers. These attacks were based on the grounds that mental illnesses are "not medical problems but rather economic, moral, social, personal and political problems . . . they are metaphorical diseases."[21] From this position, it was a short step to disqualify the purveyors of psychiatry as "experts" in and out of the courtroom. Patients were committed, so opponents declared, because they were "under psychiatric coercion," and treatment itself was "justificatory rhetoric of institutional psychiatry."

An example of dissatisfaction with psychiatrists and their methods, as voiced by a psychologist-lawyer, is:

The effectiveness of traditional therapies in changing behaviors which led to commitment . . . has yet to be clearly demonstrated. . . . those traditional forms of therapy have been living for many years on public faith and "credit" while the public, legislatures and courts have acted in reliance upon statements of therapists which indicate that treatment can in fact change behaviors.[22]

Another type of denunciation was expressed by Attorneys Roth, Dayley, and Lerner: "We urge abolition of involuntary mental hospitalization in any form. Involuntary commitment . . . depends on a medical screening . . . which is arbitrary and subjective while being rationalized as scientific and objective."[23]

Denigration of psychiatric involvement with the law reached a nadir in the conclusions of psychologists and sociologists at the University of South Dakota in a paper entitled "Involuntary Hospitalization and Psychiatric Testimony: The Infalibility [sic] of the Doctrine of Immaculate Perception."[24] The authors point out quite validly that statutory procedures have been overemphasized in involuntary commitments rather than the substantive definition of mental illess. Since the medical profession cannot produce a satisfactory definition of mental illness, these authors assert, the legal process accepts medical expertness regarding insanity in court under "a cloak of scientific credence."

The *coup de grace* on psychiatric expertise was delivered in a definitive article by Ennis and Litwack whose title flaunts the message, "Psychiatry and the Presumption of Expertise: Flipping Coins in the Court Room."[25] Their study is based on a study of reliability of psychiatric diagnoses wherein they analyze the bias, training, expectation, tradition, and psychological concepts of psychiatrists who differed in given cases. From analysis of these factors and a review of the literature on the diagnosis-making decision, they conclude, "The decision to deprive another human of liberty is not a psychiatric judgment but a social one." They further conclude that "no diagnosis should be admissible in court" and that experts have a "well meaning but contrary-to-fact belief in the reliability of psychiatric judgments."

These criticisms can be answered by the obvious, namely, that if "mental conditions," or to circumvent Szaszian "logic," "other than normative behavior and thinking" are socially induced, then society has the responsibility to deal with them. If law enforcement agencies, the guardians of our society, are ultimately responsible, the result would, in Dr. Alan Stone's words, "unwittingly reverse 200 years of progress and transform the 20th century dream of mental health . . . into the 18th century nightmare of Bedlam."[26] In the simpliest terms, it can be said that after all civil rights are observed and involuntary commitment is strictly guarded, society is still left with those "other-than-average-persons" who are blocked "by something" from the pursuit of "liberty and the pursuit of happiness." Still problems present themselves. Crucial questions are asked by judges, local scholars, and the public: "On what basis is deprivation of liberty justified? By what standard are commitable persons distinguished from those who are merely different or unwanted?"[27] Does the alleged benefit of psychiatric treatment outweigh "separation of the individual from family and friends, the stigma of being labelled 'mentally ill,' the deprivation of individual freedom?" These are very real questions and must be decided by judges who have few legislative guidelines to insure safe passage between the Scylla of help for the emotionally disturbed and the Charybdis of an indeterminate (eternal?) incarceration.

The fundamental question lays in a dichotomy: the state's duty to protect the community by confining mental patients and the individual's right to freedom. Clearly, this is the heart of the problem of involuntary confinement and preventive detention. But in trying to assess the degree of danger to society in a given mental patient, the profession is placed in a tenuous position. Dr. Diamond, among others who have surveyed the literature on the question of determination of dangerousness, agrees that "there are no real predictors of violence." As he concludes: "I know of no reports in the scientific literature . . . supported by valid . . . evidence [or] psychological or physical signs . . . reliably used to discriminate between potentially dangerous and harmless individuals."[28] The law has been concerned with this problem in its wish to preserve the rights of committable mental cases alleged to be a "danger to self or others." The situation is admittedly difficult under civil law where a person may be involuntarily committed to prevent injury to others. Many have felt that the judgment of dangerousness is beyond the scope of psychiatric judgment. Professor Dershowitz puts the dilemma thus:

[T]he business of balancing the liberty of the individual against the risks a free society must tolerate is very complex. That is the business of the law, and these are the questions which need asking and answering before liberty is denied, but they are obscured when the issue is phrased in medical terms. . . .[29]

Modern Commitment Philosophy

Mental health legislation and judicial decisions during the last decade or two have had the effect of deemphasizing psychiatric control of mental patients, whereas once, "psychiatrists, under the principle of *parens patriae*, decided what was good for their patients and prescribed accordingly."[30] This benevolent stance has now been modified. The "rights of psychiatric patients—right to freedom from confinement, right to treatment, right to refuse treatment, right to privacy and confidentiality, right to information about themselves"—must now be considered as primary. This change may be viewed as a byproduct of a new trend, characterized by Rothman as "decarceration."[31] Professor

Wexler describes this trend as one which "disfavors confinement of patients and prisoners if it is avoidable . . . disfavors lengthy periods of confinement if shorter periods might suffice . . . disfavors confinement in secure facilities if less secure facilities might be suitable."[32]

One of the early decisions that evoked the newer attitude was *Lake v. Cameron*[33] wherein an elderly woman, found wandering about the streets of Washington, D.C., was apprehended and committed to St. Elizabeth's Hospital because she was "of unsound mind." The diagnosis of chronic brain syndrome with arteriosclerosis indicated the probability of a lengthy stay in the hospital. A writ of habeas corpus presented in her behalf was denied. The case reached the U.S. Court of Appeals for the District of Columbia, on the petitioner's request for suitable alternatives in the community for the patient's care other than St. Elizabeth's Hospital. On review, Judge Bazelon remanded the case to the lower court, noting that "other alternative courses of treatment" should be sought. He commented further that "our decision does no more than require the exploration respecting other facilities . . . for the indigent appellant. . . ." Judge Bazelon, whose socially progressive opinion was not supported by some judges of the U.S. Circuit Court, indicated in his majority opinion that the testifying psychiatrists had stated that the patient needed "attention . . . whether in or out of a hospital," that was not necessarily psychiatric in nature. Following from his conclusion that the "appellant's illness [did not] require a complete deprivation of liberty that results from commitment . . . as a person of unsound mind," other resources were explored. These included foster homes, nursing homes, "a series of graded institutions . . . for the aged and infirm" (Judge Burger), none of which was appropriate for this appellant. As a result, Mrs. Lake remained in St. Elizabeth's Hospital as a mental patient where she died five years later "without an alternative domicile."[34] The least restrictive concept touched a social nerve, for in the decade to follow *Lake*, a great number of convalescent homes, halfway houses, foster homes, board and care homes, and nursing homes were developed throughout the country.

A variation of the least restrictive principle is found in *Jackson v. Indiana* 1972.[35] Here, the U.S. Supreme Court held that an accused found mentally incompetent to stand trial for a robbery could not be committed indefinitely. In this case, Jackson was a mentally defective deaf mute with "nonexistent communication skill." An order that the accused be held in a mental facility until he recovered from his mental illness would amount to a "life sentence" since the accused's mental status could never be determined in view of his inability to communicate. This "indefinite commitment" was clearly a denial of equal protection and a denial of the guarantee of due process under the Fourteenth Amendment. The court held specifically

that a person charged by a state with a criminal offense who is committed solely on account of his incapacity to proceed to trial cannot be held more than the reasonable period of time necessary to determine whether there is a substantial probability that he will attain that capacity in the foreseeable future. If it is determined that this is not the case, then the state must either institute the customary civil commitment proceeding [as] . . . with any other citizen, or release the defendant. Furthermore, even if it is determined that the defendant probably will soon be able to stand trial, his continued commitment must be justified by progress toward that goal.

The whole gamut of constitutional issues regarding involuntary commitment was examined in *Lessard v. Schmidt*, (Wisconsin, 1972).[36] The case concerned one Alberta Lessard who was taken to a mental health center in Milwaukee, detained on an emergency order, and diagnosed as schizophrenic after psychiatric examination. On the basis of mental illness and orders of the Milwaukee County Court, she was detained for a total of 145 days. A suit was brought in U.S. District Court on "behalf of Miss Lessard and all other persons 18 years or older who are being held involuntarily . . . pursuant to . . . any emergency, temporary or permanent commitment provision of the Wisconsin . . . statute." The court reviewing the case ruled as follows:

The Wisconsin civil commitment procedure is constitutionally defective insofar as it fails to require effective and timely notice of the "charges" under which a person is to be detained; fails to require adequate notice of all rights including the right to jury trial; permits detention longer than 48 hours without a hearing on probable cause; permits detention longer than two weeks without a full hearing on the necessity of commitment; permits commitment based on a hearing in which the person charged . . . is not represented by counsel at which hearsay evidence is admitted and in which psychiatric evidence is presented without the patient having been given the privilege against self-incrimination; permits commitment without proof beyond a reasonable doubt that the patient is both "mentally ill" and "dangerous" and fails to require those seeking commitment to consider less restrictive alternatives to commitment.

Although this case went up twice to the U.S. Supreme Court on procedural issues and was vacated and remanded, the prior judgment of the District Court was eventually reinstated in 1976.[37]

Criteria of Dangerousness

The concept of dangerousness enters prominently into involuntary commitment problems. Dangerousness to "self and others" has always been a criterion for involuntary commitment. Actual physical assaults or threats of assaults among mental patients have been taken as the basis of exercise of the state's police power in the commitment process. The presence of paranoid schizophrenia, a paranoid state with delusions of persecution, a personality disorder with emotional instability, and a proclivity towards aggressive behavior has been assumed to foretell further dangerousness, as have suicidal gestures. The nub of the legal and psychiatric problem is prediction prior to commitment. Even more important is prediction after release or discharge from a mental facility for both civilly or criminally incarcerated individuals. Supervision and control by chemical or physical means in an institution is no measure of the possibility of eruption of aggression in the outside world. Even amelioration or "cure" of a mental condition is no guarantee of the absence of risk. The variables of how much, how soon, how often, and where danger to others will occur are too imponderable for psychiatrists—or anyone else—to deal with in the hope of successful prediction. Perhaps computer scientists will be able to deliver an answer in the future. For the present, we can agree with Dr. Donald Kenefick of Boston, who, in relation to murder at least, stated: "We as psychiatrists are familiar enough with what little is known of . . . the individual context . . . of people capable of murder. We are, however, seldom able to tell why this or that person did or did not kill. . . ."[38]

In spite of this denial of psychiatric omniscience in predicting dangerous acts, the law needs to, and has, laid down principles governing incarceration and harmful behavior. The New York statute, which adopts standards of social risk from dangerous persons, expresses a generally held legal position.[39] Likelihood of serious harm is defined as:

1. Substantial risk of physical harm to himself as manifested by threats of or attempts at suicide or serious bodily harm or other conduct demonstrating that he is dangerous to himself, or
2. A substantial risk of physical harm to other persons as manifested by homicidal or other violent behavior by which others are placed in reasonable fear of serious physical harm.

However, situations exist and have existed where persons committed because of potential or actual dangerous behavior are presumed to continue with that potentiality because of chronic mental illess. This presumption was challenged by a U.S. Supreme Court decision in *Baxtrom v. Herold*.[40] Baxtrom, committed to New York's Dannemora State Hospital for the Criminally Insane while serving a criminal sentence, was recommitted civilly after his sentence was fulfilled. Thereupon, he tried several times to obtain a hearing on the issue of his mental illness. He was finally heard by the Supreme Court which held that Baxtrom was denied "equal protection" under the law in being denied a "jury review" of his mental condition. The decision was momentous since it permitted 967 patients held in criminally insane hospitals under the New York Department of Correction to be transferred to hospitals under the Department of Mental Health. These prisoners had been committed to Dannemora by prison officials, on psychiatric recommendation, because of "dangerous or criminal propensities." The question naturally arose as to whether these dangerous persons would continue such behavior in the civil hospital's environment or in the outside world when released. Dr. Steadman of the Research Unit of the Department of Mental Health, New York, made several followup studies of those who were returned to Dannemora because of further crime or violent acts. Over a period of five years he found only 26 (2.7 percent) of 967 patients required recommitment.[41] Either the dangerousness of the majority had dissipated, or the committing authorities had overjudged their potential behavior. In effect, Steadman's findings indicated that "false positive" prediction of violent behavior was in excess of false negatives, the false positives being those who did not fulfill the presumption of continued dangerousness. This finding was partly in accord with the general tendency of psychiatrists to be on the "safe side" with regard to bad results, i.e., violence, and partly due to the inherent difficulty of prediction.

Rouse v. Cameron (1966)[42] may be cited as one of several legal decisions that have had an important influence on the problem of involuntary commitment and dangerousness. The case was decided by the U.S. District Court of Appeals, Judge Bazelon presiding and Judge Danaher dissenting. Rouse had been committed involuntarily to St. Elizabeth's Hospital in Washington, D.C., after acquittal by reason of insanity of the charge of carrying a dangerous weapon and having large amounts of ammunition. After several years of confinement, he requested a hearing on a writ of habeas corpus. His request was denied by the District Court, but he was heard by the Court of Appeals. In the decision, several rulings were laid down bearing on psychiatric evaluation and management of such patients. These are reported in abbreviated form from the record:

The purpose of involuntary hospitalization is treatment, not punishment. The provision for commitment rests upon the supposed "necessity for treatment of the mental condition which led to the acquittal by reason of insanity."

Congress established a *statutory* "right to treatment" in the 1964 Hospitalization of the Mentally Ill Act . . . [for the District of Columbia] . . . involuntary confinement without treatment is shocking. Indeed there may be greater need for the protection of the right to treatment for persons committed without the safeguards of civil commitment and procedures,

. . . psychiatric care and treatment includes not only the contacts with psychiatrists but also activities and contact with the hospital staff designed to cure or improve the patient,

The effort should be to provide treatment which is adequate in the light of present knowledge,

Continuing failure to provide suitable and adequate treatment cannot be justified by lack of staff or facilities,

One who is "in custody in violation of the Constitution and laws" of the United States is entitled to relief in habeas corpus,

A person involuntarily committed and confined . . . is entitled to release if he has "recovered his sanity and will not in the reasonable future be dangerous to himself and others" . . . dangerous propensities do not, standing alone, warrant confinement in a government mental institution. . . . The dangerous propensities must be related to or arise out of an abnormal mental condition,

Appellant may not be held in custody for an offense of which he was not found guilty . . . his continued confinement depends not upon the fact that he committed the acts, but upon his present mental condition.

The appellant was remanded "for further proceedings" since he had improved. "The only question is whether he has reached a point at which he should be released."

The problem of dangerousness is paramount among disturbed patients, whether civilly or criminally committed. This is especially significant from the standpoint of psychiatric evaluation where a person, as formerly in Maryland under the Defective Delinquent law (Maryland Annotated Code, Article 31 B, 1971, repealed July 1, 1977),[43] can be committed for an indeterminate period because of a "propensity" toward aggressive acts. A man named McNeil,[44] convicted of assault, was committed to the Patuxent Institution in accordance with the definition that a defective delinquent is one who demonstrates "persistent aggravated antisocial or criminal behavior . . . [and] evidences a propensity toward criminal activity . . . [and is] found either intellectually deficient or emotionally unbalanced or both . . . [and] is an actual danger to society." Since McNeil's sentence had expired (the sentence for the assault would have been five years), the institution's psychiatrists endeavored to make a "valid assessment" of his status as a defective delinquent. The patient, however, refused to cooperate. After fifteen sessions in which the staff tried to communicate with him, they reported "no diagnosis . . . [possible] unless he talks." The inmate's request to be released was brought before the U.S. Supreme Court. The state of Maryland asserted power to confine

McNeil indefinitely without obtaining a judicial determination that such confinement was warranted. Speaking for the court, Justice Marshall agreed with McNeil's contention that when his sentence expired the state lost its power to hold him, and that his continued detention violated his rights under the Fourteenth Amendment. Justice Douglas, in concurring, felt that McNeil's refusal to submit to questioning was not "quixotic" but was based on his Fifth Amendment right to be silent. He stated further that the questioning of McNeil was " in a setting and has a goal pregnant with both potential and immediate danger. . . . The 5th Amendment protection . . . extends to refusal to answer questions where the person has reasonable cause to apprehend danger from a direct answer." The revised Maryland law (1977) concerning Patuxent inmates states: "A person confined at the Institution shall be released upon expiration of his sentence in the same manner . . . as if he were being released from a correctional facility."[45]

Release of an involuntarily committed offender when found to have regained his sanity after being adjudged not guilty by reason of insanity, brings up procedural questions relating to behavior on release. In a hearing on the inmate's regained sanity, the examinations by psychiatrists in the institution to which the offender was confined must necessarily evaluate dangerousness as well as the current mental condition. This brings the old and perplexing question of dangerousness to the fore. In *People v. McQuillan* (Michigan, 1974),[46] the defendant, charged with assault, rape, and "indecent liberties with a minor female,' was committed to the Center for Forensic Psychiatry for an indeterminate period after a finding of not guilty by reason of insanity before the trial court. After two years of confinement, he requested a motion to "vacate the commitment order." On a hearing, he was adjudicated sane and discharged from custody. As in *Baxstrom*, the Supreme Court of Michigan decided that "automatic commitment deprives one found not guilty by reason of insanity of due process . . . [and] equal protection of the law by not providing similar . . . release procedures found in other (e.g., civil) commitment proceedings."[47] With this finding, the Department of Mental Health in Michigan, attempting to aid the examiners, stated that "a condition of mental illness must be identified as the causative factor of potentially harmful behavior." Among other difficulties, this indicated that "in order to be involuntarily commitable, a person must be dangerous *because* of mental illness rather than dangerous *and* mentally ill," as Benedek and Farley point out in their review of the *McQuillan* decision.[48]

The Committed Patient's Right to Treatment

Even more pertinent to the psychiatrist's duty towards involuntarily committed patients is the matter of treatment. Several important decisions with regard to "human treatment" have been made during the last decade. Chief Judge Johnson of the U.S. District Court, Middle District Alabama, in *Wyatt v. Stickney*,[49] made a sweeping ruling in 1972 that Alabama's mental institutions, including the state school for mental defectives, should provide patients "with the constitutional right . . . to receive such individual treatment as would give each of them a realistic opportunity to be cured or improve his or her mental condition." To supplement this order, the judge laid down *Minimum Constitutional Standards for Adequate Habilitation of the Mentally Retarded* (and mentally ill). He stated that these standards were "mandatory and that no default can be justified by a want of operating funds." The court's ruling, a class action procedure, covered such details as

right to dignity, privacy and humane care; right to telephone communication; freedom to work in accordance with minimum wage laws or refuse to work; allowance for neat, clean, suitably fitting and seasonable clothing; assistance in grooming practices; the ratio of staff to patients; inclusion of psychologists, social workers, special educations on the staff; behavior modification programs . . . certified by a physician. . . .

The Alabama Mental Health Board and Alabama's Governor George Wallace brought separate appeals, contending that "the district court erred in holding that civilly committed mental patients have a constitutional right to treatment. . . ." The U.S. Court of Appeals, Fifth Circuit, held that the District Court did not err in finding that civilly committed patients have a constitutional right to treatment.[50]

The doctrine of right to treatment was initiated by Dr. Morton Birnbaum, a doctor-lawyer. In a pioneering paper in 1960,[51] he advanced the notion that, although the lawyer's "traditional role has been to guard against 'railroading sane persons into institutions . . . no recognition of any concept similar to the right to treatment' had occurred." Birnbaum, whom Judge Wisdom called the "father of the idea" of right to treatment, further stated in his article, "inadequate care of the institutionalized mentally ill . . . reflects a basic philosophic problem that in turn poses a legal rather than a medical problem."

The matter of right to treatment and of "whether the 14th Amendment guarantees" this right received an extensive review in *Donaldson v. O'Connor.*[52] This much-discussed case was heard by the U.S. Court of Appeals, Fifth Circuit, in 1974, reviewing judgments of a Florida court in 1971. Donaldson, civilly committed to the Chatahootchee State Hospital, Florida, as a paranoid schizophrenic, remained hospitalized for fourteen and a half years during which time, among other things, he complained of receiving no psychiatric treatment and of being housed in a "locked room." After a jury trial in the Florida courts, a jury awarded him compensatory damages of $28,500 and punitive damages of $10,000 against the superintendent of the hospital, Dr. O'Connor, and his associates. About three years later, Donaldson brought the case before the U.S. District Court of Appeals on the issue of whether he had a "constitutional right to receive treatment or to be released from the state hospital."

The Court of Appeals, in considering all details of the testimony at the trial, agreed that the plaintiff had "received only . . . subsistence level custodial care . . . perhaps less psychiatric treatment than a criminally convicted committed inmate would have received." Review of the plaintiff's accusations that Dr. O'Connor and his associates had acted in "bad faith," knowing that Donaldson was not dangerous physically to himself or others, convinced Judge Wisdom that "the jury would have been justified in finding Donaldson was nondangerous and in inferring that the defendants [the psychiatrists] knew him to be so." In relation to the "far-reaching" question posed by the case, he concluded that "a State . . . cannot constitutionally confine, without more, a non-dangerous individual who is capable of surviving safely in freedom by himself or with the help of willing and responsible family members or friends. . . ."

Following this momentous decision Dr. O'Connor petitioned the U.S. Supreme Court[53] on his contention that he should not have been held personally liable for momentary damages, since he had been acting "pursuant to state law" in his capacity as superintendent of the state hospital. The Supreme Court agreed to review the case "because of the important constitutional questions seemingly presented."

Justice Stewart's opinion, in part, stated:

The jury found Donaldson was neither dangerous to himself or dangerous to others, and also found that, if mentally ill, Donaldson had not received treatment. That verdict, based on abundant evidence, makes the issue before the court a narrow one. We need not decide whether, when, or by what procedures, a mentally ill person may be confined by the state on any of the grounds which . . . are generally advanced to justify involuntary confinement . . . to prevent injury to the public, to ensure his survival or safety, or to alleviate or cure his illness.

Given the jury's findings, what was left as justification for keeping Donaldson in continued confinement? The fact that state law may have authorized confinement of the harmless mentally ill does not itself establish a constitutionally adequate purpose for the confinement. . . .

Although one legal commentator wrote, "Because of its opacity, the *O'Connor* decision may be difficult to apply,"[54] the ruling of the U.S. Supreme Court upheld that of the Court of Appeals. Chief Justice Burger in his concurring opinion on *O'Connor* made an observation that seems to diminish the force of the "right to treatment" decision. He stated: "I . . . can discern no basis for equating an involuntarily committed mental patient's unquestioned constitutional right not to be confined without due process of law with a constitutional right to *treatment*." (Italics in original) In a not dissimilar vein, Professor Jay Katz has called attention to the possibility that the "Right to Treatment . . . once elevated to a constitutional right . . . might aggravate incarceration on therapeutic grounds."[55]

In regard to the psychiatrist's duty to treat patients in a hospital setting, Chief Justice Burger made a point that seems quite apt. In the first *Donaldson* case, the psychiatrist of the Florida State Hospital had relied to some extent on "milieu" therapy since Donaldson, as a Christian Scientist, had refused the medication prescribed for him. The doctors had mentioned the benefits of "milieu" therapy where no medication or electroshock therapy was acceptable to the patient. Justice Burger noted:

The Court's reference to "milieu therapy," (i.e., Circuit Court) may be construed as disparaging that concept. True, it is capable of being used simply to cloak official indifference, but the reality is that some mental abnormalities respond to no known treatment. Also, some mental patients respond . . . to what is loosely called "milieu treatment," i.e., keeping them comfortable, well nourished, and in a protected environment. It is not for us to say in the baffling field of psychiatry that "milieu therapy" is always a pretense.

Modern Commitment Procedures

Modern mental health laws, particularly those involving involuntary commitment, are based on two principles: (1) the substitution of the state hospital system by community mental health facilities; and (2) preservation of the legal rights of mentally ill persons in civil and penal situations. Of the two, the use of community resources has made the greatest difference in commitment and treatment of the mentally ill. Since many states—Florida, Massachusetts, Washington, West Virginia,

Michigan, and others—modified their commitment procedures from 1972 to 1976,[56] in almost the same language and with the same intent as California, California's law will be described in some detail.

The Lanterman, Petris, Short Act of 1967 stated in its preamble:

5001. The provisions of this part shall be continued to promote the legislative intent as follows:

(a) To end the inappropriate, indefinite, and involuntary commitment of mentally disordered persons and persons impaired by chronic alcoholism, and to eliminate legal disabilities;

(b) To provide prompt evaluation and treatment of persons with serious mental disorders or impaired by chronic alcoholism;

(c) To guarantee and protect public safety;

(d) To safeguard individual rights through judicial review;

(e) To provide individualized treatment, supervision, and placement services by a conservatorship program for gravely disabled persons;

(f) To encourage the use of all existing agencies, professional personnel and public funds to accomplish these objectives and to prevent duplication of services and unnecessary expenditures.

5002. Mentally disordered persons and persons impaired by chronic alcoholism may no longer be judicially committed.

Mentally disordered persons shall receive services pursuant to this part. Persons impaired by chronic alcoholism may receive services pursuant to this part if they elect to do so pursuant to Article 3 (commencing with Section 5225) of Chapter 2 of this part.

Epileptics may no longer be judicially committed.

This part shall not be construed to repeal or modify laws relating to the commitment of mentally disordered sex offenders, mentally retarded persons, and mentally disordered criminal offenders, except as specifically provided in Penal Code Section 4011.6, or as specifically provided in other statutes.

(Amended by Stats. 1970, Ch. 516; amended by Stats. 1971, Ch. 1459.)[57]

The procedure according to the California statute is initiated by an evaluation by a multidisciplinary team, usually in a "Crisis Intervention Clinic." The clinic is conducted by qualified professionals and is designed to alleviate personal or family situations which present a serious or imminent threat to the health and stability of the person or family. If necessary, the person is then asked to undergo voluntary treatment at a mental facility—a clinic or hospital. If the person declines, a mechanism is set up for his or her involuntary commitment for seventy-two hours, providing the person is "a danger to self or others or gravely disabled." The latter is defined as one who "as a result of mental disorder, is unable to provide for his basic personal needs for food, clothing or shelter." During the seventy-two hour period, an evaluation is made by the professional person in charge of the facility. If the person "no longer requires evaluation or treatment," he or she must be released.

If not, an order for fourteen-day detention and treatment must be sought from the court. The petition prepared by a family member, friend, or other person is presented to a judge of a superior court. The patient is served with a copy of the petition "as promptly as possible." If the professional person in the facility finds the patient needs further treatment, he may be *certified* for not more than fourteen days of "involuntary intensive treatment, provided the person has been advised of, but has not accepted voluntary treatment; provided he or she is dangerous to himself or others or is gravely disabled; provided the facility is designed by the county to provide intensive treatment." The certification is to be signed by a professional person, or his designee . . . and a physician, if possible a board-qualified psychiatrist. . . ."

At the expiration of the fourteen-day period, an additional period not to exceed fourteen days may occur with a service, a second certification by two individuals (professional person and physician), and a presentation to the court, with the proviso, as before, of the "right to a hearing by writ of habeas corpus." The judicial hearing may be held in the hospital or, if requested, in a courtroom by a jury. The court may release the patient or order an evidentiary hearing within two judicial days after a petition is filed. At this hearing, the patient has the right to counsel and may, upon advice, waive the presence of the professional person or physician. All aspects of due process are preserved in the hearing. Except for release of the patient at any stage of the certification periods by the psychiatrist or the court pursuant to a hearing, the total number of days for "intensive" treatment is thirty-one unless a post-certification procedure for imminently dangerous persons is invoked. This latter period lasts ninety days and is designed for patients who have

(a) threatened, attempted, or actually inflicted physical harm upon the person of another after having been taken into custody for evaluation and treatment, and, as a result of mental disorder, presents an imminent threat of substantial physical harm to others, or (b) had attempted or inflicted physical harm upon the person of another, that act having resulted in his being taken into custody and who, as a result of mental disorder, presents an imminent threat of substantial physical harm to others. . . .

This post-certification (ninety-day) procedure for dangerous or threatening persons contains all the legal safeguards described for the involuntary patient. The court may release, or remand, the dangerous patient to a state hospital or a "facility designated by the court." If the patient remains a danger, the process is repeated for an additional ninety days.

For the patient who is "gravely disabled" or a chronic alcoholic and who is unwilling or incapable of accepting treatment, a conservatorship is set up with a temporary conservator (a county official) for thirty days. The conservator will provide food, shelter, and care in a convalescent home, board and care home, or other suitable facility. A permanent conservator may be appointed by the court, and the conservatee may request a hearing at any time before a judge or at the end of six months when the conservatorship ceases, when it may be renewed. The temporary conservator investigates all aspects of the patient's medical, financial, social, and familial conditions, and reports to the court with recommendations for or against a permanent conservator and for or against certain disabilities for the conservatee: the privilege of possessing a license to operate a motor vehicle and the right to enter into a contract.

All involuntary patients including conservatees are given specific rights which shall be posted in English and Spanish. These are:

> The right to wear one's own clothes.
> The right to keep and use one's own personal possessions including toilet articles.
> The right to keep and be allowed to spend a reasonable sum of one's own money for canteen expenses and small purchases.
> The right to have access to individual storage space for one's private use.
> The right to see visitors each day.
> The right to have reasonable access to telephones, both to make and receive calls.
> The right to have ready access to letter writing materials, including stamps.
> The right to mail and receive unopened correspondence.
> The right to refuse shock treatment and any form of convulsive therapy.
> The right to refuse psychosurgery.
> The rights, as specified by regulation or which are statutory or constitutional.

In effect, the conservator has control over the patient's person or estate, or both, with permission of the court. Consultation with a psychiatrist is *only* in relation to the conservatee's mental condition. The total thrust of the new commitment law has been to limit the psychiatrist's function. The psychiatrist is permitted only to try to "intensively" treat the patient within the time allotted and to inform the conservator whether or not the patient is still "gravely disabled" in the event of a reapportionment for a second year, on the occasion of a court hearing for the discharge of conservatorship.

A further protection for the voluntary and involuntary patient relates to his or her records. Such information is confidential and disclosable only to qualified professional persons in the facility, to the courts, to attorneys, or for any purpose (insurance, medical assistance) "in the best interests of the patient." In fact, the statute provides that "any person can bring an action against an individual who wilfully and knowingly released confidential information or records . . . for the greater of . . . $500 [and] three times the damages . . . sustained by the plaintiff."[58]

The New York commitment law, passed in 1964, similarly emphasizes the patient's rights, but in a slightly different fashion, by establishing a Mental Health Information Service.[59] The service functions as a quasi-legal body to aid the court in protecting the right of patients involuntarily committed. The total thrust of the New York statute is to place a "new emphasis upon reconciling medical determination with patient's rights to due process."[60] An outstanding aspect of New York's law is the Mental Health Information Service which is empowered to

1. study and review the admission and retention of all patients.
2. inform patients, and in proper cases, others interested in the patients' welfare concerning procedures for admission and retention of the patients' rights to have judicial hearing and review, to be represented by legal counsel, and to seek independent medical opinion.
3. in any case before a court, to assemble and provide the court with all relevant information as to the patient's case, his hospitalization, his right to discharge, if any, including information from which the court may determine the need, if any, for the appointment of counsel for the patient or the obtaining of additional psychiatric opinion.[61]

As in other jurisdictions, voluntary admissions to an inpatient service are encouraged. With regard to involuntary admissions, the essential requirement is certification by two "examining physicians," together with an application executed within ten days prior to admission. At that time, a member of the inpatient psychiatric staff must examine the patient, and the Mental Health Information Service must be notified. When the patient is admitted, the following protective devices are invoked: service of notice; request for a hearing before the county court "to hear testimony and examine the patient"; decision of the court to release the patient to relatives; or an order to transfer the patient to a private or state facility for a period of not more than 6 months, with provision for request for rehearing by the patient or Mental Health Information Service within thirty days of detention.

The New York statute also provides for immediate hospitalization of a person with "likelihood of serious harm" defined as

(1) Substantial risk of physical harm to himself as manifested by threats of or attempts at suicide or serious bodily harm or other conduct demonstrating that he is dangerous to himself, or

(2) A substantial risk of physical harm to other persons as manifested by homicidal or other violent behavior by which others are placed in reasonable fear of serious physical harm.

This type of involuntary admission is subject to notice, hearing, and judicial approval as outlined above.

Problems in Modern Commitment Laws

One of the problems arising in practice is the definition of "gravely disabled" as a criterion for commitment. While "being unable to care for self" because of mental illness may be understandable from a social and legal position, it does not correspond to psychiatric concepts. Disorganized thinking, emotional flatness, delusions, hallucinations, and paranoid trends cannot always be translated into the requirement of "unable to provide food, clothing and shelter." It is conceivable that a deluded person or one emotionally withdrawn can buy food and dress him or herself. As Charles Harrington, county counsel in one of California's populous areas, states:

The term which creates the most difficulty in the courtroom is "gravely disabled." This has been defined in the code as ". . . a condition in which a person, as a result of a mental disorder, is unable to provide for his basic personal needs for food, clothing, or shelter." There are no cases construing this statutory definition.[62]

The guidelines for declaring a person gravely disturbed, "unable to provide for food, clothing and shelter," have been set forth by the California Department of Health (1978):

Food: Person is malnourished and dehydrated; little or no food in the house and the person is unable to establish where or how he obtains meals; person has no realistic plan for obtaining meals; person frequently obtains food from garbage cans or similar sources; person has been losing substantial weight without reasonable explanation; person repeatedly eats items not ordinarily considered fit for human consumption; person repeatedly steals food.

Clothing: Person repeatedly destroys his clothing; person regularly fails to wear clothing in keeping with prevailing climatic conditions; clothing repeatedly grossly torn or dirty; person has no realistic plan for obtaining needed clothing.

Shelter: Person is observed to frequently sleep in abandoned buildings, door-
ways of buildings, near public thoroughfares, in prohibited areas; person is repeatedly ejected from living quarters by landlords; person has
no realistic plan for obtaining shelter.
All such examples must be shown to be the result of a mental disorder
or chronic alcoholism and not merely the result of a lifestyle or attitude choice.

To match these guidelines to the usual "gravely disturbed patient"
seen in acute hospitals in the effort to secure conservatorship seems to
be overdramatic and nonpsychiatric. The more usual situation can be
gleaned from a court hearing petitioned by a gravely disabled person.
The patient was a young man who had been treated in a psychiatric
facility, then transferred to a convalescent home, and finally readmit-
ted to the hospital, at which time he requested a hearing regarding his
conservatorship. The direct examination by the district attorney
follows:

Direct Examination
Q. Doctor, are you familiar with the petitioner in this case, Tom?
A. I am, yes.
Q. How are you familiar with him?
A. I've known him since August the 4th, when he was admitted to this hospital
for the first time. He was admitted on six different occasions.
Q. Are you familiar with the circumstances of this admission?
A. I am.
Q. Yes, and could you describe those, please?
A. He refused to eat; he refused to move or partake in the family activity; he
stood in the yard, rigid; he's unable to take care of his own functions, body
functions, I mean, urination and so on, and take food; he was out of contact
with ordinary affairs of everyday life. He refused to listen to his parents' re-
quests which are normal requests having to do with ordinary living, and he
was completely absorbed in his ideas about his kinship with God and his rela-
tion to Him.
Q. Based on these symptoms, have you formed a diagnosis of this person?
A. Yes I have. I feel he is a catatonic schizophrenic.
Q. Do you feel if Tom was released today he could care for himself?
A. I do not think he could care for himself.
Cross-examination
Q. When you speak in terms of his being out of touch with life, are you refer-
ring specifically to his religious beliefs?
A. No, he himself is out of touch with his environment.
Q. Would you consider him gravely disabled if he decided to eat solid food as
a result of his release from this institution?
A. Well, just the consumption of food isn't the psychiatric test. The test is
whether he can arrange his life and have adequate nourishment to do what he

should do or wants to do as an independent individual, to get a job and to work at it, or to study and work at it.

Q. Exactly, and under the terms of the statute, itself, the ability for one to feed, clothe and shelter himself, have you observed any problem with Tom being unable to clothe himself properly?

A. I don't think he can clothe himself properly, independently of the hospital staff nurse. I observed him this morning, that he lay and remained in bed because God told him it was not his plan to get up. And he put his jumpers or overalls over, his body in bed, life an effigy of a body, which has some symbolic meaning to him. So, he couldn't dress himself as a young man would.

Q. Is that unusual in a hospital?

A. Definitely.

A. And has he told you that God will permit him to eat sufficient quantities of nourishment to stay alive, until he is released from the hospital?

A. God will only give him commands that I'm not aware of. They are private. In other words, he says, "I am living God's plan, not any human plan."

Q. Have you questioned my client on his church affiliation at all?

A. Yes, matter of fact I've had contact with his minister.

Q. And what was revealed in those—

A. The minister revealed the fact that he was unrealistic in his religious observances, excessive.

Q. Zealous?

A. More than zealous, deluded, in fact.

To return to the problem of continued treatment, it may be said that although community treatment of patients contributes many positive features, in the opinion and experience of the present writer, the state hospital, for all its defects, has psychological advantages. Aside from the vexing question of dangerousness, a prolonged stay in a facility relieves the patient of external pressures in his or her community and family and permits the sequestration of these pressures in order to realign ego forces for adjusting to the patient's life problems. The legal position can be interpreted from an intensive review in the *Harvard Law Review* (1974) of case and statutory law covering involuntary commitment.[63] The report concluded that "abolishing involuntary commitment would not resolve all problems of mental health."

The shift from state hospital to community mental facilities has not solved, for one, the chronic or difficult-to-treat case. Dr. Jerome Lackner, then director of the California Department of Mental Health (1977),[64] in a discussion of the American Psychiatric Association's Institute on Hospital and Community Psychiatry stated: "Older chronic patients have been transferred to nursing homes, dropping from visibility, while a new breed of younger chronic patients is appearing, traveling a circuit of acute care hospitals, nursing homes, and residential care facilities." At the same conference, Dr. Jack Weinberg, president of the American Psychiatric Association, contended that "large numbers of people are being placed in smaller facilities 'no less identifiable as institutions' and are being placed into communities that are not really communities." And finally, in defense of attacks on involuntary commitment and treatment, Dr. Jean Eisenberg of Harvard University, as quoted by Judge Bazelon,[65] wrote:

The fact that psychiatry can be abused does not make psychiatry an abuse. Scientists can be suborned, but science remains essential to human welfare. I join the call for ethical vigilance in medicine and science, not the Luddite appeal for wrecking the machinery in the vain hope of returning to a sinless Eden.

Both medically and legally, the precise definition of "dangerousness" is difficult to establish. Dangerousness to "self" is obvious. Prediction of suicide is itself a dubious enterprise (see Chapter 15, re suicide and malpractice). "Dangerous to others," however, covers a wide range of behavior. As Charles Harrington puts it:

The term "dangerous to himself or others" has not been statutorily defined, nor have any cases construed the term. In the experience of this writer, the term has included situations ranging from the obvious—e.g., where the patient is suicidal or homicidal—to the less conspicuous, where the patient uses poor judgment to the extent that traffic laws are not obeyed nor diets followed, where females become victims of predatory males, and argumentative or belligerent persons get into fights or trouble with the law.[66]

Another problem facing the psychiatrist in implementing treatment of the involuntarily committed patient is the right to refuse treatment. A crucial case in this regard is *Winter v. Miller* (1971).[67] Miss winter, an unmarried fifty-eight-year-old woman, was committed to a New York state hospital on certification of two psychiatrists in accordance with the New York Mental Health Law (Chapter 27, Section 78 [1]). In the acute psychiatric service at Bellevue Hospital where she was first confined, the patient objected to treatment by tranquilizers and to having her blood pressure taken on the grounds that she was a Christian Scientist. Her admission followed complaints by the manager of a hotel in which she had been domiciled by the Welfare Department that she had been noisy, disheveled, obstructive, and unwashed for months. On examination, the patient "berated the hospital and officials for violating her personal rights and privileges as a human being and a Christian Scientist."

After transfer to Central Islip State Hospital, she continued to be "suspicious, delusional, illogical, paranoid and evasive." A diagnosis of schizophrenic, paranoid type was made. After several months, Miss Winter was discharged as "much improved." She then requested a three-judge court hearing (federal) on the grounds that the state statute was unconstitutional in that she was "coerced into taking medication . . . and that a photograph and fingerprints" had been taken ". . . an outrageous procedure . . . and an invasion of privacy." A hearing was held by a judge of the U.S. District Court (Eastern District New York),[68] who, after full consideration of all aspects of the case, ruled that the "plaintiff's constitutional right had not been violated." The court pointed out that "the decisions of the doctors to utilize such treatment was well within the area of their competence." Her action was dismissed.

After a few years, Miss Winter appealed the case to the U.S. Court of Appeals, Second Circuit,[69] on the basis that she had been given medication in both hospitals "over her continued objections." Judge Joseph Smith wrote the opinion and commented that the appellant had never been declared incompetent, and that the New York law on commitment does not raise "even a presumption of incompetence on a finding of mental illness." On the appellees' (the New York State Mental Health commissioner) argument that the state acted as *parens patriae* with the responsibility of deciding "what was best for her under the circumstances," Judge Smith ruled that "the *parens patriae* relationship may be created if and when a person is found *legally* incompetent." He further stated that adjudication of Miss Winter as incompetent "was never sought before the doctors treated her in the way they thought 'best' for her." In disposing of the appellee's claim that the state's interest was paramount, i.e., the "overriding secular interest of public health and welfare," Judge Smith ruled: "There is no evidence in the record that in forcing unwanted medication on Miss Winter the State was in any way protecting the interest of society. . . ." Finally, in considering the appellant's claim that adherence to the Christian Science religious doctrine was violated by medical examination and treatment, the court said:

Where there is clear evidence that appellant's religious views pre-dated by some years any allegations of mental illness and where there was no contention that the current alleged mental illness in any way altered these views, there is no justification for defendant-appellees substituting their own judgment for that of their patient.

Judge Smith's opinion was negated by Judge Moore's dissent, in which Moore disagreed that the treating doctors were not justified in "concluding that medical treatment administered was in the best interests of the patient." In addition to holding that the treatment given Miss Winter was justified, Judge Moore stated:

I believe that a Sec. 78 (1) admission as well as a two physician admission under Sec. 72 (1) constitutes a quasi-judicial determination under state law authorizing medical care of an individual notwithstanding her lack of consent thereto . . . the staff of two hospitals here involved should be entitled to rely on such quasi-judicial authorization. . . .

Both opinions dealt with the problem of the mental patient who, as a result of impairment of judgment or other mental disabilities, may be unable to "seek appropriate treatment or to determine what treatment" to allow. As is discussed in a later chapter, an incompetent person cannot give consent to any given treatment under modern standards of medical practice. Hence, a physician, particularly a psychiatrist, must be aware of the limitations of treating a nonconsenting patient in his or her "best interest."

Notes

1. Lemnius Levinus, *The Touchstone of Complexions*: 23, London (1576), quoted from Hunter and Macalpine, *Three Hundred Years of Psychiatry*, Oxford U. Press, London (1963).

2. R. H. Shyrock, A. Deutsch, and G. Zilboorg, in *One Hundred Years of American Psychiatry*, Columbia U. Press, New York (1944).

3. Walter Bromberg, *From Shaman to Psychotherapist: A History of the Treatment of Mental Illness*: 97, Henry Regnery Co., Chicago (1975).

4. Albert Deutsch, *The Mentally Ill in America*: 137, Columbia U. Press, New York (2d. ed., 1949).

5. E. D. Bond, collected from the Am. J. of Insanity (1855-1876).

6. Shyrock, et al., op. cit.

7. W. C. Beers, *A Mind That Found Itself*, Longmans, New York (2d ed., 1910).

8. Thomas W. Salmon, *A Country Poor Farm*, no. 1 Ment. Hygiene 25 (Jan. 1917).

9. Bromberg, op. cit: 212

10. Notes: *Hospitalization of the Mentally Ill: Due Process and Equal Protection*, 25 Brooklyn L. Rev. 3, 187 (1968).

11. Henry Davidson, *Forensic Psychiatry*: 228, Ronald Press, New York (2d ed., 1965).

12. Thomas Szasz, *The Myth of Mental Illness*, 15 Am. Psych. 113 (1960).

13. Alfred H. Stanton and Morris S. Schwartz, *The Mental Hospital: A Study of Institutional Participation in Psychiatric Illness and Treatment*, Basic Books, Inc., New York (1954).

14. Erving Goffman, *Asylums: Essays on the Social Situation of Mental Patients and Other Inmates*, Author Books, Garden City, N.Y. (1961).

15. R. Peeler, P. Luisada, et al. *Asylums Revisited*, 134 Am. J. Psych. 1077 (Oct. 1977).

16. Victoria Graham, Assoc. Press Dispatch (Dec. 1977).

17. Title II, Public Law 88-164—Oct. 31, 1963, 77 Stat. 290.

18. Herbert C. Schulberg and Frank Baker, 17 Arch. of Gen. Psych., 658 (Dec. 1967).

19. Richard T. Rada, Robert S. Daniels, and Edgar Draper, *An Outpatient Setting for Treating Chronically Ill Psychiatric Patients*, 126 Am. J. Psych. 57 (Dec. 1969).

20. Community Mental Health Services Act, Welfare and Institutions Code, Sec.

5000 et seq., Lanterman-Petris-Short Act, Adm. 1968, Governor's Reorganization Plan, No. 1 (1970).

21. Thomas Szasz, *Involuntary Psychiatry*, 45, no. 3 U. of Cincinnati L. Rev. 347 (1976).

22. R. K. Schwitzgebel, *The Right to Effective Mental Treatment*, 62 Calif. L. Rev. 936 (1974).

23. Robert Roth, Melvin Dayley, and Judith Lerner, *Into the Abyss: Psychiatric, Liability and Emergency Commitment State*, 13, no. 1 Santa Clara Lawyer 400 (1972).

24. Dale Albers, Richard A. Paseward, and Philip Meyer, *Involuntary Hospitalization and Psychiatric Testimony: The Infallibility of the Doctrine of Immaculate Perception*, 6 Capital U. L. Rev. 11 (1976).

25. Bruce J. Ennis and Thomas R. Litwack, *Psychiatry and The Presumption of Expertise: Flipping Coins in the Court Room*, 62 Calif. L. Rev. 693 (1974).

26. Alan A. Stone, *Recent Mental Health Legislation: A Critical Perspective*, 134 Am. J. Psych. 273 (Mar. 1977).

27. Mary B. Troland, *Involuntary Commitment of the Mentally Ill*, 38 Mont. L. Rev. 309 (1977).

28. Bernard Diamond, *The Psychiatric Prediction of Dangerousness*, 123 U. of Penn. L. Rev. 439 (1974).

29. Alan Dershowitz, *Psychiatry in the Legal Process: A Knife That Cuts Both Ways*; A. Sutherland, *The Path of the Law from 1967*, 71 (1968): 4 Trial 29 (1968).

30. Robert L. Sadoff, *Changing Laws and Ethics in Psychiatry*, 5, no. 1 Bull. Am. Acad. of Psych. and L. 34 (1977).

31. D. Rothman, *Decarcerating Prisoners and Patients*, Civil Liberties Rev. 20 (Fall 1973). Quoted in Wexler.

32. David B. Wexler, *Criminal Commitments and Dangerous Mental Patients*: 4, Crime and Delinquency Issues, U.S. Dept. of Health, Education and Welfare, Nat'l. Inst. of Ment. Health, Rockville, Md. (1976).

33. *Lake v. Cameron*, 364 F. 2d, 657 (1966); 267 F. Supp. 155 (1967).

34. Quoted in Alex Brooks, op. cit.: 732.

35. *Jackson v. Indiana*, 406, U.S. 715 (1972).

36. *Lessard v. Schmidt*, 349 F. Supp. 1078 (E. D. Wisc., 1972).

37. Ibid.

38. Donald P. Keneck, *Problems of Public Consultation*, 42 Am. J. Psych. 125 (1968). Medico-Legal Matters: A Symposium.

39. McKinney, New York, Mental Health Law, Sec. 31.37 (Suppl. 1972).

40. *Baxtrom v. Herald*, 383 U.S. 107 (1966).

41. Henry J. Steadman, *Follow-up on Baxstrom Patients Returned to Hospitals for the Criminally Insane*, 130 Am. J. Psych. 317 (Mar. 1973).

42. *Rouse v. Cameron*, Supt. St. Elizabeth's Hosp., no. 19863, 387 F. 2d 241.

43. Maryland Annotated Code, Vol. 31B (1976), Art. 31B, Sec. 9(b).

44. *McNeil v. Director of Patuxent Institute*, 407 U.S. 245 (1972).

45. Maryland Annotated Code, Art. 31B, Sec. 11 (1977).

46. *People v. McQuillan*, 221 N.W. 2d 569 (1974); 392 Mich. 511.

47. Elissa Benedek and Gail Farley, *The McQuillan Decision: Civil Rights for the Mentally Ill*, 5, no. 4 Bull. Am. Acad. of Psych. and the L. 438 (1978).

48. Ibid.: 443.

49. *Wyatt v. Stickney*, 344 F. Supp. 387 (1972).

50. *Wyatt v. Stickney*, Appendix A.

51. Morton Birnbaum, *The Right to Treatment*, 46 Am. Bar A. J. 499 (1960).

52. *Donaldson v. O'Connor*, 493 F. 2d, 507 (1974).

53. *O'Connor v. Donaldson*, 422 U.S. 563 (1972).

54. K.A.H., *Recent Developments—Constitutional Law—Right to Liberty—Involuntary Confinement of Mental Patients*, 43 Tenn. L. Rev. 366 (1976).

55. Jay Katz, *The Right to Treatment: An Enhancing Legal Fiction?*, 36 U. of Chi. L. Rev. 744 (1969).

56. Mental Disability Law Reporter, 2, no. 1 Am. Bar A. 80 (July-Aug. 1977).

57. Community Mental Services (Lanterman-Petris-Short Act), Div. 5, Chap. 1667 (1967); Chap. 1374 (1968).

58. California Welfare and Institutions Code, Sec. 5001 et seq. (amended 1968).

59. Consolidated Laws of New York, McKinney, Mental Hygiene Law, Book 34A, Art. 29 et seq., amended 1972, with revision (1977).

60. *Mental Illness and Due Process: Involuntary Commitment in New York*, 16 N.Y. L. F. (1970).

61. New York Mental Hygiene Law, Sec. 29.09.

62. Chas. Harrington, *Involuntary Commitment of Mentally Disordered Persons Under the Lanterman-Petris-Short Act*, 6 Lincoln L. Rev. 55 (1973).

63. *Developments in the Law: Civil Commitment of the Mentally Ill*, 87 Harv. L. Rev. 1190 (1974).

64. 29th Inst. on Hospital and Community Psych., 12 Psychiatric News 14 (Nov. 1977).

65. Quoted in Kenneth Donaldson, *Insanity Inside Out*: xi, Crown Publ. Co., New York (1976). Foreword by Judge Bazelon.

66. Harrington, op. cit.

67. *Winter v. Miller as Commissioner of Mental Hygiene*, New York, Cir., E. D. New York, 306 F. Supp. 1158 (1969).

68. *Winter v. Miller*, 2d Cir., 446 F. 2d 65 (1971).

69. *Winter v. Miller*, 2d Cir., 404 U.S. 985 (1971).

13

Personal Injury

In recent decades, litigation concerning personal injuries due to negligence has increasingly come to occupy medical and legal practitioners. The medical and legal complexities that arise in this type of tort action are considerable. Legal intricacies are beyond the scope of this work, but the somatic and psychologic result of injuries involving the nervous system will be described. At the outset, the physician should be warned that injuries have a different connotation for the lawyer than is implied in medical management. The statement of an older medical-legal expert (1940), Dr. Moses Keschner of New York, will serve as an introduction to this question: "A physician equipped with (technical) knowledge will soon realize that facts and circumstances that are ordinarily of little or no significance in the diagnosis and treatment of an injury may be most significant in determination of the liability of the party through whose negligence the injury occurred. . . ."[1]

In a word, the legal concepts of negligence and proximate cause take precedence over the anatomy and pathology of the case explained by the neuropsychiatric expert in court. *Negligence* has been defined as "the neglect or failure to exercise the care imposed by law as a duty. It becomes actionable when the neglect or failure proximately causes damage to one in whose favor the duty is imposed."[2]

According to ordinary usage, proximate cause means "coming next in a chain of causation" (Oxford English Dictionary). In the law, proximate cause of an injury is defined as "a cause which, in the natural and continuous sequence, produces an injury, and without which the injury would not have occurred."[3] In the California Book of Approved

Jury Instructions, negligence is related to proximate cause (1975 revision): "A plaintiff who was injured as a proximate result of some negligent conduct on the part of a defendant is entitled to recover compensation. . . ."[4] In recent years the phrase "substantial factor" has been substituted for "proximate cause" in order to reduce whatever confusion the term *proximate* may arouse in the jury. Thus, an appellate court judge in a personal injury case in California held that "a defendant may be liable if his negligence is a substantial factor in causing the injury."[5]

The issue of negligence, of course, falls within the preserve of the law. However, causation of an injury, while essentially a legal problem, does become part of a medical analysis of an injury. In fact, the doctor, whether in a written report or testimony from the witness chair, is obliged to give an exact description of the physical and mental results of an injury, an opinion of the causes thereof, and a prognosis, including the effect on the future life of the claimant.

It will be noted that in the preceding paragraph the term *doctor* or *physician* has been used in connection with injuries because virtually every type of medical specialist is currently utilized in studying industrial, automobile, and household injuries. The list extends from surgeons to neurologists, neurosurgeons, orthopedic specialists, psychiatrists, electromyographers, electroencephalographers, nuclear medicine specialists (brain scan and tomography), plastic surgeons, otolaryngologists, opthalmologists, radiologists, dermatologists, internists, psychiatrists and clinical psychologists. Medical and emotional problems arising from trauma involve every organ and tissue in the body. One can paraphrase an old clinical axiom attributed to Osler—"Know syphilis and you know medicine"—in saying "trauma is no respecter of the human organism." For this reason, the mental specialist, in approaching traumatic problems, should have an appreciation of surgery and a knowledge of neurology.

It will be noted that the term *neuropsychiatrist* is used throughout this work. Although the term was more popular during the first two decades of this century when neurologists were the psychotherapists of the day,[6] it has been revived because of the intimate relation of emotional problems to the nervous system. Changing fashions in psychotherapy have not dimmed the need for a dualistic approach toward humans as modern work in psychopharmacology and neuroscience attests. As Dr. Charles Poser, professor of neurology at the University of Vermont puts it, the term "neuropsychiatrist died after World War II. . . . It should be revived."[7]

Types of Nervous System Injuries

The most frequent types of brain injury are skull fractures, cerebral concussion, brain contusion and laceration, and sub- and epidural hemorrhage. Since these conditions are seen and treated by the neurosurgeon or general surgeon, the classification given by Dr. S. Mullen, writing on neurosurgery, is illustrative:

> Bruise of scalp
> Laceration of scalp
> Depressed fracture—closed or open externally
> Linear fracture
> Concussion of brain
> Contusion of brain
> Laceration of brain
>
> *Complications:* Extradural hemorrhage
> Subdural hemorrhage
> Cerebro-spinal fluid leak
> Meningitis and abscess
> Post-Concussive syndrome
> Organic brain damage
> Cranial nerve damage
> Post-traumatic epilepsy

Spinal injuries are listed similarly by this author:

> *Cervical and lumbar spine:* Simple Crush Fracture
> Comminuted Fracture
> Fracture-dislocation
> Subluxation
>
> *Complications:* Spinal Shock
> Minimal compression of spinal cord
> Severe compression of spinal cord or transection of cord.[8]

Others classify gross head trauma more simply: (1) closed head injuries (with or without linear fractures); (2) depressed or compound fractures; (3) concussion; and (4) contusion and/or laceration. The emphasis by neurologists and neurosurgeons concerning head injuries differs somewhat from that of psychiatrists since the acute phase is treated by the former and the remote effects are more likely to be managed by the latter. This change in emphasis is reflected in a classification developed by Drs. Karl Bowman and Abram Blau in 1940 and modified by Dr. Branch Hardin in 1961, covering the range of mental disorders associated with trauma:

Acute brain syndromes associated with trauma
   Simple or minor concussion
      Concussion syndrome
Major concussion
   Traumatic coma
   Traumatic delirium
   Korsakoff's syndrome
Chronic brain syndromes associated with trauma
   With psychotic reaction
   With neurotic reaction
   With behavioral reaction (personality deterioration)
Postconcussion syndrome
Secondary traumatic mental disorders
   Terror or traumatic neuroses
   Secondary psychoneuroses
   "Compensation" neuroses (Workmen's compensation cases)
   Malingering
   Functional psychoses (the affective psychoses and schizophrenia)[9]

Practically speaking, the neuropsychiatrist is called upon in concussion cases which pass beyond simple concussion with stunning but without unconsciousness, or amnesias. This condition usually features a transitory headache and no complications. However, brain concussion (sometimes called *Commotio Cerebri*) lasts a longer time, from three to five days to months, may be accompanied by brief unconsciousness, and may be followed by amnesia and a train of symptoms which come to full flower within three to five days. These symptoms may be headache, which is intermittent or constant, band-like or at the vertex of the skull, lack of concentration, poor memory, irritability, photophobia, blurring of vision, sensitivity to noises (hyperaccusis), tinnitus, dizziness, nausea, decrease in appetite, fatigue, depression with crying spells, restlessness and/or apathy, anxiety, and feelings of dis-ease. Male and, to a lesser extent, female concussion patients complain of decrease in sexual libido. This symptom is especially prevalent in industrial accidents (See Chapter 14). The effects of concussion may last up to one or two months, and then gradually fade. If the symptoms do not subside, or if they even increase, the clinical picture of post-concussive syndrome supervenes. If impaired consciousness with lapses into coma persists for more than a few days, with or without focal neurological signs, contusion and laceration of the brain tissue are possible. A worsening situation with development of paralysis, aphasia, and delirium may signal brain hemorrhage of epidural, subdural, or intracranial type. This outline of the possible results of trauma to the skull—the closed head injury—is succinctly covered by Hardin's statement:

About one half of the patients suffering concussion will recover within a few days, while the remainder will show the sequelae generally called "post-concussion syndrome."

The serious brain injury regularly follows the pattern of recovery outlined by Schilder and Symonds: coma, followed by stupor (deep clouding of unconsciousness with general resistiveness), delirium (moderate clouding of consciousness with disorientation, bewilderment and helplessness), eventuating in a state of Korsakoff's psychosis before recovery.[10]

Of greater interest to the neuropsychiatrist is the post-concussive syndrome which is frequently encountered in litigation cases. Because it merges into neurosis after trauma, or is interlaced with what are commonly called "nervous" symptoms, this condition deserves special consideration. An overview of the background is necessary to appreciate current concepts of concussion and post-concussive states.

Historical Background: "Nervous" states and Trauma

Brain injury resulting from direct blows have been known for millennia. During the eighteenth century, surgeons were occupied with understanding the nature of contra-coup skull fracture and subsequent brain injuries. Concussion was diagnosed as distinct from skull fracture as early as the 1700s,[11] but an appreciation of "nervous symptoms" following injury to the skull or spine received beginning clarification with Erichsen's description of the syndrome of spinal concussion in 1875. The condition known as "railroad spine," or Erichsen's disease,[12] was characterized by nervous symptoms after trauma in the absence of organic injury to the nervous system. This inexplicable condition was observed in the American Civil War by Dr. Weir Mitchell, America's leading neurologist of the time. He called the "states of exhaustion" incurred by Union soldiers in battle evidences of neurasthenia.[13] A few years before, Dr. George Beard developed the concept of neurasthenia as one aspect of "nervous weakness" in men;[14] until then the condition was believed to be the sole province of women. Neurasthenia and Erichsen's disease were thus linked, Erichsen theorized, because of chemical or molecular changes in the nervous tissue. Other neurologists of the 1880s supported Erichsen's ideas, but the existence of this syndrome in industrial accidents was disbelieved in American courts, and it was usually attributed to malingery.

In pre-World War I Germany, where workingmen's insurance had developed, attention was focused on industrial accidents in which nervous symptoms were prominent in the absence of physical injury. In his classic text on neurology (1889), Oppenheim introduced the term *traumatic neurosis* from experience he had had with civilian injuries in Germany. He adopted the idea that microscopic "molecular" changes in the nervous tissue underlay the symptoms presented. But the flood of "shell shock" cases in World War I convinced both British and German military psychiatrists that tissue changes in the nervous system did not explain the irritability, restlessness, anxiety, tension, headache, and dizziness suffered by soldiers far behind the lines of active combat.[15] As a result of this experience, both in cases under fire and those in the rear echelons, "traumatic neurosis" lost favor. However, German authorities concluded a symposium on the subject of concussions and traumatic neurosis of war in 1931 by writing: "The traumatic neurosis [induced] by accidents meant . . . mental elaborations based on alleged injury. . . . The greatest number of war neuroses resulted from 'wish-determined mental elaboration' . . . a smaller number constituted 'organic sequellae of brain concussion'."[16]

The post-concussion versus neurotic question again came to the fore in the 1930s and 1940s when there occurred an increase in concussion cases due to civilian accidents and a concomitant increase in litigation. The few cases of concussion available for pathological study did produce evidence of petechial hemorrhages in the cortex of the brain (white matter). These findings buttressed the notion that symptoms of concussion, in varying degrees, were the result of minute lesions in the brain. Dr. Karl Von Hagen, an experienced neurosurgeon, summed up his study of brain concussion cases as follows:

Physically there is a change in the cell structure. There is (as Courville has demonstrated) some lack of tigroid material in the cells weeks and months after a so-called concussion. If the injury is severe enough there are vascular changes, both arterial and venous. . . . Chemically there is some change in the pH, and a retention of lactic acid and even disturbances in the sugar metabolism, or oxygen supply, early in the injury.[17]

Because of extensive experimental work with animals and improved microscopic techniques, the view of cellular changes in the concussed brain is now accepted, as witness the statement of two neurosurgeons describing the post-traumatic syndrome: "[T]he syndrome can be viewed as representing the effect of complex causal chains powered by neuro-physiological, psycho-physiological, psychiatric and probably some unknown factor."[18] The importance of these pathological findings relates to earlier views that prolonged concussion symptoms were hysterical or at least "psychiatric" in nature.

Analysis of the psychological aspects of trauma and recognition of the bias of doctors towards symptoms of head injury were somewhat innovative during the 1940s and 1950s. Dr. Maier Tuchler summed up the latter aspect of the post-traumatic syndrome when he indicated the "decided bias" which physicians exercised in viewing emotional reactions in such patients.[19] The complaints of concussion patients were assumed (and still are assumed) to fade within three or four months; any residual symptoms were considered "emotional" or as evidence of malingery. The studies of Paul Schilder at Bellevue Hospital in New York on head trauma cases have called attention to the profound effects of such injuries on the mind of the patient.[20] He notes that the body image, "the three-dimensional picture we have of ourselves," is affected: the victim of an injury overvalues the "head . . . an outstanding part of the body image." The injury disrupts our body image, giving rise to anxiety, panic, and obsessive symptoms. Schilder also points to the feeling of "social injustice" which victims of accidents entertain, a tendency that "facilitates an hysterical attitude . . . with a tendency to masochistic subjection." He shows how the various layers of the psyche respond to injury, thus forming the neurotic reaction variously called traumatic neurosis, neurosis after trauma, stress reaction, or simple psychoneurosis.

Yet, the concept of a nervous reaction of some kind after trauma was and remains suspect in many quarters. Some feel such a claim is meretricious. According to Dr. Walter Alvarez, a widely respected physician and medical publicist: "They [traumatic neurosis cases] develop from unwise suggestions by interns, doctors, nurses, physiotherapists, lawyers . . . [in whom] recovery usually occurs only after a remuneration has been satisfied."[21] Others with a sounder psychiatric background question how far the specific mental constellation of the victim should be compensated for. Dr. Hubert Smith and Dr. Harry Solomon of the Harvard medical and legal faculties phrased the legal question as follows: "Assuming there was an impact produced by the defendant, to what extent shall the law protect the idiosyncratic or excessively vulnerable person in allowing him damages."[22] The American Psychiatric Association did not include the term *traumatic neurosis* in its official *Diagnostic Manual* (1968 edition), although a glossary published by the association in the same year does include its definition:

The term [traumatic neurosis] encompasses combat, occupational or compensation neurosis. These are neurotic reactions that have been attributed to or follow a situational traumatic event, or series of events. Usually the event has some specific or symbolic emotional significance for the patient. The neurosis may be reinforced by *secondary gain*.

The courts have recognized the general principle that mental symptoms may follow trauma to the head or other parts of the body. For example, in a 1917 case in Texas,[23] a woman was struck by a brake handle as she was alighting from a streetcar. The permanence of the plaintiff's injuries was in question. The judge confirmed the award of damages, stating: "There is sufficient evidence to sustain the finding that she was suffering from a traumatic neurasthenia from which she would never entirely recover." In a more recent Texas case,[24] testifying psychiatrists diagnosed a woman injured in a motorcar accident as "neurotic reaction . . . reactive-depressive type." The reviewing judge ruled that her symptoms of "fright, nervous seizures, severe headaches, dizziness, crying spells, irritability . . . strange mental sensations [and] fear that she might lose her mind" were the "proximate result of negligent conduct" on the part of the defendant. The judge underlined the position of the court: "It is well established in this jurisdiction that the law will support recovery for physical or bodily injury or illness produced by fear or mental shock, when the fear or shock . . . are proximate results of negligent conduct. . . ."

While the injured plaintiff is permitted demonstration of his or her "fear or mental shock" deriving from an injury, the defendant is less favored. In a complex case involving a bus and tractor collision, heard by the U.S. District Court (for South District, Indiana),[25] both parties claimed negligence. The tractor company sued the bus line and its employee, the bus driver, alleging he had poor eyesight. The judge, after a showing of "good cause," followed Rule 35 of the Federal Code and ordered medical examinations of the defendant bus driver by nine physicians, including internists, opthalmologists, neurologists, and psychiatrists. The bus company and driver objected, asking the U.S. Supreme Court to review the granting of this order.

Justice Goldberg in the majority opinion ruled that examination of the driver's mental and physical condition was not in order since they "were not in controversy" sufficient for "wide-ranging neurological or psychiatric examinations." The court then added, "considering . . . we would be hesitant to set aside a visual examination if it had been the only one ordered." In a dissenting opinion, Justice Douglas took occasion to review the consequences of a "wide-reaching" neurological or "psychiatric probing" of a defendant. The justice wrote of this unusual situation:

If defendant is turned over to the plaintiff's doctors and psychoanalysts to discover the cause of the mishap, the door will be opened for grave miscarriage of justice. . . . A doctor for a fee can easily discover something with any patient. . . . Once defendants are turned over to medical or psychiatric clinics . . . the effective trial will be held there and not before the jury. . . . The doctor or psychiatrist has a holiday in the privacy of his office. The defendant is at the doctor or psychiatrist's mercy and his report may . . . overawe or confuse the jury and prevent a fair trial.

Before scrutinizing the medico-legal complexities of injury on the mind and body, a definitive review of medical experience with these conditions might be illuminating. Since the gross forms of skull and spine injuries are cared for by neurosurgeons, we will focus on those which come to the attention of the neuropsychiatrist.

Concussion and Post-Concussion Syndrome

Concussion and the post-concussion syndrome constitute significant aspects of personal injury litigation. Symptoms that last from three months to five years or longer become the basis for law suits inasmuch as the partially disabling effects interfere with the plaintiff's life activities. The symptoms of concussion enumerated above persist in a pattern that does not deviate from case to case, although all symptoms are not necessarily represented in a given patient. Conversely, patients who start with a full gamut of complaints may lose some of them gradually, while headache, dizziness, nervous tension, and weakness may persist for years. The degree of unconsciousness apparently bears little relation to the number or degree of symptoms in post-concussion syndrome, nor do age, previous personality makeup, cultural background, or other social factors. This specificity of symptoms can reasonably be related to the presumed petechial hemorrhages in the cortex of the brain. The only plausible evidence of macroscopic or microscopic alterations in the cerebral tissue in concussion could come from electroencephalographic studies or tomography. The former do show slow waves during the first three months after the injury but not uniformly; the latter is regularly negative. According to Curran, 63 percent of concussion cases show positive brainwave tracings during the first three months, while 38 percent show changes after two years.[26]

In the present author's experience, positive electroencephalogram findings are less frequent after the third month.

A case of simple brain concussion extending into the post-concussion syndrome is represented in the following case:

M. G. involved in a rear-end auto accident. The car which he was driving apparently overturned; the patient was aware only of a sensation of falling and did not remember whether he struck any part of the car. When the car came to rest, he felt nauseous and had pain in the right side of the head; a laceration appeared in his scalp. X-rays of the skull were negative.

Complaints which followed the accident were: Dizziness which developed spontaneously, especially when patient rose from a sitting or lying position. At times it almost amounted to a "blackout" in which his vision blurred to the point where he could not see. Ordinarily the dizziness cleared up in a few seconds; headaches—frontal in nature, lasting for a day to a month; nausea, occurred in the morning accompanied by vomiting. The patient felt butterflys in his stomach and had a general feeling of tension which was not present before. He said he was "leery" and "didn't trust it," meaning that he was worried lest the dizziness and blackout spells come when he was in a vulnerable position. He did not feel "sure" of himself.

Six months later the patient showed improvement as prognosticated. Headaches no longer present; nausea reduced but dizziness occurred about once a week. When he got up quickly, he would black out for a few seconds.

During the year that followed the patient still suffered from occasional dizzy spells and headaches and often vomitted (dry heaves) in the morning—but felt generally better.

Eighteen months after the accident he still complained of headache, dizzy spells and morning nausea. He occasionally had difficulty in depth perception while driving.

Concussion can occur indirectly as a result of a "whiplash," or more accurately, a craniocervical syndrome. In addition to injury of the posterior neck muscles with extension and flexion of the head on the neck, a concussion within the skull may occur. In rear-end collisions, for example, the head is rocked back and forth several times. As a consequence, the brain as a whole may be "slapped" against the interior of the skull. The brain and its envelope (the meninges), according to some investigators, are subject to a shearing action against the internal, irregular, bony surface of the skull. The concussion that ensues may cause symptoms indistinguishable from those resulting from direct trauma to the external surface of the skull. The acute symptoms of pain and disability in the neck muscles and tendons often overshadow, for a time, the occurrence of the concussion.

Aside from this often-unrecognized type of concussion, other factors require consideration. The fact that the post-concussion syndrome does not always occur in "pure culture" makes the medico-psychological evaluation difficult. Assignment of the role played by previous physical and mental deficits, if any, and those secondary to the injury can be uncertain. This is particularly true where functional (mental) elements are superimposed upon the post-concussion syndrome, which may merge into neurosis after trauma in cases that display a mixture of organic (objective) and functional (subjective) signs and symptoms. Beyond these difficulties, conscious and unconscious attitudes of the neuropsychiatric examiner towards the patients' persistent complaints may obfuscate the clinical picture. The examining physician is subject to biases of training and personal feeling, varying from the view that patients demanding help are "hysterical or malingering" to an over-solicitous posture. The neurosurgeon has a bias towards "hard signs" of neurologic deficit. The dynamic psychiatrist tends to see unconscious symbolism in the patient's complaints. The defense attorney may be biased in deciding that a "greenback poultice" will cure the patient. The plaintiff's attorney is biased against the third party's tight-fistedness and for his own yearning for justice. Finally, the admixture of emotional symptoms combined with pain and physical disabilities increases fear and foreboding in the patient, further distorting the picture.

Psychological Aspects of Concussion

Other factors supervene in prolonged concussion cases: there is often a history of prior accidents in cases coming to litigation; the fact that a patient has to prove his illness before attorneys, judges, and jury tends to increase the complaints induced by the original accident; and, finally, there is the question of settlement.

The main problem, however, is the clinical course of concussion. The symptoms begin to recede within eighteen to twenty-four months; however, they may last for years in milder form. When they do persist, a psychologic reaction develops which is often called "neurotic" or malingery, but which is in fact an intrapsychic defense against recognizing the possibility of permanent damage to the brain and nervous system. This reaction is added to by a "personality change" described below. Since the brain is an emotionally charged organ (highly "cathected" in technical terms), injury to the head arouses fears of annihilation, helplessness, and inability to control the environment. As the disabling symptoms continue to disturb the patient, a querulous, hypochondriacal attitude supervenes. The fear of lifelong suffering from headache, dizziness, tinnitus, blurred vision, fatigue, and decreased sexual libido induces a loss of drive, an apathy, and persistent irritability that approaches a change of personality. Patients describe this eventuality in such terms as "I am not the same man I was . . . I can't do what I used to do." This type of reaction, puzzling to the examiners and attorneys involved, and disappointing to the patient who is urged to overcome it, deserves explication.

Nowhere was this unconscious defensive mechanism more evident than in shell shock cases in World War I and combat fatigue situations in World War II. The threat of annihilation through bombing and gunfire, with or without physical injury, assailed the integrity of the ego to produce a helpless, disorganized state. In his extended psycho-analytic study of war neuroses from both wars, Dr. Abram Kardiner noted that the acute symptoms of combat stress included those associated with panic: tachycardia, palpitation, precordial discomfort, nausea, diarrhea, desire to urinate, dyspnea, and a feeling of choking or suffocation.[27] "The pupils are dilated, the face is flushed, the skin perspires, the patient suffers paresthesias, tremulousness, feels dizzy or faint, and often has a sense of weakness and of impending death." Most of these symptoms reflected changes in the vegetative nervous system associated with acute anxiety similar to that reported in civilian concussion cases. It is the chronicity of such acute situations that is involved in the post-concussion syndrome. Whether these reactions were, and are, secondary to the older notion of a sensitive "traumatic constitution" or a personality lacking in ego strength, they have been expressed in the lay phrase, "each man has his breaking point." Whatever the basis, the efforts of the ego to master the shock accompanying an injury determine the clinical features. Following the shock of a military or civil accident, the ego strives to regain its integration; nightmares repeating the accident, obsessive preoccupation with its details, and generalized anxiety reflect this inner psychological struggle. As the overwhelming episode retreats in time, phobias (in the case of a civilian happening, car phobias) and plaguing anxiety remain in the form of a psychoneurosis. Indeed, the symptom groupings in post-concussion and neurosis are often indistinguishable.

Beyond these intrapsychic aspects of the concussion-turned-neurosis lie socio-psychological factors. The patient suffering from trauma spreads his feelings beyond his body to the environment. His symptoms are colored by his attitudes towards doctors, insurance carriers, employers, and society in general. The patient projects his hostility to the "enemy," the driver of the vehicle that injured him or the insurance company behind the negligent driver. Accompanying this hostility, which may be well founded, are special attitudes towards his physician and lawyer. The traumatic patient is either cloying and insistent, belligerent and disgusted, or depressed and irritable. He addresses himself to the community, through prolongation of the symptoms, making it clear that he is suffering for no reason of his own making. One consequence of this attitude is the eruption of irritability, often uncontrollable in the home arena. In the examiner's office, emotional irritation assumes the form of lack of cooperation during the interview and examination, a questioning of the examiner's competence, or open opposition. Referrals to a series of specialists by attorneys for the plaintiff and defense increase the irascibility. This type of reaction signals the patient's seething anger at his fate. Time-consuming negotiations necessary in settling complex cases and the attendant legal maneuvering exacerbate the behavior described. Emotional extensions stimulated by the legal process tend to support a suspicion of exaggeration, malingery, or excess interest in remuneration. This leads to what is often described by relatives of the patient as a "personality change." Alternately, it cannot be denied that interest in damages from the negligent party or his representative often rests on a rational base if the shock of an unexpected accident is considered. The victim does have to face his life problems equipped with fewer resources than were available prior to the injury.

Post-Concussive State Versus Traumatic Neurosis

Whether the sheaf of symptoms outlined can be called a traumatic neurosis may be a matter of semantics. Many workers in this field consider a predisposing "neurotic" makeup to underlie the neurosis following trauma; hence, they do not agree that a traumatic neurosis per se exists. Dr. Herbert Modlin feels that the term *traumatic neurosis* is "inexact and jargonish": "[T]he laws seems to have acquired, and entrenched, a diagnostic concept of traumatic neurosis and to have accorded it status of an officially recognized illness, even though medicine does not."[28] He suggests that the syndrome is a "fundamental, nonspecific organismic reaction to severe external stress of a frightening or life-threatening kind." Dr. George Thompson analyzed 500 cases of what he freely called post-traumatic psychoneurosis[29] and concluded that it was the "most misunderstood condition in medico-legal cases." In classifying the specific neurotic pictures in order of frequency, i.e., anxiety, hysteria, phobia, mixed, obsessive, compulsive, hypochondriasis, and depression (superimposed on all groups), Thompson still stated parenthetically: "that they were predisposed . . .

goes without saying." The presumption that victims of injury who develop a neurosis after trauma are basically neurotogenic, if one may use the term, is a common one. However, courts have recognized the term, as witness a Louisiana case (1933)[30] in which the plaintiff, struck by a piece of falling plaster in his office with a minor injury to his scalp, claimed "permanent traumatic neurosis." On review, the judge stated in his ruling: "All of the doctors concede that medical science recognizes traumatic neurosis resulting from mere fright unaccompanied by physical or organic injury."

Before analyzing the concept of neurosis without physical injury, it should be noted that many clinical pictures closely resembling neurosis are found to emerge from the post-concussion syndrome. This progression seems to indicate that a neurosis, anxiety, hysteria, and the like can follow a direct impact.

R.D. aged 39, foreman in a machine shop, was struck by a heavy steel door as he left the premises. A steady worker for 20 years, regarded as a good father and husband with no medical history except nasal polyps and a back injury some years previously, R.D. described the accident as a sudden stunning. "I was aware of walking through the exit and the next thing I knew I was lying on the ground. I wondered what I was doing there. There was no pain at first but I felt groggy and then felt a lump on my head and some bleeding from the nose. I continued to work after the bleeding stopped. That night pain in my neck down to the shoulders, a severe headache and a feeling of being washed out and tired came on."

The next day R.D. saw his physician who diagnosed Cerebral Concussion, ordering him off the job for a month. By the time the patient came under medical care he complained of dizziness, fatigue, headache, numbness in the hand, wobbly sensations and impatience, sensitivity to noise, poor coordination with the right hand.

Nine months after the accident, the patient complained of a lengthy series of symptoms: pain in the back near the right shoulder, stiffness and pain in the neck, low back pain with a feeling of tight back muscles, fatigue and irritability. (According to his wife, the patient made life miserable at home because of his excitability "about trivial things and he won't let go." The patient agreed but stated he could not control himself.) Periods of "blanking out" . . . when nothing exists "for me" which his wife called "day dreaming." He had difficulty with memory, reduction in sexual interest, and a disturbing symptom in that he could not stand friends with whom he had been most congenial. R.D. was embarrassed to relate that he was suddenly aware of a rotten odor "like a person who had not washed" when no-one was around him.

A neurological examination at nine months proved negative.

During the next three years, R.D. was examined by several psychiatrists, orthopedic surgeons and neurologists. Electroencephalograms were negative but a brain scintigram indicated a "possible lesion in the left occipital parietal region." However, no neurological deficits appeared; a psychometric test revealed anxiety and dependency feelings but no intellectual impairment.

Re-examination after three years yielded a picture of a man regressed in behavior and personality but still neurologically negative and intellectually intact. His complaints were unabated, even increased in relation to back, neck and shoulder pain. Family members united in describing "a drastic change in his personality," citing, "The patient is dirty, he refuses to bathe and has to be forced to bathe at least once a week. He collects trash and has deteriorated and shows a weight loss of thirty pounds in the past year and is impossibly irritable and aggressive, even punishing the grandchildren and the children in the area and those around him. He is depressed and seems to 'put down everyone' and is, as the wife stated, 'Full of hatred as a criminal.' There are times when he bursts out against trivia and is almost irrational in his behavior."

Reexamination four years after the accident showed improvement from his childish regression, some hysterical behavior with a paranoid tendency, but no true delusions or intellectual deficits. It was apparent that the patient was somewhat motivated in his objectionable behavior by continued irritability, hostility, and self-indulgence. Disinterest in work, inability to concentrate, and restlessness were seen as extensions of intolerance to pain and disability, with a degree of conscious exaggeration. R.D. was able to "work on [his] irritability" by a self-taught maneuver which he called "evasive," meaning he would "walk away when I feel my temper rising."

After four years of observation, the final evaluation of R.D. combined the post-concussive state with a personality change and a neurosis of anxiety and hysterical elements.

Personality changes as evidenced in the case of R.D. are not uncommon among individuals who have suffered skull fractures or brain contusion and sometimes severe concussions. This clinical picture has been comprehensively described by Hardin:

There is decreased energy output, decreased work level, decreased ability to concentrate, and a decline in attention and memory. Depending upon the severity of the condition, retardation, and impoverishment of thinking appears. . . . Interests are constricted, with the patient clinging to safe familiar settings. The patient may appear egotistical, self-centered, willful and selfish. With social isolation, paranoid ideation may appear. Some may overcompensate with aggressiveness, to hide their fears; others may regress to infantile dependency and "demandingness." The picture is often complicated with symptoms of post-concussion syndrome, with headaches, sensitivity to loud noises, heat, or bright lights, intolerance to alcohol and exertion and dizziness.[31]

A long period of disabling symptoms may initiate a neurotic train of phobias, chronic anxiety, and depressive tendencies that for practical purposes amount to a change in personality function which could conveniently be called "neurosis after trauma." In addition, as will be discussed below, an impact of minor degree or none at all may initiate a phobia or other neurosis. The problem of differentiating these conditions falls to the neuropsychiatrist almost daily. Some time ago, Ebaugh and Benjamin suggested a paradigm to help in this differentiation:

The Injury was a true causative factor;
The Trauma was a major precipitating factor;
The Trauma was an aggravating factor;
The Trauma was a minor precipitating factor;
The Trauma had no demonstrable relation to the mental disorder.[32]

It is of historical interest that a half century ago the courts easily granted permanent disability awards for a nervous condition following injury. A 1926 Illinois case[33] illustrates this attitude. A man of subnormal intelligence suffered a cut finger, "sore spine and nervous condition" in an industrial accident. Five years later, he claimed to be a "nervous wreck" and applied for permanent disability. The defense objected to the diagnosis of "hysterical neurosis" which his psychiatrist had applied to him. On review, the Supreme Court of Illinois found for the plaintiff that permanent disability resulting from a "mental disorder resulting from an injury" was as compensable as a disability resulting from a physical injury. Nearly forty years later, the U.S. Court of Appeals agreed in *Leatherman v. Gateway Transport* (1964)[34] that the mental condition arising from a truck accident "could be of traumatic origin." In this Indiana case, the defendant had argued that the plaintiff had induced a state of hysterical conversion by "brooding on his injury," and therefore the mental condition he claimed disabled him arose from an "aberration of his own mind." In his decision sustaining the award, the justice pointed out that, although the plaintiff had not claimed "neurotic impairment" following the trauma of the truck accident, the evidence supported it. The court tacitly acknowledged the fact of traumatic neurosis, or rather neurotic symptoms after trauma, when the justice stressed the finding that "psychoneurosis as an element of injury" had not been brought forth by the plaintiff.

Emotion and Trauma

The validity of a traumatic neurosis diagnosis can be more clearly seen in cases where no physical impact occurred, but where a witness to injury to another suffered shock, fright, and mental anguish, thus experiencing an emotional "trauma." Such a situation is judged differently in different states. In California, the law allows recovery for damages to the plaintiff if it can be shown that the emotional distress was "caused by observations of injury or death to another," where contemporaneous observation of the immediate consequences of a negligent act which was the proximate cause of injury or death to another person in a particular close relationship. . . . [35]

The issue of emotional distress after witnessing an accident brings to the fore nice distinctions of legal and psychiatric significance. This issue was met in *Tobin v. Grossman* (New York, 1967),[36] wherein the witness to the tragedy was neither physically injured nor endangered. Following the California case of *Dillon* (see below), the trial court ruled that "close proximity to the accident" would justify an award to the mother who alleged she witnessed her two-year-old-son struck down by a car "in full view." The plaintiff also alleged that she suffered "severe shock to the nervous system . . . became mentally ill, underwent emotional and personality changes," and was diagnosed by her psychiatrist as "psychotic depression." The trial court ruled that these allegations in the complaint did state a cause of action, but "it would seem that recovery must be limited to those persons who can demonstrate that they were in a position physically to have been affected or influenced directly and not vicariously by the tortious act." The defendant appealed the case when further information arose showing the mother was inside the house at the time of impact, heard the brakes squeal, and rushed out to find her son lying on the lawn. The Supreme Court, Appellate Division (New York),[37] denied recovery, whereupon the plaintiff appealed the case to the Court of Appeals (New York).[38] This review finalized the denial in ruling that the mother had no cause of action where there was "unintended harm sustained by one, solely as a result of injuries inflicted directly upon another, regardless of the relationship and whether the one was an eyewitness to the incident which resulted in the direct injuries." The court, laying aside the fact of the mother's psychotic depression, stated that "the solution does not depend on advances in medical science . . . mental traumatic causation can now be diagnosed almost as well as physical traumatic causation." It decreed that causation of mental conditions in one witnessing an injury to another was a "legal problem."

More specifically, a claimant who is physically present in the "zone of danger . . . [or] area of physical risk" and who, although not physically hurt, is subject to emotional distress, has been awarded recovery from nervous symptoms. The oft-quoted case of *Dillon v. Legg* (California, 1968)[39] demonstrates the "zone of danger" principle. A mother saw her infant daughter killed by a car as she crossed at an intersection. The Supreme Court of California overturned a trial court decision based on the existing precedent that no cause of action was stated unless the plaintiff's shock resulted from fear for her own safety. In reversing the decision, the Supreme Court set forth guidelines for determining liability for emotional trauma. Foreseeability of injury, which is determinative of liability, was to depend upon

such factors as . . . (1) Whether plaintiff was located near the scene of the accident as contrasted with one who was a distance away from it. (2) Whether the shock resulted from a direct emotional impact upon the plaintiff from the sensory and contemporaneous observance of the accident, as contrasted with learning of the accident from others after its occurrence. (3) Whether plaintiff and the victim were closely related, as contrasted with an absence of any relationship or the presence of only a distant relationship.

One of the issues confronting the law in cases where plaintiffs succumb to emotional trauma on witnessing injury to another is the establishment of "boundaries of liability for mental distress following injuries." Guidelines for decisions in cases of this type are indicated in a Washington decision[40] by the Supreme Court of that state which noted that this was a "divided, confused, and unsettled area of the law." The case involved a woman sitting in her living room where she heard an "explosive sound."

Rushing in the direction of the sound she saw her neighbor's car in the middle of their back porch, two walls had been knocked down, windows shattered, articles damaged, the floor collapsed. Plaintiff's immediate concern was her husband's fate—he was teaching piano in an adjoining room—and that of her neighbor whom she knew to have some physical problems. On entering the porch, she fell through the collapsed floor and sustained minor bruises. Soon after, she experienced pain in the chest and breast, numbness in the arms and mental distress, partly because she had had a lobectomy in the lung some years before and feared further damage to her ribs. Her physician diagnosed "severe heart stress" consequent on witnessing the damage made by the intruding car.

The trial court instructed the jury that if they find the sole proximate cause of the stress was plaintiff's fear for the safety of the defendant and/or her fear for the safety of her husband and/or the damage to her home, then the verdict should be for the defendants; but if they find that a proximate cause of the stress was the noise the plaintiff heard and/or the scene which confronted her when she observed the defendant's car in her home and/or the fall plaintiff sustained and the bruises if any, resulting therefrom, and if they find that this stress proximately caused injury to the plaintiff, then the verdict should be for the plaintiff.

The Supreme Court on review found this instruction to be in error, ruling that "negligently caused mental distress" can constitute liability, and that "It is not necessary that there be any physical impact or the threat of immediate physical invasion of the plaintiff's personal security." The case was remanded for a new trial.

Not only fear and shock in witnessing a tragic situation, but also frustration, disappointment, and even strong resentment, can lead to hysterical reactions that might well qualify as traumatic neurosis without physical injury. Such cases arise especially in workmen's compensation or personnel board hearings where conflict in an office, undue criticism of a worker, or prejudiced handling of a work situation initiate a neurotic reaction (see Chapter 14). As might be expected, undue sensitivity, possibly a paranoid tendency, may be present in order for the plaintiff to develop a neurosis under stress. In the case presented below, a complication in the form of a physical component, which could or could not have been organic, entered the clinical picture but did not detract from the psychogenicity of the resulting mental condition. As noted, few psychological problems finding their way into litigation are seen in "pure culture."

A 37-year-old worker in a large manufacturing plant appeared in a local hospital following an episode of "passing out." The admission note stated: "He apparently had had an aura of his mind going blank, then had walked into his house where relatives had observed his right arm shaking. Seconds later he fell on the floor. He was unresponsive, cyanotic, and puffing. His wife noted that his jaw was rigid and that his right arm was rigid and flexed at the elbow. His eyes were open. He was not responsive and did not realize what was going on around him until 30 minutes later."

Neurological work-up at a Medical Center to which he was transferred revealed decreased power in the right arm, diffuse slowing the electroencephalograph in the left temporal area but negative vascular blood studies, and carotid angiogram studies.

The past history indicated three prior episodes of the nature described, six months before examination. A tentative diagnosis of Jacksonian epilepsy was suggested on the basis of "soft signs." Scrutiny of his emotional state, however, revealed emotional pressures secondary to difficulties with his supervisors on his job.

Having attained seniority and a foreman's rank he was transferred to towns distant from his home. This led to altercations with the management which led him to feel he was being "used" by the management, causing him insomnia, nervousness, and a feeling of helplessness. The patient felt his supervisors were "two-faced." At the same time, the cut in expense account from $15 a day to $7.50 bothered him excessively.

It was with this background that he developed the first arm "shaking" which had the character of a protesting forward movement. Much time was spent in the interview describing his movements of involuntary nature. He also spoke of the spinal tap which he received at the hands of an "interne" caused him great back pain and stiffness which he feared meant some permanent injury to his spinal cord.

On examination nine months after the original seizure, the patient's complaints centered on nervousness, apprehension, and a constant underlying worry about having a tumor of the brain, even though he was assured the brain scan was negative.

Neurological examination done on two occasions indicated no difficulty in power in lower or upper extremities. A second EEG examination was done with a normal finding. There were "no focal, lateralized or epileptiform features" noted.

The analysis of the patient pointed towards the absence of signs of organic mental dysfunction in the face of a moderate intelligence and signs of neurotic interference with his mental capacity. The preoccupation with brain disease and the constant worry that he is "incurable" in the face of medical reassurance, points to a definite depression of neurotic type.

Hysteria Versus Malingery

Dramatic reactions of this sort, as an aspect of neuroses or psychoses, raise the question of malingery or simulation. Historically, medical examiners have been partial to finding malingery or hysteria where tests reveal few correlations between anatomical or pathological expectations and the complaints, or where symptoms appear excessive. In the past, the examiners' negative attitudes often determined the diagnosis in an era when drastic methods were used to rule out malingery; for example, a blind man would be made to walk into a wall to test whether he was feigning blindness.

In malingery, a symptom is feigned or simulated. Thus, a patient will act confused, mix up his statements to indicate poor comprehension, or hold an arm in a bizarre manner to indicate paralysis. Such symptoms tend to appear childish, exaggerated, and even contrived. Simulation is a studied attempt to mimic the condition claimed. On the other hand, hysteria represents a pathological process of the mind and emotions, wherein painful or unacceptable ideas and emotions are excluded from consciousness. The modern view of hysteria considers an emotionally laden idea to be split off from consciousness and to be converted into a physical symptom—hence the term *conversion hysteria*. One mechanism is automatic (hysteria); the other is contrived (malingery). In hysteria, the ego cannot accept the experience of a threatening or painful object. Thus, a fright may result in hysterical aphonia; a distasteful scene can cause hysterical blindness; overwhelming fear often leads to hysterical paralysis; and severe insecurity can result in hysterical staggering or weakness.

Older authorities felt that simulation was an element of every neurosis, following the outworn theory that weakness "of mind" and the wish to gain attention lay at the base of hysteria. Dr. Walter Schaller, writing in 1939, stated: "Every post-traumatic neurosis is not malingery but a sub-conscious simulator . . . every hysteric is a simulator [representing] a milder implication of motive and conduct [than found in] the malingerer."[41]

The more moderate current view, as stated in Noyes' classic psychiatric text, is that "some hysterical phenomena are on the borderline between psychoneurotic reactions and simulation and therefore come close to malingering. Just where as to awareness, the line between simulation and hysteria should be drawn is therefore often arbitrary."[42] As Noyes hinted, malingery is itself a kind of neurosis.

The appearance of hysterical conversion symptoms in a man severely injured in an industrial accident illustrates the profound effect of fear in repressing some bodily functions.

The impact to Bill's back was severe. While working on a railroad car, he was pinned between a forklift and the inside wall of a warehouse in such a way as to have been jammed against and through the plywood wall. His first reaction was "I'm finished." Bill was finally able to attract the attention of fellow workers who pulled the forklift from his body. He fainted. When he came to, his thought was that his legs had been broken, that he had internal injuries. The pressure of the machine had been against his legs, pelvis, and back. Emergency examination and X-rays revealed no fracture. Bill was sent home. "They just dropped me on the couch at home . . . nothing was done although I had severe pain."

For the next three months the patient was treated conservatively, mostly with medications and rest. He felt he was not receiving the treatment his serious condition deserved, especially since he had urinated blood immediately after the accident and complained of urinary hesitancy, later. Examination by orthopedic and neurologic surgeons uncovered no gross pathology including a negative electromyographic test and myelogram.

Tranquilizing drugs and codeine for pain had produced no improvement; the patient was hospitalized for further observation. Immediately he developed a delirium, complaining in obvious fright of ants and roaches crawling about the room, of water dripping from the ceiling, of two "toughs" accompanied by large dogs surrounding his bed, attempting to pull his Foley tube out. Whether the delirium was secondary to codeine use or hysterical in nature (the patient had a completely negative history for alcohol), could not be decided. Within three days the delirium subsided but Bill's agitation continued.

For the next six months the patient remained under close observation. New symptoms appeared—complete impotence, a tilt of the head presumably due to spasm of the neck muscles, spasm of the back muscles, and hoarseness which increased to aphonia. Within a year the loss of voice for which no organic basis in the larynx was uncovered, became complete at intervals. When Bill was able to speak, an explosive quality of his speech was noted along with tremors of the face and tongue and what appeared to be a brain stem lesion. However, thorough neurological study, including an electromyograph at the University Medical Center, disproved any organic pathology.

Prolonged and thorough physical therapy was instituted with some improvement of his back and neck complaints. Still by the fourth year after trauma, the hysterical aphonia persisted, when fatigued, the sexual inadequacy remained. A thorough study of his background for years prior to the accident failed to provide any support for nervous symptoms or neurotic predisposition prior to the frightening, almost catastrophic accident in the railroad yards from which he emerged with no fractures or permanent physical injury.

The symptoms in this case involved conscious and unconscious sexual fears on a hysterical basis.

In addition to malingery and hysteria, other reactions to pain and disability require consideration. Exaggeration of symptoms or, more accurately stated, overvaluation of complaints lies close to the normal reactions of injured persons. In general, a hurt or deficiency for a time becomes all-engrossing to the sufferer, especially if a diagnosis establishes the hurt as a medical entity. Exaggeration rapidly diminishes as the reality, i.e., seriousness or triviality, of the injury asserts itself. When complaints continue beyond their physiological needs, the notion of overvaluation is descriptive. If excessive emotion is added to the victim's perception of his or her symptoms, the stage of functional overlay is reached. This phrase was designed to indicate persistent emotional preoccupation with a part of the body beyond its physiological impairment. Functional overlay must be distinguished from malingery in that the emotional overflow is not consciously motivated. In this case, some disturbance of function is observable, whereas in malingery no pathological condition exists. Functional overlay can be expressed by the technical term *psychophysiological disorder or somatization*, a term contrived to encompass both mental and physical bases for complaints. It might be helpful to regard malingery, overevaluation, functional overlay, and hysteria as constituting a gradient moving from conscious to unconscious denial of bodily integrity.

To summarize this complex and often baffling train of reactions to trauma: *Simulation* is an assumed state of pain and disability, an imitation of illness without any etiological or organic basis. *Malingery* is also an assumed state which feigns illness but may be built on an historical event preceding it, i.e., an actual injury. For practical purposes the terms are synonymous. *Exaggeration* is a magnification of pain and disability. *Overvaluation* represents an individual reaction to pain which may appear feigned but is not. *Functional overlay* is an emotional superimposition on the original symptoms of an injury or illness. *Hysteria*, i.e., conversion hysteria, is a physical representation of an emotional conflict.

One further condition requires consideration in this differential, namely *psychophysiological disorders*, defined in the American Psychiatric Association's DSM II as "caused by emotional factors . . . usually under autonomic nervous system innervation . . . ": examples are paroxysmal tachycardia, hyperventilation, irritable colon, etc. Here the autonomous nervous system produces symptoms commonly associated with anxiety where the "pathology" is neurogenic not primarily psychogenic.

Obviously, overlapping occurs in these conditions in infinite variety. The first three steps in the gradient are characterized by primary gain goals; the last three by secondary gain. The legal problem is the validity of each reaction in relation to court settlements and awards. The psychiatric problem, more narrowly, becomes the degree of ego stress caused the patient by the injury or illness.

Spinal Injuries and Neurotic Reactions

Injuries to the spine result in somewhat different clinical syndromes, both physical and mental. The immediate injuries—vertebral fractures, subluxations, spinal shock, and compression of the cord—are cared for by neurosurgeons. Of interest to the neuropsychiatrist and orthopedic surgeon are lumbosacral sprains with impingement on the sciatic nerves and a great variety of "low back" injuries resulting from lifting, falls, direct blows to the sacroiliac joint, and so forth. Our concern here is chiefly with the psychological consequences of this latter type of back injury. Just as the head is overvalued, so the spinal column, the axis of the body, is thought of as the seat of motion of the extremities and therefore the integrator of bodily function. A suspicion of ruptured disc or indication of pinched or compressed lumbosacral plexus nerves confers a feeling (or fantasy) of complete and final impairment of mobility. Often, however, constant pain in the low back and pelvis does interfere with movements of the trunk and extremities for which treatment provides little relief. The structural difficulties following back injuries constitute a large, and not entirely solved, group of orthopedic problems. For our present purpose, attention will be limited to psychological reflections on back injuries.

The back is an area sensitive to unanticipated blows. These blows are common enough when one is "slapped in the back" in social relationships and are doubly irritating when the back is injured as in a rear-end motor accident. Being "attacked from the rear" mobilizes old paranoid sensitivities (which are possibly reactions to unconscious fears of anal penetration) and feelings of unfairness because of inability to defend oneself. Moreover, persistence of the muscular pain intensifies the anxiety. Announcement of a lack of pathological findings on X-ray accentuates the fear that a hidden calamity has been glossed over with the doctor's report, "I find nothing wrong." When a stationary car is struck in the rear and a whiplash or, more accurately, a craniocervical syndrome results, definite injury to the muscle, ligaments, and emerging nerve roots compound the "assault." Torsion, pulling, or stretching of the muscles involved painfully restrict movements of the entire body. To the actual injury is added the anxiety that a permanent "crippling" will result. The constant gnawing pain and discomfort of the lumbosacral sprain and fibromyositis often give rise to an attendant car phobia in which a patient is in a panic while riding in a car, watching the traffic behind in dread of another rear-end collision.

It is highly significant, both in clinical diagnosis and in testifying on the relation of the trauma of a motorcar accident to the physical pain and mental disturbance suffered, that many competent physicians do not recognize "fibromyositis" (or simply stated "tendon-muscle" injury) as an entity. Much experimentation by orthopedic experts and rheumatologists has failed to reveal any "inflammation" in muscles subject to injury. In a recent review of the entire subject, Weinberger calls the term *traumatic fibromyositis* a "medical myth making up the folklore of trauma."[43] Reviewing the literature extensively, he feels that the common symptoms in whiplash or back injuries have been "exploited by psychiatrists who state that an actual physical injury, 'fibromyositis' provides the organic nidus around which a 'neurotic psycho-physiologic reaction' develops . . . [and] an overview of the history of 'fibrositis,' spontaneous or traumatic, suggests that it is no more than a medicalization of the common aches and pain of mankind." Weinberger quotes other rheumatologists and orthopedic specialists who believe "the tendentious and monotonous complaints of muscle pain and tenderness either express a neurotic preoccupation with the body or are examples of hysterical body language." Weinberger's claimed lack of scientific validation of muscle pain and disability by chemical, histologic, enzyme, hematologic, or other methods in no way negates the empirical fact of the physical or mental results of trauma to the back. Until a definitive explanation of the pathology underlying muscle and tendon pain after trauma is presented, the enormous number of motorcar accidents, with their resulting disability, must be evaluated in relation to claims for distress and disability.

Psychosis After Trauma

Other sequellae of head trauma, though relatively rare, are encountered. These comprise organic conditions such as post-traumatic epilepsy, mental retardation as the result of gaseous poisoning, accidental electrocution, or hemorrhages and thromboses in individuals in older age groups. The psychoses of nonorganic nature are represented in schizophrenic episodes or autistic regressions. The medico-legal problem in these as in other traumatic cases is the assignment of injury effects in contrast to preexisting or predisposing disabilities. Two functional psychoses following trauma may be cited to demonstrate brief traumatic psychoses:

Craig, a child of six, was said to have been normal physically and mentally prior to the accident which occurred when he was struck by a motorcar, knocked down and for a few moments lay under the motorcar. He immediately began to cry. Several injuries to the ribs, abdomen, and liver were sustained for which surgical treatment was given.

For two months following release from the hosptial, the child was nervous, had tantrums and nightmares and talked in an irrational manner. He said he wanted to "get the moon and the stars"; he said he was dead and was in Heaven and wanted to bring the moon and the stars with him. He was fearful of cars and panicky when touched at the site of the abdominal scar.

Examination revealed a smallish but well-developed boy, showing fear when examiner approached him with a flashlight. He was distractable, running back and forth, flashing on the overhead light, paying little attention to the examiner. He resisted even simple maneuvers such as looking in his mouth, eyes, etc. He talked in a disconnected, irrational way, often repeating simple statements the examiner had made. When asked his name, would say "I don't want to give my name."

Equally dramatic was the situation in a young woman of twenty-six who was injured in a club car of a train carrying a theatrical company to Boston. As secretary to the director of the troupe, she had been interested in a theatrical career and looked forward to an enlivening experience.

The patient fell in a railroad car following a jolting of the cars, striking her cheek bone on the right and suffered other contusions and injuries. X-rays of the skull revealed fractures of right zygomatic arch, and anterior wall of the maxillary sinus.

One and a half years later the patient developed an acute mental condition which necessitated her being committed to a State Hospital. There she was treated for schizophrenia, paranoid type, being released after four months as "improved." Three years after the accident the patient still suffered from dizziness almost daily in occurrence; headache, frontal in position, occurring about once a week, accompanied by a feeling of "heaviness" in the head; poor balance, disturbed sleep due to restlessness with occasional nightmares.

The psychiatric examination 3 years post-accident showed a tense, agitated young person, preoccupied with the accident, somewhat aloof with a tendency towards depersonalization and a paranoid attitude. The acute psychotic episode had left in its wake a subdued, tense but not actively ill young woman.

The types of injury precipitating or directly causing mental conditions are legion, while the kinds of clinical illnesses are relatively few—mainly depressive, schizophrenic episodes and chronic brain syndromes. They usually occur in persons sensitized by prior organic states or unstable emotional situations. An example of the former is a lady of sixty-six years who suffered a basilar artery thrombosis three months after an impact injury and then developed an overt paranoid psychosis.

The plaintiff fell against the metal binding of a seat in a bus that stopped abruptly while she stood in the corridor. She hurt her head, back and shoulder on direct impact. Conservative treatment for a musculo-ligamentous sprain rendered her moderately comfortable until she suddenly lost vision when her head was extended, looking upward. Neurological examination disclosed a basilar artery obstruction. A cervical collar was prescribed to prevent further head extension.

About a year later she developed paranoid delusions: she was "forced into the Symbionese Liberation Army," she was involved in the Patty Hearst case whom she believed lived in above her room in a cheap hotel. From then on, her delusional system extended to her attorneys, the examiner, the courts, and the F.B.I. She fought litigation of her accident case because "it would crack things wide open and they will name names." The delusional system remained active particularly regarding psychiatric intervention or any testimonial aid to her attorneys. The paranoid trend was considered to have been caused by the head injury and subsequent vascular problem.

The legal problem here related to proximate cause of the psychosis and the possibility of obtaining recovery for a client who regarded her attorney as one of her malefactors. A settlement was arranged to the relief of the attorneys on both sides.

More common than paranoid psychoses are depressions which mount in intensity, achieving the level of a psychotic depression. This development usually occurs in a wrongful death case.

Depression and Other Reactions After Injury

A serious depression develops in persons who are affected by wrongful death accidents in which a close relative succumbs. The tragedy causes grief, often protracted over months and years, that becomes interlarded with obsessive preoccupation with details of the accident.

Cases have been observed wherein a state of depersonalization is super-imposed on the depression, an emotional withdrawal that outlasts the expected grief reaction. This was the situation in a young matron, se-verely injured in a head-on collision in which her two infants, three years and fourteen months, respectively, sitting beside her, were killed outright.

Mrs. R. remembered nothing of the head-on collision for 20 minutes before the impact (retrograde amnesia) and nothing until she awoke in a hospital 6 days later (antrograde amnesia). She had sustained a cerebral contusion. Upon re-covery from the brain injury, the mental picture emerged. She was informed of the children's deaths while in the hospital.

The patient became aware of memory gaps. Apathy, with disinterest in eat-ing or any of her previous activities, developed. She began to puzzle about God and why He killed her children if He was a good God. It occurred to her that God ordered her suicide to bring her children back. "Why did God not protect her children" ran through her mind constantly.

Chiefly, Mrs. R. suffered in silence, remaining aloof and distant. When Mrs. R. was able to speak about her two children, when she gathered up their play-things or discussed the family life before the accident, her productions had a split-off, isolated, depersonalized quality.

Depositions, settlement conferences, discussion with attorneys made little dif-ference in her feelings. Her mental flatness persisted long after the legal case was settled.

Although emotional distress is readily understood, it is difficult to define. It runs on a gradient from anxiety, despair, despondency, heartache, wretchedness, and grief to depression and anguish. Ad-mittedly, the psychiatrist has difficulty in drawing a line between normal mourning and the emotional dis-ease of depression and mel-ancholia. Even more difficult is the apportionment of damages to match the degree of distress which a given plaintiff suffers. In the case just cited, the plaintiff suffered in her social and domestic life by virtue of grief added to a pathological emotional state.

In the case below, a woman in the "zone of risk" but relatively un-hurt witnessed the sudden death of her husband with resultant grief and bitterness but no mental illness. Her anguish was controlled by the efforts of a strong ego.

The victim had been standing in front of the car on the roadside, checking the motor; the patient was within. They were suddenly rear-ended by a speeding car driven by a drunken youth. When the plaintiff got out of the car after it had been pushed across the road and looking backward, saw her husband's slippers where the car had been standing. He had been virtually "lifted out of his shoes." When she knelt by his side, his dentures were on the ground, blood issuing from his mouth; he was dead. The picture was engraved on her mind.

With an act of will, she surmounted the shock and returned to work within two months.

As a person with a positive outlook, she successfully suppressed the incident, would not permit it to interfere with her life but was aware of a pervading sense of loss.

Interviewed one year later, the plaintiff showed remnants of depression but was able to discuss the accident. She was particularly incensed because the "accident should never have happened." Their car was well off the road; there was no occasion to be struck. Her main problem was the injustice of the accident and subsequent death. She tried not to think about the wreck, continued her social and work life, saw friends but the vision of her husband lying on the side of the road, his dentures nearby, blood coming off his mouth, his left eye bulging out of a fractured face, haunted her. The image and details of the accident became a preoccupation. Although she displayed normal behavior, inwardly she ruminated—"it was too sudden . . . it was entirely preventable. . . ."

In cases such as the one cited above, the nature of the neurotic reaction following accidents may partake of the character of the injury suffered. The anxiety evoked is colored by the circumstances of the catastrophic event. Examples are found among children who frequently suffer animal phobias, terror reactions, and sleep disturbances for months or years after an attack by a large dog or other animal. Child psychiatrists are well aware of such problems. A Canadian psychiatrist reported a 3½-year-old boy, "bitten by a small leopard in a pet shop, to awake from frequent nightmares involving animals and monsters" which required months of therapy to quiet. The stimulus of the accident may be prolonged into a phobia which lasts for years.

A young man working on a dredging operation from a barge, developed severe and intractable claustrophobia after an accident to his associate. The latter was in the hold of the barge when he lost consciousness from lack of oxygen. The patient descended into the close compartment, endeavoring to help his fellow worker. Working in close quarters to remove the associate, he himself was overcome by anoxia. Finally, both men were removed from the compartment and rushed to a hospital.

The patient recovered from his unconscious state. He was informed of the death of his fellow-worker. He immediately left his job, with which he had several years experience, became unable to work in any occupation. His anxiety and tension became chronic. After several years, the phobia obsessed him to the point where he was unable to work, dissolved his marriage and remained unnerved. At a deposition and during the court hearing, his tension mounted to the point of inability to express himself.

Burn victims from automobile accidents become fearful of appearing in public because of disfigurement, even after plastic surgery has restored the lesion. A litigant whose eyelid was torn by a large dog whom she bent over to pet while waiting in a veterinarian's office developed a chronic phobia. She imagined that her eyelid, which had been narrowed slightly by the surgical repair, gave her a "sneering" expression. She became depressed, cut short her social life, and became a recluse because she thought her eyes gave her a "sinister" appearance. Another patient, a young black woman, received a bruise on her leg which healed, leaving a darker pigmented area about four inches long over her shin bone. Previously a model, this attractive young woman became obsessed with the attention she felt had been drawn to her skin color. She developed an anxiety reaction that forced her to change her ordinarily stylish mode of attire. These reactions, although probably not sufficient to be dignified with a diagnosis of neurosis, are sufficient to insure years of unhappiness and anxiety following mild or serious disfigurements. In such cases, the psychiatrist may be requested to make an evaluation of the depth of psychic injury and the permanence of the phobias induced by the injury.

Notes

1. Moses Keschner, *Medico-Legal Aspects of Injuries to the Skull, Brain and Spinal Cord*: 567, ed. by S. Brock, Williams and Wilkins Co., Baltimore, Md. (1940).

2. Joseph T. Mirabel and Herbert A. Levy, *The Law of Negligence*: 41, Acme Book Co., Amityville, N.Y. (1962).

3. California Book of Approved Jury Instructions (BAJI): Part 3, Sec. 3.75, West Publ. Co. (1975 rev.).

4. BAJI: Part 3, Sec. 3.00 (1975 rev.).

5. *Flournoy v. State of California*, 275 Calif. App. 2d 806 (1969).

6. Walter Bromberg, *From Shaman to Psychotherapist: A History of the Treatment of Mental Illness*, Henry Regnery Co., Chicago (1975).

7. Annual Meeting, Am. Acad. of Psych. and the L. Montreal, Oct. 1978, Sec. IV. Neuro-Forensic Psychiatry.

8. Sean Mullen, *Essentials of Neuro-surgery*: 138, Spring Publ. Co., New York (1961).

9. Quoted from C. H. Hardin and Nyla Cole, *Mental Disease and Injury*: 20, in *Disease and Injury*, ed. by L. Brahdy, J. B. Lippincott Co., Philadelphia (1961).

10. Ibid.: 25.

11. Israel Wechsler, *History of Neurology*: 657, in *Textbook of Clinical Neurology*, W. B. Saunders Co., Philadelphia (7th ed., 1953).

12. John E. Erichsen, *On Concussion of the Spine, Nervous Shock and Other Obscure Injuries of the Nervous System in Their Clinical and Medico-legal Aspects*, Wm. Wood Co., New York (1975).

13. Weir Mitchell, *Fat and Blood, An Essay on the Treatment of Certain Forms of Neurasthenia and Hysteria*, J. B. Lippincott Co., Philadelphia (ed. 1877-1905).

14. George M. Beard, *A Practical Treatise on Nervous Exhaustion (Neurasthenia)*, Wm. Wood Co., New York (1880).

15. Sir David Henderson and R. D. Gillespie, *A Text-Book of Psychiatry*: 602, Oxford U. Press, London (8th ed., 1956).

16. Symposium, *Die Unfall Kreigs Neurose* (from German translation), 25 Arch. of Neur. and Psych. 29 (1931).

17. Karl Von Hagen, *The Neurological Approach to Traumatic Neurosis*, 1 J. For. Sci. 85 (Jan. 1956).

18. R. L. McLaurin and J. O. Titchener, *Post-Traumatic Syndrome*, 2: 1023, *in Neurological Surgery*, ed. by J. Woumans. W. B. Saunders Co., Philadelphia (1973).

19. Maier Tuchler, *The Traumatic Neurosis. A Perspective*, 1, no. 1, J. For. Sci. 80 (Jan. 1956).

20. Paul Schilder, *Neuroses Following Head and Brain Injuries*: 275, in *Injuries of the Skull, Brain and Spinal Cord.*

21. Walter C. Alvarez, *The Neurosis*, W. B. Saunders Co., Philadelphia (1951).

22. Hubert W. Smith and H. C. Solomon, *Traumatic Neurosis in Court*, 21 Annals of Int. Med. 367 (Sept. 1944).

23. *Houston Electric v. Pearce*, 192 S.W. 558 (Tex., 1917).

24. *Sutton Motor Company v. Crysel*, 289 S.W. 2d 631 (Tex., 1965).

25. *Schlagenhauf v. Holder*, 379 U.S. 104 Cir. for S.F. Ind.

26. William J. Curran, *Law and Medicine*: 266, Little, Brown & Co., Boston (1960).

27. Abram Kardiner, *The Traumatic Neurosis of War*, National Research Council, Washington, D.C. (1941).

28. Herbert C. Modlin, *The Trauma in "Traumatic Neurosis,"* 24 Bull. of the Menninger Clinic 49 (1960).

29. George Thompson, *Post-Traumatic Psychoneurosis. A Statistical Survey*, 121 Am. J. Psych. 1043 (May 1965).

30. *Klein v. Medical Building Realty*, 147 So. 123 (La., 1933).

31. Hardin, op cit.: 32.

32. F. C. Ebaugh and J. D. Benjamin, *Trauma and Mental Disorders*, Lea and Febiger, Philadelphia (1937).

33. *Armour Grain Company v. Industrial Commission*, 153 N.E. 699 (Ill., 1926).

34. *Leatherman v. Gateway Transportation Co.*, Cir. A. (7th Circuit), 331 F. 2d 241 (Ind., 1964).

35. California Book of Approved Instructions (BAJI): Part 12, Sec. 12.83 (1975 rev.).

36. *Tobin v. Grossman*, 284 N.Y.S. 2d 997 (1967).

37. *Tobin v. Grossman*, 291 N.Y.S. 227 (1969).

38. *Tobin v. Grossman*, 301 N.Y.S. 2d 544 (1969).

39. *Dillon v. Legg*, 68 Cal. 2d 728; 69 Cal. Reptr. 72 (1968).

40. *Hunsley v. Giard*, 553 P. 2d 1096 (Wash., 1976).

41. Walter F. Schaller, *After Effects of Head Injury*, 113 J.A.M.A. 1779 (1939).

42. A. Noyes, *Modern Clinical Psychiatry* 422, W. B. Saunders, Philadelphia (8th ed., 1973).

43. Laurence M. Weinberger, *Traumatic Fibromyositis: A Critical Review of an Enigmatic Concept*, 127 West. J. of Medicine 99 (Aug. 1977).

14

Workers' Compensation and
Other Tort Actions

In recent years, compensable industrial accidents and tort actions of personal injury, as discussed in the last chapter, have extended from obvious injuries to limbs, body, and head to less definitive mental difficulties called "intangible impairments." Early English and American legal authorities did not countenance damages for psychic (i.e., mental and emotional) injuries. An older opinion that "normal persons do not suffer injury from fright," enunciated in *Coultas v. Victorian Railway* (England, 1888),[1] remained legal dictum in this country until the turn of the century. In 1944, Hubert Winston Smith exhaustively analyzed the evolution of the emotional injury concept from the 1880s to 1940 in America, noting how the general acceptance of psychic or psychologic injuries made allowances first for the 'idiosyncracy" of the plaintiff (i.e., "predisposing neurotic background") reacting emotionally to injury.[2] As Smith noted in his review, the question then became "what constitutes psychic injury?" The evolution he traced brought the courts face to face with minor complaints in those seeking compensation for industrial injuries; complaints such as "highly nervous states, insomnia, fears" were difficult to translate into compensable damages until the introduction of a dynamic psychiatry. Although we like to think that psychiatry has become more alert to emotional defenses which become symptoms in injured patients, the courts are still wary of psychiatric subtleties in terms of causation, aggravation, and precipitation of emotional troubles in conjunction with injury or stress. David Saxe's comment not withstanding on the "uneasy attitude concerning psychiatric methodology that affects courts unfamiliar with dynamic strides in the development of modern psychiatric techniques,"[3] the courts are charged with the responsibility of fairly estimating cause and effect in claims for the disabling emotional effects of injury.

The procedure known as workmen's compensation (the term *workers' compensation* will be used hereafter in appreciation of the large number of women in the labor force) is a creature of statutory law. Prior to such statutes, employees could be charged with contributory negligence if they showed even slightly negligent conduct, and hence, they could be barred from recovery. Under workers' compensation statutes, the concept of negligence is disregarded to permit workers to obtain compensation for injuries which reduce their working capabilities. The basic principles underlying modern workers' compensation laws are represented in the following general statement:

Compensable disability is the inability, as a result of work-connected injury, to perform or obtain work suitable to the claimant's qualifications and training.

Total disability may be found . . . if the claimant's physical condition is such as to disqualify him from regular employment in the labor market.[4]

A large portion of compensable industrial injuries are surgical and medical: amputations, crush injuries, chemical intoxications, cardiac problems, and so on, but in this discussion, neurological and psychiatric sequellae of industrial injuries will be emphasized. As noted above, the so-called intangible impairments form a large part of neuropsychiatrist's concern in workers' compensation cases. California law states this aspect of the problem succinctly: "[T]o the extent that such intangible impairments to health [psychic] are disabling and attributable to effects of occupation, strain or activities, they are to be treated as injuries under Compensation Law."[5]

Once established by compensation boards, benefits for physical and mental disabilities are in terms of wage loss payments, coverage of medical expenses, and, if a permanent disability is involved, a lump sum or monthly settlement. In contrast to civil tort liability, awards are made only for the work disability produced by the injury, not for the injury as such. The legal handling of compensation claims differs from the legal process in civil accident litigation chiefly in accordance with this principle. The types of neuropsychiatric injuries encountered are similar to those discussed in the preceding chapter: head, brain, and nerve root problems, neurotic and hysterical reactions, functional overlay, symptom overvaluation, and transitory psychoses. However, the main evaluative question relates to whether the worker can resume full- or part-time work, the duration of the disability, the psychological effect on his or her truncated industrial life, including the resentment against the corporate or individual employer, and the elements of secondary gain resulting from the illness. Commentators have signalized these intervening factors in the phrase "compensation neurosis," by which is meant the compounding of original complaints arising from the injury by resentments and unconscious dependency elements. According to Tourkow and Tattan, "the injured patient relates to the Company as to a gigantic parent figure at whose hands she could not tolerate frustration. . . ."[6]

Psychological Factors in Industrial Accidents

The intimate psychological relationship between the injured and the injurer deserves attention; it is an integral part of the financial award or settlement that is fought over in workmen's compensation hearings. It is presumed that settlement of a case will bring about a cessation of symptoms in a wide variety of injuries. This is not always automatic. Often, the stress of preparation for trial, and the trial itself, so unnerve the claimant that he unconsciously places the disability in the background of current interests. The shifting attention from concern with disabilities to future problems to be encountered is a subtle reorientation within the patient which may be misinterpreted as "compensation neurosis"—or "greenback neurosis," that is, a primary interest in financial awards. The injured worker's ego shifts back and forth between concern for his pain and disability and for his bleak industrial future. This automatic mental mechanism is reminiscent of the Gestalt principle of figure-ground alternation in perception; "only one event can occupy the foreground of attention,"[7] as Max Wertheimer phrased it. Indeed, Gestalt psychotherapy[8] operates on this principle: attention is invited away from phobias and anxieties in the foreground to the healthy parts of the ego in the background. To call this "compensation neurosis" is to misunderstand automatic psychologic movements that take place in every injured worker's ego. When improvement has been observed after a settlement award, it is not only the money received that brings about subsidence of symptoms.

Other factors are involved in the resolution of symptoms upon accepting settlement for claims. Disabilities often fit in with retirement plans which had already been vaguely or concretely elaborated to coincide with the end of a working career, a factor not uncommonly found among workers nearing retirement age. The retirement design is not a conscious wish but an inner perception of waning powers and alertness that seems to find confirmation in the accident. Without willing it, the injured worker's position in the labor market and his or her future become urgent problems for which no ready solution looms. A case bearing on this point is that of Francis H.

Francis H. a 60-year-old widower, was struck at work by a piece of lumber falling a distance of 12 feet. He developed a concussion without unconsciousness with the usual post-concussive complaints of headache, dizziness, tinnitus, head noises, insomnia, blurred vision, depression and pains in the hands. Thorough and prolonged examinations by 6 specialists revealed no organic findings. The majority opinion indicated an agitated depression superimposed on the post-concussion, although some examiners felt the concussion was too mild to be causative of his prolonged symptoms. A sclerotic mastoid and chronic otitis media, preexisting, was felt to add substance to the claimant's dizziness and tinnitus.

Two years after the industrial accident the patient complained even more vividly, of being disgruntled, depressed, unhappy with "no pleasure in life." He complained of how "strong" he had been before the accident, embittered because, as a laborer, he had been effectively removed from the labor market. He grudgingly planned to retire.

A second powerful factor indirectly influencing work-related accidents is the boredom and monotony created by assembly-line labor situations. It is as if the worker appreciated John Ruskin's noble sentiment, expressed a century ago, "Life without industry is guilt, industry without art is brutality." In heavily industrialized areas, sophisticated employers have begun to take measures to reduce the monotony of labor. Furthermore, preexisting impairments in the worker, i.e., arthritis, arteriosclerosis, unstable back (lumbosacral sprain), or personality type, i.e., depressive disposition, inadequate or schizoid character type, may surface after an injury. These defects, unnoticed in the routine of life, may color the clinical picture.

Finally, "secondary gain" often strongly influences the clinical symptoms. Secondary gain is a recognized reaction wherein the symptoms suffered convey the advantages of being cared for, freed from responsibility, or thrust into the center of attention, by virtue of a medical condition. Every ill or injured person can be shown to experience this secondary gain in minute degrees; every patient from any cause wishes to be regarded as an unfortunate victim of fate, thus extracting sympathy from his or her medical attendants. Depending on "ego strength"—an abstract notion indicating the capacity to absorb emotional nurturance from the environment with its implied promise of furnishing other avenues for gaining self-esteem—the injured person may or may not give up "secondary gain." This uncertain resolution also depends on social factors, namely, the brute expectation of living on a subsidy or welfare, with its demoralizing effect, in place of the heartening effect of work.

Hirschfield and Behan, two physicians functioning in a highly industrialized area, Detroit, have examined this complex series of psychological facets of industrial accidents.[9] Based on a study of 300 accident cases in industrial plants, these authors call the events leading up to the injury the *accident process*. They point to a general pattern, as follows:

Before the accident occurs there is a state of conflict and anxiety within the patient. As a result of this condition the worker finds a self-destructive, injury-producing act which causes his "death" as a worker. From this moment the patient reacts exactly as do other psychiatrically ill people, except for the character of his symptom. Instead of having a presenting complaint of anxiety, depression, or other classical psychiatric symptom, he has the physical disorder which is the result of his accident.

These investigators point out the difficulty of "curing" such patients, particularly those labeled "accident prone": "[U]nder special circumstances when certain conflicts exist many individuals tend to cause their own accidents and probably will hold onto the injuries they sustain because the accidents solve their life problems."

There is considerable truth in these assertions, but it must not be forgotten that "pure accidents" resulting from malfunctioning machines or equipment do occur among previously healthy, well-motivated workmen. Reactions in these situations vary with the bodily area affected, but they also extend to generalized anxiety and/or depression.

For example, a thirty-one-year-old man working on an elevator was rendered unconscious for seventy-two hours by discharge of electric current through his body. Upon his improvement from an electric burn after nineteen days of hospitalization, he complained of headache, dizziness, blurred vision, poor memory, insomnia, and restlessness—a typical picture of anxiety neurosis. More distressing is the case of a young man working at a tire spreader which exploded, fracturing his arms with a tearing of the nerve trunks in his left shoulder. Because of the destruction of the radial and ulnar nerves, rendering his hand useless, an amputation at the wrist was finally performed. The emotional reaction, lasting two years when last examined, combined bouts of rage in which he shouted at himself, expressed "hate" for his family without reason, and exhibited embittered feelings of self-rejection and depression. Catastrophic dreams were especially prevalent during the first year after the accident: he would relive the accident and see himself as dead at a funeral or trapped in a car and drowning. This formerly active, athletic young man was reduced, in his own words, to a "grumbly" person convinced that the "future has gone from me," his life irreparably ruined.

Traumatic Neurosis in Workers' Compensation

As in personal injury cases, in workers' compensation cases, the courts are beginning to recognize traumatic neurosis as a palpable entity. A legal commentator stated in 1970:

Against the rather old-fashioned clinging to some shred of the "physical" in these cases, must be balanced . . . recognition of some of the most sophisticated theories of the interaction of mind and body . . . of complex neurotic conditions, including "compensation neurosis." . . .

The single question [in the future] will be whether there was a harmful change in the human organism—not just its bones and muscles, but its brain and nerves as well.[10]

The main body of cases indicates that emotional shock without physical injury when related to employment may establish total disability. However, the courts are concerned with the indices of proximate cause, possible predisposition to emotional problems, and the employment relationship to the effective shock at the time of the alleged disabling event. An Illinois case (1976)[11] illustrates these principles. A female worker, teaching a new employee how to operate a machine, turned away; on hearing a scream, she returned to find that the new employee had caught her hand in a press. The worker turned off the machine and, attempting to help, reached in to take out a severed hand. She fainted at the sight and soon developed anxiety symptoms, fear of machines, numbness of hands and feet, headaches, and nervous tension; these complaints persisted for more than a year. The Industrial Commission awarded her "temporary total disability," but when the company brought the case to a trial court, the company decided that the Industrial Commission's award "was contrary to the weight of the evidence." Psychiatric and neurologic testimony differed on her complaints about the numbness of her hand and her headaches. A neuropsychiatrist testified that the plaintiff did not receive physical injuries on the day of the accident but did suffer a great mental shock and was continuing to experience "residual anxiety . . . from the tremendous impact on her consciousness" of the gruesome accident a year prior. The second expert, a neurologist, testified that the complainant's numbness of the hand was "fictitious," while a third expert, a neuropsychiatrist, concluded that "there may be some anxiety residual in her memories from the accident but I don't believe that is her disability." The Supreme Court of Illinois, reversing the lower court, said:

We do not judge the award here was contrary to the manifest weight of the evidence. The claimant experienced a sudden severe emotional shock . . . the reaction of a person of normal sensibilities who, attempting to aid an injured co-worker, reached in and drew a severed hand from the press. . . .

Emotional trauma sufficient to cause disability in a worker depends on many factors, some of which are not readily visible on the surface. In Kansas, a jurisdiction where traumatic neurosis is recognized as a possible result of nonphysical injury, the court insisted in *Rund v. Cessna Aircraft* (1974)[12] that "emotional problems" exacerbated by an injury were "not traceable directly to an accident." This complicated situation started with the complaint of a woman employee who slipped on a wet floor in the plant while pushing a cart. She claimed a "twisted foot and knee injuries," swelling of the extremities, back pain, and hip pain radiating down her legs. Examinations by the company nurse, several doctors, an orthopedic specialist, and eventually a psychiatrist disclosed no injury to the leg or foot, and a release to return to work was ordered three months after her accident. She claimed she was too sick to work. The District Court awarded her a "running award for temporary total disability . . . with past and future medical benefits."

The company appealed the "sizeable award" for psychiatric problems. The Supreme Court of Kansas reviewed the case, including the testimony of the various doctors that her complaints were "out of proportion to what was evident" and that a preexisting "spondylolysis" of congenital type had been found by an orthopedic surgeon. At the trial, this colloquy with the orthopedist ensued:

Q. Now would it also be correct to say in this particular case you had superimposed over that pre-existing defect the back strain of which she complained? . . .
A. This would be the probable diagnosis . . . more on the history than anything else. Her examination revealed no neurologic changes to indicate nerve root compression or disc pathology. . . . she stands in lordosis . . . that is, swayback and that tends to close the disc space posteriorily . . . which gives one a headache.

The psychiatrist's testimony in part was:

A. My impressions are that her emotional problems have been of long standing —for years . . . the emotional problems exacerbated by this accident.
Q. Now you use the term "hysterical reaction" . . . could you explain more fully?

A. Well, an hysterical reaction may be demonstrated in various ways. In fact, the most common way and the way I mentioned here is the conversion reaction. In fact, it is diagnostically called an hysterical reaction, and it is described in all the literature and in our diagnosing manuals.

I should qualify that . . . our formal diagnosis is anxiety neurosis with hysterical features. . . . she is not an out and out full-blown case of hysterical conversion neurosis but she has a tendency towards it.

Q. . . . there was feeling on the part of some of the workers . . . there might have been an element of malingering involved. Have you ruled out the possibility of malingering?

A. . . . I would like to qualify that impression of malingering. . . . it is not a conscious intent on her part . . . merely an unconscious level that is unknown to her. . . . her present physical symptoms do award her secondary gains; that is, special awards, in a physical and emotional sense, insurance wise, sympathy-wise, so on.

The doctor explained that the claimant resisted returning to work because being disabled emotionally gave her gratification as secondary gain. "There are some sexual matters that she has strongly requested be kept confidential, which would impose a mental hardship on her in her present state of mind, to return to work. She avoids sexual tensions in her relationship with male employees by simply remaining away," he said.

On cross-examination, the psychiatrist was asked about the sexual implications of the claimant's job. He then testified:

Q. Now, what, in general terms, what is it about the job that creates the sexual implication? Is it the presence and contact with other men in general?

A. Well, Mrs. R. is morally a very proper and upright individual. That is how she sees herself. At her place of employment there is much going on of a sexual nature that she finds threatening.

Other witnesses testified that when the claimant came to work she would wear very tight clothing, usually black. Her body figure was described as short and "very well endowed on the top half." She wore a "lot of cake make-up," and she would go to the restroom about three times a day and completely redo her make-up, "Down to putting clean Arrid under her arms, armpits," and work on her hair. The company nurse testified that the claimant "chased men," especially one man who "rejected" her. The foreman testified that the claimant's manner of dress forced him to institute a ban on tight-fitting clothes at work. The claimant had put another face on the issue of sexual provocation, testifying:

[Y]ou have to know what Cessna is like in order to know how a woman feels out there. . . . the minute a woman walks by all work automatically stops and every eye goes on that woman. . . .

Q. Did you find that something you didn't like?
A. Well, it isn't that you don't like it exactly . . . when you look terrible and
   feel terrible . . . you don't want everybody watching you.

On analyzing the evidence for traumatic neurosis or conversion
hysteria, the presiding justice observed that the psychiatrist had actually diagnosed the claimant as "obsessive-compulsive . . . with immaturity to a surprising degree." He further noted that the psychiatrist
had testified that "the claimant had unconsciously resolved her guilt
feelings about sexuality by simply remaining away from the plant . . .
the injury enabling her to remain away," i.e., through secondary gain.
This analysis placed a different accent on the plaintiff's complaints of
back and extremity pain and her emotional "problems." On reviewing
the entire case, the Supreme Court of Kansas reversed the original
award of "temporary total disability," ruling that the award was to be
"based solely upon her disability resulting from the physical injury."
The court concluded that there was "no evidence . . . that the claimant's 'emotional problems' were caused by the accident."

Emotional Distress and Legal Decisions

In civil cases, the task of the courts is to determine matters of law
where accidents involve emotional distress, whereas the jury must
determine matters of fact and assign monetary compensation. The
courts must balance fairness to the injured plaintiff with "safeguards
against boundless liability" for a negligent act, as expressed in *Hunsley
v. Giard* (1976),[13] wherein a woman suffered physical injury and mental distress as she witnessed a car crash into her home. (For full details
of the case, see Chapter 13.) This balance has been achieved since the
early case of *Mitchell v. Rochester Railway* (1896)[14] in which a pregnant woman became trapped between two horses, sustaining a miscarriage consequent to her extreme fright, although no bodily contact
with the horses had occurred. In conformity with the old precedent,
the judge ruled that no recovery was forthcoming for "mere fright" or
"for injuries resulting therefrom." His rationale was that it would lead
to a flood of litigation "based on fictitious and speculative claims";
hence, he stated, it was contrary to public policy.

The influence of more careful psychiatric evaluation and testimony
or a liberalizing social atmosphere may have softened such judicial cau-
tion. By the 1940s, decisions in personal litigation and workers' compensation cases ran in favor of compensating emotional distress without
physical impact. In *Burlington* (Virginia, 1941),[15] a young female
worker, frightened by an electric flash in a machine fifteen feet from

her post, fainted in fright. She was awarded damages for an "irritated condition of her nervous system."

After appeal by the defendant, the Appellate Court of Virginia affirmed the award, thereby overthrowing the impact rule. The court accepted the psychiatrists' testimony that the patient suffered from anxiety neurosis precipitated by the shock of the short-circuited machine. In a similar situation (Massachusetts, 1947),[16] a woman worker eating lunch at her machine was frightened by a bolt of lightning which struck the building, causing three motors in the factory to blow out. The employee suffered no burn or physical injury, but the loud noise and the flash shocked her; she developed paralysis of the left leg. The Appellate Court in this case ruled that the "paralyzing injury produced by fright was causally connected with her employment."

More striking was an award to a workman whose foot had been run over nine years prior to his claim that it formed the basis for the development of paranoid psychosis. His award was for work-connected mental illness. The issue to which the Appellate Court addressed itself in this case, *Schneyder v. Cadillac Motors* (1937),[17] was "whether and when disability arising from a mental disorder growing out of an accident is compensable." The answer of the court was in the affirmative: "[T]he disability was a direct result of the injury . . . excluding the consequences of mental disturbances collateral to and not arising directly from the physical hurt."

The precipitation of a psychosis through work-induced stress received approval in the landmark case of *Carter v. General Motors* (Michigan, 1960).[18] *Carter* established the precedent that a worker unable to withstand the "pressure" of a job routine may be compensated for the incidence of a mental disease, in this case, schizophrenic, paranoid type. The claimant worked on an assembly line in a motorcar plant where he was required to repeat a simple operation on a metal case and then to place it on a conveyor belt. Unable to keep pace with his fellows and reprimanded for falling behind, Carter felt his foreman was "riding him." After two weeks on this job, he became aggressive towards his foreman and was diagnosed as schizophrenic, a condition that required hospitalization and electroshock treatment. Psychiatric testimony before the Compensation Appeal Board affirmed the psychiatrist's statement that Carter had "shown instability earlier in life . . . inflexibility of personality . . . [and] predisposition towards development of his illness for years." Nevertheless, the board found a causal connection between the job and the mental illness, for the plaintiff had presented no obvious mental symptoms before the job assignment.

When the case came to the Supreme Court of Michigan, it was agreed that Carter's "personality configuration . . . makes him more susceptible than others to psychotic breakdowns which could develop under pressure" of a routine job. It was further agreed that "competent expert opinion testimony . . . found a causal connection" between his job and the resultant psychosis. The legal question of proximate cause being settled, the problem of apportionment arose, i.e., whether greater weight should be given the pressure of assembly-line routine or the potentiality of Carter's personality "inflexibility." Justice Souris, writing for the majority of the court, asked:

The question then becomes, must industry, under our laws, bear the economic burden of such disability?
Implicit in the question as stated is the further question: Is the worker unable to work because of a mental injury caused by his employment to be treated differently from a worker unable to work because of a physical injury caused by his employment?

His answer was that the industry must bear the burden of the mentally ill. On the other hand, in his dissent Justice Kelly decided that Carter's basic predisposition, rather than the "causes and conditions peculiar to his employment," caused his disability. But the question has not been definitively settled for all cases, either in psychiatry or in the law.

The courts have not uniformly agreed that emotional distress following industrial accidents is compensable. For example, in *Saunders v. Pool Shipping* (Florida, 1956),[19] while on a ship a longshoreman suffered a severe head injury from a falling metal pipe. He managed to return to work within a month but continued to complain of headache, dizziness, and mental symptoms. On the basis of a "woefully inadequate" original compensation award, the plaintiff appealed to the U.S. District Court of Appeals. The testimony of the two psychiatrists who had examined the plaintiff was in direct conflict: one diagnosed "organic brain damage" caused by the original trauma, and the other, "paranoid schizophrenia not caused by the injury with no brain damage." The judge said: "Here was a struggle of complex, competing theories couched by protagonists in the weird jargon of their calling." The skepticism of judges towards psychiatric testimony in accident cases is not confined to this country. Professor Strauss, writing from South Africa, quotes an esteemed judge of the South African Appellate Division: "[P]sychiatry [is] an empirical and speculative science with rather elastic notation and terminology which is usually wise after the event."[20]

In a less testy vein, the Wisconsin Supreme Court, in reviewing an industrial accident case,[21] decided against a claimant-worker who claimed total permanent disability when squeezed between two cars. Although the accident resulted in only "minor abrasions" to the worker, he had been awarded a total disability allowance until the employer appealed eight years later on presentation of new psychiatric evaluations. On the basis of a past history of behavior disorders, time served in a penitentiary, and "immature and unreliable" conduct prior to the accident (in the face of an IQ of 122), two psychiatrists agreed that the claimant's diagnosis lay between "hysterical or neurosis with malingery or a constitutional psychopathic personality . . . [with] the greater probability of malingery." The claimant's own psychiatrist had diagnosed the subject as having had a "psychoneurotic reaction to trauma." The Supreme Court of Wisconsin, indicating that "uncertainties so completely predominate" in the conflicting opinions of the medical experts, dismissed the permanent award. The court pointed to the "entirely subjective" nature of the complaints "where examination by psychiatric experts have produced no credible evidence with sufficient positiveness to attribute claimant's psychoneurotic condition to the slight trauma he received in . . . 1945." The court framed a general principle in deciding cases with conflicting evidence:

Before it may decide to make an award, the commission must be convinced by substantial evidence. It is not too high a test to require, in treating with expert testimony that evidence, to some degree of reasonable certainty, of a relation between an injury and a result be shown by a competent opinion.

From a psychiatric point of view, a "competent opinion" depends in part on the experiential orientation of the examiner, his or her differing interests, the differing emphasis placed on the patient's complaints, and the period of the patient's life during which the examinations are made. The courts may well be wary of the kaleidoscopic picture presented by the injured worker, for the variety of reactions to industrial accidents are infinite as they invade the life pattern of the patient-claimant.

Back Injury in Industrial Accidents

As in nonindustrial cases, work-related back injuries impose both a mental and physical disability on the patient. The history often presents a background of minor lumbosacral sprains which have a cumulative effect on the current injury. A laminectomy to correct an earlier disc problem may result in increased pain and disability to the current injury which extends the pain and discomfort for years. The total effect of all back sprains, whether or not they involve a degenerated disc, is to limit activities—walking, sitting, climbing, bending, and squatting. This condition exerts a demoralizing effect on the sufferer, especially among men who took great pride in their previous strength, agility, and sexual capacity. In this latter respect, a history of partial or complete sexual impotence after a back injury is frequent. If impotence is not total, such patients report lack of complete gratification in intercourse.

Complaints of sexual inadequacy in men after a back injury following industrial accidents are so common that one must look beyond the obvious discomfort of muscle spasm and torsion of the pelvis to psychological factors. Many authors, including Modlin, Fenichel, Braverman, and Hacker, have posited some reasons for this phenomenon. Some experts indicate that sexual interest falls off in view of the influence of back pain on total movements of the body; others maintain that the "ego boundaries" are restricted by virtue of the back injury, and sexuality unconsciously recedes in importance to the patient. The second hypothesis is advanced by Braverman, Hacker, and Shor who studied 362 cases of industrial accidents.[22] The present author regards impotence in such cases as issuing from the demoralizing effect of lowered self-esteem, the loss of the sense of masculinity and mastery which productive work and a meaningful position in the economic world supply.

In addition to anxiety engendered by decrease in sexual capacity, the male back-injured patient struggles to maintain his stability in the face of increasing muscle spasm, low-back pain, and interference with the entire muscular organization. In men in the thirty- to fifty-year-old range, this feeling of ineffectiveness leads to a sense of hopelessness which develops into depression and personality changes, as indicated in reduced social contacts and irritability over trifles. Paranoid attitudes towards their wives are common, being the result of real or fancied reduction in sexual potency. The general demoralization, buttressed by actual shrinkage of income with a corresponding dwindling of industrial usefulness, leads to depression with suicidal threats.

In the case of Earl T., aged thirty-nine, self-destructive impulses following an industrial accident actually led to suicide. Since his suicide occurred about a year and a half after the original industrial back sprain, the question became one of apportionment of liability for his death among several causative factors; namely, his basic personality, his back disability with subsequent laminectomy, and "job pressures."

The deceased, whose wife sought legal redress from the insurance carrier for the original accident, was reported as having been a healthy man, without previous emotional problems, a veteran of the Korean war, active in the Alcoholics Anonymous organization after an earlier period of alcoholism.

Earl's first injury occurred while lifting a box from an awkward position in the office of an automobile parts firm. It was characterized as a spinal sprain and treated conservatively. Earl, employed as a bookkeeper, complained of continued pain and stiffness while sitting at a desk. He sought further orthopedic help: examination revealed a pre-existing spondylolisthesis in the low lumbar area (L-5). Pain, fatigue, irritability continued: it became increasingly difficult for Earl to do his work. After three months, surgery was performed with the hope of stabilizing the lumbosacral joint.

The patient returned to work but complained of pain, emotional stress and sought further medical help. A second myelogram was done but no further surgery was contemplated. The slippage of L-5 on S-1 was confirmed. The examining physicians felt the complaints were more psychiatric than physical. The symptoms, lasting a year, began to increase: Earl complained of excessive neck and back pain. He spoke of "never working again." It was obvious to his wife that his pain tolerance was low, that complaints about job-pressure were exaggerated, that his depression had increased. A year and 4 months after the original sprain, Earl killed himself.

The case of Earl T. was settled out of court for an undisclosed amount.

Cultural and Ethnic Factors

In assessing the weight of the injured claimant's personality against the consequences of the injury, the mind-set of the individual must be considered in arriving at the "cause"of mental distress following an accident. By mind-set is meant those expectations which the victim of an accident brings to his injured state, the threshold of his aggressive/passive impulses, his ideas and attitudes. In this mind-set constellation, the cultural patterns to which the person has been exposed is a potent factor. Some persons are expected to handle injury impassively and stoically; some are permitted intolerance to discomfort. It is not too much to say that cultural and subcultural patterns form a matrix on which social aspects of personality develop. In the present context, the significance of this factor is that the judicial system, whose mission is to conduct trials and hearings in fairness to plaintiff and defendant under the Constitution, cannot take these sociopsychological considerations into account in judging liability and damages for disability. Neuropsychiatrists, however, must necessarily be aware of mind-set in estimating overvaluation or minimization of symptoms and disability. The experienced physician makes this calibration automatically, excluding it in his diagnosis except in cases peculiar to a geographic location. The psychiatrist, however, looks more closely at cultural facets in personality analyses. Cross-cultural studies of mental illness have been made for years, but studies of injury-reaction in various cultures and subcultures have been neglected. It would be clearly unfair to single out any one group as illustrating typical injury reactions. For one thing, typology, or categorization of a group type, is subject to distortions and skewed conclusions. Acknowledging this defect, we will present a distinct mind-set characteristic of injured workers of Mexican origin for whatever clinical value it contains. The case histories are of a Mexican national and an Americanized worker of Mexican extraction.

Jose, born in Mexico, living in the United States for 18 years at the time of his accident. His schooling in rural Jalisco was minimal, he spoke Spanish exclusively but had a good work record for a railroad, having been the recipient of Safety awards in his 13 years of steady employment as a track laborer. The accident that prevented him from further work occurred when a 78-foot steel rail he was handling lurched and pushed Jose backward, injuring his back. For two years his complaints of back pain, of inability to move, dress himself, sit or stand did not yield to conservative treatment. Examination disclosed only tenderness in the paravertebral muscles with no neurological findings, no fractures or other spinal abnormalities.

The psychologic situation was explored in depth with the aid of a competent interpreter. The patient discussed his attitudes, complaints and feeling forthrightly in Spanish. He did not understand why his back stiffness, inability to move or lift or bend, was so unrelenting and impervious to the recommended treatment he received over two years. As a fervent religionist, he prayed that God would heal him if whatever skill the doctors possessed in Mexico and this country did not prevail. Jose regarded his injury as fate's decree: there was no hint of supernaturalism or mysticism in his reliance on Deity. Pain and suffering were, to him, matters of fact beyond analysis.

At the trial, Jose's attorney presented the facts: a 50 year old Mexican laborer, afflicted after an injury with lumbar pain and a sciatic syndrome. His lack of education and inability to communicate in English foreclosed any attempt to find work other than laboring. The particular psychologic picture, of a man without flexibility, with complete acceptance of his physical disabilities as God-given, characterizing a certain cultural pattern, was presented to the jury, by his attorney as a specific ethnic syndrome.

The defense attorney based his case, in the absence of neurological findings, on the inference of malingery or over-valuation of symptoms.

The jury found for the defendant.

The second case is that of another Mexican-born but assimilated workman, whose current environment and education were bilingual. He had worked for the railroad as a truck laborer for six years without incident until he was struck by a steel bar in the low back while lifting a tie. The injury was diagnosed as musculo-ligamentous sprain. In spite of conservative but rigorous treatment, the symptoms of pain, muscle stiffness, and disability in bending, walking, and sitting persisted for eighteen months. Thorough examinations revealed no permanent organic damage. The psychiatric findings mirrored those observed in the preceding case. Although this plaintiff was young (early twenties) and more attuned to the American cultural scene, he displayed the same, flat, factual acceptance of his disabilities, the same acceptance of irreversibility discussed in the case above. The injury was conceived as God's verdict, an immutable thought pattern that left little room for introspection or comparison with others. He showed none of the hope or none of the grinding despair that disabled persons of other cultures experience, no defense mechanisms as in a neurosis, no dramatization as in hysteria. The attitude could be paraphrased as "whatever happened resulted in a fixed impairment. Until it disappears with or without God's or the doctor's help, it is accepted as one of the vicissitudes of life."

These observations were testified to at the trial as descriptive of the plaintiff's mental state. The defense attorney pointed to the lack of neurological findings, interpreting the claimant's attitude as evidence of his exaggeration of symptoms. The jury again found for the defense.

A not dissimilar reaction was encountered in two women, one an Egyptian in this country for sixteen years and the other a Moroccan of Jewish extraction married to and deserted by an American serviceman. Both had fallen at work in a food-processing plant at different times, landing on the shoulder, hip, and lower extremity. Complete orthopedic and neurologic examinations revealed no organic basis for complaints of "paralysis" of the shoulder, arm, and leg muscles. In the first case, the plaintiff felt she had "lost her arm"; in the second, a complete (hysterical) hemi-anesthesia of the right arm and trunk with "paralysis" of the arm was encountered. Intensive physiotherapy availed little in either case. Fear of permanent injury to the "nerves" of the extremities pervaded their thinking. A fixed notion of irreversibility of the injuries colored the reactions to soft tissue contusions of the shoulder in the first and bursitis of the subacromial area in the second patient.

Suicide and Compensability

The psychiatric evaluation of a suicide becomes legally significant in three general areas: (1) where there is a request for benefits on an insurance policy, by relatives of a suicide, (2) where a suicide is said to have resulted from an injury or wrong because of someone's negligence in industrial or civil situations, and (3) where suicide was the result of an injury intentionally inflicted upon the deceased by the defendant in an action. In the first instance, the psychiatric problem may be to estimate the degree of mental illness preceding the self-destructive act. It may be a depression of psychotic proportions, the result of emotional pressure, a sense of futility and worthlessness, or a conscious wish to die as a philosophic answer to life itself. In older days, if a suicide was the result of "insanity," the beneficiaries of a policy could recover. For example, in an 1898 Illinois case, *Nelson v. Equitable Life Assurance Society*,[23] a man who killed himself in a delirium was held not to appreciate his self-destructive act and hence not to be a legal suicide. The older cases[24] maintained that "self-destruction while insane is not suicide . . . unless the person committing the self-destructive act could form a conscious intention to kill himself, and carry out the act, realizing its moral and physical consequences."

In response to such court rulings, insurance companies began to add the words "sane or insane" as an exclusion to recovery. All insurance policies at present exclude suicide, sane or insane, from death benefits to survivors, at least for a fixed period of time. In combatting this insurance company doctrine, it became important then to show, in accordance with judicial decisions, that suicide had not in fact occurred because the decedent (insured) at the time he destroyed himself was "so insane as not to be able to appreciate or comprehend the physical nature and consequences of the destructive act." The courts, as summarized in the American Law Reports discussion, "have reached widely opposed results." Some have "held lack of such comprehension is immaterial, and that recovery is barred if the act committed was of such character that if performed by a sane person, would be regarded as suicidal."[25] Others have contended that "if the insured did not comprehend the act would be fatal because of insanity, it could not be suicide"; hence, recovery is possible. In some areas, this view is upheld in the form of the decision in an Ohio case (1935),[26] wherein the court stated that the mental derangement "must go to the extent of destroying the free moral agency of the actor and be of such potency as to prevent him from fixing in his mind the purpose to commit self-destruction. . . . If his mentality is such that he cannot will or purpose, then it is not his act, because he has not willed it."

In recent years, the majority view was expressed in *Aetna Life Insurance Company v. McLaughlin* (Texas, 1964).[27] The insured died when he was struck by a school bus. His policy excluded "suicide, sane or insane." The trial court entered a judgment for the widow because the definition of suicide given the jury required that "he understand the nature and probable consequences of his act." Evidence apparently showed McLaughlin to be a "deeply troubled man immediately prior to his death." He had been drinking heavily and "lunged . . . or fell . . . in front of a moving school bus." After the widow's victory based on the husband's "insanity," the insurance company brought the case to the Court of Civil Appeals and finally to the Supreme Court of Texas. Here Judge Norvell reversed the judgment to the widow, ruling that the "suicide, sane or insane" exclusionary clause in the policy be upheld. He said:

> [I]t is not necessary for the decedent to have realized the physical nature or consequences of his act, nor that he have had a conscious purpose to take his life, the loss occasioned thereby comes within the exclusion, regardless of whether the insured decedent . . . [knew] that such act would cause his death.

In laying down the majority rule, the court pointed to the minority or so-called Kentucky rule that "consciousness of the physical nature and consequences of the act and an intention to kill oneself are essential to invoke the 'suicide, sane or insane' exclusion." He further stated that the majority rule "accepts a broad popular definition . . . [whereas] the minority view is essentially a criminal law or technical concept. . . ." It is interesting to note in this case that opinion evidence (presumably of doctors) was considered "superfluous" if the "tribunal was in possession of the same information as the witness" and that "expert testimony invades the province of the jury" (Texas Law of Evidence).

In the second area of suicide, where an injury results from someone's negligence and is not intentionally inflicted, the problem becomes whether the wrong or negligence was a "proximate cause of the suicide." This situation could occur in workers' compensation cases or civil suits for infliction of emotional distress. Here, the degree of mental illness, such as a depression, at the time of suicide must be weighed by the court with the aid of psychiatric testimony. The case of D.G., a laborer, was studied by two psychiatrists, neither of whom had seen the decedent in life. The issue to be decided was whether the motor-car accident which injured the decedent had produced a mental illness, a depression, which catapulted him to suicide. The widow's expert testified that the motor accident developed into a mental illness following infliction of physical (back injury) and emotional distress, and that, while suffering therefrom, the decedent was overcome by an uncontrollable urge to commit suicide which he successfully executed. The defendant's psychiatrist interpreted the self-destruction to be a conscious choice after twelve years of suffering. The suicide, it was felt, was a matter of choice, a decision to cease living rather than to experience a life of pain and disabilities.

D.G. had suffered five accidents over 12 years. Two laminectomies had been performed for an original disc herniation: a sympathetic nerve block and a long period of physical therapy for a fractured leg occasioned by falling out of a tree, a foot-drop and constant pain in the back were his lot since then. The whip-lash injury from the last motor car accident occurred five weeks before his suicide.

The defendant's expert concluded that the subject's behavior just prior to his demise, during the last month of life, after the accident at issue, were significant. On the day of the suicide, D.G. had gone to a friend's house where his shotgun had been lodged for some time, retrieved it, laughing and joking with his friend as he did so. His last remark was, "I'll see you later." The actual suicide was accomplished by parking his car on a roadside, lying on the ground, placing the gun between his knees, the muzzle pointing to his head in such a way as to insure a fatal shot.

The plaintiff's expert concluded that D.G.

was not predisposed to the development of depressive symptoms as a response to stress as evidenced by his ability to cope adequately with prior accidents and injuries of a severe nature during his adult life.

It is more likely than not that he would not have suicided had he not been involved in the car accident and with reasonable medical certainty, one can state that his suicide was caused by the most recent car accident.

Both psychiatrists noted he acted "out of character" during those 5 weeks, preceding the suicide, that he was depressed, uncommunicative and irritable with his grandchildren with whom he had good relations previously.

The defendant's psychiatrist, in investigating D.G.'s personality among family and neighbors found that he was disinclined to complain about physical discomfort or distress even when severe; he was habitually conscientious, perfectionistic, valuing hard work, well done; put much emphasis on being law-abiding in the community; was reliable, in his personal relationships and as an individual, physically active, adequate, capable and self-disciplined.

The case was settled out of court for an undisclosed amount.

In the third area, where suicide results from an injury intentionally inflicted upon a deceased, the law was stated in a slightly different way in a New York case (1959). This case involved a wrongful death action (*Cauverien v. DeMetz*).[28] The deceased, a diamond broker, gave a stone to a dealer for prospective sale. The dealer refused either to purchase or to return the diamond, thus "blackening the broker's reputation" and "maliciously, without justification" causing "extreme apprehension and emotional distress" . . . [and] an irresistible impulse to take his own life," which he did. Justice Nathan of the Supreme Court, Special Term, New York, commented that "this is a novel and extraordinary complaint seeking damages for wrongful death." He ruled as follows:

The overwhelming weight of authority is to the effect that a suicide—absent insanity—is a new and independent agency which breaks the causal connection between wrongful act and death, precluding an action under wrongful death statutes. . . .

However, where the suicide is committed in a state of insanity in response to an uncontrollable impulse, recovery may be had if the mental state of the deceased was caused by the defendant's wrongful act.

If the intentional act is not intended to injure the plaintiff (as it apparently was in *Cauverien*), and the defendant's act is negligent, then "the act of committing suicide is generally found to be independent intervening cause which frees the defendant from liability."

The intentional acts driving a person to suicide may be of a purely mental nature. For example, in *Tate v. Canonica* (California, 1960),[29] the widow of a man in business claimed that his associates made "threats, statements against him" for the "purposing of harrassing [sic], embarrassing and humiliating him" and that as a result the injured party underwent mental and physical harm culminating in his suicide. The widow of the deceased who had also been involved in the business claimed damages of $490,000 and punitive damages of $25,000. The alleged accusations, not specifically named, "were negligently done and sufficient cause for a breakdown ending in suicide." The defendants, in opposition to the complaint, averred that suicide was "always an impending, intervening cause." When the case reached the Supreme Court of California, it was noted that the acts of harassment and humiliation were not done for the purpose of causing suicide but for the purpose of harassment per se, and therefore there was "a nucleus for a cause of action" in the intentional and negligent acts of the defendants. In supporting this cause of action, Justice Duniway wrote:

Where the defendant intended by his conduct, to cause serious mental distress . . . and does so, and such mental distress is shown by the evidence to be a substantial factor in bringing about the suicide, a cause of action for wrongful death results, whether the suicide was committed in a state of insanity, or in response to an irresistible impulse, or not.

The judgment against the widow was reversed and remanded for trial to develop the cause of action.

It is a clinical axiom that mental states of various kinds are multi-determined; suicides may well fit this formula. Chief Judge Breitel of the New York Court of Appeals recognized the truth of this axiom:

"A suicide is a strange act and no rationalistic approach can fit the act into neat categories of rationality or irrationality."

This comment was made in the case of a surgeon who was injured in an auto accident by striking his head against a car door (*Fuller v. Preis et al.*, New York, 1964).[30] The doctor felt no symptoms at the time, but soon developed convulsive seizures which, after hospitalization, proved to be secondary to subdural hemorrhage with brain contusion. Seven months after the accident, his seizures continued unabated, in spite of competent treatment. He committed suicide, leaving a note saying "I am perfectly sane in mind" and directing his family regarding his will and certain business matters. The trial court awarded the family $200,000 in a wrongful death action. On appeal by the defendants, the Appellate Division set the judgment aside as "contrary to the weight of credible evidence." The case then came before the Court of Appeals, which, in reviewing the proceedings, reversed the lower court, ordering a new trial. Chief Judge Breitel noted that the neurologist who treated the deceased had testified that brain hemorrhage and contusion caused "post-traumatic focal seizures" which continued to the extent of three a day on the day he shot himself. The doctor had lost his practice, developed a depressed state with "deterioration and gradual contraction of his professional and private activities." At the trial, the defense objected to the neurologist's testimony on the grounds that the neurologist "did not practice the closely related specialty of psychiatry" and did not diagnose the patient as "mentally ill." Chief Judge Breitel, however, found the neurologist's testimony "credible," ruling that the suicide was the "immediate consequence of traumatic epilepsy."

There are limits to which a tortious act can precipitate a person into a mental condition for which a suit for recovery is brought. A recent case involves a woman whose son and daughter-in-law were killed in a major airplane crash and who committed suicide because of "shock, depression, melancholia and an uncontrollable urge to join her son and daughter-in-law in death" (*Saxton v. McDonnell Douglas Aircraft Co.*, 1977).[31] As a result of taking depositions, appearances in court, cross-examination, and the publicity given the Paris crash of an aircraft killing 346 passengers, the plaintiff developed an agitated depression. An award of $11 million, including "punitive damages of $10,000,000," had been asked on the basis of products liability, i.e., a faulty cargo door and faulty design of the airplane. The U.S. District Court (Central District California) ruled that the liability of the airplane manufacturer did not extend to the suicide of the mother since her "unstable mental capacity" was not a foreseeable factor in that the "shock of a death [would] compel" her to commit suicide. No psychiatric testimony to establish the depth of the depression preceding her demise was utilized in the case.

Emotional Injury from Legal Harassment

Harassment and humiliation in a sensitive person may have consequences as serious as suicide (cf. *Tate*, above) or as generalized as mental distress. Legal redress for such consequences may be sought if the "mental anguish" is sufficient to interfere with the plaintiff's ordinary life and socioeconomic functions. The plausibility of this kind of lawsuit depends in large part on whether the alleged condition amounts to a diagnosable illness or is simply a matter of life stress which the average person is able to withstand. In the event that legal damages are sought for humiliation, actual or fancied, the psychiatric task is first to evaluate the personality and the mental state of the complainant, and second, to establish the degree of ego strength or weakness which permits the hurt to reach the level of a neurosis or psychosis. This psychological exploration was carried out in the case of Carol T., a forty-four-year-old matron accused of first degree arson.

The immediate basis for the arson charge was ignition of her living room drapes from a match which Carol used to light a cigarette while standing close to the window. The drapes blazed, then the wainscoting of the wall burned and then the entire house was gutted.

She ran into another room to call the fire department, picked up a few clothes and ran out of the house as the flames engulfed the building. Investigation by the insurance underwriters was thorough with a resulting charge of arson, first degree. Carol was arrested, booked and released on $5,000 bail.

An additional charge of "defrauding an insurance company" was made when an organ valued at $1,100 which had been loaned her was destroyed and a $1,000 ring and a valuable mink stole were claimed to have been lost in the fire.

Subsequently the charges of arson and fraud were dismissed for lack of evidence. However, the court action had been given wide publicity locally to the embarrassment of Carol T. Her friends joked about her court involvement with the usual jibes about a "fire sale," etc.

As a result Carol suffered a gradual loss of friends, was resentful of insurance company detectives who "shadowed" her before the trial, became tense and emotionally upset by people's references to her arrest. The main target of gossip by acquaintances was her reputation as a "swinger." Carol had been married five times, had been a cocktail waitress in a prominent club in town and was subjected to various innuendos by her wide acquaintances.

The insurance investigators attempted to obtain proof of her alleged profligacy, following her into stores, shadowing her near home and so on. She became irritable, tense, insomniac, upset by sounds of fire sirens on the street or stories of fire. Anxiety was reflected in stomach pain, headaches and nausea. As Carol put it: "I became unglued . . . I could trust no one, even my attorney."

Personality study showed Carol to be an attractive, well-groomed woman, of high average intelligence with a frank, open attitude towards sexuality and social freedom. She was particularly distressed at the insurance investigators' attempts to discredit her socially. The tension she felt was directed chiefly at the insurance company's legal representative, his success in "stalling" legal action, and her fear of public obloquy. There was no evidence of psychosis: the anxiety was determined solely by her arrest and subsequent court action. The publicity given the case was especially trying.

As a consequence of the mental strain imposed by the continued innuendos and covert shadowing by the insurance company, Carol sued the insurance company for malicious prosecution and asked damages for breach of contract for $3,000,000. This tort action was denied by the county court. On appeal to the Appellate Court, the plaintiff's case was reinstated but a long delay of five years ensued before the case was reheard.

On this second trial, psychiatric testimony indicated that the anxiety and other nervous symptoms were specifically based on the harassment Carol suffered over a prolonged period. The jury brought in a verdict awarding the plaintiff compensatory damages for $20,000 and punitive damages for $10,000.

Workmen's compensation law has slightly different aims than personal injury tort law. Yet, its slow development has encompassed many of the features exemplified in tort law, particularly the accent on emotional distress and mental illness. Greater clarity of the relation between industrial injuries and resulting "nervous" conditions has been achieved during the last few decades. In this respect, psychiatry has been called upon to differentiate between many shades and nuances of emotional reactions. It is to be expected that, with the increase in complexity of modern technology, this field will demand even more sophisticated attention. In relation to both personal injury and workers' compensation cases, it might be said that a new branch of neuropsychiatry will come into being, best described, for want of a better term, as *traumatic psychiatry* or the *psychiatry of trauma*.

Notes

1. *Coultas v. Victorian Railway* (England) 13 A.C. 222 (P.C.) (Austl.).

2. Hubert W. Smith, *Relation of Emotion to Injury and Diseases: Legal Liability for Psychic Stimuli*, 30 Va. L. Rev. 193 (1944).

3. David Saxe, *Psychotherapy and Malpractice*, 58 Ken. L.J. 467 (1970).

4. Arthur Larson, *Laws of Workman's Compensation* 2: 1, Chapt. 10, Sec. 57, M. Bender, New York (1969).

5. California Law of Employee Injury and Workmen's Compensation, 2d Sec. 11.01, ed. rev., W. L. Hanna, M. Bender, New York (1969).

6. L. P. Tourkow and J. V. Tattan, *Some Problems Confronting the Psychiatrist and Psychologist in Compensation Work* 4 J. For. Sci. 292 (1969).

7. Max Wertheimer, *Gestalt Theory*, 11 Soc. Res. 78 (1944).

8. F. Perls, R. Hefferline, and Paul Goodman, *Gestalt Therapy*: 26 et seq., Dell Publ. Co., New York (1951).

9. A. H. Hirschfeld and R. C. Behan, *The Accident Process, Part I. Etiological Considerations of Industrial Injuries*, 186 J.A.M.A. 113 (Oct. 19, 1963).

10. A. Larson, *Mental and Physical Injury in Workmen's Compensation*, 23 Vanderbilt L. Rev. 1243, 1260 (1970).

11. *Pathfinder Company v. Industrial Commission*, 343 N.E. 2d 913 (Ill., 1976).

12. *Rund v. Cessna Aircraft*, 518 P. 2d 518 (Kans., 1974).

13. *Hunsley v. Giard*, 553 P. 2d 1096 (Wash., 1976).

14. *Mitchell v. Rochester Railway*, 45 N.E. 354 (1896).

15. *Burlington Mills Corporation v. Hagood*, 13 S.E. 2d 291 (Va., 1941).

16. Charon's case, Sup. Jud. Dist. Mass., 75 N.E. 2d 511 (1947).

17. *Schneyder v. Cadillac Motor Car Company*, 273 N.W. 418 (1937).

18. *Carter v. General Motors*, 361 Mich. 577; 106 N.W. 2d 105 (1960).

19. *Saunders v. Pool Shipping Company*, 255 F. 2d 729 (1956).

20. S. A. Strauss, *Psychiatric Testimony with Special Reference to Cases of Post-Traumatic Neurosis*, 1 J. For. Sci. 77 (1972).

21. *Miller Rasmussen Ice & Coal Company v. Industrial Commission of Wisconsin*, 57 N.W. 736 (1953).

22. Melvin Braverman, Frederick J. Hacker, and Joel Shor, *Psycho-traumatic Sexual Response*, 18 J. of For. Med. 24 (Jan. 1971).

23. *Nelson v. Equitable Life Assurance Society*, 73 Ill. App. 133 (1898).

24. 9 ALR 3d, 1015, Insurance—Suicide—Sane or Insane, Sec. 2(a).

25. Ibid.: Sec. 5.

26. *Industrial Commission of Ohio v. Brubaker*, 129 Ohio 617; 196 N.E. 409 (1935).

27. *Aetna Life Insurance Company v. McLaughlin*, 380 S.W. 2d 101, ALR 3d, 1005 (1964).

28. *Cauverien v. DeMetz*, 188 N.Y.S. 2d 627 (1959).

29. *Tate v. Canonica*, 180 C.A. 2d 898; Calif. Rptr. 28 (1960).

30. *Fuller v. Preis et al.*, N.Y. Ct. App., 363 N.Y. Supp. 2d 568; 35 N.Y. 2d 425 (1964).

31. *Saxton v. McDonnell Douglas Aircraft Company*, 428 F. Supp. 1047, Cir., C.D. Calif. (1977).

15

Professional Liability

Up to this point, discussion of psychiatric involvement in the legal process has covered indicted offenders in criminal actions and plaintiffs in civil situations. The role of psychiatry in the legal process has concerned examinations, evaluations, and expert testimony regarding the abnormalities and disabilities, responsibilities and competencies, of persons enmeshed in litigation. To this end, life reactions, behavioral patterns, emotional reactions, intellectual capacities, and disabilities have been our subjects of inquiry. This chapter reverses the direction of such inquiries, turning to the physician's and psychiatrist's own misbehavior before legal tribunals.

Beyond the citizen's obligations as imposed by law and social polity, mental specialists along with other licensed professionals have a particular ethic peculiar to their professions which they must observe. These ethical precepts have been laid down by recognized professional associations and have been rendered into law by state boards established in each state by statute. Infractions of such rules lead to legal censure of all medical and health practitioners, but especially the psychiatrist and psychologist because of his or her subjective relationship to the patient. All professionals licensed by the state—physicians, attorneys, engineers—are subject to legal censure, but the first two named are especially sensitive to ethical principles. Derelection of duty through incompetence or acts of moral turpitude may result in revocation of their license to practice their professions.

Revocation of License

Since the right to practice a profession is a "valuable property right" conferred by statute which creates this right by issuance of a license, revocation of the license is also provided for.[1] The reasons for revocation may be criminal and ethical, but other grounds for charges of unprofessional conduct of an administrative or business nature include use of a false or assumed name; misrepresentation of a "cure" to a patient; advertising or soliciting; and signing false documents. Any of these actions may be considered a cause for revocation of license. Our present concern is more narrow, restricted to those infractions or crimes wherein psychiatric opinion is sought in defense or prosecution.

The usual arena in which revocation of license is considered is in medical boards, variously named, by the several states. These disciplinary proceedings represent a "special, somewhat unique action" in a tribunal for physicians, in that "the medical profession inquires into the conduct of members of the profession . . . in order to maintain sound professional standards of conduct for the purpose of protecting the public and the standing of the medical profession in the eyes of the public."[2] The accent on ethicality serves the purpose of upholding the high standard of the learned professions. The hearings are administrative in format, and the board has discretionary powers to determine suitable penalties which may be brought before a court of record for review. It is worthy of note that in such hearings, the physician-patient privilege is not available to the licensee.[3]

Grounds for suspension or revocation of medical license throughout the country are similar to those of California. Under the heading of unprofessional conduct, as amended in 1978,[4] these are:

(a) Violating or attempting to violate . . . any provision of this chapter.
(b) Gross Negligence
(c) Repeated similar negligent acts
(d) Incompetence
(e) Gross Immorality
(f) Commission of any act involving moral turpitude, dishonesty or corruption. . . .
(g) Any action or conduct which would have warranted denial of the certificate.

Additionally, if a certificate holder becomes mentally ill to such an extent as to effect his ability to conduct with safety the practice as authorized . . . the Division of Medical Quality may take action by . . .

Suspending judgment
Placing him on probation

Suspending right to practice . . . not to exceed one year
Revoking his certificate
Taking such other action . . . as the Board deems proper.

The majority of disciplinary actions are meted out for drug violations, unlawful dispensing or prescribing of controlled drugs, and acts
involving sexual relations, identifiable as moral turpitude. Although
self-administration of drugs, fraudulent Medicaid claims, and deceptive advertising are causes for license revocation, they are in the minority.[5] More important are those of a sexual nature where a charge
of rape can easily be made in view of the close physical contact between a female patient and male physician with one draped during an
examination. For these reasons, an in-depth scrutiny of the complainant regarding her veracity may be sought.

In a 1966 California case,[6] a physician was charged with the rape
of a patient to whom he allegedly administered an intoxicating drug
or anesthetic substance in order to prevent her resistance. The defendant physician petitioned for a writ of mandate to compel certain
pretrial discovery, including a psychiatric examination of the complaining female witness. The Supreme Court of California, which
heard the appeal, noted that although

> authorities have suggested that the prosecution in a sex case should always be
> compelled to submit to a psychiatric examination . . . a general rule requiring
> psychiatric examination of complaining witnesses in every case, or . . . in
> any such case that rests upon the uncorroborated testimony of the complaining
> witness, would in many instances, not be necessary or appropriate. Moreover,
> victims of sex crimes might be deterred by such an absolute requiring from dis-
> closing such offenses. . . .[7]

Justice Tobriner wrote the court's opinion and agreed that the trial
judge should be authorized to order a psychiatric examination of the
complainant "if the circumstances indicate a necessity" for such examination. These included "little or no corroboration" to support the
charge, or if the defense raised the issue of the witness's mental or
emotional condition. In the case under discussion, the court unanimously agreed there was no necessity for an examination of the prose-
cutrix and that a "psychiatric examination is not absolute but only
relatively illuminating."

Requests for psychiatric examination of a complainant in cases where
a professional person is convicted of a sexual offense are not common.
Contests concerning the conviction are apt to be on legal (evidentiary)
grounds. In *People v. Bernstein* (California, 1959),[8] a neuropsychiatrist
was convicted of statutory rape of a sixteen-year-old patient whom he

treated for promiscuity and juvenile delinquency. The psychiatrist had progressed from "therapy across the desk to a kiss on the forehead (and later) fondling and sexual intercourse." The trial court convicted him of statutory rape, sentencing the doctor to six months in jail. He appealed to the District Court of Appeals on grounds that a phone call between himself and the complainant in which admission and denial of the acts were presented as evidence was inadmissible. This appeal was rejected.

Following his conviction, the Board of Medical Examiners revoked Dr. Bernstein's license to practice medicine. The doctor again appealed to the District Court of Appeals on grounds that statutory rape does not "per se involve moral turpitude," which was the basis for the board's revocation of the doctor's license.[9] On this writ to annul the decision of the medical board, the court admitted that the appellant's contention "may be true in general" but indicated that the board was authorized to inquire into the circumstances surrounding the crime in order to fix the degree of discipline or to determine if such offense involved moral turpitude. Here, where the victim was brought to the appellant's office for treatment for sexual promiscuity and "where the appellant held himself out as a psychiatrist licensed to rehabilitate such people, and where his license placed him in a position of trust which he violated," the court concluded that the criminal trial record reflected the fact that "statutory rape in this case involved moral turpitude."

Sexual intimacies with patients or clients, if proved, ordinarily support charges of unprofessional conduct, a basis for revocation or suspension of license. Beyond that, the Supreme Court of Kansas[10] upheld the revocation of a psychologist's license following "sexual intimacies" with patients on the grounds that sexual improprieties were unprofessional, negligent, and wrongful acts. In this case, *Morra v. State Board of Kansas* (1973), it was pointed out on appeal that the board failed to promulgate the code of ethics of the American Psychological Association until after Dr. Morra's hearing. In the original trial court hearing which approved the Kansas Board of Examiners' revocation of Dr. Morra's license, Dr. Morra had indicated the complainant's "unreliability." Because of this factor, the psychologist accused the board of acting as "investigator, grand jury, prosecutor, judge and jury . . . and other prejudices." In reviewing the proceeding, the Supreme Court of Kansas upheld the charge of unprofessional conduct and subsequent revocation of license, based "solely on negligence and wrongful actions" in the performance of his duties.

The charge of moral turpitude in a professional person can encompass other than sexual misbehavior. In another California case, *Grannis*

v. Board of Medical Quality Assurance (1971),[11] a physician appealed
to the Superior Court for review of the revocation of license which
had been based on two convictions on drunken driving. The trial court
confirmed the board's decision. Dr. Grannis then moved to the Court
of Appeal on the grounds that one of the convictions had been made
on his plea of *nolo contendre*, which was not a conviction within the
meaning of the Business and Professional Code (Section 2361, 2390).
Under this code, a doctor's conviction of more than one misdemeanor
involving the use, consumption, or self-administration of alcoholic
beverages would constitute "unprofessional conduct." This legal claim
was upheld by the Court of Appeal. The issue then became whether
the second count of the accusation—the use of alcoholic beverages to
the extent, or in such manner as to be dangerous or injurious to the
licensee, to any other person or the public—constituted unprofessional
conduct. Testimony of the appellant's psychiatrist bore on this point.

At the trial, Dr. Grannis was described as an alcoholic "who with
relatively minute quantities of alcohol, suffers an impairment of his
neurophysiological system so he loses contact with the changes in his
personality . . . and ability to judge [his] impairment of motor function. . . ." (Apparently, this corresponded to a diagnosis of pathologic
intoxication.) On cross-examination, the expert was asked:

Q. Now this impairment of or gradually lessening of anxiety . . . heightened in
   an alcoholic . . . this in turn has a direct relationship to . . . what we call
   good judgment?
A. Yes, it does.
Q. And that in turn . . . would have a definite relationship to the quality of
   patient care which Dr. Grannis could give a patient if he had any alcohol
   whatsoever?
A. That is correct.

The court upheld a stayed revocation of license, with a five-year
probation period imposed by the Board of Medical Examiners, on the
grounds that Dr. Grannis' use of alcohol was to the extent of "being
dangerous or injurious to a person holding a certificate . . . or other
person or to the public" and did indeed constitute unprofessional
conduct.

Instances of revocation of license due to "gross negligence" or "incompetence" do not involve psychiatric testimony when they move
into the realm of surgical, obstetric, or other malpractice. However,
it is worth noting that even if a psychiatrist has not engaged in surgery
or other specialties in medicine than his own, he is entitled to testify
as an expert in view of his medical training and knowledge of "standards and procedure" through study and observation. In a Florida case,

a specialist in neurology and psychiatry with proper qualifications and who professed knowledge of standard procedures was permitted to testify in a surgical malpractice case by the District Court of Appeals, notwithstanding that he had not performed such an operation. The operation in question was surgical removal of a lymph node from the posterior triangle of the neck. His testimony "could have a bearing on the weight and credibility given his opinion but did not render him incompetent to express an opinion as an expert."[12]

The topic of testimony by an expert witness in areas other than those of his own competence has been discussed by legal authorities. Wigmore suggested that the issue of expert witness qualifications should be the exclusive prerogative of the trial judge and that the rule ought to be, "The experiential qualifications of a particular witness are invariably determined by the trial judge and will not be reviewed on appeal.[13] However, neither Maryland[14] nor California[15] follows the rule suggested by Wigmore. The California Supreme Court stated: "Indeed, the exclusion of the sole expert relied on by a party because of an erroneous view of his qualifications is, in a case where expert testimony is essential, an abuse of discretion as a matter of law requiring reversal."[16] Although several earlier decisions required a showing of personal performance of the specific operative technique involved in surgical cases, the recent trend has been that a medical witness should be permitted to testify in medical malpractice actions "if it is shown that he knows the required standard of care . . . based on his professional knowledge, training and experience . . . [that] he is familiar with the techniques claimed to have been negligently performed."

By far the most common reason for revocation of medical license among physicians revolves around the use of narcotic drugs, violation of the Controlled Substance Act, and prescribing for an addict-patient without a "good faith prior examination." Whether the physician supplies the needy addict through carelessness, altruism, or even greed, the majority of physicians suffering a suspension or loss of license become involved because they have not examined their patients in "good faith." The following case illustrates this principle. A family physician

prescribed for a number of addicts without an examination on the presumptive diagnosis of obesity. The doctor asserted he made a diagnosis of obesity on inspection for which he prescribed 100 tablets of amphetamine, and a "headache" for which he prescribed codeine, 100 tablets at a time. His defense was that headache being a subjective symptom, no examination was necessary. This physician had been a successful surgeon who had suffered financial reverses in the recent past.

Detailed history of the physician, however, revealed an attack of depression five years before the instant offense for which treatment was sought in a psychiatric sanitarium, and a hypomanic attack just prior to the drug charge on the occasion for an arrest for insufficient funds. A psychiatrist diagnosing manic-depressive psychosis treated the doctor following incarceration in jail on an insufficient funds charge. Although the Board of Medical Quality Assurance (California, 1976) revoked his license, appeal was made to a court of record resulting in a stay of execution pending a trial on the grounds of mental illness as a mitigating circumstance.

Traditionally, medical personnel with easy access to drugs have treated themselves with sedatives and narcotics for minor complaints. Such unregulated use of drugs may stem from a personality problem, a neurosis, or the so-called masked depression. As in the case just cited, the doctor may struggle to maintain his professional activities in the face of a mental illness with the aid of self-administered controlled drugs. A family practitioner brought before the Board of Medical Examiners (California) for excessive use of benzedrine showed a similar history of mental illness complicated by alcoholism.

Dr. B., 45 years of age, had been given Benzedrine over a period of 22 years for a "heart condition". He continued its daily use, adding alcohol during the past three years until summoned before the California Medical Board for disciplinary action, which gave him suspension of license and three years probation.
He had been treated by a psychiatrist for depression three years before being placed on probation. During the probation period the doctor began heavy use of alcohol necessitating a hospital admission. His behavior showed belligerence, his mental state was confused and a final diagnosis of Chronic Brain Syndrome, Hepatitis, Peripheral Neuritis was made. Under treatment, the doctor cleared up, began to appreciate the effects of drugs and alcohol on his behavior and entered into psychotherapy. Insight developed into his basic sense of insecurity for which he attempted to compensate by the use of drugs and alcohol.

License revocation because of a mental illness also occurs among other than medical professionals. A lawyer was recommended for disbarment by the Disciplinary Board of the State Bar (California) because he had misappropriated funds belonging to a client. As is so often the case with medical men whose licenses are revoked by the medical board, the lawyer petitioned for a review of the disbarment action. He petitioned the California Supreme Court (1977) because of "mitigating matters,"[17] i.e., the presence of a manic-depressive psychosis at the time of the crime. Three psychiatrists testified before the board that the attorney's illness "would not allow him to appreciate the moral and legal implications of his acts at the time." The experts who had examined him several times before the offense testified that he was in a "borderline . . . state of remission," but they left open the question of further manic attacks. Although the petitioner had an excellent record as a lawyer and was reported upon favorably by the probation officer and several judges, the Supreme Court ordered disbarment: "While we sympathize with him regarding his psychiatric problems, our primary concern must be the fulfillment of proper professional standards, whatever unfortunate cause. . . ."

Moral turpitude as a basis for a charge of unprofessional conduct has been extended in the case of a physician who files fraudulent income tax returns. In a Washington case (1958),[18] a physician's license was suspended for eight months by the Board of Medical Examiners in that state. An appeal to the Supreme Court of Washington was rejected with this opinion: "In our judgment a wilful and intentional attempt to avoid payment of all or a part of one's income tax with intent to defraud the government involves moral turpitude. Such fraud is unprofessional conduct as that term is defined in the medical disciplinary act."

The court's further comment on the Medical Disciplinary Act was that while the proceeding is civil, not criminal, yet it is quasi-criminal . . . [since] it is for the protection of the public. . . ."

Psychiatric Malpractice

If revocation of a professional license signifies the death of one's practice, malpractice is its wounding. Malpractice actions come to public attention in the press, casting an unwarranted shadow on any physician. Furthermore, since malpractice is a tort action, all proceedings are moved from administrative bodies into the courtroom under legal rules of an adversary proceeding. Psychiatric malpractice constitutes only a fraction of the total tort cases for medical negligence. In his pioneer paper on psychiatric malpractice (1962) revised in 1965, Dr. William Bellamy estimated that psychiatric issues made up only 4 percent of the total medical malpractice cases in the 1946-1965 period.[19] The five areas of risk at that time were (1) treatment, including electroshock, (2) commitment, (3) suicide, (4) patient's assaultiveness and (5) psychic injury, i.e., mental anguish. These figures did not include those subject to arbitration or out-of-court settlement. Current figures analyzed by Drs. Hirsch and White (1978)[20] present a somewhat different picture in regards to bases for psychiatric malpractice. These authors analyzed 1,556 cases of medical malpractice from April 1971 to November 1977. Of these, psychiatric litigation constituted 3 percent of all medical malpractice actions. They also did not consider cases settled out of court, drawing their cases from the files of the general counsel of the American Medical Association which covered mainly Appellate Court decisions. Among other cogent comments, Hirsch and White note a "numerical increase each successive year of their study" among psychiatric malpractice complaints. Their breakdown showed that suicide precipitated 50 percent of all psychiatric actions; negligence in treatment procedures, including unnecessary treatment, defective informed consent, and inadequate followup, made up the remaining 50 percent.

The changes in bases for psychiatric malpractice over the past two or three decades reflect a change in practice. Litigation resulting from electroshock therapy due to fractures during the convulsion have been minimized through improvements in technique with anectine and brevital and, more significantly, through reduction in the number of shocks given patients.

During 1940-1971, electroshock treatments were liberally bestowed on mental patients in office and hospital practice. (One young woman received 200 such treatments for homosexuality!) In recent years, pressure from consumer groups, especially in California, has reduced electroshock treatments drastically (Vasconcellos bill, 1976),[21] and psychiatrists have adopted other forms of treatment, notably psychotropic drugs. Professor Dawidoff has studied psychiatric malpractice intensively[22] and indicates that the adoption of informed consent as to the "risks involved" has decreased the incidence of suits. Early occurrences as in *Quinley v. Cocke* (Tennessee, 1946),[23] where a patient suffering from severe pain in the hip after electroshock treatment was not X-rayed until the third day post-treatment, are not apt to occur presently.

Of all the malpractice risks facing the practicing psychiatrist, suicide is unquestionably the most distressing and most unpredictable. The law covering liability for a physician or institution in a case of suicide can be stated from a New York decision, *O'Neill v. State of New York* (1971),[24] as follows:

In a claim for wrongful death where the decedent committed suicide, in order for liability to attach to a physician or an institution, there must be a showing that there was negligence—a breach of the duty to exercise the requisite care and skill that is consonant with accepted medical procedure . . . and that this negligence was the proximate cause of death.

The court in *O'Neill* explained:

A mistaken judgment or an honest error in professional judgment by qualified doctors may not be determinative, however . . . the exercise of reasonable and ordinary care requires the physician to make a properly skillful and careful diagnoses ... and if he fails to bring to that diagnosis the proper degree of skill and care and makes an incorrect diagnosis, liability may attach.[25]

The elements of "ordinary skill and care" were factors in a New York case of suicide decided in the widow's favor.[26] A patient known to be depressed and suicidal was admitted to a New York state hospital and was placed on a ward without bars on the windows or without supervision. He jumped out of the window from the second floor, sustained a fractured neck, and died therefrom. On review of the case, the Court of Claims, New York, ruled for the deceased's wife in her claim that her husband's suicidal tendencies were neglected and the state was negligent in placing the patient on an open ward on the second floor. In rendering the judgment, the court pointed to the "important element of foreseeability" as a necessary aspect of application of skill and care. When there is knowledge that the patient entertains suicidal ideation, both hospitals and psychiatrists have the duty to exercise "reasonable care" to prevent its culmination.

The situation in *Johnson v. Grant Hospital* (Ohio, 1972)[27] appeared to be blatant. A female patient was admitted to a hospital with a history of nervousness, depression, and hallucinations that "television told her to kill herself." Her husband, after a visit, warned the nurse to "watch her." The patient was placed in a quiet room, but the door was left open. Twice Mrs. Johnson attempted to injure herself, and twice she was placed in a security room on psychiatric orders. The third time the door was left open, the patient walked out and jumped from the ninth floor to her death. The diagnosis on admission varied from schizo-affective state to depression, with the question of hallucinations and reality contact apparently unsettled. In any event, the patient was not considered insane or incompetent. On this basis, the suicide was considered a "voluntary act," and the trial court found for the defendant. An appeal was taken to the Ohio Court of Appeals which separated out three issues for its decision:

(1) Whether the decedent's emotional and mental condition as known to the defendant, was such that a reasonable prudent person would have anticipated that she would commit suicide at the time she did unless prevented, and if so, (2) did the defendant exercise reasonable care under the circumstances, and if not, (3) was this failure or negligence, on the part of the defendant, a proximate cause of the decedent's death?

The defendant-hospital argued that no expert-opinion evidence relative to the proneness of the patient to suicide was advanced at the trial which would establish the standard of care for a person not insane. In discussing this point, the Court of Appeals propounded the principle that expert witnesses are not necessary when

the subject of inquiry is within common, ordinary and general experience and knowledge of mankind . . . [and] not a highly technical question of science. . . .
  [It was] the duty of the hospital to [exert] reasonable care . . . [that] a reasonably prudent person would anticipate suicide . . . even though the patient was not insane or incompetent.

In reversing the lower court and remanding the case for trial, the majority opinion concluded that negligence was a proximate cause of the suicide. This decision typifies the generally held view that "the court's duty is to discover the probable cause of a suicide [with the] objective of determining the defendant's negligent act in the chain of causation."[28]

Complexities in Suicide Prediction

It is admittedly very difficult, sometimes impossible, to foretell a successful suicide from clinical examinations and history. Self-destructive tendencies range from adolescent identity crises and reasoned suicides at different crucial ages in life to those secondary to neurotic depressions, psychotic depressions and reactions, to grave or disfiguring physical illnesses. The distance between suicidal threats, gestures, impulses, and plans, and actual self-destruction can be great or minute. That every suicidal indication should be taken seriously is self-evident. In suicides claimed to result from psychiatric negligence, however, clinical judgment cedes to the legal test of "reasonable care . . . consonant with accepted medical practice."[29] The parameters of "reasonable care" can be quite elastic, as seen in the following case.

A patient admitted to the Veterans' Hospital in New Orleans for chronic colitis was observed to be visibly depressed. His physician requested a psychiatric consultation, which was not made until eight days after the request was filed. Before the psychiatrist visited the patient, the patient had cut a screen with a pocket knife and jumped from the sixth floor to his death. The suit for negligence and wrongful death was dismissed in the lower court.[30] The decedent's relatives appealed on the grounds of negligence on the part of the defendant and its agents for "failing to detect the suicidal intent and in not removing him to a psychiatric ward or taking other measures for his security." In analyzing the appeal, the U.S. District Court decided that psychiatric testimony at the trial by several experts with long experience and expertise in suicidology indicated that the "depression was mild." The warning signs of potential suicide, agreed upon by psychiatric experts, were not evident in the patient prior to his executed plan. Absence of tell-tale signs—previous attempts at self-destruction, depressed feelings, insomnia, hopeless feelings, frequent mention of suicide, and changes in behavior and attitude—did not allow a prediction of danger. Possession of a pen-knife, with which the deceased cut the screen, did not present any warning signal. In view of the absence of *foreseeability* of the suicide, the court relieved the hospital of responsibility.

A similar legal resolution of a suit for negligence damages against the New York Psychiatric Institute occurred in *Katz v. State of New York*.[31] A patient admitted after rectal surgery in another hospital was diagnosed as psychoneurosis, conversion hysteria The patient was in an open ward staffed by four attendants to twenty-seven patients. He was not considered a suicidal risk, even though the decedent's wife had warned of his suicidal threats. The patient left the ward, walked to the nearest subway station, and then threw himself in front of an oncoming subway train. The court found for the hospital-defendant on the basis of lack of foreseeability of the suicide.

The judiciary is aware of the complexities of managing mental patients in modern mental hospitals. For example, the "open door" policy, adopted to encourage socialization of patients and to remove the unnecessary stigma of restraint through locked doors, is praiseworthy from a therapeutic point of view, but it allows impulsive suicides to occur. Recognizing that "the open ward is too valuable a treatment method to be endangered through unjust litigation,"[32] judges have carefully analyzed its potential for suicide. Justice Tobriner of the California Supreme Court in *Meier v. Ross General Hospital* (1968)[33] aptly phrased the premise of the open door policy: "The policy rests upon the premise that freedom of movement and personal responsibility of patients, even potential suicides, improve the process of their rehabilitation and reduce possible emotional stress." *Meier* illustrates the complications arising from the open door policy as acceptable psychiatric practice and the legal intricacies of accommodating this policy to the doctrine of *res ipsa loquitor* as applied to jury instructions at the trial.

The facts in *Meier* were that the patient was admitted to a psychiatric ward in a general hospital after slashing his wrists in a suicide attempt. He was placed in a room without bars or screen and was treated with tranquilizers which he refused. The window could be opened by a crank; it also could be kept at a fixed width with the crank removed. Eight days after admission, the patient plunged headlong out of the "openable" window. The relatives brought an action against the hospital and the psychiatrist for wrongful death of a mentally disturbed patient, known to be suicide-prone, who was left in a room with a "fully openable window." At the trial, the plaintiffs "characterized the openable window as an invitation to commit suicide, a patent violation of defendant's duty of care . . . 'wholly unrelated to the open door' policy." Expert witnesses testified for the hospital that the open door policy as administered at Ross Hospital complied with accepted professional standards. They suggested that the "openable window" constituted as much a part of "open door" therapy as unlocked doors.

The trial judge gave the jury instructions that "if it is the kind of accident which ordinarily does not occur in the absence of someone's negligence: [if] it was caused by an agency . . . in the control of defendants: [if] the accident was not due to voluntary action or contribution . . . on the part of the decedent," the jury could infer that negligence was a proximate cause of the death. The plaintiffs' attorneys maintained that this instruction gave the jury the impression that "voluntary action" of the decedent was the deciding factor, whereas they felt the fact of an openable window exceeded the standard of care and in fact constituted negligence. The psychiatric issue then resolved itself into an interpretation of the open door policy and whether an openable window was properly part of treatment planning. The "probabilities of negligence" required the assistance of expert testimony to determine whether the window was left open for a "good faith medical reason." Dr. James Stubblebine testified at the trial that an openable window "did not constitute an essential . . . element of the 'open door' policy and was not essential to treatment procedures." At the trial, the jury decided the suicide was voluntary.

The plaintiffs appealed to the Supreme Court of California on the basis of legal technicalities relating to the trial judge's instructions to the jury and the "inference" of the decedent's voluntary act. Justice Tobriner and the court *en banc* ruled the judge's instructions had been in error and ordered a new trial. In so doing, they held that

the trial court must submit a conditional res ipsa instruction, even absent expert testimony on the 'probabilities of negligence,' when the evidence supports a conclusion that the cause of the accident [the openable window] was not inextricably bound in a course of treatment involving the exercise of medical judgment beyond the common knowledge of laymen.

Negligence and Malpractice

The need to observe "requisite learning and skill" and acceptable medical procedures is crucial in avoiding negligence actions. While an honest error of professional medical judgment does not constitute liability, the nonuse of learning and skill "in accord with sound professional practice" may be recoverable. The case of *O'Neill v. State of New York* mentioned above accentuates the responsibility of physicians to diagnose their cases properly in consonance with "sound professional practice." Briefly stated, *O'Neill*[34] involved a claim for the wrongful death, pain, and suffering of a woman known to have used barbiturates for years. Her private physician, having diagnosed her as overdosed with Nembutal, recommended commitment to the Creedmore State Hospital of New York. The state hospital physician considered her epileptic because of convulsions, but he did not inquire into her addiction to drugs nor did he read records of previous admissions because of overdosage. The patient died of barbiturate intoxication within three days of admittance. The clinical diagnosis was schizophrenia, schizo-affective type, and the cause of death, "cerebral vascular accident resulting from epilepsy." On the issue of whether a diagnosis of epilepsy in the face of a long history of drug addictions with barbiturates was an honest error of professional judgment, the court ruled in the negative. In fact, the court's conclusion was that the proximate cause of the patient's death was "palpable negligence" and that, "patients . . . are not responsible for diagnosing their own ailments." The death was judged as obvious malpractice and negligence; the plaintiff was awarded damages for pain, suffering, and wrongful death.

The case just cited could have been avoided by more careful history-taking, but other tragic eventualities are not so easily adumbrated. Disastrous situations are sometimes foreseeable, but they are more often unexpected, even remote. For example, a patient in a Virginia mental hospital (1969), after a period of stability, was given leave to visit his wife at home. There he brutally beat her with a claw hammer. She sued the hospital and the psychiatrists for negligence on releasing the patient, but the county court denied her claim. She next turned to the U.S. District Court, but her appeal was again denied.[35] The judge, after carefully reviewing the hospital record, stated that Virginia statute authorized temporary leave for mental patients and that negligence could not be sustained. In reaching this conclusion of no negligence on the part of the hospital or its staff, the U.S. Circuit Court judge discussed the open door policy as "practiced in a great many mental institutions . . . throughout this country, agreeing that calculated risks are involved in pursuing such a policy" which include home visits. As he explained:

Briefly stated, this policy is one whereby selected mental patients, those who do not indicate a tendency or inclination to do physical harm to themselves or others, are permitted trial visits to their homes and families . . . such visits constitute excellent therapy which is necessary if there is any reasonable possibility that the patient will ever again be able to mix with society and become a useful citizen. Such a therapy program entails risks to the patient and society as a whole, but it involves a balancing of interests which is most important in the psychiatric field.[36]

Assaultive or murderous attacks by mental patients released from state hospitals bear on psychiatric prediction of dangerousness. Such cases are usually resolved in favor of psychiatrists and state hospitals since it is necessary only to apply the standard of medical knowledge and care of the area in question. In *Orman v. State of New York*,[37] a patient released from a New York state hospital committed a wanton crime by shooting a stranger ascending the stairway in the subway; the victim was rendered paraplegic. The patient, one Neely, had been hospitalized for many years as a chronic schizophrenic of catatonic type. His early record of violence apparently ceded to lobotomy. The hospital physicians judged him sufficiently improved after sixteen years of hospitalization to change his status from an involuntary to a voluntary one. The wife of the victim filed an action for damages from his wanton assault, citing negligence by the doctors in their judgment. The Court of Claims denied her claim. The plaintiff then appealed to the Appellate Division which affirmed the lower court's ruling with the statement "[T]he State is not responsible for an honest error in professional judgment by qualified doctors in releasing a patient to the community." Review of the record, the judge commented, "showed 37 home visits which were uniformly successful." In the same vein, a patient released from a California state hospital[38] brutally assaulted and killed a young woman; the victim's father brought a malpractice action against the state in Superior Court. The patient had been committed as insane following a not guilty by reason of insanity plea to a charge of attempt to murder. He remained in a hospital for the criminally insane for four years, when he was released through medical recommendation by the superintendent, certified by the court. The plaintiff, maintaining that the murderer was still insane when released, brought the case to the Court of Appeals, Fourth District, California, which confirmed the county court's dismissal. The ruling disavowed liability of the doctors for a faulty diagnosis where an opinion was given in good faith and the Government Code (Section 820.2) had "vested discretion" in the superintendent of the hospital.

On the other hand, the courts are sedulous in guarding the rights of mental patients in relation to hospital practices. A malpractice situation arose in *Morgan v. State of New York*,[39] heard in the Court of Claims, in which a woman of sixty-nine at the time of the hearing had assaulted a man, presuming him to be the judge who dismissed her damage suit against various state officials for $8 million. Obviously grandiose and delusional, the patient was committed to a state hospital and then to Matteawan, a New York state hospital for the criminally insane, after an indictment for the assault. Her claim, now for $20 million, was based on her commitment to both hospitals. She claimed that she was illegally detained at Matteawan and that, while detained, she was assaulted with the connivance of the state's psychiatrists. During the patient's nine years of hospitalizations, she claimed she was "spread-eagled" to her cot, once for two weeks, that she was tied with a strait-jacket for two and a half days without bathroom privileges, and that, as ordered by the psychiatrists, she was frequently placed in a camisole because of aggressive behavior and suicidal threats. The rationale for such treatment became an issue revolving around the correct diagnosis of Miss Morgan. Her own psychiatrist testified that she was "psychoneurotic [with] anxiety depressive and compulsive reaction," whereas the hospital doctors considered her a lifelong schizophrenic of paranoid type. The patient's expert testified:

Q. What is your opinion as to whether she is dangerous to herself or to society in general?
A. She was highly dangerous to one man because of an episode years ago. [Stabbing a man because she thought he was the judge who dismissed her $8 million claim]. . . . The neurotic pinpoints the target. . . . Having been properly handled . . . she no longer could be considered a menace to society if turned loose.

The state's psychiatrist testified that she was a schizophrenic of paranoid type for years, that

she felt . . . a political captive, a victim of vendetta . . . she stated in writing and told us, she was a victim of the massive conspiracy of a group of politicians in and out of office who put her in Matteawan to prevent her from continued legal action against the State of New York.

The court accepted the diagnosis of the state doctors but ruled that "unnecessary punishment and cruelty . . . cannot be ignored" and that "various tranquillizers and anti-depressants could be administered . . . to restrain this ailing lady in her sixties. . . ." It was apparent, the court said, "that the kind of restraints used upon the claimant were for punishment. . . ." The court awarded the plaintiff compensation for "personal injuries including pain and suffering, which naturally flow from the assaults," irrespective of the diagnosis.

The Therapeutic Transaction and Malpractice

Some elements in the psychotherapeutic relation, not present in other physician-patient transactions, are susceptible to malpractice claims. They have to do with the deep-lying feelings that pass between healer and patient. The physician or surgeon inspires trust and affection in his patients partly because of his skill and care and partly because of the projection to him by grateful patients of the mantle of parental, almost deistic, authority and power. The psychotherapist may be similarly regarded by the patient, but he works with semimagical elements in treating his patients. Thus, he or she encourages intimate revelations of buried or half-perceived patterns of emotional reactions and interprets their meaning in terms of their current responses to the therapist; this is called the transference. But transference may be a two-way street: the therapist may react to the patient on the basis of his or her buried or half-perceived emotional reactions; this is called countertransference. The latter may interfere with the treatment process unless the therapist recognizes and deals with it. One result of the transference reaction may be the patient's falling in love with the therapist. The therapist who is blind to his own unconscious drives may respond to this love on an actual basis. Such a nonresolution of the countertransference tempts a malpractice suit; it lies outside "accepted standards of psychiatric practice." The laity may misread therapeutic kindness or affectionate sympathy as an indication of the therapist's indulgence in his or her own impulses, but the therapist's restraint is a cardinal factor in dissolving the transference.

Mishandling of this delicate emotional situation may occasionally lead to claims of negligence, as in the much discussed English case of *Landau v. Werner*[40] in which a psychoanalyst undertook to dissolve his patient's love for him (the transference) by socializing with her outside the consulting room. The patient's condition deteriorated as a result of his personal attention, and she successfully brought an action for negligence, receiving £6,000 damages. The English judge regarded the doctor's conduct as a "departure from standard practice." The psychoanalyst appealed, and the lord justice, in reviewing the award of £6,000 damages for negligence, upheld the verdict, saying "his departure from standard practice was [not] justified and [was not] a reasonable development in this young science." A similar American case, but one involving more drastic social behavior, was *Zipkin v.*

Freeman (Missouri, 1969),[41] in which the psychiatrist was found negligent of mishandling the transference. The doctor induced his patient to leave her husband, to file "spurious" lawsuits against the husband, to engage in parties with other patients, one being a nude swimming party, to take trips with him, and ultimately to engage in sexual relations. Beyond that, the patient moved into an apartment above the doctor's office with her three children and permitted him to direct her financial affairs. As a result of all these activities, based originally on the patient's falling in love with the therapist, the patient-plaintiff became depressed, moody, aloof, and socially estranged from her friends. At the trial, testimony was forthcoming from another psychiatrist that all that was done to the patient could not be considered proper psychotherapy. Both the trial court and the Supreme Court of Missouri held the plaintiff was a victim of malpractice through negligence.

But in legalistic terms, "some measure of understanding and control over counter-transference is a prerequisite to defense of a malpractice action."[42] Moreover,

A distinction [must be made] between psychoanalytic interpretation and breach of duty. Psychoanalytic interpretation is not clearly excluded from the scope of permissible expert testimony . . . [except] . . . if the treatment was an expression of his [the therapist's] own motives which fall below the standard relevant to the psychiatric community . . . [and] is an expression of his own hostility. . . .

Since the advent of various forms of "mind expansion" through "activity therapy," such as encounter groups, rolfing, primal scream therapy, marathons, and "touching" therapy to encourage "self-realization," questions have arisen as to whether innovative treatment methods are actionable. The case of *Hammer v. Rosen* (New York, 1960),[43] in which Dr. Rosen physically abused his schizophrenic patient as part of his "activity" treatment, went through the County Superior Court, Appellate Division, and the Court of Appeals in New York. Although the early decisions were in favor of the doctor, the Court of Appeals indicated that beatings by the psychiatrist constituted a "prima facie case of malpractice that should be submitted to the jury."

Beyond physical mistreatment of mental patients as a basis for malpractice actions, questions arise as to the untoward results of medication, especially the phenothiazine, butyrophene, and piperazine classes —Thorazine, Haldol, Prolixin, and the like. These drugs may produce a condition known as tardive dyskinesia, which could be the subject of a malpractice suit. This dramatic and severely uncomfortable complication is featured by involuntary movements of the tongue, cheek, neck, and limbs, resulting in uncontrollable smacking movements of the tongue, grimaces, and unintelligible speech. The tongue often becomes thick, occasioning severe panic on the part of the patient who, overwhelmed by the involuntary movements, feels he is choking. The condition usually subsides with discontinuation of the drug, but it may not, leaving open the possibility of an irreversible reaction.

The incidents of tardive dyskinesia have stimulated a large literature warning psychiatrists of the danger involved. One observer remarks[44] on the "doctor's dilemma . . . with more antipsychotic medication, Tardive Dyskinesia symptoms may worsen; without it the patient may relapse to his original psychotic state." Various methods have been suggested for control of this adverse reaction,[45] but psychiatrists generally concede that there is "no satisfactory therapeutic agent" available at this time.[46] Adverse reactions to psychotropic medication used for mental illness, in combination with a consumerism that tends to be antipsychiatric, led a group in California to file a suit in the federal court (1978).[47] The suit asked for limitations on the use of antipsychotic drugs in both voluntary and involuntary committed patients. The purpose of this suit was to forestall the prescribing of psychotropic drugs which may be dangerous, may suppress freedom of thought, may be used for punishment, and are contrary to the First, Eighth, and Fourteenth amendments to the Constitution. This case, *Jamison v. Edmund Brown*, which sought to virtually wrest the use of tranquilizing drugs from physicians, was thrown out of court after argument (Fall 1978).

The California legislature had already placed stringent safeguards, which function almost as restrictions, around the use of electroshock and psychosurgery (lobotomy) in mental patients. The act, passed in 1974,[48] mandated that the patient and/or responsible guardian or relative be given a full explanation of the procedures to be carried out, the possible risks and side effects, the degree of uncertainty and hazards of the procedures, and reasonable alternative therapies, and be apprised of the fact that all appropriate modalities had been exhausted. Violation of these strictures made a physician liable to civil penalty of $10,000 for each violation, revocation of license, or both, and the possibility of a civil suit for damages.

On objections by many psychiatrists and psychiatric organizations acting as Amicus Curiae, as to the act's difficulty of implementation, a remedial bill was enacted in 1976[49] amending some of the more stringent features. It differentiated electroshock from lobotomy and removed the requirement that "all possible risks and side effects" be disclosed to the patient, substituting the requirement that "the nature, degree, duration and probability of side effects and significant risks, commonly known to the medical profession" should be explained to the patient. In addition, it laid down certain procedures safeguarding the patient, namely, observation of due process through quarterly reports to the state director of health and the local mental health directors containing full documentation of the need for electroshock treatment in each patient (written consent and examination by three psychiatrists in the case of an involuntary patient); petition and hearing within three days by the Superior Court if the patient is unable to give written consent; review by a court of capacity to give informed consent of a patient who regains competence during the treatment; prohibition of electroshock treatment for minors under twelve years of age; and provision of a "qualified committee" in each licensed facility to review all such treatments. The civil penalty for violations of the law was reduced to $5,000 per violation, but the grounds for revocation of license remained. The bill also empowered a review committee to audit such treatment given in a private office or in the patient's home. The modified act represented some improvements, but the muting of psychiatric clinical and therapeutic judgment is still effective. Dr. Rudin and Attorney Zimmerman call attention to the final provision, that treatment in private offices shall be audited by a review committee: "These requirements are significant for all medicine. They replace professionally developed peer review . . . with state-required audits."[50]

Psychiatrists' objections to the limitations imposed on electroshock treatment assumed a concrete form in 1976 through a petition submitted to the Court of Appeals in California challenging the legislative act (Welfare and Institutions Code, Sections 5000-5405), particularly the sections which laid down conditions under which electroshock and psychosurgery could be performed.[51] The petition, a class action on behalf of Jane Doe and Betty Roe, was brought by a qualified psychiatrist and was supported by Amicus Curiae briefs. The Court of Appeals, Fourth District, California, Judge Brown presiding, reviewed the entire act, finding several sections unconstitutional. Recognizing that the legislature intended electroshock and psychosurgery to be the treatment of "last resort," the court found the criterion for therapy—a "critical need for the patient's welfare"—to be "imprecise and vague"; the review system to contradict the right to privacy for competent, voluntary patients who had been given informed consent; the requirement for a "responsible relative" to give informed consent for voluntary patients to invade the right to privacy; and the failure to provide adequate hearings for competent and voluntary patients to be a denial of due process. The court also found the penalties to be assessed against physicians who did not conform to the requirements to be invalid. Since these sections were found unconstitutional, the court stated that a rewriting of the unconstitutional sections was beyond the court's function.

Abandonment

One further duty is incumbent upon the psychiatrist as with any physician, namely, the duty not to abandon a patient once he or she is engaged to treat a case. The majority of abandonment cases where negligence is claimed occurs in obstetrical or surgical practice. Among psychiatrists, abandonment is infrequently charged since their contacts with patients may come under the "special circumstances" rule, i.e., "that a physician has been employed only for a specific occasion or service . . . [and] is not liable for abandonment if he ceases treatment after performance of the specific service."[52] In general, a physician may withdraw from a case after he has given the patient reasonable notice and has secured the services of another physician, may remove himself by mutual consent with the patient, may refuse to treat at a certain time or place, or may limit his service to a specialty without incurring abandonment. This rule is based on the "implied contract" which the physician makes with the patient. As stated in the American Law Reports: "That one who engages a physician to treat his case impliedly engages him to attend throughout that illness or until his services are dispensed with or he is dismissed by the patient."[53] The courts have interpreted this contract to lie upon the foundation of "public considerations which are separable from the nature and exercise of his calling," as explained in a Georgia case (1955).[54]

Breach of this rule may result in negligence and/or malpractice suits, especially if an injury or unusual pain is proximately caused by abandonment. According to case law, to constitute abandonment, the termination of the therapeutic relationship "must have been brought about by a unilateral act of the physician."

Abandonment has occasionally been charged in a psychiatric case as witness *Brandt v. Grubin* (New Jersey, 1974),[55] in which a general practitioner treated an anxious, depressed man with Thorazine, before referring him for psychiatric evaluation. Dr. Grubin gave the patient 10 mgs. of Thorazine. On the advice of the doctor, the twenty-one-year-old patient went to a psychiatric clinic and then to a general hospital where he was again advised to seek psychiatric help. Finally, he was admitted to a psychiatric ward of a general hospital where he committed suicide, one month after Dr. Grubin's initial contact. At the trial, the plaintiffs secured a psychiatric expert whose report stated that Dr. Grubin was guilty of "departing from accepted standards of practice is not adequately assessing the seriousness of the situation. . . ." The expert further stated in his report: "Simply to give the patient a small dose of Thorazine and tell the patient to get psychiatric help was clearly inadequate for the needs of the situation." Both negligence and abandonment were charged; the trial court returned a verdict of guilty against the doctor.

The doctor appealed to the Superior Court of New Jersey (Law Division), which decided that Grubin had not abandoned his patient and granted the physician's motion for summary judgment. They ruled:

A physician who upon initial examination determines that he is incapable of helping his patient, and who refers that patient to a source of competent medical assistance, should be held liable neither for the actions of subsequent treating professionals nor for his refusal to become further involved with the case.[56]

A species of abandonment can occur wherein followup treatment of a case is inadequate or poorly advised. When an untoward result is obtained or a serious complication ensues, the physician may be charged with negligence for improper followup instructions. A Minnesota psychiatrist (1970) dismissed a patient after a period of hospital treatment with electroshock and sleep-inducing drugs. The patient had a history of periodic intemperate consumption of alcohol and medications; he had been admitted to the hospital because of a postoperative depression. After treatment, the psychiatrist dismissed the patient over the telephone without specific instructions to the family; he did, however, prescribe paraldehyde to be taken at home. Subsequently, the patient took an excess amount of paraldehyde, became stuporous, and in this state burned himself, as a result of which ten surgical grafts over his body were needed and his right elbow became nonfunctional.

An attorney to whom the family brought the malpractice suit allowed the statute of limitations to lapse, whereupon both he and the psychiatrist were sued, the first for malpractice, and the second for negligence.[57] After reviewing the case of the psychiatrist, the Supreme Court of Minnesota affirmed the verdict of negligence because the doctor "failed to warn against excessive use of drugs used by the patient at home." The higher court further declared:

[I]t is the duty of a physician or surgeon, in dealing with a case, to give the patient or his family or attendants all necessary and proper instructions as to the care and attention to be given the patient and the cautions to be observed, and a failure to give such instructions is negligence which will render him liable for resulting injury.

The possibilities for legal sanctions against neuropsychiatrists are less broad than those which face physicians and surgeons, but they are equally onerous. As with everyone who deals with difficult and sometimes intransigent human beings, the psychiatrist's best protection against claims of negligence and malpractice is the care and thoughtfulness he brings to his patients. Beyond these obvious guidelines lie larger factors related to the public's increasing criticism of medical and psychiatric examination and treatment methods. Increasing exposure to the public, through the press and other media, of all branches of medical practice has produced what amounts to an intrusion into the traditional authoritarian medical stance towards patients. Objective scrutiny confirms the fact that physicians have long worn the mantle of authoritarianism conferred by their lineage through shamans, medicine men, up to the time of modern medicine. This critical trend has yielded beneficial results in terms of democratizing what was once held to be esoteric knowledge. This diffusion of knowledge is sound, but it must be recognized that the bond between healer and patient may sometimes be tenuous and impalpable, and not readily explainable. It is in this area that the mental sciences may aid the court when it is confronted by complex problems of human interrelatedness.

Notes

1. Am. Juris., 2d ed., Vol. 61, 167, Sec. 44, op. cit.

2. Am. Juris., Vol. 61, Sec. 48, op. cit.

3. Arnold G. Regardie, *If Unprofessional Conduct Is Charged by the California Board of Medical Quality Assurance*, 127 West. J. of Med. 438 (Nov. 1977).

4. California Business and Professional Code, West Annot, Calif., Code 1974: Pocket Part. 1978, Art. 13, 2361, 2417.

5. Board of Medical Quality Assurance, Department of Consumer Affairs, California Action Report (May 1977).

6. *Ballard v. Sup. Ct. San Diego County, Calif.*, 410 P. 2d 838 (1966), 64 Calif. 2d 159; 49 Calif. Rptr. 302.

7. Ibid.: 848.

8. *People v. Bernstein*, 340 P. 2d 299 (1959).

9. *Bernstein v. Board of Medical Examiners*, 22 Calif. Rptr. 419 (1962).

10. *Morra v. State Board of Examiners of Psychologists*, 212 Kans. 103; 510 P. 2d 614 (Kans., 1973).

11. *Grannis v. Board of Medical Quality Assurance*, 96 Calif. Rptr. 863 (1971), 19 Calif. App. 3d 551.

12. *Hawkins v. Schofman*, 204 So. 2d 336; Cir. 3d Dist. Fla., 1967).

13. *Wigmore on Evidence*, Sec. 561, Vol. 2 (3d ed., 1940).

14. In Harold Radman, 366 A. 2d 477, Ct. Spec. App. (Md., 1976).

15. *Brown v. Colm*, 11 Calif. 3d 639; 114 Calif. Rptr. 128 (1974).

16. Ibid.

17. *In re Abbott*, 19 C. 3d 249; 137 Calif. Rptr. 195 (1977).

18. *In re Kindschi*, 319 P. 2d 824 (Wash., 1958).

19. William Bellamy, *Malpractice in Psychiatry*, 118 Am. Psych. 709 (1962).

20. Harold Hirsch and Edward White, *The Pathologic Anatomy of Medical Malpractice Claims. Legal Aspects of Medical Malpractice*, 6, no. 1 J. of Legal Med. 25 (Jan. 1978).

21. Vasconcellos Bill, 1976. W. & J. Code, Sec. 5325 et seq., Calif.

22. Donald J. Dawidoff, *The Malpractice of Psychiatrists*, Duke L. J. 696 (1966).

23. *Quinley v. Cocke*, 192 S.W. 2d 992 (Tenn., 1946).

24. *O'Neill v. State of New York*, 323 N.Y.S. 2d 56, 60 (1971).

25. Ibid.: 60.

26. *Lawrence v. State of New York*, 255 N.Y.S. 2d 129 (1964).

27. *Johnson v. Grant Hospital*, 286 N.E. 2d 308 (Ohio, 1972).

28. Victor Schwartz, *Civil Liability for Causing Suicide: A Synthesis of Law and Psychiatry*, 24 Vanderbilt L. Rev. 217 (Mar. 1971).

29. *O'Neill v. State of New York*.

30. *Frederic v. U.S.*, 246 F. Supp. 368 (E.D. La. 1965).

31. *Katz v. State of New York*, 248 N.Y.S. 2d 912 (1965).

32. Bellamy, op cit: 907.

33. *Meier v. Ross General Hospital*, 69 C. 2d 420, 71 Calif. Rptr. 903, 44 P. 2d 519 (1968).

34. *O'Neill v. State of New York*.

35. *Eanes v. U.S.*, 407 F. 2d 823, 4th Cir. (1969).

36. Ibid.: 824.

37. *Orman v. State of New York*, 322 N.Y.S. 2d 914 (1971).

38. *Kravitz v. State of California*, 8 Calif. App. 3d 301, 87 Calif. Rptr. 352 (1970).

39. *Morgan v. State of New York*, 319 N.Y.S. 2d 151 (1970).

40. *Landau v. Werner*, 105 Sol. Jour. 1008 (London, 1961).

41. *Zipkin v. Freeman*, 436 S.W. 2d 753 (Mo., 1969).

42. Dawidoff, op. cit.

43. *Hammer v. Rosen*, 198 N.Y.S. 2d 65 (1960).

44. *Preventing Drug-Induced Dyskinesia*, Med. World News, 76 (Feb. 6, 1978).

45. John A. Chiles, *Extrapyramidal Reactions in Adolescents Treated with High Potency Antipsychotics*, 135 Am. J. Psych. 239 (Feb. 1978).

46. Eric Caine, David Margolin, Gerald Brown, and Michael Ebert, *Giles de la Tourette Syndrome, Tardive Dyskinesia and Psychosis in an Adolescent*, 135 Am. J. Psych. 241 (Feb. 1978).

47. *Barbara Jamison et al. v. Edmund G. Brown, Jr., et. al.*, No. C 78-0445 WHO (Feb. 1978).

48. California Welfare and Institutions Code, Amendment to Sec. 5325, 5326; added Sec. 5326.3, 6326.4 and 5326.5 (1974).

49. AB 1032, Calif. Chap. 1109, Welfare and Institutions Code, Sec. 5326.2 (d).

50. Edward Rudin and Rick Zimmerman, *Psychiatric Treatment. General Implica-*

tions and Lessons from Recent Court Decisions in California, 128 West J. of Med. 459 (May 1978).

51. *Aden v. Younger,* 47 Calif. App. 3d 662 (1976).
52. Am. L. Rev., 2d 439, Sec. 3.
53. Ibid.: Sec. 460.
54. *Norton v. Hamilton,* 89 S.E. 2d 809 (Ga., 1955).
55. *Brandt v. Gruber,* 131 N.J. Super. Ct. 182: 329 A. 2d 82 (N.J., 1974).
56. Ibid., 329 A. 2d 89.
57. *Christy v. Saliterman,* 179 N.W. 2d 288 (Minn., 1970).

16

Privacy, Confidentiality, and Consent

Basic Right to Privacy

The right to privacy, although not specifically written into the Constitution, is nevertheless guaranteed to all citizens of the United States. In a case relating to the right to abortion,[1] the Supreme Court stated: "The Constitution does not explicitly mention any right to privacy. In a line of decisions, however, going back as far as ... 1891, the Court has recognized that a right of personal privacy, or a guarantee of certain areas or zones of privacy does exist under the Constitution." The opinion goes on to indicate that the Fourth, Fifth, Ninth, and Fourteenth Amendments permit an interpretation that "personal rights ... can be deemed ... implicit in the concept of ordered liberty." Indeed, the Supreme Court noted that privacy was recognized as lying "in the penumbras of the Bill of Rights." However, there are restrictions to this general statement. In a Connecticut case heard by the U.S. District Court in 1970,[2] wherein a physician claimed that the request to report a drug-dependent person to the Department of Health was unconstitutional, the court said: "There is no constitutional foundation for the cloak of confidentiality which gives a patient the privilege to exclude communications to physicians in judicial proceedings."

Further, where a criminal defendant was required to submit to a psychiatric examination, his claim that this represented an "invasion of the privilege against self-incrimination" was discussed at length in the *Harvard Law Review* (1970).[3] An examination of this type "impinges on values protected by the privilege, i.e., the right of persons

to lead private lives . . . respect for inviolability of the human personality. . . ." In a similar vein, the Supreme Judiciary of Massachusetts
ruled that a motion picture taken of patients at the Bridgewater State
Hospital, a maximum security institution, was an invasion of privacy.[4]
The producer, Frederick Wiseman, made a documentary film, *The
Titicut Follies*, after securing releases from eleven patients. The film
involved sixty-two committed patients shown in their cells, in the
shower, in the yard, and other areas. The court "enjoined the showing
of the film to the general public," but permitted its exhibition to professionals in the mental health field.

One basic consideration bearing on privacy rights is the fiduciary
(trust) relation established between a patient and his physician. The
court in *Hammond v. Aetna Insurance, Ohio* (1965)[5] stated: "[T]he
patient's privacy is no mere ethical duty upon the part of the physician;
there is a legal duty as well . . . ," that is, the physician has a trust responsibility as to information entrusted to his care. The case related
to a physician who divulged confidential material to an attorney on
the attorney's pretext that the patient intended to sue his doctor for
malpractice. The doctor, being the victim of a trick by the attorney,
was absolved from wrong-doing, but the U.S. District judge (Ohio)
reminded the physician of his "duty of undivided loyalty" to his patient. In all medicine, and especially in psychiatric and psychotherapeutic areas, privacy covering a patient's condition and utterances can
involve "an interweaving of the three ethical-legal concepts of informed consent, confidentiality and privilege."[6]

Our present concern is with the right to privacy of communication
of sensitive information given by a patient to an examining or treating
physician or psychotherapist. The law protects the privilege of such
communication between physician and patient, between priest and
penitent, and between attorney and client. The basic reason for such
privilege is to prevent the disclosure of experiences, feelings, or ideas
recited to the physician by a patient that would cause shame, disgrace,
or humiliation to the patient. This privilege belongs to the patient with
the exceptions to be noted and is statutory in thirty-six states.[7] Funda-
mentally, however, the physician-patient privilege has its roots in the
Hippocratic Oath to which all physicians subscribe. This time-honored
oath ends in these words: "All that may come to my knowledge in the
exercise of my profession or outside of my profession or in daily commerce with men, which ought not to be spread about, I will keep secret
and never reveal."

The confidentiality which the law allows thus arises out of the tradition of medicine. In this respect, the psychotherapist or treating psy-

chiatrist (this includes psychologists in the California and other states' Codes)[8] carries a great responsibility.

Physician-Patient Privilege in Court

The confidentiality which the physician-patient privilege confers is subject to many exceptions. Although given "statutory recognition," the privilege does not hold water where an accused raises the defense of insanity, or where "the evidence relating to the mental competency or sanity of an accused" is at issue and disclosure of mental tests is "in the interests of public justice." These exceptions arose in *U.S. v. Carr*,[9] a Washington, D.C., case in which the accused (Carr) claimed insanity in the stabbing death of his enamorata. The defense counsel requested a psychiatrist to examine Carr under truth serum to see if his powers of recall would improve. The expert wrote a note to the defense attorney stating that he did not think that "pentothal hypnosis would give us information we don't already have. . . . It is very likely that what would come out would be he had in fact gone to [the deceased's] sister's home with the intention of forcing [the deceased] to talk to him or else he would kill her." At the trial, the prosecutor requested that the notes be read to the jury. The trial judge permitted it on condition that the jury regard its substance as to weight of credibility. The jury convicted Carr of first degree murder.

On appeal, the defense contended that the notes fell under the physician-patient privilege; the prosecution asserted that they were needed "in the interests of public justice." The case came to the U.S. Court of Appeals Washington, D.C., Cir. (1970) where the majority opinion found "no departure from . . . acceptable trial procedure" in placing the psychiatrist's notes in evidence." Chief Judge Bazelon dissented in that the psychiatrist's notes had been read in open court for "their weight" to establish the expert's credibility. (There had been inconsistencies in the doctor's testimony at trial which he expressed in his notes.) Judge Bazelon based his conclusion of reversible error on the fact that the jury could not be expected to "consider only credibility and not the substance of a critical issue in the case—appellant's premeditation and sanity."

Besides these exceptions, numerous others have been propounded. The California Code explicates the meaning of confidential communication between physician and patient in these terms:

"A confidential communication between patient and psychotherapist," means information obtained by an examination of the patient, transmitted between a patient and his psychotherapist in the course of that relationship and in confidence . . . which . . . discloses the information to no third person other than those who are present to further the interest of the patient in the consultation, or those to whom disclosure is reasonably necessary for the transmission of the information or the accomplishment of the purpose for which the psychotherapist is consulted, and includes a diagnosis made and the advice given by the psychotherapist in the course of that relationship.[10]

The Code indicates further exceptions to the privilege, namely,

(a) When the communication is relevant to an issue tendered by the patient and others in his interest. (Section 1016).

(b) When the psychotherapist is court appointed (with a condition that privilege does apply if a lawyer needs the information whether or not to enter a plea of the defendant's mental condition);

(c) In planning a crime or tort;

(d) In the case of a deceased patient or his property;

(e) In the event of a breach of duty in the psychotherapist-patient relation;

(f) In a criminal action to determine sanity;

(g) Where the psychotherapist has reasonable cause to believe the patient is dangerous to himself or to the person or property of another;

(h) In a proceeding to establish competence;

(i) Where information is required to be reported to public employee, office or record;

(j) For a child under age sixteen or where patient has been victim of a crime;

(k) Unless psychotherapist is authorized to practice medicine or psychology.

The privilege against communicating confidential information gained by a physician in the performance of his profession in New York[11] is closely similar to that outlined for California, as it is in other states. The privilege was upheld in a New York case,[12] wherein a plaintiff who lost a suit for damages in a personal injury case appealed to the Appellate Division of the New York Supreme Court on grounds of "prejudicial conduct" by the defense attorney. The defense attorney had called a psychiatrist who had treated the plaintiff some ten years prior to testify as to a "lying problem" affecting his children. The Appellate Division considered this action improper "because it would involve disclosure of confidential information." The court ruled that counsel had engaged in "prejudicial questioning . . . [which] . . . deprived plaintiff of a fair trial."

Conversely, the New York Court of Appeals[13] denied the privilege to a defendant in a murder trial on his appeal. Originally found incompetent to stand trial, the defendant was transferred to Matteawan State Hospital for the criminally insane until certified as able to confer with counsel in his defense. At the trial where the defendant was convicted of killing his wife, the state hospital psychiatrist who had studied the case testified that the defendant was "sane and a malingerer." The defendant then sought an appeal, contending that his "physician-patient privilege was violated" when his psychiatrist testified that he was sane at the time of the homicide. The court stated: "Where insanity is asserted as a defense . . . the defendant offers evidence to show his insanity in support of his plea . . . a complete waiver is effected, and the prosecutor is then permitted to call psychiatric experts to testify regarding his sanity."

The crucial test of whether a psychiatrist or psychotherapist has an absolute privilege concerning all communications from the patient during therapy contacts was met in *In re Lifschutz* (1970).[14] In this much discussed case, Dr. Lifschutz, a psychiatrist, was subpoenaed for a deposition on a patient he had treated ten years prior to the current case in which the patient, Joseph Housek, brought suit against one John Arabian for an assault causing him "physical injuries, pain, suffering and severe mental and emotional distress." The psychiatrist refused to be deposed or to produce records on the grounds that "an absolute privilege of confidentiality is essential to the effective practice of psychotherapy." After moving through the lower courts, the Supreme Court of California agreed to hear the case because of its "far-reaching questions of constitutional law." Dr. Lifschutz had contended, after being held in contempt of court and ordered to serve in the county jail for refusal to be deposed, that his "personal constitutional right to privacy," his right to effectively practice his profession, and the constitutional right to privacy of his patients had been infringed. He also "attacked" the statute which compelled him to testify as "unconstitutionally denying him equal protection under the law" since "clergymen" are protected from revealing confidential communications from penitents.

Dr. Lifschutz's position received considerable support from the psychiatric profession, chiefly on the basis of the delicate relationship of the therapeutic transaction, as described by Guttmacher:

> [T]he patient's statements may reveal to his therapist much more than the patient intends or realizes. . . . [He] confides more utterly than anyone else in the world. He exposes to the therapist not only what his words directly express; he lays bare his entire self, his dreams, his fantasies, his sins, and his shame. . . . Most patients [find] it extremely hard to bring themselves to the point where they are willing to expose the dark recesses of their mind to the psychiatrist. . . . It would be too much to expect them to do so if they knew that all they say . . . may be revealed to the whole world from a witness stand.[15]

This passage, written in 1952, aptly expresses the personal situation of the psychotherapeutic transaction. However, in the twenty-seven years since it was penned, there has been a loosening of the taboo among the public concerning exposing the "dark recesses of the mind" in favor of acknowledging the universality of private thoughts and fantasies. In spite of these claims, the Supreme Court of California ruled that "no constitutional right enables the psychotherapist to assert an absolute privilege concerning all psychotherapeutic communications." The court decreed that communication "lost its privileged status" when the patient claims recovery in a personal injury action for "mental and emotional distress." The court recognized "the justifiable expectations of confidentiality that most individuals seeking psychotherapeutic treatment harbor" but these were waived when emotional complaints were put at issue. Finally, in denying Lifschutz' claim of "absolute privilege," the court said no "constitutional privacy rights of the psychotherapist" were violated. It should be noted at this point that California has enlarged the term "psychotherapist" to legally include school psychologists and clinical social workers, as well as, marriage, family, and child counselors (Evidence Code, Calif., Sec. 1010, 1970 amendment). Judge Tobriner, who wrote the *Lifschutz* decision, commented that "until twenty years ago no statutes dealt with privilege for psychotherapeutic communications," thus accenting the viability of psychotherapy.

Confidentiality and Public Disclosure

The Lifschutz case brought the problem of intimate disclosures in communications between psychotherapists and patients forcibly to the fore. In 1973, a New York court in *Doe v. Roe*[16] touched on this sensitive relationship by sustaining a complaint that a book written and published by a psychotherapist, virtually a "case history of the patient and her family," should be enjoined from distribution. The plaintiff-patient claimed that the "near verbatim record of the treatment was an invasion of privacy and a breach of confidence," in spite of the author's attempt to disguise the identity of the patient. The author replied to the complaint that the purpose of the book was the advancement of scientific knowledge. The court observed that the "manner of advertising contradicts" the stated purpose. It affirmed the preliminary injunction against distribution of the book as laid down by the lower court.

The author of the book brought the case to the U.S. Supreme Court on the issue of violation of First Amendment rights to freedom of speech and of the press. The subject of the book, Jane Doe, had meanwhile suffered "embarrassment, insomnia, shame and declining health" because the material had been recognized by her friends as patently from her life. The Supreme Court did not hear the case but returned it for retrial in the New York courts on the issues of consent and "disguise of the case." Judge Martin Stecher of the New York Supreme Court, New York County (1977),[17] after hearing from Jane Doe and reviewing the total situation thoroughly, enjoined a "permanent injunction from further circulation of the book" (200 copies had been sold). In ruling against the doctor-author, Judge Stecher concluded that "the physician-patient relation is contractual . . . [with] the implied promise to obey the Hippocratic Oath." He also said that "a physician's obligation of confidentiality is not absolute but must give way to the general public interest," i.e., "the scientific value" of the work, which in this case he had already ruled to be grossly inadequate.

The more immediate question of invoking the communication privilege on the witness stand, as in *Lifschutz*, aroused the American Psychiatric Association to appoint a Task Force on Confidentiality, consisting of five eminent psychiatrists, to study the subject. Their report[18] made certain recommendations, including one to the Senatorial Committee that was considering the Federal Evidence Code's Rule 504 concerning the psychotherapist-patient privilege (1974). Dr. Maurice Grossman, chairman of the task force, representing American psychiatrists through the association, pleaded for a broadening of the privilege before the Senatorial Committee. He stated that if the privilege were not strengthened in the Federal Evidence Code, "Every physician's file and mind would be unlocked about every patient's innermost fantasies, dreams, secrets and sorrows and make them available to any lawyer or prosecuting attorney for whatever righteous or unrighteous reason he may have." The fear voiced in the name of psychiatrists, concerning the evaporation of the therapist's privilge to refuse to reveal material developed during intensive psychotherapy, was stimulated by the *Lifschutz* decision. In the dramatic terms of Dr. Grossman, "the patient-litigant exception has been used repeatedly to act as a barn door opening to attack the protection of the whole record in spite of a California Supreme Court ruling that disclosure must be limited and discreet." Yet, in spite of the accepted principle that "effective psychotherapy rests on the patient's ability to unburden every thought, fantasy, feeling or wish to his therapist without restraint," the Supreme Court in *Lifschutz* "struck a highly desirable balance between protection of and flow of information needed to make litigation fair and accurate," as phrased by Louisell and Sinclair, 1971.[19]

Still, the fear of disclosure of confidential information passed from patient to psychotherapist in a public forum alarmed many therapists. The increasing requests of third parties—insurance companies and the

like—for detailed information on patients came to be viewed as a threat
to the privacy of the therapeutic transaction. Dr. Grossman, in a paper
in the *American Journal of Psychiatry* (1971),[20] called attention to
the possibility that reports going through "many unsophisticated
hands" would leak confidential information to office personnel, thence
to attorneys and others. On this point, the task force suggested ways
of safeguarding sensitive information about patients to insurance carriers, employers, governmental bureaus, computer banks, and, with an
eye to the future, national health care proposals: "That the American
Psychiatric Association adopt a position recommending its members
to refuse to channel any sensitive reports through employer agencies;
and that reports to medical directors of insurance companies be noted
'any divulgence to other parties or for other purposes will constitute
a breach of the release waiver and of medical ethics.' "[21]

Following Dr. Lifschutz' attempt to modify privilege rules in favor
of the psychotherapist as well as the patient, another California psychiatrist, Dr. George Caesar, in *Caesar v. Mountanos* (1976),[22] refused
to obey court instructions to answer questions about his patient with
whom the doctor had a psychotherapeutic relationship. He was cited
for contempt of court. On appeal to set aside the contempt sentence,
the U.S. District Court ruled that there was no absolute constitutional
protection of such communication privilege when the patient "tendered the issue of her mental condition and mental suffering" as the
result of an accident. The court based its lifting of the privilege on the
general concept that "the harm done to the cause of justice through
suppression of the truth is infinitely greater than any harm . . . done
to the physician-patient relationship."[23]

Privilege, Privacy, and Dangerousness

Dangerousness in the mentally ill has been discussed in Chapter 12
as it relates to commitment procedures. However, a patient who admits or proclaims an intent to harm another during the course of psychotherapy or during a psychiatric examination presents a distinct
problem involving confidentiality on the part of an expert. The definition of dangerousness itself varies in the various jurisdictions.[24] Some
states use the phrase "dangerous or a menace if left at large"; Minnesota defines a dangerous person as one whose "conduct might reasonably be expected to produce a clear and present danger of injury to
others"; Massachusetts speaks of "likelihood of serious harm" in its
codes for commitment of insane persons; California uses the phrase
"[one] who has threatened, attempted or inflicted physical harm upon

the person of another . . . or presents an imminent threat of substantial harm to others. . . ."[25] The real problem of the psychotherapist is whether the threat of injury to another is fact or fantasy, whether it is real or an aspect of the unfolding therapy. If the former, the responsibility of divulging this confidence is indeed awesome. And it is generally acknowledged that the psychiatrist or psychologist has no infallible dangerousness-prediction methods at his or her disposal. The real question that flows from such threats or vaporings, whichever they may be, is whether the psychotherapist has the right to so invade the patient's privacy as to repeat intentions to harm those outside the therapeutic situation. Guidelines for therapists in this precarious position have been laid down in the crucial case of *Tarasoff*.[26]

The case concerned a patient under treatment at Cowell Memorial Hospital at the University of California, at Berkeley, who confided to his therapist, Dr. Lawrence Moore, a psychologist, that he intended to kill his fiancée. The psychologist requested that the campus police detain the patient, one Poddar, but the chief of psychiatry, Dr. Harvey Powelson, countermanded the order. Subsequently, Poddar killed his fiancée, Tatiana Tarasoff. Her parents brought suit against the university, the doctors, and campus police, which was heard by the Supreme Court of California. In an amended complaint, the parents stated four causes of action: "Failure to detain a dangerous patient"; "Failure to warn on a dangerous patient"; "Abandonment of a dangerous patient"; "Breach of primary duty to patient and to the public." The court concentrated on the second cause of action, i.e., failure to warn, since "failure to bring about Poddar's confinement" was barred by governmental immunity. The defendants (the doctors and the police) contended they "owed no duty of care to Tatiana or her parents."

The reasoning of the court bears a direct relation to a psychiatrist's or psychologist's duty towards a patient and towards confidentiality. The justices first engaged the issue of "foreseeable harm," which traditionally (in common law) imposed liability "if the defendant bears some special relationship to the dangerous person or potential victim." The doctor-patient relationship satisfied this requirement. They next recognized the difficulty of predicting danger in a patient in a therapeutic contact. Their answer was "the ultimate question of resolving . . . the conflicting interests of patient and potential victim is one of social policy, not professional expertise." The court acknowledged the position of the American Psychiatric Association, representing psychiatrists generally as Amicus Curiae, that psychiatrists cannot accurately predict violence. Nevertheless, it decided that "once a therapist does in fact determine, or under applicable professional standards reasonably should have determined, that a patient poses a serious danger of violence to others, he bears a duty to exercise reasonable care to protect the foreseeable victim of that danger."

Justice Tobriner, who wrote the majority opinion, assented to the need to protect "the rights of the patient to privacy" and the consequent public importance of "safeguarding the confidential character of psychotherapeutic communication." Against this interest, the justice stated that "We must weigh the public interest in safety from violent assault." To put it more succinctly, he wrote: "The protective privilege ends where the public peril begins." The other issues discussed in the opinion, such as the immunity of the campus police and Dr. Moore and the liability of Dr. Powelson, his associates, and the University of California, are of less psychiatric import in relation to the main thrust of the opinion. The case was remanded for further proceedings.

Justice Mosk, in concurring and dissenting, made a point based on the agreed-upon fact that "psychiatric predictions of violence are inherently unreliable." He wrote:

I would restructure the rule designed by the majority to eliminate all reference to conformity to standards of the profession in predicting violence. If a psychiatrist does in fact predict violence, then a duty to warn arises. The majority's expansion of that rule will take us from the world of reality into the wonderland of clairvoyance.

In his dissent to the majority opinion, Justice Clark reviewed the provision of the Lanterman-Petris-Short Act that provided for confidentiality.[27] The provision states that "all information and records obtained in the course of providing services to either voluntary or involuntary recipients . . . shall be confidential [except to] qualified professional persons." This, he remarked, "balanced these concerns," i.e., adequate treatment, safety for society, and individual liberty, "thereby promoting effective treatment, reducing over-commitment, and ensuring greater safety for our society." Criticism of the "duty to warn" was also forthcoming from psychiatrists.

Dr. Alan Stone of the Harvard Medical School and chairman of the American Psychiatric Association's Commission on Judicial Action and Confidentiality (1976)[28] commented that "California's tort law has always been at the extreme end of the spectrum in its effort to compensate everyone for everything. . . . I hope that other states would not accept this as precedent." Dr. Jerome Beigler, chairman of the association's committee, observed that confidentiality in a therapeutic relationship is "the only thing that helps the patient. . . . the duty to warn immediately ruptures that." Both commentators agreed with Justice Clark's dissent. Beigler wrote: "Given the importance of confidentiality to the practice of psychiatry, it becomes clear the duty to warn imposed by the majority will cripple the use and effectiveness of psychiatry . . . forcing the psychiatrist to violate the patient's trust will destroy the interpersonal relationship by which treatment is effected."

Although a psychotherapist is enjoined (in California at least) to disclose potential threats of injury to a person confided by the "dangerous" patient, California courts have cautioned therapists "not to disclose a confidence unless such disclosure is necessary . . . even then he [should] do so discreetly."[29]

The general rule of "duty to warn" does not apply when the psychiatrist is aware of suicidal tendencies and does not restrain the patient from a lethal act. The courts have not extended the *Tarasoff* decision, where the danger was that of self-inflicted harm or suicide, according to a California case, *Bellah v. Greenson* (1977),[30] decided by the First Appellate District. The patient was under the care of Dr. Greenson who recorded that she was prone to suicide. Subsequently, Bellah did die of a self-administered overdose of drugs. Two years later, the parents sued the doctor for wrongful death and for failure to take measures to prevent their daughter's death. The Appellate Court considered the pertinent issue to be "whether plaintiffs have alleged facts sufficient to give rise to a duty on the part of the defendant [psychiatrist] to disclose to plaintiffs [the likelihood] of suicide . . . and whether he was under a duty to restrain [patient] from so doing." Relying on *Tarasoff*, the court ruled that "disclosure of a confidential communication . . . is not required . . . where the risk of harm is self-inflicted harm or . . . property damage."

Privilege Claimed by the Patient

That the patient is entitled to the physician-patient privilege is well known, but not infrequently an accused refuses to answer questions posed by the examining psychiatrist on grounds of invoking a privilege, i.e., his constitutional right against self-incrimination. The courts have ruled that the subject of a mental examination may remain silent, standing on the Fifth Amendment, unless the patient interposes an insanity defense which of itself waives the privilege. In *People v. Danis* (California, 1973),[31] the offender was convicted of car theft. His psychiatrist had offered material to support a diminished capacity plea because the defendant could have had no specific intent to steal in virtue of a diagnosis of personality disorder, antisocial type, with a background of deprivation and instability. The prosecution psychiatrist agreed with the diagnosis but denied diminished capacity to form an intent for the crime. On appeal, the Court of Appeal, First District, stated that the appointment of the state's psychiatrist did not violate the defendant's privilege because he "waived the Fifth Amendment by presenting his own testimony urging the diminished capacity plea." The Appeals judge affirmed the trial court's decision of no privilege when the court had kept the prosecution expert from testifying "to any statements made by the defendant."

In a plea of not guilty by reason of insanity, a defendant refused to answer psychiatrists' questions on the grounds of self-incrimination. In a New York case, *Lee v. County Court* (1972),[32] the defendant was indicted for the murder of two women two days after his release from a mental institution. Three psychiatrists who examined the defendant before the trial found him to be schizophrenic; a fourth declared him sane. The jury found the defendant guilty. On appeal, the Appellate Division ordered a new trial because the People had "not proved sanity beyond a reasonable doubt." The defendant again pleaded not guilty by reason of insanity. A new mental examination was ordered, but the defendant refused to submit, "asserting his privilege against self-incrimination." However, the court ordered that "the defense counsel and district attorney could be present at the examination . . . and that if this defendant shall refuse to answer questions deemed pertinent by the designated psychiatrist," the court would strike the defendant's defense of insanity. The defendant again refused. His plea was stricken, and the whole issue came before the Court of Appeals, which soberly observed that the questions raised did not "lend themselves to facile solutions."

The issue before the court was precisely whether, during examination by psychiatrists, the defendant should answer questions about his conduct during the crime, thus destroying his privilege against self-incrimination. This situation sometimes occurs when an expert examiner is attempting to understand the accused's mental state at the time of the crime. The psychiatrist is usually prevented from testifying to any material that might touch on the guilt or innocence of the defendant; he can testify only "on the facts which formed the basis of his medical opinion as to sanity," as the New York court ruled. As a practical matter, an examiner cannot, in some cases, form an adequate opinion without going into the facts surrounding a crime. At any rate, the Court of Appeals ruled that the defendant had "waived his privilege" when he interposed an insanity defense.

Another concern to psychiatrists in *Lee* decided by this court was the right of the defendant to have his counsel present at the examination. The dissenting Chief Judge Fuld and Judge Brietel raised several points in their opinions in this regard. Judge Brietel noted that the refusal to cooperate with examining doctors may itself be "evidence of insanity just as much as it may be evidence of feigned insanity." Judge Fuld brought up the need not only to have counsel present at the examination, but also to benefit from the attorney's advice in answering questions. As one judge put it, "Questions, . . . seemingly innocuous . . . can be aimed at eliciting the most dangerous responses. Without benefit of counsel to advise him, it is quite likely that the accused will unknowingly provide the prosecution with sufficient evidence to . . . defeat his defense of insanity."

The rules of evidence govern whether an accused or the psychiatrist shall claim self-privilege. It will be recalled in *Lifschutz* that the doctor contended that the Constitution granted him an absolute right to refuse to disclose information about a patient for reasons of his own. This claim was rejected. The court in that case made the pertinent observation that the "depth and intimacy of the patient's revelations" were significant rather than the "psychotherapist's own deep involvement in the treatment." In other words, if the patient does not claim the privilege of confidential communication, the physician cannot assert it. It is also the rule that where a psychotherapist or psychiatrist is appointed by the court, i.e., an examining physician as opposed to a treating doctor, no privilege obtains since a "court-appointed [doctor] does not create a confidential relationship."[33] If the court appointment is made on the request of the defendant's lawyer in order to give him information whether to "enter an insanity plea or . . . a defense based on mental or emotional condition," the privilege is restored.[34]

Prerogatives and Obligations of the Expert

The rules of evidence restrict psychiatric testimony to utterances made by the patient and observations of his or her behavior, gestures, and demeanor. Generally, reports of relatives or friends fall under the hearsay rule unless admitted as evidence. However, during an examination of an accused or a plaintiff, the expert may consult hospital records made by himself or other doctors, reports of their examinations, school records, psychologic reports, and even the result of interviews with relatives and friends or the police to help form this opinion. For example, the American Law Institute's Model Penal Code[35] recommends that in a psychiatric examination, "any method may be employed which is accepted by the medical profession for the examination of those alleged to be suffering from mental disease or defect." This was the basis for an appeal from a murder conviction in New York where a defendant had made a plea of not guilty by reason of insanity (*People v. Sugden*, 1974).[36] A youth of twenty murdered a boy of thirteen, one of his "gang," hoping in the judge's words "to elevate his status as a criminal . . . [with] a test run to see if he had the professional capacity" to kill. The defendant appealed on the basis that the prosecution psychiatrist, Dr. Zoltan, had based his opinion of sanity, in part, on an out-of-court statement by a witness, one of the group present at the time of the crime. In addition, in forming his opinion Dr. Zoltan had used a psychologist's report of the defendant when he was seven years old, medical reports of other physicians, the defendant's written confession, and written statements of four persons involved in the crime. The expert had examined the defendant for three hours. In overruling the issue of hearsay evidence as part of the psychiatrist's testimony, Chief Judge Brietel agreed that at one "time in this state, the court prohibited an expert from expressing an opinion based on material not in evidence."

The examining psychiatrist is handicapped when he has to rely on information given only by the defendant; the history of his background and precrime behavior is often of decisive help. The court recognized this fact in a recent New York case (1974),[37] *People v. Stone*, when Dr. Jaenicke, a state psychiatrist, was permitted to develop his opinion on the basis of a total of twelve interviews with the defendant, police physicians who dealt with the accused, and friends. Dr. Jaenicke, in finding defendant Stone sane, explained that he "did not want to isolate the individual from the rest of the people who knew him." In his testimony, he said he used information so gathered, ordinarily considered hearsay, to "crystallize and confirm" his opinion after the examination. Similarly, the Court of Appeals, in *Sugden* agreed to this procedure. It affirmed the trial court's permission to have Dr. Zoltan testify as to information obtained from sources other than the defendant, but "only as to its weight, not admissibility."

All physicians are obligated to act in good faith towards their patients.[38] Failure to do so opens the possibility of a charge of fraud and deceit. Good faith is defined as disclosure to the patient of the "medical condition, the possibilities of cure, the risks involved in a given treatment," and the like. This legal principle brings up the question of informed consent. Justice Mosk of the California Supreme Court developed the principles of good faith and informed consent in *Cobbs v. Grant* (1972).[39] The case involved a complex surgical situation in which the plaintiff sued for malpractice. During a gastric operation, the splenic vessels had been nicked, necessitating removal of the spleen. The patient brought an action for malpractice and battery based on negligence and lack of consent for the splenectomy. The preliminary consent had been for the surgery of a stomach ulcer; the splenic hemorrhage was an added complication. The trial court found for the plaintiff. On appeal by the surgeon, Justice Mosk's analysis, conceding it was a "close case," ruled out battery and agreed that negligence had not been proven. In reversing the finding against the doctor, the judge recognized that the complication could not have been foretold. However, he stated that a "physician's obligation is the reasonable disclosure of choices, inherent dangers [in proposed surgery], and potential complications."

The general rule of "good faith" obtains for oral as well as written communications about patients. Such reports should not expose the patient to public ridicule or humiliation which might result from future court or other public appearances. A Utah case illustrates this type of unforeseen psychiatric complication. In *Berry v. Moench* (1958),[40] a psychiatrist treated with electroshock therapy and psychotherapy a young man whom he had diagnosed as a manic depressive psychosis in a psychopathic personality. A second psychiatrist in another city who was counseling a relative of the patient's fianceé requested a report from his colleague concerning the patient. The first doctor complied but added allegedly "false and derogatory information" to an account of the diagnosis and treatment. The patient-plaintiff claimed damages for "libel and defamation." The report contained a description of the patient's "psychopathic" behavior—his card playing, his refusal to pay the therapist's fee, his extravagance in buying expensive cars, and his general indolence and involvement in "constant trouble." When the letter fell into the plaintiff's hands, he married his fianceé and immediately brought suit against the doctor. Upon learning the contents of the letter, the bride's family promptly disowned her. The plaintiff won his suit when the letter was revealed in court.

The psychiatrist then appealed, basing his contention on a "conditional privilege" in that he was communicating with a colleague. The Utah Supreme Court felt this was a situation wherein "reasonable minds might differ" and remanded the case back to the trial court for a new trial, ruling that a "conditional or qualified privilege . . . must be done in good faith and fairly" and then only as to "limited information."

Informed Consent

The doctrine of informed consent rests on the right to privacy, the "right to be left alone," and the corollary right not to have a "doctor substitute his own judgment" for that of the patient. The privilege of choosing or rejecting one's own treatment, unless forbidden by a "compelling state interest," is and has been recognized in law.[41] A California case brought this issue to the fore in *People v. Privitera* (1977)[42] wherein a doctor asserted that the prohibition against Laetrile was an unconstitutional invasion of the cancer victim's rights. Laetrile is an alleged cancer-curing drug which has been in controversy for some time; claims of its effectiveness have been negated by the medical profession but are supported by a few physicians and a large segment of the population. In this case, Dr. James R. Privitera contended that the patient had "the right to control one's body . . . and to determine what should be done with his own body." The court agreed with the appellant that the rights of patients and the doctor's duty to obtain consent for medical or surgical treatment are embedded in Anglo-American law for all branches of medical practice. The court added, apparently in consideration of the medical establishment's refusal to recommend Laetrile for cancer patients, "the right [of a patient] is not restricted to the wise; it includes the foolish refusal of medical treatment."

The urgency of applying informed consent in psychiatric practice surfaced during the last four decades with the introduction of drastic treatment methods—insulin shock therapy, electroshock therapy, psychotropic drugs, and psychosurgery. In contrast to other physicians, the psychiatrist is in a special position in that the nature of mental illness does not always permit the patient to make an "intelligent decision" as to whether or not to submit to the doctor's proposed course of treatment. Furthermore, it might be "ill-advised" to seek consent from a disturbed person who may become increasingly anxious or depressed over the proposed treatment, particularly if the possibility of injury is discussed. In *Lester v. Aetna Casualty Company* (Louisiana 1957),[43] a patient claimed malpractice against a psychiatrist for injuries sustained as a result of electroshock therapy. The U.S. Court of Appeals held it was not prejudicial error where the jury was instructed that it was "commonly accepted and proper practice among qualified psychiatrists . . . not to disclose the possibilities [of injury] . . . and that it was in the best interest of the patient that the matter be handled in such fashion." In *Lester*, the psychiatrist was careful to explain that it would be "unwise and unsafe to require him [the patient] to undergo the strain of discussing . . . the probable hazards of the treatment." On review of the patient's appeal, the U.S. District Court upheld the Louisiana court's dismissal of the malpractice suit in favor of the doctor.

Before anectine was utilized (a drug which "softens" the force of the convulsion on the muscular-skeleton system), the severity of shock treatment with its attendant fractures and dislocations in a sense forced informed consent to the fore. For example, in *Mitchell v. Robinson* (1951)[44] Dr. Jack DeMott and G. Wilse Robinson treated a "severe emotional illness" in a thirty-five-year-old man with the the new insulin "sub-coma" treatment alternating with electroshock. The patient developed compression fractures of three vertebrae. In the malpractice suit, the defendant doctors asked for a directed verdict since there was no "expert testimony to show that . . . the therapy . . . failed to conform to the required standards of an ordinarily careful and prudent neurologist or psychiatrist in the community." A judgment of malpractice was obtained by the plaintiff, and the doctors took an appeal to the Supreme Court of Missouri. This court reviewed the situation in extenso, citing cases of this type occurring in the late 1950s. Their discussion centered on the "really meritorious question" of whether "the doctors were under a duty to inform the plaintiff that one of the hazards of insulin treatment is fracture of the bones. . . ." Their answer was that "the doctor owes a duty to his patient to make reasonable disclosure of all significant facts . . . [including] the more probable consequences and difficulties inherent in the proposed operation." They agreed with the general proposition that a doctor "who fails to perform this duty is guilty of malpractice."

The need for testimony regarding community medical standards where doctors are accused of malpractice negligence, an issue in *Mitchell*, again arose in a Missouri case, *Aiken v. Clary* (1965).[45] Here, a patient diagnosed as paranoid schizophrenic was treated with insulin shock therapy and as a result "lapsed into a coma and suffered organic brain damage, resulting in total disability." A malpractice suit based on negligence was entered in a trial court with a jury verdict for the defendant-doctor. The patient-plaintiff appealed to the Supreme Court of Missouri; its review turned on the question developed in *Mitchell*, i.e., whether expert testimony was required to explain the community standards of reasonable care in treating the patient. This had not been done in *Mitchell*. In the current case under consideration, the Supreme Court decided that matters such as the dangers of prolonged coma, paralysis, epilepsy, or even death which might follow insulin coma therapy were "beyond the common knowledge and experience of laymen." The case was reversed, and the court noted that physicians have a clear duty to inform patients of *all* the complications and dangers that might ensue from any given treatment.

The landmark case covering informed consent in involuntarily committed patients is *Kaimowitz v. Michigan Department of Mental Health* (1973).[46] A John Doe, charged with the murder and rape of a student nurse in a Michigan state hospital, had been civilly committed as a criminal sexual psychopath under a law, since repealed. After seventeen years in the state hospital, the inmate-patient was included in an experimental study of criminal psychopaths aimed at devising methods of violence control. The research project had been duly authorized to the Lafayette Clinic in Detroit. A well-prepared plan had been developed which envisaged brain surgery, using depth electrodes in the limbic area to determine the suitability of destroying that part of the brain thought to control "rage and antisocial" conduct. A writ of habeas corpus to release John Doe, one of the proposed subjects, was entered. The proposed psychosurgery was claimed to be "cruel and unusual punishment" in contradiction to the Eighth Amendment. John Doe was released by the court, the issue being "constitutionality of detention of John Doe and adequacy of informed consent for an experimental surgical procedure on the brain." A panel of three judges heard the case, and the arguments of the opponents and proponents of psychosurgery for violent behavior were presented. After a prolonged hearing with testimony from leading neurosurgeons, psychiatrists, neuroscience specialists, and other experts, the judges deciding on the constitutionality of the proposed surgery said: "Intrusion into one's intellect, when one is involuntarily detained and subject to the control of institutional authorities, is an intrusion into one's constitutionally protected right of privacy. . . ." In relation to the "informed consent" problem for involuntarily committed patients, they ruled:

When the state of medical knowledge develops to the extent that the type of psychosurgical intervention proposed here becomes an accepted neurosurgical procedure and is no longer experimental, it is possible, with appropriate review mechanisms, that involuntarily detained mental patients could consent to such an operation . . . that an involuntarily detained mental patient today can give adequate consent to accepted neurosurgical procedures.

The Lafayette Clinic pilot study was discontinued after the *Kaimowitz* decision, but the controversy remains, mainly on a theoretical level. One of the questions is whether amygdalotomy (destruction of impairment of a nucleus near the thalmus, removal of which releases violent rage reactions in experimental animals) is legal or ethical, even with informed consent. A thorough study by Samuel Shuman of Wayne State University, Department of Law and Psychiatry, deals in depth with the ethical and legal problems of psychosurgery.[47] In attempting to find whether legal approval of psychosurgery when properly safeguarded matches medical certification of such procedures, Shuman felt that medical opinion against the implantation of electrodes in the brain was "guided by emotion more than scientific reasoning."

One reason why medical science hesitates to approve of psychosurgery for misbehavior patterns is that the question of whether the brain tissue in the part to be excised or chemically altered is diseased or normal is still unresolved. Explanations of the "cause" of violence are too obscure to assure that psychosurgery will attain the wished-for-result. Informed consent for such treatment rests on a truly tenuous base. In any event, the political and legal implication of "scientific manipulation" of behavior through psychosurgery is beyond our current interest.

There are many areas in which consumer interests conflict with medical innovations in treatment. In such situations, the courts may be called upon to adjudicate the conflicts evoked. It is expected that, in the future, consumer groups that wish to protect the rights of potential mental patients will bring more of these problems to the courts. As a result, legislative and administrative regulations have increased, and will increase, bringing further control to medical practice. In a sense, this activity already revolutionized medical and psychiatric practice during the past decade. Disturbing as this trend may be, it must be realized that slow and inexorable changes are inevitable in a world where the interdependence of all of us dictates control measures in social life. Many of these changes will come about through legal decisions, for the law is designed, in part, to make final judgments on technological acts that affect the public. Such an evolution is especially significant for psychiatry because this discipline will, as Adolf Meyer, one of America's pioneer psychiatrists, predicted in 1928,[48] become "assimilated in the common sense of tomorrow."

Notes

1. *Roe v. Wade*, 410 U.S. 113:93 (1973).

2. *Felber v. Foote*, Commissioner Dept. of Health, Conn. 321 F. Supp. 85 Dis. Conn. Cir. (1970).

3. Note: *Requiring a Criminal Defendant to Submit to a Government Psychiatric Expert: An Invasion of the Privilege Against Self Incrimination.* 83 Harv. L. Rev. 648 (1970).

4. *Commonwealth v. Wiseman*, 249 N.E. 2d 610 (Mass., 1969).

5. *Hammond v. Aetna Insurance Company*, 243 F. Supp. 793 (Ohio, 1965).

6. Robert L. Sadoff, *Informed Consent, Confidentiality and Privilege in Psychology and the Law*, 2, no. 2 Bull. Am. Acad. of Psych. and the Law 101 (June 1974).

7. Robert J. Joling, *Informed Consent, Confidentiality and Privilege in Psychology Legal Implications*, 2, no. 2 Bull. Am. Acad. of Psych. and the L. 107 (June 1974).

8. California Evidence Code, Art. 7, Sec. 1072 (1967).

9. *U.S. v. Carr*, 437 F. 2d 662 (D.C. Cir. Ct., 1970).

10. California Evidence Code, Art. 7, Sec. 1010-1028 (1967).

11. New York Civil Procedure Rules, Art. 45, Sec. 4504.

12. *Gorman v. Goldman*, 321 N.Y. Supp. 2d 296.

13. *People of New York v. Abdul Karim-Al Kanani*, 307 N.E. 2d 43, N.Y. Ct. App. (1973).

14. *In re Joseph Lifschutz*, Calif. Sup. Ct., 85 Calif., Rptr. 829, 467 P. 2d 557 (1970).

15. Manfred Guttmacher and Henry Weihofen, *Psychiatry and the Law*: 272.

16. *Doe v. Roe*, 345 N.Y. Supp. 2d 560 (1973), N.Y. Sup. Ct. App. Div., 1st Dept. (1973).

17. *Doe v. Roe*, 400 N.Y. Supp. 2d 668 (1977).

18. Task Force Report, no. 9, Confidentiality and Third Parties, 23 Am. Psych. An., Washington, D.C. (1975).

19. David W. Louisell and Kent Sinclair, *Foreword: Supreme Court of California, 1969-1970*, 59 Calif. L. Rev. 30 (Jan. 1971).

20. Maurice Grossman, *Insurance Reports as a Threat to Confidentiality*, 128 Am. J. Psych. 96 (July 1971).

21. Task Force Report, no. 9: 53.

22. *Caesar v. Mountanos*, 542 F. 2d 1064 Cir., 9th Cir. (1976).

23. Quotation in: Elyce Z. Ferster, *Confidential and Privileged Communications*: 153, in *Readings in Law and Psychiatry* by Allen, Ferster and Rubin, Johns Hopkins Press, Baltimore (1968 ed.).

24. Quoted in Alexander Brooks, op. cit.: 677.

25. California Welfare and Institutions Code, Art. 6, Sec. 5300 et seq. (1967).

26. *Tarasoff v. Regents, University of California*, 551 P. 2d 334 (1976).

27. California Welfare and Institutions Code, Sec. 5328.

28. *The Tarasoff Decision*, Psych. News 1 *Am. Psych. A.* (Aug. 6, 1976).

29. B. Witkin, California Evidence, 2d 1977, Supp. Sec. 861.

30. *Bellah v. Greenson*, Sup. Ct. 463051, Calif. 1st App. Dist. Div. 2 (Oct. 1977).

31. *People v. Danis*, 31 C.A. 3d 782 (Calif. 1973).
32. *Lee v. County Court, Erie County*, 318 N.Y.S. 2d 705 (1972).
33. California Evidence Code, Sec. 993.
34. California Evidence Code, Sec. 1017.
35. American Law Institute, Model Penal Code, Art. 4, Sec. 4.05 (1961).
36. *People v. Sugden*, 363 N.Y.S. 2d 923 (1974).
37. *People v. Stone*, N.Y.S. 737 (1974).
38. Am. Juris., 2d 61 Sec. 99 (1872).
39. *Cobbs v. Grant*, 104 Calif. Rptr. 505 (1972).
40. *Berry v. Moench*, 331 P. 2d 814, Utah Sup. Ct. (1958).
41. 79 Am. L. Rev. 2d 1028.
42. *People v. Privitera*, 74 C.A. 3d 836 (1977).
43. *Lester v. Aetna Casualty*, 240 F. 2d 676, Cir., 5th Dist. (La., 1957).
44. *Mitchell v. Robinson*, 334 S.W. 2d 11 (Mo., 1960).
45. *Aiken v. Clary*, 396 S.W. 2d 668 (Mo., 1965).
46. *Kaimowitz v. Michigan Department of Mental Health*, Unreported: Cir. Ct., Wayne Co., Mich., 1973, reprinted in Brooks, op. cit.: 902.
47. Samuel I. Shuman, *Psychosurgery and the Medical Control of Violence*, Wayne State U. Press, Detroit (1977).
48. Adolf Meyer, *The "Complaint" As the Center of Genetic-Dynamic and Noso-logical Teaching in Psychiatry*, 199 New England J. of Med. (1928).

Landmark Cases of Forensic Psychiatric Interest

Section I: Commitment

1. *In involuntary civil commitments, proof must be beyond reasonable doubt rather than preponderance of the evidence.*

In re Ballay, 482 F. 2d 648 (D.C. Cir., 1973), 157 U.S. App. D.C. 59

Petition for commitment to a mental hospital of allegedly mentally ill person; trial court ordered commitment. *Although subsequently discharged*, he appealed. Commitment reversed on appeal, holding: (1) the issue was not moot because of the discharge; and (2) proof of mental illness and dangerousness in involuntary civil commitment proceedings must be beyond a reasonable doubt rather than by a preponderance of the evidence.

2. *Involuntary civil commitment, following criminal insane confinement, may only be had with hearing and right to trial by jury.*

Baxstrom v. Herold, 383 U.S. 107; 86 S. Ct. 760 (1960) 15 L.Ed.2d 620

Petitioner, while a prisoner, was certified insane by a prison physician and transferred to a state institution under the jurisdiction of the New York Department of Corrections (Dannemora). When his sentence expired, director of institutions filed a petition requesting he be civilly committed. Administrator determined ex-parte that petitioner was not suited for care in a civil hospital; he remained at the state institution for mentally ill prisoners. The state court dismissed his Writ of Habeas Corpus and request for transfer to civil hospital. On appeal, the U.S. Supreme Court (Warren, Ch.J.) held: Petitioner had been denied equal protection of the law by the statutory procedure by which he was committed at the expiration of a prison sentence without the jury review available to all other persons civilly committed in New York and by his commitment to an institution maintained by the Department of Corrections beyond the expiration of his prison term without the judicial determination that he is dangerously mentally ill.

3. *Commitment of defendant found not guilty by reason of insanity requires hearing similar to civil commitment.*

Bolton v. Harris, 395 F. 2d 642 (D.C. Cir., 1968), 130 U.S. App. D.C. 1

Appellant attacks a District of Columbia statute which makes commitment mandatory after a voluntary plea of not guilty by reason of insanity. Court held on appeal: Persons found not guilty by reason of insanity must be given a judicial hearing with procedures substantially similar to civil commitment proceedings. After any commitment, a patient is entitled to periodic examinations by the hospital staff and has a right to be examined by an outside psychiatrist, as to present mental capacity.

4. *Recommitment unconstitutional without hearing.*

Dixon v. Attorney General of Pennsylvania, 325 F. Supp. 966 (M.D. Pa., 1971)

Appellant acquitted by reason of insanity; committed to Farview State Hospital for criminally insane. Class action brought challenging Pennsylvania statutes re: commitment of mentally disabled persons. Biggs, J. (of Federal District Court, following *Baxtrom*) held: Pennsylvania Mental Health Act unconstitutional when the defendant recommitted by "paper notation" approved by the superintendent without hearing as to present mental condition of patient. Also, appellate court noted no "alternative facility" for offenders acquitted NGRI after involuntary commitment. Judge Biggs ordered the release of all patients from Farview when sentences expired.

5. *Adequate treatment of involuntarily committed person.*

Rouse v. Cameron, 373 F. 2d 451 (D.C. Cir., 1966)

Petitioner was involuntarily committed to St. Elizabeth's Hospital, on being acquitted of an offense by reason of insanity, and given group and milieu therapy. Court of Appeals held: One involuntarily committed because acquitted of offense by reason of insanity has a constitutional right to treatment. Hospital need not show that the treatment will cure or improve him, but only that there is a bona fide effort to do so. Hospital must determine whether treatment is suitable for specific patient.

6. *Patients involuntarily committed constitutionally require treatment adequate to their needs.*

Wyatt v. Stickney, 325 F. Supp. 781 (M.D. Ala, 1971) and 344 F. Supp. 373 (M.D. Ala, 1972)

Class action by guardians of patients confined in Alabama state hospital attacking a program of treatment in use at the hospital resulting in a "unit-team" approach. Court held: When patients are involuntarily committed to state mental hospital for treatment purposes, they have a constitutional right to receive such individual treatment as will give each of them a realistic opportunity to be cured or to improve his or her mental condition. Court found the program of treatment at the Alabama state hospital to be scientifically and medically inadequate and deprived the patients of their constitutional rights (but reserved a ruling thus affording state officials an opportunity to promulgate and implement proper standards).

7. *Mentally retarded patients involuntarily committed have a constitutional right to treatment supervised by the courts.*

Wyatt v. Alderholt, 530 F. 2d 1305 (5th Cir., 1974)

A class action against the Alabama State Commission of Mental Health alleged that the state hospital designed to habilitate the mentally retarded operated in a constitutionally impermissible fashion. Held: The constitution grants persons civilly committed to state hospitals a right to treatment. The right to treatment could be implemented through judicially controlled and fixed standards.

8. *Continued retention in state hospital when not dangerous is unconstitutional. Superintendent and associates assessed compensatory and punitive damages.*

Donaldson v. O'Connor, 493 F. 2d 507 (5th Cir., 1974)
O'Connor v. Donaldson, 422 U.S. 563; 95 S. Ct. 2486 (1975)

Plaintiff, who was confined almost fifteen years as a mental patient in a Florida state hospital, brought this action for damages under 42 U.S.C. Section 1982, against the hospital's superintendent and other staff members alleging that they had intentionally and maliciously deprived him of his constitutional rights to liberty. The evidence showed that plaintiff, whose frequent requests for release had been rejected by hospital staff, notwithstanding testimony by responsible persons that they would care for him if necessary, was dangerous neither to himself nor to others, and if mentally ill had not received treatment. The superintendent's primary defense was that he acted in good faith, since state law (which he believed valid) authorized custodial confinement of the sick. The jury found for plaintiff and awarded compensatory and punitive damages. The Court of Appeal affirmed.

The U.S. Supreme Court vacated the judgment and remanded. Stewart, J., expressing the unanimous opinion of the Court held: (1) a state cannot constitutionally confine in a mental hospital, without more, a nondangerous individual who is capable of surviving safely in freedom by himself or with the help of willing and responsible family members or friends, (2) the Court of Appeals must consider, in light of this decision on qualified immunity possessed by state officials under 42 U.S.C. Section 1983, whether the trial judge's failure to instruct with respect to the superintendent's claimed reliance on state law rendered inadequate the instructions on compensatory and punitive damages.

9. *Due process safeguards provided for mentally ill persons held in involuntary detention.*

Lessard v. Schmidt, 340 F. Supp. 1078 (E.D. Wis., 1972)

Class action brought in behalf of petitioner and other persons eighteen years and older who are being held involuntarily pursuant to any emergency, temporary, or permanent commitment provisions of the Wisconsin involuntary commitment statute. Federal court held: (1) it failed to require effective and timely notice of "charges" justifying detention; (2) it failed to notify of right to trial by jury; (3) it permitted detention longer than forty-eight hours without a hearing on probable cause; (4) it permitted detention of more than two weeks without a full hearing on the necessity of commitment; (5) it permitted commitment based on a hearing in which the person charged was not represented by adversary counsel; (6) it admitted hearsay evidence; (7) it denied the privilege against self-incrimination; (8) it did not require proof of dangerous or mental illness beyond a reasonable doubt; and (9) it failed to provide least restrictive alternative.

10. *Civil commitment of juvenile required constitutional safeguards.*

Kremens v. Bartley, 431 U.S. 119; 97 S. Ct. 1709 (1977)

Appellees, five mentally ill individuals who were between the ages fifteen and eighteen, brought this action to challenge the constitutionality of a Pennsylvania statute governing the voluntary admission and commitment to a state mental hospital, which provided that juveniles might be admitted upon a parent's application, but were free to withdraw only with consent of the parent admitting them.

Appellees also sought to represent a class consisting of all those under the age of eighteen. District Court held provisions violative of due process although after commencement of the action, regulations were promulgated to substantially increase procedural safeguards afforded juveniles. (After District Court's decision, a new Pennsylvania statute was enacted repealing provisions held to be unconstitutional.) Held, also, appellees did represent the class.

U.S. Supreme Court vacated and remanded for reconsideration, held: (Rehnquist, J.) The new statute, which provided that a juvenile between the ages of fourteen and eighteen may voluntarily commit himself (substantially as the adult procedure), but his parents could not commit him, rendered the case moot as to the named plaintiff.

11. *Offender committed as incompetent to stand trial must be treated to prepare for release.*

Nason v. Supt. of Bridgewater State Hospital, 353 Mass. 774; 233 N.E. 2d 908 (1968)

Nason, who had been indicted for murder but never tried, because he was committed to a state mental hospital as mentally incompetent to stand trial, sought Habeas Corpus. (Earlier the Massachusetts Supreme Court at 351 Mass. 94, 98, 217 N.E. 2d 733, held that the court could not order Nason to have proper treatment.) Now, Supreme Court of Massachusetts held: Where patient, involuntarily committed, had received only inadequate treatment in a state hospital with a view to prepare the patient for release, the court ordered medical treatment to be set up immediately to prepare for eventual release; remanded to trial court to supervise that program.

12. *A juvenile has constitutional rights to due process and procedural safeguards.*

In re Gault, 387 U.S. 1; 87 S. Ct. 1428 (1967)

Juvenile Court of Arizona committed a fifteen-year-old boy to State Industrial School, as a juvenile delinquent, for a period of his minority, unless
sooner discharged by due process of law, after the boy was taken into custody by the county sheriff without notice to his parents, for making an
obscene telephone call. Petition which was filed on the hearing day, and
not served on or shown to the boy or his parents, makes no reference to
the factual basis for the judicial action, stating only the boy was a delinquent minor; the complainant was not present at the hearing. The parents'
petition for the habeas corpus was dismissed; affirmed by the Arizona Supreme Court.

On appeal, the U.S. Supreme Court reversed. Fortas, J., expressing the
views of five justices, held that the juvenile was denied due process of law
because juvenile delinquency proceedings which may lead to commitment
in a state institution must measure up to the essentials of due process and
fair treatment, including: (1) written notice of the specific charge or factual
allegations, given to the juvenile and his parents or guardian sufficiently in
advance of the hearing to permit preparation; (2) notification to the child
and his parents of the juvenile's right to be represented by counsel retained
by them or appointed; (3) application of the constitutional privilege against
self-incrimination; and (4) absent a valid confession. . . . opportunity for
cross-examination in accordance with constitutional requirements.

13. *Experimental psychosurgery on involuntarily committed insane person:
alleged cruel and unusual punishment and lack of consent.*

Kaimowitz v. Michigan Dept. of Mental Health, No. 73-19434-AW Mich.
Cir. Ct., Wayne Co., July 10, 1973, unreported, but text available in 1 Mental Disability Law Rptr. 147 (1976)

Proposed study (1972) of medical treatment and surgery (depth electrodes
for amygdalotomy) to control violence in experimental subjects.

Under that, the initial subject selected was a thirty-six-year-old male, confined to a state institution for criminally insane under the criminal sexual
psychopath law, having raped and killed a young nurse while an involuntarily committed patient in a state hospital. The patient has been treated with
electroshock therapy; he had a history of hyperactivity as a child and a
possible measles encephalitis.

Before experimental surgery was done, Attorney Kaimowitz, a fellow patient, representing the Medical Committee for Human Rights, brought suit
to release the selected subject alleging: (1) illegal detention in the state hospital under a repealed statute; (2) lack of fully informed consent of risks inherent in research operation; (3) lack of consultation with parents; and
(4) the state legislature had not been fully informed that psychosurgery was
contemplated when research grant was submitted. (Also raised were doubts
about the scientific validity of the research.)

Issues raised at trial: (1) If the state can compel a committed patient to undergo therapy, can the state command submission to psychosurgery? (2) Is there duress when such patient gives knowledgeable consent? (3) Is confinement so inherently coercive that a committed patient can never give a knowledgeable consent, as the institutional physician-managers can impose sanctions at their whim or discretion?

The three-judge trial court determined that it was a denial of due process and was illegal detention because the criminal psychopath law was unconstitutional; and he was released.

The judicial panel decided that when the experimental operation had been validated scientifically, it might then be tried with due safeguards and consent.

14. *Recommitment (in Wisconsin) of sexual deviate after conviction for treatment in a prison (sex deviate facility) must have evidentiary hearing.*

Humphrey v. Cady, 405 U.S. 504; 92 S. Ct. 1048 (1972)

Petitioner was convicted in Wisconsin of contributing to the delinquency of a minor, a misdemeanor, punishable by a maximum of one-year sentence. Under another statute, in lieu of sentence, he was committed to the "sex deviate facility" for a potentially indefinite period, allowing the court to consider whether the crime was "probably motivated by a desire for sexual excitement," and on such finding may commit the criminal for a social, physical, and mental examination. If there is a recommendation for treatment, the court must hold an evidentiary hearing on the need for treatment, and if such need is found, must commit for treatment in lieu of sentence for a period equal to the maximum sentence for the crime, renewable at five-year intervals if he is a danger to the public. After one year, court ordered recommitment; defendant's counsel argued this would be second punishment for a single offense, hence violation of constitutional rights. Writ of Habeas Corpus dismissed by Wisconsin Supreme Court.

He petitioned U.S. District Court (8th Cir.) arguing double jeopardy, that commitment was essentially for compulsory treatment for which he should have right of jury trial; deprivation of due process because he was confined in a prison not a mental hospital.

U.S. District Court, without an evidentiary hearing, held: Claims were lacking in merit as a matter of law . . . and refused to certify for probable cause for appeal.

On certiorari, U.S. Supreme Court reversed and remanded to the District Court. Marshall, J., for a unanimous court, held: (1) petitioner's claims were substantial enough to warrant evidentiary hearing; and (2) the state on remand should be given opportunity to develop relevant facts relating to waiver at the evidentiary hearing.

15. *Inadequate housing, lack of treatment for committed juveniles is unconstitutional.*

Morales v. Turman, 430 U.S. 322; 97 S. Ct. 1189 (1977) [lower court's opinion 535 F. 2d 864—5th Cir., 1976]

Suit brought against Texas state officials in Texas U.S. District Court, alleging unconstitutional conditions in state institutions for juvenile delinquents (including housing, not providing for rehabilitation or treatment which justified their confinement). The single-judge District Court determined that juveniles' constitutional rights had been violated. (383 F. Supp. 53). The U.S. Court of Appeals reversed on ground that a three-judge (not one-judge) District Court should have been convened.

The Supreme Court reversed and remanded in a per curiam decision expressing unanimous view holding that a single District Court judge could properly exercise full jurisdiction.

16. *Inmate of prison transferred to criminally insane hospital must have hearing on insanity.*

    U.S. ex rel. Schuster v. Herold, 410 F. 2d 1071 (U.S. Ct. of App. 2d Cir., 1969)

    Schuster, a convicted murderer, diagnosed as "paranoid" when complaining of "corruption of prison education program," was transferred to Dannemora State Hospital, New York, for criminally insane. Writ of Habeas Corpus challenged legality of transfer from Clinton prison without evidentiary hearing (subjecting him to additional deprivation and deprived him of opportunity for parole).

    On appeal, to Court of Appeals, held that where he was transferred without notice or under procedures according civilians undergoing commitment, he was entitled to a hearing on question of his sanity with all procedures granted noncriminals who are involuntarily committed. Reversed and remanded to District Court.

Section II: Insanity Plea

17. *M'Naghten's Case*, 8 Eng. Rep. 718 (1843)

    [Opinion of fifteen judges of common law courts, called in extraordinary session, at Queen's direction, to the House of Lords]

    "To establish a defense on the ground of insanity, it must be clearly proved that at the time of committing the act, the party accused was labouring under such a defect of reason, from disease of the mind, as not to know the nature and quality of the act he was doing, or [if he did know that] as not to know what he was doing was wrong."

18. *Expert opinion does not decide presence of mental disease or defect: this is province of the jury.*

    McDonald v. United States, 312 F. 2d 847; 114 U.S. App. D.C. 120 (D.C. Cir., 1962)

Defendant convicted of manslaughter; appealed as not guilty by reason of mental defect. Circuit court held: The issue of mental defect should be submitted to the jury, and jury should be instructed that "a mental disease or defect or any abnormal condition of the mind which substantially affects the mental and emotional processes and substantially impairs behavior control," could be a defense. Defendant, on request, is entitled to an instruction that if he is acquitted by reason of insanity he would be confined in a mental hospital until it was determined that he was no longer dangerous to himself or others. Even if there is *uncontradicted* medical evidence sufficient to indicate that he was not guilty by reason of insanity, the question of disease or defect is entirely the province of the jury, the trier of fact.

19. *Product test (Durham) (1953)*

Durham v. United States, 214 F. 2d 862; 94 U.S. App. D.C. 228 (D.C. Cir., 1954)

Defendant was convicted of housebreaking and appealed. Reversed on appeal, the court adopting a *new* test of criminal responsibility—that if the defendant's unlawful act was the product of mental disease or a mental defect, he was not criminally responsible. Reversed and remanded for new trial.

20. *Discussion of M'Naghten's shortcomings: recommendation of A.L.I. test.*

United States v. Freeman, 357 F. 2d 606 (U.S. Ct. of App. 2nd Cir., 1966)

Defendant was convicted of selling narcotics. A confirmed addict, Freeman claimed "not sufficient capacity and will to be responsible for the crime." U.S. District Court (S. D., New York) utilized M'Naghten, finding him sane. One psychiatrist diagnosed: "episodes of toxic psychosis"; second diagnosed: "dulling of thinking process." Both agreed he was sane under M'Naghten. Circuit Court of Appeals reversed and remanded, ordering employment of "criteria of Model Penal Code test (A.L.I.)."

21. *Acceptance of American Law Institute test v. Durham.*

United States v. Brawner, 471 F. 2d 969 (D.C. Cir., 1972) 153 U.S. App. D.C. 1

Following *McDonald*, court ruled that "product" test of Durham is "undesirable . . . [because] it gives undue dominance by experts giving testimony." Accepted A.L.I. test and "substantial capacity both to appreciate the wrongfulness of his conduct and to conform it to the requirements of law." Reversed and remanded.

22. *Currens test: psychopathic personality and mental illness.*

United States v. Currens, 290 F. 2nd 751 (3rd Cir., 1961)

Defendant convicted of Dyer Act by U.S. District Court of Pennsylvania. Appealed, that jury was charged under M'Naghten whereas psychiatrists found him "hysterical, emotionally unstable to degree of affecting his judgment." Other experts found him "explosive . . . irrational . . . possible disintegrating personality." Biggs, J., held: Sociopathy was sufficient to "put insanity at issue." Stated "all pertinent symptoms . . . should be put before court and jury." Enlarged A.L.I. test by replacing "capacity to appreciate criminality" with "capacity to conform conduct to . . . law." Dissent noted closeness to "irresistible impulse" theory, in Bigg's decision.

23. *Conclusory testimony by psychiatrists prohibited: may confuse jury.*

Washington v. U.S., 390 F. 2d 444 (U.S. Cir. D.C., 1967)

Defendant was convicted of rape, robbery, and assault with deadly weapon. Appeal on grounds that judge should have acquitted by reason of insanity because psychiatrists evaluated defendant with labels, as "schizophrenic . . . neurotic" etc. Appellate Court held: trial court should not allow expert witnesses to use technical, psychiatric terms since "labels are uninformative . . . and distract jury's attention from . . . underlying facts." Unexplained labels are not enough. Opinion of Barzelon, Jr., include instructions to expert witnesses in insanity cases.

24. *"Mental disease or defect" should not exclude psychopathic personality in A.L.I. insanity test.*

Wade v. United States, 426 F. 2d 64 (U.S. Ct. of App. 9th Cir., 1970)

Defendant, a psychopathic personality, was convicted in a federal trial court, as sane. On appeal, it was held the M'Naghten rule was not in force, and he was entitled to the test of criminal responsibility in terms of the Model Penal Code Section 4.01 (1)—a person is not responsible for criminal conduct if at the time of such conduct, as a result of mental disease or defect, he lacks substantial capacity either to appreciate the wrongfulness of his conduct or to conform his conduct to the requisites of the law. Ely, J., held trial court should not instruct that A.L.I. test includes . . . "abnormality manifested by repeated criminal acts or otherwise antisocial conduct" . . . does not confer irresponsibility. Conviction reversed. Dissenting opinions maintain psychopathic exclusion should be maintained in jury charge.

25. *Liberal interpretation of M'Naghten* (California).

People v. Wolff, 61 Cal. 2d 795, 40 Cal. Rptr. 271 (1964)

Fifteen-year-old boy convicted of first degree murder of his mother. Psychiatric examination revealed "bizarre ideas, sexual confusion, impulsive behavior, impaired judgment." On appeal, California Supreme Court ruled, in spite of 4 psychiatrists who called the boy "schizophrenic," the reviewing court was limited to determining whether there was substantial evidence in record to support the verdict of sanity; the jury could find the defendant sane because he knew right from wrong; that they could not entirely reject psychiatric testimony. However, the court broadened the M'Naghten test to include "appreciation" of crime, beyond "knowing" test. Modified by reducing first degree to second degree; affirmed as modified.

26. *California adopts A.L.I. test: abandons M'Naghten.*

People v. Drew, 22 Cal. 3d 333, 149 Cal. Rptr. 275 (1978)

Defendant charged with battery on police officer. Court-appointed psychiatrists diagnosed "latent schizophrenia." Previous record of mental illness. Jury convicted of assault. Defendant appealed he was "not guilty by reason of insanity." Supreme Court of California held four to three the M'Naghten test, defining the defense of insanity was "deficient" as a test of insanity, because of its exclusive focus on the knowledge of right and wrong. (The M'Naghten test was adopted by California in 1864.)

Vigorous dissent: Major change in law (M'Naghten) should be made by the legislature. A.L.I. test still a "vague behavioral test to be determined by psychiatrists."

Section III: Diminished Capacity

27. *Diminished Capacity Due to Abnormal Mental State.*

People v. Wells, 33 Cal. 2d 330, 202 Pac. 2d 53 (1949)

Defendant, while serving indeterminate sentence of "life" (Folsom Prison) threw a heavy cuspidor injuring a guard, resulting in a conviction under statute providing death penalty for assault by life prisoner likely to produce great bodily injury; affirmed by Court of Appeals. On appeal to Supreme Court of California, petitioner asserted psychiatric finding that "malice aforethought" was negated by "abnormal mental state . . . [because] of fear and state of tension" disallowed by trial court. Supreme Court ruled psychiatric evidence was admissible; that fear amounting to lack of mental capacity to have malice aforethought "which did not permit requisite mental intent." Ruled unconstitutional as denial of due process, but "error not prejudicial."

28. *Diminished Capacity Due to "Dissociative Reaction" not acceptable.*

U.S. v. Pollard, 171 F. Sup. 474 (Mich., 1959)
U.S. v. Pollard, 282 F. 2d 450 (6th Cir., 1960)

Defendant, a policeman, who was depressed after wife and child were killed wantonly two years before, charged with robberies. Changed plea to NGRI. Found sane by trial without jury (District Court E. D. Mich.). Psychiatric report—"diseased mind which produced irresistible impulse." Other reports—"dissociative reaction . . . actions not consciously motivated." Study at Federal Medical Center agreed—"depression with unconscious desire to be punished."

Levin, Jr., of U.S. District Court confirmed, saying: "I have great respect for profession of psychiatry . . . yet [there are] compelling reasons for not blindly following opinions of experts . . . and for not disregarding my own experience and collective conscience."

29. *Mental abnormality not amounting to insanity may negate specific intent— a partial defense.*

People v. Gorshen, 51 Cal. 2d 716; 336 Pac. 2d 492 (1959)

Defendant appealed after being convicted of second degree murder. California Supreme Court, affirming, held: (1) that in a prosecution for murder, the opinion of the doctor of the medical essence of malice aforethought was not objectionable on the ground that such testimony was a medical interpretation of a legal principle; (2) that where the defendant claimed he did not intend to take human life, or at least did not act with malice aforethought, medical testimony that defendant had "uncontrollable compulsion based on sexual delusion" of schizophrenic nature, negated the specific intent of murder with malice aforethought, being a partial defense to a murder charge but is not a test of the legal defense of insanity.

30. *Diminished Capacity due to intoxication.*

People v. Conley, 64 Cal. 2d 310, 49 Cal. Rptr. 815, 411 Pac. 2d 911 (1966)

Defendant found guilty on two counts of first degree murder, and appealed. He killed a girl friend, who had reconciled with her husband (whom he also killed). He had been drinking steadily for three days before the act. Supreme Court of California ruled, evidence of diminished mental capacity, whether caused by intoxication, trauma, or disease, can be used to show that a defendant did not have a specific mental state. Malice aforethought is a specific mental state and defendant may show that he lacked that mental state. In the absence of malice, a homicide cannot be an offense higher than manslaughter. A person who intentionally kills may still be incapable of harboring malice aforethought because of mental disease, defect or intoxication, hence such a case is voluntary manslaughter.

31. *Diminished Capacity v. Heat of Passion.*

People v. Berry, 18 Cal. 3d 509; 556 Pac. 2d 777, 134 Cal. Rptr. 415 (1976)

Defendant convicted of murder first degree and assault with great bodily harm. Choked wife with telephone cord after prior assault. Wife taunted defendant with love and "sexual favors" to another man while stimulating defendant, tormenting him with both divorce-wish and sexual advances. Appeal on ground of error in refusing voluntary manslaughter charge on "heat of passion" theory. Expert psychiatrist testified that homicide due to "uncontrollable rage under provocation" by victim produced an "altered mental state," not psychosis. Supreme Court of California ruled not sufficient for diminished capacity plea, but error in not instructing on "heat of passion" theory, of a reasonable man (killing under provocation in heat of passion). Hence voluntary manslaughter correct charge.

Section IV: Civil Rights: Criminal's Rights

32. *Fundamental Decision of Civil Rights. Separate but equal educational facilities unconstitutional.*

Brown v. Board of Education of Topeka, 349 U.S. 294; 75 S. Ct. 753 (1954)

The principle that racial discrimination in public education is unconstitutional was announced by the Supreme Court in this and three companion cases.

In a supplemental opinion by Warren, Ch. J., the Supreme Court unanimously reversed those courts below which had permitted racial segregation in public schools, and remanded the cases with directions that these courts, in fashioning and effectuating the decrees, should be guided by equitable principles; that is, prompt and reasonable start toward full compliance with the decision requiring desegregation.

33. *Miranda Rights defined: extension of Escobedo.*

Miranda v. State of Arizona, 384 U.S. 436; 86 S. Ct. 1062 (1966)

The right to counsel of a person during interrogation was first stated in *Escobedo v. Illinois*. Extended in *Miranda*: a suspect must be apprised of his rights and exercise of those rights must be fully honored. The following safeguards must be observed (U.S. Supreme Court):

> He must be informed of right to remain silent.
> Any statement he makes may be used as evidence against him.
> He has the right to presence of counsel; and if he is unable to afford an attorney, one will be appointed for him; and
> He has the right to stop interrogation, by any indication thereof; and thereafter he can remain silent; the right to counsel continues.

34. *Legal rights of convicted sex psychopath.*

Specht v. Patterson, 386 U.S. 605; 87 S. Ct. 1209 (1967)

Specht was convicted on Indecent Liberties (Colorado) for which the maximum sentence of ten years could be imposed. Under the state's Sex Offender Act (1963), he could be sentenced without a hearing to indeterminate term of one day to life, if found by a psychiatrist to constitute a threat of bodily harm to the public or was a habitual offender and mentally ill. Petitioner challenged constitutionality of Sex Law on grounds of denial of hearing and right of confrontation. Denied by Supreme Court of Colorado.

U.S. Supreme Court reversed. Douglas, J., expressed unanimous view of the court that the failure to grant such procedural safeguards violated due process requirements of the XIV Amendment.

35. *Incarceration of chronic alcoholic is cruel and unusual punishment.*

Driver v. Hinnant, 356 F. 2d 761 (4th Cir., 1966)

Offender arrested for public drunkenness in North Carolina whose statute provided that any person found drunk or intoxicated on a public highway or public place or meeting was guilty of a misdemeanor. Appealed that law as unconstitutional under VIII Amendment. U.S. 4th Circuit Court agreed: violation of VIII Amendment (cruel and unusual punishment) as applied to chronic alcoholic, who is powerless to stop drinking and whose drinking was compulsive. Such a person lacks evil intent (mens rea).

36. *Chronic alcoholic suffers from a disease and cannot be punished therefor.*

Easter v. District of Columbia, 361 F. 2d 50 (D.C. Cir., 1966) 124 U.S. App. D.C. 33

Defendant was convicted in Washington, D.C., of public intoxication and appealed. On appeal, it was held that chronic alcoholism is a defense to a charge of public intoxication and is not itself a crime—expert medical and psychiatric evidence established that the defendant was a chronic alcoholic, who had lost control over his use of alcohol. While an alcoholic may be committed for treatment or may be released, he may not be punished therefor.

37. *Punishment for "status" of addiction is cruel and unusual and violation of VIII Amendment.*

Robinson v. California, 370 U.S. 660; 82 S. Ct. 1417 (1962)

Defendant convicted in Los Angeles of being *addicted* to the use of narcotics, and affirmed on appeal to Appellate Department of Los Angeles Superior Court. Appealed to Supreme Court of the U.S. resulted in reversal. California statute making it a criminal offense to be "addicted to the use of narcotics" is cruel and unusual punishment because the "addict is a sick person . . . [addiction is a status,] not a crime." Justice Douglas. Hence, VIII Amendment is violated. Dissent: Power to punish or treat belongs to the state; is not a constitutional issue. (Justices Clark and White)

38. *Chronic Alcoholism is a voluntary act; no defense for drunk charge.*

Powell v. State of Texas, 392 U.S. 514; 88 S. Ct. 2145 (1968)

Defendant was charged with being drunk in a public place; trial court noted his defense for compulsive alcoholism was cruel and unusual punishment, contrary to VIII Amendment. Ruled that since defendant was afflicted with the disease of chronic alcoholism and his appearance in public was of his own volition, his condition not a defense to the charge. Trial court found defendant guilty.

On appeal to the U.S. Supreme Court, on a five to four decision, upheld Texas court. Dissenting opinion stated defendant should not be punished for being in a condition he was "powerless to change," and his appearance in public was due to a compulsion. However, Texas statute was directed against socially offensive behavior.

Section V: Competency to Stand Trial

39. *Standard test for competency to stand trial.*

Dusky v. United States, 362 U.S. 402; 80 S. Ct. 788 (1960) See also 271 F. 2d 385 (8th Cir., 1959)

This case involved the validity and application of federal statutes providing for pretrial determination of mental competency to stand trial. Defendant convicted of transporting a girl from Kansas to Missouri unlawfully, that is, kidnapping. Psychiatric examination at U.S. Medical Center, diagnosed "schizophrenia, chronic." After conflicting testimony, trial court stated: "since he is oriented for time and place . . . he is competent to stand trial." Appealed to U.S. Court of Appeals who affirmed.

On certiorari, U.S. Supreme Court reversed, stating: An accused is not mentally competent merely because he is oriented to time and place and has some recollection of event. The test must be whether the accused has sufficient present ability to consult with his lawyer "with a reasonable degree of rational understanding and whether he has a rational as well as a factual understanding of the proceedings against him."

40. *Defendant incompetent to stand trial must have opportunity to regain capacity in foreseeable future or be committed civilly or released.*

Jackson v. Indiana, 406 U.S. 715; 92 S. Ct. 1845 (1972)

In a robbery prosecution in the state trial court, court found the accused incompetent to stand trial, and ordered him committed until certified sane. Because accused was a deaf-mute, mentally defective, and unable to read or write, and able communicate only through limited sign language, his counsel claimed commitment would amount to a "life sentence." Motion for new trial denied; upheld by Supreme Court of Indiana.

Appeal to U.S. Supreme Court, Blackmun, J., expressed unanimous view of court and reversed, holding that accused's commitment violated equal protection since he was committed solely on incompetency to stand trial without probability that he would ever attain that capacity in the foreseeable future. As he is a deaf-mute, the state must either release him or institute civil commitment proceedings.

41. *Psychiatric examination for competency to stand trial a constitutional right.*

Pate v. Robinson, 383 U.S. 375; 86 S. Ct. 836 (1966)

Robinson tried and found guilty of murder in Illinois: Sentence was life imprisonment. Long history of psychopathic behavior (one prior infanticide). Four witnesses testified he was insane, although counsel did not demand hearing on competency. At trial, continuance for psychiatric testimony further denied. On appeal, Supreme Court of Illinois affirmed, judging defendant as "mentally alert" in court.

Petition to U.S. District Court against Warden Pate denied without a hearing, but U.S. District Court of Appeals (7th Cir.) reversed holding that Robinson was convicted in an "unduly hurried" hearing. Further appeal to U.S. Supreme Court, Clark, J., affirmed, holding that defendant was constitutionally entitled to a hearing on competency to stand trial.

Section VI: Confidentiality and Privilege

42. *Psychotherapist's duty to warn potential victim of patient's expressed intention to harm others.*

Tarasoff v. Board of Regents of the University of California, 17 Cal. 3d 425; 551 Pac. 2d 334, 131 Cal. Rptr. 14 (1975)

One Poddar, student at the University of California, was in treatment as out-patient in mental health clinic. He told his therapist he intended to kill his fiancee. No order for seventy-two hour detention period was ordered. Subsequently, Poddar killed Miss Tarasoff. Her parents brought suit for wrongful death, accusing, among other things, "failure to warn of a dangerous patient" or to order a detention period. Case dismissed for lack of cause of action. On appeal to Appellate Court, dismissal was affirmed.

Supreme Court of California reversed on appeal. Recognizing the difficulty of "predicting danger in a therapeutic context," they ruled that "once a therapist . . . determines . . . that a patient poses a serious danger of violence to others, he bears a duty to exercise reasonable care to protect the forseeable victim . . ."

Against objection by psychiatrists through amicus curiae that the confidential character of psychotherapeutic communications should be maintained, the court (Tobriner, J.) held: "the protective privilege ends where the public peril begins."

43. *Duty to warn does not hold in suicide.*

Bellah v. Greenson, 81 Cal. App. 3d 604, 146 Cal. Rptr. 535 (1978)

Patient, under care of psychiatrist, took overdose of sleeping pills and died. Psychiatrist had notes indicating suicidal intent of patient while under treatment. Two years after death, parents brought malpractice action, "failure to warn" for wrongful death. Trial court found for defendant doctor. Court of Appeal (California) First Appellate District held: (distinguishing *Tarasoff*) that "disclosure of a confidential communication . . . is not required . . . where the risk of harm is self-inflicted . . . or where the danger . . . [is] of property damage."

44. *Limitation of psychotherapist-patient privilege.*

In re Lifschutz, 2 Cal. 3d 415, 85 Cal. Rptr. 829, 467 Pac. 2d 557 (1970)

Dr. Lifschutz, a psychiatrist, was subpoened to depose on a patient he had treated ten years prior to this suit brought by the patient who claimed severe emotional and mental distress following an accident. The psychiatrist refused to be deposed or produce records on grounds of "absolute privilege of confidentiality and right to privacy of his patient as constitutional right." The doctor was held in contempt and jailed.

On Writ of Habeas Corpus, Supreme Court of California ruled that psychotherapist privilege was not absolute: That when the patient tenders his mental and emotional condition in issue, it becomes an automatic waiver of privilege . . . patient may apply for order to limit the scope of inquiry.

45. Psychotherapist-patient privilege not absolute.

Caesar v. Mountanos, 542 F. 2d 1064 (9th Cir., 1976)

Dr. Caesar refused to answer questions in court at deposition regarding patient he treated. Held in contempt. On appeal, U.S. District Court held that where plaintiff tendered issue of her mental condition and suffering as a result of accident, psychotherapist-patient privilege is waived: Justified by compelling state interest; "the harm done to the cause of justice through suppression of the truth is infinitely greater than any harm . . . done the physician-patient relationship." (Wigmore)

Section VII: Personal Injury

46. Emotional Trauma without physical injury, compensable.

Christy Bros. Circus v. Turnage, 38 Ga. App. 581, 144 S.E. 680 (1928)

Petitioner stated a good cause of action by pleading that a horse was backed against the audience and evacuated on the lap of a patron of the circus, in full view of the audience, including many of her friends. Recovery denied in trial court. On appeal, held: that though the physical touching of a person's body (which violates a personal right, and is therefore "a personal injury") does not cause injury, yet recovery could be had for mental suffering alone, without showing there was physical injury out of which the mental suffering arose.

47. Psychiatric illness as a result of emotional stress on job, compensable.

Carter v. General Motors, 361 Mich. 577, 106 N.W. 2d 105 (1961)

Workmen's Compensation proceeding for benefits for psychosis resulting from emotional pressure encountered in daily work on assembly line. Patient fell behind and foreman "rode him." Worker developed paranoid ideas, diagnosed as schizophrenia for which he was treated in a hospital with electroshock. Compensation awarded for "pressure" on job as cause of mental illness. Psychiatric testimony stated patient had an "inflexible personality" before mental illness. Appeal was before Supreme Court of Michigan: Agreed the proximate cause of psychosis was the assembly-line routine, in spite of patient's basic predisposition to mental illness. Awarded compensation for the psychotic period.

48. *Harassment causing emotional distress recoverable as wrongful death.*

Cauverien v. De Metz, 188 N.Y.S. 2d 627 (1959)

A diamond broker gave a dealer a stone for prospective sale. Dealer refused to purchase or return diamond, thus "blackening the broker's reputation." Malicious behavior caused "extreme emotional distress" to the latter who took his own life on an impulse. Wrongful death held to result when the suicide was committed in response to "irresistible impulse . . . founded on a state of insanity," that is, emotional distress.

This case was contrary to the usual rule that "a suicide—absent insanity—is a new and independent agency which breaks the causal connection between wrongful act and death, precluding an action under wrongful death statutes."

Section VIII: Child Custody Problems

49. *Child Custody in conventional v. Bohemian household.*

Painter v. Bannister, 248 Iowa 1390, 140 N.W. 2d 152 (1966)

Mother of child aged seven years died; child given to maternal grandparents by father. Subsequently he requested child be returned to him; grandparents (Bannisters) refused. Action sought for custody; awarded to father by trial court. Grandparents appealed to Iowa Supreme Court. Psychiatric report stated no psychiatric problem in either party but "divergent life patterns." Child psychologist advised best interests of child was in "safe, dependable, conventional, middle-class" home of Bannister versus "arty, unconventional, Bohemian" home of father (Painter).

Stuart, J., reversed trial court stating that child had established a "father-son relationship with Bannister" which outweighed probably the more intellectually stimulating home with father.

50. *Best interest of child served by custody remaining with mother although latter may show mental illness, if juvenile not neglected.*

Todd v. Superior Ct., 68 Wash. 2d 578, 414 Pac. 2d 605 (1966)

Deborah, aged thirteen, declared a "dependent" child by Juvenile Court because mother was declared unfit due to persecutory delusions. Psychiatrists and social welfare workers on many occasions found mother to be paranoid schizophrenic. Supreme Court of Washington affirmed finding of "dependency" as best interests of child.

Dissent by Rosellini, C.J., stated that juvenile made good grades in school, was no disciplinary problem, and mother was devoted and not neglectful of Deborah. Question of whether trial court may declare a child dependent . . . on sole ground parent is mentally disturbed, answered in the negative. If mother's illness has not caused mistreatment of child, custody should be returned to mother.

Bibliographic Essay

A comprehensive bibliography covering the field of forensic psychiatry would involve dovetailing legal decisions by the courts with clinical experiences in legal matters by psychiatric practitioners. To join these areas in a common bibliography foreshadows difficulties, because legal writings derive from judicial decisions developed into case law, while psychiatric writings represent individual reactions to contacts with defendants, plaintiffs, attorneys, and judges. To consider legal bibliography first, it should be noted that cases condensed into legal principles are widely distributed in time and space, sometimes covering centuries of jurisprudence. On the other hand, medico-legal opinions voiced by physicians extend not much more than a century in time.

In the body of legal decisions and writings regarding psychiatry, the main emphasis has been on rules for estimating the effect of mental disease or defect on criminal responsibility. Thus the M'Naghten Rule and its modifications (Durham, Currens, American Law Institute tests), the irresistible impulse theory, diminished capacity, and competency to stand trial tests have received analysis both in court decisions and in reasoned expositions of legal theory. Where the *not guilty by reason of insanity* plea is offered in close cases, decisions follow a thorough review of the virtues or liabilities of the M'Naghten Rule or the A.L.I. test. Hence, such decisions are recommended reading.

In the Nineteenth Century, for example, criticism of M'Naghten by Isaac Ray culminated in Judge Doe's discussion of the problem in detail in *People v. Pike* (1869), a New Hampshire case. More recently *People v. Wolff* (1978) 78 Calif. App. 3d 735, 144 Calif. App. 3d 735, 144 Calif. Rptr. 344, a California case, broadened the then legal M'Naghten test, and analyzed intensively the defects of the older rule.

Even more recent was the thorough review of M'Naghten and its derivatives in *People v. Drew* (1978) 22 Calif. 3d 333, 149 Calif. Rptr. 275, 583 Pac. 2d 1308, wherein the A.L.I. test was accepted, with four dissenting voices, for the State of California. One can do no better than read the detailed analysis given by the majority, with the dissenting opinions. Beyond judicial decisions, the literature on insanity tests in law journal reviews, textbooks, and monographs has been vast since the time of Isaac Ray's celebrated *A Treatise on Medical Jurisprudence of Insanity* (5th ed. 1871; recently reissued New York: Arno Press, 1976).

Although the number of legal scholars discussing the M'Naghten test has been legion, the writings of Professors Jerome Hall, Abraham Goldstein, Herbert Fingarette, Henry Weihofen, Wilbur Katz, Edward de Grazie, Livermore and Meehl, and a host of others, have been significant. Judges of the United States Courts of Appeals—David L. Bazelon, Chief Judge of the District of Columbia Judicial Circuit; John Biggs, Jr., of the Third Judicial Circuit; and Irving R. Kaufman, Chief Judge of the Second Judicial Circuit— and the Justices of the United States Supreme Court have discussed, in decisional writings and lectures, their analyses of tests for mental irresponsibility. The proceedings of the American Law Institute (for which Professor Herbert Wechsler was the Recorder) discussed the issue of insanity and the law in extenso before enunciating the A.L.I. test. Law journals of practically all law schools, from Harvard and Yale down to less renowned institutions, have carried articles and monographs on the legal tests for insanity (some annotated in the present text). Many of these articles citing major decisions and works analyzed the defects and virtues of the various tests with recommendations that have added little to the practical resolution in actual cases before the bar.

Books and monographs by lawyers and by older legal authorities (such as Professor Edwin Keedy), in pointing out defects in the M'Naghten rule, repeat criticisms of the ruling. Among current writings are the American Law Reports, 2d and 3d series, that review specific topics, including the insanity defense, in case law with annotations, buttressed by "Practice pointers" giving definite suggestions for lawyers.

During the past two decades increasing attention has been paid by legal authors to psychiatric diagnoses, evaluations, and testimony in criminal cases. Spurred by Thomas Szasz's attack on the validity of psychiatry as a discipline in *The Myth of Mental Illness* (New York: Harper and Row Inc., 1961), *Law, Liberty and Psychiatry* (New York: Macmillan, Inc., 1963), and a flood of anti-psychiatric articles by Szasz and followers, lawyers have attacked psychiatric testimony. Jay Ziskin in *Coping with Psychiatric and Psychological Testimony* (Beverly Hills, Ca.: Law and Psychology Press, 1970) has detailed methods of challenging testimony of experts in court. He has also marshaled much criticism on the confused state of psychiatric diagnoses and court testimony collected from writings by psychiatrists and psychologists. In the same direction, Richard Arens's *Insanity Defense* (New York: Philosophical Library, Inc., 1974) criticized psychiatric concepts of insanity and hospital practice particularly related to St. Elizabeth's Hospital, Washington, D.C. during the 1960s. A less contentious and more sober volume discussing forensic psychiatric issues is that by L. R. Tancredi, J. Lieb, and A. E. Slaby, *Legal Issues in Psychiatric Care* (New York: Harper and Row, Inc., 1975). Similarly, Professor R. J. Bonnie edited a compendium in *Psychiatrists and the Legal Process* (Charlottesville: University Press of Virginia, 1977) which contained seminal articles by leaders in both fields covering the period 1973-1977, a period of growth of forensic psychiatry. This is an up-to-date, balanced presentation. An indepth study of the influence of psychoanalysis in legal practice by J. Katz, J. Goldstein, and A. M. Dershowitz, *Psychoanalysis, Psychiatry and the Law* (New York: Free Press, 1967) is a carefully written, thoroughly documented presentation. C. G. Schoenfeld's *Psychoanalysis and The Law* (Springfield, Ill.: Charles C Thomas, 1973) reviews psychoanalysis as applied to medico-legal thinking, emphasizing the need for lawyers to learn more of modern-day psycho-dynamics.

Other recommended readings, written chiefly by attorneys, are included in *Mental Disability in Civil Practice* by Sidney Asch (Rochester, N.Y.: Lawyers Co-operative Publishing Co., 1973). Full reviews of pertinent literature, with controversial views by lawyers and psychiatrists, are found in Alexander Brooks's *Law, Psychiatry and the Mental Health System* (Boston: Little, Brown & Co., 1974) and to a lesser extent in Ralph Slovenko's *Psychiatry and the Law* (Boston: Little, Brown & Co., 1973). *Readings in Law and Psychiatry* by Richard C. Allen, Elyce Z. Ferster, and Jesse G. Rubin (Baltimore: Johns Hopkins Press, 1976) contains excerpts from various authors and judges without much explanatory material. The text of William J. Curran and E. Donald Shapiro's *Law, Medicine and Forensic Science* (Boston: Little, Brown & Co., Law School Case Book Series, 2nd ed., 1970) contains a large chapter on forensic psychiatry built around several prominent cases. The casebooks mentioned cover both criminal and civil areas where psychiatry is involved. Texts by and for lawyers covering malpractice—*Trial of Medical Malpractice Cases* by D. W. Louisell and H. Williams (New York: Matthew Bender & Co., Inc., 1960) and *Doctor, Patient and the Law* by R. C. Morris and A. R. Moritz (St. Louis, Mo.: C. V. Mosby Co., 1971)—deal chiefly in forensic pathology in criminal and civil cases, but contain brief chapters on the psychiatric aspect of litigation.

In relation to other problems such as "competency to stand trial" rulings of judges in particular cases have constituted law: i.e. *Dusky v. U.S.* (1960) 362 U.S. 402, 80 S. Ct. 788. Reading the decisions permits a view of the thinking that goes into decision making among the judiciary.

The question of the release of those ruled "not guilty by reason of insanity" and committed to a hospital for insane criminals has been discussed in detail in various jurisdictions, for example in New York's *Baxstrom v. Herold* (1966) 383 U.S. 105, 86 S. Ct. 760. This issue joined with the question of treatment of involuntarily committed persons—*Rouse v. Cameron* (D.C. Cir., 1966) 373 F. 2d 451, 125 U.S. App. D.C. 366—has led to much comment in law journals.

The psychiatric literature is rich in criminologic material which is tangential to forensic psychiatry. Aside from older material published during the first half of this century, David Abrahamsen's *Psychology of Crime* (New York: Columbia University Press, 1960), Manfred Guttmacher's *The Mind of the Murderer* (New York: Farrar, Strauss and Cudahy, 1960), Walter Bromberg's *Crime and the Mind* (Philadelphia: Lippincott, 1948, revised edition, New York: Macmillan, 1965), John Macdonald's *Psychiatry and the Criminal* 2nd ed. (Springfield, Ill.: Charles C Thomas, 1969) are chiefly clinical studies. Beyond these are myriad articles in professional journals for psychiatrists, psychologists, penologists, criminologists, probation and psychiatric social workers that deal with delinquents and criminal offenders and their treatment and management. These, again, are tangential to forensic psychiatry but provide insights of value. Among the latter, Karl Menninger's book *The Crime of Punishment* (New York: Viking Press, Inc., 1968) deserves mention as does the comprehensive review of sexual psychopathology in Ben Karpman's *The Sexual Offender and His Offenses* (New York: Julian Press, Inc., 1954) which contains a complete bibliography of works on sexual criminology up to the 1950s.

In the specific field of forensic psychiatry, several older works deserve mention: G. Zilboorg's long article on "Legal Aspects of Psychiatry" in *One Hundred Years of American Psychiatry* (New York: Columbia University Press, 1944), *Psychiatry and the Law* (New York: W. W. Norton & Co., 1954) by Henry Weihofen and M. Gutt-macher and Professor Weihofen's standard work *Mental Disease as a Criminal Defense* (Buffalo, N.Y.: Dennis & Co., 1954). Two modern texts, *The American Handbook of Psychiatry* 2nd ed. (New York: Basic Books, 1971, edited by S. Arieti) and *Comprehensive Textbook of Psychiatry* 2nd ed. (Baltimore: Williams and Wilkens, 1975, edited by Alfred Freedman and associates) contain chapters on criminologic and forensic psychiatry by recognized experts. These chapters represent currently acceptable attitudes and practices in the field.

Specific areas in criminal law, such as: competency to stand trial, personal injury including head injuries, drug intoxication, and alcoholism have been discussed extensively in the *Journal of Forensic Science, The American Journal of Psychiatry, Bulletin of the American Academy of Psychiatry and Law, Alcohol Quarterly, Psychological Bulletin* and so on. The National Institute of Health and the Group for Advancement of Psychiatry and various committess of the American Psychiatric Association have published monographs on forensic subjects: "Competency to Stand Trial" (1974), including L. McGarry's extensive study on the same subject, "Confidentiality and Third Parties" (1975), "Juvenile Delinquency" (1976), and other germane topics. Alan Stone, Bernard Diamond, Seymour Halleck, Herbert Modlin, Andrew Watson, Seymour Pollack, Jonas Rappeport, Jacques Quen, and a host of others have published seminal articles in recent years on vital issues in forensic psychiatry.

Textbooks of forensic psychiatry are relatively few. Henry Davidson's *Forensic Psychiatry* 2nd ed. (New York: Ronald Press, 1965) covered all areas of the legal process in which psychiatrists were involved, including advice on evaluating and testifying, with a glossary for physicians and lawyers of their opposite fields. Andrew Watson's *Psychiatry for Lawyers* (New York: International Universities Press, 1968, 2nd ed., 1978) is concerned with human behavior and its changes as reflected in legal problems. The personality development and its vagaries are clearly spelled out in this volume as they appear in a lawyer's work. M. Blinder's *Psychiatry in the Everyday Practice of Law* (Rochester, N.Y.: Lawyers Co-Operative Publishing Co., 1973) contains case reports and a review of testimony at trial with practical suggestions for the expert. There is also adequate consideration given neurologic and mental sequellae of injury. Robert Sadoff's *Practical Guide for Lawyers and Psychiatrists* (Springfield, Ill.: Charles C Thomas, 1975) covers practical aspects of forensic psychiatry and includes a glossary of psychiatric terms for lawyers.

Books, of which there are many, dealing with medico-legal aspects of celebrated trials, contain valued materials not always present in judicial reports. For example, *The Trial of Jack Ruby* (New York: Macmillan, 1965) by John Kaplan and Jon Waltz, Elmer Gertz's *Moment of Madness* (Chicago: Follett Publishing Co., 1968), as well as Melvin Belli's personal account *Dallas Justice: A Real Story of Jack Ruby* (New York: David McKay Co., 1964) provide insights into legal strategy and philosophy concerning psychiatric testimony. In addition, novels and fictionalized accounts of criminal trials, often shed dramatic light on technical aspects of medico-legal activities.

Index

About the Author

Walter Bromberg is a practicing neuro-psychiatrist and is currently Adjunct Professor of Legal Medicine at McGeorge School of Law, University of the Pacific, Sacramento, California. He was formerly Director of the Psychiatric Clinic, Criminal Court, New York County and Senior Psychiatrist at the Bellevue Psychiatric Hospital, New York City, prior to locating in California.